Contemporary European Politics

A Comparative Perspective

THOMAS M. MAGSTADT

THOMSON
™
WADSWORTH

Australia • Brazil • Canada • Mexico • Singapore • Spain
United Kingdom • United States

Contemporary European Politics: A Comparative Perspective
Thomas M. Magstadt

Executive Editor: David Tatom
Development Editor: Scott Spoolman
Associate Development Editor: Rebecca Green
Editorial Assistant: Eva Dickerson
Technology Project Manager: Michelle Vardeman
Senior Marketing Manager: Janise Fry
Marketing Assistant: Teresa Jessen
Marketing Communications Manager: Nathaniel
  Bergson-Michelson
Project Manager, Editorial Production: Marti Paul
Creative Director: Rob Hugel

Art Director: Maria Epes
Print Buyer: Doreen Suruki
Permissions Editor: Kiely Sisk
Production Service: Aaron Downey, Matrix Productions Inc.
Copy Editor: Victoria Nelson
Illustrator: International Typesetting and Composition
Cover Designer: Jeanette Barber
Cover Photographer/Artist: Digital Vision
Cover Printer: Malloy Incorporated
Compositor: International Typesetting and Composition
Printer: Malloy Incorporated

Printed in the United States of America
1 2 3 4 5 6 7 10 09 08 07 06

Library of Congress Control Number: 2005938014

ISBN 0-534-57776-8

Thomson Higher Education
10 Davis Drive
Belmont, CA 94002-3098
USA

For more information about our products, contact us at:
Thomson Learning Academic Resource Center
1-800-423-0563
For permission to use material from this text or product,
submit a request online at
http://www.thomsonrights.com.
Any additional questions about permissions can be
submittted by e-mail to
thomsonrights@thomson.com.

For Barbara, who lived in Italy; Rebecca, who lived in Belgium;
Michael, who lives in the Czech Republic; and my mother, Esther, who lives in my heart.

About The Author

Thomas Magstadt earned his doctorate at the Johns Hopkins Schools of Advanced International Studies (SAIS). He is the author of *Understanding Politics: Ideas, Institutions, and Issues*, 7th edition (Thomson/Wadsworth, 2006), *Nations and Government: Comparative Politics in Regional Perspective*, 5th edition (Thomson/Wadsworth, 2005), and *An Empire If You Can Keep It: Power and Principle in American Foreign Policy* (Congressional Quarterly Press, 2004). He has also published numerous scholarly papers and articles. Magstadt was a tenured professor and political science chair at the University of Nebraska–Kearney and Augustana College in Sioux Falls in the 1970s and 1980s. He served as an intelligence analyst (1983–1986), a visiting professor at the Air War College (1990–1992), a Fulbright Scholar in the Czech Republic (1994–1996), and taught at the University of Missouri–Kansas City (1997–2001), before turning to full-time writing. He lives in Westwood Hills, Kansas.

Contents

List of Tables and Figures

List of Maps and Boxes

Preface

This first edition of *Contemporary European Politics: A Comparative Perspective* has two main purposes, to examine contemporary politics within key European nation-states and to look at Europe's progress toward a goal that is ultimately incompatible with the nation-state system. The first purpose necessarily focuses on the habits of thought and behavior, as well as governmental institutions and processes, long associated with sovereign states; the second underscores the degree to which sovereignty and nationalism have been superseded without being formally relinquished.

American school children learn at an early age that Europe has a special place in American history. The first colonists who settled along the Atlantic seaboard in the early seventeenth century were Europeans. The vast majority of immigrants to the Americas during the next three centuries crossed the Atlantic to get here. They were Europeans of all nationalities. Today, immigrants to the United States come mainly from the Western Hemisphere—especially Mexico and Central America. With few exceptions, these new arrivals also speak a European language—Spanish, Portuguese, or perhaps French. They, too, have historic and cultural ties to Europe (especially the Iberian peninsula).

At the time of the American Revolution, the colonies were huddled on the European side of the Atlantic. That was no mere accident. America's cultural and political orientation, not surprisingly, was toward the Atlantic coastal cities of New York, Philadelphia, and Boston, and, beyond America's shores, toward the British Isles and Europe. Despite the fact that Asia is on the rise today and that Asians comprise prominent immigrant communities in contemporary America, Europe is still the most important region of the world—politically, strategically, and economically—for the United States.

Europe's special importance to America is a good reason for American college students to learn more about it, but it's not the only one. Europe looms very large on the world stage—and it is going to loom even larger in the decades to come. Indeed, Europe today "has more people, more wealth, and more trade than the United States of America."[1] No fewer than twenty-five countries from all parts of the Continent now belong to the European Union (EU). For anyone familiar with modern European history, it is nothing short of amazing to learn that "the citizens of the EU use a standard license plate, birth certificate, and passport. . . . The EU has its own flag, its own anthem, and its own national day."[2]

The population of the European Union now exceeds 450 million (by comparison, the population of the United States is something under 300 million in 2006). The EU's combined gross national product (GNP) has drawn roughly equal with America's. Even though most people know that Japan's economy was sluggish throughout the 1990s and that China's was racing along, the fact that Europe was quietly reinventing itself often went unnoticed. But it is a safe prediction that it will not go unnoticed in the coming decades. It is no secret these days that China is one of Asia's awakening giants (India is another) or that Europe's former great powers (Austria-Hungary, Britain, France, Germany, Russia, and Spain) are no longer giants on the world stage. But the European Union *is* a giant. True, it is a different sort of giant. It is not "awakening" or "emerging" (like China and India) or militarily muscle bound (like the United States). Economically, the EU is already a superpower—a clumsy giant, to be sure, one still in its infancy and unsteady on its legs. But then much the same could be said of the United States between 1776 and 1865. We know relatively little about the birth or death of superpowers because so far there have been only two, and one of them (the Soviet Union) no longer exists. To comprehend what is going on in Europe today we have to broaden the old Cold War definition of the word *superpower* and consider the possibility that old ways of looking at power itself are no longer entirely adequate in the Age of Globalization. Indeed, studying the new Europe is essential for understanding the emerging world order and the challenges both pose for the United States in the years ahead. In the future, we will need to know more—a lot more—about Europe than we do today. This volume is devoted to that end.

I have divided Europe into west (Part I) and east (Part II), and given the European Union separate treatment (Part III). In so doing, I do not mean to imply that Europe continues to be politically divided as it was during the Cold War—that unnatural state came to an abrupt end in 1989, a fact that was confirmed in the 1990s when the Soviet state collapsed, the two German states merged into one again, several former Soviet satellite states joined NATO, and the European Union began accession talks with Poland, Hungary, Czech Republic, Estonia, Slovenia, and Cyprus. (All six countries, plus Latvia, Lithuania, Slovakia, and Malta, joined the EU in 2004.) Indeed, Europe is perhaps becoming less divided along an east-west axis that ever before in its history. Nonetheless, there remain significant differences between the eastern and western regions of Europe to justify using the old political geography for purposes of comparative analysis. Readers are invited to judge for themselves, preferably *after* they have read the book.

---

[1] T. J. Reid, *The United States of Europe: The New Superpower and the End of American Supremacy* (New York: Penguin, 2004), p. 1.

[2] Ibid., p. 3. The author writes: "When I drove recently from the Arctic Circle to the Mediterranean, I passed through eight countries, never saw a border guard, and never had to bother with foreign exchange."

I will not sketch the outlines of the book here. Anyone interested in getting a general idea about what is inside has only to turn to the table of contents. The only way to find out in greater detail is to keep turning the pages. Each chapter has a brief overview at the beginning and a Summary and Conclusions section at the end. In addition, I have highlighted key terms in the text and listed them at the end of each chapter, along with suggested readings. All these features are offered as learning aids, but in the end there is no substitute for reading and reflection.

Also, students and instructors who use the first edition of *Contemporary European Politics* will be able to get periodic updates to the country studies, European Union, and suggested readings by visiting my website at www.worldviewwest.com. As this non-partisan website is my own personal project, I am solely responsible for its content. Its purpose is to promote public interest in the study of foreign policy, international affairs, and comparative politics in the conviction that knowledge of the world beyond our borders is vital to America's future and that a politically illiterate citizenry is a standing invitation to demagoguery. As time goes by I will add content and links specifically designed as learning aids for college students and teaching aids for college instructors. Suggestions and questions from both students and teachers are welcome.

Books do not just happen. Writing a book is hard work, but the actual writing is only part of the process—the tip of the iceberg, as it were. What the reader does not see—the big invisible mass beneath the surface—is the most important part. From the research to the reviewing, editing, fact checking, proofreading, and printing, any book worthy of publication requires teamwork. As the author I accept the blame for any errors or deficiencies in this volume, but I want to share any credit with two individuals in particular: David Tatom, executive editor at Thomson Wadsworth, who first started me thinking about doing a book of this nature during a pleasant lunch at the Country Club Plaza in Kansas City several years ago, and Scott Spoolman, a fine editor who always takes whatever I give him and makes it better.

I also want to thank the following scholars for reviewing and critiquing the manuscript: Celine A. Jacquemin, St. Mary's University–San Antonio; Karl W. Ryavec, University of Massachusetts–Amherst; Mitchell P. Smith, University of Oklahoma; and Guy D. Whitten, Texas A & M University.

Any author who claims to enjoy being reviewed is either a liar or a masochist. Reviewers can be cruel, conceited, petty, and nitpicking, but the good ones are just the opposite: knowledgeable, generous, meticulous, and constructive. And they work for small compensation. Over the years I have had both the best and worst of reviewers, but I have never failed to benefit from the expertise of each and every one who put forth a sincere effort. Several reviewers made detailed page-by-page comments and offered excellent suggestions for this first edition. Rest assured that I am grateful for your efforts.

Inevitably, there are many others who have made important contributions but with whom I personally have no contact. Wherever and whoever you are, I thank you one and all.

Author's Note on Statistical Sources: The statistics used throughout this book are the most current available. The numbers for national populations, GNP, and the like are elusive and impossible for any individual researcher to verify. Wherever possible, I have crosschecked numbers using various sources (government statistics, the World Bank, various other international organizations, etc.). Where I have cited a specific source, it is for purposes of attribution only. No one can say for certain whether the statistics published by governments, including the United States government, are accurate or tell the whole story. In fact, it is this writer's opinion that they typically do not. Sources for the statistical profiles at the beginning of each of the three parts of this book are as follows: *The World Bank Atlas 2000, The World in 2005, The World in 2006, The World Almanac 2005,* and the monthly statistical abstracts ("Economic and Financial Indicators" and "Emerging Market Indicators") published at the back of each issue of *The Economist*.

EUROPE

F.Y.R.O.M - The Former Yugoslav Republic of Macedonia

SOURCE: Adapted from the University of Texas Libraries, The University of Texas at Austin.

1

The European Dilemma
Unity or Diversity?

T *he theme of this chapter is captured in the title: Europe is a paradox. On one hand, it is possible to think of Europe as a single entity—a "civilization" set apart from all the rest. On the other hand, Europe is characterized by great diversity—a hodge-podge of rival ethnic groups speaking a babble of tongues and representing a wide spectrum of distinctive cultures. Similarly, starting in the middle of the twentieth century, Europe became a proving ground for a process called* integration *aimed at creating a community in Europe (later upgraded to a* union*), but during the first half of the twentieth century Europe was the scene of two catastrophic world wars. Thus, two opposite tendencies—discord and collaboration—are clearly present in modern European history.*

The chapter asks, "What is Europe?" It begins with a brief introduction to the contemporary scene, accenting important aspects of Europe's political geography. It notes that Europe exists both as an abstraction and as a concrete reality. In the abstract, Europe can be viewed as a unit—a single geographic and cultural expression with a common body of literature, music, art, science, ethics, and religion. As a concrete reality, the history of modern Europe is the story of fragmentation, not unity—several dozen states of varying sizes and shapes organized on the principle of ethnicity or nationality (hence the term nation-states).

In the modern era Europe's ethnic diversity and political fragmentation, despite shared experiences and traditions, gave rise to vigorous competition and, not infrequently, conflict, culminating in two so-called world wars in the period 1914–1945. The role of revolutionary mass movements, messianic ideologies, and totalitarian states in shaping Europe's recent political history is also highlighted in this chapter.

After World War II, the Cold War between the United States and the Soviet Union radically redrew the political map of Europe. For more than four decades to follow, Europe was effectively cut in half, with Eastern Europe under Soviet domination and Western Europe under American patronage and protection. The chapter explores the causes and consequences of this abnormal state of affairs, noting that postwar Europe displayed two contradictory tendencies: one toward division, the other toward integration. Ironically, the east-west conflict in Europe lent credence to the need for unity on both sides of the Iron Curtain. In the East, the unity was imposed by Moscow. In the West, it was negotiated via a series of historic treaties that gave birth to the North Atlantic Treaty Organization (NATO) and the Rome Treaty (the Common Market) among others. Thus, the process of economic integration at its inception can be seen as a response to Europe's divided condition.

The Soviet Union was not postwar Europe's only nightmare, however. Europeans were all too familiar with the horrors of war in general. Thus, leading politicians and thinkers in Western Europe sought a way to break the cycle of war after 1945. The first major step came in the form of a coal and steel community among six West European states in the early 1950s. The European Union is discussed in greater depth and detail in the last two chapters of this book, but it is important to note at the outset that economic integration has been one of the major themes of European politics for more than half a century now.

The end of the Cold War brought new possibilities and challenges. Europe was once again transformed. The Soviet threat vanished overnight. Communism ceased to be a threat at home or abroad. Former communist states turned westward and it was now possible to imagine a unified Europe. But as we shall see in subsequent chapters, attempts to move in this direction have caused nationalism to resurface in many countries. And the recent attempt to win popular approval for a European constitution came to grief when voters in France and the Netherlands rejected the proposal in 2005.

Returning to the twin themes of discord and collaboration, the chapter ends with a brief discussion of sovereignty and the limits of Europe. It suggests that these limits are not exclusively (or even primarily) geographic, but also political, religious, cultural, and psychological.

Europe is the westernmost part of Eurasia, a region of many distinctive cultures, rich in history and steeped in political traditions that collectively define what it means to be European. But Europe is also a region of distinctive subregions—Latin, Germanic, and Slavic; Roman Catholic and Eastern Orthodox; Iberia, Scandinavia, and the Balkans, and so on. Thus, it is hardly surprising that Europe means different things to different people, not least to Europeans themselves, or that visualizing the political map of contemporary Europe is a little like looking at a holograph: the image changes depending entirely on the viewer's perspective.

On the most rarified level, there is a single metaphysical Europe, one that defies easy description and (by definition) cannot be fully captured in words or pictures. It is the Europe that Europeans love to claim, the abstraction they universally embrace when they contrast the way Europeans think, look, behave, or eat with the way, for example, Americans do. This abstract Europe exists only in the mind, but the mind is a powerful thing, especially when it is multiplied by 450 million.

Four hundred and fifty million: that was the approximate population of the **European Union** (EU) in the summer of 2005, one year after the accession of 10 new member states. Oddly, that mark of success pointed to the schizophrenic tendencies of contemporary Europe. On one hand, Europe is integrating into a single regionwide market. The gradual process of melding governmental powers has been going on for well over a half century with results that over time are transforming Europe and, in consequence, the global power balance.

On the other hand, there are still the two Europes of old—**Western Europe** and **Eastern Europe**—the Europe of predominantly Latin persuasion, Roman Catholicism, and the **Protestant Reformation** versus predominantly Slavic Europe, where strong currents of religious and political intolerance and autocratic rule, historically speaking, run deep and wide. Incorporating eight former communist states with centrally planned economies into the common market of the EU is, without question, a step of historic significance. But it is not going to be easy, for there are no precedents on which to draw, and it cannot be accomplished over night. The accumulated psychological, cultural, and political effects of disparate national experiences during centuries of largely separate development cannot be erased simply by enacting new laws and treaties. Nor are all states in either half of Europe members of the EU—in the west, Norway and Switzerland remain on the outside by choice; in the east, Albania, Belarus, Bulgaria, Croatia, Macedonia, Moldova, Montenegro, Romania, Russia, and Serbia all remain on the sidelines. Of these outsiders, Russia is the major potential spoiler, a geopolitical giant with temporary feet of clay but nuclear fists. (Russia's economy went into a steep decline in the decade after the collapse of the Soviet state; as we shall see later, however, the sharp rise in the price of oil and natural gas on the world market after September 11, 2001, proved to be a bonanza for Russia, which is the world's leading exporter of natural gas and the second largest oil exporter, after Saudi Arabia.)

The rapid expansion of the EU raises an even more fundamental set of questions: What is Europe? Who is European? Where does Europe end and Asia begin? It is easy to forget that Europeans share a landmass with Asians, and that Spaniards, Italians, and Norwegians live on the same extended piece of real estate as Chinese, Koreans, and Malaysians. Not to mention Turks. Indeed, whether or not to admit Turkey to the European Union is a major question facing Brussels at present, one that is proving to be controversial and potentially divisive.

Even if Europeans were to agree on where to draw a line around Europe, the boundary lines that have divided the Continent internally for centuries would still remain. These boundaries are multidimensional—cultural, economic, political, and psychological. They exist on at least two levels, national and regional—they also exist on the local level in many places (especially border areas). Nationally, Europe continues to be divided into states that are most readily identified by a dominant ethnic or national group—Britain, Denmark, France, Germany, Greece, Italy, Spain, and so on. Even the most ardent Europhile will readily concede that after a half-century of steady progress toward a single economy, Danes are no less Danish than they were before they joined the EU.

The same is true of the rest of Europe, with one possible exception—Germany. The majority of Germans are conscious of the fact that Germany's best hope of overcoming the triple stigma of World War II (the Holocaust, Nazi rule, and military aggression) and allaying any fears that history might repeat itself is to work for something larger and less threatening than the nation. That "something" is Europe.

The rest of Europe lacks Germany's lingering sense of national shame. On the contrary, evidence of persistent **nationalism** is not hard to find anywhere in Europe (even, truth to tell, in Germany). Although extreme nationalism caused alarm bells to go off in several European countries (including Germany) in the 1990s, the most common form of nationalism by far is not the militant or xenophobic variety. Rather, it is the nationalism of the British, for example, who are perennially divided over whether or not the benefits of "wider and deeper" integration within the European Union are worth the costs—above all, the loss of national control over economic and trade policy; or the French, whose enthusiasm for the EU and other European projects varies in direct proportion to France's influence; or the Poles, for whom EU membership, ironically, is a giant step toward erasing Poland's humiliating past, a tale of woe that goes back more than two centuries and includes partition, military conquest, and more than four decades of unwilling fealty to Moscow.

There is rich symbolism, and no little irony, in the fact that the EU and the bureaucracy it commands are headquartered in Brussels, the capital of Belgium (population: 10 million), a country that despite its diminutive size contains two culturally and linguistically distinct ethnic groups.* Much the same can be said of the former Czechoslovakia, which bore a striking demographic resemblance to Belgium. Like Belgium, Czechoslovakia was a very small country (about 15 million) and, also like Belgium, it was divided between two major groups—the Bohemian-Moravian (Czech) majority and the Slovaks (about 5 million).

---

*Belgium is divided between a Flemish-speaking majority closely related to the Dutch in the north and French-speaking Walloons in the south (about a third of the total population); in addition, there is a tiny German-speaking region in the far east of Belgium.

Unlike Belgium, Czechoslovakia split into two separate states, the Czech Republic and Slovakia.

The breakup of Czechoslovakia, accomplished without violence in 1992, is a useful reminder that there are two opposing tendencies playing out in contemporary Europe. One tends to unite, the other to divide.

The continuing reality of a de facto east-west divide is also important to our understanding of contemporary Europe. The Cold War is long gone and with it the so-called **Iron Curtain,** military-strategic rivalry, and mutually exclusive trade blocs, but the reality of two Europes persists. Thus, when the EU expanded in 2004, the *New York Times* noted: "The result looks dangerously like a Europe with different tiers of citizenship. Although Poland, Hungary, the Czech Republic, the Baltic states and the others will reap immediate benefits from joining a common market of 25 nations and 450 million people, their citizens will initially not enjoy the freedom to work in any member nation, a freedom enjoyed by current union residents. They will not share fully in Europe's lavish system of farm subsidies, nor receive anywhere near as much in development aid as nations like Spain and Ireland did when they joined."[1]

This two-tier arrangement reflected the simple truth that a rich Europe exists alongside a poor one and that parts of the latter would now be cautiously and gradually assimilated into the exclusive economic club created by and for the former. The average gross domestic product of the ten new EU members was less than half that of the fifteen West European members already in the club. At current growth rates it would take the Czech Republic about forty years to catch up with Western Europe and Poland would need nearly sixty years. Even Slovenia, with a considerable head start, would not catch up for more than three decades. In addition, surveys show that East Europeans generally do not live as long, smoke more, are not as happy, and have less trust in government than West Europeans. Ironically, East Europeans tend to express greater enthusiasm for Europe than West Europeans.[2]

A glimpse of the political distance separating Eastern and Western Europe appeared in the aftermath of the U.S. invasion of Iraq in 2003 when West European public opinion turned decisively against Washington—as did the governments of several key NATO countries including France, Germany, Belgium, and Turkey—while the nations and governments of Eastern Europe, with the major exception of Russia, strongly supported the American cause.* In the words

---

*NATO stands for North Atlantic Treaty Organization. Bulgaria, Estonia, Latvia, Lithuania, Romania, Slovakia and Slovenia joined NATO in 2004, bringing the total membership to 26. The other 19 members include Belgium, Canada, Czech Republic, Denmark, France, Germany, Greece, Hungary, Iceland, Italy, Luxembourg, Netherlands, Norway, Poland, Portugal, Spain, Turkey, United Kingdom, and United States.

of a noted British journalist writing in the *Economist* in November 2003, "Central Europeans want an EU in which they are respected, not one in which they are bossed around casually by top dogs such as France and Germany. President Jacques Chirac's outburst in February—when he said that the central Europeans should have 'shut up' instead of supporting United States policy on Iraq—betrayed just the patronizing and bullying attitude which the EU's future members least want to encounter in Brussels."[3]

It is true that some West European governments, most notably Italy and Spain, also sided with the United States, but it is important to remember that they did so despite overwhelming popular disapproval. In Spain, on the eve of general elections in March 2004, train-station bombings—apparently carried out by members of the al-Qaeda terrorist network—rocked Madrid, killing more than 200 people, and brought a Socialist government to power on a platform that, among other things, pledged to withdraw all Spanish troops from Iraq. In Western Europe, that left only Britain's Tony Blair and Italy's Silvio Berlusconi still actively backing American foreign policy in the Persian Gulf. President George W. Bush's high-profile visit to Italy in June 2004 provoked massive street demonstrations in Rome, thus underscoring the political hazards facing any European government seen as too friendly to the United States. Even the redoubtable Tony Blair saw his popularity plunge in the aftermath of the invasion, telling delegates to the annual Labour Party meeting in September 2004, "I know this issue [the war in Iraq] has divided the country," and admitting that many Britons believed he was "pandering to George Bush" in a cause "that's irrelevant to us."[4]

Europe's east-west split over Iraq was not a freak accident but instead reflected a difference in outlook and interests, as well as an undertow of mutual mistrust. Poles, Czechs, and Hungarians, like others in Eastern Europe, are well aware of the fact that West Europeans harbor certain prejudices against "Slavs" and that westerners tend to lump all easterners together even though Hungarians, for example, are not Slavic, Czechs are not eastern (just ask them!), and Slovenes are far better off than, say, Latvians. In general, West Europeans tend to look eastward with a certain sense of superiority. Slavic languages are foreign to West Europeans in a way that English, French, German, Dutch, Italian, and Spanish are not. Even the best-educated westerners rarely speak a Slavic language, whereas virtually all university-educated easterners speak English, French, or German, if not all three.

The source of West European condescension toward Slavs is not entirely, or even primarily, cultural. To some extent, it is a lingering aftereffect of the

Cold War, when age-old biases were reinforced by political and ideological antagonism. But it is the economic gulf that best explains the disdain Europe's rich nations have so often shown toward Europe's poor ones. Anyone who has not seen West Europeans (and Americans) happily strolling on the enchanting streets of Old Town Prague, dining in expensive restaurants that few Czechs can afford to patronize, or shopping in fine boutiques and upscale department stores that cater almost exclusively to foreigners, will have difficulty appreciating how conspicuous or humiliating the east-west income gap is to many East Europeans. By the same token, when Polish, Czech, and Hungarian tourists travel in Italy or France, for example, they frequently go in large groups, follow a tight itinerary, keep moving, sleep on the bus, take enough food for the entire trip, and buy precious little along the way. For anyone who has traveled in this way in Europe, as I have (with Czechs), it is painfully apparent that compared to Eastern Europe the middle class in Western Europe is far larger and better off.

A word is in order about the frequent conflation (and confusion) of **Central Europe** with Eastern Europe. First, they are not the same geographically although there are no boundaries drawn on any map that clearly delineate where one begins and the other ends. Indeed, the Czech capital, Prague, is actually further west than Vienna, the Austrian capital. As one eminent authority has noted, "Czechs, in particular, emphasize that historically and culturally they belong to Central Europe and not to Eastern Europe. Such classifications often have great symbolic value, speaking to deep-rooted identities of a country. Visiting Prague, I hear time and again that Eastern Europeans are people such as Bulgarians and Romanians. This is always said in a pejorative way. The implication is that Prague is an old cultural city at the center of Europe, not to be mixed up with the supposedly less cultured people living more to the east."[5] Seen in this light, the Czech rebellion in 1968 (the so-called Prague Spring) was cultural and psychological, as well as political, the daring attempt of an oppressed nation to reconnect with its collective self-image and its historical roots after two decades of obeisance to a master (Russia) from the wrong side of Europe's east-west divide.

Second, Central Europe includes Austria, Germany, Poland, Lithuania, and the former Czechoslovakia (now the Czech Republic and Slovakia), countries situated on opposite sides of the Iron Curtain during the prolonged Cold War separation. Though the **east-west divide** in Europe is real, its significance can be exaggerated. Focusing on Central Europe is a useful corrective. Historically speaking, the middle of the Continent has seen a great deal of interpenetration and interdependence.

The distinction between Central and Eastern Europe may be lost on most Greeks, Italians, and Spaniards, but it is second nature to Austrians, Czechs, Germans, Lithuanians and Poles.

Third, historical east-west patterns of migration both within Europe and between Europe and the United States reveal a significant fact, one that Americans of European ancestry will easily recognize. In the first instance, ethnic Germans are quite common throughout Eastern Europe. In the eighteenth century, for example, many land-hungry German farmers (including my paternal ancestors) settled in western Russia and the Ukraine at the invitation of Catherine the Great. Under the **Hapsburg Empire,** German was the official language of Bohemia and Moravia (currently the Czech Republic). Poles and Germans intermingled and settled on both sides of a shifting border, and Bavarians settled in large numbers in western Bohemia.

Then, between the American Civil War (1865) and World War I (1914), Central Europeans mass-migrated to the United States. Wave upon wave of Germans, Poles, Czechs, and Slovaks as well as Dutch, Greeks, Italians, Scandinavians, Irish, and others crossed the Atlantic in search of a better life in the New World. Significantly, Czechs, Slovaks, and Poles joined Germans—Central Europeans all—in coming to America. East Europeans—Bulgarians, Romanians, Russians, and Serbians—came in far smaller numbers. Many emigrants from Russia were not ethnic Russians at all, but Germans whose ancestors had been offered free land and exemption from military service to settle in Russia a century earlier and who now lacked similar incentives to stay. Large German, Czech, and Polish communities still exist in Chicago and elsewhere, and the Midwest features towns with names like Prague (Oklahoma), New Prague (Minnesota), Tabor (South Dakota), and Warsaw (Indiana and Illinois).

Finally, many Central Europeans feel they have the right to rejoin the West. They argue that had it not been for Soviet domination after World War II, they would have developed right alongside the West Europeans. After all, they point out, Western Europe received a great deal of Marshall Plan aid from the United States, which Stalin forbade the Central Europeans to accept.

In sum, despite the end of the Cold War, the emergence of a **single market** and the creation of a **euro zone,** and the EU's great leap eastward, Europe today still comprises many regions, nations, cultures, and languages, even as it is rapidly changing, integrating, and redefining itself. In other words, the new Europe has not totally eclipsed the old Europe. It remains to be seen whether the former will prove to be as resilient in the decades to follow as the latter has been over a far longer time span—one measured not in decades but centuries.

WHAT IS EUROPE? CIVILIZATION, CULTURE, AND IDENTITY

The meaning of Europe has been the subject of considerable philosophical and literary interest for a long time: What is Europe? One simple answer is that Europeans innately know what it is and that try as they might, non-Europeans will never understand. This answer begs the question, of course, and sounds a lot like a copout. If Europe exists in reality and not just in the imagination, it must have certain definable characteristics, dimensions, and features common to the whole. Indeed, it does. Apart from geography (Europe is often called the "Continent," as though there were only one), Europeans share a religious heritage, namely, **Christianity.** True, Europe is split one way between **Roman Catholic** and Protestant branches and another between the Roman and **Eastern Orthodox** traditions, but the vast majority of Europeans share a Christian heritage. The at times acrimonious debate over whether or not to include mention of God or Christianity in the preamble to the ill-fated EU constitution illustrates the continuing political importance of religiously rooted values in the political life of Europe. The fact that such mention was ultimately left out illustrates the tension in contemporary Europe between old values and new ones, between secular and religious elements in society, and between conservative (right-wing) and socialist (left-wing) tendencies.[6]

Even so, the legacy of a common religious heritage is plainly visible across the landscape of Europe: everywhere the first signs of human habitation on the horizon are the spires of the great centuries-old cathedrals that dominate the town squares. By the architecture alone, there is no mistaking the region or the religion of the people who live there.

Stepping inside a cathedral in Europe is quite different from entering a typical church or synagogue in the United States. Americans are struck by the impressive dimensions of many European cathedrals, even lesser ones, but no less impressed by the artwork. Everywhere there are exquisite frescoes, statues, stained glass, and oil paintings—all of course rich in religious significance and symbolism. Go from a cathedral to a museum of art and it quickly becomes apparent even to the uninitiated that until quite recently (the late nineteenth century) most of Europe's great works of art were inspired by religious themes. Much the same can be said of Europe's most famous and lasting music. There is no question that the works of the great European composers—Bach, Beethoven, Chopin, Dvorak, Mozart, Schubert, Verdi, and many others—in a very real sense belong to Europe as a whole, not to any one nation.

Europe also shares a common social and political history, in particular the medieval institutions of **absolute monarchy** and **feudalism** based on social class, a landowning **aristocracy,** guilds, and serfdom.[7] In premodern Europe heredity, not merit, determined one's place in society; rarely did anyone rise above (or fall below) the accidents of birth, family, and social class. Male succession, the rules of inheritance (primogeniture), and knight errantry all point to the importance of gallantry, chivalry, virility, and military prowess. Joan of Arc, an anomaly in fifteenth-century Europe, was burned at the stake for heresy, but her greatest crime was crashing through the gender barrier at time when women did not take up arms. Medieval Europe was a man's world—a rich man's world, to be more precise.

On The Importance of Being First

Why did Europe take off some time around the fifteenth century, surpassing other regions and eventually colonizing much of the non-European world? There is no short answer to this question, but Providence appears to have played a prominent role—a conjunction of favorable circumstances including a temperate climate, fertile soil, an ecology favorable to agriculture, science and technology borrowed from the great civilizations that flourished in the Middle East first under the Arab-Islamic caliphates and later under the Ottoman Turks, and so on.[8]

The great seafaring explorations that proved the world was not flat and opened it up to exploitation catapulted Europe into the modern age. Social and political conditions that allowed and even encouraged the rise of a new entre-preneurial middle class with a vested interest in the free market (capitalism) helped to further accelerate the West's economic development. So, too, did the eighteenth-century philosophical revolution known as the Enlightenment, which called established beliefs about the world into question. The liberating effects of the Enlightenment on the minds, morals, and manners of Europeans created a climate conducive to invention and innovation and thus helped set the stage for the industrial revolution. For these and other reasons, Europe jumped ahead of other regions and, as a consequence, was able to develop in its own way and at its own pace.*

This "modernization from within" contrasts sharply with the externally induced social and political change that occurred in the last century or so in the Middle East, Africa, Asia, and Latin America. In the **Middle Ages** Europe was much like today's developing countries were prior to World War II (patriarchal, steeped in tradition, and dependent on agriculture, hunting, and fishing), although, unlike Latin America, Africa, and Asia, Europe as a whole was not conquered and colonized. (Spain under Moorish rule for some seven hundred years is a notable exception.) The Chinese and Ottoman empires were both ahead of medieval Europe in state organization, science and technology, economic development, and military prowess. Indeed, the Ottomans invaded Europe, reaching the outskirts of Vienna in the sixteenth century before they were finally stopped.

Nonetheless, Western Europe is a rare exception in the modern world insofar as the existing political traditions and institutions were not imposed from without. The European countries most immune to outside invasion (Britain and Scandinavia) evolved quite differently from Germany and Italy, which in turn have followed paths different from Eastern Europe and the **Balkan Peninsula.** Whereas in Britain,

---

*Some of the material here and elsewhere in this volume is adapted from my *Nations and Government: Comparative Politics in Regional Perspective,* 5th ed. (Belmont, CA: Wadsworth, 2004).

limits on monarchical authority in the form of parliamentary institutions and an independent judiciary gradually tipped the balance of power between government and society in favor of society, in Prussia (and Imperial Germany after 1871) the opposite happened. Only after the Third Reich's defeat in World War II, and then only under the watchful eye of the Allied Occupation, did West Germany embrace liberal democracy. In Russia, there was never a question of balance between government and society until the Soviet state, successor to Tsarist absolutism, collapsed in 1989. Even now, the Russian state under President Vladimir Putin dominates Russian life to a degree that would be considered intolerable in Western societies.

Feudalism and Aristocracy

Constitutional democracy never had any serious rivals in the United States. It is true that some detractors *accused* John Adams (among others) of being a monarchist, but that accusation flies in the face of all the evidence; in fairness, Adams ranks with Benjamin Franklin and George Washington as one of the heroic figures of the American Revolution.[9] By contrast, "None of the European countries has as long and continuous a history of elected representative government as the United States, although they are generally much older countries. France, as a result of its 1789 revolution, was the first European country to adopt a modern form of democracy. But that attempt ended quickly in failure. . . . Great Britain has the longest uninterrupted history of democracy. But, although some democratic notions can be traced as far back as medieval times, it took the British until the latter part of the 19th century to implement universal manhood suffrage, and female suffrage was achieved only after World War I."[10]

The twin legacy of aristocracy and feudalism is a relic of the past, but a relic that continues to cast shadows across the political landscape of Europe. It is difficult for most Americans to imagine a society locked within the confines of a rigid class structure, but in Europe that was the reality until quite recently. Europeans thus remain class conscious even though the rules have changed and upward mobility is now possible. (The main barrier today, as we shall see later, is economic rather than social or political.)

Because feudalism never existed in the New World, Americans often too easily dismiss the importance of social class in politics both at home and abroad. Thus, "in Europe, the ideas of democracy had to overcome a highly stratified feudal system in which the notion that all human beings have equal rights was alien. Even today the feudal heritage has an impact on European societies . . . [and] although the rich have lost much of their wealth because of steep taxes and other factors, many of them retain a distinct lifestyle that differentiates them from the lower strata of society. Speech patterns, for example, tend to differ from the highest to the lowest levels of European societies." In both France and England, it is still true that the way someone looks, acts and speaks are indicators of social class. And whereas all titles of nobility were abolished in the United States at the founding, "there are still people in England who are addressed as 'my lord' or 'my lady.' In Germany, some families still use the title *Graf* (count), because they stem from nobility."[11] In addition, the title "Baron" is still used in many European countries and addressing academicians as "Herr Doktor" or "Frau Doktor" or (an even higher distinction) "Herr Professor" or "Frau Professor" is still required by the rules of academic decorum in German-speaking countries.[12]

The feudal heritage, combined with the rise of absolute monarchies and the machinations of a corrupt papacy, eventually led to struggles over class and religion in Western Europe and to the rise of church-based and class-conscious political parties. By contrast, there is no feudal or aristocratic tradition in the United States and the constitutional separation of church and state has limited the role of organized religion in American politics. It is a striking fact that the socialist labor parties so common in Western Europe have no counterpart in American politics. The absence of such a party in the United States results in part from the early establishment of universal white male suffrage and a more forgiving educational system that not does bar the door to higher education and its benefits by tests administered at an early age, among other things. In Europe, with the major exception of France, the working class had to fight for the franchise, and to this end it supported political movements that persisted for decades afterward.

Another striking difference between Europe and America is that European democracies typically have many political parties rather than just two. European parties span a far wider spectrum of ideology and opinion than the two major parties in the United States. Indeed, both major parties are umbrella parties that try to appeal to the broadest possible cross-section of the electorate. Moreover, American "liberals"—essentially the backbone of the Democratic Party—would be considered either centrist or right-of-center in the European context. European political parties are more prominent but less permanent than in the United States. Also, voters tend to identify more strongly with a particular political party and are less likely to put the personality of rival candidates above party allegiance than in the United States. This difference, however, does not mean that personal leadership qualities are unimportant in Europe—witness the political careers of Margaret Thatcher and Tony Blair in the United Kingdom, Konrad Adenauer, Willy Brandt and Helmut Kohl in Germany, and Charles de Gaulle and Francois Mitterand in France, to name but a few.

From Renaissance to Revolution

One good way to gain a deeper understanding of these differences is to place contemporary European politics in historical and cultural perspective. In many ways, the story of modern Europe begins in the fourteenth century with the dawning of the Italian Renaissance.

The **Renaissance** changed Europe forever. Its earthly focus on "man as the measure of all things" represented a radical departure from the prevailing beliefs of medieval times.[13] Whereas Christianity stressed that Divine will sets the shape and course of history, the giants of the Renaissance believed in the surpassing powers of the human spirit and intellect. Although the Reformation was a time of great tumult, it revitalized Christianity and reaffirmed its dominance of the West's moral and spiritual life. Moreover, the movement Luther launched turned into a social upheaval with political ramifications that surprised and alarmed Luther himself. (Luther bitterly denounced the violent excesses of rampaging anti-papists).

The Renaissance and the Reformation together fed into powerful new intellectual, economic, and political undercurrents that emerged in the form of mercantilism, the scientific revolution, the Enlightenment, the industrial revolution, and imperialism. First we look at the role of mercantilism in modern Europe.

Mercantilism was a response to the challenge posed by Dutch maritime trading prowess in the seventeenth century. As formulated in France under Louis XI (1643–1715), it was a policy aimed at impeding or preventing the importation of Dutch products by imposing high tariffs, banning the use of third-country ships in foreign trade and commerce, and subsidizing domestic shippers and manufacturers. Mercantilism reflected the desire to promote national producers and manufacturers (an early version of the "infant industries" development strategy associated with the early stages of the industrial revolution).

In Holland, England, and France, mercantilism also provided the impetus for the acquisition of colonial empires. The instruments of this early empire-building rivalry were the great merchant companies, notably the Dutch East India Company and the English East India Company. (A similar French trade monopoly was also established later.) Thanks to broad charter authority granted by home governments, these great companies not only "conducted the business" of shipping and trading but also "exercised rights of sovereignty" in the colonies.[14]

The urge to conquer new worlds in the sixteenth and seventeenth centuries was no less evident in domestic than in international affairs. The **scientific revolution,** as this period has come to be known, was a time of tremendous intellectual vitality. Pioneers of modern science like Copernicus, Galileo, Descartes, Francis Bacon, and Isaac Newton gave new meaning to the humanistic impulses associated with the Renaissance. In little more than a century and a half, they revolutionized our understanding of the physical world and laid the foundations of the natural sciences, including physics, chemistry, biology, and astronomy. In so doing, they also laid the foundations of modernity, with all its implications for good or evil. They gave future generations the tools to conquer nature and paved the way for the **secular humanism** of today, a philosophy that stresses the potential of humankind, using scientific as well as political means, to solve social and economic problems.

Understanding the idealistic roots of democracy or socialism (or democratic socialism) in the modern world is impossible without appreciating the tremendous impact of science on the way people think, work, live, and die in the modern era. In eighteenth-century Europe, the **Enlightenment** provided a presentiment of the power of science to change how we think and live, culminating in two revolutions that rocked the old world to its foundations. This sequence of events—a revolution in ideas about the world followed by bold attempts to change it—was no mere coincidence.

As an intellectual movement, the eighteenth-century Enlightenment was a significantly new way of looking at humanity and the world, emphasizing reason over religious faith. Indeed, this period is also known as the Age of Reason. The morality linked to Enlightenment ideas and ideals was readily identifiable in the

Judeo-Christian tradition and the ethical systems of Greek and Roman antiquity: the Golden Rule of the New Testament, the Golden Mean of the Greek philosophers, the emphasis on honesty and other conventional virtues. Two elements of Roman Catholic dogma, however, were rejected. One was the key role of the holy sacraments (such as the ritual breaking of bread and drinking of wine known as Holy Communion, and the giving of last rites at the time of death) as the path to salvation; the other was the central importance of asceticism, self-deprivation, and resistance to temptation (broadly defined as worldly pleasures). In place of the notion that suffering and self-sacrifice were divinely ordained tests of faith, Enlightenment thinkers (principally the French *philosophes*) developed the doctrine of **ethical hedonism,** which held that ordinary human desires were natural and good, not things to be denied or ashamed of. The orthodox Christian teaching on the inherent evil in human beings (the doctrine of original sin) was replaced by a belief in humanity's innate goodness. The high-minded idealism that pervaded the Enlightenment's intellectual and political crosscurrents, as well as the serious call for far-reaching changes in government and society based on reason, distinguishes it from other historical periods in the modern era.

By focusing on the workings of the empirical world (fact and experience) and seeking the truth about human nature and social behavior through introspection, the **French *philosophes*** did for the social sciences what the giants of the scientific revolution did for the natural sciences. The *philosophes* developed trenchant critiques of established social values and political institutions. The overriding aim, however, was not to disparage existing customs and beliefs but rather to make the world a better place for the majority of human beings, rich and poor alike.

Politically, the *philosophes* seem surprisingly moderate (and modern) by today's standards. In general, they did not advocate anything so radical as the dismantling of the nation-state system or even the overthrow of Europe's absolute monarchs. Instead, they envisioned a new social order in which the rule of law bound rulers and ruled alike and all citizens were guaranteed equal rights. The *philosophes* did not seek economic equality or common ownership of property—indeed, they seldom called for the abolition of noble titles and ranks—but they did favor eliminating aristocratic powers and privileges.

Eighteenth-century Europe's rational thinkers did not envision a bloody transformation, nor were they preoccupied with the possibility of violent revolution. In retrospect, of course, they badly misjudged the dangers of mass movements. The first upheaval occurred in France.

The **French Revolution** of 1789 was not the inevitable result of the Enlightenment but rather the product of a complex set of interrelated circumstances, including social injustice, economic disarray, and political ineptitude. It began as a rebellion of the nobility against what this class regarded as unfair and onerous taxation imposed by King Louis XVI and metamorphosed into a popular uprising that quickly turned into the first (but by no means the last) modern Reign of Terror. The execution of Louis XVI in 1793 was a turning point in French (and European) history. Radicals called Jacobins gained control and set about creating a "republic of virtue"—a thinly veiled tyranny run by zealots in search of utopia.

The fever stage of the French Revolution did not last long: it soon gave way to a reactionary regime that rejected both popular government, which came to be equated with mob rule, and absolute monarchy rooted in heredity and privilege. Under the guise of republicanism, they set up a kind of ruling committee known as the Directory. This regime lasted about five years before giving way to the dictatorship of Napoleon Bonaparte.

The French Revolution makes for a fascinating study. For our purposes, the essential point is that this revolution, despite its ultimate failure in France, was a harbinger of things to come. Popular demands for democracy and social justice would accompany another kind of revolution, namely, the industrial revolution. This revolution would change the way work and workers were organized, what they produced, where they produced it, when, and how. And, in the process, it would transform one European society after another.

The new technologies associated with industrialization in turn facilitated the rise of liberalism in nineteenth-century Europe. Likewise, the socioeconomic transformation associated with modernization made constitutional democracy attractive to the rising commercial middle class, which would now have the political means to protect and expand its economic interests. At the same time, the factory system fostered by expanding markets and new technologies, created a new class of wage laborers, which transformed the structure of previously rural, agriculturally based, aristocratic societies, with consequences that could hardly have been imagined at the time.

The use of mechanical energy to increase labor productivity was a key feature of the **industrial revolution.** Textile manufacturing and mining were the first industrial sectors to be mechanized; virtually all others followed. One of the early social consequences was the exploitation of workers—including children—for profit; another, as Karl Marx noted, was the concentration of labor, which in time gave rise to new social forces that changed Western European politics forever.

The coming of age of coal-fueled, steam-powered machines provided the impetus for the construction of railroads and canals, revolutionizing modes of transportation and communication, and making farming far less labor intensive in the process. The mass internal migration from rural to urban settings is associated with the larger phenomenon of technological change in nineteenth-century Europe and America. Industrialization led to the rise of modern urban centers—a process that occurred in a relatively short time span, especially in the United States, Germany, Russia, and Japan. These four rising powers were to play the major roles in the unfolding drama of world politics in the twentieth century.

Today the results of the industrial revolution—the good, bad, and the ugly— are widely apparent in Europe. Urbanization and its accompanying ills have changed the landscape. Big cities, elaborate highway systems, mammoth shopping malls, a depopulated countryside, air and water pollution, massive industrial parks and power plants side by side with drab housing complexes, traffic congestion, and high crime rates—these are just a few of the economic and social consequences of the industrial revolution.

The State and Society

Along with socioeconomic changes came changes in political thinking. Three competing public philosophies—or ideologies—competed for the hearts and minds of the people in the nineteenth century (and, for the matter, still do): liberalism, socialism, and conservatism. The key issue in all three revolves around the proper relationship between the state and society. Should the state shape society or should society shape the state? Is economic prosperity more likely to result from state action or inaction? Does social justice require the state to redistribute wealth or is economic inequality desirable, natural, and inevitable?

At the time of its inception in revolutionary France, **liberalism** represented a middle way between the extreme egalitarianism of the Jacobins and the inherited wealth, power, and privilege of the old aristocratic order. It was ideally suited to the interests of the emerging middle class, for whom liberty ranked above equality in the hierarchy of political values. Politically, liberalism decried arbitrary and repressive rule, press censorship, laws conferring special privilege on hereditary aristocracies, and discrimination against individuals on the basis of race or religion. Economically, it stressed property rights and other middle-class interests.

Influenced by Adam Smith and others, nineteenth-century liberals embraced the view that free competition among nations and individuals, unrestrained by tariffs and monopolies, would inevitably produce the greatest prosperity for the largest number; that unemployment, hunger, and deprivation were nature's way of regulating population growth; and that wages are determined not by capitalists seeking to maximize profits and minimize costs but by the "iron law" of supply and demand.

Because liberalism represented rather narrow economic interests by contemporary standards, advocates of democracy and republicanism stepped forward—in England they were called radicals. And as the industrial revolution came of age, the working class also came of age. For the champions of this underclass, "bourgeois" democracy was too cautious and too compatible with capitalism. Instead, they turned to **socialism.** In so doing, they founded a movement that continues to have millions of followers in many European countries right down to the present.

There are many varieties of socialism, but—with the notable exception of social democrats—all share distaste for private ownership of the means of production (that is, "free enterprise"). Money (the object of capitalist enterprise) is viewed as the root of all evil in society. Socialism disdains the profit motive and advocates basic equality in the distribution of material goods. It takes an optimistic view of human nature, and it blames greed, envy, corruption, and crime on injustices built into the nature of capitalistic society. Remove the social causes of antisocial behavior, in this view, and domestic tranquility will surely follow.

In the United States, socialism is often erroneously equated with one of its offshoots, namely communism. Communism, however, is an extreme brand of socialism often associated with the advocacy of violent revolution. Contrary to common belief (at least in the United States), not all communists are revolutionaries. Adherents of *evolutionary* communism, for example, believe that capitalism can be defeated via free elections in which informed voters choose socialism. Indeed, something resembling that process has occurred at various times in various countries, including many in Western Europe, although the result in virtually every case has been to place more moderate Socialist parties in power rather than Communist parties per se.

While liberalism, republicanism, and socialism were vying for the allegiance of newly emerging social forces in Great Britain and on the Continent, the advocates of **conservatism** were trying to preserve traditional values and protect the old order. The most important conservative thinker was Edmund Burke (1729–1797). In his book *Reflections on the French Revolution* (1790), Burke warned that when nations discard customs, beliefs, and institutions rooted in the past in the vain hope of building a perfect society, they risk chaos and political catastrophe. No doubt the victims of the Jacobin terror would have agreed.

Against the background of the advancing industrial revolution, these crosscurrents—liberalism, socialism, and conservatism—competed for primacy in Western Europe during the nineteenth and most of the twentieth centuries. Democracy did not become the norm in Europe until the twentieth century. The existing democratic constitutions in Western Europe are not very old (see Table 1.1), and until the late twentieth century there were no liberal democracies anywhere in Eastern Europe with the exception of Czechoslovakia, which adopted a democratic constitution when it achieved independence in 1918.

As noted earlier, the political spectrum in Europe is much broader and more diversified than in the United States. The conventional American understanding of social class can be misleading when applied in the European setting. There social class has played a major role in defining ideological positions and creating political parties. To a much greater extent than in the United States, class consciousness has long been a motive force in European politics, and ideological divisions are often as important in election campaigns and outcomes as policy differences.

Culture and Identity

The focus in the preceding pages has been mainly on European civilization defined as those facets of collective historical and cultural experience that transcend political boundaries—in other words, on what Europeans have in common. But for all its commonalities, Europe has been a patchwork of warring **nation-states** since the beginning of the modern era, characterized by its divisions and disunity far more than its comity. The nation-states of Europe all represent distinct cultures with languages, manners, artistic styles, cuisine, traditional dress, and the like that set them apart from one another. Although most European countries play host to more than one culture and several are home to more than one nation, typically the dominant group defines the national culture.[15]

For good or ill, Europeans long ago learned to pay first allegiance to a single nation. Most Europeans today still express far greater love for the language and territory and symbols of the nation-state than for Europe. It is possible that the texture of European nationalism will change eventually, that it will become more a matter of cultural predilection than political allegiance, but there is little solid evidence to prove it. Tendencies toward supranationalism are still largely confined to

TABLE 1.1 Dates of Current Constitutions of EU Member States in 2004

Country	Date
Austria	1929
Belgium	1994*
Britain	(no written constitution)
Czech Republic	1992
Cyprus	1960
Denmark	1953
Estonia	1992
Finland	1919
France	1958
Germany	1949
Greece	1975
Italy	1948
Hungary	1949†
Ireland	1937
Latvia	1922‡
Lithuania	1992
Luxembourg	1868
Malta	1964
Netherlands	1815
Poland	1997
Portugal	1976
Slovakia	1992
Slovenia	1991
Spain	1978
Sweden	1975*

*The constitutions of Belgium and Sweden represent revisions of earlier democratic constitutions.
†Amended after 1989.
‡Amended in 1933 and six times after 1989.

Europe's elites; at the grass roots level, the idea of creating an "ever closer union" headquartered in Brussels still has a quite narrow appeal, as voters in France and the Netherlands showed in May 2005 (and as voters in Denmark, Ireland, Norway, Sweden, and Switzerland have shown on previous occasions in the past). Polls in the United Kingdom also consistently point to a lack of public support for a stronger and more tightly integrated European Union.

Nationalism is a homegrown product of European civilization even though it is no longer confined to Europe. Volumes have been written about nationalism.

Significantly, few scholars look with favor on the fruits of nationalism, yet there can be no doubt as to its popular appeal in the modern world. There is no denying the positive force of nationalism in mobilizing societies to face an external threat or to undertake great projects at home. But there is also no denying that the fruits of nationalism in Europe and elsewhere have more often been bitter, even deadly.

Imperialism, militarism, and **totalitarianism** were intimately associated with nationalism, starting with the Napoleonic Wars of the early nineteenth century, followed by the race for overseas colonies later in the same century, followed in turn by the rise of totalitarian movements in Russia, Italy, and Germany between the two world wars in the first half of the twentieth century, and then finally (perhaps even fatally) infecting the decolonization process after World War II.

The Turkish Question

What to do about Turkey has become an urgent political question for Europe in recent years. Europeans have misgivings about the current direction of the EU and the pace of change many see as being forced by the governments of two big EU countries (France and Germany). Popular alarm at the prospect of having to assimilate a new influx of non-European (especially Muslim) immigrants into secular Western societies with a common Christian heritage, chronically high unemployment, and continuing concerns terrorist infiltration through notoriously porous borders appear to account in no small measure for the rising public anger directed both at Brussels and national leaders who campaigned for passage of the proposed EU constitution in 2004–2005.[16]

We will discuss the dilemma Turkey presents to the European Union in greater detail later in the book. For now, suffice it to say that Turkey is a big country with a tradition of greatness (epitomized by the Ottoman empire), a Muslim population, and a history entangled with Europe's own, even though Turkey is not, as a matter of culture, religion, language, or geography, European. Thus, to bring Turkey into the European family means to open not one door, but many. Indeed, if Turkey can be reinvented as a European state, what then are the boundaries of the New Europe and, in a larger sense, what *is* Europe? Otherwise put, if Europe can be anything politicians want it to be, does it not stand in danger of losing its identify, of becoming nothing?

But Turkey is not so easily dismissed. Turkey is a charter member of the quintessential Western club of the postwar era, the North Atlantic Treaty Organization (NATO), along with twenty-five other countries, all but two of which are located in Europe. Moreover, Turkey's proximity to Europe is closer than that of the other two non-European NATO members, the United States and Canada. Hence the dilemma: to admit Turkey is to move forward but into uncharted waters; to reject Turkey is to risk moving backward into a world of national, ethnic, and religious antagonisms, rivalries, and conflicts.

EUROPE'S DARK SIDE: WAR AND TYRANNY

The second half of the nineteenth century is often called the **Age of Imperialism,** for at this time began a new wave of European colonial expansion. Expansionism was the order of the day in North America too, although the United States was engaged in carving out a continental rather than an overseas empire and the territories it annexed became states rather than colonies. Earlier in the same century, people had become disillusioned with empires and colonies, partly because of successful revolutions in the Americas against England, Spain, and Portugal. Industrialization diverted attention from external expansion in favor of internal development, and the new emphasis on free trade removed much of the rationale for global empire building. British Prime Minister Benjamin Disraeli expressed the tenor of the times in 1852. "These wretched colonies," he said, "will all be independent too in a few years and are a millstone around our necks."

Theories of Colonial Rule

As industry grew, Europe's economic and political leaders began to seek new sources of raw materials and new markets for their products. After 1870, protectionist policies came into vogue in many countries and soon a race for new colonies began. A plethora of theories defending colonial expansion were expounded. The American Admiral Alfred T. Mahan's geopolitical concepts were used to "prove" that great powers could not survive without overseas possessions. The British scientist Charles Darwin's concept of the survival of the fittest was used to "prove" that **colonialism** was in accordance with the inexorable laws of nature. The English writer Rudyard Kipling wrote about the "white man's burden" (to spread civilization to a benighted world). Even U.S. President McKinley claimed that God had spoken to him on the eve of the Spanish-American War (1898), commissioning the United States to take the Philippines and Christianize "our brown brothers."

By the end of the nineteenth century, **imperialism** had redrawn the geopolitical map of the world. Most of Asia and Africa had been colonized. Even China had lost its sovereign status: it was subjugated through a series of treaties that gave the imperialist powers special rights and prerogatives. Africa in 1914 was under the colonial sway of no fewer than seven European nations—Belgium, France, Germany, Great Britain, Italy, Portugal, and Spain. In fact, only two independent nations remained—Ethiopia and Liberia.

The Balance of Power System

Paradoxically, as Europe approached the zenith of its power, it was also reaching the end of its preeminence in world affairs. For centuries the international system had been synonymous with the European system. Since the **Treaty of Westphalia** (1648), the rulers and statesmen of Europe had recognized the existence of a **balance of power,** a system that preserved order and prevented the hegemony of any one state over the others.

This uniquely European system grew out of shared values forged over the centuries. In 1871, Edward Gibbon, author of *The Decline and Fall of the Roman Empire,* proposed "to consider Europe as one great republic, whose various inhabitants have attained almost the same level of politeness and cultivation. The balance of power will then continue to fluctuate, and the prosperity of our own or the neighboring kingdoms may be alternately exalted or depressed; but these events cannot essentially injure our general state of happiness, the system of arts, and law, and the manners which so advantageously distinguish, above the rest of mankind, the Europeans and their colonies."[17]

During the heyday of the European balance-of-power era, many of the great thinkers made implicit reference to the intellectual and moral foundations that underpinned a de facto political unity. For example, a French thinker named Fenelon, noted, "Christendom forms a kind of general republic which has its common interests, fears, and precautions." Rousseau asserted, "The nations of Europe form among themselves an invisible nation"; and the great Enlightenment philosopher of international law, Vattel, wrote, "Europe forms a political system, a body where the whole is connected by the relations and different interests of nations inhabiting this part of the world."[18] In sum, the fuel that kept "the motor of the balance of power moving," according to this thesis, "is the intellectual and moral foundation of Western civilization, the intellectual and moral climate within which the protagonists of eighteenth-century society moved and which permeated all their thought and action."[19]

Beyond a common worldview, the main features of the European balance-of-power system can be summarized as follows:

1. Numerous sovereign powers—five to ten significant state actors are present at any given time.

2. Flexible alliances—state actors are pragmatic and unencumbered by ideological baggage.

3. Limited objectives—state actors do not pursue goals that threaten the existence of other states.

4. Limited means—strategies, tactics, and armaments employed in pursuit of national interests are circumscribed by both the state of technology and moral constraints.

5. A keeper of the balance—as an island power aloof from the affairs of the Continent, Great Britain was ideally situated to play the role of "honest broker" by intervening on the Continent to prevent France or any other great power from establishing an empire that would pose a threat to the British isles.

The Demise of the Eurocentric System

Ironically, the globalization brought about by imperialism hastened the demise of this Eurocentric international system. In the years leading up to World War I, the European system showed signs of decrepitude: alliances turned rigid, an unrestrained arms race occurred, ideological divisions sharpened, and nationalism spread.[20]

This process continued relentlessly until, on the eve of World War II, the United States ranked first or second in nearly every measure of economic power, including total population (size of available labor force), urbanization, per capita levels of industrialization, iron and steel production, energy consumption, total industrial potential, and, finally, relative shares of world manufacturing.[21]

President Woodrow Wilson conceived of the **League of Nations** as an alternative to nationalism and the European balance-of-power system. Although it never worked, it prefigured the emergence of a new global system with the two rising non-European powers, the United States and Japan, joining Britain, Germany, and Russia as the major actors. Strangely, in the runup to World War II the two future superpowers, the United States and Soviet Russia, were both reluctant to confront Japan and Germany. In the aftermath of that war, Japan and Germany in defeat would cease to be independent actors and the United States would emerge in a preeminent position, rivaled only by the Soviet Union.

The Totalitarian Interlude

A dark shadow fell across the political landscape of Europe after World War I. An extreme left-wing ideology, the Marxist-Leninist form of **communism,** triumphed in Russia in 1917, and an extreme right-wing ideology, **fascism,** gained ascendancy in Italy a few years later. But it was in Germany between the two world wars that the battle lines between extremist left and right ideologies were drawn most sharply and fatefully.

In retrospect, World War I led to World War II. Following an **unconditional surrender,** Germany was forced to accept full responsibility (and liability) for the death and destruction caused by the war. In addition to this **"war guilt" clause,** the **Treaty of Versailles** also assessed heavy reparations and indemnities against Germany and called for permanent unilateral German disarmament. In the words of historian John Keegan:

> Forced to disgorge the conquests of 1870–71 in Alsace and Lorraine and to surrender to an independent Poland the historic areas of German settlement in Silesia and West Prussia, humiliated by a compulsory disarmament that reduced its army to a tiny gendarmerie, dissolved its battlefleet altogether and abolished its air force, and blackmailed by the continuation of starvation through blockade into signing a humiliating peace treaty, republican Germany came to nurture grievances stronger by far than those that had distorted its international relations and domestic politics before 1914.[22]

Although pro-democratic parties in the Weimar Republic initially enjoyed the wide support in Germany, the Versailles Treaty was an easy target for demagogues and extremists. To the extent that the Weimar government was fragmented and ineffective, it deserved much of the blame for Germany's collapsing economy in the 1920s, but the harsh peace imposed on Germany made it all too easy for xenophobes and extreme nationalists in Germany to concoct self-absolving conspiracy theories that put all the blame on "foreigners" (communists, Jews, et cetera). Thus, the punitive peace helped set the stage for the rise of Adolf Hitler's Nazi party.

In the early 1920s, hyperinflation (skyrocketing prices) left the German middle class impoverished. The worldwide stock market collapse of 1929 delivered the deathblow to Germany's faltering democracy. Foreign banks called in their loans to Germany, and a wave of protectionism brought international trade to a near standstill. Repression spread across the industrialized world, and unemployment grew to epidemic proportions. In the chaos and despair that ensued, extremism found fertile soil. Germany became a hothouse for radical ideologies, especially **National Socialism.**

National Socialism (Nazism) had much in common with other extreme right-wing (fascist) ideologies. It was ultranationalistic, glorifying the German *Volk* as a chosen people and enshrining a mythical *Volksgeist* (popular spirit) as the force that defined, united, and guided the German nation. Among its highest values were loyalty to the leader, obedience to authority, and courage in the face of danger. The **Nazis** glorified power; for true believers, violence was a virtue, and war would bring triumph rather than tragedy.

Hitler came to power legally. His Nazi party had a larger following in the early 1930s than any of its competitors. The Nazi leader was popular in part because he told the German people what they wanted to hear. For example, he attributed Germany's defeat in World War I not to German failings but to a stab in the back by Communists and Jews (he tended to equate the two). He also pandered to German prejudices, particularly anti-Semitism. Jews became a convenient scape-goat for nearly everything that was wrong with German society. In sum, National Socialism was a doctrine of hatred, prejudice, violence, and revenge.

Such dark sentiments were not confined to Germany. The roots of European fascism were in Italy, and its branches reached far and wide. Fascism triumphed in a relatively mild form in Spain in the 1930s. It also took hold in Eastern Europe; fascist regimes in Hungary, Romania, and Bulgaria collaborated with Hitler in the early stages of World War II. Moreover, even where fascism failed to gain the upper hand, its sympathizers occasionally made their presence felt. In southern France, for instance, the so-called Vichy regime collaborated with Hitler during the war. On the other side of the globe, a militaristic, expansionist, and fanatically nationalistic regime closely resembling the fascist model came to power in Japan in the 1930s.

Why did fascism arise so suddenly and virulently in both Europe and Asia between the two world wars? First, fascism's successes in the interwar period owed much to the failings of liberal democracy.[23] Second, the results of World War I, as we have seen, set the stage for Germany's attempt to redeem itself for the humiliating defeat it suffered; in Asia, China's ongoing political turmoil was an open invitation to Japanese aggression. Third, leaders in democratic countries placed too much faith in the capability of an untested international organization (the League of Nations) to maintain the peace. Fourth, the United States, the dominant power of the twentieth century, did not join the League of Nations, thus insuring that it would be ineffective as a restraint on future aggressors. Finally, the Great Depression shattered national economies, caused societies to turn inward (for example, adopting high protectionist tariffs), and created conditions in which demagoguery and political extremism thrived.

We turn now to a brief consideration of the recurrent problems of war and revolution in European history. These violent episodes form a bloodstained backdrop to the study of Europe's political experience prior to 1945.

WAR AND REVOLUTION:
AN AMBIGUOUS LEGACY

One thing is certain: war has played a major role in shaping the modern history of Western Europe. As we have seen, revolution—the domestic equivalent of war—has also been an integral part of European history during the past two centuries. (More recently, terrorism has intruded on the political scene as well.) The conclusion cannot be escaped: collective violence is a European tradition, despite its civilization.

The implications of this dark side of Europe's heritage are not obvious. Perhaps a violent history predisposes individuals or societies to violence. But this is not necessarily the case. In fact, the cataclysmic events that tore Europe asunder in the twentieth century could just as well have the opposite effect in the twenty-first century: to make succeeding generations determined not to repeat the same mistakes.

Similarly, the nations of Western Europe have firsthand experience with the burdens of imperialism and with the pitfalls of unrestrained nationalism. It may be that these lessons will be forgotten or that they were never properly learned. From the vantage point of the present, however, it appears as though Europeans, chastened by Europe's violent past, are eager to find a different pathway to the future. (It is a different story in the Balkans, as bitter ethnic conflicts in the former Yugoslavia recently demonstrated.)

World War II sealed the fate of the European system and, for a time at least, relegated the former great powers (and colonial overlords) of Europe to second-rate status. As a result of two devastating wars on the Continent, France, Germany, and Great Britain—the core countries of Western Europe—were forced to turn to the United States for succor and security. The Marshall Plan (see Chapter 2) and the North Atlantic Treaty Organization, two American postwar initiatives, symbolized the decline of Europe's core countries.

But obituaries for Western Europe were premature. The recovery of the Continent, highlighted by economic miracles in Germany and Italy, the resurgence of democratic rule, and the integration of national economies into a single trading bloc now called the European Union (formerly known as the Common Market), the collapse of Communism and the subsequent opening up of Eastern Europe to trade and investment—all these momentous developments have combined to bring into being a new economic superpower and a new dispensation.

POSTWAR EUROPE

The two world wars changed Europe by splitting it in two and changed the world by ending Europe's ascendancy and leaving the former Great Powers minus Soviet Russia dependent on the United States. The new dispensation in Europe did not completely wipe out all traces of the old Europe; indeed, the postwar Europe bore a clear—if somewhat superficial—resemblance to the prewar lines of demarcation. The most notable exceptions were in Central Europe, where Stalin grabbed part of Poland and compensated Poland with German land. Also, Germany was divided into eastern and western parts, with the Soviet Union controlling the former and the United States (along with Britain and France) controlling the latter.

The Long Winter: Cold War, Iron Curtain

Onset of the Cold War signaled a new era in European history. For the first time ever, an insuperable barrier cut one half of Europe off from the other half. This abnormal condition (what Winston Churchill famously called the Iron Curtain) came about as a result of the power vacuum in the heart of Europe in 1945 resulting from the utter devastation wrought by a half-decade of total war. Only two powers were capable of filling that vacuum: one was a democracy, the United States, and the other was a dictatorship, the Soviet Union. The United States wanted to rehabilitate Europe; the Soviet Union, it was feared, wanted to dominate it. The American people wanted nothing more than to "bring the boys back home" in 1945, with the result that a rapid demobilization occurred; the Soviet Union did not demobilize because Stalin, as the head of a totalitarian state, had long ago silenced all opposition and did not have to contend with public opinion. That Soviet advantage was offset, however, by one of even greater importance on the American side. The United States alone emerged from World War II with its economy intact. Indeed, the American economy dwarfed its Soviet counterpart and placed the United States in a position of economic and diplomatic dominance on the world stage (see Table 1.2). Except in the realm of conventional military strength ("troops on the ground") in Europe, the Soviet Union would not be a true rival of the United States for more than a decade.

We cannot retrace the history of the Cold War in detail in this slender volume. Suffice it to say that the Soviet Union acquired nuclear weapons and the technological know-how to deliver them over long distances by the end of the 1950s—sooner than American defense policy experts had expected. The Cold War moved into a new stage as the short-lived American nuclear monopoly gave way to the era of mutual deterrence in the 1960s. By this time, the North Atlantic Treaty Alliance (NATO) established in 1949 to counter the Soviet threat was matched on the other side of the Iron Curtain by the Warsaw Pact, and the Common Market, launched in 1958, had its counterpart in the Council of Mutual Economic Assistance (COMECON). In short, Europe's splitup was institutionalized on various levels—military and economic, as well as political—and seemingly permanent.

T A B L E 1.2 American Economic Dominance in 1950 (1964 US$)

	Total GNP	Per Capita GNP
United States	381 billion	2,536
USSR	126	699
United Kingdom	71	1,393 (1951)
France	50	1,172
West Germany	48	1,001
Japan	32	382
Italy	29	626 (1951)

SOURCE: Paul Kennedy, *The Rise and Fall of the Great Powers* (New York: Vintage, 1989), p. 369, n. 77.

But Europe's bipolar configuration was never balanced. Soviet military strength created a kind of façade that for a time concealed the economic inadequacies of the Stalinist model of central planning. While the economies of Western Europe, energized by the revitalizing effects of open and increasingly integrated markets, experienced strong and steady growth, the opposite was happening in Eastern Europe, where a prolonged slowdown turned into sudden stagnation in the 1980s and plunged the entire Soviet bloc into a crisis from which it did not recover.

Europe after the Cold War

Few expected the Cold War to end when it did or the way it did. No one knew exactly what it would mean for Europe or the world, but the mood of euphoria—optimism mixed with joy and celebration—was nearly universal. The Soviet state was unloved even at home. Russians never stopped loving Mother Russia, but the silent majority remained deeply divided over Stalin and his legacy, Stalinism. For East Europeans, Moscow was an oppressive Big Brother; for West Europeans, an omnipresent threat. When the Berlin Wall came down, the images of Germans dancing in the streets flashed across television screens around the world and captured the spirit of the moment.

But when the big party was over and the new day in Europe dawned, there were many urgent questions to be answered. Would the breakup of the Soviet Union be peaceful or violent? Would strategic nuclear weapons from the vast Soviet arsenal remain in the hands of newly independent states such as Ukraine and Kazakhstan? Should the former communist states of Eastern Europe be invited to join NATO and the EU? Would Russia allow them to join? Was NATO still relevant or could it be safely disbanded now that the Soviet Union had self-destructed? And so on. How and when these questions were answered would determine the shape of the new Europe.

Nonetheless, the prospects opening up before Europe could hardly have been brighter or more exciting. For five decades, from 1939 to 1989, Europe had been

TABLE 1.3 The European Balance of Power

	Potential Power in 2005		Actual Power in 2001*	
	GNP (US$)	Population	Army size	Nuclear weapons
United Kingdom	2.35	61 million	113,900	185
France	2.22	61 million	150,809	470
Germany	2.93	83 million	211,800	0
Italy	1.83	58 million	137,349	0
Russia	0.62	143 million	321,000	10,000

* The size of the active-duty armed forces of France, Germany, and Italy decreased significantly after 2000 as the governments of these countries faced chronic budget deficits.

SOURCE: GNP and population estimates are in *The World in 2005* (an annual publication of *The Economist*), pp. 88–90. Figures on army size are in IISS, *The Military Balance, 2001/2002;* see also, Andrew Cordesman, "Western Military Balance and Defense Efforts," CSIS, January 2002, pp. 22–24. Numbers for nuclear weapons in national arsenals are found in Robert S. Norris and William M. Arkin, "French and British Nuclear Forces, 2000," *Bulletin of Atomic Scientists,* vol. 56, no. 5 (September–October, 2000), pp. 69–71; and Norris and Arkin, "Russian Nuclear Forces, 2000," pp. 70–71.

at war—first hot, then cold. Then came the revolutions of 1989, ending communist rule in Eastern Europe. (In the Soviet Union, Mikhail Gorbachev, the reform-minded Kremlin boss who had started the ball rolling, managed to hang on a little longer). Suddenly the unthinkable became thinkable. There was, first of all, the possibility of becoming whole again. Germany's astonishingly rapid reunion paved the way and set the pace. Indeed, after decades in the deep freeze, Europe's political landscape was changing by the day. Second, the end of the ideological rivalry between the superpowers—between "capitalism" and "communism"—meant that the nuclear sword of Damocles dangling so menacingly over Europe was at long last safely sheathed. Remarkably, even though nuclear weapons continue to exist in large numbers in Europe (see Table 1.3), the sense of threat associated with these horrific weapons has virtually disappeared.

Third, the fading away of the Soviet threat brought a dramatic lessening of European diplomatic and military dependency on America. Economically, the European Union's Big Four (Britain, France, Germany, and Italy) dwarfed Russia in the 1990s. What is surprising, however, is that except for nuclear weapons the Big Four also overmatched Russia *militarily*. Thus, as Western Europe had long ago achieved its economic independence, the stage now appeared to be set for a major redefinition of trans-Atlantic relations.

Finally, the end of the Cold War served to underscore the changing nature of sovereignty in the European context in two contradictory ways. On one hand, it expanded and accelerated the processes of economic integration within the European Union (as we will see in Part III of this book). On the other, it gave East European states political independence for the first time since World War II. Many West Europeans feared that admitting new states to the EU would unduly burden the existing member states; at the same time, not a few East Europeans were reluctant to surrender full sovereignty so soon after having regained it (although it is important to note that all new member states from the former

Soviet bloc overwhelmingly voted in favor of joining the EU in national referenda). When Vaclav Klaus, the often-abrasive president of the Czech Republic, voiced grave reservations about the direction the EU was heading in 2004, he was both a pariah and a prophet. But no one knew that the following year it would be voters in France and the Netherlands, not Czechs, who would vindicate him.

Sovereignty and the Nation-State

The EU's recent setbacks attest to the fact that no study of modern Europe can be complete without a close look at the idea of **sovereignty** and what it means in the context of European politics and history. Sovereignty denotes a supreme decision-making authority and is generally considered indivisible. Sovereignty is inconceivable apart from the state, defined as a population and territory under a common political authority or government. "The doctrine of sovereignty implies the decentralization of power in the community of states and legitimates the freedom of the individual state to make independent decisions."[24]

Sovereignty was not always what it is today. In fact, it did not exist as a concept until about the sixteenth century, when it arose as a defense of the monarch's sole right to rule over a given territory in opposition to the claims of local princes, the papacy, or the Holy Roman Empire. Thus, sovereignty is a *European* idea with deep roots in *European* politics. It plays a major political and legal-administrative role in the formation of the nation-state system.

It is easily forgotten today that countries like Britain, France, Germany, Italy, and Spain did not emerge full blown as nation-states. On the contrary, all were cobbled together from various provinces, duchies, principalities, and the like, often involving related but distinct population groups—that is, groups speaking different languages or dialects, displaying different folkways, adhering to different religions, and the like. The country we know today as Italy did not exist until the 1860s, and Germany only emerged as a unified state in 1871. These two "nation-states" were both forged in the fires of war and revolution; it took the resulting authoritarian states (monarchies) many years to complete the nation-building process. As in other countries (for example, Austria, Belgium, and Spain), it is doubtful whether this process was ever really completed. In any event, both Germany and Italy succumbed to demagoguery and totalitarianism in the interwar period (1919–1939). Only in abject defeat did they embrace democracy.

After September 11, 2001, there was much talk in Washington about "nation building" in places like Afghanistan and Iraq, but unfortunately no mention was made of the trials and tribulations associated with nation building in Europe, where it all began. Had decision makers in the White House bothered to check, they would have found that Europe's own experience with nation building was a rather long and bloody process. Only at the end of the Thirty Years' War (1618–1648) was the doctrine of sovereignty accepted as a legal and political fact by the signatories to the Treaty of Westphalia. Thereafter, the nation-state became almost synonymous with modernity (as in the familiar phrase "modern nation-state system"); more important, it also became the basic unit of political organization, for good or ill, first in Europe and eventually the entire world.

That the rise of the **nation-state system** coincides with Europe's rise to preeminence on the world stage is no mere coincidence. European dynamism was no doubt spurred in part by the Great Powers' felt need to compete with each other. This competition assumed many forms, including mercantilism, royal patronage of the arts and sciences, espionage, alliances, arms races, war, and imperialism (the race for overseas colonies). However, competition in Europe's classical multipolar balance of power system did not preclude cooperation, especially (but by no means) exclusively in the realm of international trade and finance. Peace treaties were hardly less common than acts of war in old Europe, and there was even an attempt to create a kind of international organization (the Concert of Europe) after the Napoleonic Wars in 1815. In addition, the German *Zollverein* (1819–1844), a customs union, can be viewed as a precursor of the Rome Treaty (1957) establishing the six-member European Economic Community (EEC) that we know today as the EU.

In sum, the nation-state system is associated with both the best of times and the worst of times in European history. It witnessed Europe's unprecedented ascendancy in the world. Never before in world history had a single region comprising a single civilization colonized all corners of the globe. At the same time, this decentralized, anarchic system brought untold misery, violent mass revolutions, and world wars, culminating in the Stalinist reign of terror, the Holocaust, and old Europe's Armageddon in 1939–1945.

The Limits of Europe

We fast-forward now to May 1, 2004, "an extraordinary moment" in European history—namely, the admission of ten new member-states, including eight from Eastern Europe. Only time will tell exactly what it meant for Europe, much less America and the world. In the words of one noted authority, "It's been said that Europe has had a name for 2,500 years but is still in the design stage."[25] Indeed, Europe has always resisted grand designs. Philosophers, kings, popes, poets, dreamers, and demagogues have tried unsuccessfully to move Europe past the "design stage" for centuries to no avail.

Even the Roman Empire at its zenith did not conquer and control all of Europe. No European empire ever grew so large or lasted so long as the Chinese empire. No foreign invader was ever able to conquer and rule Europe—not the Mongols who invaded Ukraine (Kievan Russia) and Hungary or the Moors (Muslims) who invaded Spain or the Ottoman Turks who invaded the Balkans and Austria. After the fall of the Roman Empire, Charlemagne (771–814) came as close as any European ruler to conquering Western Europe. At its height, his Frankish Empire included all of modern-day France, most of modern-day Germany, and much of modern-day Italy. But it did not include the territories of modern-day Britain, Spain (except for a narrow strip in the northeast part of the country), southern Italy, Scandinavia, or Eastern Europe (Poland, Russia, Serbia, and the like).

In a real sense, historic Europe is the result of horticulture, not architecture. By contrast, the United States is the work of political architects—the founders—who adopted the constitution and created a government at a precise time (1787–88) and a precise place (Philadelphia). It is possible that the emerging Europe will follow a different path, one more like the American model. Indeed, what came to be called the European Community (EC) was the brainchild of several major postwar figures, most notably Jean Monnet, Robert Schuman, and Paul-Henri Spaak.[26] Thus, the EC and its offspring, the EU, existed first in the minds of European integrationists and federalists and only later did political-administrative structures bearing these names actually come into being.

No one can say with any certainty what the future holds in store for Europe, but if "the past is prologue," it is a safe bet that nationalism will not die quietly or quickly. Whether it will ever again assume the virulent forms it did in the first half of the twentieth century is one big question. Another is whether Europe will find a way to accommodate diversity (nationalism) while pursuing common goals of peace, prosperity, and stability. We explore the obstacles, opportunities, and political choices facing Europe today in the following chapters.

SUMMARY AND CONCLUSIONS

Europe is a paradox. It is a highly diverse region of proud and independent nations conscious of the values and traditions they share in common. There is no denying that Europe has changed dramatically in the six decades since World War II, and it would be foolish to assume that the historic process of European integration set in motion in the early 1950s has run its course.

Even though the Cold War is over and the "iron curtain" between Eastern and Western Europe no longer exists, there is still an east-west divide in Europe. Western Europe comprises established democracies and is home to many rich countries; Eastern Europe, still struggling to overcome the legacy of totalitarian rule, is relatively poor.

There are two opposing tendencies playing out in contemporary Europe. One tends to unite, the other to divide. Europe shares a cultural heritage including religious, artistic, legal, and political traditions that constitute what was once commonly known as "Western civilization." In theory, these basic elements provide a foundation for building supranational institutions that could eventually lead to a political union—the dream of **Eurofederalists.** But most Europeans still pay primary allegiance to a single nation, not to Europe. Although the notion of Europe remains a distant abstraction in the popular mind, the European Union is an all too concrete reality, one that is often viewed as aloof and intrusive, despite its remarkable success as an experiment in economic integration.

Turkey's bid for EU membership raises the question: Where does Europe end and Asia begin? Whether or not to admit Turkey to the EU is highly controversial because Turkey has a large population, is predominantly Muslim, and lags behind most EU countries economically, to mention but a few causes for concern.

The limits of the new Europe are largely a function of the old Europe: the nation-state remains the principal unit of political organization. The marriage of nationalism and sovereignty has been the defining feature of the international system since the middle of the seventeenth century.

Ironically, as nationalism and the nation-state were taking root in all parts of the globe, the two world wars caused European intellectuals and leaders to have serious misgivings about both. In this sense, the first half of the twentieth century taught Europe painful lessons that a number of important West European leaders tried to apply in the second half. Undeniably, the efforts of these leaders bore fruits as evidenced by the success of the European Union, which expanded from a mere six member-states in 1958 (when it was called the Common Market) to twenty-five in 2004.

Europeans themselves—voters and taxpayers—will ultimately determine the limits of the new Europe, both politically and geographically. Whether or not the EU constitution ultimately gets approved in some form, the point is clear enough: the process of building the new Europe remains hostage to the old Europe—the Europe of separate and sovereign nation-states.

As these words were written in the summer of 2005, Europe was facing a major political challenge—namely, how to keep the EU from falling apart after the proposed EU constitution, the first of its kind in Europe's history, suddenly became moot following back-to-back negative votes in France and the Netherlands. Many observers were betting against its approval from the outset but expected the British to play the role of spoiler. But it turns out that grassroots opposition to greater centralization of political authority in Brussels (that is, within the EU framework) is widespread. The reason goes to the heart of Europe's dilemma: how to achieve lasting peace and prosperity while accommodating other long-cherished values—above all, sovereignty and diversity.

KEY TERMS

absolute monarchy

Age of Imperialism

aristocracy

Balkan Peninsula

balance of power

Central Europe

Christianity

colonialism

communism

conservativism

Eastern Europe

Eastern Orthodox

east-west divide

Enlightenment

ethical hedonism

Eurofederalists

European Union

euro zone

fascism

feudalism

French *philosophes*

French Revolution

Hapsburg Empire

imperialism

industrial revolution

Iron Curtain

Judeo-Christian
   tradition

League of Nations

liberalism

mercantilism

Middle Ages

nationalism

National Socialism

nation-state

nation-state system

Nazis

Protestant Reformation

Renaissance

Roman Catholic

scientific revolution

secular humanism

single market

socialism

sovereignty

totalitarianism

Treaty of Versailles

Treaty of Westphalia

unconditional surrender

"war guilt" clause

Western Europe

SUGGESTED READINGS

Calleo, David P. *Rethinking Europe's Future* (Princeton, NJ: Princeton University Press, 2001).

Carr, Edward H. *The Twenty Years' Crisis, 1919–1939* (New York: Harper Torchbooks, 1964).

Dehio, Ludwig. *The Precarious Balance: Four Centuries of the European Power Struggle* (New York: Vintage Books, 1962).

De Rougemont, Denis. *The Meaning of Europe* (New York: Stein and Day, 1965).

Freeman, Charles. *The Closing of the Western Mind: The Rise of Faith and the Fall of Reason* (New York: Vintage Books, 2005).

Hitchcock, Alfred. *The Struggle for Europe: The Turbulent History of a Divided Continent 1945 to the Present* (New York: Alfred A. Knopf/Anchor Books, 2004).

Judt, Tony. *A Grand Illusion? An Essay on Europe* (New York: Hill and Wang, 1996).

Keegan, John. *The First World War* (New York: Vintage Books, 1998).

Kissinger, Henry A. *A World Restored: The Politics of Conservatism in a Revolutionary Age* (New York: Grosset and Dunlap, 1964).

Marx, Anthony. *Faith in Nation: Exclusionary Origins of Nationalism* (Oxford: Oxford University Press, 2003).

Pond, Elizabeth. *The Rebirth of Europe* (Washington, DC: Brookings, 2002).

Rose, Richard. *What Is Europe?* (New York: HarperCollins, 1996).

Strachan, Hew. *European Armies and the Conduct of War* (London: George Allen and Unwin, 1983).

WEB SITES

www.historyguide.org/ (see especially European history resources)

www.rferl.org/ (Radio Free Europe)

http://news.bbc.co.uk/1/hi/world/europe/default.stm (BBC Europe)

www.europedaily.com/ (Europe Daily news)

www.searcheurope.com/ (Europe search engine)

www.lib.byu.edu/~rdh/wwi/versailles.html (Versailles peace treaty)

www.journalismnet.com/europe/searchnews.htm (Search European news)

http://library.byu.edu/~rdh/eurodocs/ (primary historical documents from Western Europe)

www.angelfire.com/ma3/moderneurope/ ("modern European history website")

NOTES

1. Editorial, "Europe Lifts the Curtain," *The New York Times,* April 30, 2004, p. 26.
2. Op-Ed, Robert Lane Greene and Nigel Holmes, "Will a Bigger Europe Be a Better Europe?" *The New York Times,* April 30, 2004, p. 27.

3. Robert Cottrell, "When East Meets West: A Survey of EU Enlargement," *The Economist*, November 22, 2003, p. 4. (Note: Surveys are published as separately numbered inserts.)

4. Patrick E. Tyler, "In Party Speech, Blair Admits Political Costs of Iraq Mistakes," *The New York Times*, September 28, 2004 (electronic edition).

5. Jürg Steiner, *The European Democracies*, 4th ed. (New York; Longman, 1998), xiii.

6. The preamble to the proposed constitution simply declares that the EU draws its "inspiration from the cultural, religious and humanist inheritance of Europe, from which have developed the universal values of the inviolable and inalienable rights of the human person, democracy, equality, freedom and the rule of law." The Vatican and several Roman Catholic countries (most notably, Poland) pressed in vain for the constitution's inclusion of a specific reference to Christianity.

7. See, for example, Edward Peters, *Europe: The World of the Middle Ages* (Englewood Cliffs, NJ: Prentice-Hall, 1977).

8. See Jared Diamond, *Guns, Germs, and Steel: The Fate of Human Societies* (New York: Norton, 1997).

9. See, for example, David McCollough, *John Adams* (New York: Simon and Schuster, 2001).

10. Steiner, *European Democracies,* xv–xvi.

11. Ibid.

12. This phrase is borrowed from Kenneth Clark's award-winning "Civilization" series.

13. Bryce, Lyon, Herbert H. Rowen, and Theodore S. Hamerow, *A History of the Western World* (Skokie, IL: Rand McNally, 1969), p. 444.

14. Some Western scholars draw a distinction between European nationalism and the "exclusionary" brand of nationalism often found in Africa and Asia, but one recent book dissents. See Mark Anthony, *Faith in Nation: The Exclusionary Origins of Nationalism* (Oxford: Oxford University Press, 2003). Anthony argues that the starting point of most histories on the subject is too recent; he finds abundant evidence of exclusionary nationalism in Europe in the centuries immediately preceding the modern era.

15. Europeans are not alone in fearing the prospect of more Muslims residing in Western Europe. See, for example, Robert S. Leiken, "Europe's Angry Muslim," *Foreign Affairs,* July/August, 2005, pp. 120–135. In the author's own words, "the growing nightmare of officials at the Department of Homeland Security is passport-carrying, visa-exempt mujahideen coming from the United States' western European allies" (p. 120).

16. Edward Gibbon, *The Decline and Fall of the Roman Empire,* vol. 3 (1781) (London: Allen Lane/Penguin, 1994), p. 511.

17. Hans Morganthau and Kenneth Thompson, *Politics among Nations: The Struggle for Power and Peace,* 6th ed. (New York: Knopf, 1985), p. 235.

18. Ibid., p. 238.

19. See Ludwig Dehio, *The Precarious Balance: Four Centuries of the European Power Struggle* (New York: Vintage Books, 1962).

20. For detailed comparative data, neatly presented in a series of statistical tables, see Paul Kennedy, *The Rise and Fall of the Great Powers: Economic Change and Military Conflict from 1500 to 2000* (New York; Vintage, 1989), pp. 199–202.

21. John Keegan, *The First World War* (New York: Vintage Books, 1998), p. 424.

22. For an excellent brief analysis of the fascist phenomenon, including its causes and characteristics, by a recognized authority, see Robert O. Paxton, *The Anatomy of Fascism* (New York: Vintage Books, 2005). Paxton underscores certain key features of fascism, including the emphasis on historical grievances, hero worship (the "cult of personality"), nationalistic militancy, intolerance of opposition, and calculated use of violence as a political tool.

23. Jack C. Plano and Roy Olton, *The International Relations Dictionary,* 3rd edition (Santa Barbara, California: ABC-CLIO, 1982), p. 286.

24. See John Darton, "Union but not Unanimity, as Europe's East joins West," *The New York Times,* March 11, 2004 (electronic edition). The "noted authority" mentioned here is Timothy Garton Ash, an Oxford professor of European studies. It was Ash who described May 1, 2004, as "an extraordinary moment."

25. See, for example, Desmond Dinan, *Europe Recast: A History of European Union* (Boulder, CO: Lynne Rienner, 2004), pp. 45–82.

Established Democracies

United Kingdom
Area: 94,399 square miles
Population: 60.3 million
Population density per square mile: 620
Language(s): English, Gaelic, and Welsh
Literacy: 99%
Major religions: Anglican, Roman Catholic
Monetary unit: pound sterling
GNP: 1998 = $1.26 trillion; 2006 = $2.34 trillion (estimate)
GNP per capita: 1998 = $21,410 (PPP adjusted = $20,314); 2006 = $38,860 (estimate)
GNP growth rate: 1998 = 2.0%; 2005 (Q3) = 1.7%
Average yearly inflation rate (1990–1999): 3.0%
Recent inflation rate: 2.1% (November 2005)
Unemployment rate: 4.9% (October 2005)

France
Area: 210,038 square miles
Population: 60.2 million
Population density per square mile: 277
Language(s): French
Literacy: 99%
Monetary unit: euro (formerly the French franc)
GNP: 1998 = $1.465 trillion; 2006 = $2.8 trillion (estimate)
GNP per capita: 1998 = $24,210 (PPP adjusted: $21,214); 2006 = $37,500 (estimate)
GNP growth rate: 2006 = 2.8%
Average yearly inflation rate (1990–1999): 1.7%
Current inflation rate: 1.6% (November 2005)
Unemployment rate: 9.6% (November 2005)

Germany
Area: 137,753 square miles
Population: 81.8 million
Population density per square mile: 594
Language(s): German
Literacy: 99%
Monetary unit: euro (formerly the Deutschmark)
GNP: 1998 = $2.179 trillion; 2006 = $3.000 trillion (estimate)
GNP per capita: 1998 = $26,570 (PPP adjusted: $22,026); 2006 = $36,290 (estimate)
GNP growth rate: 1998 = 0.9%; 2006 = 2.5%
Average yearly inflation rate (1990–1998): 2.2%
Recent inflation rate: 2.1% (December 2005)
Unemployment rate: 11.2% (December 2005)

Italy

Area: 116,305 square miles
Population: 58.2 million
Population density per square mile: 506
Language(s): Italian
Literacy: 98.6%
Monetary unit: euro (formerly the Italian lira)
GNP: 1998 = $1.15 trillion; 2006 = $1.78 trillion (estimate)
GNP per capita: 1998 = $20,090 (PPP adjusted: $20,365); 2006 = $30,630 (estimate)
Average GNP growth rate: 1990–1998 = 1.0%; 2006 = 1.1%
Average yearly inflation rate (1990–1998): 4.4%
Recent inflation rate: 2.0% (December 2005)
Unemployment rate: 7.7% (June 2005)

Spain

Area: 194,897 square miles
Population: 41.1 million
Population density per square mile: 213
Language(s): Spanish (official); also Basque, Castilian, Catalan, Galician
Literacy: 97.9%
Monetary unit: euro (formerly the peseta)
GNP: 1998 = $555 billion; 2006 = $1.21 trillion (estimate)
GNP per capita: 1998 = $14,100 (PPP adjusted: $15,960); 2006 = $27,790 (estimate)
Average GNP growth rate: 1990–1998 = 3.0%; 2006 = 3.5%
Average yearly inflation rate (1990–1998): 4.2%
Recent inflation rate: 3.4% (November 2005)
Unemployment rate: 8.6% (October 2005)

2

Western Europe
Divergent Paths to the Modern State

*A*cademicians will debate whether Europe constitutes a single civilization or a group of civilizations that happen to coexist in a single geographic area, but one thing that is not debatable is the prominent place of the nation-state in modern Europe. Some nation-states have distinctive cultures that are strikingly similar in many respects to what historians, anthropologists, and archeologists call "civilizations." In this book, we will not try to resolve the debate over where cultures end and civilizations begin, but it is important to note that ethnic and cultural distinctions do not always coincide with the boundaries of nation-states on the Continent. This fact has had profound consequences.

The political map of modern Europe looks more like a giant jigsaw puzzle than the result of any rational process. The shapes of the pieces have changed many times in Europe's history. Some have disappeared or been replaced by others altogether. Wars have been fought and revolutions inspired by a rising sense of nationalism or the desire for a national revival. The separate paths these pieces of the puzzle have taken to modernity and statehood vary greatly. Each piece—each nation-state or "country"—has a different story.

The story of a country's political struggles—its revolutions, wars, constitutional crises, reform movements, economic dislocations, political collapses, and the like—is to a large extent what history is all about. Most people feel an emotional attachment to the homeland or country where they were born. The same often applies to the country's political traditions, symbols, institutions, and the like. Ironically, the history of modern Europe is inextricably intertwined with this nonrational, primordial, or emotional dimension of human affairs— the stuff of politics that flows from the heart rather than the head. But the political boundaries of Europe have never fit perfectly with its cultural or ethnic divisions.

The shape of nation-states is based in part on ethnicity, but not entirely. To some extent, the nation-state is a hypothetical construct—a convenient political myth—rather than an accurate description of the culturally, ethnically, and religiously heterogeneous political units that comprise the crowded and relatively compact piece of real estate called Europe.

In Chapter Two we look at the political geography, culture, and history of five major West European countries—the United Kingdom, France, Germany, Italy, and Spain—in considerable detail. In the process, we will identify elements common to all five (and to most other countries in Western Europe). We will also discover some surprisingly sharp contrasts that underscore Europe's great diversity—a diversity that, as we noted in Chapter One, has been both a blessing and a curse.

In Chapter One we asked the question: What is Europe? The answer can take us in many different directions or down many a blind alley. It's the kind of question a college professor might ask on a final exam but one that hardly ever comes up in polite conversation. If it did, there would probably be more politeness than conversation.

And yet it lies at the heart of any attempt to understand what is happening in Europe today. To have an idea where Europe is going we have to know where it has been. In politics as in everyday life, antecedents matter. Just as we all have our own story (or "baggage") as adults, every nation also has its own story. But Europe is a region, not a nation. Do regions also have a story?

In fact, they do. Europe is a collection of disparate nations and cultures, as we know, but it is also a civilization exhibiting patterns of thought, belief and behavior that transcend a single culture. A glance at the bookshelves next to my desk reminds me that new textbooks based on the idea of Western civilization are coming out all the time. One of these volumes is entitled *Western Civilizations*, reminding us that historians continue to debate whether modern Europe is the embodiment one civilization or many. Are ancient Mesopotamia, Egypt, Persia, Greece, Rome, Arabia, and the Ottoman Empire best thought of as separate civilizations, or are they parts of the same story?

The answer turns on a definition. Are we talking about culture or geography? If by *Western* we mean all the cultural influences that have contributed to the way Europe thinks, lives, worships, and works, then it makes sense to speak of a single Western civilization. If, on the other hand, we are talking about geography, then it probably does not. A good map is all we need to settle the question.

Or is it? If the term *Western* is synonymous with *European*, there is no possibility to admit nations or cultures outside Europe proper. But where precisely does Europe end and the Middle East or Asia begin? We will not try to answer that question here except to say that Russia and Turkey are two major nation-states on the fringes of the Continent that illustrate the difficulty of defining Europe *even in strictly geographic terms*. We will have a closer look at the European Union (EU) later, but for now it's enough to note that as these lines are written Europe is facing this very question as a matter of practical politics. Turkey has long sought EU membership, but Brussels (the seat of the European Union as well as the capital of Belgium) was reluctant to give Europe's assent—until 2004, that is, when the EU agreed to start accession talks that may eventually bring Turkey all the way into Europe (although that result is by no means guaranteed).

Clearly, Europe is changing, and in order to understand what Europe is today—or what it is likely to become tomorrow—we (Americans) will either have to change the way we think about Europe or we will reach a point where our ignorance imperils our interests and we are seen by our one-time allies as irrelevant or anachronistic or—worse still—dangerous. How *do* we think about Europe? Even if Europe is more than the sum of its parts, we obviously need to know something about the parts. But alas, there are *too many* parts to include them all in a single text or course. Just how many depends on how we define a part. The nation-state provides the most convenient way to identify the parts of Europe, but it's not the only way. Europe can also be broken down by subregions–for example, Northern Europe, Central Europe, Eastern Europe, Southern Europe, the Iberian Peninsula, and the Balkans are among the categories most frequently encountered in the literature.

But it is nation-states that still give the map of modern Europe its familiar shape and form, still largely define its essential geopolitical realities and relationships, and still exert a powerful hold over the minds of Europeans themselves. Nonetheless, the success of the European Union would appear to argue otherwise, would it not? As already noted, by 2005 no fewer than 25 countries belonged to the EU, with two more–Bulgaria and Romania–slated to join in 2007. After that, only a few Slavic countries will remain outside Europe's big tent, including several of the former Yugoslav republics (most notably Croatia and Serbia), Russia, Ukraine, and Belarus.* Membership in the European Union, however, has not obliterated nationalism anywhere in Europe; perhaps it has caused nationalism to recede somewhat, but even that is debatable, and it could be argued that at the present time it is having just the opposite effect.

We will look at the political settings of five West European democracies–the United Kingdom, France, Germany, Italy and Spain–in this chapter. Over a period spanning nearly two millennia, from the Golden Age of Athens to the early modern era, the center of gravity in Europe gradually shifted from South to North, from bounded sea to boundless ocean, and from the sun-drenched lands bathed by moist, warm sea breezes wafting off the Mediterranean to the less salubrious forests, fields, and plains on the far side of the Pyrenees, stretching

---

*Norway and Switzerland are two notable holdouts; voters in these countries gave Europe the thumbs down. Norwegians voted against EC membership in September 1971. In 1992, the Swiss voted against membership in the European Economic Area, implicitly rejecting EU membership (the Swiss government having applied for admission in May of that year.) In November 1994, Norwegians rejected EC membership for a second time.

westward from the Alps to the Atlantic and northward across the Russian steppe to the windswept ice fields of the Artic Circle. In ancient times, first Greece and then Rome constituted the dynamic core of Western civilization. Later, Spain moved to center stage, established itself as a formidable naval and mercantile power and colonized most of Central and South America (Brazil, the major exception, was colonized by Spain's Iberian neighbor and rival, Portugal). But by the sixteenth century, Britain, France, Russia, and Sweden were rapidly eclipsing Spain as Europe's most formidable **Great Powers.**

Soon Sweden's star would also fade, but Prussia would take its place and eventually metamorphose into modern Germany. In addition, during the golden age of Europe's global ascendancy—from approximately the sixteenth to the early twentieth century—the **Hapsburg dynasty** would carve out a huge empire in the borderlands of East-Central Europe, "the lands between."[1]

Ironically, Italy would play no part in the great game of international politics until its very belated resurrection in the 1860s. By this time, there were few colonial plums remaining to be picked and, in any event, Italy would be over-shadowed and outgunned by Great Powers to the north, including Austria-Hungary, France, Germany, and Russia. Moreover, the era of European land powers was giving way to a new era of sea powers, in which the United States and Japan would challenge even the mighty British navy for control over the some of world's most vital strategic chokepoints.

The fact that Italy and Spain are now important actors in the new Europe is remarkable, especially given the depths of national disgrace and moral opprobrium to which both would plunge between 1919 and 1945. The telling of that part of our story, however, will have to wait till later.

CASE STUDIES: THE UNITED KINGDOM, FRANCE, GERMANY, ITALY, AND SPAIN

In 2004, the United Kingdom ("Britain," for short), France, Germany, Italy, and Spain had a combined population of roughly 302 million (compared to about 292 million in the U.S.) and a combined GDP in the range of 9 trillion dollars—more than four-fifths of Europe's total annual GDP and second only to that of the United States globally. Together, they form the inner core of the European Union (EU), the world's largest trading bloc. Along with Russia, they are the major European military powers. The United Kingdom and France possess nuclear weapons, Germany has the third largest economy in the world (Japan ranks second behind the United States), and Italy's economy, ranked sixth in the world, still exceeds that of China in total annual output. Although Spain ranks only fifth in the EU according to population and GDP, it plays a key role as the only true medium-sized power in Western Europe (before Poland's accession in 2004, it was the only such power in the EU). As such, it is in a unique position to act as a bridge between the major powers and the minor powers.

It is important to note that the great majority of European countries are small—a fact often overlooked or underestimated. The Netherlands, with a population of 16 million (roughly the same as that of Florida), is the next largest country (behind Spain) in Western Europe. Indeed, there is only one other state in the EU—Poland—that is bigger than the Netherlands. We will see why this plethora of small states is a crucial factor in European politics at present—indeed, more than ever before in Europe's history. But lest we get ahead of our story, let us first take a closer look at all but one of contemporary Europe's major powers. (We look at the other one, Russia, in Part II.)

THE UNITED KINGDOM: HOW DARWIN'S ISLAND EVOLVED

Roughly the size of Oregon, the United Kingdom is a relatively small island nation that has played a disproportionately large role in modern European history. The distance from the northern tip of Scotland to the southern coast of England is slightly less than 600 miles. Because the country is long and narrow, the ocean is never very far away—even in the so-called Midlands the coast is less than a two-hour drive from the deepest interior (see Map 2.1).

The United Kingdom comprises four distinct regions, the ancestral homelands of the country's four major ethnic groups: England in the south, Scotland in the north, Wales in the west, and Northern Ireland, a few miles west of Scotland across the North Channel of the Irish Sea. The island on which England, Scotland, and Wales are located is known as Great Britain. More than four-fifths of the population lives in England. With a population density greater than India's and eight times that of the United States, the United Kingdom is one of the most densely populated countries in the world. England boasts more than nine hundred people per square mile, more than in Japan. Overcrowding is now a fact of life that has serious implications for politics and public policy, as we will see later in the book.

The political, financial, and cultural center of the nation is London: in this respect, few nations are more highly centralized. With a population in excess of 7 million, London, the capital, is one of the largest cities in the world. Most of the major banks, corporations, newspapers, and television networks are also located there. So, too, are the British equivalents of Wall Street, Broadway, and Hollywood. In addition, two world-famous universities—Oxford and Cambridge—are located close to London. Finally, many of the United Kingdom's most famous historical and cultural landmarks and tourist attractions—Buckingham Palace, the Tower of London, Westminster Abbey, Big Ben, the British Parliament, St. Paul's Cathedral—are found in London.

Made in England

The historical domination of the United Kingdom by England and England by London would presumably have created strong pressures toward homogenization

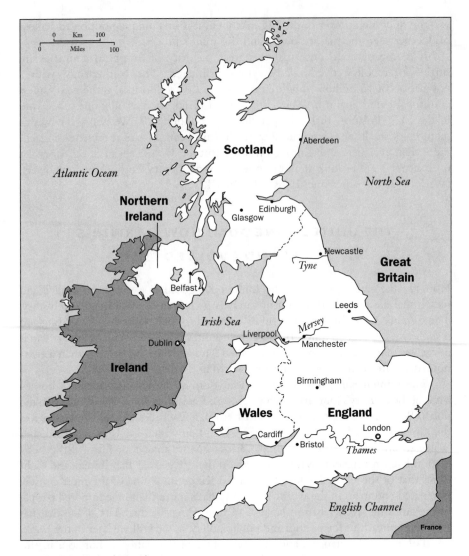

MAP 2.1 United Kingdom

and can easily give rise to the impression that the British people are, in fact, all alike; that there is an extremely high degree of social harmony; and that whatever political problems the nation might have, disunity is not one of them—all false. As noted earlier, the United Kingdom has four distinct nationality groups: the English, the Scots, the Welsh, and the Irish. Although English is spoken throughout the country and the political system is a unitary one, each region has its own separate identity, including language, history, customs, and folkways. High population density, urban crowding and the influx of immigrants from former British colonies—including Muslims from the Middle East and South Asia—have led to racial tensions and tighter restrictions on immigration, especially after the shock of

September 11, 2001, which prompted Prime Minister Tony Blair to make common cause with the United States in a so-called war on terrorism.

A Fortunate Geography

Of great importance, historically, is that England became a unified kingdom under a strong central government much earlier than most of the continental states. England was already a single kingdom before the **Norman Conquest** in 1066 (see Figure 2.1). One effect of this early unification was to give the English a more secure sense of nationality (expressed in a less fervent form of nationalism) than either the French or the Germans. Another effect is that British statesmen in modern times have been able to concentrate on taming the power of the central government rather than trying to build a state.

By contrast, France was not consolidated as a nation-state under a king until the fifteenth century, and then only after great and prolonged struggles. The French had to work long and hard at creating a state capable of overcoming the great nobles, assimilating a variety of provincial peoples, languages and cultures, and eventually imposing republican forms on conservative sections of the country that preferred the papacy and the monarchy to bourgeois politicians. Germany was unified for the first time only in 1870–71 (and reunified in 1990, having been split into two separate states in 1949).

The United Kingdom's political stability derives in part from its geography. Separated from the Continent by the **English Channel,** its internal boundaries have changed very little over the centuries. Wales has belonged to England since the thirteenth century and was formally united with England in 1535. Nonetheless, Wales has its own capital, Cardiff, and its own distinct national language, Welsh, still spoken by perhaps one-fourth of the population. Scotland was joined to England in 1707 but has its own legal, educational, and local government systems. Ireland accepted union with England in 1800, but religious differences (Ireland is Roman Catholic; England, largely Protestant or Anglican) and economic disparities made the marriage unworkable. In 1922, following years of bloody civil war, Ireland became independent, but the six northeastern counties of Ulster (Northern Ireland) remained in the United Kingdom and were granted home rule.

Historically speaking, the lack of boundary disputes and incursions by external enemies has meant that Britain has avoided the destabilizing effects of having to digest new chunks of territory, assimilate new populations, or adjust to foreign rule. Problems arising from the presence of disaffected or displaced minorities have likewise been relatively few. These circumstances created an environment conducive to the comparatively peaceful evolution of the British political system from a monarchy to a parliamentary democracy.

The English Channel, a mere twenty miles wide at its narrowest point, has played a major role in shaping British political history. For centuries it was a geographic barrier to invasion (the last successful invasion was by the Normans in the eleventh century). It also enabled England to remain aloof from many of the conflicts on the Continent. England's advantageous geopolitical position meant

1588 English naval forces defeat Spanish Armada; war between England and Spain continues until 1603

1600 Queen Elizabeth grants charter to East India Company

1607 Colony of Virginia is founded at Jamestown

1618 Outbreak of Thirty Years' War (1618–1648)

1645 Oliver Cromwell forms New Model Army; defeats Charles I, who surrenders to Scots; Scots surrender Charles I to Parliament; Charles I escapes, makes secret treaty with Scots

1648 Cromwell defeats Scots; Treaty of Westphalia ends Thirty Years' War

1649 Charles I tried and executed; England governed as a republic ("Commonwealth") until 1660

1660 Parliament restores monarchy; reign of Charles II begins

1679 Act of Habeas Corpus passed, forbidding imprisonment without trial; Parliament's Bill of Exclusion against the Roman Catholic Duke of York blocked by Charles II; Parliament dismissed; Charles II rejects petitions calling for new Parliament; petitioners become known as Whigs; Whig opponents (royalists) known as Tories

1687 James II issues Declaration of Liberty of Conscience, extends toleration to all religions

1688 England's "Glorious Revolution"; William III of Orange invited to save England from Roman Catholicism, lands in England, James II flees to France

1689 Parliament enacts Bill of Rights; establishes a constitutional monarchy; bars Roman Catholics from the throne; William III and Mary II become joint monarchs of England and Scotland (to 1694), Toleration Act grants freedom of worship to dissenters in England

1701 The Act of Settlement makes Protestant descendants of Sophia of Hanover the successors to the British throne; former King James II dies in exile in France; King William forms a grand alliance between England, Holland, and Austria to prevent the union of the Spanish and French crowns; the War of the Spanish Succession breaks out in Europe

1702 Queen Anne of England declares war on France as part of the War of the Spanish Succession

1707 The Act of Union unites the kingdoms of England and Scotland and transfers the seat of Scottish Government to London

1713 Britain and France sign the Treaty of Utrecht, concluding the War of the Spanish Succession

1719 South Sea Bubble bursts, ruining many investors who speculated with South Sea Company stock

1740 War of Austrian Succession; ends with Treaty of Aix-la-Chapelle in 1748

1756 Seven Years' War begins; Britain, allied with Prussia, declares war against France and her allies, Austria and Russia

1759 British force captures Quebec; Britain evicts France from Canada

1760 Accession of George III to the British throne

1763 Peace of Paris ends Seven Years' War

1765 Stamp Act raises taxes in American colonies in an effort to make them self-financing; new tax proves highly unpopular in colonies; repealed following year

1773 "Boston Tea Party,"—an act of colonial defiance aimed at the British East India tea monopoly

1774 Parliament passes Coercive Acts in retaliation for Boston Tea Party

1775 American War for Independence begins

1776 American colonies formally declare independence from British rule

1783 British recognize American independence at Peace of Versailles

F I G U R E 2.1 Landmarks in British History (1588–1901)

1790 Edmund Burke publishes *Reflections on the French Revolution* in defense of conservativism

1793 Outbreak of war between France and Britain

1800 Act of Union unites England and Ireland

1803 Following short-lived peace, Britain declares war against Napoleonic France

1805 Admiral Nelson destroys French and Spanish fleets at Battle of Trafalgar but is killed in the fighting

1815 Napoleon suffers final defeat; British Parliament passes protectionist Corn Laws to ban cheap imports

1821–23 Irish famine

1832 Passage of Great Reform Act, which extends vote to 500,000 people and reapportions Parliamentary following period of mass agitation and demands for reform

1833 Slavery abolished throughout the British Empire; Parliament enacts new law (called the Factory Act) prohibiting children under nine years old from working in factories and reducing working hours of women and older children

1834 A Poor Law Act is enacted, establishing workhouses for the poor

1835 Parliament passes Municipal Reform Act requiring town council members to be elected and council financial accounts to be published

1839 Supporters of People's Charter stage Chartist Riots

1846 Unpopular Corn Laws repealed

1848 Chartists lead mass demonstrations in London; revolutions in Europe; Parliament passes Public Health Act

1854–56 Crimean War; Britain and France seek to stop Russian expansion into Middle East

1870 Primary education becomes compulsory

1871 Trade union are legalized

1875 Britain purchases a controlling interest in the Suez Canal

1876 Queen Victoria declared Empress of India

1877 Britain consolidates its position of dominance in South Africa

1879 Bloody Zulu War fought in South Africa

1880–81 First Anglo-Boer War fought in South Africa

1881 Parliament passes Irish Land and Coercion Acts

1882 Britain occupies Egypt

1884 Parliament passes third Reform Act; further extends franchise

1887 The Independent Labour Party is formed

1896–98 British conquest of Sudan

1901 Death of Queen Victoria

F I G U R E 2.1 *(Continued)*

that the British crown could act as the **keeper of the balance,** choosing when and when not to get involved in the game of power politics on the Continent.

Because the threat of invasion was minimal, the British never had to maintain a large standing army on its home territory, and the military was never a serious threat to civilian rule. Instead, the nation concentrated on building a powerful naval force that enabled it to dominate the seaways in the eighteenth and nineteenth centuries. One consequence of the small-army, large-navy system was that the absolute power of the monarchy was never so absolute in England as on the Continent. Unlike armies, navies are not useful as instruments of repression or coercion at home.

A Seafaring Nation

The United Kingdom's geography goes far toward explaining its historic rise to economic prowess. A strong maritime tradition and an auspicious location at Europe's gateway to the North Atlantic placed the British in an ideal position to establish a foothold in the New World. The opening of new Atlantic trade routes made London a major international financial and commercial center. The need to protect these routes in both war and peace in turn provided the incentive to build a strong navy. Sea power made possible the growth of a colonial empire, which counteracted any temptation to lapse into the isolationism of an island fortress.

Even so, the United Kingdom did not seek to become an integral part of Europe. Instead, the British have traditionally been self-reliant and independent in both domestic and foreign affairs, viewing entanglements on the Continent with a mixture of disinterest and disdain. This tradition of aloofness helps explain why the U.K. did not join the Common Market (the present-day European Union) in 1958, when it was first formed.[2] Many British subjects continue to be **Eurosceptics** (wary of the EU) and still often question whether the benefits of membership outweigh the burdens. Thus, the opening of a railway tunnel under the English Channel (the **Chunnel**) in 1994 is important for symbolic as well as economic reasons.

Another legacy of Britain's strong maritime tradition is an attachment to the doctrine of free trade. Tariffs were steadily reduced, and by the middle of the nineteenth century, British agriculture was largely unprotected. The existence of overseas colonies, British naval supremacy, and the cost-effectiveness of oceanic transport encouraged the importation of food, and this in turn freed up domestic resources for industrialization. Today the United Kingdom is highly dependent on agricultural imports.

Not surprisingly, the British have long paid close attention to the balance of payments. Food imports must be offset by the export of manufactured goods; fluctuations in exchange rates, domestic inflation, foreign competition, and changes in consumer habits at home and abroad can all have serious political and economic ramifications in a country so deeply enmeshed in the international economy.

Absolute Monarchs Need Not Apply

British history has clearly been influenced by geography, but geography also exerts a force of its own on contemporary British politics and government. The British are not the island's original inhabitants but instead are descendents of Angles, Saxons, and Jutes from Germany. The Celts (Welsh, Scots, and Irish) were there first.

Until the eleventh century, Britain was invaded repeatedly. The Danes ruled the country from 1016 to 1042. In 1066, William the Conqueror invaded from Normandy (in what is known as the Norman Conquest), established a monarchy, and introduced the feudal system. Under this system, the nobility were granted certain rights and privileges (land entitlements, access to the royal court, and others) in exchange for loyalty to the king and the acceptance of various duties and obligations (paying taxes, defending the realm, keeping the peace). Disputes over these rights and duties were settled in a council of lords convened by the king.

In 1212 and 1213, King John summoned various clergymen, barons, knights, and other dignitaries "to speak" about the affairs of the realm. (The word "parliament" derives from the French verb *parler,* meaning, "to speak.") From these humble origins evolved the concepts of constitutionalism and parliamentary government.

In the beginning, **Parliament** was a kind of royal sounding board and advisory council rather than a check on the monarch's power and authority. In time, the right of barons to approve taxes became the right of Parliament to originate all revenue and spending bills. Along the way there were occasional battles between Parliament and the king—none more fateful than the one begun in 1629, when Charles I dissolved Parliament and proceeded to rule as a tyrant. In 1650, Oliver Cromwell led an uprising—known in history books as the **Puritan Revolution**—that overthrew the monarchy (Charles I was beheaded) and established a short-lived republic.

Religion was also a factor in the Puritan Revolution. As a result of a doctrinal dispute with the pope, the Anglican Church had replaced the Roman Catholic Church as the established religion in England more than a century earlier, but controversy over the break with Rome still raged. When James II, a Roman Catholic, tried to reopen the religious question, forcing a showdown between Parliament and the monarchy, he was deposed in a bloodless coup. Rather than abolishing the monarchy, Parliament invited the king's Protestant daughter, Mary, and her husband, William, to share the crown. By accepting, they implicitly recognized the supremacy of Parliament. Since 1689, no British monarch has challenged this constitutional principle.

In the seventeenth century, **Whigs** (liberals) and **Tories** (conservatives) evolved from factions into full-fledged political parties. Finally, the idea of cabinet rule—in which the leaders of the majority party in Parliament act as a board of directors (called the Government) to set policy, make key decisions in crisis situations, and manage the bureaucracy—emerged as an integral part of the British constitutional system. In the nineteenth century, the government gradually extended the franchise, but until 1918 males over the age of 21 were excluded unless they owned property. Women finally won the right to vote in 1918 as well, but even then only women over the age of 30 were enfranchised (lowered to 21 in 1928).

Parliamentary government is a form of indirect democracy—that is, the voters elect representatives (members of Parliament or **MPs**) who make the laws. The majority party in parliament even chooses the **prime minister,** which means that the chief executive does not have a *personal* mandate in the same sense that a directly elected president has. Traditionally, British democracy was entirely indirect—that is, based on consent via elected representatives. Unlike some parliamentary democracies, the British government did not see fit to let voters to decide an important policy issue directly until 1975, when Prime Minister Harold Wilson (Labour) kept a campaign promise to put the question of EU membership to a popular vote or referendum. (The United Kingdom had joined the EU two years earlier, but the wisdom of that decision was still being bitterly debated.) In the end, the public approved the measure by more than a two-thirds margin and British voters were given an opportunity at direct democracy on the national level for the first time in British history.

France's path to democracy is very different from the United Kingdom's—more tortuous and turbulent by far. The form of France's democracy is also quite different from the United Kingdom's, although, as we will see, it borrows heavily from the British experience.

FRANCE: IN SEARCH OF LOST GRANDEUR

About the size of Texas, France is located in a pivotal position on the Continent. Although it shares a border with six other countries (Spain, Italy, Switzerland, Germany, Luxembourg, and Belgium), France is demarcated by natural boundaries, with one fateful exception (see Map 2.2). To the north is the English Channel; to the west, the Bay of Biscay; to the southwest, the Pyrenees Mountains; to the south, the Mediterranean Sea; and to the southeast, the Alps. In the northeast, however, France and Germany have historically engaged in confrontation and conflict over disputed territories along the southern Rhine River (particularly in a resource-rich region known as the Saar) and in Alsace-Lorraine. There are no insurmountable barriers to invasion in this region: even Belgium, which poses no direct military threat, was a geostrategic liability for France before World War II because it could (and did) serve as a springboard for German armed aggression.

Internally, France has an extensive network of navigable rivers, canals, and railways, combined with a compact geography. This fact, along with natural boundaries, has contributed to a strong sense of national identity and a high degree of political and economic integration. French is the first language and Roman Catholicism is formally the religion of the great majority of the population.

Even so, the French people are far from homogenous; customs, attitudes, and opinions vary significantly from region to region. Historically, Roman civilization strongly influenced the south of France, and Germanic culture influenced the north. Economically, too, there is an important division: the south and west are rural, conservative, and relatively poor, whereas the north and east are industrially developed, growth oriented, and relatively prosperous.

France remained a nation of shopkeepers, artisans, and small farmers longer than most other Western industrial democracies. Although the actual numbers of self-employed producers and proprietors in traditional sectors of the economy have declined sharply since the 1950s, family-owned shops are still fairly common and French individualism is as vibrant as ever.

Paris: The Capital and So Much More

Paris is to France as London is to the United Kingdom. One in every six French citizens—some 10 million people—lives in Paris or its suburbs. Paris dominates the political, economic, cultural, and intellectual life of the country. It is the banking center and industrial hub. More than one-third of all commercial and financial profits are earned in Paris, which also accounts for over half of France's domestic wholesale and retail trade. Paris is also one of Europe's most popular tourist attractions, with its rich historical heritage, magnificent architecture,

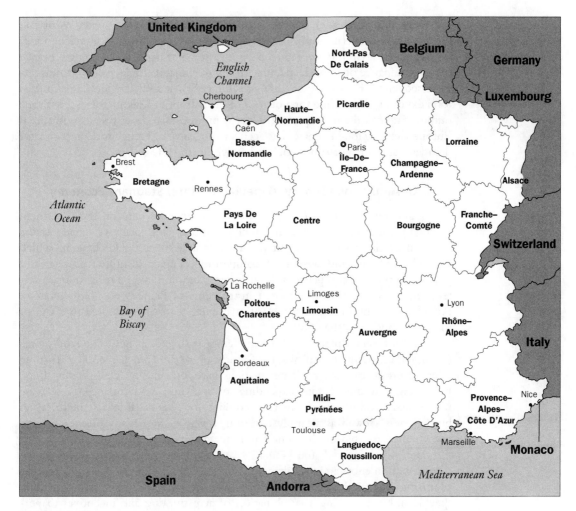

M A P 2.2 France

world-famous art museums, beautiful parks, and fine restaurants. The Louvre, the Cathedral of Nôtre-Dame, the Eiffel Tower, Montmartre, and the Champs-Élysées are only a few of the landmarks that give Paris its distinctive character.

The division between Paris and the provinces is etched deeply into French culture, society, and politics. The contrast between the high culture and hustle-bustle of Paris and the rustic and more relaxed pace of life in the provinces is made all the more significant because France remains less urban than other industrialized countries. France has only six cities with populations over 500,000, in which about one-third of the French people live; by comparison, fully one-half of the British population live in big cities. As a result, French politics continues to reflect the influence of France's traditional rural society and economy even though the latter is now mainly urban based and driven by the manufacturing, retailing and service sectors rather than farming and mining.

Despite a diversified manufacturing industry and state-initiated efforts at technological modernization, French farmers—numbering 2.5 million, or about 8 percent of the labor force—remain a powerful voice in domestic politics. France has an abundance of arable land and a variety of climates conducive to farming. As a consequence, France is not only agriculturally self-sufficient but also a major food exporter, accounting for a quarter of the European Union's total agricultural output. France's desire to protect its farm producers and buttress its position as Europe's leading food exporter has been a major *motif* of French foreign policy for decades—and a major source of tension within the EU.

An Ambiguous Legacy: Benevolent State, Stagnant Economy

Although France kept pace with industrialization elsewhere on the Continent during the nineteenth century, the French economy (and society) stagnated in the first half of the twentieth century. One reason is that, unlike Britain, which stressed free trade and welcomed competition, France instituted protectionist policies to prevent competition, both foreign and domestic. Tariffs, quotas, cartels, and subsidies were the chosen instruments of France's economic strategy. Roughly one-third of the French national budget was still allocated to direct or indirect subsidies in the 1950s.

French business practices also impeded growth and change. The family firm (along with the family farm) was the foundation of the French economy. Turning a bigger profit, capturing a larger market share, opening up new product lines, modifying consumer habits, expanding, diversifying, modernizing—these were not primary considerations. In fact, competition was regarded as unethical. A business was viewed as a family tradition, a way of life. Many businesses were owned and operated by the same family for generations, even centuries.

After World War II, the French government took the lead in directing the reconstruction effort and revitalizing the economy. Through so-called **indicative planning** and modernization commissions, the state set targets for growth in specific industries, using a combination of arm twisting and incentives to persuade the private sector to comply.

It worked a miracle—the French economic miracle, to be exact. Industrial production doubled between 1952 and 1963, and grew by another 70 percent in the next decade. By the early 1980s, the French economy had surpassed the United Kingdom's and was gaining on West Germany's. France's GNP per capita was higher than Japan's, and it was increasing faster than that of any other major Western democracy. High inflation, a recurring problem (often running in double digits between 1975 and 1984), was gradually brought under control as well, falling to a mere 1–2% in recent years.

France's economic miracle is all but forgotten now, however, as chronic double-digit unemployment has replaced chronic double-digit inflation. Meanwhile, the cost of maintaining the cradle-to-the-grave French welfare state, including rules that guarantee extraordinary job security as well as generous benefits for workers (including a 35-hour work-week!), is driving the government into debt

TABLE 2.1 **France and the Other Great Powers in 1914: A Three-Dimensional Comparison**

Country	National Income (billions of U.S. dollars)	Population (millions)	Per Capita Income (U.S. dollars)
United States	37	90	377
Great Britain	11	45	244
Germany	12	65	184
France	6	39	153
Italy	4	37	108
Japan	2	55	36

SOURCE: Paul Kennedy, *The Rise and Fall of the Great Powers* (New York: Vintage Books, 1989), p. 243.

and undermining France's ability to compete in global markets (see Chapter Three). The French economy nonetheless remains the fifth largest in the world (behind the United States, Japan, Germany, and the United Kingdom), and France continues to play a pivotal role in the world's biggest internal market—namely, the European Union. The chain-reaction urban riots that spread across the country in the fall of 2005 were a wakeup call.[3] The violence, involving mainly young, second-generation Muslims from former French colonies in North and West Africa, was a grim reminder that France faces major challenges in the coming years. But, of course, France is by no means alone in facing big challenges—much the same can be said of virtually every other post-industrial Western nation (including the United States).

Population Blues

France experienced zero population growth long before it was fashionable. Between 1860 and 1940, France's population held steady while that of surrounding countries, especially Germany, was taking off. For France this situation was particularly alarming because both its population and its per capita income had fallen far below that of Britain and France on the eve of World War I (see Table 2.1). France was the only Roman Catholic nation in the world in which population was not increasing. Between the wars, the population actually started shrinking (in part reflecting the loss of 1.5 million Frenchmen in World War I).

Most of France's population growth in recent years is the result of immigration from former French colonies in North and West Africa. Some 5 million immigrants sought refuge in France by 1990, at a time when unemployment in the nation was nearing 10 percent (it rose to around 12 percent in 1996 and remains in the double digits). The social unrest that engulfed France in October and November 2005 dramatically illustrated the destabilizing effects of this volatile mix. We take a closer look at this problem in the next chapter.

1643 Louis XIV (the "Sun King") ascends to the throne with Mazarin as his principal minister; reign marked by regal extravagance, quest for glory and continual wars

1682 Royal court moves to Versailles

1685 Louis XIV revokes the Edict of Nantes, which guaranteed political and religious right to the Huguenots (Protestants)

1715 Louis XIV dies; Louis XV accedes

1762 Publication of Rousseau's *Social Contract*

1774 Louis XVI becomes king

1778–1783 France supports the American Revolution (against archrival England)

1789 French Revolution; storming of the Bastille

1792 Louis XVI tried for treason and convicted; monarchy abolished

1793 Louis XVI and Queen Marie Antoinette are executed (by guillotine) in Paris

1794 Robespierre overthrown; Reign of Terror ends

1803–15 Napoleonic Wars

1804 Napoleon Bonaparte crowns himself Emperor of France

1814 Napoleon, defeated on the battlefield, abdicates, and is exiled to Elba; French monarchy restored; Louis XVIII crowned king (the "Bourbon Restoration"); Congress of Vienna begins task of reconstructing Europe

1815 Napoleon reenters Paris; beginning of the "100 Days"; Napoleon defeated at Waterloo; deported to St. Helena

1852 Napoleon's nephew crowned Emperor Napoleon III

1870–71 Franco-Prussian War; disastrous defeat for France; downfall of Napoleon III

1871 Third Republic established

1898–1906 Dreyfus Affair (anti-Semitism in French army)

1914–1918 France at war with Germany in World War I

1919 Versailles Treaty; France on winning side, gets back Alsace-Lorraine

1929–1939 The Depression

1939 France declares war on Germany

1940 Paris falls; collapse of Third Republic; Vichy regime (puppet government) established

1945 End of war; defeated and occupied France again come out on winning side; Fourth Republic established; General Charles de Gaulle, leader of the Free French (in exile) during the war, heads the new French government

1946–54 War of national liberation (independence) in Indochina (Vietnam)

1954–58 War of national liberation (independence) in Algeria

1958 France in crisis; rumors of a military coup; De Gaulle steps in, founds the Fifth Republic

FIGURE 2.2 Historical Landmarks: France (1643–1958)

Religion and Society   The fact that France is a predominantly Roman Catholic society today speaks volumes about French history but says little about the role of religion in contemporary France. Religion has long been at or near the center of civil strife. In the sixteenth century, French Protestants (called **Huguenots**), who wanted to bring the Reformation to France, fought church loyalists, who wanted to preserve Catholicism as the one true faith. The **Edict of Nantes** (1598) brought religious toleration and peace, but the struggle resumed in the next century, culminating in the decree of King Louis XIV that all of France would be Roman Catholic (see Figure 2.2). Religion was a factor in the **French Revolution**

(1789), but this time it was Catholics against anticlericals (opponents of the church) rather than Catholics against Protestants. Historically, the church has been a conservative force in French society, opposed to republicanism and allied with the monarch, its protector. Religious controversy in general and **anti-clericalism** in particular thus have deep roots in French political history. This fact helps explain why both the Communist and the Socialist parties have, at different times, enjoyed a large popular following in postwar France, despite the incompatibility of Marxist and Christian doctrines.

Hence the appearance of religious unity in present-day France is deceptive. The great majority of the French people are Roman Catholic (over 70 percent are baptized in the church), but most are nonpracticing. Even so, the church continues to play a significant role in French society through its extensive primary and secondary private school system. Since the early 1950s, church and state have cooperated closely in the area of education, with the state providing considerable financial support for parochial schools and the church accepting state-defined regulations and curricular standards. But in the 1980s, when the ruling Socialist party proposed further steps to integrate (and possibly absorb) the Catholic schools into the public school system, a mass protest in Paris persuaded the government to drop the idea.

A History of Triumph and Turmoil

Absolute monarchs ruled France for some eight hundred years prior to the French Revolution. This long stretch of centralized rule, which reached its zenith during the reign of Louis XIV (1643–1715), is no doubt one reason why France developed a strong sense of national identity.

But the political system degenerated under the despotic Louis XVI, and French society became increasingly polarized. A kind of representative assembly, the **Estates General,** had been in existence since the fourteenth century, and judicial bodies called *parlements* occasionally served as royal sounding boards or advisory councils. Thus the mechanisms for political accommodation were available but were little used. Unlike the British monarchy, French kings were loath to compromise with the aristocracy or the rising middle class.

Louis XVI's decision to suspend the *parlements* helped to precipitate the French Revolution, which was a watershed in European history. Its impact went far beyond France. It was the prelude to a century of turmoil, division and disunity. The short-lived First Republic soon gave way to the First Empire under Napoleon Bonaparte. Napoleon continued to pay lip service to the republican ideal and held occasional plebiscites (special issue-based elections sometimes also called referendums) to underscore his popular mandate, but in reality he established a personal dictatorship not much different from an absolute monarchy.

Prior to the 20th century, few events in European history had a greater impact in reshaping the contours of politics on the Continent than the Napoleonic wars (1803–1815). An archetypal megalomaniac, Napoleon attempted to conquer all of

---

B O X 2.1   **The Franco-Prussian War: Prelude to World War I**

The Franco-Prussian War of 1870–71 signaled the rise of German military preeminence and imperialism. The Prussian chancellor, Otto von Bismarck, wanted this war and used it to create a unified Germany. In France, Napoleon III viewed Prussia with growing alarm, especially after Prussia's victory over Austria in the Austro-Prussian War of 1866. Bismarck exploited France's fear of a German juggernaught to bring the state of southern states of Germany into a national union. Even so, it was an ill-fated France that declared war on July 19, 1870.

Having secured a pledge of neutrality from Russia, Italy, and Britain, Bismarck had good reason to be confident of another military victory. By declaring war, France had played right into Bismarck's hands: believing France to be the aggressor, the states of southern Germany joined the North German Confederation. The Germans swiftly defeated the French in a series of engagements that culminated in the decisive battle of

Sedan (September 1870), where the emperor (Napoleon III) and 100,000 French soldiers were captured. Napoleon III was deposed in a bloodless revolution. Although the German forces surrounded Paris, the French (now led by a provisional government) held out despite suffering several months of famine until February 1871.

The Franco-Prussian War led to the birth of modern Germany and the death of France's Second Empire. France was utterly humiliated. Forced to pay a billion dollar indemnity and to cede most of the territories of Alsace and Lorraine to the Germans, France plunged into civil war. Paris refused to accept the harsh terms of the peace settlement and formed the Paris Commune in defiance of the new national government. In the spring of 1871, units of the French army loyal to the government began the second siege of Paris, retaking the capital after a bloody fight.

Europe with the aim of creating a vast empire ruled from Paris. Napoleon invented a whole new system of warfare, one that mass-mobilized French society in a war fought in the name of ideals—namely, liberty, nationalism, and a potent combination of the two that came to be called national liberation. For the first time in the modern era, a universalistic secular ideology played a major role in waging a war of continental conquest. It would not be the last time.

After Napoleon's defeat in 1815, the House of Bourbon was restored to the throne. The Bourbons were said to have learned nothing and forgotten nothing. In 1848, a revolt again toppled the monarchy and led to the Second Republic, which, like the First, was short lived. Louis Napoleon, the nephew of Napoleon Bonaparte, emerged as the new popular leader; following in his uncle's footsteps, he crowned himself emperor in 1852.

The Second Empire lasted until 1870, when France was defeated by Germany in the **Franco–Prussian War** (see Box 2.1). This defeat and the election of a large number of reactionary monarchists to the National Assembly alarmed progressive elements of all persuasions. Radicals violently opposed to the monarchy and the church, perhaps influenced by Marxism, set up a rival government in the capital, the so-called **Paris Commune**. A bloody civil war ensued in which 20,000 people died during the last week of fighting alone.

The **Third Republic** came into being in 1871 and lasted until World War II—the longest-surviving political system since the French Revolution. However, divisive party politics and a weak executive impaired the workings of government and tarnished democracy's image in the eyes of many French voters.

The Paradoxes of French Politics

World War I caused great damage in France, but the Third Republic somehow survived. World War II, however, sounded its death knell. France has tried a dozen different political systems since 1789, including five republics. (We will look at France's two post–World War II republics in Chapter 4.) The contradictions of French politics over the last two centuries can be briefly summarized as follows:

- A belief in republicanism combined with a mistrust of government expressed in the insistence on a weak executive under the Third and Fourth republics

- A susceptibility to Bonapartism expressed in the occasional emergence of a "white knight on horseback" (Napoleon Bonaparte, Louis Napoleon, Georges Boulanger, and Charles de Gaulle) as well as the occasional resort to plebiscites to renew the leader's popular mandate

- A tendency toward polarization expressed in the historic dichotomies of reactionary versus revolutionary, royalist versus socialist and communist, papist versus the anticlericalist, and republican versus authoritarian

- A high level of patriotism and national pride combined with a marked tendency toward popular revolt against the symbols and substance of national authority

Compared with the United Kingdom, France has historically been less stable and cohesive. France has lacked the continuity that is the hallmark of British parliamentary rule. And France's economic policies have historically been protectionist, in contrast to the British stress on free trade and competition. Lastly, in contrast to the reserved British citizenry, the French have exhibited a capacity for impressive mass demonstrations that are quite often effective in changing government policy.

We turn now to Germany, the country that nearly conquered all of Europe twice in the first half of the twentieth century. Although utterly devastated in 1945 (at the end of WWII), Germany is again a powerhouse in Europe, but it is a different Germany than the one that twice ravaged Europe. Also, unlike France and Britain, Germany was a late arrival in the family of European nation-states. We look at the origins and development of the German nation-state next.

GERMANY: NATIONHOOD, NAZISM, AND A NEW BEGINNING

A century ago, Germany was the preeminent military power on the Continent. For forty-five years following World War II, it was divided into two distinct parts—the Federal Republic of Germany (West Germany) and the German Democratic Republic (East Germany). After a popular uprising against communist rule in East Germany and the subsequent opening of the intra-German border in 1989, the movement toward German unification proceeded rapidly and was completed in October 1990. The result was a reconstituted Germany a little bigger than Poland

M A P 2.3 Germany

and a little smaller than Montana in total area. In population, however, the new Germany, at 82 million, is easily the most populous country in the EU. Indeed, except for Russia, Germany is the largest country in Europe. In addition, German is the language of Austria and parts of Switzerland, and it is one of the three officials languages of Belgium. Finally, German is widely spoken as a second language in many parts of Central Europe, including the Czech Republic, Slovakia, and Hungary, a legacy of centuries-long Hapsburg rule.

A Crisis of Geography

Germany sits at the crossroads of Europe. Unlike the United Kingdom or France, Germany does not have natural boundaries, a fact that has shaped the nation's fate in several ways (see Map 2.3).

For centuries, whenever wars were fought in Europe, German territory was apt to be a battleground. There are at least three reasons for this: ethnic Germans predominated in Central Europe (what Germans call *Mitteleuropa*), which in the modern era was contested at various times by Sweden, Poland, Russia, France, Prussia, and the Hapsburg Empire; until late in the nineteenth century it was divided into many principalities (feudal territories ruled by princes), most of them small (Prussia was the major exception); and the absence of geographic barriers made German lands accessible to the armies of neighboring states. In the Thirty Years' War (1618–1648), many battles were fought on German soil (see Figure 2.3). This war, involving the territorial ambitions of Europe's absolute monarchs and pitting Catholics against Protestants, left Germany permanently split between Protestants (largely Lutheran) in the north and Catholics in the south. As one historian notes, "The real losers in the war were the German people. Over 300,000 had been killed in battle. Millions of civilians had died of malnutrition and disease, and wandering, undisciplined troops had robbed, burned, and looted almost at will. Most authorities believe that the population of the Empire dropped from about 21,000,000 to 13,500,000 between 1618 and 1648. Even if they exaggerate, the Thirty Years' War remains one of the most terrible in history."[4]

Having no natural boundaries, however, also meant that industrious Germans (many of whom were successful entrepreneurs) could spread out and settle in adjacent territories without being cut off from the homeland. In time, German culture became disseminated well beyond Germany proper. When Hitler seized the **Sudetenland** from Czechoslovakia in 1938, he did so on the (indisputable) grounds that most of the people living there were Germans. Hitler even sought to justify Nazi aggression by asserting Germany's ostensible need for *Lebensraum* (living space)—a patently false justification, but one that made a certain amount of sense to a nation long accustomed to migrating into neighboring areas.

Germany's geographic vulnerability influenced its history in other ways as well. If, as is often said, the best defense is a good offense, then one logical response to the danger of invasion is to go on the offensive. For hundreds of years, the fragmented Germany was unable to follow such a strategy. In the eighteenth century, however, the German state of Prussia emerged as a major power under Frederick the Great, who ruled from 1740 to 1786. Frederick enlarged Prussia considerably (he took Silesia from Austria and acquired another large chunk of territory from Poland). From this time forward, the ideal of the military state was a prominent part of the German *Weltanschauung* (worldview).

The Concept of Germany

Largely because of the struggle against the empire-hungry Napoleon, the concept of a German nation began to emerge. The **German Confederation** created at the **Congress of Vienna** in 1815 was a modest precursor of the modern German state, but rivalry between Austria and Prussia, distaste for reform, and the claims of German princes combined to block an early move toward German unification. The loose confederation, which awarded Vienna the permanent presidency, encompassed

1871 Bismarck completes drive to unify Prussia and the German kingdoms into a single nation; King Wilhelm I proclaimed Kaiser; France forced to sign humiliating treaty with Germany ending the Franco-Prussian War

1878 Treaty of Berlin divides Africa and the Balkans among the European powers for colonization

1879 Dual Alliance between Austria and Germany; two sides promise to come to each other's aid in the event of aggression

1883 Germany under Bismarck's guidance adopts first compulsory national health insurance program

1884 Bismarck implements national workers' compensation program

1885 Bismarck seizes Cameroon and Togoland

1888 Kaiser Wilhelm II at age 29 succeeds his father following untimely death of Wilhelm I

1889 Germany adopts old-age and invalidity pensions

1890 Rwanda becomes part of German East Africa

1894 The reluctant new tsar of Russia (Tsar Nicholas II) and Wilhelm II do not renew a friendship treaty, thus signaling the start of an adversary relationship

1898 Otto von Bismarck (b. 1815), former "Iron Chancellor" (1871–1890), dies; Bismarck considered creation of the German social security system as his greatest accomplishment.

1900 German Navy Law calls for massive increase in sea power

1902 Germany, Austria-Hungary, and Italy renew Triple Alliance for 12 years

1912 In November, Austria denounces Serbian gains in the Balkans; Russia and France back Serbia, Italy and Germany back Austria; in December, Germany, Austria, and Italy renew Triple Alliance for 6 years

1914 Outbreak of World War I; ignited when the German army invades Luxembourg and Belgium and Germany declares war on France in early August; Britain and Belgium declare war on Germany; U.S. proclaims neutrality; Germany declares war on Russia later in August

1918 Germany defeated, signs armistice

1919 Versailles Treaty; Germany loses colonies and lands to France and other neighbors, forced to pay reparations

1923 Adolf Hitler leads abortive coup in Munich beer hall; hyperinflation leads to economic collapse

1924 Hitler writes *Mein Kampf* in prison

1929 Global depression, mass unemployment

1933 Hitler becomes chancellor; creates monolithic state; systematic persecution of Germany's Jews escalates

1935 Germany rearmament shifts into high gear; Nuremberg Laws deprive German Jews of citizenship

1936 Berlin Olympics

1938 Annexation of Austria and Sudetenland; *Kristallnacht* (Night of Broken Glass) sees orchestrated attacks on Jews and Jewish property as well as synagogues

1943–45 Invasion of Poland triggers World War II; millions, mostly Jews but also many Gypsies, Slavs, homosexuals, and other categories slated for extermination die in Holocaust as Nazis carry out Hitler's Final Solution (genocidal mass murder) in death camps of Eastern Europe

1945 Germany defeated; divided into four zones of allied occupation

1945–46 Nuremberg war crimes trials

1949 Germany divided into two separate states; in the west the French, British, and American zones become the Federal Republic of Germany (FRG); in the east, the Soviet zone becomes the German Democratic Republic (GDR)

FIGURE 2.3 Historical Landmarks: Modern Germany 1871–1949

thirty-nine sovereign entities, running the gamut from the formidable Austrian Empire and Prussia to four free cities. For example, the diet (assembly) that was supposed to meet at Frankfurt was more a council of ambassadors than an elective assembly, and a unanimous vote was required on important matters. Also, the confederation's legislative powers were severely restricted. In practice, the league was important in German politics only on the rare occasions when Prince Metternich, the great Austrian statesman, found it convenient.

Metternich used the confederation, for example, to suppress student protests inspired by pan-German nationalism and liberalism, both despised by the ruling elites. After the assassination of a reactionary writer, the confederation was used as the vehicle to launch the draconian **Carlsbad Decrees** of 1819.[5] Although there was considerable ferment in intellectual circles, German society as a whole—still largely rural but with a growing urban-industrial labor force—remained rather more tranquil than other parts of Europe.

In Prussia, the landowning Junkers were allied with the crown. The noble *Junker* (the *j* is silent with a long *u* as in "union") class supplied most of the officers for the royal army and for the top posts in the state administration:

> Sons of burghers filled state posts in the lower echelons and shared in decision making on municipal affairs. The skillful and efficient bureaucracy of Prussia set standards that other German states sought to imitate. The peasant masses in overwhelmingly rural "Germany" seemed content to allow public business to be conducted by their social betters.[6]

Prussia was an efficient monarchy. Under the enlightened rule of Frederick William III, the state continued to support education and promote economic growth. A common tariff, established in 1818 in all its territories, lowered duties (discouraging smugglers as well as opening up the economy to competition) and allowed free entry of raw materials (a spur to industrial development). These progressive measures worked remarkably well—so well that nearly all the German states except Austria soon joined Prussia's customs union, the **Zollverein**. "By 1834 over twenty-three million Germans, living in an area larger than New York, Pennsylvania, and New England combined, were exchanging goods freely."[7] In retrospect, the Prussian experiment in economic integration can be seen as an early forerunner of the European Union.

The Zollverein was a tonic to commerce. By mid-century, manufacturing and trade were facilitated by an intricate railroad network built and subsidized mainly by Prussia. Economic integration, in turn, facilitated political unification. It is possible that the new Europe of the twenty-first century, under the impetus of the European Union, which also began as a customs union, will imitate the German experience. At the very least, there may be a parallel between the role Prussia played in the formation of the modern German state and the key role Germany is now playing in Europe.

Economic development brought social dislocations as modern factories, both foreign and domestic, displaced the old trades. Signs of popular discontent and political disturbances began to appear, rooted in a newly emerging commercial-industrial class structure as dissidents and agitators demanded what were then radical reforms, including a graduated income tax and guarantees of the right to work. In some parts of the confederation, kings and princes made limited concessions to liberalism. In Prussia, Frederick William IV, the most liberal of the Prussian monarchs, convened a united **Landtag** (a representative assembly) in 1847 but soon had second thoughts. The revolutionary turmoil that erupted throughout Europe in 1848 brought class conflict to the surface in German society. Landed gentry were pitted against the middle class (factory owners, bankers, lawyers, professors), the middle class against the workers, and peasants against liberals of all stripes. The revolts in the German states (and Austria) failed to depose the rulers, who were supported by loyal armies.

The clamor for constitutional change in Prussia and elsewhere mingled with nationalistic fervor. Talk of German unification in time became commonplace to the point where even the Prussian Hohenzollern and Austrian Hapsburg rulers paid it lip service. Ironically, dreams of a powerful and united German state continued to be associated with a desire for liberal democratic government.

From Bismarck to Hitler

Otto von Bismarck unified Germany in 1871, having gained wide popular support at home following impressive military victories over Denmark (in 1864), Austria (in 1866) and France (in 1870). The **German Empire** (also known as the **Second Reich**) was the product of triumph and the prelude to tragedy for the German people. Germany under Bismarck became the most powerful state in Europe. Over the next seventy-five years, Germany would fight and lose two world wars, undergo a tumultuous revolution, and embrace the totalitarian designs of a raving tyrant, Adolph Hitler.

Whether or not German aggression was the real cause of World War I, the allied powers placed this stigma on Germany when, as noted in Chapter One, they insisted on a "war guilt" clause as a pivotal feature of the Versailles Treaty ending that war. U.S. President Woodrow Wilson spoke for many of his contemporaries when he blamed the war on two prominent features of prewar German politics: nationalism and autocracy. He believed that one way to prevent future wars in Europe was to remake Germany (and other autocratic regimes) in the image of a parliamentary democracy. Where there are popular controls on government, Wilson theorized, war is likely to be a last resort because, if people are given a choice, they will choose not to fight and die except in self-defense.

The **Weimar Republic,** Germany's first constitutional system, was born in these inauspicious circumstances. The new German government had several marks against it from the start. First, in the mind of Germans it was forever associated with Germany's humiliating defeat in World War I. Second, it sprang full blown from the brow of Zeus, so to speak—the German people were never consulted. Third, it was un-German: Germany had no prior experience with republican government, and there was little in German history or culture to underpin any kind of democracy. Fourth, it was associated with a draconian peace that extracted onerous and punitive war reparations and indemnities from Germany. Fifth, it was powerless to protect legitimate German interests against continuing foreign encroachments (for example, Germany was required to finance an allied army of occupation in the Rhineland for fifteen years). Not surprisingly, when the economy went into a tailspin (as it did at least twice in the 1920s), popular disenchantment with the form of government opened the door to demagoguery and dictatorship.

Hitler's **Third Reich** was an aberration made possible by the impact of a worldwide depression on an already beleaguered German economy and society. Although Hitler came to power legally, he had no respect for laws and constitutions. As chancellor, he quickly obtained an enabling act from the German **Reichstag** (parliament). Thus armed with the power to rule by decree, Hitler instituted one of the most repressive and brutal tyrannies in history.

At a conference in Munich in September 1938, Hitler demanded that the Sudetenland be ceded to Germany. The following year Hitler and Stalin made an infamous deal, known as the **Molotov–Ribbentrop Pact.** Ostensibly a non-aggression pact, it was the device by which the two dictators divided up Poland and Hitler "conceded" the Baltic States and Bessarabia (now called Moldavia, at the time part of Romania) to the Soviet Union. The **Holocaust**—the genocidal murder of nearly 6 million Jews and a like number of others (including Poles, Gypsies, Magyars, and homosexuals)—stands as the most heinous symbol of Nazi totalitarian rule.

A lively academic debate about Germany's role in the outbreak of World War I continues, but there is no doubt that Germany was the aggressor in World War II. Nonetheless, the Allies (except for the Soviet Union) did not seek a punitive peace after Germany's defeat in 1945; in fact, the United States and the United Kingdom, viewing a viable Germany as a valuable future ally against Soviet military expansion, actually shielded West Germany from Soviet and French demands for huge reparations payments.

In sum, Germany's political history is much shorter than that of France and Britain, more authoritarian, more militaristic, and more aggressive (with the notable exception of Napoleonic France, which preceded the birth of modern Germany by more than half a century). Germany's geography (in the heart of Central Europe), relatively large population, and abundant natural resources needed for industrialization (especially coal and iron ore) made a policy of military expansionism possible. At the same time, Germany's geography, in contrast to Britain's, made a policy of aloofness from the affairs of the Continent infeasible.

After 1945, Germany changed dramatically, embracing democratic institutions (imposed for a second time by the victorious powers, especially the United States and the United Kingdom). However, unlike France and Britain, where democracy has deep internal roots and developed gradually over time, Germany's democracy is young, has external roots, and was created on the spot, so to speak. As we will see in the next chapter, the German people have nonetheless demonstrated a strong commitment to democracy and to the ideal of Greater Europe as opposed to the expansionist idea of Greater Germany.

ITALY: AFTER ROME AND RUIN, RESPECTABILITY

As every schoolchild knows, Italy is where the Roman Empire was born and a magnificent civilization flourished. At the pinnacle of its power, ancient Rome held dominion over the largest part of Europe ever brought under a single political authority. Modern Italy—a mere remnant of that golden age—is a boot-shaped peninsula covering an area slightly larger than Arizona and extending from the Southern Alps into the central Mediterranean Sea. The terrain is mostly rugged and mountainous, or hilly, with some plains and coastal lowland; the climate varies considerably from Alpine winters in the north to hot, dry summers in the south. The fertile Po valley accounts for over 70 percent of Italy's lowlands, which in turn constitute only about one-fifth of Italy's total land mass. Italy is strategically positioned in the middle of the Mediterranean Sea, giving it access to the rest of Europe by land and to the Middle East and North Africa by sea.

However, modern Italy has never been an important land or sea power, despite the country's considerable assets, including its strategic location, heroic past, vibrant artistic traditions, varied climates, gifted people and advanced economy. Why? We will try to answer this question in the following pages.

A Tortuous Road to Nationhood

Rome's founding in the seventh century B.C.E. to the collapse of the **Western Roman Empire** in 476 C.E. spanned more than a millennium. Significantly, the Roman Catholic Church survived the breakup of the empire intact, providing spiritual and cultural continuity wherever it had struck root and eventually becoming a major rival to temporal authority in the kingdoms of modern Europe. In Italy, however, political authority became fragmented as imperial rule gave way to feudalism. By the sixteenth century, Italy had become home to several major city-states, including the republics of Florence and Venice, the Duchy of Milan, the **Papal States** (the Vatican's precursor), among other smaller ones. This was the heyday of the Renaissance, the great flowering of the arts and literature, of Leonardo de Vinci, Michelangelo, and Niccolò Machiavelli, author of a shocking little book, **The Prince,** which is still in print and well worth reading (see Figure 2.4).

The Prince is shocking because of its remorseless political realism. Machiavelli (1469–1527) longed to see Italy united in a single sovereign state. He knew that only a wise and ruthless prince would be able to do that. Accordingly, Machiavelli set himself to the task of providing the blueprint—a kind of do-it-yourself manual for the would-be ruler of all Italy. Despite the moral teachings of the "universal Christian church" (the term *catholic* means universal), he advised the prince to give the *appearance* of honesty and morality even when lying or committing cruel acts. He argued that rulers have *no choice* but to spy on each other, to engage in plotting and intrigue, to punish or even kill opponents, and so on. To succeed in the dog-eat-dog game of politics, Machiavelli contended, the prince must constantly appear honest and upright while assiduously practicing "how not to be good."

Machiavelli also advised the prince not to keep a promise that has outlived its usefulness; to conceal his true intentions; and to cultivate the appearance of

1796 Napoleon Bonaparte conquers much of northern Italy and establishes Italian republics

1797 Pope submits to Bonaparte; uprisings against French in Verona; French enter Venice; Cisalpine Republic established in Lombardy; Venice given to Austria

1798 Roman Republic declared; Ferdinand IV enters Rome (later retaken by French); Abdication of Charles Immanuel IV of Savoy

1799 French occupation of Naples; Milan taken by Russians; Austrians enter Turin; Naples capitulates to Bourbons

1801 Napoleon occupies Milan; Kingdom of Etruria founded by Napoleon in Tuscany; Treaty of Florence between France and Naples

1802 Cisalpine Republic called Italian Republic; France annexes Piedmont

1804 Northern Italy unified as Kingdom of Italy under French rule

1805 Napoleon crowns himself King of Italy, annexes several more parts of Italy

1806 Venetia annexed to Kingdom of Italy; Joseph Bonaparte declared King of the Two Sicilies

1808 Joachim Murat becomes King of Naples; Papal States partly annexed to Kingdom of Italy

1809 Napoleon annexes Rome and Papal States to French empire

1814 Napoleon defeated; banished to Elba; Italy divided into Papal States, Austrian duchies, the Kingdom of Sardinia, and the Kingdom of the Two Sicilies

1820 Revolt in Naples

1821 Revolt in Piedmont

1831 Revolution in the Papal States; King Charles Albert becomes King of Sardinia; Young Italy Party founded by Mazzini

1845 Pius IX becomes Pope

1848 Uprisings in Palermo; constitutional edict in Naples; constitutional monarchy proclaimed in Piedmont; constitution granted in Rome, Republic proclaimed with Mazzini as head. Successful revolution in Milan; Venice proclaimed a Republic; Charles Albert [Piedmont and Sardinia] invades Lombardy; Tuscan forces invade Lombardy; Naples constitution denied; Union of Venetia and Piedmont declared, soon overthrown; Battle of Custozza, Charles Albert defeated

1849 Charles Albert abdicates in favor of Victor Emmanuel II; Sicilian revolution crushed by Naples; Austrians take Florence; Venice surrenders to Austria

1850 Cavour becomes Prime Minister in Sardinia-Piedmonte

1852 Napoleon III becomes Emperor of France

1858 Meeting of Cavour and Napoleon III

1859 War between Austria and Sardinia-Piedmont; Austria defeated by Piemontese and French; Sardinia gains Lombardy

1860 Tuscany and Emilia declare for union with Sardinia-Piedmonte; Revolution in Sicily, Garibaldi lands and is victorious; invades Italy and gains victory; enters Naples; Piemontese army under Victor Emmanuel takes over from Garibaldi; Marche and Umbria vote for annexation to Piedmont

1861 Sicily and Naples vote to join Kingdom of Italy; Kingdom of Italy proclaimed

1866 Italy joins Prussia in War against Austria; gains Venetia (Venice)

1870 Italian troops occupy Rome when French abandon city; Rome votes for union with Italy

1871 Rome made Capital of Kingdom

1912 Italy occupied Libya

1915 Although it is allied with Austria and Germany, Italy enters the war on the side of the Allies

F I G U R E 2.4 Historical Landmarks: Modern Italy 1796–1952 (*Continues*)

1922 Mussolini becomes prime minister of Italy and quickly assumes dictatorial powers

1929 The Lateran Treaty normalizes relations between Italy and the Vatican

1940 Italy enters the war, having previously formed an alliance with Nazi Germany

1943 Fascist-ruled Italy surrenders, but Germany seizes control of the country and fights the Allies until the end of the war

1946 Italians votes to abolish the monarchy and Italy becomes a republic (parliamentary democracy)

1952 Italy becomes a founding member of the European Coal and Steel Community (ECSC), which evolves into the European Union

FIGURE 2.4 (*Continued*)

generosity even while imposing painful austerities and acting out of cold-blooded self-interest. In this way, Machiavelli shifted the ethical underpinning of politics. Thus, for the true prince—one who seeks to prevail in the face of great danger and treachery, that is—generosity means giving away other people's property, while taking great care to safeguard one's own.

So it is hardly surprising that the term **Machiavellian** has come to be associated with a ruthless, amoral brand of politics. But Machiavelli did not invent the methods he prescribed. He simply systematized a set of practices that were prevalent in the governmental dealings of the city-states in sixteenth-century Italy. His grim formula for success is still widely practiced—and not only in authoritarian states. Indeed, as we will soon see, it is still practiced in Italy today even though Italians have now enjoyed well over half a century of uninterrupted republican self-rule.

It would be some three and a half centuries before Machiavelli's dream of a unified Italy would become a reality. Italy would long remain fragmented while the rest of Europe was being transmuted into a patchwork of nation-states under the consolidated rule of absolute monarchs whose legitimacy rested on two main pillars: the dynastic principle of succession and divine right. The first meant that the eldest male heir of the monarch would *automatically* inherit the crown upon the monarch's death. When there was no adult male heir, the king's eldest daughter at times ascended the throne; England's Queen Elizabeth I, Russia's Catherine the Great, and Austria's Maria Teresa are among the great female sovereigns of modern Europe. The second pillar meant the monarch claimed to be God's instrument on earth, an extraordinary assertion that quite obviously required the Pope's assent.

This cozy relationship between church and state is one key to understanding European politics in the age of royal absolutism dating from the late fifteenth century. The fact that the Pope resided in Rome gave the Papal States (and the neighboring city-states of present-day Italy) a political significance in the life of modern Europe far greater than they would otherwise have had.

Absolutism gradually gave way to constitutionalism on the Continent, but it was not finally extinguished until World War I (1914–1918) brought about the collapse of the Austro-Hungarian and Russian empires. By that time, Italy had had roughly five decades to adjust to independence and unification—two sides of the same coin in Italy's modern nation-building experience.

The reasons for Italy's belated unification are complex and beyond the scope of this book, but Italy's longtime lack of *independence* can be traced to two main causes: its disunity—fragmented as it was into five major city-states at a time when mighty nation-states were emerging in the rest of Europe—and the key role of the Papacy in European politics. From 1559 to 1704, the Pope was only too happy to have Spain as the dominant political force on the peninsula, for two main reasons. First, the Spanish House of Hapsburg acted as a barrier to the spread of Protestantism in Italy. Second, Spain and later Austria protected Europe from the Ottoman Turks—that is, non-European (Muslim) invaders. Following the War of the Spanish Succession (1701–1704), Austria replaced Spain as the protector of the Papal States, an arrangement that lasted nearly a century until Napoleon (1796–1815) conquered the peninsula, created centralized legal and political-administrative systems, and unwittingly paved the way for Italy's eventual unification in the 1860s.

Italy, at Last

As Italy's belated experience in nation building was to demonstrate, it is easier to establish a new state than it is to create a seamless new social and civil order (see Map 2.4). Like the United States of America's birth, Italy's was tumultuous and prolonged. But unlike the United States, Italy was to spend its first decades after unification sorting out what needed to be done to make constitutional government work, only to have it go terribly awry after World War I. That part of the story comes later, however.

The start of the new century was anything but auspicious: in 1900 an anarchist killed the king. It was a time when all across Europe anarchism was in the air, like a deadly contagion, and Italy was by no means immune. The assassination of King Umberto was symptomatic of the deep unresolved tensions and class divisions within Italian society. It is little short of alarming in retrospect that barely a decade before the outbreak of a world-shattering war, Italians had still reached no consensus on who should govern or how. Many of those representing the commercial-industrial-agricultural interests (or *bourgeoisie*) strongly favored protectionist policies and tough measures to curb trade unions, whereas others in the same class, especially entrepreneurial and professional interests, generally favored more liberal policies, including the right of workers to strike. Many trade unionists, in turn, were strongly influenced by socialist ideas, although there were divisions here too between Marxist extremists, one step away from the anarchists, and more moderate socialists who advocated reform rather than revolution. The latter embraced gradualist approaches to change and generally eschewed violence.

Adding still more spice to this peppery political stew was the Roman Catholic Church. Italian Catholics were split into a right wing whose adherents (correctly) associated socialism with secularization of society and a left wing who were deeply alienated by the avarice of a self-entitling socioeconomic elite in bed with corrupt politicians. The former reacted to the decay of private morality, the latter to the dearth of public morality. Both sides agreed that *morality* was the issue. Neither had any idea that Italy's moral stock would soon plunge to new depths.

M A P 2.4 Italy

SOURCE: Adapted from the University of Texas Libraries, The University of Texas at Austin.

In the years leading up to World War I, Italy's tendencies toward instability were kept in check by the mediating presence of Giovanni Giolitti. Already at this early stage, a pattern was emerging, one that was to become Italy's dubious trademark—precarious and short-lived coalition governments that in the absence of a popular leader could paralyze the political system. Happily for prewar Italy, Giolitti *was* a popular leader, resulting in such major pieces of legislation as the nationalization of the railways, legalization of labor unions, regulation of working conditions for women and children, and the introduction of universal male suffrage in 1912. These progressive measures, however, were bundled with banking and industrial policies that helped set the stage for the postwar rise of the fascist state—namely, a strengthening of the ties between banks and big business, greater concentration of enterprise ownership, and a continuation of protectionism for steel, sugar and cotton.

Italy's expansionist prewar foreign policy provided another presentiment of what was to come when, for example, Italy waged war on Turkey and annexed Libya. Earlier, toward the end of the nineteenth century, Italy had occupied Eritrea and Somalia in the Horn of Africa, but that effort came to grief—as would Italy's later militaristic adventures.

Staring into the Abyss: The Fascist Era

World War I shattered the old order in Europe and littered the political landscape with wreckage of every kind. The evidence of ruined homes, towns and cities was plain enough to see. Evidence of ruined lives, hopes and dreams was less visible to the eye but even more difficult to repair. Looking back on what happened to Europe in the nightmarish three decades after 1914, it is clear that one "world war" led to another. Without arguing that it was inevitable, there is every reason to believe that the social, economic, political, psychological and moral dislocations associated with World War I predisposed many European countries to the kind of political instability, polarization, and mass violence that occurred in Italy and Germany. This is certainly not to excuse the abominable things that happened in these two countries, only to set these things in historical context.

Benito Mussolini founded the **Fascist Party** in 1921 at a time when many Italians were gripped by anger and a sense of betrayal. After much debate, Italy had intervened on the side of the victors, Britain and France, in World War I only to be deprived of the spoils (Dalmatia, in particular) at the Paris Peace Conference. Meanwhile, economic reversals, including huge budget deficits, crippling inflation and rising high unemployment, greatly exacerbated the situation. Buoyed by this rising tide of popular discontent, Mussolini ordered his paramilitary organization, the **Black Shirts,** to stage a march on Rome in October 1922.

It was at this juncture that a showdown between Machiavelli and Mussolini might have nipped the nascent Fascist movement in the bud. But the "prince"—in actuality, the king—failed to heed the prime minister's urgent advice to declare a state of emergency. Instead, the king got a bad case of cold feet and invited Mussolini to form a new government. From this point forward, Mussolini moved methodically and relentlessly to amass total power in his own hands. How exactly did he do it?

State terror (politically motivated violence perpetrated by the government) in support of propaganda has often played a prominent role in mass movements of both the right and the left. One of the most striking examples is provided by Mussolini's *fasci di combattimento* ("combat groups"). After attempts to gain power by wooing the working class away from the Socialist Party failed, Mussolini began to cultivate the middle classes and to seek financing from the wealthy industrialists and big landowners. Convinced of the impossibility of capturing control of the Italian government by legal means, in the early 1920s he turned increasingly toward terror as a means of dealing with political opponents.

Mussolini's Fascists thus substituted arson and assassination for the normal, nonviolent means of political competition. Armed bands conducted raids—called **punitive expeditions**—against unsuspecting and defenseless communities. The local police often would cooperate by doing nothing.

The punitive expeditions mounted by the Italian Fascists demonstrated the utility of politically motivated terror in a totalitarian revolution. Cleverly employed, terrorism can create a sense of utter defenselessness in the face of an imminent but often indistinct danger. Mussolini's use of terror had a threefold purpose: (1) to create an artificial atmosphere of crisis; (2) to demonstrate that the state is no longer capable of providing law-abiding citizens with protection from unprovoked attacks on their persons and property; and (3) to prod an increasingly fearful, desperate, and fragmented citizenry to turn for refuge and order to the very same political movement that, unbeknown to most, is behind the growing lawlessness.

Once in power, Mussolini rewrote electoral laws to suit his purposes, dissolved all parties except his own, reintroduced the death penalty, and created a special category of political crimes and a secret police accountable only to him. The Italian dictator followed the classical formula for creating a totalitarian state, the same basic model Lenin and Stalin put into effect in the Soviet Union in the 1920s and Hitler would copy in the 1930s. Indeed, although they were at opposite ends of the ideological spectrum, Mussolini and Stalin were practitioners of the same dark political art. Thus, the Fascist approach to civil society, much like the Communist approach, was to abolish all autonomous associations. Mussolini forced both labor and business into new Fascist-controlled organizations, banned strikes and closeouts, created special courts to settle labor-management disputes, and the like.

Mussolini followed Machiavelli's advice in adopting some measures that appeared generous and were cleverly calculated to have wide popular appeal. He not only made the trains run on time (as legend has it), but he also instituted a pension system and a 40-hour workweek.

After the start of the depression in 1929, the Fascist Party moved toward a state-centered economic model that heavily involved the government in banking and capital allocation. Investment in the manufacturing sector in many cases targeted military and defense-related industries. The **Lateran Pacts** between the Italian government and the Vatican signed in 1929 amounted to a marriage of convenience between the Fascist state and the Roman Catholic Church: the Vatican recognized the legitimacy of the Italian state (and hence Fascism); in return, Roman Catholicism became the official state religion and its teachings were made mandatory in all Italy's schools.

Fascist ideology was ultranationalistic and extolled war as a virtue, the sure path to personal and political glory. This glorification of war permeated Mussolini's foreign policy and largely explains his penchant for adventurism. Thus, in 1935, despite French and British mediation efforts and the risk of punitive economic sanctions, Italy invaded Ethiopia. In 1939, Mussolini ordered troops into Albania.

But, as totalitarian dictators go, Mussolini was a paper tiger. Italy was never a serious military factor in World War II. In July 1943, one month after Italy capitulated, Allied troops landed in Sicily and began to move northward. It was the beginning of the end for the Italy's Fascists and for Mussolini himself: in April 1945 Italian partisans caught the fallen dictator trying to slip across the border into Switzerland and shot him.

Italy and Germany were forced to accept unconditional surrender at the end of World War II, but the settlement that followed was not the harsh peace that many Italians and Germans feared. Instead, in contrast to the Treaty of Versailles, the victorious Allied Powers did not seek to impose punitive terms on the losers. In fact, the war was never formally terminated.

Germany, Italy, and Japan were transformed into constitutional democracies under the tutelage of the Allied Occupation authorities; at the same time, in the face of a rising Soviet military threat, the United States pushed for the economic recovery and political rehabilitation of the defeated powers. Ironically, the anti-communist phobia that gripped the West in the early postwar era was a boon to Italy and Germany.

Unlike Italy, Spain remained neutral in both world wars. For reasons that will soon become clear, however, Spain would be ostracized from the rest of Europe for three decades after World War II, long after both Germany and Italy had been politically and economically rehabilitated.

SPAIN: EMPIRE OR NATION?

A glance at a map of Europe is enough to tell the story. Spain, like France, is blessed with a favorable geography that afforded it direct access to both the outer world (via the Atlantic Ocean) and the inner world (the Mediterranean Sea). The latter spawned the great empires and creative outpourings that together constitute what we commonly call Western civilization. The former lured Spain into following Portugal's lead in the great age of global exploration dating back to the late fifteenth century. Spain's modern history illustrates the importance of geography in a positive sense. By contrast, Poland's history no less vividly shows that geography can be a negative factor, and Russian history just as clearly demonstrates that it can be both negative and positive in different ways and at different times (see Chapter 5).

M A P 2.5 Spain

SOURCE: Adapted from the University of Texas Libraries, The University of Texas at Austin.

Spain's most prominent strategic features are its peninsular position, the **Pyrenees Mountains** that form a natural border between France and Spain, an interior dominated by the great **Meseta Plateau,** and the **Strait of Gibraltar** separating it from North Africa (Morocco) by a narrow ribbon of water. Spain's paradoxical geography makes it at once a part of Europe and sets it apart from Europe. To an extent often overlooked by contemporary students of comparative politics, geography determines the shape and size of the stage on which the history of nations is acted out. Spain had a large stage even before it established a world empire in the sixteenth and seventeenth centuries.

Like Britain, France, Germany and Italy, Spain is a nation of regions (see Map 2.4). First and foremost is the old Kingdom of Castile, which played a pivotal role in shaping the political map of the Meseta, including León and Old

Castile in the northern Meseta; new Castile in the center; Extremadura to the southwest; and Murcia to the southeast. Linguistically, **Castilian** is the language most people think of as Spanish. (Other important languages of Spain include Euskera, the Basque language; Catalan, the language of Catalonia; plus Gallego, Valencian, and Mallorcan.)

The southernmost Spanish province is **Andalusia,** a vast agricultural region famous for its vineyards and fine wines. Like the region of **Valencia** on the east coast of Spain, Andalusia is also a major producer and exporter of fruits (especially oranges) and vegetables.

Galicia, straight north of Portugal, is a rugged land with a rich fishing and seafaring tradition. To the east of Galicia along Spain's north coast are the mountainous provinces of **Asturias, Cantabria,** and **Euskadi** (better known as the **Basque country**). Asturias holds large coal deposits and Euskadi is the source of Basque iron. **Navarra** and **Aragón** are situated between the Pyrenees and the Meseta tableland. At the opposite (eastern) end of the Pyrenees is **Catalonia,** where both agriculture and manufacturing flourish. Catalonia's Barcelona is perhaps Spain's most cosmopolitan—and certainly one of its most beautiful—cities. Its political history is closely linked with that of neighboring Aragón and the whole of eastern Spain. Catalonia and Aragón together conquered Valencia and the **Balearic Islands** (Ibiza, Minorca, and Majorca), which were vital to the Kingdom of Aragón.

Spain is thus a far more diverse and divisible society than one might think. Roughly twice the size of Oregon, and with a population of about 40 million, it is a large country. As we will see, Spain became the scene of considerable social and political strife beginning in the nineteenth century and culminating in the bloody Spanish civil war of the 1930s—and this despite the fact that Spain has embraced but one religion, Roman Catholicism, since the end of the **Reconquest** (victory over the Moors) in 1492.

Turning Point

The year 1492 was a very big year in Spanish history. The Reconquest coincided with two other important events: the marriage of Ferdinand of Aragon and Isabella of Castile and the launching of the **Spanish Inquisition.** The former united Spain under one political authority, forging a modern nation-state that by the sixteenth century would rival Britain and France for the top ranking among Europe's great powers. The latter was aimed at nothing short of imposing cultural and religious uniformity as an integral part of the Spanish Crown's nation building strategy. The main thrust (and lasting legacy) of this strategy was to create a highly centralized political-administrative system buttressed by a national nobility loyal to the Crown but combined with confederal elements, thus reflecting Spain's regional diversity while enshrining unity as its core political value. The tension between these two implicit models of government is still evident in Spanish politics today.

Of course it was also in 1492 that "Columbus sailed the ocean blue" and "discovered" America. As Native Americans are quick to point out, Columbus was actually a latecomer. Even so, for Europeans of the fifteenth century the discovery of the Western Hemisphere opened up a brave new world of seemingly boundless wealth, and the Spanish, being the first to arrive on the scene, claimed nearly all of what is today Latin America (minus Brazil) plus the southwestern United States (including California, Nevada, Arizona, and New Mexico), as well as Texas and much of the Deep South (including Florida and Alabama).

According to many historians of the period, Spain's colonial policies exploited the conquered peoples and plundered the riches of the New World, using religion as a kind of moral cover and a means of social control, without giving anything back to the native inhabitants, whose cultures and folkways were brutally suppressed. Certainly this view is widely accepted throughout Latin America. But other scholars argue that the **Spanish Conquest,** despite admitted excesses, was also a blessing because the conquerors, however repressive, were far more enlightened (and less violent) than the indigenous rulers.[8] What is clear is that Spain's colonial empire in the New World lasted more than three hundred years, longer than that of Britain, France, the Netherlands, or Russia. The first to form, it was also the first to unravel: the U.S.'s famed **Monroe Doctrine** (1823) warning Europe to stay out of the Western Hemisphere corresponds closely with the disintegration of the Spanish Empire in the Americas.

As far back as 1588, the defeat of the **Spanish Armada** by England had signaled the beginning of Spain's long, slow decline as a great power. The eighteenth century and nineteenth centuries confirmed this trend. At the beginning of the eighteenth century, the **War of Spanish Succession** brought the Bourbon dynasty to power. A century later, in 1808, Napoleon invaded Spain and placed his brother, Joseph, on the Spanish throne. From this point forward, Spain became an arena of episodic social unrest that occasionally erupted into civil war. When the tumult finally ended on the **Iberian Peninsula,** Spain had seen no fewer than seven constitutions come and go, and the whole of Europe was about to plunge into the abyss.

First Stirrings of Democracy

During most of the turbulent nineteenth century, Spain was the crucible of class warfare with the clergy, the aristocracy, and the army facing off against the emerging industrial working class loosely allied with middle-class liberals of various descriptions (intellectuals, entrepreneurs, lawyers, doctors, teachers, and others). At bottom, it was a struggle over one of the fundamental questions facing all modern societies: what is the best form of government? Spain was deeply split between conservative monarchists and liberal constitutionalists. The former favored a restoration and continuance of a strong hereditary monarchy after Spain's humiliating defeat and subjugation during the Napoleonic wars. The latter longed for a liberal constitution that would place strict limits on the crown, expand civil liberties, extend the franchise, and transfer legislative powers to an elected assembly. Spanish politics became a seesaw battle between these two camps (see Figure 2.5).

The **Spanish Constitution of 1812** (also called the Constitution of Cádiz) marks the start of Spain's long and tortuous path to democracy. Fernando VII,

1808 France invades Spain; Joseph Napoleon is placed on the throne
1808–1814 Peninsula War
1812 Constitution of Cádiz
1833–1840 First Carlist War; Royal Statute of 1834; Constitution of 1837
1845 Constitution of 1845
1869 Constitution of 1869
1873–1874 First Republic
1870–1875 Second Carlist War
1875 Second Bourbon Restoration (Alfonso XII)
1885 Death of Alfonso XII; beginning of Regency
1876 Constitution of 1876
1898 Defeat in Spanish-American War
1902 End of Regency; Alfonso XIII crowned King of Spain
1923–1931 Dictatorship of General Primo de Rivera
1931 (April) Left wins local elections; Alfonso XIII exits Spain
1931–1939 Second Republic
1936–1939 Spanish Civil War
1939 Nationalist victory; General Francisco Franco takes power

FIGURE 2.5 Turbulent Spain (1808–1939)

upon returning to the throne two years later, abolished this constitution. There would be several more attempts to establish a constitutional democracy in Spain during the course of the nineteenth century, all ending in failure. There would also be two civil wars (1833–1840) and (1870–1875) and the occasional military coup d'etat (called a ***pronunciamento*** in Spain). Of the two nondemocratic methods of changing the guard, the *pronunciamento* has generally involved the least bloodshed by far. Indeed, in the past two centuries military intervention in Spanish politics has served to *lessen* politically motivated violence in times of governmental crisis. Spanish monarchs would have to contend with popular demands for constitutional reform throughout the nineteenth century and even share power (or give the appearance of power sharing) with the country's parliament. Monarchical dominance would be momentarily interrupted by short periods of constitutional rule (1812, 1837, 1869, and 1931). But Spain's first two attempts to establish full-fledged republics would come to grief.

Spain's First Republic (1873–74) was short-lived, giving way to the period known as the Restoration and the Regency under Alfonso XII (who died in 1885) and María Cristina (acting as Regent until 1902). The closing decades of the nineteenth century in Spain witnessed the rise of radical labor union and anarchist movements. Radical socialists, anarchists, and trade unionists joined forces, at times blurring the distinctions and giving rise to elite fears of a popular groundswell that threatened to plunge the country into chaos. Spain's loss of its remaining colonies in the **Spanish-American War** (1898) was yet another blow to Spanish patriotic pride, but the monarchy survived for another two decades after Alfonso III ascended to the throne in 1902.

The Spanish Civil War

The background to the **Spanish Civil War** is thus a prolonged period of imperial decline followed by more than a century of domestic strife with no lasting resolution of the underlying social and political conflicts that would eventually tear the country asunder. Alfonso III remained in power until 1931, but by that time he had been reduced to a mere figurehead following a classic Spanish-style *pronunciamento* in 1923 when General Miguel Primo de Rivera, colorfully described by the historian Hugh Thomas as "patriotic, comparatively magnanimous, and personally brave," assumed dictatorial powers.[9]

Primo de Rivera ruled until 1931, when he quietly stepped down when local elections resulted in an overwhelming victory for republican candidates. Alfonso III promptly fled, opening the door to the **Second Republic** and a new constitution that for a brief time made Spain one of the most democratic countries in Europe.

The ill-fated Second Republic was marked by growing tensions between the left and the right, pitting liberals of all stripes, including Socialists and Communists, against the **Nationalists,** the aristocracy, and the Roman Catholic Church. As the struggle turned violent, degenerating into fratricidal war in 1936, the army split into rival forces representing the Nationalists on one side and the Republicans on the other. General Francisco Franco, the Nationalist leader emerged as the man of the hour, leading the Nationalists to a decisive victory in 1938-39 with strong backing from Nazi Germany and Fascist Italy.

Franco would go on to rule Spain with a firm hand for the next three and half decades. But social peace, when it finally came, was bought at a very dear price in both blood and freedom, not to mention economic progress. In the words of Hugh Thomas:

> The Spanish Civil War exceeded in ferocity most wars between nations. Yet the losses were less than had been generally feared. The total number of deaths caused by the war seems to have been approximately 600,000. Of these about 100,000 may be supposed to have died by murder or summary execution. Perhaps as many as 220,000 died of disease or malnutrition directly attributable to the war. About 320,00 probably died in action.[10]

Spain would be ruled as a semifascist authoritarian state until 1975. Civil liberties would be severely curtailed and Spain would become an international pariah, excluded both from NATO and the European Community, as well as the postwar global system of trade and finance. Perhaps worse, the war would have a damaging psychological effect on a whole generation and leave a stigma that would linger for decades to come.

The causes of Spain's civil war and its authoritarian aftermath, however, lie deeper in the past. Spain peaked early as an imperial power, having carved out a vast colonial empire in the Americas in the sixteenth century. But Spain treated her colonies as spoils of war to be exploited and plundered rather than assets to be developed and nurtured. Moreover, the Spanish Crown foolishly squandered much of the wealth it extracted.

The defeat of the Spanish Armada in 1588 signaled the beginning of the end of Spain's golden age. The War of Spanish Succession (1701–1715) led to Spain's loss of the Spanish Netherlands, Gibraltar, and the island of Minorca under the terms of the Treaty of Utrecht (1713), in effect reducing Spain to the status of a second rank power. In the nineteenth century, Napoleon seized control of Spain without firing a shot. The Peninsula War (1808–1814) ensued. The British Royal Navy was crucial to the eventual success of the "hammer and anvil" campaign against Napoleon's forces in Spain and Portugal. (The hammer was the Anglo-Portuguese army commanded by Sir Arthur Wellesley, the Duke of Wellington, pounding a much larger French army against the anvil of the Spanish armies, guerrillas, and the Portuguese militia.) The consequences of that bitter conflict for Spain's future political stability were incalculable: a power vacuum lasting roughly a decade and leading to loss of colonies; turmoil for several decades after that; civil wars involving dynastic claims and succession disputes; an ill-fated republic; and finally a corrupt liberal democracy. Thus, the Spanish Civil War had deep roots in the social strife and political turmoil of the nineteenth century.

SUMMARY AND CONCLUSIONS

This chapter examined the roots of modern political cultures and parliamentary democracies in Western Europe, with special emphasis on the United Kingdom, France, Germany, Italy, and Spain as case studies. It noted that Europe is a mix of many cultures and nations with distinct languages, cultures, histories, and political traditions. Nonetheless, Western Europe has a common core of values and beliefs reflecting the pervasive and enduring influence of Christianity, the Renaissance and Reformation, the scientific revolution, the Enlightenment, the industrial revolution, and the Age of Imperialism. The salubrious climate and compact geography of the Continent and the accessibility of maritime highways to the world outside have also contributed to the development of a distinctly Western outlook among the peoples of this region. In Chapter Three we explore contemporary patterns of politics and government, the products of this heritage.

KEY TERMS

Andalusia	Cantabria	English Channel
anti-clericalism	Carlsbad Decrees	Estates General
Aragón	Castilian	Eurosceptics
Asturias	Catalonia	Euskadi
Balearic Islands	Chunnel	*fasci di combattimento*
Basque country	Congress of Vienna	Fascist Party
Black Shirts	Edict of Nantes	Franco-Prussian War

French Revolution

Galicia

German Confederation

German Empire

Great Powers

Hapsburg dynasty

Holocaust

Huguenots

Iberian Peninsula

indicative planning

keeper of the balance

Landtag

Lateran Pacts

Machiavellian

Meseta Plateau

Mitteleuropa

Molotov-Ribbentrop
    Pact

Monroe Doctrine

MPs

Nationalists (Spain)

Navarra

Norman Conquest

Papal States

Paris Commune

Parliament

prime minister

The Prince

pronunciamento

punitive expedition

Pyrenees Mountains

Puritan Revolution

Reconquest

Reichstag

Second Republic
    (Spain)

Second Reich

Spanish-American War

Spanish Armada

Spanish Civil War

Spanish Conquest

Spanish Constitution
    of 1812

Spanish Inquisition

Strait of Gibraltar

Sudetenland

Third Reich

Third Republic (France)

Tories

Valencia

War of Spanish
    Succession

Weimar Republic

Western Roman
    Empire

Whigs

Zollverein

SUGGESTED READINGS

Bernstein, Richard. *Fragile Glory: A Portrait of France and the French*. New York: Plume, 1995.

Best, Judith A. *The Mainstream of Western Political Thought*. New York: Human Sciences Press, 1980.

Bruun, Geoffrey. *Nineteenth Century European Civilization—1815–1914*. New York: Oxford University Press (Galaxy), 1960.

Bullock, Alan. *Hitler: A Study in Tyranny*. New York: Harper and Row, 1964.

Chaliand, Gérard. *Mirrors of a Disaster: The Spanish Military Conquest of America*. Piscataway, NJ: Transaction, 2005.

Dunn, Richard S. *The Age of Religious Wars, 1559–1715*. 2nd ed. New York: W.W. Norton, 1979.

Dunn, Susan. *Sister Revolutions: French Lightning, American Light*. New York: Faber and Faber, 2004.

Elias, Norbert. *The Germans*. New York: Columbia University Press, 1996.

Englund, Steven. *Napoleon: A Political Life*. New York: Simon and Schuster, 2003.

Evans, Richard J. *Coming of the Third Reich*. New York: Penguin Group (USA), 2005.

Gregor, A. James. *Interpretations of Fascism*. Morristown, NJ: General Learning Press, 1974.

Hibbert, Christopher. *The House of Medici: Its Rise and Fall*. New York: HarperCollins/ Morrow Quill, 1982.

Himmelfarb, Gertrude. *Roads to Modernity: The British, French, and American Enlightenments*. New York: Alfred A. Knopf, 2004.

Horne, John N. *De Gaulle and Modern France*. New York: St. Martin's Press, 1995.

Hobsbawm, E. J. *The Age of Revolution*. New York: Mentor, 1962.

Kennedy, Paul. *The Rise and Fall of the Great Powers: Economic Change and Military Conflict from 1500 to 2000*. New York: Random House, 1987.

Ladurie, Emmanuel L. *The Ancien Regime: A History of France 1610–1770*. Cambridge, Mass.: Blackwell, 1996.

Lovett, Clara M. *Giusepe Ferrari and the Italian Revolution*. Chapel Hill, NC: University of North Carolina Press, 1979.

Machiavelli, Niccoló. *The Prince*. Trans. Luigi Ricci, with an introduction by Christian Gauss. New York: Signet Classics, 1999.

Paxton, Robert O. *The Anatomy of Fascism*. Vintage Books: New York, 2005.

Plumb, J. H. *The Italian Renaissance: A Concise Survey of Its History and Culture*. New York: Harper Torchbooks, 1961.

Payne, Stanley G. *Spain's First Democracy: The Second Republic, 1931–1936*. Madison, WI: University of Wisconsin Press, 1993.

Potter, David. *A History of France, 1460–1560: The Emergence of a Nation-State*. New York: Saint Martin's, 1995.

Taylor, A. J. P. *Bismarck: The Man and the Statesman*. New York: Vintage Books, 1967.

Thomas, Hugh. *The Spanish Civil War*. New York: Harper and Row, 1961.

Tindall, Gillian. *Celestine: Voices from a French Village*. New York: Henry Holt, 1996.

WEB SITES

www.gksoft.com/govt/en/europa.html

www.politicalresources.net/europe.htm

www.benne.luna.nl/pp/eur/index.htm

www.democ.uci.edu/resource.htm

NOTES

1. Alan Palmer, *The Lands Between: A History of East Central Europe since the Congress of Vienna* (New York: Macmillan, 1970).

2. The British rejected membership in the Common Market in 1958; several years later, they tried to join but were thwarted by President de Gaulle of France. Only after de Gaulle's departure from government (and subsequent death) was the United Kingdom admitted to the European Community (EC) in 1973. The EC became the European Union (EU) in 1993.

3. See, for example, "France's Failure," *The Economist,* November 12, 2005, pp. 11—12; see also Mark Landler and Craig S. Smith, "French Officials Try to Ease Fear as Crisis Swells," *The New York Times,* November 8, 2005 (electronic edition).

4. Gerhard Rempel, "The Thirty-Years-War," lecture for Western Civilization course published on the Internet at http://mars.acnet.wnec.edu/~grempel/courses/wc2/lectures/30yearswar.html.

5. The Carlsbad Decrees intensified censorship, banned radical professors and students (including Karl Marx), and outlawed political clubs. They also required each member state to appoint commissioners to monitor and certify the universities for ideological reliability.

6. Arthur J. May, *The Age of Metternich* (New York: Holt, 1963), p. 40.

7. Ibid., 44.

8. See, for example, Hugh Thomas, *Rivers of Gold: The Rise of the Spanish Empire, from Columbus to Magellan* (New York: Random House, 2004). "Who can doubt now," Thomas asks, "that [the Spanish] were right to denounce the idea of religion based on human sacrifice or the simple worship of the sun or the rain?"

9. Hugh Thomas, *The Spanish Civil War* (New York: Harper and Row, 1961), p. 16.

10. Ibid., p. 606.

3

Politics in Western Europe

Triumph of Constitutional Democracy

*T*he political systems of Western Europe are not identical, but the similarities are more striking than the differences. Since the mid-1970s, when dictatorships in Spain and Portugal and military rule in Greece ended, every country in Western Europe has been governed by civilian rulers who came to power through free elections. Hence the governments of the region display a remarkably consistent pattern too uniform to be mere coincidence.

European democracies have several key features in common. They are based on clearly defined principles. Governments are elected by universal suffrage. With the exception of Great Britain, all have written constitutions.

Many also continue to have monarchs who now serve as symbols (frequently called figureheads), performing many of the ceremonial and formal functions of government, having long ago lost the substance of sovereign power. For this reason, some of these governments are described as constitutional monarchies—a term that is somewhat misleading because in actuality they are representative democracies resembling the British parliamentary model.

Spain falls into this category, as do Belgium, Luxembourg, the Netherlands, Denmark, Norway, and Sweden. In these countries, the monarch reigns but does not rule—the king or queen is the ceremonial head of state, but an elected parliament makes the laws and chooses the government, consisting of the prime minister and the cabinet, who make policy and oversee the day-to-day operations of the bureaucracy. A constitutional monarch could theoretically intercede in the political process, but to do so might place the institution of the monarchy at risk.

The countries of Western Europe enjoy a high standard of living based on liberal market economies. With the notable exceptions of Norway and Switzerland, these national economies are now integrated into the supranational economy of the European Union (EU). Some countries are, of course, more prosperous than others, and all face problems associated with a postindustrial stage of development; nonetheless, even the least prosperous West European countries (Greece and Portugal) are better off than Slovenia, the most prosperous country in Eastern Europe.

MIRACULOUS RECOVERY, POSTMODERN MALAISE

After World War II, the United States under President Harry Truman became actively involved in shaping Europe's future. First, it acted as a catalyst for economic recovery on the Continent through the European Recovery Program, better known as the Marshall Plan, approved by Congress in 1948. Second, it determined on a course of reconciliation rather than retribution toward Germany. Third, it made a long-term commitment to Western European security by creating the North Atlantic Treaty Organization (NATO), a military alliance with no expiration clause that included most major Western democracies. This initiative removed any lingering doubts in Europe about whether the United States would risk war to defend democracy and freedom on the other side of the Atlantic.

Fourth, and perhaps least appreciated at the time, the United States encouraged economic cooperation among the Western European democracies. The first manifestation of this policy was the Organization for European Economic Cooperation (OEEC), set up to administer Marshall Plan aid. (In 1961 the Organization for Economic Cooperation and Development, or OECD, replaced the OEEC; the twenty-four nation OECD included member-states of both the European Economic Community and the European Free Trade Association, popularly known as the EFTA, plus the United States, Canada, and Japan.) The OEEC countries pledged to develop intra-European trade by reducing tariffs and other barriers to trade expansion.[1] As things turned out, this lofty rhetoric foreshadowed developments that would soon transform Western Europe from a blighted region into the world's most dynamic trading bloc.

Postwar Europe's first step toward economic integration was to create the European Coal and Steel Community (ECSC) in 1952. The ECSC, which established a framework for sharing strategic resources, set the stage for formation of the European Economic Community (EEC), or Common Market, in 1958. The result was a customs union, meaning that the six charter members (France, West Germany, Italy, Belgium, the Netherlands, and Luxembourg) agreed to remove tariffs on trade among themselves and set common tariffs on trade with others. This became the nucleus of the present-day European Union (EU), which now includes twenty-five member-states (see Chapter Nine).

Europe's Postwar Economic Miracles

France, West Germany, and Italy each experienced a kind of economic miracle during the 1950s. The miracle was not that they recovered but that they

TABLE 3.1 The Changing Global Balance: Asian Challengers

	Economic Power (2004)		Military Power (2003)	
	Population	**GNP ($)**	**Active Troops**	**Nuclear Warheads***
China	1.3 billion	1.46 trillion	2.2 million	300–600
India	1.1 billion	639 billion	1.3 million	200–250
Japan	127.1 million	4.36 trillion	239 thousand	0

*These are Western open-source estimates. See, for example, the BBC news story, "South Asia's High Nuclear Stakes," May 7, 2003, at http://news.bbc.co.uk/1/hi/world/south_asia/1732430.stm. Estimates vary widely, however. Thus, the Natural Resources Defense Council (NRDC) placed the number of India's nuclear weapons at a much lower level (about 30–35) in 2002. www.nrdc.org/nuclear/southasia.asp

recovered so rapidly. Within a decade of the war's end, industry was up and running again, granaries were bulging, and roads, railways, and bridges were rebuilt. This rising tide lifted all boats—the resurgence of the bigger nations boosted economic growth in the smaller ones.

But along with prosperity came new problems. As industry became increasingly automated and the workforce shifted from manufacturing to the service sector, the challenges facing the governments of the region changed rapidly, and the very pace of change itself became a major challenge. At the same time, the Common Market—today's European Union—came of age, creating new opportunities for the member nations but also bringing new tensions and necessitating often-painful adjustments. Meanwhile, new challengers arose in the Far East. Japan advanced even more rapidly that America's European allies, becoming second only to the United States as an economic power, and a resurgent China served notice that Europe and North America would face formidable new trade rivals in the coming decades (see Table 3.1).

Next we consider some of the problems associated with what has come to be called *postmodern society*. These problems are in a sense an outgrowth of overdevelopment. Academicians and policy makers in the West have not been reticent about giving advice to "developing countries" faced with the problems of "underdevelopment." They (we) are only beginning to recognize that development is a never-ending process and that, like a double-edged sword, it cuts both ways; that there is a downside to economic growth (because solutions to one set of problems give rise to new ones); and that such postmodern afflictions as urban sprawl, energy dependency, air and water pollution, traffic congestion, and stress-related illnesses are symptoms of this postmodern syndrome. In many respects, the problems Europe's biggest and richest countries are encountering typify the whole region.

Problems of Postindustrial Society

The Industrial Revolution brought a major shift in the economic foundations of both American and European society. The transition from farming to manufacturing entailed a massive demographic shift from rural to urban settings—a shift accompanied by secularization, the breakup of the extended family, and a sharp rise in the need for governmental regulation and intervention (particularly in such areas as public utilities and social services). Major advances in living standards, political gains by organized labor (such as the right to strike), and consumer-related technological innovation offset the problems associated with industrialization.

Economically, **postindustrial society** is characterized by a whole series of demographic and macroeconomic shifts: from the manufacturing to the service sector (banking, insurance, advertising, marketing, management, and so on), from domestic to international markets, from a cash-and-carry economy to one based on credit and installment buying, from one-income to two-income families, and from a saving culture to a consuming culture. In general, a defining feature of post-industrial society is the shift in the nature of work, as fewer and fewer workers are employed in traditional blue collar jobs while more and more jobs of all kinds are outsourced to places (especially China, India, and other Asian countries) where labor is cheap and abundant. Another defining feature is an aging population, as people live and work longer, putting great pressure on private and public pension systems. Postindustrialism also brings overdevelopment or reverse development (characterized by outmigration from cities to suburbs, slums, and deteriorating inner city schools, services, and tax bases as well as outsourcing of jobs and alarmingly high rates of youth unemployment); these concepts and constructs now deserve a place alongside underdevelopment in economics and political science texts.

Overdevelopment is exemplified by the modern megalopolis: mass aggregation of people and urban sprawl. Europe as a whole is far more crowded than North America, 134 people per square mile (Europe) versus a mere 32 (North America). Surprisingly, except for Asia (203 people per square mile), Europe is the most densely populated region in the world. Such raw figures, however, are less important than population distribution—urbanization, to be precise. Thus, the most densely populated place on earth is found in Europe, not Asia: the tiny state of Monaco, with a total area of three-quarters of a square mile and a population of 32,000, has a population density of 43,000 people per square mile! But Monaco is not alone.

Paris (population 9.8 million) and London (population 7.6 million) are two more familiar examples of the modern megalopolis in Western Europe. Others include Madrid (5.1 million) and Barcelona (4.1 million) in Spain, as well as the Italian city of Milan (4.1 million). Athens, Greece, with a population of 3.2 million, is battling to preserve its ancient monuments against the ravages of time, acid rain, and air pollution, as is Rome, Italy. Germany has several large urban concentrations as well as major cities with populations of 2–3 million. In fact, one-third of the entire German population is concentrated in just eight urban areas (see Table 3.2.)

The dynamics of economic growth in postindustrial nations lure people to big cities in search of high-paying jobs, professional opportunities, social status, and cultural activities. But as cities become more and more overcrowded, population growth typically outruns the capacity of local government to maintain adequate police and fire protection, sanitation, schools, mass transportation systems, hospitals, streets, parks, and other amenities.

With overcrowding often comes a host of social and health-related problems, including traffic congestion, air pollution, crime, juvenile delinquency, drug

TABLE 3.2 Where One-Third of All Germans Live

Urban Concentrations (Main City)	Population
Rhine-Ruhr North (Essen)	6.54 million
Rhine Main (Frankfurt)	3.68 million
Berlin	3.32 million
Rhine-Ruhr Middle (Düsseldorf)	3.24 million
Rhine-Ruhr South (Cologne)	3.06 million
Stuttgart	2.68 million
Hamburg	2.67 million
Munich	2.3 million

abuse, high divorce rates, domestic violence, homelessness, and increased stress, which can exacerbate all the other problems. (The point is not that overcrowding is the primary cause of all these problems but simply that they are widely associated with urban life in postmodern societies.) A related issue is immigration, which has generated fears of an unbridled exodus of newcomers from the east (the Slavic countries) and the south (North Africa). Legal immigration to Western Europe was only a small fraction of the total, which included millions of illegal immigrants living there in the early 1990s. This influx is costly for host governments (many immigrants need health care, housing, education, and other social services), disruptive for communities, and potentially destabilizing. As we noted in the previous chapter, urban riots involving recent immigrants—who were primarily young, poor, and jobless—rocked France in the fall of 2005. These riots were an ominous symptom of a more general problem, one that is by no means confined to France. At the same time, it stands to reason that long-time citizens are more likely to resent "foreigners" when they already feel cramped for space or squeezed for jobs. Right-wing radical parties tend to grow under such conditions (as has happened in many West European countries, including Austria, France, Germany, and the Netherlands).

One reason for the job crunch is that postindustrial societies have failed to solve the economic problems associated with the capitalist business cycle. Since 1970, unemployment rates have varied from a low of less than 1.0 percent of the total labor force (West Germany, 1970) to a high of more than 21 percent (Spain, 1985). In the mid-1980s, the United Kingdom, the Netherlands, and France (plus Belgium and Spain) all hit double-digit unemployment (see Table 3.3). Today, many West European countries are struggling with this problem. Both Belgium and Germany had the dubious distinction of double-digit joblessness in 2005, and the jobless rate in France and Spain hovered right around 10 percent.[2] Youth unemployment was well over 20 percent in Italy, Belgium, France and Spain, and not much lower for the EU as a whole. Such high rates of unemployment have potentially dire social and economic consequences, as a truncated labor force is asked to support a growing number of retirees and pensioners.

TABLE 3.3 Unemployment Rates, 1970–2005: Leading Industrial
Democracies (percentage of total labor force)

Country	1970	1975	1980	1985	1990	1996*	2000	2005†
France	2.5	4.0	6.3	10.2	8.9	12.5	9.6	9.6
Germany	0.8	3.6	2.9	7.2	4.9	10.2	9.4	11.2
Italy	5.3	5.8	7.5	9.6	10.3	12.1	10.5	7.7
Japan	1.1	1.9	2.0	2.6	2.1	3.4	4.6	4.6
Netherlands	1.0	5.2	6.0	10.6	7.5	6.5	2.5	6.5
Sweden	1.5	1.6	2.0	2.8	1.5	8.8	5.1	5.0
United Kingdom	3.0	4.3	6.4	11.2	6.8	7.6	5.3	4.9
United States	4.8	8.3	7.0	7.1	5.4	5.4	3.9	5.0

*Midyear; *The Economist,* Sept. 7, 1996, p. 98.
†*The Economist,* January 7, 2006, p. 88.
SOURCE: OECD Economic Outlook 48, no. 12 (December 1990) and 51, no. 6 (June 1992).

Inflation rates have also fluctuated widely in Western Europe. Germany and the Netherlands have long enjoyed relatively stable inflation rates, but the United Kingdom, France, and Italy were on inflation roller coasters until the 1990s (see Table 3.4). These ups and downs tend to erode consumers' confidence in the economy and voters' confidence in the government. A dilemma that has plagued postindustrial democracies is the teeter-totter effect of disinflation versus full-employment policies: falling unemployment tends to be accompanied by rising inflation, whereas price stabilization (low inflation) is usually associated with rising unemployment. Unsurprisingly, therefore, inflation rates in Western Europe have remained low in recent times, averaging 2.5 percent for the European area as a whole in late 2005.

Postindustrial nations often face problems arising from past economic and technological successes. As society changes, new circumstances give rise to new political forces. For example, the increase in life expectancy (combined with an early retirement option for many employees) has created a powerful new interest group consisting of senior citizens and retirees who strongly oppose any erosion in the retirement benefits and social services they currently receive. (See Chapter Four for a more detailed discussion of this problem, which is fast becoming a crisis in many Western European countries as governments procrastinate in the vain hope of finding an easy way out.) The fact that most households now have two bread-winners, that existing labor laws make it very difficult for business enterprises to fire workers, and, finally, that globalization (that is, a highly competitive world market) has induced European companies to outsource labor-intensive functions of all kinds (both in manufacturing and services) means that even relatively robust economies in Western Europe are not immune to unemployment.

Minorities and first-time workers (often youth) tend to be hit hardest by joblessness. University-educated people may be forced to take low-paying menial jobs for which they are overqualified. Moreover, immigrants are willing—even

T A B L E 3.4 Inflation Rates, 1970–2005: Leading Industrial Democracies (percentages)

Country	1970	1975	1980	1985	1990	1995–1996*	2005†
France	5.9	11.8	13.3	5.8	3.4	2.2	1.6
Germany	3.4	5.9	5.4	2.2	2.7	1.6	2.1
Italy	5.0	17.1	21.3	9.2	6.5	3.6	2.0
Japan	7.7	11.8	7.7	2.0	3.1	nil	−0.8
Netherlands	3.7	10.2	6.5	2.2	2.5	1.8	1.8
Sweden	10.6	11.7	13.7	7.4	10.5	0.8	0.8
United Kingdom	6.4	24.2	18.0	6.1	9.5	2.2	2.1
United States	5.9	9.1	13.5	3.6	5.4	3.0	3.5

*Data in this column are for mid-1995 to mid-1996; see *The Economist,* Aug. 17, 1996, p. 80.

†Data in this column are for late 2005; see *The Economist,* January 7, 2006, p. 88.

SOURCE: International Monetary Fund, *Government Finance Statistics Yearbook* 1991, vol. 54 (Washington, D.C.: IMF, 1991), pp. 116–119; OECD, *Economic Outlook* 50 (December 1991), p. 56.

eager—to take dirty jobs and work for low wages (which they typically do out of sheer necessity). The consequences of all these factors are often disillusionment, anger, and resentment.

Threats to the environment also present new policy problems: air and water pollution, noise abatement, chemical and nuclear waste disposal, deforestation, and wildlife conservation are but a few examples. Air pollution is largely an urban scourge—it is caused by emissions from automobiles, mass-transit vehicles, and smokestack industries. But the cost of cleaning the air (and of most other environmental ameliorations) must ultimately be borne by all taxpayers and consumers, no matter where they happen to live. A basic political question in every society is who gets what, when, and how; a related question is who *pays* what, when, and how. Eastern Europe is too poor to pay, so Western Europe will have to do it or it will not get done any time soon.

It is fashionable in the United States to view Western Europe as a region afflicted with all sorts of problems attributed to the excesses of the **welfare state.** There is some truth in this critique, but there is also a good deal of self-delusion and a tendency to exaggerate Europe's problems and minimize the impressive achievements of the European democracies in the past half-century. Here again we see how beguiling demographic "facts" can be. For example, although Western Europe has a much higher population density than the United States, none of the world's largest fifteen cities is located on the Continent (see Table 3.5). New York City and Los Angeles are bigger than any city in Europe. In addition, most European cities have mass transit systems, including subways, trams, trolleys, and buses, that most American cities lack, and more often than not there are also bicycle lanes going in all directions. Compared to Americans, Europeans tend to be less—often far less—dependent on automobiles to get to work or school.

TABLE 3.5 World's Largest Cities (Europe Doesn't Make the List)

Rank, City, Country	Population (millions) 2000
1. Tokyo, Japan	34.4
2. Mexico City, Mexico	18.0
3. New York City, USA	17.8
4. São Paulo, Brazil	17.0
5. Mumbai (Bombay), India	16.0
6. Kolkata (Calcutta), India	13.0
7. Shanghai, China	12.8
8. Buenos Aires, Argentina	12.5
9. Delhi, India	12.4
10. Los Angeles, USA	11.8
11. Osaka, Japan	11.1
12. Jakarta, Indonesia	11.0
13. Beijing, China	10.8
14. Rio de Janeiro, Brazil	10.8
15. Cairo, Egypt	10.4

SOURCE: *The World Almanac 2005*, p. 850.

With few exceptions, Europeans are convinced of the benefits of the welfare state, proud of the fact that society takes care of the sick and elderly, and critical of American-style capitalism, which they tend to see as cutthroat and heartless.[3] European countries on average devote a far larger share of GNP to social spending than does the United States, and a smaller share to national defense. According to the OECD, the United States devotes about 11 percent of its GDP to income redistribution through transfer payments and other social benefits, compared to 25 percent for EU countries. Moreover, European workers enjoy greater protection and business is more tightly regulated than in the United States. For example, "the legal minimum wage in the U.S. in the 1990s was only 39 percent of the average wage, whereas in the European Union it was 53 percent of the average wage."[4] Also, generous family benefits—in particular, paid maternity leave—are the norm in Western Europe. But pro-family policies have not boosted birthrates, which remain very low (except among some immigrant groups). This pattern also holds true in Italy, despite the Vatican's adamant stand against contraception.

Redefining the role of the state in the economy, the environment, and society is a fundamental problem of postmodern development. The West's romance with the free market was rekindled by British Prime Minister Margaret Thatcher in 1979 and was reinforced by the administrations of President Ronald Reagan and

West German Chancellor Helmut Kohl. France (under a Socialist president) tried to buck the conservative trend in the early 1980s, but failed when the economy faltered badly. In 1986, a center-right coalition won control of the French National Assembly from the Socialists, ushering in center-right government. The Socialists were left with little choice but to move to the right or lose the presidency.

The taming of the French Socialists points to one other feature of post-industrial politics: a narrowing of the differences between parties of the right and parties of the left. Extremist parties at both ends of the political spectrum fell by the wayside—at least momentarily. Ideology was downplayed. Government and opposition alike advocated pragmatic solutions to economic and social problems. These trends reflected a middle-of-the-road popular consensus.

The decade of 1990s began with a disturbing tendency toward right-wing extremism in several Western European countries, including France, Germany, and Italy. Many European voters expressed growing disaffection with ossified party structures and official corruption, as well as old social injustices and new economic challenges. The end of the Cold War contributed to a climate of great expectations on the Continent, a sense that the time had come to rejuvenate Europe's established democracies as well as to encourage the emerging ones in Eastern Europe.

Germany faced the greatest immediate challenge: merging the two former German states into a single entity. But, as we are about to discover, this was only one of a number of major challenges facing Germany, most of which were (and are) common to Western Europe as a whole, although in varying forms. The rising tide of intolerance receded as the decade drew to a close only to resurge in the unsettling period after September 11, 2001.

CASE STUDIES: BRITAIN, FRANCE, GERMANY, ITALY, AND SPAIN

The five countries featured in Part I of this book had a combined population of over 302 million people in 2005 (slightly larger than the United States). These countries with a total GDP roughly four-fifths that of the U.S. form the core of a rising economic Leviathan—the European Union (EU)—but lack commensurate military power for reasons (and with consequences) that will be explored in Chapter Four. (We focus on the European Union in Part III of this book.)

France and Germany have been the prime movers behind this potential pan-European superpower since the 1950s, when the European Coal and Steel Community (ECSC) and the European Economic Community (EEC), fore-runners of the EU, were launched. The United Kingdom joined belatedly (in the 1970s), but never abandoned its "special relationship" with the United States. Italy has been part of the European project from the start, but Spain did not join until 1986. All five countries have dynamic market economies, generous social welfare programs, and stable democracies. Even so, these similarities conceal important differences—differences that continue to make all talk of creating a "United States of Europe" premature, if not altogether preposterous.

BRITAIN: MOTHER OF ALL PARLIAMENTS

In contrast to the United States, whose founders developed elaborate theoretical underpinnings for the political system, in Great Britain the political tradition is an outgrowth of centuries of history, experiment, and legal precedent. A theory of British constitutionalism can be found in the writings and speeches of Edmund Burke, who in the late eighteenth century celebrated the role of continuity and stability in the development of Britain's evolving political system. Burke credited Britain's success to the long, unbroken chain of national development during which economic equality and political liberty evolved side by side.

Constitution by Evolution

The United Kingdom—both a **parliamentary democracy** and a constitutional monarchy—has never formally adopted a constitution. Rather, it is the product of four elements: statutory law, **common law, custom and convention,** and **works of authority** (discussed later). In truth, the British constitution is so deeply embedded in the political culture that trying to write it down would probably undermine its authority by reopening political debates long settled. In stark contrast to most constitutional democracies, therefore, the British parliamentary system is the result of an evolutionary process rather than a revolution or a constitutional convention.

Today the normal method of amending and augmenting the British constitution is statutory law, which originates from acts of Parliament. The Parliament Act of 1911 that reduced the legislative role of the House of Lords is a prime example. Elected **Members of Parliament** (MPs) in the **House of Commons** (lower house) make statutory law. The role of the **House of Lords,** or upper house, in the legislative process will be discussed later in this chapter.

Common law is judge-made law. It is based on legal rulings and decisions passed down through generations that are generally upheld in the courts. At one time common law played a crucial role in the evolution of the British system. For example, it is the basis of the principle of **parliamentary sovereignty.** A. V. Dicey, a great nineteenth-century British political thinker, considered this principle one of the two main pillars of the British constitution (the other being the rule of law). Common law now plays a secondary role.

Custom and convention are longstanding practices not based on statutory or common law. Rather, they are rooted in nothing but the perceived logic of the system itself. They must be observed in order for the government to run smoothly and efficiently. For example, it is important for symbolic reasons for the Crown (Queen Elizabeth II at present) to give acts of Parliament its royal assent.

A law that did not have the royal stamp of approval would seem somehow not legitimate. The last time a British monarch refused to give assent to an act of Parliament was in the 1700s. Another custom is the monarch's dissolving Parliament and calling for new elections, at the prime minister's request, if the government receives a vote of no confidence.

Tracts known as works of authority, esteemed for the quality of reasoning they exhibit and the reputation of the scholars who produced them, constitute a final source of constitutional law. In addition to Dicey, prominent British constitutional authorities include John Austin and Walter Bagehot, among others.

There is no power of judicial review in Great Britain. Government minister, judges, and administrative officials can interpret the constitution in specific instances, but in general, acts of Parliament are supreme. And there are no extraordinary procedures for amending the British constitution; statutes and common law are changed by ordinary legislation (that is, they require a simple majority in the House of Commons). One caveat is necessary here: in specific areas, parliamentary sovereignty conflicts with the supremacy of EU law over national law. As we will note later in this book, the tension between these two principles—one national, the other supranational—goes to the root of the crisis facing the EU after French and Dutch voters rejected the proposed EU constitution in 2005. Two seminal ideas underpin British politics: parliamentary sovereignty and the **rule of law.** Dicey defined parliamentary sovereignty as "the right to make or unmake any law whatever; and, further, that no person or body is recognized by the law of England as having a right to override or set aside the legislation of Parliament." The rule of law, according to Dicey, means two things. First, "no man is punishable . . . except for a distinct breach of law established . . . before ordinary courts of the land." Second, "no man is above the law . . . whatever his rank." Dicey also observed that "the constitution is pervaded by the rule of law" in the sense that the general principles of the constitution are themselves "the result of judicial decision determining the rights of private persons in particular cases brought before the courts."[5]

The British parliamentary system has four salient characteristics. First, it is a centralized or **unitary system,** in contrast to the federal system found in the United States or Germany. The central government possesses all the powers of government and delegates to local governments only as much authority as it deems necessary and proper. Consequently, London has complete power over the local authorities; thus, the concept of reserved powers—in other words, powers residing in the individual states—has no relevance in the British system.

Second, at the national level a **fusion of powers** exists in place of the separation of powers found in the United States. The U.S. presidential system bars members of Congress from concurrently holding a cabinet office. In contrast, the British cabinet consists of the leaders of the majority party in the House of Commons. Normally, election to Parliament is a prerequisite to becoming a cabinet member. After an election, the head of the victorious party in Parliament (the prime minister) names the other members (ministers) of the new cabinet; following a pro forma vote of approval by the party's majority in the House of Commons, a government is formed. The cabinet, headed by the prime minister, is responsible for formulating and initiating legislation. Although all members of Parliament, including the opposition, are free to question and criticize the government, the majority party is virtually assured that its legislative proposals will pass.

A third key feature is **collective ministerial responsibility.** The prime minister and cabinet (the government) are members of Parliament and exercise executive power only so long as they continue to enjoy the backing of a parliamentary majority. The government must be prepared to answer the questions about its policies before both houses of Parliament. The collective aspect of ministerial responsibility relates to the fact that cabinet members are expected to support all policies, actions, and decisions of the government in public; they may dissent only behind closed doors.

Fourth, the British model features a stable **two-party system.** This does not mean there are only two political parties in existence but rather that two major parties tend to alternate in power. In a multiparty system, the government will often be formed by a coalition of two or more parties. The absence of coalitions in the United Kingdom is a product of the electoral system, which like the American system is based on single-member districts and a **first-past-the-post** rule that favors established parties. This system also greatly magnifies the effect of even a small plurality of votes. In 2005, for example, the ruling Labour party won only 35 percent of the popular vote (a mere 3 percent more than the Conservatives) but gained 55 percent of the seats in Parliament—still a comfortable (though much reduced) majority. Thus, in contrast to the situation in many parliamentary democracies (especially those that employ a system of proportional representation), the victorious party in British elections has no need to enter into coalitions with smaller parties.

Despite the tendency of the British system to shut out (or underrepresent) small parties, the two major political parties (Conservative and Labour) present relatively clear policy alternatives to the electorate to a far greater extent than do the two major parties (Republican and Democratic) in the United States. The reason clearly has more to do with differences in British and American political cultures than with the mechanics of electoral systems because both base representation on single-member districts and plurality voting (that is, the candidate with the most votes wins even if he or she gets less than half the votes cast). British political parties are more disciplined than the two major parties in the United States. Consequently, when a party wins an election and forms a government, it can almost always put its program into effect without legislative obstruction.

Westminster: Where Lower Is Higher

Westminster, where Parliament sits, is virtually synonymous with the British government. In Parliament the British have fused the political symbols, ceremonies, and conventions of the past with the changing realities of the present. The House of Commons—the lower chamber—has wielded primary legislative power since 1911; nonetheless, the House of Lords has survived, as a relic of Britain's aristocratic past.

The House of Lords long consisted of approximately eleven hundred members, of whom about four-fifths were hereditary peers. The remaining members included the bishops of the Church of England, Lords of Appeal in Ordinary (without the power of judicial review but otherwise similar in function to the U.S. Supreme Court), and other life peers (distinguished British subjects appointed by the monarch). Typically, only about two hundred to three hundred members attended sessions regularly. In 1999, the **House of Lords Act** brought about far-reaching reforms in the upper house, setting the stage for the eventual abolition of all hereditary peerages but allowing a maximum of 92 to be excluded. As these seats are vacated, they will be filled through by-elections in which members of the House of Lords rank the candidates. A candidate must be preferred by an absolute majority to win the election. If no candidate is ranked number one by a majority of the voting members, the votes of the candidate receiving the fewest first-preference rankings are redistributed. For example, say Candidate X is still in the running and Candidate Y has been eliminated. If Candidate X is the second preference on 10 ballots that originally went to Candidate Y, Candidate X gets ten more votes. This process continues until one candidate gets a clear majority. At least two such by-elections were held between 2002 and 2005.

The upper chamber has not had power to veto money bills since 1911 and since 1949 can only delay passage of other bills for one year (this limited power is called a suspensive veto). The precarious position of the lords is suggested by the fact that they rarely go against the House of Commons. Indeed, they have done so only four times in more than eighty years and only once in recent times.[6] The lords know that if they were to become too assertive in obstructing or delaying legislation, the House of Lords could quite possibly be abolished. In the British system, because there is no constitution to amend, the House of Commons can do virtually anything it wants by majority vote, so long as it has public approval.

The House of Commons approves or rejects legislation and provides a public (now televised) arena where the opposition can and often does go on the verbal offensive, forcing the prime minister and cabinet to defend the government's actions and policies. It comprises approximately 646 members elected by plurality vote in single-member districts for five-year terms, subject to dissolution by the Crown on the advice of the prime minister. The seats are apportioned according to population, so England's share is slightly more than 80 percent of the total, followed by Scotland, Wales, and Northern Ireland. (A tenacious Scottish nationalist movement seeks full independence for Scotland.)

Parliament is the sole source of legislative power in the British system. It alone can make new laws and repeal or revise old ones. This power gives the majority party enormous leverage; theoretically, it could reshape the entire political system by one simple parliamentary act. But the political obstacles to drastic structural change are formidable. The existing system has broad national support. Any attempt to reorder the system would risk a tumultuous outpouring of public indignation. In Great Britain, when the government loses public support, it is expected to resign. The major party out of power would normally join the public in protesting against any abrupt change in the British political system. In all likelihood, the minor parties would side with the major opposition party.

The role of the opposition is, quite simply, to oppose. If it does not do so, it is acting irresponsibly. Thus the majority party and the major opposition party both have a vital role to play. No major party is ever irrelevant, win or lose. This point is underscored by the traditional name given to the party out of power: the **loyal opposition** (officially known as Her Majesty's Loyal Opposition). Compare this tradition with partisan politics in the United States, where the leaders of the party in power often invoke patriotism as a means to stifle criticism and discourage "obstructionism" by members of the opposing party in Congress.

The government controls the legislative process. After a bill is formally introduced in the House of Commons, the government decides when it will be debated. Except for the nineteen **opposition days** during each session of Parliament, the government has control of the legislative agenda. Bills go through three readings—one when they are introduced, another when they are debated, and a third when they are voted on. Floor debate occurs after the second reading, a crucial point in the process. Bills approved at this stage usually have clear sailing the rest of the way. Following debate, bills go to standing committees.

In contrast to the committee system in the U.S. Congress, British committees are often very large (up to fifty members) and are not specialized. However, because the personnel of a committee changes with each bill and members can volunteer for each bill, members with expertise or special concerns do get to consider bills of particular interest to them. In this way the party leaders are able to satisfy membership demands for participation without actually conceding any power of great importance. Committees' powers are narrowly circumscribed: they refine the language of legislation, but they may not redefine the legislation itself. They rarely pass an amendment unless the minister of the relevant department proposes it. The majority party always controls the committees by the same margin that it enjoys in the full House of Commons.

Next comes the report stage, during which amendments can be approved or rejected. The government's amendments are almost always passed; any private member's amendment at this stage is generally rejected unless it has the blessing of the government. Bills dealing with constitutional issues are handled differently: they go to a "committee of the whole"—the entire House of Commons is the committee. If a bill of this nature is passed without amendments, it does not have to go through the report stage.

The **third reading** in the House of Commons occurs when a bill is voted on in final form. If it passes, it goes to the House of Lords, which can amend it, but only if the House of Commons approves. The final step is the granting of **royal assent** by the Crown—a mere formality but one that preserves the symbolism so important to the legitimization of government in Great Britain.

Is the legislative process cut and dried, with the government holding all the trump cards? Not really. The opposition has ample opportunity to criticize, embarrass, and call the government to account. The most important opposition device is question time, which is televised. Every day, Monday through Thursday, government ministers must answer questions on the floor of the House of Commons; twice a week, the prime minister must answer questions as well.

Question time makes politics something of a spectacle in Great Britain. It puts a premium on debate skills and forces policy makers to justify their actions and decisions continuously—not only to Parliament but to the British people as well.

If the government loses its popular support, it may either resign or risk a **vote of no confidence** in Parliament. If Parliament passes such a motion or defeats a government bill with a vote of confidence attached, the government must, by convention, resign and either permit another party leader to form a government or ask the monarch to dissolve Parliament and call new elections. This procedure was last invoked in 1979, when the Labour party lost on a vote of confidence, resigned, and opened the door to the Conservative party, which subsequently won the elections and held power until May of 1997. The threat of a no-confidence vote can also play a role in making or breaking parliamentary governments, but it rarely comes into play in the United Kingdom because the party in power typically has a solid majority. Even when Labour lost 47 MPs in the 2005 parliamentary elections, Prime Minister Tony Blair still had a comfortable majority in the House of Commons (356 seats out of a total of 646).

Under normal circumstances, the government need not worry about losing important votes in Parliament. The majority party members are led by the government's chief whip, who holds a salaried position. The chief whip helps the government set the schedule in Parliament and keeps the cabinet briefed on developments there. Above all, the chief whip is responsible for party discipline, which in the British context means ensuring that majority-party MPs support government policy and vote to pass government bills. (The opposition and minor parties also have whips who perform the same disciplinary functions.)

The House of Lords passes on legislation and can offer amendments, but its lawmaking powers are quite limited. It can delay money bills for no more than one month and all other legislation for no more than one year. Generally, the lords confine themselves to scrutinizing legislation, refining the language, and occasionally offering an amendment to reinforce rather than weaken the bill's original intent.

As noted earlier, the British system features a fusion of powers. This fusion is particularly evident in the judicial functions of the House of Lords, which serves as the highest court of appeals in Great Britain. In that, it is similar to the U.S. Supreme Court, except that the House of Lords does not have the power to declare legislative acts unconstitutional.

Some critics argue that the House of Lords is an anachronism and should either be abolished altogether or replaced by a democratically elected upper house. But the British remain steeped in tradition and that is not likely to happen any time soon.

10 Downing Street: Prime Minister and Cabinet

The prime minister holds the most powerful position in the British system of **cabinet government,** acting simultaneously as chief executive, majority party leader, and principal adviser to the crown. The prime minister appoints and dismisses cabinet members, sets the legislative agenda, decides major policy issues, directs the bureaucracy, and manages the nation's diplomatic affairs. Being both head of government and leader of the parliamentary majority, the prime minister has enormous authority. Some critics have asserted that the British prime minister is a virtual dictator, but this charge is greatly exaggerated.

Besides the ever-present possibility of a no-confidence vote, there are systemic liabilities that tend to offset a prime minister's powers. For instance, a prime minister cannot blame Parliament for failed government policies the way U.S. presidents can blame Congress. As British prime ministers have discovered, the more power a chief executive wields, the more responsibility he or she must bear for the outcome. One recent illustration of this point was Tony Blair's unpopular decision to take the U.K. into the war in Iraq as America's junior partner, which was followed by a sharp drop in Labour MPs (and Blair's prestige) after the 2005 elections.

British voters do not vote for the prime minister in national elections the way American voters vote for the president; rather, the majority party in Parliament chooses a prime minister. The choice is always a foregone conclusion, however, because each party selects a leader at its convention before a general election. This part of the process is similar to the nominating conventions in the United States, except that future prime ministers do not have to face grueling primaries.

The formation and functioning of the cabinet illustrate the fusion of legislative and executive powers in the British system. The prime minister chooses leading MPs to serve in the cabinet. There is no limit on the size of the cabinet; each prime minister decides which departments will have cabinet representation, although certain ministers—among them Chancellor of the Exchequer (treasury), Foreign Secretary, and Home Secretary—are always included. The cabinet's functions include final determination of proposals to be submitted to Parliament, supreme control of the national executive (that is, the power to move the government decisively in one direction or another), and continuous coordination of the administrative departments.

The cabinet operates under the principle of collective responsibility. Publicly, all cabinet members must support the government's policies without reservation, even if they disagree among themselves in private. A cabinet member who cannot support a decision is expected to resign. Individual ministerial responsibility, according to which ministers of departments are responsible for all the actions of their departments, is also an important feature of the British government. Unlike the United States, where cabinet members often "pass the buck" (witness Secretary of Defense Donald Rumsfeld in the Abu Ghraib prisoner abuse scandal), British ministers are expected to bear the consequences of any administrative failure, any injustice to individuals, or any policy that comes under verbal attack in Parliament, whether they were personally responsible or not. Again unlike the United States, most ministers are members of the House of Commons; as such, they often face hostile questioning from the opposition and must be prepared to defend themselves in open (nationally televised) debate.

The cabinet generally convenes once a week in the Cabinet Room at the prime minister's residence, 10 Downing Street. The chief whip normally attends cabinet meetings, which are chaired by the prime minister. Votes are rarely taken, the prime minister preferring instead to seek consensus or to listen to the discussion and then declare a decision. The precise nature of cabinet meetings is shrouded in mystery: tradition, self-restraint, and the **Official Secrets Act** keep leaks to a minimum.

There are two schools of thought regarding the extent of the prime minister's powers. One school views the prime minister as omnipotent, having the final authority to decide all matters and to appoint or dismiss cabinet members at will. The other school stresses that any politician who gets a cabinet post is powerful in his or her own right. Creating a cabinet is a political act: the prime minister must placate other powerful cabinet members and protect party unity. The widely reported policy differences between Prime Minister Tony Blair and Treasury Chancellor Gordon Brown in 2002 illustrates this point.[7] In recent times, there has been a widely noted tendency toward cabinet and even prime ministerial government (particularly under Thatcher and now Blair), pointing to two interesting facts: first, the British political system is still evolving; second, having no written constitution, it can change without going through any cumbersome amendment process.

Coordination and communication between the cabinet and the subordinate levels of the government are done through cabinet committees and the Cabinet Office. Originally, the committees were created to deal with particular issues; today there are about twenty-five permanent cabinet committees responsible for interdepartmental coordination and oversight in various issue areas. There are also over one hundred ad hoc committees to handle specific issues and facilitate two-way communication between the cabinet and the appropriate government departments.

The Cabinet Office also houses a secretariat that handles the cabinet's administrative affairs. It assists in coordinating the operations of government, keeps noncabinet ministers informed of cabinet decisions, prepares and circulates the agenda for cabinet meetings (and cabinet committee meetings), and the like. With the growth of the powers, functions, and responsibilities of the executive, the secretariat has become an indispensable part of the government's administrative apparatus.

Whitehall: Administrative Nerve Center

The cabinet is the pinnacle of the central government, but the departments are the building blocks. Headquartered in **Whitehall,** the departments run the day-to-day business of the government. They are supervised by a minister or by a secretary of state. (Recall that not all departments enjoy cabinet status.) Each departmental minister is assisted by at least one junior minister called a **parliamentary secretary.** The largest departments may also have parliamentary undersecretaries. All these officials (about a hundred in all, plus the cabinet posts) are members of the majority party in Parliament whom the prime minister appoints.

Department ministers are in charge of main administrative units of the government and must perform a variety of managerial functions, including motivating and monitoring the large number of civil servants who staff the department. The minister's chief aide is the **permanent secretary,** a senior civil servant who has the broad administrative experience and substantive expertise that a politically appointed minister may lack. Nevertheless, ultimate responsibility for departmental performance rests squarely on the minister's shoulders. A minister's most important and difficult task can be to persuade, bully, cajole, and otherwise induce the civil servants at the working levels of government to implement policy according to the government's wishes.

Parties and Elections

Traditionally, Great Britain has had a two-party system, but throughout most of the twentieth century there have been three major national political parties: the Conservative (or Tory) Party, the Labour Party, and the Liberal Party. For a century, control of the government has alternated between the Conservatives and Labour, but there have been various attempts to revitalize the Liberal party and, in the 1980s, even to fashion a whole new party movement from like-minded elements of Labour and Liberals. Irish, Scottish, and Welsh nationalism are also notable factors in British elections. Irish nationalism led to the creation of an independent state of Ireland after World War I and continues to bedevil the British in Ulster (Northern Ireland); a nettlesome Scottish nationalism also continues to be a burr under the saddle of Westminster politicians for whom English domination is a given.

The Conservatives ruled without interruption during the 1980s. In 1987, Margaret Thatcher became the first British prime minister in the twentieth century to lead a party to three consecutive election victories (Tony Blair has now equaled that record). Thatcher stepped down near the end of 1990 in the face of flagging popular support for her brand of conservativism. Her mild-mannered successor, John Major, was a sharp contrast in style and also proved to be surprisingly original in substance. Two years later, Major survived a major test when the Conservative party won a narrow majority in Parliament—one that nevertheless enabled the Tories to rule for another five years.

In terms of doctrine, the British Conservative party can be loosely compared with the U.S. Republican Party under President Ronald Reagan, although in contrast to conservatives in the U.S., British politicians of the center-right accept a welfare state, which even after the Thatcher reforms is still relatively generous in redistributing society's wealth from the top down. Thatcher's imprint on British society was perhaps deeper and more lasting than President Reagan's because the United States, unlike Great Britain, has never had a comprehensive cradle-to-the-grave system of social insurance (including, for example, national health care).

Prime Minister Thatcher sought to reduce the size of government, curb spending, denationalize (or reprivatize) industry, cut taxes, maintain a strong independent nuclear strike force, and remain in the European Union. **Thatcherism** also encouraged private home ownership and self-reliance, advocated partial privatization of the National Health System (NHS), and opposed modernizing Britain's state-owned railway system. In addition, Thatcher tried to break the grip of the trade unions on the nation's domestic economic policy. In relentlessly pursuing this strategy of governmental retrenchment and economic revitalization, Thatcher was aided by the fact that the Conservative Party is relatively cohesive, without deep ideological divisions or warring factions.

By contrast, the Labour party is a coalition of disparate interests. Originally an outgrowth of the British trade union movement, it was founded as the party of the working class. It became the main opposition party in the 1920s. From the outset, it distanced itself from the once-powerful Liberal party by embracing a moderate form of socialism. For example, policies advocated as recently as the 1980s included renationalization of industry, unilateral nuclear disarmament, withdrawal from the EU, closing of U.S. military bases, expansion of the social welfare system, higher taxes for the wealthy, and concessions to organized labor.

After World War I, the Labour Party became the major (and only) alternative to Tory government. But the rise of Labour in the first two decades of the twentieth century was matched by its near-demise in the last two decades of the century. Following its electoral defeat in 1979, the party was split by struggle between the left wing and moderate factions. The moderates opposed both the party's stance favoring British withdrawal from the EU and a change in the party's method of selecting its leader. The new Social Democratic Party, founded by disaffected Labourites, was the bitter fruit of this struggle. The defection weakened the Labour Party but did not give rise to a viable alternative.

In the late 1980s, following its third straight election defeat, the party began to shift toward the center in an effort to get back into the political mainstream which had moved to the right under the influence of Prime Minister Thatcher's theories and policies. Due in part to continued internal divisions over ideology and policy, however, it would be another decade before this process would finally bring Labour back to power.[8] By then Britain's main party of the left would have a whole new look—that of its youthful, moderate, and market-friendly new leader, Tony Blair.

Today Labour is no longer simply a working-class party. It is an umbrella organization appealing not only to workers but also to middle-class civil servants, teachers, housewives, peace activists, welfare recipients, students, pensioners, the jobless, the homeless, and the otherwise poor and downtrodden. Under Prime Minister Blair's leadership, Labour has also reached out to the business community and the professions. As indicated earlier, Mr. Blair's **New Labour** platform discarded "old" Labour's ideologically inspired policy objectives and downplayed ideology. Labour won the 2005 elections but lost a significant number of parliamentary seats (see Chapter Four), as Tony Blair's unwavering support for the unpopular war in Iraq, among other things, alienated many British voters.

British political parties have not shown much enthusiasm for fundamental realignments or even temporary coalitions. In the 1983 elections, for example, the Social Democrats and the Liberals formed such a coalition, which they called the Alliance. The two parties kept their campaign finances separate but issued a joint manifesto urging government action to relieve unemployment, cuts in military spending, redoubled arms control efforts, expanded welfare programs, continued membership in the EU, and incentives for private enterprise. The Alliance was designed to offer the British voters a middle-of-the-road alternative to the right-leaning Conservatives and left-leaning Labourites; it met with little success at the polls, however.

In addition to the Liberals, minor parties in Great Britain include the Greens, the Scottish Nationalist Party, the Unionist Party, the Nationalist Front Party, and the Communist Party. All third parties face two fundamental obstacles—tradition and the first-past-the-post electoral system. On tradition, Sydney Bailey's observation is apposite:

> There is nothing sacred in the number two, but the fact is that for by far the greater part of the three centuries during which parties in the modern sense have existed in Britain there have been two major parties, a Government party and an Opposition party.[9]

British voters, like voters in most countries with a history of stable government, are reluctant to vote for parties they consider untested. This rational-traditional voting behavior is reinforced by an electoral system based on single-member districts and selection by plurality vote (whoever gets the most votes wins)—a system imitated in the United States, but rarely found elsewhere in the world. The way it works is quite simple. Each voting district is given one seat in the legislature (or parliament) and one seat only. (In proportional representation systems, multimember districts typically have three to five seats.) Thus, all the candidates in each district are vying for that one seat. But to win, a candidate need only receive a plurality of the votes, not a majority. If there are, say, six parties with candidates in the race it is quite possible that the winning candidate will poll no more than 25 percent, and maybe less. Theoretically, if the votes were evenly distributed in a six-way race a candidate could win with less than 17 percent of the vote—by simply getting one more vote than any of the other five.

Always a Winner: First Past the Post

In the British system, parliamentary elections must be held at least every five years, but the prime minister has the prerogative of calling elections sooner. Negative circumstances, such as a vote of no confidence or a scandal, can force early elections. More often, the prime minister will try to capitalize on a momentary surge in public approval to win another five-year term. For example, in 1983, when the British defeated Argentina in a war over the Falkland Islands, Prime Minister Thatcher called early elections to take advantage of the resulting surge in her personal popularity. By contrast, John Major did not call early elections in 1991 because public displeasure with the Tory government at that time was high (as evidenced by the large loss of town hall seats in local elections). By waiting to hold parliamentary elections until the spring of 1992, Major was able to ride out the storm, and the Conservatives won a fourth consecutive term in office—the first British party to do so in 150 years.

British elections are short and simple compared with those in the United States. In the United States, president, senators, and representatives are elected to terms of different lengths, and national elections are staggered, taking place every two years. As a result, campaigns are frequent, and it seems as though one election barely ends before the next begins. In Great Britain there is normally one national election every four or five years.

Elections take place when the prime minister formally asks the monarch to dissolve Parliament, a procedure that usually takes about ten days. Balloting occurs no more than three weeks after a royal proclamation summons a new Parliament. As a rule, the prime minister dissolves Parliament before the five-year term is up. Because the government can decide precisely when the next election is to be held, however, the party in power has an advantage over the opposition.

All British subjects 18 years of age or older are eligible to vote, provided that they have registered. Because voting registers are produced only once a year now, it can take up to sixteen months for a voter to qualify. In Great Britain, however, local officials have an obligation to get everybody registered, which is not the case in the United States. The result is that virtually every adult is registered in the United Kingdom, in sharp contrast to the United States, where only half the eligible voters may be registered at any given time.

The British invented the first-past-the-post system. As noted earlier, each party in a voting district (called a *constituency*) fields a single candidate, and whoever gets a plurality of the votes wins. It is common to win this type of election with less than an absolute majority of the popular vote (the more candidates the less likely it is than anyone will receive more than half the votes cast). This system—which is also used in the United States—has been widely criticized on the grounds that it distorts the actual voting results. In 1979, for example, the Conservative Party won 339 seats in Parliament, a clear majority; if the seats had been distributed in proportion to the votes, however, the Conservatives would have won only 279, well short of a majority. Labour won in 2005 with the smallest plurality on record—little more than a third of the popular vote. Only in 1900, 1906, 1931, and 1935 would the government have won a working majority in Parliament if the seats were distributed in direct proportion to the votes.[10] On the other hand, the British have not been plagued by weak minority governments, which are quite common in many other parliamentary democracies.

Critics of the current system generally favor some form of **proportional representation.** (The PR system has, in fact, been introduced to British voters in elections to the European Parliament.) The British affinity for tradition is a formidable obstacle to any such change, however. Another is the logic of parliamentary rule, which works best when there is a majority party able to form a unified government and implement a consistent set of policies. As we have seen, the British system tends to magnify the winning party's parliamentary majority.[11] Changing the system would reduce the odds that any single party would win a working majority. Parties would be forced to enter into coalitions in order to form a government.

In sum, the British and American electoral systems are alike (single-member districts and whoever gets the most votes wins), but that is where the similarities end. British national elections are more party oriented than those in the United States, where the personality, reputation, and charisma of the individual candidate are often paramount. Also, British elections are much shorter and less costly.

Public Opinion and Pressure Groups

We have already alluded to the role of public opinion in the British system. Prime ministers often decide when to call new elections on the basis of opinion polls. Conversely, when a government's popular approval rating falls, it may be forced to resign. Thus public opinion is likely to have a more direct impact on government in Great Britain, where the prime minister and cabinet have an indefinite term of office, than in the United States, where the president and administration have a fixed term.

Public opinion polling can be critical in any democratic society, but it is especially important in the British system, where success or failure in elections is often a question of timing. It is also important because a steady or sudden drop in the government's popularity can induce it to resign or prompt a confidence vote in Parliament. Consequently, the accuracy of polls is more than a matter of theoretical interest. The 1992 elections demonstrated that polls and pollsters are no more infallible in Great Britain than elsewhere. All the polls on the eve of the elections predicted that the outcome would be very close and that Labour would have the edge. They also predicted that the outcome might be a "hung Parliament," with neither major party attaining a clear majority in the House of Commons.[12] These predictions all turned out to be wrong.

Pressure groups began gaining influence in the United Kingdom after World War II. In fact, prior to the Tories' victory in 1979, the trade unions and big business had become so powerful that some experts began to describe the system as "corporatist." The heralds of the **corporatist model** argued that a new triple alliance of government, big business, and organized labor was becoming more powerful than Parliament. However, there is little reason to believe that the parliamentary system itself is in jeopardy. Indeed, Prime Minister Thatcher greatly reduced organized labor's clout in economic policy formulation, and union membership declined by more than 20 percent between 1979 and 1986 in the United Kingdom.[13] Critics note that organized labor's loss has been big business's gain—a lament also heard in the United States dating back to the early 1980s.

In the British system, pressure groups are most effective when they can establish lines of communication with the civil service. For the most part, it is the executive branch (the cabinet and the various ministries and departments) that formulates public policy in the British system, in contrast to the United States, where lobbying Congress is as important as establishing contacts within the bureaucracy. British pressure groups therefore generally bypass Parliament altogether.

In the next chapter, we turn from institutional patterns to the challenges facing British government in recent years. We also will assess the performance of the government and consider Britain's prospects for the future in the light of current problems and available policy choices (solutions). But first we look at political institutions in France, Germany, Spain, and Italy.

FRANCE'S FIFTH REPUBLIC

France witnessed the rise and fall of four republics and fifteen constitutions between 1789 and 1958. The Fifth Republic has now survived for almost half a century—a noteworthy achievement, considering that its predecessor, adopted in the wake of World War II, endured a scant twelve years. During that time, French governments lasted an average of only six months. So it is small wonder that political instability was both the cause of the Fourth Republic's early demise and the principal malady the Fifth Republic's Constitution was designed to cure.

A Hybrid System

The Constitution of the **Fifth Republic** is a composite of France's earlier constitutions. It incorporates presidential, parliamentary, and plebiscitarian features, along with certain "Gaullist" innovations—elements associated with the personality and political philosophy of the Fifth Republic's founder and first president, General Charles de Gaulle.

The hallmark of the current Constitution (adopted in 1958) is the pivotal role of the president, which contrasts sharply with its predecessors. Under the Third and Fourth Republics, the president was little more than a figurehead who rubber-stamped measures passed by the parliament. Chosen by the legislature acting as an electoral college, presidents were captives of that body. French parliaments were notoriously fragmented and ineffectual, which meant that the French government was often adrift. Presidents had the power to appoint prime ministers (with legislative approval) and to dissolve the parliament, but that was all. Real power, to the extent that it existed at all, was lodged in the prime minister and cabinet, who were often paralyzed by a perpetually divided parliament.

To remedy this situation, de Gaulle stressed the need for a strong and dignified president who would be aloof from fractious party politics and could guide the nation, mediate among the parties, and discipline (or circumvent) the parliament in the interests of unity, stability, and efficiency. As a champion of French nationalism who despised the narrow particularism of petty politicians, the controversial de Gaulle was both admired by many for his leadership abilities and reviled by others for his allegedly Bonapartist tendencies.

The *plebiscitarian* aspect of the present Constitution has its historical roots in the populist nature of Napoleon Bonaparte's rule and, more specifically, in the French Constitution of 1852. A **plebiscite** (or referendum) is a way to let the people decide politically charged questions facing the nation by a direct vote. The idea of taking issues directly to the people appeals to egalitarian instincts in a democratic society, but in the hands of a charismatic demagogue it can be a means of subverting democracy. A popular president can use the referendum to get around the parliament, in effect establishing a personalistic (and deliberately antirepublican) form of rule. The problem with direct votes of this kind is something such illustrious political thinkers as James Madison, John Stuart Mill, and Alexis de Tocqueville have all warned against—namely, the tyranny of the majority. The idea of a republic (or *representative* democracy) is to place a buffer of popularly elected legislators between the people and the power of government as protection against mob rule. In direct democracy, the majority can too easily trample minority rights into the ground—so goes the theory.

But a would-be Bonaparte has the potential to bully the legislature in other ways. One example of how Charles de Gaulle used the expansive (and expandable) presidential powers at his disposal was the 1962 referendum on the direct election of the president. De Gaulle decided somewhat belatedly that it would strengthen the hand of the French president (namely, himself) to be directly elected to a seven-year term. (Originally in the Fifth Republic, an electoral college indirectly elected the French president to a shorter term.) De Gaulle was a peculiar combination of autocrat, democrat, and populist. Most important, the French nation saw him as the savior of French democracy (which he was) and a great leader who above all personified the idea of France.

To nobody's surprise, the referendum passed—this result was expected in part because de Gaulle had threatened to resign if it failed, thus presenting French voters with a kind of ultimatum. Arguably, the amendment was unconstitutional because the constitution contains no provision for amendment by referendum; in any event, the law was changed in 2000. France's presidents now serve five-year terms, but before the law was changed, the political deck was stacked in favor of a strong executive to a degree not found in any other West European country. Thus President François Mitterrand held office from 1981 to 1995 but only had to run for re-election one time.

The republican facet of the system is embodied in the parliament, or **National Assembly,** whose members are directly elected by secret ballot on the basis of universal suffrage. But under the Fifth Republic's constitution, the legislative branch can be bullied—or even circumvented—by a strong-willed and popular chief executive, as President de Gaulle demonstrated.

Finally, the quasi-parliamentary nature of the system can be seen in the presence of a cabinet-style executive in which the leader of the majority party in parliament (or of a coalition) chooses a cabinet and forms a government (as in Great Britain). The constitution divides executive powers between the prime minister and the president. This divided (dual) executive arrangement can give rise to a constitutional crisis if the two executives are not on parallel tracks (discussed later in connection with the term cohabitation).

The present constitution has weathered several decades of storm and stress. Longevity begets legitimacy. The mix of authoritarian, populist, republican, and parliamentary characteristics mirrors both the complexities of France's political history and the ideological diversity of the French electorate.

Who Rules? President and Prime Minister

France has a unique dual executive: a president with ample constitutional prerogatives to act and a prime minister who is the head of the government. However impracticable on its face, this arrangement has worked reasonably well compared with others the French have tried.

Almost all West European governments conform to the familiar parliamentary model in which the prime minister is normally the leader of the largest party or faction in the parliament and the cabinet is, in effect, a roster of notable legislators from the majority party (or the parties in a governing coalition where no single party has a clear majority). Parliamentary rule can lead to governmental instability, especially where a multiparty system and an ideologically fragmented or polarized electorate prevent any single party from gaining a clear majority. Coalition governments are often vulnerable to votes of no confidence about controversial issues. Under some conditions, coalitions can even produce the expectation of instability, which may in time become a self-fulfilling prophecy.

In a presidential system, the chief executive is chosen by popular vote for a fixed term. Except in extraordinary circumstances using cumbersome procedures, the legislative branch does not have the power to oust the president. Thus in one sense the presidential system has greater stability than the parliamentary system. By contrast, presidential government lacks the flexibility of the parliamentary system. In the former, if a scandal occurs or public support wanes, the government cannot simply resign and call for new elections; it can do so in the latter.

The French system aims for the best of both worlds, combining a strong president with a parliamentary form of government. Both fusion of powers and separation of powers are present: the prime minister and cabinet are linked by party ties and constitutional logic to the National Assembly, but the president is elected separately and is not directly affected by the vicissitudes of parliamentary politics. The government can be censured and forced to resign. Also, the president can dissolve the parliament as often as once every twelve months, but this power has been used very sparingly.

In general, the constitution positions the president as an arbitrator charged with settling differences among conflicting interests. Elected for a five-year term (a seven-year term was the norm until recently) and eligible for reelection, a popular president may dominate the political system for many years without facing the rigors of frequent campaigning or the vagaries of party politics. To win, a presidential candidate must gain an absolute majority of the votes cast. If no candidate wins such a majority, a runoff election is held. This **two-ballot system** ensures that whoever is elected will be the first or second choice of the majority of voters and thus that the president will have a national mandate. Having a president endorsed by only a minority of the electorate would not be an auspicious start for a new government, especially in a country like France with a tradition of divisive politics.

Today, thanks to de Gaulle, the French president possesses powers the British monarch now has only in theory. These include the power to appoint the prime minister (although the president must carefully weigh the balance of power among the parties in the parliament before making this choice). The president also has the power to dissolve the National Assembly, declare a state of emergency after consulting with the Constitutional Council, and issue decree laws in a crisis. The power to call a national referendum also gives a popular president the option of going directly to the people, thus ignoring the political parties and circumventing the National Assembly—an option not available to American presidents.

In dealing with a fractious or immobilized National Assembly, the executive branch (when united) has several constitutional weapons at its disposal. For example, the prime minister (most likely in close consultation with the president) could ask for *decree* powers and combine such a request with a vote of confidence. The National Assembly would then face a stark choice: either to grant the request, which would mean that the government could make laws by fiat (without parliamentary approval), or face dissolution. The government can also put a controversial bill into a bundle with other bills and demand a **package vote.** This tactic forces the National Assembly either to approve a measure many members may oppose or to vote against legislation that the majority (and the public) favors. The actual value of these weapons in the executive arsenal exists primarily in the realm of deterrents and safeguards, however, because any systematic attempt by the chief executive to frustrate the will of the majority in parliament is obviously at odds with the basic rules of political life in a democratic republic.

In the Fifth Republic, prime ministers have played a subordinate role to presidents. Even so, the prime minister's powers today are greater than they were under the Third and Fourth Republics. Presidents and prime ministers can cooperate to push legislation through the National Assembly or can block measures they oppose.

Although prime ministers play second fiddle to presidents in the French system, they have important political and administrative functions. The prime minister typically supervises and coordinates the work of the cabinet ministers, acts as the principal liaison between the executive and legislative branches, and, in the absence of a parliamentary majority, mediates among the parties in the governing coalition. This was one of the main responsibilities of Michel Rocard, who became prime minister in 1988 after the Socialists won in parliamentary elections but fell short of a clear majority. Another normal function of the prime minister is to direct and lead the election campaign in the National Assembly; it is politically risky (and perhaps undignified) for the president to get personally involved in legislative elections.

How independent or assertive a prime minister is depends on personalities and circumstances. If the president and prime minister are from the same party, the prime minister can be reduced to a largely advisory role in policy under a commanding figure like Charles de Gaulle or François Mitterrand. If the two chief executives are from different parties and embrace different ideologies, the prime minister will have the lead in policy matters because his or her party has a popular mandate and controls a majority of the votes (if not seats) in the parliament.

Unlike presidents, prime ministers have precious little job security. Hence Rocard's term in office was plagued by economic problems. He resigned in May 1991 and was replaced by Édith Cresson, France's first female prime minister. Cresson was controversial from the start. Having failed to halt a downslide in Socialist popularity, she resigned ten months later, after the Socialist party made its worst showing since World War II in local and regional elections. Similarly, Conservative Prime Minister Alain Juppé had no choice but to relinquish power to a Socialist rival, Lionel Jospin, in June 1997 after a center-right defeat in early elections called by President Chirac. As this election shows, a government in a parliamentary system can miscalculate its strength, so that the right to call elections early is not an unmitigated asset.

The Fifth Republic constitution reduced the power of the French cabinet as well as that of the prime minister. As a rule, cabinet members owe their positions and the scope of their power to the president. The cabinet grew in both size and importance after de Gaulle's departure in 1969. Cabinet members are drawn from diverse walks of life; many come from the elite ranks of the civil service. Unlike their British counterparts, members of the National Assembly must formally resign from the legislature to take a cabinet position. In practice, however, cabinet ministers only temporarily relinquish their parliamentary seats to a surrogate; as soon as they leave the government, they typically go back to the National Assembly. Another French wrinkle is that ministers are often simultaneously mayors of major cities as well. Thus, when Jacques Chaban-Delmas was prime minister (1969–1972), he continued as mayor of Bordeaux; and when Jacques Chirac became prime minister for the second time (1986–1988), he stayed on as mayor of Paris.

French Technocracy: An Elite Civil Service

The basic components of the French civil service are known *as **les grands corps**,* which include the Council of State, the Court of Accounts, the Finance Inspectorate, two corps of engineers, and the diplomatic service. The civil servants in these organizations are graduates of prestigious public policy and engineering schools known as ***les grandes écoles,*** of which the most famous is the ***École Nationale d'Administration*** **(ENA).** They dominate virtually all segments of the French administration.

In many cases, top officials in the government (and chief executive officers of major French corporations as well) are recruited from the elite ranks of the civil service (about one-third of France's ambassadors are graduates of ENA, for example). It is not fanciful for these French **technocrats** (professional public administrators with strong science backgrounds) to imagine becoming president or prime minister some day—ENA graduates have risen to both of these top positions in the past. (The French invented the term *technocrat*—it combines *bureaucrat* with *technical* or *technology* and underscores the French emphasis on mathematics and engineering.)

Until recently, France's highly centralized unitary system precluded any large role for local government. In the classical French system, most decisions were made in Paris, and prefects (officials appointed by the government) supervised the mayors of municipalities in the various *départements* (intermediate administrative districts). In this traditional **tutelage system,** prefects were powerful links between Paris and the provinces, but decentralization has resulted in more power being transferred to municipal and regional governments. In France, big-city mayors are often major political players even on the national level.

France's civil service is a reassuring institutional presence in a country where party politics has historically often been chaotic. Since the advent of the Fifth Republic, however, the National Assembly has operated under constitutional rules that give it an important role in governing while minimizing its potential for mischief.

The Taming of Parliament

The French parliament wielded most of the power under the Third (1871–1940) and Fourth (1946–1958) Republics. The instability and paralysis of parliamentary government during that often turbulent era led directly to the curbing of the powers of the parliament by the present Constitution. The fulcrum of French government moved to the presidency under the Fifth Republic.

The legislature comprises an upper and a lower house—the National Assembly and the Senate, respectively. With two exceptions, the National Assembly and the Senate share power equally. The former has the right to examine the budget first, and the cabinet is responsible to the National Assembly rather than to the Senate.

The French use a unique double-ballot method of election. Deputies run for office in single-member districts; if no candidate wins an absolute majority (a likely outcome), the two highest vote getters on the first ballot then compete in a runoff election to determine the winner in each district. This system has an interesting twist, one that stands in sharp contrast to the British and American systems: parties can form alliances for the second vote, in effect dividing up voting districts according to which party's candidate has the best chance of winning in each district. In the 1997 elections, for example, between-election alliances enabled the Communists to win 38 seats in the National Assembly with a share of the popular vote only about half as large as Jean Le Pen's extreme right National Front, which won only one seat.

France has a **rationalized parliament,** one that unlike the American and British systems is noteworthy for the powers it does *not* have. First, it cannot meet for more than six months each year. Second, almost all legislation originates in the executive branch. The National Assembly has absolutely no power to introduce budget measures. If it fails to approve the government's budget by a certain deadline, the budget can be enacted by executive decree. (In parliamentary systems, individual members are often forbidden to introduce money bills or reduce taxes.) Moreover, as noted earlier, the parliament can be compelled by the executive to cast a package vote on several pieces of legislation at once. Also, the government can make any particular vote a vote of confidence. In a confidence vote, a measure is considered approved unless the National Assembly passes a censure resolution by an absolute majority of the members. This means that only the votes in favor of censure are counted; abstentions have the effect of opposing censure. The deck is stacked, so to speak, in favor of the government.

At times, President de Gaulle creatively combined provisions of the Constitution to maximize presidential leverage over the parties in the parliament. Thus, for example, he was not above calling for a package vote on some part of his overall program and then making the vote itself a matter of confidence!

The committee system in the Fifth Republic is a cross between the U.S. Congress and the British House of Commons. As in the British system, there are only six standing committees. But as in the United States, they are specialized. Most committees have more than one hundred members. Membership on committees is apportioned according to party strength in the parliament. Committee assignments are used as a means to distribute power among the parties and to give the opposition a formal role in the political process.

In the U.S. Congress, committees have a great deal of discretion in dealing with legislative proposals from the executive branch. Not so in France.

Committees in the French parliament cannot change the substance of government bills. There are other differences as well. Investigative committees can be created to probe government actions, but they have limited powers. The length of time they may investigate is set, they cannot investigate matters that are being handled by the judiciary, findings must be reported to a standing committee for approval or rejection, and, to minimize leaks, they may meet only in closed sessions. An electoral college consisting of members of the National Assembly and representatives of local governments indirectly elects the Senate. Its 300-plus members serve nine-year terms, and Senate elections are staggered at three-year intervals. The Senate is autonomous and cannot be dissolved by the president.

The French Senate gives disproportionate representation to rural areas and thus acts as a counterweight to the urban-oriented National Assembly. Although it is weaker than the Assembly, the Senate may reject government bills. (The Assembly can override a Senate veto, however.) The Senate's chief role is to keep the government honest by using question time to challenge the prime minister and key cabinet members.

Unlike Great Britain or the United States, France has frequently had a problem with governmental instability sometimes instigated by quarrelsome and uncompromising political parties and other times by demonstrative segments of society (students, workers, farmers, or recent immigrants). Even so, when the French public becomes disaffected (as is frequently the case) there is a popularly elected president who can replace the prime minister without undue disruption to the normal functioning of the political system—exactly what happened following the referendum on the proposed EU constitution in May 2005 in which the voters embarrassed the government, decisively rejecting a measure enthusiastically endorsed by both Prime Minister Jean-Pierre Raffarin and President Chirac. In this sense, France has a big advantage over most other parliamentary democracies.

The French parliament typically has at least five or six political parties represented at any given time and no one party has a clear majority. The volatility of French politics adds drama to parliamentary elections, even though the presence of a strong, directly elected chief executive (the president) minimizes the danger of party-induced governmental gridlock. We look at spectrum of political parties in contemporary France next.

A Multiparty System

France continues to have an array of political parties ranging across the spectrum from extreme right to extreme left. Traditionally, the Socialists and Communists have been the two main parties on the left. From the end of World War II until the late 1970s, the Communist Party generally garnered around 20 percent of the popular vote. The 1980s saw a steady erosion of Communist support and a rise in the popularity of the Socialists.

It was in the 1980s that the center-left (led by the Socialist Party) finally tipped the scales against the center-right. In 1981, the Socialists not only won the presidency but also gained a clear majority in the National Assembly. Although support for the Socialist Party dropped in the 1986 elections, France's Socialist president, François Mitterrand, easily won reelection to a second term in 1988.

By 1990, rising unemployment and budgetary constraints that hit traditionally left-leaning lower-income groups hardest sent the Socialists' popularity into a nosedive (discussed later).

On the political right (which stresses French independence and a competitive economy), **Gaullist** parties under various names predominated in the decades after the Fifth Republic's inception. De Gaulle himself never founded a party; indeed, he was contemptuous of political parties in general. Nonetheless, his followers kept the Gaullist legacy alive for a time under the banner of the Gaullist Union of Democrats for the Republic (UDR) and later under a neo-Gaullist party, the Rally for the Republic (RPR), headed by Jacques Chirac.

In 1978, then President Valéry Giscard d'Estaing created a new political formation, the Union for French Democracy (UDF), a coalition of several center-right parties and some smaller groups. An RPR-UDF alliance produced a center-right victory in the 1978 national elections, despite a determined effort by the Socialists and Communists to close ranks and enforce "republican discipline" in the second round of balloting. The RPR and UDF shared many elements of a common political philosophy, both favoring strong presidential government, a centralized administrative system, and free-market economic policies, but personal ambitions and myopic leadership prevented them from cooperating fully and helped the Socialists gain power in the 1980s. As we shall see, the Gaullist parties made a strong comeback in the 1990s.

In addition, splinter parties on both the left and the right have arisen from time to time. One such party, the **National Front,** has become firmly rooted in a disenchanted segment of the French electorate. The leader of this movement, Jean-Marie Le Pen, did surprisingly well in his first presidential bid in 1988. In the subsequent legislative elections, the extreme-right Front—which espouses nationalistic, racist, anti-immigrant policies—made a poor showing, but in the 1992 balloting it bounced back, finishing only a little behind the governing Socialist Party. At the same time, the two environmental parties together garnered slightly more votes than the National Front, prompting at least one commentator to suggest (prematurely, in retrospect) that France's party system was being transformed.[14]

From de Gaulle to Chirac: Testing the System

In 1964, then Prime Minister Georges Pompidou described the delicate institutional balance of the Fifth Republic:

> France has now chosen a system midway between the American presidential regime and the British parliamentary regime, where the chief of state, who formulates general policy, has the basis of authority in universal suffrage but can only exercise his function with a government that he may have chosen and named, but which in order to survive, must maintain the confidence of the Assembly.[15]

The Fifth Republic has provided France with unprecedented political stability. The personality of de Gaulle was certainly a factor in the early years. De Gaulle's influence extended well beyond his presidency. His opposition to domestic communism, his emphasis on France's sovereign independence (symbolized by the French nuclear strike force), his concern with enhancing French prestige in Europe and beyond, and his desire for economic growth without extensive nationalization of industry were all continued by his two presidential successors, Georges Pompidou (1969–1974) and Valéry Giscard d'Estaing (1974–1981). National Assembly and the French voters have also broadly supported these policies.

But in 1981 this national consensus fell away when, for the first time ever, the Socialist Party won a clear majority in the National Assembly and a Socialist, François Mitterrand, was elected president. The Socialist victories portended a turn to the left in the form of expanded welfare programs, deficit spending on a grand scale, greater nationalization of French industry, worker participation in management, administrative decentralization, and abolition of capital punishment. The realization of this agenda, however, was hampered by deepening domestic difficulties—in particular, high unemployment and economic stagnation—that adversely affected the Socialists' popularity.

Mitterand: Short-Lived "Rupture with Capitalism"　In February 1982, the Socialist government nationalized the "commanding heights" of the economy— that is to say, it took over key industries as well as banks and lending institutions. Although these policies were not a radical break with France's postwar past even under Gaullist (or center-right) governments, the newly nationalized industries employed hundreds of thousands of workers and represented a significant slice of France's total gross national product (GNP) and exports. After the new nation- alizations, the public sector accounted for nearly one-third of industrial sales and nearly a quarter of the French work force. In addition, the state gained near-total control of France's banking and credit systems. This "rupture with capitalism" cost French taxpayers well over 40 billion francs, as the state bought its way back into key sectors of the economy. (France no longer uses the franc, having swit- ched to the euro in 2002; in the summer of 2005 one euro was worth $1.21, but exchange rates fluctuate over time.)

The idea behind the nationalization program was to enhance the state's power to bring about rapid capital formation, economic modernization, and state- managed growth. The plan foundered when the government allowed state- owned enterprises to pursue their own strategies rather than conforming to a central plan. At the same time, the Mitterrand government, anxious to avoid embarrassment, poured money into the newly nationalized industries through budget allocations and loans from state-owned banks. These transfusions depleted the treasury but did not revive the patients, as one industry after another sank into the rising sea of red ink.

But the consequences of Mitterrand's false start in 1981 could not easily be swept under the rug. The budget deficit rose sharply, inflation remained high when it was falling elsewhere in the EU, and the trade deficit suddenly mush- roomed. In the face of these rapidly deteriorating conditions, Mitterrand bit the bullet: in 1983, the government reversed engines and adopted a tough austerity program (called "rigor" by crow-eating Socialist politicians).

The austerity measures involved holding wages down, curbing budget increases, and strictly controlling the money supply. But the response was sluggish. France's growth rate fell below that of most other Western European nations while inflation stayed high. At the same time, France endured several consecutive "double deficits" (simultaneous budget and trade shortfalls). The chronic trade deficit was particularly troubling because it suggested a loss of French competitiveness in the world market.

To make matters worse, unemployment climbed steadily under Socialist rule (although it did not rise as rapidly as it did in the United States and the United Kingdom under conservative governments of Reagan and Thatcher, respectively). Even a state-mandated job creation program had little effect. If the Socialist Party, with its strong commitment to the working class, could not even guarantee jobs for people who wanted to work, the voters were almost certain to punish its candidates at the polls.

Soon the president and then the political system itself came under fire. The president was criticized for being too aloof from political pressures and public opinion, and the system was criticized for being overly politicized. Because presidential elections were held every seven years until recently and parliamentary elections at least every five years, elections—and preparations for them—came to dominate French politics. Legislative or presidential elections were held twelve times between 1962 and 1988. One authority asserted that "long-range programs gave place to expediency, and party alignments obeyed the logic of electoral tactics rather than policy making."[16]

A severe test of the system came in the 1986 national elections, when the center-right parties won a narrow majority. Compelled by that outcome to choose a conservative prime minister, Socialist President Mitterrand asked the leader of a neo-Gaullist party, Jacques Chirac, to form a new government. The Fifth Republic had been created with a built-in time bomb that seemed about to detonate: a divided executive was in power. The president and the prime minister belonged to opposing parties, had different agendas, and looked to different constituencies.

Cohabitation: The Taming of the Left   With the economy still in a slump, the Socialists lost the 1986 election to a center-right coalition headed by Jacques Chirac. The French constitution, with its unique dual executive, was now put to one of its most severe tests: Could two leaders with radically different philosophies share power without bringing the country to a constitutional crisis? Prime Minister Chirac sought to denationalize firms and banks that the Socialists had earlier brought under state control. His more general aim was to deregulate the economy and return the initiative to the private sector.

To no one's surprise, this "cohabitation" amounted to little more than treading water until the 1988 presidential election. President Mitterrand campaigned for reelection on a pragmatic, market-oriented platform that closely resembled that of his principal center-right opponent, Prime Minister Chirac. Mitterrand promised voters that there would be no repeat of the failed Socialist experiment of 1981—no nationalizations, no new corporate taxes, and no quixotic measures like his earlier attempt at shortening the workweek.

Voters believed him, and Mitterrand won a second term by a comfortable margin. Pollsters predicted that the Socialists would win a clear majority (289 seats) in National Assembly elections the following month, but they were wrong. Contrary to expectations, the center-right parties captured enough seats to leave Mitterrand's party 13 seats short of a majority. The message of the electorate was fairly clear: Give us a middle-of-the-road government and cut the ideological rhetoric. Clearly, Mitterrand's triumph over Chirac in 1988 was indicative of the huge advantages accruing to the incumbent of France's republic rather than a mandate for the Socialists.

President Mitterrand got the message. His moderation in domestic policy was matched by prudence in foreign policy, including firm support for NATO (in contrast to the Gaullist tradition, which stressed strategic self-reliance and a special role vis-à-vis the two superpowers). At the same time, he pursued defense policies long popular in France, bolstering the nation's independent nuclear strike force (the third largest in the world) while promoting strategic and conventional arms reduction in Europe and beyond. Under Mitterrand, France played a leadership role in the European Union as well.

In general, foreign policy differences between left and right in France have been minimal—in essence, all the main parties have embraced the Gaullist formula (opposed to American dominance, distrustful of the "special relationship" between the U.S. and the U.K., bent on close collaboration with Germany, committed to an independent French nuclear deterrent, and so on).

The Rise of the Extreme Right   Despite the resounding vote for moderate parties and policies, the surprising popularity of right-wing extremist Jean-Marie Le Pen in the 1988 presidential race struck a discordant note. Le Pen campaigned on a nationalistic and racist platform that critics denounced as a new form of fascism. The target of his wrath was the influx of immigrants from France's former colonies in Africa and Asia. In the end, his neo-Fascist message struck a responsive chord with hundreds of thousands of French voters.

Why? The rise of the National Front was a reflection of social and economic troubles facing France in the late 1980s and early 1990s. Unemployment and underemployment aggravated racial and ethnic tensions in French society, as did urban overcrowding, rising crime rates, drug abuse, and traffic congestion. A growing number of French voters conveniently blamed immigrants from North Africa (especially Algeria, Tunisia, and Morocco) for France's social and economic problems. Many of these immigrants also happened to be Muslims, a fact that was bound to lead to some friction in a traditionally Roman Catholic country like France (even though France is a fairly secular society now and regular attendance at mass is uncommon). By 2005, there were an estimated 4–5 million Muslims living in France, constituting the second largest religious community in the country. Muslims were also the fastest-growing segment of the population thanks to a high birthrate as well as new arrivals from abroad.

The National Front did not fade out of the picture in the 1990s, as has often happened with upstart political parties in France. When he again ran for president in 1995, Le Pen did slightly better than he had done seven years earlier. In response, both Mitterrand's Socialists and later Chirac's Gaullists tried to preempt the extreme right and satisfy a spreading xenophobia within French society by adopting tough measures aimed at curbing illegal immigration.

Cohabitation: Acts II and III   History repeated itself in 1993, when the center-right again won a majority (roughly 80 percent) of the seats in parliamentary elections and Mitterrand was again forced to name a leader of the archrival neo-Gaullist RPR, Édouard Balladur, to head a new government. The Mitterrand era came to an end in 1995. Chirac was elected president in a close race, defeating the Socialist candidate, Lionel Jospin. At the time of Chirac's victory, the center-right not only claimed four-fifths of the National Assembly seats and two-thirds of the Senate but also controlled twenty of twenty-two regional councils, most departmental councils, and many of the larger municipal councils. In 1997, President Chirac called surprise parliamentary elections in the expectation of receiving a mandate for his conservative economic policies. The French electorate once again surprised the politicians and pundits by handing the parties of the left, led by the Socialists, a resounding victory. The result was to force Chirac to accept a Socialist government headed by his political rival, Lionel Jospin, the man he had narrowly defeated in his quest for the presidency two years earlier. Cohabitation between Chirac and Jospin was uneasy. France's government was perhaps not adrift but it was going nowhere.

The Elections of 2002 and 2005

The presidential election of 2002 was bizarre, even by French standards. In the first round of balloting, the electorate expressed its extreme displeasure in two ways, first by staying away from the polls (voter turnout was unusually low) and second by saying to Chirac and Jospin, in effect, "A plague on both your houses." Chirac outpolled the others but received only one in every five votes cast—a dismal result for the incumbent president. For Prime Minister Jospin, however, the outcome was humiliating: he finished behind the extreme right-wing candidate Jean-Marie Le Pen. Most incredibly, Le Pen came within three percentage points of beating Chirac! The results stunned France (and Europe). In the second round of balloting, however, Chirac received four out of five votes cast (82 percent), the largest margin of any president in the history of the Fifth Republic.[17] Thus, the ultimate result was an outpouring of support for French democracy, as the electorate voted against Le Pen (rather than for Chirac) in overwhelming numbers.

The parliamentary elections in June left no doubt that France was fed up with "cohabitation." Chirac's center-right coalition (called the Union for the Presidential Majority or UMP) won a decisive victory, garnering 357 seats to the second-finishing Socialist Party's 140 seats. But the UMP received only about a third of the votes cast and nearly two-fifths of the electorate stayed home. The message of these two elections was mixed but clear: on the positive side, no more divided government; on the negative side, little confidence in the president. Nonetheless, the extreme right was shut out of the National Assembly, having failed to win a single seat (thanks to the peculiar arithmetic of the French electoral system).[18]

And despite the fact that President Chirac's personal mandate was suspect, it appeared as though he could look forward to five more years in office with a prime minister of his own choosing and a compliant National Assembly.

But the French referendum on the EU in May 2005 changed the picture once again. Leading up to the vote, polls in France showed deep dissatisfaction with France's prime minister, Jean-Pierre Raffarin (who replaced Jospin in 2002), as well as with President Chirac, whose popularity fell to the lowest level of any French president on record. When the French electorate voted the new EU constitution down, it was a direct slap in the face of President Chirac, who had campaigned tirelessly on behalf of the measure. As noted earlier, Chirac promptly dismissed Prime Minister Raffarin, replacing him with Dominique de Villepin a former foreign minister and longtime Chirac loyalist. Chirac's decision to name de Villepin as France's new prime minister was widely criticized in France. One big strike against de Villepin as critics were quick to point out was that he had never held an elective office. And although his standing in the polls climbed for a time in 2005, he did not escape unscathed from the urban riots later that year (see Chapter Four.)

GERMANY'S UNIFIED FEDERAL REPUBLIC

On October 3, 1990, West Germany and East Germany were united as one country after more than four decades as separate entities. The East German communist regime was swept away, and the West German system of government was extended throughout the new nation. Thus despite a tradition of autocratic rule, Germany is today a thriving democracy. Before unification, the **Federal Republic of Germany (FRG)**—or West Germany, as it was commonly known—comprised ten states, or *Länder* (singular *Land*), plus West Berlin.[19] It encompassed an area about the size of Oregon. The new unified Germany encompasses sixteen *Länder* and a land area of 137,838 square miles, slightly larger than Montana. Its population has gone from just under 62 million to just over 82.5 million. The capital has been officially moved from Bonn back to Berlin, historically the center of Germany's political life.

The *Länder* are the building blocks in a system designed to ensure a high degree of political decentralization. Land governments have the primary responsibility to enact legislation in specific areas such as education and cultural affairs. They alone have the means to implement laws enacted by the federal government, to command most of the administrative personnel to accomplish this task, to exercise police power (taking care of the health, welfare, and moral well-being of the people), to direct the educational system, and to ensure that the press does not violate constitutional rules.

Although the *Länder* have considerable clout, the federal government is the main repository of political authority in the constitutional system. The central government has the exclusive right to legislate in foreign affairs, citizenship matters, currency and coinage, railways, postal service and telecommunications, and copyrights. In other areas, notably civil and criminal law and laws relating to the regulation of the economy, the central government and the *Länder* share power.

Compared to the United States, Germany's federalism leaves more power in the hands of the "states"; the *Länder* run more of their own affairs and receive a larger proportion of taxes than American states do. For example, individual and corporate income taxes are split between Berlin and the *Länder* in equal 40-percent shares; the cities get 20 percent. The *Länder* also receive one-third of the value-added tax (VAT), the major source of tax revenue used in Germany and throughout Europe. (The VAT is a turnover tax levied on all transactions; it is based on the incremental price of an item as it goes from manufacturer to distributor to retailer, paid by the buyer, and collected by the seller.) Thus, the *Länder* in Germany are not reduced to begging the national government for money, as U.S. states so often are.

In sum, German federalism was modified to fit Germany's unique set of circumstances and, no doubt, to please the Allied powers that occupied the country at the end of World War II (especially the United States). The dilemma was this: West Germany would need a constitution if it was to function as a federal republic, but to adopt a formal constitution was to give implicit recognition to the permanency of Germany's postwar division. To get around this dilemma, West Germany gave its political charter a most unusual name: it was not to be dignified as a "constitution" but simply called the "basic law."

The Basic Law

Germany's charter is called the **Basic Law** rather than a Constitution because it was designed as a temporary document after World War II to be supplanted by a formal constitution (with a capital *C*) at such time as the two Germanys were reunified. Its last article states, "This Basic Law loses its validity on the day on which a Constitution that has been freely decided on by the German people comes into effect." That day has not yet arrived even though Germany is now unified because the German people are quite satisfied with what they have now and because no German government has wanted to open up a Pandora's box by initiating a process that would have an unpredictable and potentially divisive outcome.

The drafting of the Basic Law was extraordinary in part because it was done under the watchful eyes of the powers occupying Germany after World War II. The United States, Great Britain, and France served as models from which the West Germans borrowed freely. From the United States they took the principles of federalism (dividing governmental responsibilities between a national government and state governments) and true bicameralism (having two legislative chambers elected in different ways and playing distinctive constitutional roles). From Great Britain they adapted the parliamentary system. They imitated the French electoral system, using proportional representation to fill some of the seats in the **Bundestag** (lower house). The preamble to the Basic Law proclaims West

Germany's right of self-determination, and there is no mention of the Allied occupation. Remarkably, one decade after World War II, a sovereign, independent, and democratic government became fully operational in West Germany.

Protection of Individual Rights   Significantly, the first nineteen articles of the Basic Law deal with the inalienable rights of every West German. As one student of German politics has observed, "The relevant historical experience was that of the Third Reich with its oppressive flouting of all human liberties."[20] The Weimar Constitution (imposed by the victorious powers after Germany's defeat in World War I) made it possible for the government to suspend constitutional rights during times of emergency. Abuse of these emergency powers by the Nazi regime eventually led to the revocation of the constitution itself. Accordingly, Article 19 of the Basic Law proclaims, "In no case may the essential content of a basic right be encroached upon." The guarantees contained in the first nineteen articles are entrenched: no act of the executive, legislative, or judicial branch of government can revoke or abridge them. If a question arises about whether or not a statutory law conflicts with the Basic Law, the Federal Constitutional Court resolves the issue.

The rights guaranteed under the Basic Law include equality before the law; freedom of speech, religion, assembly, and the press; academic freedom; freedom of association; freedom from unlawful searches; private property rights; the right of asylum; freedom from discrimination based on race, sex, or political convictions; and the right to refuse military service as a matter of conscience. Article 18 attaches a caveat to these rights, stipulating that they cannot be used "to attack the democratic order." This provision was clearly aimed at the two extremes of left and right, communism and Nazism, which have so afflicted German life in the twentieth century. It also reflected the postwar preoccupation with Soviet communism that prevailed throughout the Atlantic community and was particularly pervasive in West Germany. However, fear of the reawakening of neo-Nazi ultranationalism has never been far beneath the surface in the Federal Republic, as evidenced by the fact that neo-Nazi activity has generally been interpreted as constituting an attack on the democratic order.

It is not easy to amend the Basic Law. In fact, some key parts of the German constitution are irrevocable (they cannot be changed, period). Can you guess why? (Never fear, the answer is near.)

The Amendment Process and Article 23   Amending the Basic Law requires a two-thirds majority vote in both houses of the parliament, but the fundamental principles and guarantees cannot be revoked or amended. In addition to the civil liberties enumerated in the first nineteen articles, the federal, republican, democratic, and welfare state features of the political system are deliberately set in stone to prevent a recurrence of the Nazi nightmare.

From its inception, the Basic Law of the Federal Republic looked ahead to a time when Germany would be united. Under Article 23, East Germany (the German Democratic Republic or GDR) could be merged with West Germany at any time, the only proviso being that the GDR accept the Basic Law. Before 1989, this part of the Basic Law seemed irrelevant in the context of the Cold War. But with the overthrow of communist rule in East Germany at the end of 1989, Article 23 became the vehicle by which the two states merged.

The Chancellor

Germany has a parliamentary form of government with a dual executive. The president is a figurehead, indirectly elected and endowed with ceremonial powers. The true chief executive is the **chancellor,** who obtains the position in the same way as the British prime minister—by being leader of the majority party in the lower house (the Bundestag). If no one party enjoys an absolute majority, as has often been the case in Germany, the leader of the major party in the ruling coalition (that is, a government comprised of two or more parties) becomes the chancellor.

The chancellor, with parliamentary approval, appoints and dismisses cabinet members. Together with the cabinet, the chancellor sets policy guidelines and proposes legislation. As the head of government, the chancellor is responsible for translating policies into operational programs. The chancellor has the power to veto budget measures. In a national emergency, the chancellor becomes commander in chief. In short, the chancellor, like the British prime minister, is the dominant figure in the government.

The Basic Law contains a provision, called the constructive vote of no confidence that makes it very difficult to remove a chancellor or dissolve parliament. Indeed, this very rule allowed Konrad Adenauer (Germany's first chancellor after World War II) to rule in difficult times with only a one-seat majority and, more recently, led Chancellor Gerhard Schröder, faced with declining public support for his policies, to *engineer* a no-confidence vote so he could call early elections. Three of Germany's five chancellors—Adenauer (1949–1963), Ludwig Erhardt (1963–1966), and Willy Brandt (1969–1974)—resigned between elections when they became a liability to the party they headed. (Similarly, since World War II, no fewer than four Conservative British prime ministers have stepped down between elections to make way for new party leadership.)

In Germany, as in other parliamentary democracies, the leader gets most of the credit when the party's fortunes are rising (often a reflection of a robust economy), and all the blame when they are falling. In the United States and other presidential democracies, by contrast, the president takes all the credit in good times but often blames others (the legislative branch, the party out of power, foreign enemies, and domestic troublemakers) when things go wrong. And though leaders in Germany and other parliamentary democracies are not above trying to do the same thing, they are less likely to get away with it because the principles that underpin the parliamentary model of government (such as party discipline and collective responsibility) make it very difficult. Thus, voters can see through any attempt to deflect blame and it can easily backfire.

The chancellor chooses cabinet members in close consultation with the party's executive committee. Seldom does one of the two major parties win a clear majority in the Bundestag, so it is usually necessary for either the Christian

Democratic Union (CDU) or the Social Democratic party (SDP) to enter into a coalition with the small Free Democratic Party (FDP) or, after the 1998 elections, the Green Party. As a consequence, the allocation of cabinet posts typically reflects the need to entice the coalition partner with some key ministerial appointments. For example, Hans-Dietrich Genscher, leader of the FDP, was for many years the Federal Republic's foreign minister, first as the junior partner in a coalition with the SDP under Helmut Schmidt and then, after FDP broke with the SDP in 1982, in a coalition with the CDU under Helmut Kohl. (Genscher, in poor health, resigned in 1992.) In 1998, Green Party leader Joshka Fisher became the foreign minister in the government headed by the SDP.

Almost all cabinet members are also members of the Bundestag and are active in both roles. In contrast to British cabinet members, German ministers are almost always chosen for their expertise in a particular policy area. There are generally about seventeen cabinet members, the most prominent being the ministers of finance, foreign affairs, defense, and interior. Cabinet members participate in decision making, advise the chancellor on policy matters, direct the formulation of policy proposals and legislation within their own departments, and oversee the implementation of policy by their subordinates.

Directly below the chancellor and the cabinet are the parliamentary secretaries (who are members of the federal legislature) and state secretaries (career civil service employees). The parliamentary secretaries are considered junior ministers—they leave office at the end of the term of the cabinet member they serve. The state secretaries, as professional bureaucrats, provide some continuity from one government to the next—they stay on after cabinet members leave office. The departments tend to be small (in contrast with British departments) because the *Land* governments, as we noted earlier, actually administer most federal programs and enforce federal as well as state laws.

Today in Germany, the power of the executive branch is counter-balanced by the legislative branch. A popularly elected legislature with a vigorous opposition is one key to protecting individual liberties and preventing an adventuristic foreign policy (for example, one seeking to conquer neighboring states by force of arms no matter what the costs and risks). Given its history of political extremism, which led to totalitarian (Nazi) rule between the two world wars, the newly unified German state definitely needs a pro-active parliament. Such a body is necessary not only to ensure democracy at home, but also to *assure* the rest of Europe that Germany no longer poses a threat to stability and peace on the Continent. Hence, it is especially important in Germany's case that its parliament, to which we now turn, can make or break governments—and has done so.

The German Parliament

Unlike Great Britain, Germany lacks a great parliamentary tradition. Bismarck largely ignored the Reichstag (the forerunner of the Bundestag), and during the Weimar period it was ineffectual. Even after 1949, the Bundestag lacked prestige and was treated with a certain disdain by Chancellor Adenauer (who resembled France's authoritarian President Charles de Gaulle in this respect).

The German parliament is bicameral. The lower house (Bundestag), consisting of 672 members, is directly elected; the 69-member upper house—known as the **Bundesrat**—is indirectly elected. The Bundestag is the primary law-making body, although the Bundesrat also plays an important legislative role. The chancellor initiates most bills, but before any bill can become law, the Bundestag must vote its approval. Thus it functions as one of the principal mechanisms in the constitutional system of check and balances. The Basic Law underscores the independence of the Bundestag by stipulating that its members are "not bound by orders and instructions and shall be subject only to their conscience."

The Bundestag   In addition to choosing the chancellor, the Bundestag acts as a watchdog over the government. The Bundestag has the power to oust a chancellor at any time with a constructive vote of no confidence. On its own initiative, it can also enact legislation binding on the government, conduct public debates on government policy, investigate government actions, and directly question the chancellor and cabinet members. (The latter can be summoned to appear before the Bundestag, but they cannot be forced to disclose information.)

Voting patterns in the Bundestag reflect a strict party discipline. Parliamentary parties are organized into *Fraktionen* (factions). The *Fraktionen* meet frequently to decide how to vote on upcoming bills and to discuss legislative strategy and determine the specific responsibility each deputy will assume on each piece of legislation. The assignments and instructions even include the precise arguments that deputies will make. The *Fraktionen* are built into the parliamentary structure: only parties with a bloc of deputies large enough to form a *Fraktion* (at least 5 percent of the total membership) can be represented in committees.

In Germany, as in the United States, committees are a principal source of legislative power. Committees generally meet in private, and the opposition has ample opportunity to participate. Most of the nineteen standing committees have identical counterparts in the cabinet. This arrangement facilitates the flow of communications between the government and the Bundestag because cabinet officials are usually deputies in the Bundestag as well. Normally, committees in Germany do not have the kind of investigatory powers found in the U.S. Congress, but the Bundestag can establish special committees of inquiry on the recommendation of one-fourth of the deputies.

The Bundestag elects a presiding officer or president through a secret ballot. In practice, the majority party actually decides who will be the Bundestag president. There are also three vice-presidents selected from opposition parties. Together with other party leaders, these officials form the Council of Elders, which acts as an advisory board to the president of the Bundestag, schedules debates on pending legislation, and allocates speaking time to the parliamentary parties.

The Bundesrat   Also known as the Federal Council, the Bundesrat—the upper house of the legislature—is the main institutional mechanism for adjusting and regulating relations between the Bund (federal government) and the *Länder.* Intended as a bulwark against excessive centralization, it is perhaps the most distinctive feature of the German federal system. Unlike the relatively powerless British House of Lords, the Bundesrat is a powerful body with exclusive constitutional functions. Directly responsible to the state governments, it has wide-ranging influence on federal policies and procedures, making it the most imposing institutional expression of German federalism.

The Bundesrat is not popularly elected; the various *Land* governments, which have three to six seats each (depending on population), appoint its members. Each *Land* government must vote as a block—a provision that reinforces the federal character of the German parliament.

The Bundestag is constitutionally required to submit the legislation it passes to the Bundesrat. All bills that directly affect the *Länder* must be approved by the Bundesrat to become law; in other words, the Bundesrat can veto such legislation. Other bills do not require its approval, but any objections raised by the Bundesrat must be debated in the Bundestag before the bill becomes law. The influence of the Bundesrat over federal policy has increased steadily, giving the *Länder* a role in the political system far exceeding that of the state governments in the United States.

Because the composition of the Bundesrat is not affected by national elections, this house has a special aura of stability. It is also more streamlined and more efficient than the lower house because most of its members hold ministerial posts in their respective *Land* governments and can use their own administrative staffs to help them prepare legislation. Often bureaucrats by profession, Bundesrat members tend to have more technical expertise than Bundestag deputies do, and they can be more specialized. This fact naturally facilitates the implementation of laws, which is the purview of the *Länder* (state governments).

Finally, party influence is muted in the Bundesrat. Members are expected to represent the interests of the *Länder* without regard for party preference. The strict party discipline found in the Bundestag is matched by the tight control *Land* governments exercise over their representatives in the Bundesrat. In sum, the Bundesrat gives the German states a powerful weapon to protect themselves against federal encroachment.

How Laws Are Made in Germany

The Basic Law divides legislation into three categories: exclusive, concurrent, and framework law. Article 30 lodges state legislative authority firmly in the *Länder,* and Article 70 stipulates that the *Länder* have all legislative powers not expressly conferred on the federal parliament. Exclusive legislative authority, assigned solely to the Bund (federal government), is limited to foreign affairs, defense, currency, and foreign trade. Concurrent legislative authority applies in such areas as criminal and civil law, trade and commerce, and public roads. The *Länder* may legislate in these areas so long as the Bund has not already done so. (All federal legislation in this category must be approved by the Bundesrat to become law.) Framework legislative authority limits the Bund to providing only outline bills, leaving the details up to the *Länder.* This category includes public services, the environment, and regional planning. Although the most important legislation is given to the

Bund, administration of programs and implementation of policy are left largely in the hands of the *Länder*.

Bills in the parliament run a familiar gauntlet: formal introduction, committee review, several readings, debate, and final vote. Individual lawmakers in both chambers may introduce measures. The executive branch drafts most legislation. All government bills must be sent to the Bundesrat first, and any changes to a bill must accompany it to the Bundestag. Because the Bundesrat has veto power over all concurrent legislation, the government normally works closely with this body in the drafting stages to avoid potential problems. (On some issues, the Bundesrat has only a suspensive veto—meaning that it can delay passage of a bill but cannot defeat it.)

After a bill has been introduced, it goes to the Bundestag, where it is debated. Next it is sent to a standing committee, where most of the detail work is done. A committee member is usually assigned to prepare a report about the bill, which then goes back to the full house for further debate. This stage is known as the second reading. A third reading usually follows shortly thereafter, and the measure is voted on. If it passes, it is sent to the Bundesrat. In the case of legislation introduced by the government, the Bundesrat gets two reviews. If the Bundesrat and the Bundestag do not agree on the form or substance of a particular bill, the bill goes to a conference committee, as it might in the U.S. Congress. The conference committee has twenty-two members, half from each house of the parliament. Differences in language are usually reconciled through this mechanism. Once a bill has been passed by both houses and has been signed by the president and the chancellor, it becomes law.

Parties and Elections

Under the Weimar Republic, left- and right-wing parties were separated by a yawning ideological chasm. The resulting instability led to the Holocaust and World War II—twin calamities on a scale unprecedented in modern European history. Today the vast majority of German voters, mindful of Germany's descent into the totalitarian abyss in the 1930s, have crowded around the political center, choosing moderation over extremism.

Since 1949, the Federal Republic has had just two major parties, the center-left Social Democratic Party (SDP) and the center-right (or conservative) Christian Democratic Union (CDU). The latter has formed a permanent alliance with the Bavarian Christian Social Union (CSU). In addition, the relatively small Free Democratic Party (FDP) has shown remarkable staying power and has played a strategic role as the holder of the balance. Because the two major parties are frequently represented almost equally in the Bundestag, the Free Democrats have often controlled the decisive votes; as a result, the FDP's influence historically has been disproportionate to its size, and it has frequently been a junior partner in coalition governments.

Although the SDP started out as a socialist party closely aligned with the labor-union movement, it recast itself as a social democratic party (the Godesberg Program) in 1959. The CDU-CSU caters mainly to business interests and social conservatives; both are relatively moderate. Indeed, the two parties shared power from 1966 to 1969 in what was known as the Grand Coalition.

Smaller parties have a better chance of surviving in Germany than in Great Britain because half of the Bundestag is chosen by proportional representation. Even so, the party system was consciously designed to keep the number of parties at a reasonable level and to prevent small extremist groups from disrupting the orderly democratic process. Parties must receive a minimum of 5 percent of the national vote or win seats in a minimum of three electoral districts to gain Bundestag representation.

The Greens are a rising leftist party that focuses almost exclusively on environmental and antinuclear issues. In the spring of 1987, the Greens led a counterculture coalition in protest against a nationwide census. The ostensible issue was the right to privacy; the real issue was the authority of the state, which the Greens generally regard with fear and loathing. With the reunification of East and West Germany, another political party, the Party of Democratic Socialism (PDS)—the renamed former ruling party in the old GDR—entered the picture. In regional and local elections in the former GDR, the PDS has consistently demonstrated strong popular support (attaining 20 percent of the vote and winning four Bundestag seats in 1994). Moreover, it showed resiliency and resourcefulness in subsequent elections, polling 5.1 percent of the votes—enough to meet the threshold for forming a *Fraktion* (gaining PR seats) in the Bundestag—in the 1998 elections. Thus, the PDS is a significant force in German politics; its strength at the state level in the eastern *Länder* was underscored when it formed a coalition government with the SPD in the *Land* of Saxony in 1994.

National elections normally occur every four years in Germany. Two different electoral systems are used to choose the Bundestag's deputies—a first vote and a second vote. Half are elected by a simple majority (a *plurality*) in single-member districts (the first vote); the other half are elected by proportional representation, the second vote. In the first vote, the individual candidate is featured; in the second vote, the party is paramount. Thus each voter casts two votes, one for an individual and one for a **Land** list put together by the party. The second vote is crucial because it determines the total number of seats a party receives in each *Land*. The party decides who is at the top of the list and who is at the bottom, a practice that enhances the role and importance of political parties in Germany.

A Limited Government

Weighing the cumulative effects of the system prescribed by the Basic Law (federalism, the unique organization of the legislature, the carefully structured party system, the independent judiciary, and the explicit guarantees of civil liberties), it becomes apparent that one of the main purposes of the Basic Law was to arrange the institutional furniture in postwar Germany to preclude a repeat of the horrors associated with the Nazi era. Limited government, more than any other facet of constitutional democracy, was central to the drafters of the Basic Law, who deliberately sought to build into the system safeguards against the concentration of power that had caused so much turmoil leading up to World War II.

The democratic performance of the Federal Republic of Germany (FRG) since World War II has indeed been impressive. The experience of Weimar has not been repeated. Though the Weimar Republic was largely undone by severe economic distress, West Germany's rapid postwar recovery and sustained industrial growth since 1949 have frequently been described as an economic miracle. Spurred on by a remarkable economic resurgence and a firm commitment to constitutional government, the present generation of Germans has given democracy a new lease on life in a land where it was once thought to be unworkable. Moreover, West Germany's economic success helped to spur East Germans' dissatisfaction with a communist regime that denied them freedom (including the freedom to travel in the West or even visit relatives in West Germany) and failed to provide a standard of living anywhere close to that of the West Germans'.

Germany had been a microcosm of the Cold War for over forty years. The collapse of communism in East Germany symbolized the end of an era in international politics and a new beginning for the German people. We will examine the new Germany's problems and prospects in Chapter Four.

ITALY'S FRACTIOUS DEMOCRACY

World War II was a watershed in the history of modern Italy. King Victor Immanuel III failed in his effort to salvage the monarchy in 1945. His decision to depose Mussolini and declare war on Germany came too late to hasten the end or effect the outcome in any significant way. The fact that the Italian Communists had led the Resistance to Mussolini's **Fascist** regime and the Nazis throughout the war proved to be exceedingly important after the war. In general, it was the Left (Communists and Socialists) who fought the fascism everywhere in Europe; Italy and Spain exemplify this legacy but they are not unique. As a result, political parties of the Left were popular in many West European parties after the war; wherever democracy was restored, these parties were rewarded at the polls. Italy was one of these countries.

The 1948 Constitution: Too Much of A Good Thing?

The Italian constitution of 1948 established a democratic republic. It abolished the monarchy and in its place created an indirectly elected presidency with limited but not insignificant powers, including the suspensive veto (sending a bill back to parliament for reconsideration) and nominating prime ministers. In this respect, the Italian parliamentary system differs from the British system. Most executive power belongs to the prime minister and cabinet. As insurance against the rise of another Mussolini, the principal of collective responsibility was enshrined in the constitution. Consequently, in Italy, the *cabinet,* not the prime minister, must win Parliament's approval.

Legislative power resides in the parliament, consisting of a lower house, the Chamber of Deputies (630 seats), and an upper house, the Senate (315 seats).

The two legislative chambers in Italy have equal powers. The drafters of the 1948 constitution bent over backwards to make the government responsive to the people; one of the unintended consequences, as we will see, was to make it ineffective.

How is it possible to design a representative democracy so as to maximize responsiveness? The way Italy tried to do it in 1948 provides clues but unfortunately not a good solution. First, local authorities were charged with responsibility for mailing voting cards to all eligible voters. Second, suffrage was extended to all Italians.[21] Third, members of both houses of parliament were elected by proportional representation. The Chamber of Deputies was divided into thirty-two voting districts; the number of seats apportioned to each district depended on population. Each party made up lists of candidates in each district. Following the balloting, seats were distributed according to the percentage of votes cast for each party list in that district (voters could also write in the names of favorite candidates on each list). Senators were elected in single-member districts, but here again the seats were distributed according to a proportional-representation formula on a regional basis.

The net result was to give many political parties an opportunity to win at least a few seats but to make it highly unlikely that any single party would win a clear majority. Multiparty coalition governments are often unstable and short lived, leading to chronic governmental paralysis. Postwar Italy illustrates the perils of partisan politics in a parliamentary democracy with no built-in safeguards against party proliferation. Finally, in April 1993, after four-plus decades of bitter experience, Italy held a national referendum on political reform. The results of the referendum would have potentially far-reaching consequences for the future of Italian politics. Before we discuss the verdict of the voters, however, let us take a closer look at what led up to it.

Economic Success, Political Morass

In 1946, when Italy awoke from the long nightmare of Fascism, the Italian people voted in favor of creating a republic. Two years later, as we know, the republic was formally launched as a parliamentary democracy designed to prevent a recurrence of totalitarianism through free elections, universal suffrage, and proportional representation. The idea was inspired by good intentions, but the result was a political system poised on the edge of a cliff. Thus, between 1946 and 2000, Italy witnessed the rise and fall of nearly fifty-nine governments—more than one per year. No fewer than twenty-three different prime ministers headed governments during this period. Most of these governments were coalitions under the leadership of the Christian Democratic Party. Obviously, many of these coalitions were unstable. Even so, the Christian Democrats acted as a kind of balance wheel, consistently winning around 40 percent of the popular vote until the national elections of 1983 when the CD's popularity began to spiral downward. But the critical force holding coalitions together was anti-communism and a popular revulsion in Italy's post-Fascist era against all forms of political extremism. It is important to recall that Italy was the scene of several spectacular terrorist acts in the 1970s and 1980s (see Chapter Four).

Italy's economy has proven surprisingly vibrant in spite of the country's chronic political mess. Indeed, Italy was transformed economically as well as politically after World War II—so much so that observers, as with Germany, took to referring to Italy's economic miracle. Before the war, agriculture was the backbone of the economy. Today, agriculture employs less than one worker in ten, and Italy boasts one of the largest and most modern economies in Europe, ranking sixth in the world. Compared to Russia, for example, Italy has well under half as many people, but its economy (GDP) was three times larger than Russia's in 2004. Remarkably, Italy's GDP was still substantially larger than that of China, whose population was more than twenty times larger than that of Italy.

Even so, frequent political scandals have accompanied Italy's economic success. Not surprisingly, these two phenomena—one as negative as the other is positive—are linked.

The Road to Reform

In a sense, the seeds of reform in Italy were embedded in the constitution itself—or, more specifically, in its flaws. We cannot cover the entire sweep of Italy's postwar political history in detail here. Instead, a brief sketch of the prereform era will precede a more detailed treatment of the institutional reforms undertaken in 1990s.

A Plethora of Parties . . .   Italian governments until very recently were typically short lived. There are all sorts of reasons why governments fall in parliamentary systems. Sometimes an unexpected event jolts the whole society and the public rightly or wrongly blames the government. Or a cabinet member gets embroiled in a scandal over money or sexual improprieties, and the government is forced out by a parliamentary vote of no confidence.

The problem of party proliferation was not immediately apparent in Italy, although there was a tendency toward unstable coalitions from the outset. Thus, in the 1948 elections the Christian Democrats won nearly half the popular vote; the Italian Communist Party (PCI) came in second with nearly a third of the popular vote. Four other parties were represented, but the Christian Democratic Party (DC), by far the strongest party, formed a middle-of-the-road coalition government with the backing of three smaller parties. During the first two legislative terms (1948–1953 and 1953–1958), however, there were a total of nine governments, three in the first term and six in the second. That pattern was to carry through until the 1990s (see Table 3.6), when popular discontent and official corruption created the kind of political chemistry that often leads to revolution or reform. In Italy's case it did lead to reform, but whether or not it went far enough to fix the country's problem-ridden political system remains to be seen.

. . . And Unstable Governments   To say that Italy's political system was "problem ridden" requires some explanation. Over a period of more than four decades, not one government stayed in power for the full five years—the normal lifespan of each parliament under Italy's constitution. Indeed, not only were

TABLE 3.6   The Great Shuffle: Italy's Short-Lived Governments (1948–1992)

Parliament (dates)	Governments	Coalitions*	Leading Party
First Parliament (1948–1953)	3	3	Christian Democrats (DC)
Second Parliament (1953–1958)	6	2	Christian Democrats (DC)
Third Parliament (1958–1963)	5	2	Christian Democrats (DC)
Fourth Parliament (1963–1968)	4	3	Christian Democrats (DC)
Fifth Parliament (1968–1972)	6	3	Christian Democrats (DC)
Sixth Parliament (1972–1976)	5	4	Christian Democrats (DC)
Seventh Parliament (1976–1979)	3	1	Christian Democrats (DC)
Eighth Parliament (1979–1983)	6	6	DC or Republican (PRI)†
Ninth Parliament (1983–1987)	3	2	Socialists (PSI)‡
Tenth Parliament (1987–1992)	4	5	Christian Democrats (DC)
Total =	45	31	

*The reason for the difference in numbers of governments and coalitions is that the Christian Democratic (DC) party formed governments without coalition partners 14 times between 1948 and 1992. Most of these single-party governments were short lived; the Andreotti government (July 1976 to January 1979) lasted the longest.

†The first three governments were led by the DC, the next two led by the Republican (PRI) party, and the last one (April 1962–May 1963) by the DC again.

‡ In April 1987, the Christian Democrats formed a minority government for the short interregnum between the fall of the Socialist-led government of Bettino Craxi and the national elections in July of that year.

governments chronically unstable, but it also happened that the situation went from bad to worse: in one fifteen-year span between 1968 and 1983, Italy had twenty different governments and nine different prime ministers. During a similar period, Britain had four governments and prime ministers (Edward Heath, Harold Wilson, James Callahan, and Margaret Thatcher).

But the fact that the Christian Democrats continued to poll nearly 40 percent of the popular vote until 1983 softened the political impact of such an otherwise bewildering procession of governments. Party fragmentation became a major problem after 1983 in large part because the Christian Democrats, the holder of the balance, began to falter. When that happened, it left a deepening void at the center that no other party could fill (see Box 3.1).

At the beginning of the 1980s, a dozen parties were represented in the Parliament; a decade later the number has risen to sixteen. At the same time, the share of the popular vote going to minor parties rose from about a tenth in the early 1980s to nearly half in 1994. What caused this deterioration in the consensus that had kept the Christian Democrats in the driver's seat for so long?

External factors played a major role in bringing about the crisis of Italian democracy in the 1990s. First, the fact that the DC's precipitous decline in popularity between 1987 and 1992 coincided with the disintegration of the Soviet bloc cannot be ignored. During the Cold War, anticommunism was often a tempting political tactic at election time in the West. The socio-moral context was particularly conducive to anticommunist appeals in Italy, the motherland of the Roman Catholic Church. The frequency of terrorist attacks between 1969

B O X   3.1   **Politics in Italy: Exceptional, Abnormal, or Exceptionally Abnormal?**

Starting in the late 1980s, and rising to a crescendo in the 1990s, the cry has gone up that Italy must, at last, become "a normal country." Such was the title of the manifesto produced in 1995 by the leader of the former Italian Communist Party: *Un paese normale*. But the phrase was a leitmotif of speeches and articles across the spectrum, and remains an obsessive refrain in the media to this day. Its message is that Italy must become like other countries of the West. "Normality" here, as always, implies more than just a standard that is typical. What is not typical may be exceptional, and so better than it; but what is not "normal" is infallibly worse than abnormal or subnormal. The call for Italy to become a normal country expresses a longing to resemble others who are superior to it.

The full list of the anomalies that set Italy apart varies from one account to another, but all highlight three central features. For forty years of continuous Christian-Democratic hegemony, there was no real alternation of government. Under this regime, political corruption acquired colossal proportions. Intertwined with it, organized crime became a power in the land as the operations of the Mafia extended from Sicily to Rome and the North. Other national shortcomings are often noted: administrative inefficiency, lack of respect for the law, want of patriotism. But in the widespread conviction that the condition of Italy is abnormal, immovable government, pervasive corruption and militarized crime have had pride of place.

SOURCE: Excerpted from Perry Anderson, "Land without Prejudice," *London Review of Books*, vol. 24, no. 6, March 21, 2002 at www.lrb.co.uk/v24/n06/ande01_.html.

and 1983; the abduction and murder of former Prime Minister Aldo Moro by **Red Brigade** terrorists in 1978; and the bloody 1985 terrorist massacres in the Vienna and Rome airports—all reinforced public fear of the far left.

But as the 1980s progressed, the receding Soviet threat and the general withering away of Communism in Europe weakened the incentive for Italian voters to stick with a safe choice at the polls. It is no mere coincidence that the Communists, whose share of the popular vote fell from 26 percent in 1987 to 16 percent in 1992, lost even more ground than did the Christian Democrats at this time. But there were more specific, internal causes of the sea change in voter attitudes as well.

Another external factor that will be taken up in greater depth later in this book was the accelerating pace of European integration. As the EU economies became more and more intermeshed, policies and rules made in Brussels placed constraints on the national governments of member states. In order to qualify for membership in the European Monetary Union (EMU), for example, EU countries were expected to keep budget deficits under 3 percent of GDP and hold down inflation at or near levels achieved by the best-performing member states; also a country's public debt ratio could not exceed 60 percent of GDP. There were other criteria, as well, involving interest rates and the EU's exchange-rate mechanism.[22] Recall that the 1980s coincided with a conservative resurgence in the West: the Reagan era in the United States, the Thatcher era in Britain, and the Kohl era in Germany. Italy's governing consensus and profligate public spending policies were out of step with this trend. Moreover, they were out of step with the demands of the new era of global competition. Italy's old ways of doing things came to look more and more outmoded under these circumstances.

Two Cheers (and Votes) for Change

In the early 1990s, government scandals and corruption magnified this generalized sense that the old ways were no longer working and that the system needed fixing. In northern Italy, various separatist Leagues—the so-called *Lega Nord*—suddenly appeared in areas that were traditional DC strongholds. This largely spontaneous movement was not centralized or even organized, but it was clearly directed against the established parties, against Rome, and against corrupt politicians—hence its separatist character. The power of popular disenchantment was also used to force key changes in the electoral system in the early 1990s through the crude device of the abrogative referendum (a direct vote abolishing an existing law). The first referendum, held in 1991, did away with the worst features of the proportional representation (PR) system. The second one, in 1993, converted the PR system for Senate elections into one closely resembling a British-style first-past-the-post system. The size of the vote in favor of these reforms was even more impressive than the reforms themselves: 96 percent in 1991 and 83 percent in 1993.

The impact of these changes on the electoral fortunes of the Christian Democrats and the Socialists—the two leading parties in the governing coalition at this time, was devastating, at least in the short run. Although the coalition parties narrowly won the 1992 elections, the campaign brought out revelations of corruption that shocked even voters accustomed to corrupt officials. It was so bad that Italians dubbed it **Tangentopoli** ("Bribesville"). Giuliano Amato, a Socialist untainted by the charges of corruption flying in all directions, formed a government and launched an anticorruption drive dubbed **Operation Clean Hands,** but within six month five ministers were facing criminal prosecution and resigned. By 1994, it was becoming increasingly difficult to distinguish lawmakers from lawbreakers—about one-fifth of the Italy's parliamentarians were under criminal investigation. Italy was now facing its worst political crisis since World War II, one on a par with the fall of France's Fourth Republic in 1958 or President Richard Nixon's resignation in 1974 following the Watergate affair.

Although his government lasted only one year, Prime Minister Amato virtually saved Italy from financial collapse. After the lira's nosedive forced Italy to withdraw from the European Monetary System (EMS)—the forerunner of the monetary union now in effect—Amato pushed an austere budget through Parliament and in so doing set the country back on a bumpy road to recovery. Belt-tightening budgets are never painless and often very unpopular, and this one was no exception. But Italians knew the situation called for drastic action. Thus, Amato's successor was a caretaker: former governor of the Bank of Italy, Carlo Azeglio Ciampi—a distinguished banker, not a "crooked" politician. Putting a professional banker in charge of the government calmed international financial markets and reassured Italy's business community. Ciampi was the right choice at the right time, but it was clear that his appointment was only a temporary expedient: Italy needed a new face and a new start. The stage was set for something dramatic to happen. That something turned out to be a new slate-clearing round of national elections called less than two years after the previous round. The new face belonged to a flamboyant business tycoon named Silvio Berlusconi. But the telling of this part of the story is best left to the next chapter.

SPAIN'S REJUVENATED POLITY

Spain's war injuries in the twentieth century were entirely self-inflicted. Spain was neutral in both world wars but endured a bloody civil war in the 1930s. That bitter experience would color Spanish politics for many decades to come. The immediate upshot of the Spanish Civil War was to wipe out all traces of democratic rule. Out of the wreckage of that war stepped a strongman, Francisco Franco, who instituted a personal dictatorship that remained basically unchanged and unchallenged until his death in 1975. Franco ruled Spain in the manner of an autocrat, but he did create a pseudolegislative body, the **Cortes,** to rubber-stamp his policies. Ironically, the Cortes would prove to be instrumental in the creation of Spain's new parliamentary democracy in October 1976. Here is how it happened.

A Belated Economic Miracle

The Cortes under Franco was not a real legislative body; when Franco was alive, it represented no one except Franco. That was its great failing as a tool of popular self-government but ironically it was also a key to the future. With Franco gone, the Cortes represented nobody and nothing. Without Franco, it had no purpose or direction. It would find a new purpose and in so doing play a key role in creating a new political order in Spain.

The Spanish monarchy also had a major role in this drama. When Alfonso III fled the country as it was plunging into civil war, he left the throne unoccupied but not vacant—that is, he never abdicated. Franco later promised to restore the monarchy but did not do so; he did not want a rival with a strong claim to political legitimacy around, especially not one with liberal inclinations. Alfonso died in exile; it was his son and successor, Don Juan, who was known to have liberal views. Finally in 1969, Franco directed the Cortes to name Juan Carlos, Alfonso's grandson, the Prince of Spain and heir to the throne. With this one masterstroke, Franco skipped Don Juan and named his own successor—Juan Carlos would become king upon Franco's death.

Two days after Franco died in November 1975, the Cortes dutifully named Juan Carlos King of Spain. It was as though Spain was turning back the pages of history. But soon it became apparent that Juan Carlos himself has something else in mind—namely, leading Spain forward, not backward. First, in July 1976 Juan Carlos got the Cortes to put Adolfo Suárez on its short list of candidates for the office of prime minister. Once in office, Suárez, working closely with the popular monarch, devised a package of democratic reforms and deftly guided them through the Cortes.

In October 1976, the Cortes that had faithfully served Franco for so many years did something quite unexpected and remarkable: it voted itself out of existence.

It did so by voting overwhelmingly, 425 in favor to 15 against, with 13 abstentions—to approve the proposed **Law on Political Reforms.** This law created a bicameral legislation and laid the groundwork for the drafting of a new constitution. In December 1976, the Spanish people approved a referendum on the new law by a landslide. The door to democracy was now flung wide open.

Events now moved rapidly. The new parliament drafted, debated, and passed a new, democratic constitution that was submitted to a popular referendum in December 1978. To nobody's surprise, it, too, passed by a lopsided majority. The following year, Adolfo Suárez and the Democratic Center Union (UCD) won reelection. Spanish democracy was up and running.

A People's King: The Failed Coup of 1981

Spain's political system is correctly but confusingly called a constitutional monarchy. This label is correct because under the Spanish Constitution, the monarch serves as the head of state; it is confusing because the same charter also makes Spain a parliamentary democracy. In this respect, Spain resembles several other West European countries, including Belgium, Denmark, Great Britain, Norway, the Netherlands, and Sweden. But there is a difference: the Spanish monarch, unlike his counterparts in these other countries, is more than a figurehead. In 1981, for example, when a military coup was attempted, it was King Juan Carlos who saved Spain's infant democracy. The drama of this event has been told elsewhere and often. The Civil Guard had no qualms about seizing control of Parliament and holding the entire body hostage at gunpoint for 18 tense hours. But when the popular monarch told General Alfonso Armada—one of the leading coup plotters—that if the army intended to terminate Spanish democracy they would have to kill him first, they backed down.

A Parliamentary Democracy Fit for Europe

Spain's parliamentary democracy is very similar to the British model; even the subordinate seconding role of the upper house (called the Senate in the Spanish Parliament) parallels that of the British House of Lords. But there are a few notable differences. Unlike the British system, the Spanish prime minister and cabinet are invested (voted on) separately in the 350-member House of Deputies. Also, Spain borrowed the idea of a constructive vote of no confidence from Germany. Designed as a safeguard against the kind of chronic governmental instability that has plagued Italy (and France prior to 1958), this device prevents Parliament from dismissing an existing government (a negative vote) unless it simultaneously offers an alternative. Finally, Spain's method of electing the House of Deputies—a PR (proportional representation) formula that disadvantages minor or fringe parties—also creates a systemic bias in favor of stability.

A big question in all democracies, especially those in which governments are made and unmade by parliaments, is the party system. Like virtually all other European countries, and in contrast to the United States, Spain has a multiparty system. The now-extinct centrist party that played the key role in the transition to democracy and the formation of the first freely elected government was the Democratic Center Union (UCD)—the party of Adolfo Suárez. For reasons that are still not entirely known, Suàrez quit the UCD in 1981and formed a new centrist party the **Social and Democratic Center** (CDS). This maneuver did get him a seat in the parliament but the center parties thereafter lost ground to two other parties, the center-right **Popular Party** (PP) and the center-left **Spanish Socialist Workers' Party** (PSOE). Both of these parties moved toward the center in the 1980s, capturing many votes that formerly went to the UCD or the CDS. With the string of Socialist Party victories in 1982, 1986, 1989, and 1993, the PSOE emerged as a mainstay of Spanish politics, eclipsing the UCD/CDS. Its main rival was the center-right Popular Party. As we will see in Chapter 4, the center-right Popular Party came on strong in the 1990s to win two successive elections, one narrowly and the other—in 2000—by a convincing margin. That, in turn, set the stage for the dramatic events that followed.

SUMMARY AND CONCLUSIONS

At present, the political systems of Western Europe display a remarkable consistency: all are based on the principle of government by consent, all are ruled by civilians who came to power by free elections based on universal suffrage and the secret ballot, and all protect personal freedoms and civil liberties from infringement by the state. This consistent pattern is no doubt one reason why the West has been able to move farther and faster toward economic unity (and perhaps political union) than any region of the world.

The early stages of economic integration accompanied a rapid rate of economic growth in Western Europe, including miraculous postwar recoveries in West Germany, France, and Italy. The West German "economic miracle" was especially impressive because wartime Germany had suffered enormous damage to massive Allied bombing during World War II. West Germany became the Continent's showcase market economy in contrast to East Germany, a Soviet-style centrally planned economy that lagged far behind. The generally high level of prosperity achieved in Western Europe from the 1950s on pointed to the efficacy of open, competitive economies. Although correlation and causation are two different things, membership in the European Economic Community (EEC)— the precursor to the European Union (EU) was quite clearly associated with economic success. (We focus on the EU in Chapters Eight and Nine.)

The success of Western Europe's market economies has gone hand in hand with a high level of political stability in the region. Even in Italy, where governments have often been short lived, no serious threats to the country's basic institutions have arisen in the postwar era. However, none of this good news has prevented problems associated with the postindustrial stage of development from arising and nothing precludes future crises of an even more serious nature. In Chapter Four we explore the challenges Western Europe will face in the coming years.

KEY TERMS

Basic Law

Bundesrat

Bundestag

cabinet government

chancellor

collective ministerial
responsibility

common law

corporatist model

Cortes

custom and convention

*École Nationale
d'Administration* (ENA)

Fascist

Federal Republic of
Germany (FRG)

Fifth Republic

first past the post

Fraktionen

fusion of powers

Gaullist

House of Commons

House of Lords

House of Lords Act
(1999)

Land list

Länder

Law on Political
Reforms

Lega Nord

les grandes écoles

les grands corps

loyal opposition

Members of Parliament

National Assembly

National Front

New Labour

Official Secrets Act

Operation Clean Hands

opposition days

overdevelopment

package vote

parliamentary
democracy

parliamentary secretary

parliamentary
sovereignty

Permanent secretary

plebiscite

Popular Party (PP)

postindustrial society

proportional
representation (PR)

question time

rationalized parliament

Red Brigade

royal assent

rule of law

Social and Democratic
Center (CDS)

Spanish Socialist
Workers' Party (PSOE

Tangentopoli

technocrats

Thatcherism

third reading

tutelage system

two-ballot system

two-party system

unitary system

vote of no confidence

welfare state

Westminster

Whitehall

works of authority

SUGGESTED READINGS

Alford, B. W. *Britain in the World Economy since 1880.* White Plains, NY: Longman, 1995.

Dorey, Peter. *British Politics since 1945.* Cambridge, MA: Blackwell, 1995.

Geppert, Dominik. *The Postwar Challenge: Cultural, Social, and Political Change in Western Europe, 1945–1958.* New York: Oxford University Press, 2004.

Ginsborg, Paul. *Italy and Its Discontents.* New York: St. Martin's Press, 2002.

Kavanagh, Dennis. *British Politics Today,* 7th ed. Manchester, UK: Manchester University Press, 2004.

Keating, Paul. *Class and Inequality in Britain: Social Stratification since 1945.* Cambridge, MA: Blackwell, 1997.

Parkes, Stuart. *Understanding Contemporary Germany.* New York: Routledge, 1996.

Putnam, Robert D.; Leonardi, Rafaella; and Nanetti, Y. *Making Democracy Work: Civil Transitions in Modern Italy.* Princeton, NJ: Princeton University Press, 1994.

Romero-Salvado, Francisco, J. *Twentieth Century Spain: Politics and Society in Spain, 1898–1998.* New York: St. Martin's Press, 1999.

Sowerwine, Charles. *France since 1870: Culture, Society, and Politics.* New York: Palgrave Macmillan, 2001.

Stevens, Anne. *Government and Politics of France.* New York: Palgrave Macmillan, 2003.

WEB SITES

www.keele.ac.uk/depts/por/ukbase.htm (British government and politics website, excellent)

www.historylearningsite.co.uk/gbpolitics.htm (United Kingdom)

www.gksoft.com/govt/en/fr.html (France)

http://europa.eu.int/abc/governments/index_en.htm (European governments online, links)

www.discoverfrance.net/France/DF_govt.shtml (France)

www.electionworld.org/spain.htm (elections around the world website)

www.abacci.com/atlas/economy.asp?countryID=325 (Spanish politics)

www.gksoft.com/govt/en/es.html (governments on the WWW—Spain)

www.italyemb.org/government.htm (Italian government—embassy website)

www.gksoft.com/govt/en/it.html (governments on the WWW—Italy)

www.abacci.com/atlas/politics3.asp?countryID=229 (Italian politics)

www.gksoft.com/govt/en/de.html (governments on the WWW—Germany)

www.germany-info.org/relaunch/index.html (German government—embassy website)

http://europa.eu.int/abc/governments/germany/index_en.htm (European governments online—Germany)

www.bundesregierung.de/en (official German government website)

NOTES

1. For more information, visit the website of the Organization for European Cooperation and Development (OECD) at www.oecd.org/about/origins/oeec.htm.

2. "France's Riots: An underclass rebellion" (Special Report), *The Economist,* November 12, 2005, pp. 24–26.

3. See T. R. Reid, *The United States of Europe: The New Superpower and the End of American Supremacy* (New York: Penguin, 2004), especially chap. 6 ("The European

Social Model"), pp. 144–176; see also Jeremy Rifkin, *The European Dream: How Europe's Vision of the Future is Quietly Eclipsing the American Dream* (New York: Tarcher/Penguin, 2004), especially the second and third chapters ("The New Land of Opportunity" and "The Quiet Economic Miracle"), pp. 36–85.

4. Rifkin, *European Dream,* p. 43.

5. Sydney Bailey, *British Parliamentary Democracy,* 3rd ed. (Westport, CN: Greenwood, 1978), pp. 4–5.

6. The House of Lords locked horns with the House of Commons in 1991 over a controversial measure (called the War Crimes Bill) that cleared the way for prosecution of several alleged Nazi mass murderers living in Great Britain. That was the first time the Parliament Act of 1911 had been invoked in four decades.

7. See, for example, Bagehot, "A Dangerous Game," *The Economist,* December 7, 2002, p. 56. One issue they disagreed about was whether or when the U.K. should adopt the euro (Blair pushed for it, Brown opposed it). Another issue was whether to give universities authority to set and collect tuition fees (Blair for, Brown against). Normally, policy disputes within the government are kept from public view. There is much speculation that Brown's true ambition is to be the next prime minister. That speculation continued in late 2005 after Blair's popular image was badly tarnished by what critics termed his "lap dog" support for U.S. President George W. Bush's decision to invade Iraq even after it had become clear that the reasons for going into Iraq were false, the war was unwinnable, and there was no easy way out.

8. Alexander MacLeod, "Britain's Labour Party Faces Watershed Battle," *Christian Science Monitor,* Apr. 15, 1992, p. 1.

9. Bailey, *British Parliamentary Democracy,* p. 131.

10. R. M. Punnett, *British Government and Politics,* 5th ed. (Prospect Heights, IL: Waveland, 1990), p. 68.

11. For example, in 1983 the Conservatives won an overwhelming 144-seat majority with well under half the popular votes. In the 1987 elections, they captured only about 43 percent of the popular vote but still ended up with a 101-seat majority in Parliament. In the 1992 elections, by contrast, the Conservatives won roughly the same percentage of the popular vote but gained only a 22-seat majority—a much smaller magnifier effect but enough to give the Tories more than half the seats. In 1997, the same type of effect worked in favor of the victorious Labour Party.

12. See, for example, Craig R. Whitney, "British Race Is Neck and Neck at the Finish," *The New York Times,* Apr. 9, 1992, p. A4.

13. "One More Defeat on Long Retreat," *The Economist,* May 7, 1988, pp. 51–52.

14. Howard La Franchi, "French Say 'Non' to Traditional Political Parties," *Christian Science Monitor,* Mar. 24, 1992, p. 1.

15. Suzanne Berger, *The French Political System,* 3rd ed. (New York: Random House, 1974), p. 368.

16. Roy Macridis, ed., *Modern Political Systems: Europe,* 6th ed. (Englewood Cliffs, NJ: Prentice-Hall, 1986), p. 120.

17. "Jacque Chirac Wins by Default," *The Economist,* May 11, 2002, pp. 48–49.

18. To qualify for round two in France's parliamentary elections, a party either has to come in first or second or win on the ballots of at least 12.5% of the registered voters. A low turnout thus hurts smaller parties because it means they must secure a larger share of the vote actually cast to clear the 12.5 percent hurdle.

19. The term *unification* here is used in preference to *reunification* because the latter suggests a return to the Germany of Hitler's Third Reich, which would be misleading and provocative.

20. Guido Goldman, *The German Political System* (New York: Random House, 1974), p. 56.

21. The legal voting age for lower-house elections is 18; for the upper house (Senate) it is 25.

22. Desmond Dinan, *Europe Recast: A History of the European Union* (Boulder: Lynne Rienner, 2004), pp. 248–249.

4

Western Europe Today
Democracy in Postmodern Societies

C hapter Four looks at the policy agenda in Western Europe, where many of the world's wealthiest postmodern societies are found today. The striking fact that these societies are so-called welfare states and that they are all facing some of the same problems is interesting from both a theoretical and practical (policy) standpoint.

This chapter begins by exploring the meaning of postmodern *as a concept commonly applied to Western societies. Just as there is no single, all-purpose formula for comparing political systems, there is also no universally accepted definition for postmodern.*

Chapter Four also explores the concept of liberal democracy and the elements of liberal economic policy—based on competition and unregulated markets—before moving on to a brief survey of the problems facing many Western societies going through the throes of postmodern development. It then examines the problems facing each of the featured countries in Part I as well as policy responses. A brief assessment of the prospects for successful outcomes will identify some of the stumbling blocks to quick and straightforward solutions facing political decision makers in these countries.

What *does* it mean to say that France and Germany are **postmodern** societies but Bulgaria and Romania are not? (See Box 4.1) To answer this question, we have to understand what it means to be *modern*. The word itself is politically loaded. What is the opposite of modern? Tribal, traditional, superstitious, primitive, backward, agrarian, underdeveloped, less developed, and so on—none of these alternative labels is flattering to so-called premodern societies. Because the West created what we think of as the modern world, the West has also defined what it means to be modern. Modern means "like us." Everything that is not like us is, by definition, not modern.

B O X 4.1 The Postmodern Paradigm Shift

The word *postmodern* has many meanings but always denotes something that comes after—or grows out of—modern states and societies. The latter have certain things in common, including bureaucratization, industrialization, urbanization, and secularization. In traditional societies, most people live on farms or in rural villages and see the world through the prism of religion, legend, and superstition. When societies go from traditional to modern, people are uprooted, forced to move to cities, work in factories, and live in crowded and often squalid conditions. A burgeoning new urban working class emerges alongside a smaller entrepreneurial and professional middle class, thus setting the stage for the postmodern phase of development.

Postmodern societies continue to produce food and fiber (like traditional societies) and manufactured goods (like modern societies), but services (banking, insurance, law, medicine, education, accounting, advertising, retail sales, and computer programming, to name but a few) grow in importance and eventually eclipse the production of tangible goods. The ratio of blue-collar workers to white-collar workers falls sharply as factories downsize or close, and high-rise office buildings spring up along multilane beltways that encircle sprawling metropolitan areas. Traffic congestion, air pollution, and the familiar background noise of the city become facts of life. In addition to major environmental issues, postmodern societies face an array of problems (violent crime, illegal drug use, AIDs, to cite a few examples) related to overcrowding, immigration, the growth of an urban underclass, and youth unemployment.

Globalization is also a phenomenon closely linked to this postmodern syndrome. In postmodern societies, companies are often saddled with a high-cost labor force. Wage earners typically receive benefits (health insurance, paid sick and maternity leave, pension plans, and the like) as well as union-backed protection against job loss. These conditions—long associated with social progress—now create huge incentives for Western companies to relocated to low-wage areas (such as China and India) where labor is superabundant and there are far fewer rules (minimum wage, child labor laws, occupational safety, toxic waste disposal, et cetera). The resulting rush to outsource means that more and more jobs are exported while more and more products are imported, that investment capital flows in ever greater amounts from Western economies to Asia, and that the postmodern West faces the prospect of chronic trade imbalances.

Advanced technology, a trademark of modernity, is no longer the monopoly of the richest countries. Thus, postmodern development involves a paradigm shift in which old problems of underdevelopment persist in the poorest countries but new problems of overdevelopment appear in the richest ones.

THE DOWNSIDE OF MODERNITY

Recognizing the bias in this definition, however, does not make it go away, nor does it change the fact that **modernity** is more than an idea; it is also an ideal, a goal, a thing much to be desired in the minds of people everywhere. Or not. Those who do not admire or desire to be more like modern (Western) societies are sometimes violently antimodern (anti-Western). That rueful fact nonetheless can help us to clarify in our own minds what the word *modern* has come to mean in the eyes of the world. In the West, modernity is now associated with all sorts of gadgets and conveniences, with automobiles and air travel, computers and mass communications. But in fact it is older than any of these things. As we noted in the last chapter, modernity begins with the rise of the nation-state itself, encompassing the European exploration of the New World, the Enlightenment, the scientific and industrial revolutions, the Age of Imperialism, and, last but not least, the triumph of **liberalism** and democracy in the West.

Liberalism. It means different things to different people, but there is no question that this word implies freedom, including freedom for a few to get rich and freedom for the many to vote, strike, protest, or emigrate. In other words, modernity is not just about utopian dreams; it's about real-world possibilities and the chance to go to school, to make a living, to raise a family, to be safe from harm, and to live in peace. All these things are implied in the term *modernity* because all are associated (rightly or wrongly) with the established democracies of Western Europe, the United States, and Canada (the "West").

Why, then, are some people violently opposed to all things modern? What is wrong with this picture? Part of the answer is very straightforward: the West (and therefore modernity) is widely associated with colonialism in the minds of non-Westerners. Colonialism is a controversial topic in the West; some argue it was not all bad, others that it was all a dreadful mistake. Outside the West, however, there is very little argument: it was a bad thing and a stain on Europe's reputation. Other things as well about modernity do not always go down well outside Europe. For example, modernity is associated with scientific inquiry, rejection of superstition, and secularism (the view that religion is a personal matter and has no place in the affairs of government or the making of public policy). Secularism in particular has been one of the most divisive and controversial aspects of modernity.

In the non-Western world, modernity is often associated with exploitation in various forms—of indigenous peoples, local conflicts, natural resources, and the environment. But the advances in living standards that modernity brought to the West and the promise it held out for the newly independent nations following decolonization more than offset these failings, at least until recently.

WELFARE STATES: BROKEN BEYOND REPAIR?

What has changed? Western Europe is more prosperous than ever. The European Union now encompasses twenty-five countries, 450 million people, and boasts a combined gross national product slightly larger than that of the United States. Every EU member state is a functioning democracy with universal suffrage, a free press, and the like. Every one holds free elections, protects the civil and political rights of its citizens, and nurtures a competitive economy. Per capita incomes in Western Europe are among the highest in the world. Surely there is a great deal to admire and emulate. So we return to the question asked earlier: What is wrong with this picture?

All the familiar features of the modern welfare state are still in place. Social benefits—including health insurance, old-age pensions, maternity leave, subsidized housing, unemployment compensation, and free public education—are far more generous than in the United States. Life expectancy is high throughout Western Europe. Infant mortality and childhood poverty rates are among the lowest in the world (in many cases, lower than in the United States). But tax rates and consumer prices in many countries are significantly higher than in the United States (see Figure 4.1). Here is where clouds begin to darken the political landscape.

Cost of Living Index

New York = 100, Spring 2005

FIGURE 4.1 Cost of Living Index

Taxes are never popular. In countries where voters are given an opportunity to elect a new government every four or five years—possibly more frequently in parliamentary systems—there is always political pressure to lower taxes. If the government resists this pressure for the sake of a balanced budget or because cutting social benefits would be political suicide, there are likely to be opposition leaders who will not resist. Promising to cut taxes is not a foolproof way to win elections, but it is always a temptation for politicians seeking office. It is especially tempting (and likely to succeed) in countries where taxes take half the average worker's take-home pay.

In Western Europe, taxes generally range from 45 to 50 percent of GDP. Among the twenty-seven OECD countries, the lowest tax rates are found in the United States—29 percent of GDP in 2004. By comparison, in Sweden, the highest of the OECD[1] countries, taxes equaled 54 percent of GDP in 2004; in France, the figure was 46 percent. But, as will be seen later in this chapter, even these astronomical tax rates are proving inadequate to cover the rising costs of welfare state social benefits in many of these countries.

Citizens are likely to accept high taxes so long as social benefits are generous. Indeed, Europeans express pride in a society that takes care of its less fortunate members, and often decry what they see as a sink-or-swim social ethic existing in the United States. But what happens when chronic budget deficits lead to mounting public debt, despite high taxes? The government is then forced to raise taxes or cut spending. Raising taxes when they are already very high is politically inexpedient. But the other alternative—cutting expenditures—is also likely to create a backlash at election time unless the government can find a relatively painless way to do it. "Painless" means not cutting social benefits because the **welfare state** is what justifies high taxes in the first place.

If this policy dilemma is posed to Americans as a kind of theoretical exercise, they are likely to say, "Okay, if country X can't cut social programs for political reasons, how about making cuts in defense spending?" The defense budget normally accounts for 5–6 percent of GNP in the United States.[2] Not so in Europe, where most countries spend far less on national defense, not only in absolute terms, but also relatively speaking (slightly less than 1.9 percent of GNP for NATO's European members as a whole). Spain, for example, spent just 1.2 percent of its GNP on defense in 2002. On the other hand, European countries spend far more on social programs than do governments on all levels in the United States-an average of 26 percent compared to 11 percent.[3]

People naturally come to see social benefits as **entitlements**—rights rather than privileges or perquisites. Governments cut social benefits at their own peril. At the same time, where taxes are already very high, governments cannot raise taxes without incurring the wrath of the voters and, what is worse, undermining the economy.

How does raising taxes undermine the economy? It does so in a variety of ways: by undercutting business and consumer confidence, taking money away from investment (supply) and consumption (demand), discouraging foreign investment, and making exports less competitive (higher priced) on the world market. Generally speaking, economists agree that low taxes on profits, incomes, and consumption are more compatible with rapid and sustained economic growth than high taxes. However, low taxes are not possible in a welfare state. But very few taxpayers are economists (and even economists are not necessarily in favor of dismantling the welfare state). Polls (as well as election results) show that Europeans in overwhelming numbers favor the preservation (if not extension) of the welfare state.

Still, facts are stubborn. Overall economic growth rates in the EU are sluggish compared with other competitive economies in the world. After 1945, average income in West European countries rose from around 40 percent of American levels to slightly over 70 percent by 1973. Since then, however, Western Europe has not succeeded in closing that gap; in fact, the gap began to widen again in the 1980s, a trend that became even more pronounced in the 1990s. The US economy has outperformed the EU by two or more percentage points in recent years, while China has been quietly catching up with sustained growth rates averaging 9–10 percent a year.[4]

In 2005, the American economy achieved an impressive growth rate of 3.5 percent; by comparison, France's economy was sluggish (1.3 percent) and the economies of Germany and Italy inched along at a snail's pace (a mere 0.6 and 0.1 percent, respectively). Although Great Britain did slightly better (1.6 percent), China—the EU's main challenger after the United States—easily outperformed them all (9.1 percent).[5] And although it is true that China started from a much lower level and is still a developing country, the implied loss of competitiveness does not bode well for the West in an era of global markets and liberal trade regimes. Unless something happens (or is done) to reverse this trend, it could ultimately prove to be the undoing of the welfare state.

TABLE 4.1   Idle in Europe: Unemployment in
Selected Countries (2004)

Country	Unemployment Rate (%)
Belgium	12.8
Denmark	6.2
France	9.9
Germany	10.8
Italy	7.7
Netherlands	6.4
Spain	10.5
United Kingdom	4.7
Euro area	8.9

Evidence that there are structural (or fundamental) problems in these economies is not hard to find. For example, unemployment rates are alarmingly high in many countries, averaging 9 percent in the euro area in 2004–5 (see Table 4.1).[6] Compare these figures to the United States, where it was 5.1 percent, or Switzerland, where it was only 4.0 percent. (The unemployment rate in the U.S. is probably higher than reported, however, since those no longer seeking work are not counted. In general, official government statistics often do not tell the whole story; unfortunately, there are few if any alternative sources of macroscopic social and economic data.)

Joblessness on this scale is particularly troubling to countries unaccustomed to high unemployment rates. The tight job market has hit university graduates and other new entrants or recent entrants into the labor force the hardest. It has also created a backlash against immigrants and acted as a spur to ultranationalist movements in many Western European countries, including France, Germany, Italy, the Netherlands, and Spain.

France presents a textbook example of a society struggling with both of these postmodern problems. Indeed, they have manifested themselves in the most acute forms in France, as the recent rise of an extreme right-wing political movement (see Chapter Five) and the 2005 urban riots attest. But these and other challenges are facing nearly all of Europe's established democracies at present.

Paradoxically, Europe is facing a population *implosion*.[7] According to the UN projections, the world's population will grow from slightly over 6 billion in 2000 to slightly under 9 billion by 2050. Under this gloomy forecast, however, the population of the EU countries would fall by 6 percent during that same period. For the countries with the lowest fertility rates, the decline would be breathtaking: Italy's population, for example, would free-fall from 58 million to 45 million if nothing changes. Still more incredible, Germany's population (currently at 82–83 million) would dwindle to a mere 25 million by the end of the century. But there is always a danger in projecting short- or medium-term trends too far into the future. It seems highly unlikely that modern governments—faced with a demographic doomsday scenario of this magnitude—would not adopt policies aimed at boosting birth rates, enticing more immigrants, and the like.

As Europe's population is shrinking, it is also aging, thanks to rising life expectancy. The upshot is a corresponding rise in the number of retirees and a falling ratio of wage earners to retirees. Across Western Europe (as in the United States), the rising cost of old-age pensions is a major issue. The causes are well known, starting with the fact that people live longer. Though no one denies that a problem exists, most everyone agrees that high (and rising) life expectancy is desirable and that it would be wrong to place the burden of structural adjustments in the economy or spending cuts to balance the budget on the elderly. Doing nothing is fast becoming a formula for financial collapse.

Europeans generally pay a lot more into state pension funds than Americans do. Social Security contributions in the United States are around 12 percent of wages and salaries. In Germany, the figure is close to 29 percent; it is even higher in Italy (about 33 percent). Moreover, as noted earlier, the demographics will go from the bad to worse—much worse—in the decades to come. Europe's population will age at a record rate. The ratio of elderly (aged 65 plus) to the working-age population (aged 20 to 64) will double.[8] What this means is that benefits must be cut in half or the contribution rate (already high in Western Europe) must double or the retirement age will have to go up.

None of these alternatives is likely to prove popular with voters or painless for senior citizens (a large and growing part of the voting population). But if nothing is done, "some countries in the EU, where pensions are especially generous, could pile up liabilities on the scale of war debts. By 2050, nine of the EU's 15 member states would have accumulated gross debt of 150–300% of GDP."[9] When countries pile up public debt, foreign lenders begin to run for cover. That, in turn, contributes to the kind of downward spiral that can easily culminate in a political and economic crisis.

The demographic question, and its political consequences, provides one example of a postmodern problem that afflicts all or most European democracies today. Ironically, many of the challenges facing European societies at present are the unintended consequences of technological advances and public policies that have brought great benefits to these countries. The critical need for pension reform illustrates how yesterday's solutions often give rise to today's problems.

THE BUMPY ROAD AHEAD

Other postmodern challenges that require creative public policy responses include the changing labor market, the environment, immigration, integration, and **globalization.** Each of these challenges is associated with a set of specific problems and issues—the labor market with unemployment, job security, and the right to strike; the environment with air and water pollution, hazardous waste disposal, and energy conservation; immigration with border controls, race relations, and alien rights; integration (membership in the European Union) with nationalism, a desire to keep decisions as close to the people as possible, and popular resistance to American-style federalism; globalization with the need to compete against Asian countries where labor is cheap and abundant.

The case studies to follow will elucidate the nature of these challenges and show how they impinge on politics in contemporary Europe. They will also underscore the fact that many of these problems are interconnected. Thus, to cite one example, anti-immigration sentiment is often most pronounced in countries where unemployment is highest. It is easy to blame foreigners (who often take jobs nobody else wants) for all sorts of social and economic ills. Newcomers are either "lazy" if they cannot find work or "scabs" if they can (because they are willing to work long hours for low pay). Right-wing extremism feeds on such racial stereotypes and prejudices.

Finding the connections between these supposedly separate phenomena is one key to understanding what is actually going on in a given place and time. This is what the empirical science of politics (as distinct from normative political theory) is all about.

We will also encounter problems found in some countries but not in others, whereas other problems are entirely unique to a particular country. Regionalism, for example, remains a major issue in Britain, Belgium, Italy, and Spain, but not in Denmark, the Netherlands, Portugal, or Sweden. It is also an issue in Germany, but there it results from circumstances imposed from outside, namely the fact that from 1945 to 1989 Germany was divided into two very different states with very different forms of government, economic systems, and different standards of living. France, on the other hand, has largely overcome its problems of regionalism, although there are still echoes of a time when the provinces were linguistically, culturally, and politically distinct. France certainly has no disruptive regional problems to compare with those of Spain (the Basque separatist movement) or Belgium (the French-speaking Walloons versus the Dutch-speaking Flemings) or Britain (what to do about Northern Ireland) or Italy (the rich north versus the poor south).

In contemporary Europe, there is a facet of the postmodern paradigm that is not present anywhere else in the world, namely, the process of deconstructing the nation-state, otherwise known as integration. What was once an experiment in economic integration is evolving into a new political structure known as the European Union (EU). Traditionally, states operated mainly on two levels—national and international. In Europe, the twenty-five EU member-states operate on *three* levels—national, supranational, and international. One way to think about it is to imagine politics in Europe as a triple chess game involving three matches being played at the same time. On the top (international) board, nation-states continue to conduct international diplomacy in time-honored ways; on the bottom (national) board, they still make and enforce laws, collect taxes, and, in general, carry on as though nothing has changed; but on the middle (supranational) board, rules and decisions previously considered to be the exclusive preserve of sovereign national governments are being hammered out on a daily basis by career EU bureaucrats—called **Eurocrats**—in Brussels.

In postmodern Europe, what happens on the middle chess board increasingly influences—or drives—what happens on the bottom and top boards. On the bottom one, EU member states no longer exercise exclusive control over domestic economic policy—indeed, the very distinction between domestic and foreign policy has become blurred. In some areas, it is disappearing altogether. Even at the top level—international relations—the EU members do lip service to a Common Foreign and Security Policy (CFSP), although that declared goal was placed in serious question when French and Dutch voters rejected the proposed EU constitution in 2005. These developments will be explored and explained in Part III of this book, but the reader should keep in mind that the EU is now a pervasive force in European politics. Suffice it to say that no comparative analysis of politics in Europe today can ignore the impact of Brussels (the EU) on national politics in the twenty-five EU member states.

But the EU *itself* has been (and continues to be) the focus of vigorous debates on the Continent. It is no exaggeration to say that the growth of the EU—how far, how fast, how deep, and how wide—is a burning question in Europe. The demise of the proposed EU constitution in 2005 dashed all hopes of building momentum toward some form of political union (for example, a "United States of Europe" advocated by some Eurofederalists). As a result, the old Europe of great-power rivalries and sovereign nation-states is moribund but a new Europe—one capable of speaking with a single voice on the world stage—is still struggling to be born. Another related question involves the United States. The context of transatlantic ties changed greatly after the fall of communism in Europe. Was there still a need for the North Atlantic Treaty Organization (NATO) when there was no longer a Soviet threat? Few were prepared to declare against NATO, but nearly all recognized it would have to change. Behind all the talk was a more basic issue, namely, the nature of Europe's relationship with the United States. Should Europe continue to follow America's lead in the world or should it strike out on its own? The 9/11 crisis for a brief time galvanized a new sense of unity in the West, but the question of whether or not to invade Iraq opened deeper divisions in NATO than ever. France, Germany, and Belgium opposed the United States; Great Britain, Spain, and Italy backed the United States. (Most of the East European newcomers to NATO also backed the United States.)

Everywhere in Western Europe, however, public opinion was overwhelmingly against the invasion. Whether America was a positive or a negative force in the world became a front-burner political issue in many European countries. In Spain, a pro-American government was voted down in 2004; the new government promptly withdrew from the Western coalition in Iraq.[10] In Britain, Prime Minister Tony Blair came under heavy public criticism for siding with President Bush; although Blair managed to stay in office, his popularity plummeted. In January 2005, at the prestigious World Economic Forum in Davos, Switzerland, even Blair began to distance himself from the United States, declaring, "If America wants the rest of the world to be part of the agenda it has set, it must be part of their agenda, too."[11] Nonetheless, when British voters punished Blair's Labour party in parliamentary elections held in May of that year, the harsh verdict was widely interpreted as a reflection of public opposition to the Iraqi war.

Although neither NATO nor the nation-state itself can be taken for granted in the new Europe, it is way too early to pronounce NATO dead or dismiss the nation-state as a relic of the past. In all probability, both will remain prominent features on the European political scene for a long time to come. In many ways, postmodern Europe is a paradox—a recently dynamic region in danger of becoming a futuristic valley of the dinosaurs (dysfunctional old nation-states) if current economic and demographic trends persist.

Western Europe was the place where economic miracles occurred after World War II. Asia has earned that distinction more recently. The world has changed dramatically in the span of a few decades. Indeed, change is the name of the game in the postmodern era, but change gives rise to dislocations and necessitates adjustments. Will continued integration revitalize or stultify Europe's economies? How will Europe's welfare states respond to the challenges of globalization? In the pages that follow, we will look at how five leading democracies in Western Europe, buffeted by gale-force winds of change since 1989, are coping—some better than others.

BRITAIN: THE GREAT DILEMMA

The most persistent policy problem in Great Britain for much of the postwar period was the disappointing performance of the economy. After World War II, the British people were asked to sacrifice for the future: those with more would be asked to sacrifice more. A welfare state would be created with the available resources—that would be society's reward. Marshall Plan funds would be used for capital investment rather than current consumption. These policies were widely hailed by outside observers as a shining example of the regenerative powers of democracy. Yet the long-term result was not an economic miracle like those that occurred in West Germany and Italy but rather economic decay, despite the fact that the U.K. received more Marshall Plan aid than any other country—nearly 3.2 billion dollars (see Table 4.2).

Britain's Early Postwar Blues: A Stalled Economy

The United Kingdom stagnated as Germany, Italy, and France made a rapid economic recovery in the 1950s and 1960s. When OPEC oil prices skyrocketed in the early 1970s, inflation soared in Western Europe. In Great Britain, the annual inflation rate exceeded 20 percent at one point. Voters wondered whether any government, Conservative or Labour, could revive the British economy. The discovery of oil and gas in the North Sea brought the prospect of energy self-sufficiency— one of the only bright spots in a gloomy picture. A new economic phenomenon called **stagflation**—stagnating growth accompanied by high inflation—appeared. According to **Keynesian economic theory,** market economies can be expected to go through business cycles of boom and bust. In periods of rapid growth, inflation is a problem (prescribed cure: budget cuts, higher taxes and interest rates); in periods of recession, unemployment is a problem (prescribed cure: deficit spending, lower taxes and interest rates). But in the 1970s, the British economy was hit by inflation and recession at the same time.

Following the Great Depression and World War II, full employment became a permanent priority. Indeed, the jobless rate has been a key measure of governmental performance in Great Britain ever since. Starting in the 1970s, however,

TABLE 4.2 Marshall Plan Aid to Europe, 1948–1952 (millions US$)*

COUNTRY	Total	Grants	Loans
Austria	677.8	677.8	—
Belgium-Luxembourg	559.3	491.3	68.0
Denmark	273.0	239.7	33.3
France	2,713.6	2,488.0	225.6
Germany, Federal Republic of	1,390.6	1,173.7	216.9
Greece	706.7	706.7	—
Iceland	29.3	24.0	5.3
Ireland	147.5	19.3	128.2
Italy (including Trieste)	1,508.8	1,413.2	95.6
Netherlands	1,083.5	916.8	166.7
Norway	255.3	216.1	39.2
Portugal	51.2	15.1	36.1
Sweden	107.3	86.9	20.4
Turkey	225.1	140.1	85.0
United Kingdom	3,189.8	2,805.0	384.8
Regional	407.0	407.0	—
Total for all countries	**$13,325.8**	**$11,820.7**	**$1,505.1**

*Economic assistance provided April 3, 1948 to June 30, 1952 according to the Statistics and Reports division of the Agency for International Development (AID).

unemployment inched steadily upward, and by the mid-1980s hit record levels. Public opinion polls reinforced the impression that the state of the economy was a potential time bomb for the government.

Yet the British economy bounced back in the 1980s under the free-market policies of Prime Minister Margaret Thatcher's Conservative government. The official index of leading economic indicators (stock prices, interest rates, housing starts) rose faster during the six months leading up to the 1987 election than at any time since the early 1970s and propelled the Conservatives to a third straight victory at the polls.

Because the government can put its programs into effect in the British system, the party in power is held strictly accountable for the condition of the country. That is why in 1979, when the British economy was in the doldrums, the voters ousted the Labour party and put the Conservatives (Tories) in power. That is also why in 1997 the voters ousted the Tories.

The Politics of Economic Policy

In 1979, Prime Minister Thatcher had focused on one fundamental question: What is the proper balance between government intervention and free enterprise?

She blamed Great Britain's sagging economy on the excesses of a cradle-to-the-grave welfare state in which an ever-expanding public sector encroached on and undercut the private sector. Elect a Conservative government, she vowed, and things will be different.

Thatcher kept her promise: she denationalized industry, gave big business new investment incentives, cut taxes, and curtailed welfare spending. The British economy did revive, but there was little cause for celebration. "Amid a revivified economy, Britain's decaying inner cities are the worst blot on eight years of Tory government," proclaimed *The Economist,* a conservative British newsweekly.[12] In the 1987 campaign, Thatcher promised to rehabilitate inner cities, correct chronic housing problems, liberate schools from heavy-handed local controls, and reform local taxes. But some of these problems proved intractable, and at least one of her solutions, a new poll tax, drew jeers from the public and provoked mass protests in Trafalgar Square and elsewhere. This controversy contributed to Thatcher's growing unpopularity and, along with internal party dissension over Britain's strained relations with Europe (the EC), also contributed to her eventual ouster from the Conservative Party leadership (and thus from her position as prime minister).

Making a "Major" Change

When John Major replaced Margaret Thatcher as prime minister in November 1990, he seemed uncertain whether to stay the course Thatcher had charted or chart a new one. He chose the latter in June 1991 when he told members of his ruling Conservative party that he would attend the European Union summit at Maastricht and play a constructive role in negotiating a treaty aimed at establishing a common currency. Declaring "Britain must not be sidelined," Major threw in his lot with the pro-Europe faction against Thatcher's anti-federalists. Although he did not commit the United Kingdom to a Europe-wide currency immediately, his acceptance in principle of a monetary union cleared the way for the next giant step toward a unified Europe. This strategy was designed, in Major's words, to prevent Britain from remaining Europe's "odd man out."

Recession returned in the early 1990s, with inflation approaching double digits, unemployment on the rise, and burgeoning budget deficits. These disturbing trends forced John Major's Tory Government to introduce tough austerity measures. Major's tight fiscal and monetary policies brought down inflation and unemployment levels significantly, but the sacrifices implicit in these measures—for example, reduced public spending—led to public dissatisfaction and mounting criticism even within the Conservative party. Major hung on by a thread until the 1997 elections, when Labour galloped back into power with one of the largest landside majorities in modern British history.

Northern Ireland: Peace at Last?

Violence and civil strife in Northern Ireland continue to divert attention, energy, and resources from domestic ills. Militant Irish nationalists, claiming to represent the Roman Catholic minority, have waged a guerrilla war against Protestant-backed

British rule since the late 1960s. The **Provisional Irish Republican Army (IRA)** used terrorist tactics to achieve its objective of separation from the United Kingdom and union with the Republic of Ireland. Such a union would transform the Protestant majority in **Ulster** (Northern Ireland) into a minority in Roman Catholic Ireland. Radical Ulster Protestants have also used terrorism against Catholics in Northern Ireland. Despite a recent reduction in violence, there is still no end to the deadlock in sight.

Although its strategy and tactics are focused more on conventional political methods than terrorism these days, the IRA is not likely to abandon the struggle. In February 1991, IRA terrorists carried out a mortar attack on 10 Downing Street, the prime minister's official residence, while the cabinet was in session there. Although nobody was hurt, the terrorists had tried to decapitate the British government. Heroic efforts by Peter Brooke, Great Britain's secretary for Northern Ireland, led to a new round of talks in April and May 1991 among all parties except **Sinn Fein,** the political wing of the outlawed IRA, but the talks broke down the following July.

In the ensuing years, Northern Ireland remained a combat zone. Peace talks bore fruit in 1994 when the IRA and Protestant military groups agreed to a ceasefire, but a permanent settlement eluded the parties. The hopes raised by President Bill Clinton's visit in late 1995 quickly evaporated. The leadership of Sinn Fein continued to demand "inclusive" dialogue without preconditions. For its part, London was loath to pressure union loyalists into negotiating with Sinn Fein unless or until the IRA promised to stop killing people. In early 1997, bombing attacks against Ulster Catholics, apparently the work of loyalist guerrillas, resumed. Both sides were once again sinking into the murderous morass of terrorism.

In the late 1990s, Protestants and Catholics, weary of the violence, finally came to terms. Some 3200 people had been killed in three decades of civil strife. Following lengthy negotiations led by U.S. Ambassador George J. Mitchell, the parties agreed to a settlement, the so-called **Good Friday Agreement.** In the referenda that followed (May 1998), huge majorities in both Northern Ireland and Ireland endorsed the proposed settlement. After a false start and a new round of negotiations, a twelve-member cabinet responsible to an elected Assembly replaced direct British rule at the end of 1999. Northern Ireland would remain in the United Kingdom but assume responsibility for schools, public transportation, finance, and the like. London would continue to set policy in the areas of taxation, foreign affairs, defense, and external trade.

Two major questions remained unanswered: First, when and how would a surrender of weapons (called "decommissioning") on the part of Protestant and Catholic paramilitary groups take place? In the years following the Good Friday Agreement, Ulster Unionist leaders continued to insist that the IRA was not following through on its promise to disarm while Sinn Fein charged that hardline Protestant leader David Trimble was trying to sabotage the peace process, using the decommissioning issue as a pretext. Second, given a chance would the people of Northern Ireland vote to stay in the United Kingdom or to merge with a newly rich and rejuvenated Republic of Ireland? Significantly, Ireland has enjoyed one of the highest growth rates in the West in recent years and ranks 4th in the world in per capita GDP (using purchasing power parity as a yardstick), according to OECD estimates. The fate of Northern Ireland's 1.6 million people turned on whether these two looming issues could be addressed without triggering a new round of violence.

The Democratic Republic of Scotland

Demands for greater local autonomy (independence from London) dating back to the 1960s led Prime Minister Tony Blair to present new proposals for **devolution** (downward transfer of power) to Scotland and Wales in 1997. Although some leaders of the **Scottish National Party** favored outright independence, most Scottish voters were leery of such a drastic measure. In September 1997, the Scottish electorate overwhelmingly approved the Blair government's plan calling for a Scottish legislature and a chief executive to be known as the first minister. In the first separate Scottish elections (held in 1999) the Labour party won the most seats, but not enough seats to form a government outright. The Scottish National Party finished second, enough to serve notice that the political idea of an independent Scotland was alive and well. Devolution also occurred in Wales in the late 1990s, but Welsh voters are wary of big changes in this direction and are content with limited local self-rule.

Foreign and Defense Policy

Long before the 2003 war in Iraq caused a political furor in the United Kingdom, British foreign and defense policy have fueled a good deal of controversy. When the United Kingdom joined the United States in a faceoff with France and Germany over how to handle the Iraqi problem, it was a case of déjà vu for Europeans with a memory. In the 1960s, France under de Gaulle loudly denounced Britain's **special relationship** with the United States (based on America's origins as a British colony, a common language, common legal traditions, and, finally, the close Anglo-American alliance during World War II).

The fact that London at first chose not to join the Common Market underscored the British desire to remain aloof from the Continent. When the United Kingdom belatedly applied for membership, French President Charles de Gaulle vetoed it. Not until de Gaulle was gone from the scene was the U.K. finally admitted, along with Ireland and Denmark, in 1973. But lingering doubts about British loyalties and London's own ambivalence toward the Common Market, reinforced by Margaret Thatcher's personal anti-European stance, continued to obstruct efforts to build bridges (figuratively speaking) across the English Channel.

John Major attempted to mend fences with Europe but not to take them down. This new dispensation was called into question in 1996, however, when a major controversy arose over the European response to mad cow disease (a deadly illness traced to British cattle and transmitted to humans through the consumption of beef from infected animals). It would fall to a new government unencumbered by all the baggage of the recent past to redefine the United Kingdom's relationship to Europe.

Blair in the Chair: A New Look for Labour

The Conservatives paid dearly in the 1997 general election for equivocating and fighting among themselves on the question of Europe and whether to support the **European Monetary Union (EMU).** The British electorate, weary of the Tories after eighteen years of Conservative rule, gave Tony Blair's Labour party a landslide victory. With 45 percent of the popular vote Labour won almost two-thirds of the seats in Parliament. The vote swing in the 1997 election was extraordinary: Labour gained 10 percentage points over the previous (1992) election, and the Conservatives lost 11 percentage points. At age 43, Blair became the youngest British prime minister in nearly two hundred years and headed the largest Labour majority ever.

In power, Blair quickly established a distinctive leadership style, pursuing market-friendly economic policies designed to stimulate growth, create jobs, boost productivity, and fight inflation. His social policies aimed at reducing crime and improving education. In foreign policy he adopted an activist stance that included a major British role in the Balkans plus a commitment to sort out Britain's ongoing problems within the European Union—above all, whether and when to join the **euro** (the single currency in which eleven EU members including Germany, France, and Italy currently participate).

On the home front, Blair did not undertake bold new initiatives or set about systematically undoing Margaret Thatcher's handiwork, but rather sought to tackle high-priority problems by setting specific targets in various policy areas. At first, he demonstrated a preference for accommodation over confrontation but later showed another side of his character: stiff resolve in the face of criticism and growing public disenchantment with his policies.

The question of Europe loomed large. Blair appeared ready to push for British membership in the **euro zone,** but the events of 9/11 sidetracked British politics, and the renewed tensions between the United Kingdom and France (as well as Germany) over the war in Iraq rekindled distrust on both sides of the English Channel. Within his own party he faced a challenge from skeptics (including Chancellor of the Exchequer Gordon Brown) who questioned the wisdom of surrendering control over British monetary policy to the European Union until the new European Central Bank had proved itself capable of maintaining price stability and stimulating growth on the Continent.

Blair at War

By the summer of 2000, more than a year before 9/11 intruded, Blair's honeymoon with the British electorate was over. Most damaging were leaks to the press that included a candid political strategy memo written by Blair himself and another written by the prime minister's pollster.[13] Even more damaging than the contents of the leaked memos was the impression they conveyed of a prime minister dithering and a government spinning out of control. The Blair government stood firm when lorry (truck) drivers, angry at having to pay over $4.30 a gallon for diesel fuel, staged a blockade of refineries and oil depots and traffic slowdowns throughout the country, briefly crippling the economy and causing a great deal of inconvenience all around. Blair refused to lower the stiff British tax at the pump (the highest in Europe), which the public blamed for the problem. He showed a tough streak in foreign policy as well at this time, ordering British commandos into Sierra Leone, where rebels had brutalized the civilian population and threatened the stability of neighboring states.

In 1997, Blair had led Labour back to power promising closer ties to Europe, but that policy was put on the back burner after September 11, 2001. When U.S. President George W. Bush declared a "war on terrorism" following the 9/11 attacks, Blair pledged the British government's full support. At a special ceremony commemorating those who died in the attacks (including British citizens), the royal band played the "Star Spangled Banner"—a rare show of sympathy and solidarity in the annals of international diplomacy. Blair followed up by committing British troops to the American-led invasion of Afghanistan later in 2001, at times appearing to be a step ahead of President Bush in the rush to retaliate against the perpetrators of the 9/11 terrorist acts.

Despite antiwar demonstrations in the United Kingdom and strong opposition from France and Germany, Blair backed the U.S. position as President Bush called for a preemptive war against Iraq. The war came in March 2003, and British troops again joined the U.S.-led invasion. British participation in the Iraq war was never popular in the United Kingdom (discussed later), but Blair stayed the course despite mounting criticism (particularly damaging to his image was the charge that he had become President Bush's "lap dog").

The occupation of Iraq turned out to be a messy affair. Questions about the truthfulness of the Blair government in presenting evidence of Saddam Hussein's alleged efforts to obtain uranium from Niger in West Africa embarrassed Blair in the summer of 2003. Nonetheless, he vigorously defended the decision to go to war and stood by secret information (intelligence reports) that, he said, proved it was the right decision.

Labour won the 2005 elections but with a much diminished majority in Parliament (see Table 4.3). Although Blair remained as prime minister, his mandate was significantly weaker than after Labour's previous two wins and his prestige at home and abroad was damaged. Most pundits agreed that the outcome of the election reflected disarray within the Tory (Conservative party) leadership rather than popular approval of Blair's policies. Rumors abounded. Many observers doubted that he would complete a third term.

The deadly terrorist bombings in London that killed some fifty-five morning commuters in July 2005 were apparently linked to British foreign policy in the Middle East and, in particular, to British military involvement in Iraq.[14] The bombings pointed to a number of unresolved social and political issues facing British society. First, these were *suicide* bombings, the worst and deadliest form of terrorism. Second, the perpetrators were reportedly British citizens. They did not infiltrate from a foreign land. Third, they were Muslims, and Muslims from Africa, the Middle East, and Asia represent the largest (and fastest-growing) religious

TABLE 4.3 British Parliamentary Elections: May 2005

Party	Percent	Seats (646 total)
Labour	35.2	356
Conservative	32.2	197
Liberal Democrats	22.0	62
Others	10.6	31

Turnout = 61.3%
SOURCE: BBC.

minority in the United Kingdom (there were an estimated 1.5 million Muslims residing in the United Kingdom in 2001). According to the British Housing Corporation, Muslim children were almost three times more likely than the rest of the population to live in overcrowded accommodations.[15] (The Muslim minority has the youngest age profile of all British religious groups; about one in three British Muslims is under the age of 16.)

As a group, Muslims remain outside the mainstream of British society. Many are poor by British standards. Muslim youths in particular often express feelings of alienation. Most British Muslims decry violence in the name of Islam, but that is little comfort to the families of innocent victims nor does it make the daunting social, economic, and political problems associated with assimilating a large Muslim minority into traditional British society go away.

In sum, Tony Blair brought a fresh, new look to British politics, but the old problems did not go away. Many of these problems were similar to those found in other high-income, postindustrial societies and none appeared likely to precipitate a crisis in the near future. The prospects for the United Kingdom appear to be good, but just how good depends in no small part on how the British ultimately balance nationalism and supranationalism. Given the potential for *four different brands* of nationalism in Britain—Irish, Scottish, and Welsh as well as English—any tilt toward nationalism is fraught with political dangers. The other course—fully joining Europe—is a better bet to pay big dividends. That, however, remains Britain's great dilemma.

FRANCE: MODEL OR RELIC?

After World War II, the French adopted an economic strategy that was exactly the opposite of Great Britain's. The working class was made to sacrifice most, and the rich got richer. Marshall Plan aid was used in part for current consumption and indirectly to pay for the Indochina War (which cost more than the Marshall Plan contributed). General de Gaulle rejected the proposal of Prime Minister Pierre Mendes-France to break inflation after the Liberation, so the value of the franc plummeted. Economists in France and abroad wrote the country off. Yet after an initial expansion of the communist vote in a burst of working-class anger, France eventually did achieve its own economic miracle of sorts, and it is now richer than Great Britain.

The French postwar economic miracle gave way to a time of troubles in the 1980s. By odd coincidence, France's economic fortunes started to sputter just as the British economy began to crank up. France's difficulties deepened under Socialist economic reforms aimed at enlarging the role of the state and cutting the size of the private sector. In the early 1980s, France under Mitterrand and Great Britain under Thatcher were moving in opposite directions. However, as we have seen, by the end of the decade, President Mitterrand was looking and sounding a lot like a born-again Reaganite. (Recall that President Ronald Reagan was generally opposed to state regulation of the economy).

With the movement from community to union in Europe, President Mitterrand assigned high priority to preparing France for a competitive future, one without the protectionism and state intervention (*dirigisme*) that have been hallmarks of the French economy. It was one of history's ironies that this job fell to a Socialist leader; it was a sign of the times that he seemed to relish the prospect.

Why was it a sign of the times? Because in the United States and United Kingdom market-friendly, pro-business economic policies appeared to be working; the electorate was moving to the right; and left-of-center political parties (the Democrats in America and Labour in Britain) were following. This tendency was evident beyond the two countries in which it started. In the ensuing years it turned into a major trend.

Chirac and France's "Highs"

The election of Jacques Chirac as president in 1995 appeared to signal a mild shift toward the right in French politics. During the campaign, Chirac pledged to undertake fiscal reform and reduce France's high unemployment rate (which had skyrocketed in recent years). Nor was unemployment the only "high" problem Chirac faced. High taxes and bloated budgets were part of Mitterrand's legacy. But the high jobless rate made it difficult to cut France's budget deficit, as did high wages and pensions for France's five million public-sector workers.

Another "high," the high cost of welfare in France—including health benefits, generous unemployment compensation, family allowances, and housing subsidies—also complicated efforts at reform. Between 1990 and 1995, France's welfare system accumulated a huge debt. Attempts to cut welfare benefits were vigorously resisted by workers, but failure to cut the cost of these benefits to business and industry, while keeping the minimum wage at high levels, discouraged employers from hiring new workers. (The system is funded by employers and employees as well as by the state.)

Meanwhile, three weeks of public-sector strikes in late 1995 crippled the economy and cost the country dearly. The strikes were precipitated by the Bank of France's decision to hike interest rates sharply in response to a run on the franc. But workers were also disgusted with government efforts to reduce the budget deficit while doing little to ease the double-digit jobless rate. For President

Chirac, who had promised to make unemployment his "priority of priorities and reduce the budget deficit," it was not a promising start.

In April 1997, Chirac dissolved the National Assembly and called new elections, hoping to achieve a larger center-right majority and fortify his own popular mandate in the face of continuing labor unrest and obstruction from both the left- and right-wing opposition over key issues such as unemployment, immigration, and the planned European Monetary Union (EMU). The combined left, led by the Socialists, won a clear majority in the National Assembly. The Socialists alone won significantly fewer votes than the combined total for the center-right (RPR-UDF), but in the arithmetic of parliamentary politics the election added up to a big victory for the left.

What accounted for the swing to the left? No single problem can explain voting behavior anywhere, but in France it was a knot of interrelated issues with the workplace at the core. French workers are traditionally demonstrative. Organized labor has declined dramatically in numbers, but damaging strikes are still common. The Socialists won the election in 1997 by promising a 35-hour work week—less work at the same pay. Not surprisingly, it was a popular measure. But it was not sound policy (for reasons that will become clear later).

As mentioned earlier, France's "highs" (for example, high unemployment and high levels of public debt) complicate efforts to deal with pressing social problems. But another "high"—namely, the high expectations and volatility of the workforce, is often the biggest political challenge facing the government. Indeed, implementation of the 35-hour work in early 2000 actually prompted a series of protests by some workers loath to give up a two-hour lunch break or unhappy about having to work Saturdays, others (such as postal employees) who objected to having to do the same amount of work in less time, and still others (such as truck drivers) who would lose hours and overtime. To make matters worse, it was not at all clear that the main argument in favor of a shorter workweek—that it would boost productivity and employment—would prove to be true. In May 2005, the French National Assembly passed a new law that set the stage for a general lengthening of the workweek, without actually repealing the old law.

An "Old" Problem

Like other postmodern societies, France's population is aging. One huge public-policy dilemma facing France today involves pensions. At the core of the pension problem is the fact that the state provides generous benefits to France's retirees—that, plus the fact that the money for public pension funds has to come from somewhere. The favored source in France (and nearly everywhere else) has been taxes. But today's taxpayers do not want to pay more today for less tomorrow—and that is precisely what the taxpayers in France feared they would be asked to do. There are only so many ways to keep a sinking ship afloat: the same can be said of a pension fund. Besides raising taxes (always politically risky), the retirement age can be raised or the benefits reduced (for example, by excluding bonuses from the definition of income or calculating payments on the basis of the highest-paid twenty-five years of service rather than the highest paid ten years).

But none of these solutions is likely to be popular with French employees for obvious reasons. Moreover, ideology always conditions the search for policy prescriptions, and France is certainly no exception. Hence, no Socialist government is likely to tamper with the **special regimes** that give public sector employees generous pension terms compared with private-sector employees. Nor are the Socialists likely to consider moving toward a system of individual (private) pension funds. (It was adoption of just such a plan in 1995 that led to the conservative defeat two years later.)

The question of pension reform is emblematic of the type of policy dilemmas facing not only France but also most other modern, postindustrial societies. It remains to be seen whether France will be on the cutting edge—helping to show the way—or get mired in the kind of endless debate and rancor that will give France's friendly competitors in the New Europe an advantage.

The Ghost of de Gaulle: French Foreign Policy

President Charles de Gaulle set France on an independent course in the late 1950's and 1960s. He sought to restore the *grandeur* of old France at the height of its power and prestige. To that end, he at times opposed the United States, decried the special relationship between London and Washington, committed France to developing an independent nuclear strike force (the *force de frappe*), and cultivated a closer relationship with Moscow than any other member of the Western alliance. In the mid-1960s, de Gaulle pulled France out of the "O" in NATO (meaning Paris withdrew from the NATO organization but not from the alliance itself),[16] and NATO headquarters was moved from Paris to Brussels. Relations between the United States and France were further strained in the 1960s by President de Gaulle's criticism of U.S. policy in Indochina.

France and America have long had a love-hate relationship and still do today. Franco-American relations can best be viewed in the broader context of France's postwar foreign policy rather than as a manifestation of French anti-Americanism. The desire to pursue an independent course in foreign policy, to view Moscow as a potential counterweight to Washington rather than a pariah state during the Cold War, to take the lead in promoting Europe's (and France's) interests within NATO, combined with a tendency to denounce American military intervention at times (the Vietnam War and the invasion of Iraq) and support it at other times (Bosnia and Afghanistan) can easily give rise to the false impression that France is the scene of rampant anti-Americanism. If that were the case, however, it would be impossible to explain the outpouring of pro-American sympathy in France after 9/11, when a front-page headline in France's leading newspaper (*Le Monde*) declared, "We are all Americans now."

After the 9/11 attacks, President Chirac pledged French support for America's "war on terrorism." Accordingly, France joined the coalition of states that actively aided the American invasion of Afghanistan 2001. But France strongly opposed the invasion of Iraq without a second UN resolution, threatening to use its veto in the United Nation Security Council if necessary. As a result, the Bush administration decided not to seek UN approval. This incident left a bitter taste in the mouths of many Americans (some even urged a boycott of French wines). Perhaps more than anything Washington officials said or did, this public response, which threatened to harm one of France's key farm exports, made Paris take notice. President Chirac subsequently endeavored to smooth relations with the United States, without, however, recanting or expressing any regrets publicly.

The French government has long been firmly committed to the EU. (The outcome of France's referendum on the EU constitution on May 29, 2005, revealed that French society is not in full accord with the government on this issue, however.) French farmers benefit from the system of price supports (subsidies) and tariffs called the Common Agricultural Policy (CAP), which was adopted at French insistence in the 1960s. In the 1990s, France strongly backed creation of the new European monetary system (the euro), as well as EU enlargement.

The unification of Germany after 1989 inevitably raised old fears in France, which lost three wars to Germany between 1871 and 1945. The Franco-German agreement to create a joint army corps separate from NATO reflected France's anxiety over the twin prospects of German resurgence and American retrenchment. The launching of the euro (single currency) and creation of a European Central Bank (headquartered in Frankfurt, Germany) has helped reassure France that Germany is permanently enmeshed in Europe.

President Jacques Chirac strongly backed the proposed EU constitution in 2004–2005, as did Prime Minister Jean-Pierre Raffarin. (Recall that Raffarin was Chirac's choice to replace Socialist Prime Minister Lionel Jospin following the elections in 2002). In May 2005, French voters were asked to vote yes or no on the EU constitution. Shortly before the French referendum, Spanish voters had approved the measure. But any momentum Europe had gained in Spain it lost in France where the measure was decisively defeated. The outcome was widely interpreted as a vote against the French government—perhaps even more than against the EU. Having been chastised by the voters, President Chirac promptly sacked Prime Minister Raffarin and reshuffled the cabinet, naming Dominique de Villepin, foreign minister in the previous cabinet, to head the new government.

Critics question the choice of Prime Minister de Villepin on the grounds that de Villepin had never held an elective office and his popularity with the voters had therefore never been put to the test. But he did well enough in his first few months in office to start a buzz about a possible run at the presidency in 2007 when Chirac's term expires. That was before a fateful few days in the fall of 2005 when two incidents sparked riots in a Paris suburb; the rioting then "spread around the capital's periphery" and eventually engulfed scores of cities and towns around the country.[17]

When President Chirac's public appeal for calm fell flat, de Villepin declared a state of emergency, invoking a 1955 curfew law that, ironically, dates back to France's war with Algeria (then still a French colony seeking independence.) France's colonies are history, but the urban riots of 2005 showed that the legacy of French colonial rule is still alive—in the ethnic ghettos of Paris and other cities. The *banlieues* (the French word for the rundown housing projects that ring the capital) are home to many of the 5–6 million Muslims living in France. These so-called "sensitive urban zones," a feature of cities and towns all over

France, are breeding grounds for violent crime and social unrest. In 2004, for example, some 333 cars were burned on New Year's Eve alone. And during the first seven months of 2005, another 21,900 cars were set afire. To be sure, car burning is a crime, but in France's volatile suburbs it was becoming a form of social protest.

The French continue to call Muslims and other minorities "immigrants" even though they are citizens. France officially maintains a fine façade of social and political equality, but Paris banned the Muslim headscarf in state schools in 2004, and aside from representatives of France's overseas territories, there were no minorities (and, thus, no Muslims) in parliament in 2005 when the riots broke out. The same color barrier was evident in other high-profiles professions— television news anchors, police officers, lawyers, judges, and the like, are over-whelmingly white.

The de facto segregation of France's large Muslim minority in suburban slums is not simply a matter of social acceptance (or the absence thereof): it has economic causes and consequences. In a word, Muslim youth in France appear to be the victims of job discrimination on a vast scale. The overall unemployment rate for the country as a whole in late 2005 stood at about 10 percent. But the youth unemployment rate was more that twice as high—around 23 percent. The rate for young Muslims, however, approached a "staggering" 40 percent.[18]

Coping with changes at home and abroad will present challenges to France in the coming years. Dealing with such daunting problems as social inequality, economic stagnation, a loss of competitiveness, youth unemployment, and the creeping demographic crisis resulting from an aging population is costly in fiscal and cultural terms; not dealing with them may be even costlier in political terms, as the rise of a xenophobic right-wing party on one hand and the urban riots of 2005 on the other clearly attest. We look next at government and politics in Germany.

GERMANY: BEYOND UNIFICATION, WHAT?

After World War II, the Allies imposed deflationary policies on West Germany. The Germans in turn imposed austerity and hard work on themselves—in contrast to the British, who fell to taking more and more from the state while giving less and less. Helped in part by the American decision to extend Marshall Plan aid to Germany, the German economy revived very quickly. In short order, the Federal Republic created a welfare state far more lavish than anything in Great Britain or France. The West Germans came out winners.

In the 1950s, West Germany's economy surged ahead of most of its neighbors' on the Continent (Italy alone kept pace for a time). In the decades that followed, Germany became the standard by which other Western industrial democracies measured their own economic performance. West Germany's extraordinary and sustained record of economic growth would not have been possible without an equally extraordinary record of political stability that lasted through the 1980s.

The Kohl Era

In 1982, the center-right Christian Democratic Union–Christian Socialist Union (CDU-CSU) formed a coalition government with the Free Democrats (FDP), who decided to break a thirteen-year alliance with the left-leaning Social Democrats (SDP). Six months later, German voters gave a solid mandate to Helmut Kohl's conservative government.

The victory of Chancellor Kohl's Koalition der Mitte (center coalition) in 1983 followed Germany's worst economic slump since the Great Depression of the 1930s. Many German voters blamed the recession on the generous but expensive welfare-state programs favored by the SDP. Kohl and the Christian Democrats promised to reverse the course with a combination of tax cuts, investment incentives, and budget reductions. Although less drastic, Kohl's approach vaguely resembled Reaganomics and the supply-side prescriptions of Great Britain's Prime Minister Thatcher.

Kohl's economic program produced generally positive results: economic growth stopped its downslide, inflation was brought down to its lowest point in thirty-four years, and budget deficits were sharply curtailed. In addition, spending for social welfare programs was curbed significantly. The German economy rebounded: by mid-1986, German factories were operating at 85 percent of capacity, and in some heavy industrial sectors could not keep pace with demand. Capital investment perked up as well. Plant modernization accelerated rapidly— particularly the use of computers and robots. To top it all off, the balance of payments showed a record surplus in 1986. The one low mark on Kohl's report card was unemployment, which remained high.

In the 1987 parliamentary elections, the CDU came out on top, but the **Greens**—an antinuclear, environmental party—garnered a million votes more than they had four years earlier. Environmentalists and peace activists got a boost in that election from the 1986 Chernobyl nuclear accident in the Ukraine. The Greens sought to capitalize on popular fears, calling for West Germany's imme- diate withdrawal from NATO, unilateral disarmament, and the dismantling of all nuclear power stations in West Germany. In so doing, they struck a responsive chord within a slim but significant minority of the German electorate, winning a small block of Bundestag seats in the 1987 elections.

Although Germany is an affluent society, the struggle over how wealth and power are (or ought to be) distributed intensified as a result of German **unifi- cation.** Strains in the German economy became ever more apparent as century drew to a close. Organized labor charged that the Kohl government was blatantly partial to big business, while big business countered by pointing to Germany's extremely high labor costs even relative to other leading EU countries (including wages, benefits, and pensions). (See Figure 4.2)

A related problem was the presence of poverty amid plenty. The long-term unemployed, divorced women with children, elderly pensioners, and refugees seeking asylum were hit especially hard by what Germans call the **new poverty.** Some of Chancellor Kohl's critics claimed to see a relationship between poverty and policy. For example, the percentage of long-term unemployed rose sharply during the 1980s, a

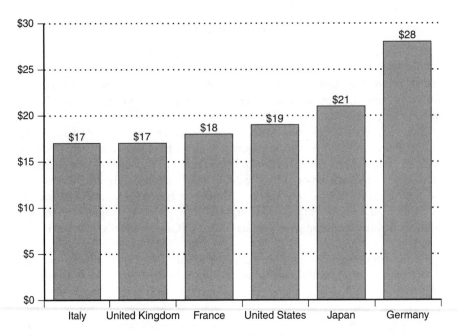

FIGURE 4.2 Germany's Labor Pains in the Late 1990s (manufacturing labor costs, wages, and benefits, in U.S. Dollars per hour, 1999 estimate)

SOURCE: Organization for Economic Cooperation and Development.

trend that feeds into the poverty issue in Germany because, under existing rules, the longer an individual is unemployed, the less he or she receives in public assistance.

Nonetheless, it is worth noting that the Kohl government's approach to cutting social programs was decidedly more restrained than that of Ronald Reagan or Margaret Thatcher. Kohl's softer touch reveals a crucial feature of Germany's postwar political system, namely, that the policy-making process in Germany tends to be more cooperative and less adversarial than in most other Western democracies. Why? The answer most likely has something to do with Germany's turbulent history in the first half of the twentieth century, which created a strong incentive in postwar Germany to avoid polarization of the kind that preceded Hitler's rise to power and that in retrospect was a prelude to disaster. No doubt there are other reasons as well, including the precedent set by Otto von Bismarck, who, it will be recalled, was the author of Europe's first welfare state system.

In 1989, West Germany's political world changed abruptly. For several years, all previous policy debates were overshadowed by one overriding concern—how to happily remarry the two Germanys after a half-century of bitter separation.

German Unification

The unification issue moved front and center following the dramatic toppling of the communist regime in East Germany at the end of 1989. The conservative East

German Christian Democratic Union, which won a plurality (41 percent) of the votes in March 1990, campaigned on a platform calling for rapid merger of the two German states. With his popularity high and rising, West German Chancellor Helmut Kohl went to East Germany and campaigned for the conservatives and for early unification. On October 3, 1990, the two German states formally merged into a single entity. Two months later the first free, all-German elections in fifty-eight years were held. The center-right coalition by the ruling Christian Democrats received a strong mandate to continue in power. The Social Democratic Party received only one-third of the popular vote.

Unification added 16 million Germans to the Federal Republic literally overnight. What would be the political implications of suddenly incorporating so many people who had never lived under constitutional democracy or coped with a free-enterprise system? How long would the process take? How much would it cost? How would it be financed? What sort of compromises would be necessary? The problems associated with making the two states into one were daunting even for a country like Germany with a stable government and a strong economy. Transforming the former East Germany from a police state with a centrally planned economy to a democratic society with a free-market economy proved to be a very costly and rancorous enterprise.

The pace of unification was a primary issue in the early 1990s. The CDU on both sides of the border favored a merger "as soon as possible" pursuant to Article 23 of the Basic Law, which allows regions of prewar Germany to join the Federal Republic upon acceptance of the Basic Law. The SDP, however, called for a new constitution. Drafting such a constitution would obviously take time and involve careful negotiations between the two German governments. The timetable for unity was thus a key question. A closely related issue was how much West Germany would compromise with its GDR "poor relation" in negotiating the precise terms of unification. For example, would West Germany agree to modernize the Basic Law by including such themes as environmental protection?

Having dreamed of a united Germany for four decades, however, West Germans quickly discovered that the dream came with a staggering price tag. Absorbing the influx of East Germans and modernizing the GDR's outmoded factories would be expensive. In addition to unemployment, adjustments associated with a quick monetary union (using the West German mark in all German territory) brought the risk of inflation and recession. Predictably, the government was forced to raise taxes.

Divisions between Germany's western and eastern populations widened at the outset of the 1990s. The economy continued to boom in the west, while unemployment rose rapidly in the east; fully one-third of the work force was either unemployed or employed part time. *Ossis* (easterners) received less than half the average wages of *Wessis* (westerners). Many *Ossis* felt like second-class citizens because they were poor by comparison with *Wessis,* dependent on former West Germany for development funds, and newcomers to a political system they had nothing to do with designing. In addition, reclaiming of expropriated eastern properties by affluent *Wessis* was particularly galling to many *Ossis.* This situation was exacerbated by a sharp decline in eastern Germany's GDP.

The deepening economic crisis in the east led to angry anti-Kohl demonstrations in eastern cities in March and April 1991, as well as outbreaks of right-wing racist violence (discussed later). At the same time, Kohl came under attack in West Germany for allegedly breaking his promise not to raise taxes to rebuild the former GDR. It was the kind of dilemma that is often the undoing of a democratic leader. Indeed, the Christian Democratic Union (CDU) did suffer losses in state elections in the spring of 1991. Perhaps the most humiliating defeat for Kohl came in his home state (Land) of Rhineland Palatinate, one that cost the CDU the majority it had held in the Bundesrat since October 1990.

Having embarked on unification, there was no turning back for the Kohl government. But the realities were daunting. For example, East Germany under communist rule had become an ecological nightmare, and the cleanup costs alone were staggering. The states that once comprised East Germany have 25 percent of the Federal Republic's population and 33 percent of its territory, but in the early 1990s accounted for only about 7.5 percent of its total output. Closing down inefficient enterprises and modernizing others was essential but could not be done without causing high unemployment in the former GDR. After reunification, the jobless rate in Germany as a whole (but highest by far in the east) steadily rose until it reached double digits.

In the meantime, the Federal Republic struggled to absorb the flood of immigrants from Eastern Europe. Some came as asylum seekers; others were ethnic Germans who could expect immediate citizenship under a policy carried over from the Cold War. In all, some 2.5 million people poured into Germany after 1989, including 775,000 Eastern Europeans of German descent and a large number of refugees (former East Germans constituted the majority of new arrivals). This invasion was unsettling and unwelcome to many West Germans—so much so that it opened a debate on the nation's asylum laws and immigration policies. Many observers attributed the rise of an ultraright nationalist movement in Germany in the early 1990s to Germans' growing fear that their country would be overwhelmed by a human tidal wave from the east. The neo-Nazis committed a spate of violent crimes against foreigners, especially Turks, in 1991 and 1992—behavior reminiscent of Nazi attacks on German Jews in the late 1930s. Popular indignation both within Germany and from the international community prompted a government crackdown on the far right at the end of 1992.

In the 1994 elections, a resurgence of the German economy helped the CDU-CSU overcome Chancellor Helmut Kohl's fading popularity. The center-right coalition won but ended up with a precarious ten-seat majority in the Bundestag and a net loss of 57 seats. But Kohl's political troubles were far from over. In early 1995, Kohl banned neo-Nazi groups in an effort to curb continued far-right racial violence. It was a sign of the times. In December 1995, unemployment reached a postwar high of 3.8 million—another sign of the times. The likelihood that these two developments were related was particularly disturbing to students of history who recalled the circumstances leading to the Holocaust—the polarization of German society associated with severe economic dislocations of the 1920s and 1930s.

Exit Kohl, Enter Schröder

German voters ended Chancellor Kohl's 16-year rule in 1998 when a center-left coalition led by the Social Democrats resoundingly defeated the CDU-CSU. The SDP joined forces with the Green Party to form a government. The new chancellor, Gerhard Schröder, chose Joshka Fisher, leader of the Greens, to head the foreign ministry. For the first time ever, a major European power had a Green foreign minister. Given the Greens' history of vociferous opposition to nuclear weapons and the use of military force, there was a question whether Germany would become a less reliable ally of the United States in future crises.

Schröder's most controversial appointment was the new finance minister, Oskar Lafontaine (popularly known as "Red Oskar"). Under Lafontaine's influence, German economic policy at first tilted sharply to the left (reminiscent of what happened in France under Mitterrand in the early 1980s). Not only was spending hiked, but also a large ecological tax was put on gasoline. At the same time, changes in workplace rules favored labor and had a chilling effect on the business climate. As economic conditions worsened and his government's popularity plummeted, however, Schröder abruptly changed directions, adopting a more centrist economic policy called the *Sparpaket* (austerity package). The German economy rebounded briefly, but then slowed to a crawl. Meanwhile, some four million Germans were unemployed (about 9 percent of the worker force). For Germans, accustomed to being Europe's economic leader, the decline during the 1990s under both the Kohl and Schröder governments was a rude awakening.

In foreign policy, Chancellor Schröder's response to the 9/11 terrorist attacks removed any doubt about Germany's continued commitment to NATO and close relations with the United States, as Germany committed more troops to Afghanistan in 2001–2002 than any other ally. However, when George Bush decided to confront Iraq's Saddam Hussein in the spring of 2003, it was a different story. By this time, Chancellor Schröder's popularity was eroding and most Germans were opposed to the war in Iraq

The SDP barely kept control of the government in the 2002 elections, polling just 6,000 votes more than the CDU-CSU (out of a total electorate of 61.4 million). Schröder capitalized on the antimilitarism of most German voters by opposing the U.S. policy of confrontation with Iraq. In addition, the FDP stumbled going into the 2002 elections. As a result, the Greens finished third in the balloting (ahead of the FDP) supplying the governing coalition with a slim majority in the Bundestag.

The 2005 Election: And The Winner Is . . .

As Germany's flagging economy failed to revive under Schröder's leadership, the government's popularity fell steadily. In the summer of 2005, Schröder set the stage for early elections with a deliberately orchestrated no-confidence vote in the Bundestag. That accomplished, the Chancellor was then in a position to ask the president to dissolve Parliament and call new elections. (The Basic Law makes it difficult for a Chancellor to maneuver in this way.)

The September 2005 election was inconclusive. The outcome left Germany in a temporary state of political limbo. The Social Democrats had lost but there was no clear winner. Early polls showed Angela Merkel, the leader of the opposition CDU-CSU, with a huge twenty-point lead over the incumbent Schröder, but Merkel stumbled badly on the campaign trail. The election was a virtual dead heat. The CDU-CSU garnered only 35.2 percent of the vote (a smaller share than it had gotten in 2002). The SPD won 34.3 percent of the vote—its lowest total since 1990, but better than polls had predicted. Three small parties split the other nearly one-third of the votes: the Free Democrats (9.8 percent), the upstart New Left party (8.7 percent), and the Greens (8.0 percent).

The outcome of the election had clarified nothing—in fact, it had muddied the waters more than ever. Schröder was out but Angela Merkel had failed to get anything resembling a mandate to govern. There was much talk of a "grand coalition" of the two big parties with Merkel at its head, but Schröder initially rejected that possibility out of hand. The suspense built through the months of September and October; finally in November, after much wheeling-and- dealing, the SPD agreed to a coalition that many observers considered "grand" in name only. Angela Merkel became the new Chancellor and the SPD leader Franz Müntefering became vice-chancellor and labor minister (a particularly key post in the context of German politics and Germany's well-entrenched unions).

At 51, Merkel thus became Germany's youngest Chancellor, and the first East German, the first woman, and the first scientist to make it to the pinnacle of German politics. But she would have her work cut out for her. The coalition she led was untested and possibly fragile. She campaigned on a platform that included strong support for U.S. foreign policy in Iraq and for President George W. Bush personally. She also promised to push pro-business economic policies, including tax reform (eliminating a tangled mass of loopholes and subsidies) and labor-market reforms designed to reduce unemployment and make the German economy more competitive. Her solution to the problem of large budget deficits (projected at $75 billion for 2006) is to spur the economy by keeping interest rates down and encouraging investment rather than by raising taxes. One of her boldest stands on the campaign trail was to oppose Turkey's admission to the EU.

Politicians are frequently better campaigners than chief executives. Perhaps Angela Merkel will prove to be just the opposite—a better chief executive than campaigner. But she faces a tough test: how to revive Germany's sick giant economy without causing a rupture in the delicately balanced coalition on which her success—and perhaps her political survival—depends.

Germany's Economy: A Miracle No More

Germany remains Europe's economic giant, accounting for nearly one-third of the euro-area GDP today. The German economy—which ranks third in the world behind only the United States and Japan—continues to have many underlying strengths which include large well-established multinational corporations with brand names recognized around the world, a well-trained workforce, among the highest GDP per capita in Europe, a comprehensive system of social welfare, and a stable democracy. Germany's economy not only generates investment capital itself, but also attracts venture capital from abroad—especially when the economy's vital signs are strong. Some of its recent troubles stem from the fact that it absorbed a failed state (the former East Germany) in the 1990s—a remarkable achievement by any standards. The eastern *Länder* will eventually catch up and cease being a liability, becoming an asset instead.

In the meantime Germany's current malaise is likely to deepen unless the growing contradictions between the economy (greater efficiency, lower labor costs, higher productivity) and society (welfare-state benefits, pensions, job security) can be resolved. Despite the sullen mood of many German voters that led to the SPD defeat in the 2005 elections, there were signs that the German economy was beginning to recover. In particular, unit labor costs—a primary measure of competitiveness—fell significantly in Germany between 1999 and 2005; meanwhile, they stayed the same in France, and rose steadily in Italy and Spain. At the same time, Germany was outperforming France and Spain as an exporter of goods and services as well (while Italy's export curve remained flat).

If, as the saying goes, the "past is prologue," the worst may be yet to come, however. When ousted Chancellor Gerhard Schröder launched a bold blueprint for reform (called Agenda 2010) in 2003, it caused a furor that badly crippled the program and was possibly "the straw that broke the camel's back" (cost him his job). Even so, Agenda 2010 did achieve some positive results, including a major restructuring of the unemployment benefit and social security (the so-called Hartz IV law). This measure—considered a radical departure from Germany's trademark "social-market economy"—for the first time makes continued benefits dependent on a means test. In a society where some 1.8 million unemployed (nearly 40 percent of the total) are long-term cases, there was (and is) obviously a strong possibility that some idle "workers" were making no effort to find a job. Although it is too soon to say whether this new law will have the desired effects, it represents a step in the right direction—or, to be more exact, the center-right direction.

Balancing economic imperatives and social goals is a key test of the new German government. Whether Angela Merkel will be equal to the test remains to be seen. As suggested earlier, the inconclusive results of the 2005 election insured that whoever became chancellor would be forced to do a high-wire act. The big question mark hanging over German politics is all the more critical because of the even bigger question marks hanging over German society and Germany's economy. As we are about to see, Italy (like France and others) is facing many similar problems.

ITALY: REFORM OR RELAPSE?

Fascist Italy was allied with Nazi Germany in World War II. Italy was thus on the losing side and bore the shame of being in league with the perpetrator of the Holocaust. Many Italians, however, did not support Mussolini and, in fact, there was an active underground fighting against the Fascist dictatorship throughout the war.

At the end of the war, Italian partisans caught Mussolini hiding in the back of a truck in a German convoy. He was trying to flee to Switzerland. They executed the cowardly dictator, his mistress, Clara Petacci, and other leading Fascists, then hung the bodies by one foot (a fate reserved for crooks and embezzlers in medieval Italy) from a steel girder at an Esso gas station in the Piazzale Loreto in Milan.

Some American GIs heard about it and went to see the gruesome scene for themselves. They were witnesses after the fact: it was the Italians themselves who had delivered the final deathblow to the hated Fascists. Symbolically, it was less an act of vengeance than one of national redemption.

Italy's Postwar Economic Renaissance

With American help, Italy set about rebuilding the country. Talk of reconstruction typically conjures up images of damaged buildings and bridges, and that was true of Italy after the war. But Italy also had to rebuild its entire economy from the ground up, create a new political order, and overcome the social and psychological effects—as well as the moral stigma—of Fascism. What happened in Italy in the 1950s paralleled what happened in West Germany—a so-called economic miracle transformed both countries in a decade or so, erasing the scenes of devastation and replacing them with new roads, schools, hospitals, factories, and the like.

Italy's gross national product climbed steadily after 1950, doubling by the early 1960s. Unemployment fell to 2.5 percent. Statistics can never quite capture the human drama, however. In the early 1950s, many Italian families were living in abject poverty. Half the homes did not have indoor toilets and more than 60 percent did not have clean running water. Two decades later, Italy was a different place. Illiteracy was drastically reduced. Agriculture (while still important) was no longer the backbone of the economy. Many people owned cars, televisions, and telephones. Italy was no longer a poor country—or rather *northern* Italy was no longer poor.

The Italian economy is highly diversified. Major industries include iron and steel, machine tools, engineering, motor vehicles, chemicals, food processing, textiles, clothing, and leather goods. Tourism has also been a bonanza for postwar Italy, which until quite recently was the world's number one tourist destination. Italy derives at least a quarter of its GDP from services, including restaurants, hotels, and other businesses that cater to tourists and sightseers, but complacency and high prices have hurt Italy's tourism industry. (As a tourist destination, Italy now ranks fifth, behind France, Spain, the United States, and China.)

Italy is divided into north and south; the north is rich and industrial, the south is poor and agricultural. Italy's eight southern regions comprise 40 percent of the territory and one-third of the population but they account for only about one-fourth of the GDP. Italy is one of the world's top-ranking wine and cheese producers. Other important agricultural products include wool, wheat, corn, rice, fruits, and olive oil, making Italy virtually self-sufficient in food and fiber.

Rich Italy, Poor Italy

In the decades after World War II, the manufacturing north raced ahead while the farming and fishing south fell farther and farther behind. The result is that today there is not one Italy, but two—a rich urban-industrial Italy (north) and a relatively poor agrarian Italy (south).[19] In terms of economic development, northern Italy clearly belongs in Western Europe; by contrast, the economic profile of southern Italy more closely resembles that of some countries and regions in Eastern Europe.

Not surprisingly, this situation has reinforced the regionalism inherent in the geographic shape of the country. (Italy bears a striking resemblance to an elongated boot.) Northerners are sophisticated and famously fashion-conscious; southerners are often provincial and tradition-bound. Sharp north-south contrasts in culture and climate render the glaring disparity in wealth and living standards all the more divisive.

A Passion for Politics

To outsiders, Italy often appears to be a country in perpetual chaos.[20] Apathy is not the Italian way. Italians approach life with gusto (the word itself is one of Italy's gifts to the world). Not surprisingly, Italians tend to approach politics with the same kind of passion. Strikes and mass demonstrations are a normal part of political life in Italy. In liberal democracies, the judicial system provides an alternative to direct political action; in Italy, nearly everybody goes on strike sooner or later. In February 2004, for example, thousands of doctors and airline pilots staged a one-day strike. In May 2004, judges and prosecutors went on strike to protest against a judicial-reform measure proposed by Prime Minister Silvio Berlusconi (who was being tried on corruption charges that spring).[21] Politics in Italy is rarely dull.

Why? Culture is part of the answer; injustice is another part. Crime and corruption have long been part of the Italian political scene. But cause and effect are difficult to sort out. In many ways, the story of Silvio Berlusconi—how he amassed a personal fortune, his rise to power, and the use (or misuse, say his detractors) of private enterprise in the pursuit of public office—is a kind of parable. If we study the parable, we can better understand the polity.

Berlusconi's Debut: The 1994 Election

As we noted earlier, scandals involving high-ranking government officials led to a public clamor for political reforms in the early 1990s. The Christian Democrats and the Socialists were punished at the polls; the former would not recover, but the Left bounced back in two important local elections (Rome and Milan) at the end of 1993.

The 1994 election was a trial run for a new electoral system aimed at reducing the number of political parties and, in theory, making elections more rational and conducive to stable governments. Under new system, 75 percent of the parliamentary seats would be elected on a first-past-the-post basis. The new system did not prove to be a magic bullet, but it induced the parties to form two electorate alliances—center-right and center-left—thus greatly simplifying the choice given to the voters. (In theory, presenting voters with fewer choices will produce a more rational outcome; the more choices voters are given, the less likely it is that any single party will get a popular mandate.)

The stage was thus set for Silvio Berlusconi to make his political debut. The richest man in Italy, Berlusconi was a well-known media tycoon who owned the three largest private television networks in the country. With the collapse of the political center and the resuscitation of the Left, Italian politics had become suddenly very fluid. The neo-Fascist **Italian Social Movement (MSI)** party had made a surprisingly strong (and, for many Italians, alarming) showing in the elections in both Rome and Milan. The center-right needed a party and a candidate to fill the vacuum.

Berlusconi would become that candidate; he would create a new party called **Forza Italia (FI),** "Go Italy," the cheer for Italy's national soccer (European football) team. Berlusconi owned the highly successful AC Milan football team; the name of his new political party thus created a clever psychological association—politics, nationalism, a winning team, and the man who would be Italy's new leader.

Berlusconi emerged the winner in the 1994 election with the help of the three national television networks he owned (all of which aired flattering daily news stories about the candidate who happened to be the same person dispensing the paychecks). A conflict of interest, perhaps, but Italy is by no means the only Western democracy where the line between politics and business is often blurred.

In winning the election, Berlusconi's upstart political party, Forza Italia garnered about one vote in five (21 percent). He became prime minister by forging a political alliance—the so-called Freedom Pole—with two other parties of the right, the neo-fascist **Northern Alliance (AN),** formerly the MSI, and the **Northern League** (*Lega Nord*), a grass roots movement fueled by popular disgust with Rome. In all, Berlusconi's **Freedom Pole** captured a combined total of 301 seats (the left bloc or "Progressives" won 164 seats).

Berlusconi could form a government only with the cooperation of the other right-wing parties, so he did what politicians often do best—he cut a deal. The Northern League would get 70 percent of the candidacies in the north (a total of 106 single-member seats with only 8.4 percent of the vote) in return for backing Berlusconi. The Northern Alliance received 85 single-member seats with 13.4 percent of the vote. Together, these two parties claimed 40 percent of the single-member seats with less than 22 percent of the vote. Although his own party, Forza Italia, ended up with only 14 percent of these seats, Berlusconi got the grand prize—he was Italy's new prime minister.

But not for long: The Freedom Pole proved to be a flash in the pan, forced out after only eight months in office. Both political blocs were unstable, camouflaging the fact that there were more political parties in the 1994 elections than there had been in 1992. When the League pulled out of the coalition, Berlusconi resigned without a vote of confidence. The crisis in Italian politics appeared far from over.

The Center-Left Takes a Turn

A stopgap government lasted a little more than year, followed by new elections. This time the center-left bloc, renamed **Uliva** (Olive Tree), headed by PDS leader Romano Prodi, eked out a victory.[22] Prodi stepped down in 1998 following a vote of no confidence and was succeeded by another center-left government under Massimo D'Alema. Together, the Prodi and D'Alema governments remained in office for the full five-year election cycle. The new electoral system appeared to be working more or less as its reformers had intended, producing an alternation in power if not a reduction in the number of political parties. Finally, despite the unstable nature of the two ruling coalitions in 1996–2001, the Prodi and D'Alema governments managed to push through a number of important reforms in education, health, and public administration.

In addition, Italy's budget deficits and interest rates were brought into line with the EU's criteria (see Chapter 11) for joining the European Monetary Union (EMU), commonly known as the euro zone. For Italy, burdened with a bloated and inefficient bureaucracy and addicted to budget-busting social programs, this was a signal achievement. It also presented a major challenge. In the past, Italy had paid for its extravagant public spending with high inflation and frequent devaluations. As a member of the euro zone, Italy would be forced to practice fiscal discipline or face the consequences.

When Prodi was pushed out of office, due largely to his unpopular spending cuts and deficit reduction efforts, the EU heads of government elected him president of the European Commission: a reward for his un-Italian display of austerity. (Italy's extremely high government debt-to-GDP ratio dropped steadily from 135 percent of GDP in 1997 to under 120 percent of GDP in 2004, when it began to rise once again.) As the 2001 elections approached, Italy was at a crossroads—would the economy regain its lost momentum? Would politics in Italy become normalized at long last? The stage was set for yet another uniquely Italian drama, half tragedy, half comedy—a kind of Berlusconi burlesque.

Berlusconi's Second Coming

The 2001 elections put Forza Italia ahead of the pack and Berlusconi in the driver's seat. FI won nearly 30 percent of the popular vote—easily outpolling all other parties. PDS/DS, Forza Italia's main rival, finished a distant second with 16.5 percent of the vote. Once again, the reforms had worked: the election had been fought between two rival blocs of parties. But this time, voters had given one party within one of these blocs a mandate. That party, of course, was Berlusconi's FI.

Italy's problems did not evaporate with the 2001 elections. There was (and is) still much to be done. The state is too heavily involved in the economy, the labor market is rigid, the welfare state is profligate, and the like. Berlusconi campaigned as a classic liberal (that is, he promised more local control, less government, fewer rules and regulations). His mandate appears to have been a vote for change, but what kind of change? Obviously, cutting back on government means cutting back on government spending. In Europe's welfare states, the biggest budget item is not defense spending, but *social* spending. Rather than stressing the need for cutbacks in popular social programs, however, Berlusconi promised tax cuts. His message to the voters was: "Make me your leader and I will put more money in your pockets (by cutting taxes)." What he did *not* say was, "I will also take money out of your pockets (by cutting social benefits)"—a page right out of *The Prince*.

The Character Issue

When Berlusconi won the second time, Italian voters knew he was not squeaky clean. He had been indicted and convicted of tax fraud and other fraud-related crimes three times. True, he was acquitted on appeal in all three instances, thus avoiding lengthy jail sentences. But prosecutors also alleged that Berlusconi had bribed the judges. These charges were pending and other criminal investigations were underway in 2001, when the voters of Italy gave Berlusconi a second chance at running the government.

Why? To some extent, Italians are inured to corruption. Politicians have often been caught lying or cheating or taking bribes. It is nothing new and there is little the average citizen can do to stop it. Italians have thus learned to look past the private dealings and personal lives of public figures (in marked contrast to the British or Americans). Another part of the answer is that judges and prosecutors have also been tainted by corruption at times. This does not mean that all public figures in Italy are corrupt, which is certainly not true. Nor does it mean that Italians are indifferent to official corruption—witness the public outrage over the **Tangentopoli** ("Bribesville") scandals in the early 1990s. But what passes for a political scandal in Britain or America—sexual misconduct, for example—is unlikely to cause a ripple in Italian politics.

A Higher-Profile Foreign Policy

During the Cold War, Italy generally maintained a low profile in external affairs. Membership in NATO (and friendship with the United States) was the first pillar of Italy's foreign policy. Unlike France, Italy was content to rely on the American nuclear umbrella and to remain a **security consumer** so long as the Soviet-American rivalry dominated the east-west strategic relationship in Europe. The second pillar was support for European integration in partnership with Germany and France, the other two original large member states. Italy was a charter member of the coal and steel community and the Common Market in the 1950s, and played a positive role at each stage in the evolution of what is now the European Union. Thus, Italy has pursued a cautious and pragmatic foreign policy that balances trans-Atlantic and European ties—the former serve Italy's security interests, and the latter serve its economic interests. What this meant was that Italy had a vital interest in *not* taking sides when tensions rose between the United States and France. The utility of a low profile in these circumstances is fairly obvious.

Since the end of the Cold War, Italy has pursued a more active and independent course in foreign affairs, acting the part of a **security producer** for the first time in the post-Fascist era. In this regard, Italy has supported the proposal for a European Security and Defense Policy (ESDP) but unlike France views it as a complement to NATO, not an alternative. Italy also supports some **out-of-area operations** by NATO but unlike the United States wants military action to have prior U.N. authorization.

The Berlusconi government lent strong support to the Bush administration's war on terrorism after 9/11, making available 2700 troops for "Operation Enduring Freedom" (the invasion of Afghanistan) in 2001. Although Berlusconi expressed a preference for "constructive engagement" with "rogue states" (such as Iraq under Saddam Hussein, Iran, and North Korea) even after President Bush's "axis of evil" speech, he backed the U.S. decision to invade Iraq in the spring of 2003, making some 3000 troops available to participate in the U.S.-led invasion and occupation.

The Iraq war was never popular in Italy. In the spring of 2005, as the conflict dragged on, Berlusconi announced that Italy would begin a partial withdrawal of its troops before the end of the year. The timing was significant: parliamentary elections loomed on the horizon.

An Embattled Leader

The end of Berlusconi's story had not yet been written as 2005 neared an end. He had managed to avoid conviction on the many criminal charges against him. But he had used his supreme political office to pressure the judiciary, change laws for his personal benefit, and manipulate the legal system.[23] Among other things, he pushed a law through parliament in June 2003 that exempted holders of "high state roles" from criminal prosecution, raising suspicion that his main motivation for seeking control of the government in the first place had been to stay out of jail.[24] In 2005, with parliamentary elections fast approaching, the Berlusconi government moved to reverse the electoral reforms of the 1990s, restoring the very system of proportional representation that had produced Western Europe's most chaotic parliamentary democracy.

Preoccupied with his legal problems, Berlusconi achieved little of his promised reform program. He had exemplified many of the worst features of Italian politics—favoritism, cronyism, corruption, and the mixing of political and business interests on an unprecedented scale. But despite it all, he had managed to survive in office for the full constitutional term—the first prime minister to do so since World War II. Whether the embattled prime minister would survive the parliamentary elections of April 2006, only time would tell. But nobody was counting him out.

SPAIN: NATION OF REGIONS OR REGION OF NATIONS?

Spain's debut as a parliamentary democracy came late in the game by Western standards. Until Franco's death in 1975, Spain was shunned as a pariah state, diplomatically isolated, and left to fend for itself—economically, militarily, and diplomatically. Spain was excluded from the North Atlantic Treaty Organization (NATO), the Common Market (European Economic Community or EEC), and the General Agreement on Trade and Tariffs (GATT). As punishment for Franco's collaboration with Nazi Germany and Fascist Italy in World War II, Spain was even shut out of the United Nations until 1955. Ironically, both Italy and Germany were welcomed back into the Western family of nations while Spain remained ostracized.

The stigma is gone now for the most part, thanks to Spain's rebirth as a true republic (technically, a constitutional monarchy) after 1975. Spain joined NATO in 1982 and is now a member of all the major international bodies. The final step in the long journey back to Europe came in 1986, when Spain joined the European Community, renamed the European Union (EU) in 1993.

That Spain's "long journey" involved a detour lasting many decades and that democracy was kept on hold during this time only to burst out the instant Spain's aging dictator breathed his last is a curious thing. Why did Franco cling to personal power (like Fidel Castro in Cuba, for example) until the bitter end despite the isolation and moral opprobrium it brought upon him? Unlike Castro before the collapse of the Soviet Union, Spain did not have a superpower patron or protector. Spain paid a heavy price for taking "the road less traveled" under Franco.

We are left to wonder: Why did the Spanish people not revolt? Franco was a dictator, to be sure, but he was no Stalin. He did not stage show trials and carry out mass purges. One has an uneasy sense that Spanish society was somehow not without guilt. When does compliance cross the line and become complicity? At the same time, it is all too easy for outsiders to criticize from a safe distance—and often unfair. What do we really know about Spain? Unless we understand Spanish history and culture, we are almost certain to get it wrong.

When we think of Spain, we think of a country—that is, one nation with one history speaking a single language. But Spain is not nearly as simple as that. Neither, of course, is Belgium, Britain France, Germany, or Italy. To some extent, the idea of the nation is political propaganda rather than fact. Monarchs of old assembled disparate lands and peoples into states or empires, then set about nation building—that is, getting conquered people(s) to switch allegiance. Spain was not a blank canvas at the dawn of Europe's modern era. Today's Basques and Catalans, for example, are the descendents of the ancient inhabitants of the Basque country and Catalonia. By definition, if you are Spanish, you come from some part of Spain. Whether the part or the whole is more important is the question.

The point is not that Spain is likely to collapse, but it is worth recalling that it *did* collapse in the 1930s—the Spanish Civil War was a cataclysmic event in Iberian (and European) history. What happened then was not inevitable. How was it possible?

Spain is a patchwork of peoples with local or regional languages, cultures, and loyalties. There are over 41 million people living in Spain who have at least one thing in common: they are Spanish citizens. But some of them are from Andalusia, others from Galicia, and so on. Recognizing the importance of these regional differences and how they shaped Spanish politics provides clues as to why the Spanish people abided a dictator like Franco for so long. One hypothesis is that after the trauma of the civil war people believed that acquiescing in a centralized authoritarian government was the only way to ensure peace and tranquility in Spain.

TABLE 4.4 Who's the Best in the West?

Country	Rank	Estimated per capita GDP (2006)
Britain	1	$38,860
France	2	$37,500
Germany	3	$36,290
Italy	4	$30,630
Spain	5	$27,790
... And then there's the U.S.		$44,180

SOURCE: "The world in 2006," *The Economist,* pp. 92–96.

Given this background, it is all the more remarkable that Spain adopted democracy and never looked back. In fact, looking back is one thing nearly all Spaniards, no matter what part of the country they come from, are reluctant to do. Thus, "by 1975 Spanish society had managed to reach agreement, not on an uncontested account of what happened during the civil war, but at least on some lesson to be drawn from it. The main one was that two warring sides were equally responsible for the barbarism, and neither bore more guilt than the other. The episode was simply the result of 'collective madness.'"[25]

An Economy Fit for Europe

When the ruling **People's Party (PP)** was defeated in March 2004, it was not because the economy was sputtering under the stewardship of Prime Minister José María Aznar. On the contrary, Spain's economy grew at an overall rate 3.2 percent a year during Aznar's tenure—although not spectacular, better than most other EU countries. Unemployment, though still too high, had been cut in half (from 22 percent to 11 percent). Inflation was a tame 2.6 percent in 2003. And countries like France, Germany, and Italy could only look at Spain's modest budget deficits with envy. All in all, Spain's economic vital signs were positive.

Spain was a far richer country in 2004 than it was 30 years earlier. Democracy had opened the door to Spain's entry into the European Union. The challenge facing the government was to bring the economy and public finances into line with the EU's growth and stability pact. This challenge was met in time for Spain to participate in Stage Three of the European Monetary Union (EMU) launched in January 1999.

No one questions whether Spain belongs in the new Europe now. Nonetheless, Spain lagged far behind the European democracies during the Franco period and consequently still has some catching up to do. Without minimizing the very real progress Spain has made since the mid-1970s, it still has a ways to go before it pulls even with the EU's leading national economies. Spain's per capita GDP in 2004 was considerably below that of Britain, Germany, France, and Italy (see Table 4.4).

Without a remarkable economic revival in the 1980s and 1990s, Spain would almost undoubtedly rank with Greece and Portugal, the poorest countries in

Western Europe. But to get into the first rank with Britain, France, and Germany, Spain will have to do two things: first, stay the course in terms of general economic policy (budgetary restraint and low inflation); second, additional market reforms aimed at improving competitiveness, innovation, and productivity.

The Franco regime created a **corporate state** in which monolithic business and labor organizations served as instruments of social and political control rather than independent pressure groups. State-owned monopolies controlled the commanding heights of the economy, including radio and television, public utilities, railroads, airlines, and much more. On paper, the Aznar-Popular Party (PP) government privatized these state-owned enterprises after 1996, but the so-called privatization involved a sleight-of-hand: "the state kept golden shares (since ruled illegal by the EU), picked the bosses, and, directly or indirectly, appointed most of the directors."[26]

Housing is a huge problem in Spain, but not for want of supply or demand—indeed, there is plenty of both. In 2003, for example, there were four times as many housing starts in Spain as in richer, more populous Britain, but despite this supply prices for new Spanish houses rose 18.5 percent. At the same time, 3 to 4 million houses stood empty and a similar number were second homes (vacation getaways).

Clearly, there is something seriously amiss when young people cannot afford even a tiny flat and thousands of employees turn down better jobs in other places that involve a move because they cannot find affordable housing in those places. Meanwhile, housing debt has climbed sharply and now devours nearly half of the average family's disposable income. One piece of this puzzle has to do with rich foreigners buying vacation homes in Spain—a relatively rare phenomenon until Spain opened its doors to Europe (and vice versa). That obviously adds an external variable, increasing demands and driving the price of both new and existing homes up. Another piece is cultural: renting a place to live is not a common or customary practice in Spain. Nearly nine out of ten houses are owner occupied.

Unemployment is also a continuing problem in Spain. Although, as noted earlier, it was cut in half after 1996, it remains among the highest in Western Europe. The roots of the problem again go back to the Franco era, when independent unions did not exist, workers could not engage in collective bargaining, and the main purpose of labor policy was full employment. Wages and working conditions were not on the bargaining table in Franco's Spain, but the government made it almost impossible for employers to fire anybody. With workers' rights came higher wages after 1975, but there has been no corresponding change on the flip side of Franco-era labor policy: it is still extremely difficult to dismiss unproductive employees in Spain. One result is high unemployment; another is dampened productivity.

Productivity is one of the keys to economic success. In the absence of steady productivity gains, it is impossible to compete in European or global markets. But productivity ultimately depends on such disparate factors as education, women's rights, and how much is spent on research and development (R&D) to develop new products and product lines, more efficient production methods, better marketing tools, state-of-the-art information management systems (a la Wal Mart), and the like. As a share of GDP, Spain devotes only half as much as the

EU average to R&D and only a third as much as the U.S. One telltale sign of a technological time lag is the fact that less than a fourth of households in Spain were wired for the Internet as late as 2002.

Demographic trends in Spain, as elsewhere in Western Europe, are also troubling. Spain's fertility rate has dropped sharply in recent decades and is now among the lowest in the world, whereas life expectancy is stretching out, the population is aging, and the age profile of Spanish society is changing dramatically. There were about 700,000 babies born in Spain in 1976; for the past twenty years, that number has averaged between 400,000 and 450,000.

Immigrants are taking up the slack. Of the 2.7 million foreigners said to be residing in Spain in 2004, nearly two-fifths came from Latin America, about a fifth from Western Europe (the pre-2004 EU members) and Africa, and the rest from Eastern Europe and elsewhere. For Spanish policy makers, this influx is a double-edged sword, presenting opportunities (a more competitive and youthful labor market leading to potential productivity gains, for example) and new challenges (discussed later).

At the beginning of the 1990s, immigrants constituted only about 1 percent of Spain's population; by 2004, that figure had jumped above 6 percent. The Spanish government faces a dilemma: Spain needs the demographic boost young immigrants provide, but Spain's immigration policies and related legal and social support systems are not in place to deal with a rapid influx—including an estimated 800,000 illegals in 2003. The newcomers include some 600,000 Muslims. Over half are from neighboring Morocco, separated from Spain by a thin ribbon of water at the gateway between the Atlantic Ocean and the Mediterranean Sea.

So far, Spain has not experienced the kind of xenophobic stirrings that have surfaced in France, Germany, Austria, and even the Netherlands, where tolerance has long been a trademark of Dutch society. How to assimilate culturally and religiously diverse minorities and keep the doors open to legal immigrants and seekers after political asylum while dealing with the attendant risks to society in areas such as public health, crime, and terrorism will continue to rank high on Spain's political agenda in the years to come.

Turnabout: The 2004 Elections

Prior to the March 2004 elections, Spanish foreign policy under the center-right government of José María Aznar was more closely aligned with the United States than with Germany and France or, for that matter, with Spanish or European public opinion. When Aznar's People's Party lost the elections, the proximate cause was widely believed to be the terrorist train bombings in Madrid that occurred three days before the balloting (on March 11). In fact, what angered voters most was the government's initial claim that these bombings were the work of **ETA,** the Basque separatist group linked to acts of violence in the past. Spanish voter certainly were not expressing sympathy for the ETA; rather, they were outraged at the blatant attempt to manipulate the outcome of the election.

How would blaming the terrorist bloodletting on the Basques rather than al-Qaeda help the ruling PP? The Spanish government strongly backed the U.S.

decision to invade Iraq. It did so in the face of overwhelming public sentiment against the war. During the campaign, José Luis Rodríguez Zapatero, the Socialist Party leader, warned that Aznar's pro-American foreign policy was placing the Spanish people at risk by making Spain a prime target of international terrorism and that if the Socialists won the election they would withdraw from the U.S.-backed coalition. The March 11 terrorist attacks that targeted commuter trains in the morning rush hour made that warning appear prophetic. (France and Germany both strongly opposed the invasion; Tony Blair backed American policy all the way, but British public opinion did not.)

As it turned out, the alleged perpetrators were Moroccan Muslims with ties to al-Qaeda, not Basque terrorists at all. Unsurprisingly, this revelation only further damaged the PP's standing in the eyes of many Spanish voters, especially young people adamantly opposed to the war.

Aznar's uncompromising streak was also evident in his government's dealings within the EU. The qualified majority voting (QMV) formula adopted at the Nice summit in 2000 gave Spain eight votes in the Council of Ministers, a disproportionate number compared to voting weights (ten votes each) assigned to Britain, France, Germany, and Italy, the four largest member states. (The population of each of the Big Four EU members except Germany exceeds Spain's by about 20 million, or roughly 50 percent; Germany's population is twice that of Spain.

When the EU enlarged for the fifth time in 2004, one of the ten new members, Poland, happened to be almost identical in size to Spain. Aznar refused to agree to a new QMV formula based on population alone, as that would have diminished Spain's voice in the Europe. Poland followed Aznar's lead. Aznar's recalcitrance paid off, at least in the short run: both Spain and Poland received 27 votes under the new formula to 29 votes for the Big Four. Thus, Poland (a newcomer) and Spain (a relative newcomer) had almost as great a voice in European affairs as Britain, France, Germany, and Italy. (Population aside, these four countries also have much bigger economies than Spain, and they literally dwarf Poland.)

Aznar's detractors portrayed him as "arrogant"—a charge his public demeanor often appeared to support. Nothing Aznar did, however, was more controversial or in the end more damaging to him politically than his unwavering pro-American stance. In particular, Aznar's decision to side with the United States and Great Britain against France and Germany over the war in Iraq opened a chasm between the Spanish government and the Spanish people. The terrorists who set off the bombs that killed Spanish commuters on that tragic morning in March 2004 were in fact targeting the government, which they knew to be highly vulnerable. The PP—and José María Aznar—paid the price at the polls. Unfortunately, a lot of innocent people paid a much bigger price.

Spain's Regions

To say someone is a nationalist in the Spanish context really begs the question. If the person in question is from the Basque country, for example, it probably means he or she is a *Basque* nationalist (that is, one whose first and fiercest loyalty is not to Spain).

Even then we would have to inquire further to know what *kind* of a nationalist we were talking to (or about), whether this particular Basque nationalist supported the separatist ETA and its political wing, **Batasuna,** or the moderate **Basque National Party (PNV)** of regional premier Juan José Ibarretxe.

ETA is an extremist group. Like the IRA in Northern Ireland, ETA has carried out numerous terrorist acts against innocent civilians, assassinations of politicians, officials, and judges, and other violent crimes. Batasuna is to ETA as Sinn Fein is to the IRA: the political wing of an urban guerrilla movement. The goal of the PNV is similar to ETA's, but Ibarretxe and his followers eschew violence.

Exactly what would satisfy the majority of Basques, though, is difficult to say. This question was once again placed on the front burner of Spanish politics at the end of 2004, when the Basque parliament narrowly voted to approve a controversial plan that would redefine relations between the Basque country and Madrid and set the stage for a referendum on becoming "a free state associated with Spain." The outcome is still uncertain, but the new bid to enhance Basque autonomy could be akin to opening up a Pandora's box in a country where ethno-regional loyalties abound and nationalism means different things to different people.

Spain's regionalism is hardly different from that of multinational states like Belgium or Russia insofar as it too arises from ancient ethnic, linguistic, and cultural patterns deeply rooted in the history and political geography of the area. Although it does not formally create a federal structure, Spain's current constitution clearly reflects this social and cultural diversity by dividing the country into seventeen "autonomous communities." That ambiguous concept leaves a great deal of latitude for the central and regional governments to work out mutually acceptable terms on a case-by-case basis. These **intergovernmental compacts** ("statutes") vary from region to region.

Thus, if Spain is not quite federal, neither is it entirely unitary. We are familiar with Basque nationalism, but Catalonia is also a bastion of nationalism— *Catalan* nationalism. Other regions with distinct national identities and political histories include Navarre, Aragon, Galicia, and Andalusia, among others. Even artificial political-administrative regions such as Cantabria, Madrid, and Murcia have become more region conscious in order to compete in what amounts to a region-based political marketplace. That, in turn, rankles with Basque and Catalan nationalists because it muddies the waters and dilutes the message that "*We* are unique."

Both the Basque region and Catalonia are demanding a revision in the statute defining the intergovernmental relationship with Madrid. The Basque plan for a referendum on changes to the statute (what critics say is a referendum on self-determination but the PNV denies) is the most far reaching. The Basques already control nearly all tax collection, spending (except for foreign affairs, defense, and pensions), and law enforcement. For its part, Catalonia wants much of what the Basque region already has (including extensive control over tax collection) plus changes in the Senate in Madrid to make it more of a regional body (recall how the German Bundesrat is designed to give the states a clear voice at the center and legislative powers to match).

The Basque country and Catalonia are featured here as examples of nationalism on a regional level. These two examples illustrate the ambiguity of the word *national* in the Spanish context. (Belgium is another country with regions that break down along national or ethnic lines, as did Czechoslovakia and Yugoslavia before they broke up in the early 1990s.) Region-based nationalism is not confined to Basques and Catalans. One fear is that if the center grants these two regions more and more autonomy, other regions will demand the same, leading to a spiraling descent into the abyss. Another fear is that no matter how many concessions Madrid makes to the regions, it will never be enough, that a soft policy only serves to whet the appetite of firebrands who are rewarded by mandates from local voters.

Aznar's policy was not soft, especially when it came to dealing with ETA. Aznar's successor, José Zapatero, was beholden to Catalonia's Socialists after the 2004 victory, but his government made it clear that "the Socialist Party will never accept self-determination for any part of Spain." In any event, the question remains: What is Spain? Is it one nation encompassing many regions, or many regions pretending to be one nation? Either way, Spain is faces major challenges of integration on two levels: within the EU and within itself.

SUMMARY AND CONCLUSIONS

Theorists in the subfield of comparative politics look for patterns and trends that, in turn, direct attention to interesting questions. Finding the right answers—or refuting wrong ones—is what scientific research is all about. To the extent that comparing political systems can help to identify common problems and isolates the causes, it is not only a path to greater understanding (an end in itself) but also potentially of great value to policy makers (a means).

The British economy failed to revive as rapidly as the economies of Germany, France, and Italy after World War II. Prime Minister Margaret Thatcher pursued market-friendly pro-business policies that spurred economic growth in the 1980s. These policies have been kept in effect by Labour Prime Minister Tony Blair. Recently, the British economy has outperformed the EU as a whole, moved well ahead of France, and gained on Germany relative to GDP. In fact, British per capita GDP is now higher than Germany's.

In France (as in Germany), postwar economic success has given way to a postmodern malaise. Though France's economy has not stagnated, it has lost its dynamism. The population is aging and the working age population is shrinking as the number of pensioners keeps going up. This situation, along with generous social (family and health) benefits, is placing ever greater strains on France's public finances. Chronic budget deficits, high unemployment, and a rigid labor market all point to the need for major reforms, but any attempt to dismantle the welfare state in France is almost certain to meet with fierce popular resistance.

The German economic miracle after World War II gave rise to the most dynamic economy in Europe. West Germans enjoyed a standard of living that was (and is) among the highest in the world. In the 1990s, East Germans began catching up (thanks mainly to huge and unprecedented capital transfers from the western part of Germany to the eastern part). Germany displays many economic and social problems common to other postindustrial countries in Europe, but nothing has marred Germany's postwar record of political stability thus far. The indecisive outcome of the 2005 election, however, raises serious doubts whether Germany's new and untested Chancellor, Angela Merkel, can act to carry out the program of far-reaching reforms she outlined in the campaign.

Germany is no longer a threat to France, thanks in large part to the American military presence there, but centuries of rivalry between the two countries have left a legacy of mistrust. Germany's leadership role in building the European Union and its success in building a stable democracy, however, have done much to reassure France and the rest of Europe that the German threat is a thing of the past. Beginning in 2002, Germany openly opposed the United States (over the war in Iraq) for the first time since World War II. Precisely what this newfound foreign-policy independence means for the future of Germany (and Europe) is an open question.

Italy also experienced an economic miracle after World War II. Italy's high partisan politics meant that governments were often short lived. In the early 1990s, political reforms designed to defragment the party system, rationalize elections, and stabilize the government were put into effect. The reforms have not brought about a transformation (no major party has emerged and governing coalitions are often fragile), but they have encouraged political parties to engage in coalition formation and compromise to a greater extent than before. Italy, too, faces the problems of postmodern development but continues to struggle with several preexisting problems, such as the yawning wealth gap between the rich north and the poor south, political scandals, a splintered party system, fragile coalitions, governmental paralysis, and a disenchanted electorate unwilling or unable to make corrupt politicians pay for their misdeeds.

After World War II, Spain remained a pariah state until Franco's departure from the scene in the mid-1970s. With the flowering of Spanish democracy came membership in the European Union, which in turn boosted Spain's economy. Spain comprises various distinct populations and territories with unique cultures and languages—historically, it was a region (Iberia) of nations rather than the other way around. Today, several centuries of nation building has created a new nation—Spain—but it has not erased preexisting cultures and political loyalties. For the most part, these nations within a nation pay primary allegiance to the government in Madrid. The Basque country is one notable exception; Catalonia is another. Although most do not back the violent ETA separatists, Basques have long expressed a desire for independence.

Spain was among the major West European countries to back President Bush's decision to oust Saddam Hussein from Iraq in 2003. The pro-American stance of the Spanish government contrasted sharply with the anti-American sentiment of the Spanish people. The train bombings in Madrid in March 2004 were in retaliation for Spain's participation in the invasion of Iraq. Spanish voters swung to the left, electing a Socialist government headed by José Zapatero (who opposed the war in Iraq) to replace the center-right People's Party (PP) and its leader José María Aznar.

KEY TERMS

Basque National Party (PNV)

Batasuna

corporate state

devolution

entitlements

ETA

euro

Eurocrats

European Monetary Union (EMU)

euro zone

Forza Italia (FI)

Freedom Pole

globalization

Good Friday agreement

Greens

intergovernmental compacts

Italian Social Movement (MSI)

Keynesian economic theory

liberalism

modernity

new poverty

Northern Alliance (AN)

Northern League

Ossis

out-of-area operations (NATO)

People's Party (PP)

postmodern

Provisional Irish Republican Army (IRA)

Scottish National Party

security consumer

security producer

Sinn Fein

Sparpaket

special regimes

special relationship

stagflation

Tangentopoli

Uliva

Ulster

unification (Germany)

welfare state

Wessis

SUGGESTED READINGS

Brenner, Michael and Parmentier, Guillaume. *Reconcilable Differences: U.S.-French Relations in the New Era.* Brookings Institution: Washington, DC: 2002.

Foster, Christopher. *British Government in Crisis.* Oxford: Hart Publishing, 2005.

Ginsborg, Paul. *Silvio Berlusconi: Television, Power, and Patrimony.* New York: Verso, 2004.

Gunther, Richard; Monetero, Jose R.; and Botello, Joan. *Democracy in Modern Spain.* New Haven, CN: Yale University Press, 2004.

Ireland, Patrick. *Becoming Europe: Immigration, Integration, and the Welfare State.* Pittsburgh: University of Pittsburgh Press, 2004.

Schmidt, Manfred G. *Political Institutions in the Federal Republic of Germany.* New York: Oxford University Press, 2003.

WEB SITES

www.gksoft.com/govt/en/

www.electionworld.org/

www.pbs.org/wgbh/commandingheights/lo/countries/index.html

www.oecd.org/home/

iris.sourceoecd.org/

www.worldbank.org/data/

www.electionsineurope.org/links.asp

NOTES

1. This acronym stands for the Organization of Economic Cooperation and Development. Established in 1960, its membership in 2005 included all the West European countries plus Australia, Canada, the Czech Republic, Hungary, Japan, New Zealand, Poland, Slovakia, South Korea, Turkey, and the United States

2. Defense spending in the United States fell below that level in the 1990s but shot up again after September 11, 2001 and the subsequent invasions of Afghanistan and Iraq.

3. These are OECD figures. Cited in Jeremy Rifkin, *The European Dream: How Europe's Vision of the Future Is Quietly Eclipsing the American Dream* (New York: Tarcher/Penguin, 2004), p. 43.

4. Gideon Rachman, "A Divided Union: A Survey of the European Union," *The Economist,* September 25, 2004, p. 9. (Survey are published as inserts and numbered separately.)

5. According to most Western estimates and World Bank annual statistical abstracts, China's double-digit annual growth rates are part of a pattern going back to the early 1990s.

6. Rachman, "Divided Union," p. 8.

7. Charlemagne, "Europe's Population Implosion," *The Economist,* July 19, 2003, p. 42.

8. In 2005, there were 35 senior citizens for every 100 working-age adults in Europe; in 2050, there will be 75 seniors for every 100 workers. According to *The Economist,* "In Spain and Italy, the ratio of pensioners to workers is projected to be one-to-one." Ibid.

9. Paul Wallace, "Time to Grow Up: A Survey of Pensions," *The Economist,* February 16, 2002, p. 6.

10. The leader of the winning Socialist party, José Luis Rodríguez Zapatero, had made a campaign promise to pull Spanish troops out of Iraq; the Socialist victory was tragically aided by the bloody terrorist bombings at Madrid's central train station on the eve of the elections. See Elaine Sciolino, "Following Attacks, Spain's Governing Party Is Beaten," *The New York Times,* March 15, 2004 (electronic edition).

11. See Alan Cowell, "Blair Calls on United States to Cooperate with Rest of the World," *The New York Times,* January 27, 2005 (electronic edition).

12. *The Economist,* June 27, 1987, p. 60.

13. "Tony Two-Timed," *The Economist,* July 22, 2000, p. 53. In his memo, Blair admitted to "a sense" that the government was "somehow out of touch with gut British instincts," while his pollster characterized the government as "drifting, growing almost monthly weaker and more diffuse."

14. For details, see the cover story in *The Economist,* "London under Attack," July 9–15, 2005, pp. 9–11, and in the same issue, "Murder in the Rush Hour," pp. 47–48.

15. Housing Corporation, Document 48/04, released September 24, 2004. (Available online at http://www.housingcorplibrary.org.uk/housingcorp.nsf/AllDocuments/ B8641D52D5FA61B880256F1D005A4154.)

16. The "O" (organization) in this case means the integrated military command structure and the bureaucracy that supports it.

17. "France's Riots: An Underclass Rebellion," special report, *The Economist,* November 12, 2005, pp. 24–26.

18. Ibid., p. 24.

19. See John Peet, "Addio, Dolce Vita" (A Survey of Italy), *The Economist,* November 26, 2005, especially pp. 13–15. Note: A map on p. 14 of this article shows the extremely uneven distribution of per capita GDP between the North and the South.

20. For example, in the article cited in note 19, the author entitles one section "Why Italian politics is impossible." Unfortunately, the explanation proffered is circular: the mess he describes is the result of the mess he describes.

21. Magistrates (judges and prosecutors) went on a three-day nationwide strike to protest against certain proposed judicial reforms in May 2004. See Francis Kennedy, "Italian Magistrates Go on Strike," BBC World News, May 25, 2004 (at http:// news.bbc.co.uk/2/hi/europe/3745119.stm).

22. PDS = Democratic Party of the Left. The other main parties of the left include the Italian Communist Party (PCI) and the Italian Socialist Party (PSI).

23. For more details on Berlusconi's shady affairs, see Addio Peet, "Dolce Vita," p. 12. See also "He's Not Safe Yet," January 19, 2002, p. 42, and "Italy and Corruption: Is There less than Before?" *The Economist,* February 16, 2002, p. 47; Charlemagne, "Silvio Berlusconi, Italy's Would-be Napoleon," *The Economist,* March 24, 2001, p. 40, and "Comparative Corruption," *The Economist,* May 17, 2003, p. 47.

24. "Italy's Prime Minister: Off the Hook, At Last," *The Economist,* June 21, 2003, p. 42.

25. John Grimond, "The Second Transition: A Survey of Spain," *The Economist,* June 26, 2004, p. 15.

26. Ibid., p. 9.

PART II

Emerging Democracies

Russia

Area: 6,592,812 square miles

Population (2005): 143,700,000

Density: 21–22 per square mile

Languages: Russian, many others

Literacy: 99.6%

Female school enrollment: 100%

Major religions: Russian (Eastern) Orthodox, Islam

Monetary unit: ruble

GNP (2004): $623 billion (estimate)

GNP per capita (2005): $4,300 (estimate)

Average per capita GNP growth (1990–1998): −7.2% Recent GNP growth rate: 5–6% (2004)

Inflation (1990–1998): 230%

Recent inflation rate (2005): 13–14%

Computers per thousand (1998): 40.6

Poland

Area: 120,728 square miles

Population: 38,100,000

Density: 329 per square mile

Languages: Polish 98%, German 1%

Literacy: 99.8%

Female school enrollment: 100%

Major religion: Roman Catholic 95%

Monetary unit: zloty

GNP (2005): $279 billion (estimate)

GNP per capita (2005): $7,300 (estimate)

Average per capital GNP growth (1990–1998): 4.4%

Recent GNP growth rate (2004): 2.1%

Inflation (1990–1998): 26.9%

Recent inflation rate (May, 2005): 2.5%

Computers per thousand (1998): 43.9

Ukraine

Area: 233,090 square miles

Population: 46,900,000

Density: 205 per square mile

Languages: Ukrainian (official), Russian, Polish

Female school enrollment: 100%

Literacy: 99.7%

Major religions: Ukrainian Orthodox, Uniate, Greek Catholic, and Roman Catholic

Monetary unit: Hryvnia (UAH)

GNP (2005): $77 billion (estimate)

GNP per capita (2005): $1,630 (estimate)

Average per capita GNP growth (1990–1998): −11.4%

Recent GNP growth rate (2005): 7.0% (estimate)

Inflation (1990–1998): 440 percent

Recent inflation rate (2005): 8.0% (estimate)

Computers per thousand (1998): 13.8

Czech Republic

Area: 49,373 square miles
Population: 10,200,000
Density: approximately 340 per
  square miles
Language: Czech
Literacy: 99.9%
Female school enrollment: 100%
Major religions: Atheist
  (predominant), Roman Catholic,
Protestant
Monetary unit: Czech koruna (crown)
GNP (2005): $122 billion (estimate)
GNP per capita (2005): $11,960
  (estimate)
GNP per capita growth (1990–1998):
  −0.2%
Recent GNP growth rate (2004): 4–5%
Inflation (1990–1998): 13.7%
Recent inflation rate (May, 2005):
  1.3%
Computers per thousand (1998): 97.3

Yugoslavia (Serbia and Montenegro)

Area: 39,435 square miles
Population: 8,000,000
Density: 266 per square mile
Languages: Serbo-Croatian (majority),
  others
Literacy: 98%
Female school enrollment: not
  available
Major religion: Eastern Orthodox
  (50%), Roman Catholic (30%),
  Islamic (9%)
Monetary unit: dinar
GNP (2003): $19.2 billion (estimate)
GNP per capita (2003): $2.370
Average per capita GNP growth
  (1990–1998): not available
GNP per capita growth (2003): 3.4%
Inflation (1990–1998): not available
Recent inflation rate: 11.2% (2003)
Computers per thousand: not
  available

5

Eastern Europe
The Slavic Zone

*I*n this chapter we examine the setting of politics in the predominantly Slavic eastern half of
Europe. It traces both the precommunist history of the region in broad outline and the
communist era, which now has also passed into history. It focuses special attention on five
countries (Russia, Poland, Ukraine, the Czech Republic, and Serbia-Montenegro). The end
of Pax Sovietica—a term once used to describe Moscow's hegemony (political-military
domination) in Slavic Europe—ushered in a period of ethnic conflict and political instability,
which is simply another way of saying that the natural contours of history and political
geography, obscured for four decades by the false uniformity of totalitarian rule, have
reappeared.

On March 5, 1946, Winston Churchill gave an address at Westminster College in
Fulton, Missouri, in which he spoke darkly of the danger posed by Soviet
communism:

> From Stettin in the Baltic to Trieste in the Adriatic, an iron curtain has
> descended across the Continent. Behind that line lie all the capitals of the
> ancient states of Central and Eastern Europe. Warsaw, Berlin, Prague,
> Vienna, Budapest, Belgrade, Bucharest, and Sofia, all these famous cities
> and the populations around them lie in what I must call the Soviet
> sphere, and all are subject in one form or another, not only to Soviet
> influence but to a very high and, in many cases, increasing measure of
> control from Moscow.[1]

Whether we regard Churchill's words as alarmist or prophetic, the political
geography he traced remained a fact of life for more than forty years.

Behind that **Iron Curtain** lay the former Union of Soviet Socialist Republics
(USSR), more commonly known as the **Soviet Union,** plus Bulgaria, Hungary,

Poland, Romania, and what were until recently Czechoslovakia, East Germany, and Yugoslavia. Eastern Europe (or Slavic Europe) today refers to the lands of Central Europe and the Balkans. It encompasses not only the former Soviet republics of Russia, Ukraine, Belarus, and Moldova but also Latvia, Lithuania, and Estonia. It does not include the former Soviet republics of Georgia, Armenia, and Azerbaijan, located in the **Caucasus,** wedged between Europe and Asia. These countries are geographically and culturally part of no larger region (neither European nor Asian). They exhibit the historical influences of Russia and the Islamic cultures of the Middle East (including Turkey). Tiny Albania has a geographic and political relationship to the **Balkans;** ethnic Albanians constitute the majority of people living in the tinderbox province of former Yugoslavia (now Serbia) known as Kosovo.

SLAVIC EUROPE

Two-thirds of the peoples of Russia and Eastern Europe are of **Slavic** origin. Slavs have been the predominant group there since at least the seventh century. They can be divided into three major subgroups: eastern Slavs (Great Russians, Ukrainians, White Russians, and Ruthenians); western Slavs (primarily Poles, Czechs, and Slovaks); and southern Slavs (Serbs, Croats, Slovenes, Montenegrins, and Bulgars).

The Slavic nations are extremely diverse. Cultural and linguistic traditions vary considerably. Christianity spread throughout the region but took different forms: eastern and southern Slavs embraced the **Eastern Orthodox rite** (related to Greek Orthodoxy and once based in Byzantium or present-day Istanbul), and the western Slavs looked to Rome and the Pope. This explains in part why western Slavs use the Latin alphabet, whereas eastern and southern Slavs use Cyrillic (based on the Greek alphabet).

The non-Slavic groups of Slavic Europe are likewise diverse. The three largest are the Magyars, Moldavians, and Germans (see Box 5.1). Others are the Gagauz, Latvians (Letts), Lithuanians, Estonians, Finns, Jews, Tatars, Bashkirs, Chechens, Ingush, Abkhazians, Meshketians, Albanians, and Mongols. (Georgians, Armenians, and Ossetians live primarily in the Caucasus and therefore do not belong to Slavic Europe as defined earlier.) These groups generally resented Moscow's **Russification** policies of the past (imposing Russian culture on non-Russian peoples) and now abhor the pan-Slavic sentiments often expressed by Russian nationalists. The impact of this non-Slavic presence, particularly in periods of social decay and political instability, is greater than the sum of its parts.

The mutual antagonisms so common to this region have not been confined to relations between Slavs and non-Slavs. What has been variously called the

---

B O X 5.1 Magyars in a Slavic World

What is a Magyar (pronounced MADJAR)?
Clue: Hungary.

Hungary is a country in Eastern Europe with a population of about 10 million. Most Hungarians are not Slavs — the language they speak is related to Finnish and Estonian. It has no more in common with Slavic languages than with, say, German or French. Hungarians make up nine-tenths of the population of Hungary and one-tenth of the population of Slovakia and Romania. There are also tens of thousands of Serbs, Romanians, and Slovaks—as well as large Romany (Gypsy) and German minorities—mixed into Hungary's population along the borders it shares with those two countries. Two-thirds of the population is Roman Catholic and about one-third is Protestant (Calvinist, Lutheran, or something else), whereas the Eastern Orthodox Church (the Greek branch of Catholicism) is prevalent in Russia, Ukraine, and the Balkans.

How did so many Hungarians happen to settle outside Hungary? Why do so many people who are not ethnic Hungarians live in Hungary? To answer these two questions is to explain a great deal about the history of Eastern Europe—a history of changing borders and ethnic conflict. From the sixteenth century to the twentieth century, Hungary was part of the Hapsburg (or Austro-Hungarian) Empire, which contained many large and distinct ethnic groups. After World War I, Hungary, Czechoslovakia, and Yugoslavia emerged from the ruins of the defeated Austro-Hungarian monarchy. Both Czechoslovakia and Yugoslavia broke apart after 1989. Hungary has stayed together but has traded allegations of ethnic discrimination with Slovakia, Romania, and Serbia.

These problems are rooted in a time when nation-states did not exist in Europe or anywhere else and when borders were not clearly defined and tightly controlled. From the Golden Age of Rome to the heyday of the Soviet Union, the great empires of Europe were multinational entities. The emergence of nation-states in the modern era awakened nationalistic stirrings throughout Europe—including among ethnic groups (nations) within the Hapsburg Empire. The Hapsburg rulers suppressed nationalism, sometimes brutally. When Austria-Hungary broke up, there was no script to follow in creating new nation-states in its place. Instead, a ragtag process of political bargaining, improvisation, and compromise gave rise to boundary lines that did not always make sense—a problem complicated by a history of settling ethnic and political differences by the sword.

Hungary has several advantages over some other emerging democracies in Eastern Europe. First, it was ruled as a monarchy (by Magyar kings) long before it became part of the Hapsburg Empire—thus, Magyars have a clear sense of who they are and deep roots where they are. Second, Magyars greatly outnumber Hungary's ethnic minorities. Moreover, the presence of ethnic minorities, paradoxically, gives the majority an incentive for solidarity. Third, Hungary has a long tradition of looking West rather than East. As a result, it has moved quickly to reestablish cultural and commercial ties with Europe's prosperous democracies and jumped on the fast track to join the European Union. Finally, Hungary's transition to a market-based liberal democracy after 1989 was faster and smoother than that of most of its neighbors.

---

buffer zone or *shatter zone* of Slavic Europe encompasses a wide array of deep-rooted ethnic conflicts. The Balkan region, in particular, has historically been a hotbed of ethnic and religious rivalries pitting Serbs against Albanians, Slavs (mostly Christians) against Turks (Muslims), and so on. The violence and "ethnic cleansing" that occurred when Yugoslavia disintegrated in the early 1990s was tragic but hardly unprecedented.

Although the nations of Eastern Europe are diverse in many ways, their fates have been interwoven. Besides linguistic links and the political fortunes (or misfortunes) that have fused them together in one empire or another at different times, in some cases they have shared religious and cultural experiences. Above all, the forces of history and geography have intruded on these nations and shaped a destiny that is uniquely Slavic.

The Influence of Geography

Early in the nineteenth century, France's most famous student of American democracy, Alexis de Tocqueville, predicted that the United States and Russia were apparently "marked out by the will of heaven to sway the destinies of half the globe."[2] Tocqueville anticipated the bipolar world that emerged after 1945 because he understood the importance of geopolitics: the United States and Russia, he observed, would be able to expand over relatively empty landmasses and incorporate or annihilate the indigenous populations, whereas the Europeans would have no choice but to attempt to knock together overseas empires, which were more difficult to keep under firm political-administrative control for obvious geographical reasons (they were scattered, distant, and inaccessible except by marine transport).

For most of the twentieth century, the Soviet Union dominated the map of Eurasia. Occupying more than 8.6 million square miles (one-sixth of the earth's total landmass), it was by far the largest country in the world, more than twice the size of the United States. (About 25 percent of the USSR was in Europe.) Accounting for about half of the Soviet Union's total population and slightly more than three-fourths of its territory was Russia proper. Russia's 6.6 million square miles dwarf the United States' 3.6 million, but in terms of population the situation is reversed: the United States has nearly 300 million people, whereas Russia at present has only about half that number (less than 144 million). Moreover, Russia's population is declining and America's continues growing.

Russia and Ukraine

If Eastern Europe was dominated by the Soviet Union, the Soviet Union was in turn dominated by Russia (see Map 5.1). Geography has played a major role in shaping the political traditions of the Russian people. One authority on Soviet politics has written:

> It is indeed easy to see how Russia's geography has influenced the course of its history. To begin with, Russia's original location on the East European plain contributed directly to many of its important historic events. Being relatively close to Byzantium, for example, influenced Russia's choice of Eastern (Greek) Orthodoxy as its state religion (988). Two and a half centuries later, because of its location, Russia fell prey to the Mongol invasion and remained for several centuries almost completely isolated from Europe, which was then going through the Renaissance and Reformation. A result of this isolation was Russia's lagging behind Europe in technology and industrialization.[3]

Three facts of life determined by geography have been crucial in shaping Russian history and culture. First, Russia lies in the northern latitudes, where it is cold much of the year. Second, it is mostly flat (much like Kansas and Nebraska in the United States) and thus presents no natural barriers to invasion or expansion. Third, it is immense, spanning no fewer than eleven time zones.

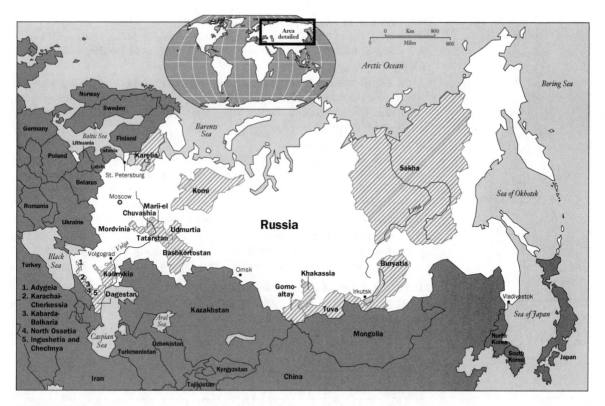

MAP 5.1 Russia

Russia has an abundance of mineral resources and boasts several mighty rivers. Nature yields her bounties grudgingly on the Russian steppe, given the relatively short growing season and the long, cold winters. And although Russia has a lot of land, only 15 percent of it is suitable for agriculture. The Ukraine was the breadbasket of czarist Russia and then of the Soviet empire (because of a growing season long enough for grain crops to mature), but its location on the globe corresponds to that of Ontario, Canada—meaning that it typically experiences long, cold winters. The storied resilience of the Russian people in the face of adversity no doubt owes much to the rigors of the climate.

Empire or Power Vacuum?

The sheer size of Russia, resulting in a need to protect boundaries thousands of miles long, and the absence of natural barriers, which leaves the nation open to attack from any direction except the north, have contributed to a pervasive sense of insecurity. This insecurity reaches as far back as the thirteenth century (see Figure 5.1), when the Mongols invaded, pillaged, and plundered the land of the **Kievan Rus** (modern Ukraine). The Mongol yoke was not removed for nearly two hundred and fifty years.

860–1698 Kievan and Appanage Periods

Rurik dynasty. Period of Kievan Rus state, destroyed by Mongol-Tatars in 1240. Reign of Ivan III (1462–1505), rise of Moscovy to recentralize demolished empire.

1698–1917 Imperial Period

Romanov dynasty. Peter the Great (1682–1725) Westernizes Russia. Catherine the Great (1762–1796) expands Russia's borders. Napoleon invades but fails to conquer Russia. Reign of Nicholas I (1825–1855): time of discontent and repression. October Revolution (1917), overthrow of Nicholas II.

1917–1991 Soviet Period

Communist one-party state called Union of Soviet Socialist Republics (USSR) established. Stalin collectivizes agriculture and institutes centrally planned economy. Soviet Union survives World War II intact; Moscow carves out exclusive sphere of influence in Eastern Europe; Cold War rivalry with United States. Collapse of Soviet state in 1991, USSR dissolves into 15 separate and independent states.

1991–present Post-Soviet Period

Russia undergoes troubled transformation from one-party totalitarian state to constitutional democracy and market economy with mixed results.

FIGURE 5.1 Landmarks in Russian History

In the early sixteenth century, danger came from the opposite direction: Poland. The result was another humiliating defeat and another foreign occupation, this time for only three years. In 1709, Sweden attacked, under Charles XII, a military genius. Russia's Peter the Great, soon to become an empire builder in his own right, rose to the challenge. Under his command, the defending Russian forces defeated the Swedes at Poltava in the Ukraine.

A century later, Napoleon Bonaparte of France invaded Russia and marched all the way to Moscow. However, the harsh winter climate and Russia's sheer physical size proved to be too much even for the brilliant Napoleon and his formidable army. According to historian Nicholas Riasanovsky, "More soldiers of Napoleon died from hunger and epidemics than from cold, for the supply services, handicapped by enormous distances, insecure lines of communication, and bad planning, failed on the whole to sustain the military effort."[4]

Germany invaded twice in the twentieth century. In World War II, Hitler conquered and occupied much of historic Russia west of the Urals. Kiev was destroyed, Leningrad was besieged for two and a half years, and Moscow came perilously close to falling. Twenty million Soviet citizens died; cities, towns, and villages were reduced to rubble and ash; the foundations of the economy were obliterated.

The same geography that has made Russia vulnerable to invasion and instability has also afforded opportunities for expansion. Thus, "when not being invaded, Russia itself was often invading neighboring countries, annexing them, building an empire, and pursuing territorial expansion in the quest for greater physical security."[5] Russian rulers themselves thus created stability problems in bordering areas by incorporating non-Russian groups into the empire. The czars never achieved full Russification of these groups.

Aside from the quest for security, there were powerful economic and commercial incentives to engage in empire building, many of them also affected by geography. For example, the desire to gain access to warm-water ports, a major objective of Russian foreign policy, can be traced directly to Russia's geographic predicament. This drive for trading outlets and the strategic importance of the Bosporus straits (the passage between the Black Sea and the Mediterranean) motivated a push to the south that provoked tension between Russia and the Ottoman Empire (now Turkey) and a war with two other Great Powers in the mid-nineteenth century. Russia's humiliating defeat by Great Britain and France in the Crimean War (1853–1856) was a classic example of the danger of "imperial overstretch."[6]

Geography has also influenced Russian political culture. A famous Russian historian, Vasili Kluchevsky, identified "forest, steppe and river" as "the basic elements of Russian nature" and asserted that they "played an active and unique part in the formation of the life and ideas" of the Russians.[7] Many Russians, for example, have a very romantic view of nature, and associate the Russian landscape closely with love of country or the "motherland". This emotional attachment explains why millions of Russians fought so bravely in World War II. Russians did not love Marx or Lenin, nor were they willing to die for an alien ideology (communism). Significantly, even Russia's brutal dictator, Joseph Stalin, urged Russians to fight for "mother Russia"—not for Marx or Lenin.

Another scholar, Nicholas Berdyaev, argued that "the immensity of Russia" has also left a deep imprint on the culture, society, and general outlook of the Russian people. What is particularly fascinating is the way Berdyaev links geography and politics:

> A difficult problem presents itself ceaselessly to the Russian—the problem of organizing his vast territory. The immensity of Russia, the absence of boundaries, was expressed in the structure of the Russian soul. . . . It might be said that the Russian people fell victim to the immensity of its territory. Form does not come easily, the gift of form is not great among the Russians. Russian historians explain the despotic character of Russian government by this necessary organization of the boundless Russian plain. Kluchevsky, the most distinguished of Russian historians, said, "The state expands, the people grow sickly." In a certain sense this remains true also of the Soviet-Communist government, under which the interests of the people are sacrificed to the power and organization of the Soviet state.[8]

Geography and environment have not predetermined Russia's history, but these physical factors have undoubtedly conditioned and constrained the development of Russian institutions, traditions, and values. The great constants in Russia's history are environmental in the broadest sense of the word: its vast space and daunting distances; its majestic forests; its smooth, flat plains; its harsh winter climate.

THE IMPRINT OF HISTORY

Just as geography influences history, the past (particularly memories of a nation's finest and darkest moments) leaves a deep imprint on political culture. History is relevant to politics for as long as it is remembered (a good example is the Mongol invasion of Russia). Moreover, what is remembered is more important than what actually happened. For example, the Russians and neighboring peoples have very different collective memories of the beginning of World War II. The actual events are much less important, politically speaking, than the prevailing cultural mythology about those events.

Decline of the Romanov Dynasty

When Czar Nicholas II abdicated in 1917 amid the turbulence of war and revolution, he brought to an end three centuries of **Romanov** rule in Russia. Nicholas and his predecessor, Czar Alexander III, had been obsessed with unifying the multinational empire they inherited. However, unlike Peter the Great (1682–1725), Catherine the Great (1762–1795), Alexander I (1801–1825), or Nicholas I (1825–1855), the last two Romanov rulers were unequal to the challenges they faced.

And challenges sprang up like crocuses in spring. First, there were external threats on two sides: to the west, a united Germany, to the east, Japan. Germany had shown its military prowess in victories against Austria in 1866 and France in 1870. Japan's emergence as a great power caught Russia by surprise. In the Russo-Japanese War of 1904–1905, Japan destroyed Russia's Far Eastern fleet with a surprise attack in the outer harbor of Port Arthur. When Czar Nicholas II ordered the Baltic fleet to sail around the globe to save the day, the Japanese dealt Russia's antique armada another crushing blow in the battle of Tsushima Strait in 1905.

The Age of Anarchism: Prelude to Revolution

The Far Eastern debacle set the stage for Russia's first revolution, just as the October Revolution would do twelve years later. The **Revolution of 1905** was precipitated by defeat in war, but war alone does not explain the revolutions. The forces of rebellion and violence had been stirring within Russian society for decades before they erupted in 1905. They first appeared in the 1870s, when anarchism (opposition to all rules) and nihilism (advocacy of destruction for its own sake) mixed with populism (closeness to the people) to produce a homegrown ideology called *narodnichestvo* (derived from the Russian word for "people" or "nation"). The leaders of this movement came to be known as *narodniki;* some of the most prominent were Alexander Herzen, Michael Bakunin, Nicholas Chernyshevsky, Peter Lavrov, and Nicholas Mikhailovsky.

The *narodniki* inspired a group of fanatical revolutionaries, the **Narodnaya Volya** ("People's Will"), who launched an offensive against the government of Alexander II. Members of this group believed that "because of the highly centralized nature of the Russian state, a few assassinations could do tremendous damage to the regime, as well as provide the requisite political instruction for the educated society and the masses."[9] Alexander II, who had freed the serfs, had the misfortune to become the revolutionaries' chief target: the ringleaders of Narodnaya Volya condemned him to death and began what has been described as an "emperor hunt":

> The Executive Committee of the "Will of the People" included only about thirty men and women.... Although the police made every effort to destroy the revolutionaries and although many terrorists perished, the "Will of the People" made one attempt after another to assassinate the emperor. Time and again Alexander II escaped through sheer luck. Many people were killed when the very dining room of his palace was blown up, while at one time the emperor's security official refused to let him leave his suburban residence, except by water![10]

An anarchist finally succeeded in killing Alexander II in 1881. Several years later, revolutionaries also made an attempt on the life Alexander III. The plot failed, but one of the conspirators arrested by the **Okhrana** (the czar's secret police) was Alexander Ilyich Ulyanov, the brother of Vladimir Ilyich Ulyanov, who became known to the world as Lenin. Without Lenin, there would probably not have been an October Revolution; without the October Revolution, there would certainly not have been a Soviet Union.

THE ORIGINS OF SOVIET TOTALITARIANISM

Lenin's ideas about revolution were a mixture of Russian populism, anarchism, and Marxism. As a self-styled champion of Russia's oppressed masses, Lenin had a certain kinship with the old *narodniki;* as an advocate of revolutionary violence (though not assassination), he was a soulmate of the anarchists; and as the founder of the Communist Party of the Soviet Union, he was a disciple of Marx.

Lenin and the Bolsheviks

Lenin split the Russian Social Democratic party in 1903 over the issue of revolution. One faction of the party known as the **Mensheviks** opposed subversion and revolution, arguing that socialism and democracy could be achieved in Russia without violence. The **Bolsheviks,** Lenin's faction, insisted that only a conspiratorial vanguard party, secretly laying the groundwork for all-out revolution, could bring the corrupt czarist order down. Lenin explained this idea in a famous 1902 essay, "What Is to Be Done?"

The working class exclusively by its own efforts is able to develop only trade union consciousness. . . . Modern social consciousness can be brought to them only from without. . . . [It] can arise only on the basis of profound scientific knowledge. The bearers of science are not the proletariat but the bourgeois intelligentsia. It is out of the heads of members of this stratum that modern socialism originated. . . . Pure and simple trade unionism means the ideological subordination of the workers to the bourgeoisie. . . . Our task is to bring the labor movement under the wing of Social Democracy.

Lest anyone miss the point, Lenin added, "aside from the influence of Social Democracy, there is no conscious activity of the workers."[11]

The working class had become a potent base of power. In the decades leading up to World War I, western Russia had undergone rapid economic growth, thanks to inflows of European capital and to government-promoted industrial development (including state ownership). If the rate of growth had been maintained, and if the Great War had not intervened in August 1914, Russia would have been a major economic power even without a revolution. But Marx's observation that capitalists would be their own gravediggers (by creating an underclass of exploited assembly line workers) turned out to be particularly prophetic in the case of Russia, where the growth of a manufacturing sector created centers of large-scale industry in key cities such as Saint Petersburg and Moscow. In these cities, the Bolsheviks found the **proletariat** (urban working class) Marx praised in his writings and Lenin needed to make a revolution.

The October Revolution

Lenin, with the help of fellow Bolshevik Leon Trotsky, masterminded the **October Revolution.** Never known for political moderation, Lenin moved quickly to consolidate his power by scrapping the elected **soviets** (governing councils), banning or suppressing all opposition groups, and putting Bolsheviks in control of the military, the police, the state administration, and the economy. He also established his own dreaded secret police, the **Cheka.** The Cheka imitated the czarist Okhrana but went further in perfecting a system of state terrorism that included purges against all alleged counterrevolutionaries, expropriations of property, and tight control of all mass communications (radio, newspapers, journals, and publishing houses). Thus Lenin and Leninism set the stage for Stalin and Stalinism.

The Bolsheviks faced a variety of challenges in the first few years after seizing power. The national government was embroiled in a civil war with the so-called white (anti-Bolshevik) armies during this period, commonly known as **War Communism.** The Western Allies—including the United States, Great Britain, and France—intervened indirectly with military and economic aid. They also intervened directly, if halfheartedly, on the pretense of recovering war supplies given earlier to the czarist government. The main aim, however, was to assist the "Whites" (the czarists) in overthrowing the Bolshevik Reds." (The United States intervened on the side of the Whites, but there was little if any fighting between the American soldiers and armed Bolsheviks. Most Americans who died in Russia died of disease and exposure, not from enemy fire.)

Lenin's government managed to survive the civil war and Allied intervention, but the harsh policies of War Communism alienated many former supporters of the October Revolution. In 1921, when sailors (who had played a key role in the revolution) mutinied at Kronstadt—a naval base near Saint Petersburg in the Gulf of Finland—Lenin crushed the rebellion. However, the incident apparently made a deep impression on Lenin, who subsequently relaxed the stringent measures imposed earlier. The result was the **New Economic Policy (NEP),** which allowed limited private enterprise, involvement of foreign managers in industry, farming for profit, and considerable literary and artistic freedom.

The Stalin Era

To most objective observers, **Stalinism** and totalitarianism are synonyms. Stalin was one of Lenin's close associates. After the October Revolution, he became Commissar for Nationalities, a key position in the sprawling multinational Soviet empire. One of Stalin's jobs was to keep a close eye on non-Russian nationalities and to prevent any organized opposition from developing on the Soviet periphery, which, of course, included the vital border zones. Thus, Stalin played a key role in the maintaining internal security and in building organizational-administrative ties between the Kremlin (the seat of the central government in Moscow) and the capitals of the so-called soviet republics.

When Lenin became incapacitated following an assassination attempt that nearly cost him his life and then a severe stroke, there ensued a ferocious power struggle behind the scenes. Stalin was considered one of the least likely to succeed Lenin. Paradoxically, the fact that his colleagues on the Politburo (the supreme decision-making body in the Communist Party) underestimated him probably helped him outmaneuver them. As General Secretary of the party, Stalin had a post that none of the ruling party's leading lights wanted. It was a low-profile clerical job that involved keeping party files and shuffling papers.

Within a few short years of Lenin's death, however, Stalin would consolidate his power, redefining the role of General Secretary, creating a **cult of personality** in the process, and becoming one of modern history's most notorious totalitarian dictators. In the late 1920s, he initiated a brutal campaign (discussed later) designed to transform a backward country into a modern military-industrial state at breakneck speed.

The Great Terror

At the height of the Stalin terror in the mid-1930s, nobody was safe. Nearly all the party's old guard—comrades of Lenin—fell before Stalin's firing squads. Most of the military high command met a similar fate. Guilt by association became the order of the day. Anyone who was connected in any way with the old czarist government—anyone who had ever held a position of responsibility in the economy or been recognized in any professional field (science, education, letters) before the revolution—was purged.

Stalin even invented subversive groups as a pretext for purging whole categories of "enemies." One class of prosperous peasants known as **kulaki** was completely wiped out; the kulaks were either killed or sent into exile in Siberia. Millions more peasants perished in the early 1930s in a famine actually worsened by Stalin's brutal policy of diverting capital from agriculture to industry and confiscating crops to feed city dwellers. Despite the domestic famine, Stalin still exported grain to the West to earn hard currency during this period.

Why did Stalin wage war against his own society? What did the resulting bloodbath accomplish? Was there a method in his madness? When Lenin became incapacitated by a stroke in 1922, Stalin knew that a succession struggle was inevitable. On Lenin's death in 1924, Stalin began maneuvering against top Bolshevik leaders.

His first victim was Trotsky, whom he condemned for advocating "permanent revolution" (working for the overthrow of bourgeois capitalist governments) and expelled from the party with the support of Lenin's other lieutenants. Using "salami" tactics, he cut the Bolshevik old guard to pieces, cleverly playing one faction against another, denouncing first the leftists, then the rightists, until he had vilified and discredited them all.

By 1928, Stalin had succeeded in turning the obscure position of General Secretary of the Communist Party into a vehicle of autocratic power. But achieving personal sway over a weak nation did not satisfy Stalin's lust for power, nor did it assuage his obsessive insecurity. Russia was weak, he reasoned, because it was economically backward. It would never be strong until it industrialized. In the modern age, industrial development was the key to military prowess and national glory: that was the lesson to be learned from Japan, Germany, and the United States. In Stalin's own words: "We are fifty or a hundred years behind the advanced countries. We must make good this lag in ten years. Either we do it or they crush us."[12] But how could the Soviet Union industrialize? It was poor and agrarian. Worse, it was surrounded by hostile capitalist states. Under these unfavorable circumstances, Stalin argued, a policy of "socialism in one country"—a euphemism for his highly nationalistic economic development strategy—made more sense than Trotsky's call for worldwide "permanent revolution."

Collectivization and the Gulag Archipelago

Stalin's solution was simple but brutal: if the West could not be trusted (or was not willing) to provide the capital for Soviet industry, Stalin would squeeze it out of Soviet society. Given that the Soviet economy was largely agricultural, Stalin's go-it-alone strategy—a policy generally known as **autarky**—meant that the Soviet farmer would have to bear the brunt of the industrialization drive. But Stalin knew that the peasants would resist confiscatory taxes or forced deliveries to the state. So he decided to collectivize agriculture (take land away from the peasants and reorganize agriculture into large state-controlled farms) more for economic expediency than out of ideological conviction. **Collectivization** was Stalin's way of extracting capital from agriculture for investment in industry—collectivization and forced industrialization were two sides of the same coin.

Stalin's economic development strategy also prompted his bloody campaign against the kulaks. Because the kulaks were the richest farmers, they had the most to lose from collectivization and were therefore the most likely to resist or obstruct. Stalin's *dekulakization* campaign thus appears to have been launched because the hapless kulaks were inconvenient (not, as Stalin claimed, because they were "capitalist bloodsuckers"). Imposing party control over a widely dispersed rural population (the peasantry) was another reason for collectivizing agriculture and sending all who dared to resist to an early grave or the **gulags** (forced-labor camps).

It is no coincidence that **central planning** and the collectivization of Soviet agriculture were inaugurated in the same year, 1929.[13] (The Soviet Union based all of its economic activity—including production, investment, and consumption—on so-called **Five-Year Plans,** which were broken down into yearly and monthly plans, containing specific quotas or targets for all enterprises, including industry, agriculture, and services.) Henceforth Stalin would let nothing (and nobody) get in the way of his crash industrialization program.[14]

The impact of the collectivization drive on Ukraine, Russia's breadbasket, was nothing short of cataclysmic: "A tremendous resistance developed. About a million of the so-called kulaks, some 5 million people counting their families, disappeared in the process, often having been sent to concentration camps in far-off Siberia or Central Asia. A frightful famine swept the Ukraine. Peasants slaughtered their cattle and horses, rather than bring them into a *kolkhoz* (collective farm). Thus from 1929 to 1933 in the Soviet Union the number of horses, in millions, declined from 34 to 16.6, of cattle from 68.1 to 38.6, of sheep and goats from 147.2 to 50.6, and of hogs from 20.9 to 12.2. Droughts in 1931 and 1932 added to the horrors of the transition from private to collectivized farming."[15]

In retrospect, the **Great Terror** of the 1930s can be seen as part of Stalin's mad dash for modernization. Millions of citizens were arrested on the flimsiest of pretexts and were sent off to labor camps run by the secret police. Prison-camp labor built a major part of the USSR's industrial infrastructure (roads, canals, bridges, railroads, dams, power grids). In Siberia, forced labor opened new mines and built new towns. In Moscow, forced labor built the impressive subway system—one of the marvels of the Stalinist era proudly shown to all visitors from abroad.[16]

Forced labor is slave labor. Much of the terror Stalin unleashed in the 1930s was in reality an excuse for enslaving much of the Soviet work force in order to industrialize the nation without having to pay for it. Is this scenario too diabolical to be true? No one familiar with the show trials of the 1930s, in which the old Bolsheviks who had been Lenin's comrades in arms publicly confessed to heinous crimes and denounced themselves as spies and traitors, would doubt Stalin's capacity for cruelty. (After they had confessed, Stalin's rivals were taken out and shot.)

In sum, Stalin created a rigidly centralized system of rule in which state terror was used to mobilize society and enforce strict conformity with his will. He brought the entire economy under a central plan that consistently gave greater priority to industrial development than to agriculture or the production of consumer goods. This dogmatic insistence on the primacy of heavy industry became one of the hallmarks of Stalinist economy policy. After World War II, Stalin would leave his totalitarian stamp not only on the Soviet Union on also on the rest of Eastern Europe as well; and not only on the economies but also on the societies and political cultures of the region.

The Soviet Phoenix

In Egyptian mythology, the phoenix is a magnificent bird that lives for five hundred years before voluntarily consuming itself in flames, only to emerge from the ashes and start a new life cycle. The legendary rebirth of the phoenix is an appropriate metaphor for the Soviet experience in World War II.

On June 22, 1941, Hitler's army invaded the Soviet Union and rolled relentlessly toward Moscow. By October, German forces had encircled the city on three sides at a distance of twenty miles. Although Hitler's troops did not actually enter Moscow, they came much too close for comfort.

Without question, the Soviet Union was the main victim of German aggression in World War II. The Red Army did emerge victorious, but as historian Isaac Deutscher noted:

> Against this backdrop must be set the price Russia paid for the victory: the seven million dead, officially counted—the losses may in fact have been much larger [twenty million]; the uncounted millions of cripples; the devastation of most cities and towns, and of much of the countryside in European Russia; the destruction of industry, exemplified by the total flooding of the coal-mines of the Donets; the complete homelessness of twenty-five million people, living in caves, trenches, and mud huts, not to speak of the latent homelessness of many more millions of evacuees in the Urals and beyond.[17]

Soviet industry, bought at a terrible human price in the 1930s, lay in shambles. Between 1941 and 1945, Soviet industrial might was cut nearly in half; despite the Stalinist emphasis on steel production, the USSR was producing only about one-eighth as much steel as the United States in 1945. Soviet agriculture, too, had to be rebuilt "almost from scratch."[18]

But for all the death and destruction, the Soviet Union did not disintegrate. On the contrary, the war strengthened Soviet patriotism and made the survivors determined to do whatever was necessary to rebuild the country. West Germany's postwar reconstruction is generally considered an economic miracle. Similar comebacks occurred in Italy and Japan, but what is more remarkable (though less frequently remarked on) is the Soviet economic miracle. Soviet workers, unlike the Germans, Italians, and Japanese, had to rebuild without foreign aid. (The Truman administration offered—but Stalin refused to accept—Marshall Plan aid. Still, the United States supplied the Soviet Union with 11 billion dollars worth of Lend Lease aid during World War II, including B-29 bombers. Also, the Soviets engaged in a systematic and massive theft of property and resources from Germany and Eastern Europe at the end of the war.)

Most of the Soviet recovery is attributable to two factors: Stalin's draconian system of labor conscription (the war and its aftermath provided a steady flow of fresh recruits to the **gulags**) and a centrally planned economy that permitted all resources and energies to be concentrated on strategic industries (coal, steel, electricity, machine tools, armaments).[19] By 1950, the Soviet Union had consolidated its hold on Eastern Europe, successfully tested an atomic bomb, and rebuilt much of its heavy industry. Stalin had the largest standing army in Europe (indeed, the largest in the world), and the Soviet Union was less than a decade away from entering the space age. (In 1957, the USSR became the first country to put a satellite—its name was Sputnik—into orbit.)

THE COLD WAR ERA (1945–1991)

The Cold War had a major impact on Soviet and Eastern European politics after World War II. The tenor of relations between the United States and the Soviet Union set the limits of east-west cooperation in all areas, including trade, tourism, technology, and cultural exchange. For this reason, we need to look at the general pattern of superpower relations since 1945.

In retrospect, the Cold War began before the Great Patriotic War (as the Soviets call World War II) ended. The Big Three—Churchill, Roosevelt, and Stalin—met several times as the war wound down, at Tehran, in Persia (Iran); Yalta, Ukraine; and Potsdam, Germany. On the surface, these meetings were conducted in a spirit of mutual trust as befits allies in a great and noble cause. Below the surface, mistrust guided the maneuvers of both Stalin and Churchill. Only Roosevelt appears to have entertained illusions about the possibilities for postwar collaboration between the Soviet Union and the West.

President Roosevelt did not live to see the end of World War II or the visible outbreak of the Cold War; he died suddenly in April 1945. His successor, Harry Truman, took a dim view of Stalin from the start. When the United States dropped the atomic bombs on Hiroshima and Nagasaki in August 1945, stopping the Russian advance into Manchuria (northern China) may have been a factor (even the United States pressured Stalin to enter the war in Asia). Defeating Japan without having to invade the main islands was undoubtedly President Truman's primary aim.

The Red Zone

The United States abruptly cut off aid to the Soviet Union and turned down a Soviet loan request. Stalin then refused to withdraw Soviet troops from northern Iran and reneged on wartime promises to allow free elections in Soviet-occupied Eastern Europe. Instead, Stalin moved to consolidate Soviet control over Poland, East Germany, Romania, Hungary, Bulgaria, and, finally, in early 1948, Czechoslovakia.

Against the backdrop of Stalin's expansionism in Eastern Europe, a great debate unfolded in the United States about policy toward the Soviet Union. The Cold War would not emerge clearly until 1948. But a telegram dispatched by George Kennan from the U.S. embassy in Moscow in February 1946 presaged the policy of **containment,** which after 1948 became the cornerstone of the United States' national security strategy for four decades.

Stalin's actions in Poland and Czechoslovakia were particularly alarming to the American public. There was a sizable Polish community in the United States—Chicago still boasts the second-largest concentration of Polish people in the world (exceeded only by Warsaw). Stalin had assured Roosevelt that the Soviet Union would respect Polish sovereignty. Czechoslovakia was a special case because it had been a showcase of democracy between the two world wars. In early 1948, leaders of the Czechoslovakian Communist Party, subservient to Stalin, staged a coup—with Stalin's backing and very likely on his orders. In the course of the Communist takeover, Jan Masaryk, the country's popular foreign minister and son of the beloved first president of Czechoslovakia, Thomas Masaryk, died under mysterious circumstances—he fell or was thrown from a window. President Truman, capitalizing on the furor created by the latest Soviet land grab, asked Congress to back the Marshall Plan (a massive, multibillion aid program aimed at speeding the economic recovery of Western Europe from the devastation of World War II). Though it was by far the biggest foreign-aid package ever proposed, funding was approved in short order.

The year 1948 also saw the first Berlin crisis. Before World War II, Berlin had been the capital of Germany. After the war, when Germany was divided into zones occupied by each of the victorious Allies, Berlin, located inside the Soviet-occupied eastern zone, was likewise divided. Stalin wanted all of Berlin under East German (Soviet) jurisdiction. He decided to force the issue by blockading Berlin. The United States responded with an airlift that kept West Berlin alive. Stalin was checkmated: either he could shoot down the U.S. supply planes and touch off a new hot war, or he could back off. He backed off.

In 1949, the United States established the North Atlantic Treaty Organization (NATO), the first peacetime U.S. alliance in 150 years. The Soviet Union responded by forming the **Warsaw Pact.** In 1949, two other landmark events occurred: the Soviet Union conducted its first successful atomic bomb test, and the pro-Western government of Chiang Kai-shek was driven off China's mainland onto the island of Taiwan by the forces of Chinese Communist leader Mao Zedong.

Stalin's Heirs

Stalin's death in 1953 provoked a succession crisis. Following several years of bitter infighting, Nikita Khrushchev emerged as the winner. He lost little time in distancing himself from the deceased dictator.

At the Twentieth Party Congress in 1956, Khrushchev delivered his famous **Secret Speech.** The four-hour address contained a blockbuster: the pronouncement that Stalin had made serious errors in the 1930s and had committed excesses in the name of building communism. Of course, many who heard this shocking "revelation" already knew about the Stalin terror (not a few from firsthand experience). But before Khrushchev's speech, nobody in the Soviet Union dared whisper a word about it.

Khrushchev's **de-Stalinization** drive was his most significant contribution to the development of the Soviet state. Not only did he denounce government based on fear and Stalinist terror, but he also emptied the labor camps and dismantled most of the vast camp system (the "gulag archipelago," as survivor and author Alexander Solzhenitsyn has called it).

Other attempts at reforming the Stalinist state, however, were destined to fail. In agriculture, Khrushchev launched the **virgin lands** campaign under which millions of hectares of land in Kazakhstan and eastern Russia were to be plowed and planted for the first time. It seemed like a good idea at the time, and at first it seemed to be working. But within a decade the campaign turned to disaster as the fragile topsoil was blown away by fierce winds. In the spring of 1963, according to one account:

> Dust clouds hid the sun for several days, irrigation canals were choked, and along some stands of trees drifts of soil more than two meters high were formed. Many towns and villages were covered with dirt, and from thousands of hectares the arable layer was so completely removed by the winds that the underlying bedrock was exposed. Precise data on the damaged areas were not published, but millions of hectares were involved. . . . It will take at least one to two centuries before the arable layer is restored to these areas.[20]

Khrushchev's other attempts at economic and administrative reform were equally ill fated. In an effort to decentralize the cumbersome state bureaucracy, he abolished most of the Moscow-based economic departments, creating regional economic councils (*sovnarkhozy*) in their place. But officials with a vested interest in preserving the power and status of the center, Moscow, resisted this change. Khrushchev also introduced a plan for the regular rotation of party personnel (thus threatening the job security of party bosses) and tried splitting regional party committees into agricultural and industrial sectors, again in the name of increased efficiency.

What resulted was confusion and probable sabotage by disgruntled functionaries and administrators. When Khrushchev was ousted in 1964, his successors cited his "hare-brained schemes" as justification. His detractors also accused him of trying to create a cult of personality (a Stalinist sin) and thus violating the Leninist principle of collective leadership. Accordingly, Leonid Brezhnev, Khrushchev's successor as general secretary, did not assume the post of premier. (Khrushchev, like Stalin, had simultaneously held the top post in both party and government.) Alexei Kosygin became the new premier, while Nikolai Podgorny served as the new president. Thus a kind of triumvirate, with Brezhnev as "first among equals," replaced one-man dictatorship for the first time in Soviet history. (Brezhnev ousted Podgorny and assumed the post of president, as well as party chief, in 1977.)

Toward the Prague Spring

Following Stalin's death in 1953, east-west relations improved in Europe. No one was prepared to declare the end of the Cold War. Instead, it was called a "thaw."

The Soviet Union faced major challenges at home and abroad. After Communist Party Secretary Nikita Khrushchev renounced Stalinism in 1956, uprisings against communist rule occurred in Poland and Hungary. Khrushchev sent troops into Hungary in 1956; the communist government in Poland weathered the storm without direct Soviet intervention. But the lessons on both sides were clear: Moscow would not permit defection of the Eastern European satellites, from the Warsaw Pact; for Moscow, the price of empire was eternal vigilance.

Between 1958 and 1961, the issue of Berlin heated up again, resulting in an on-again, off-again crisis that culminated in August 1961 in the building of the Berlin Wall to stop the flood of escapees to the West. A year later came a crisis over Soviet offensive missiles stationed in Cuba that brought the two superpowers to the very brink of nuclear war. The confrontation had a sobering effect on both sides. The upshot was the establishment of a telephone hot line between the White House and the Kremlin and the signing of the Partial Nuclear Test Ban Treaty in July 1963.

But as tensions were stabilizing with the West, they were heating up on the other Soviet flank. In the early 1960s, a rift in relations between the USSR and its former communist ally, the People's Republic of China, escalated into a war of words. Throughout the 1960s, the two communist giants traded insults. The spat turned ugly in 1969, when fighting broke out along the border demarcated by the Amur and Ussuri rivers. There were relatively few casualties, but Sino-Soviet relations remained frigid, and Moscow found itself engaged in two cold wars at once.

Even within Eastern Europe—Moscow's own special sphere of influence— the Soviets faced challenges. As early as 1948, Yugoslavia had split with the Soviet Union when Tito, the national hero of the Yugoslav resistance movement in World War II, refused to kowtow to Stalin. A decade later, Hungary and Poland had made unsuccessful bids for independence from Moscow. In 1968, it was Czechoslovakia's turn, as the spellbinding Prague Spring brought the flowering of a mass movement embracing "socialism with a human face." Led by Alexander Dubcek, the communist regime proposed to open up the political system to opposition parties. Moscow would not tolerate such "bourgeois" heresy. At the order of General Secretary Leonid Brezhnev, Soviet troops rolled into Prague and crushed the Czech rebellion. Brezhnev justified the intervention on the grounds that socialist states have an obligation to aid any member of the socialist commonwealth beset by counterrevolution. In other words, once a socialist state, always a socialist state. Elsewhere this policy, which came to be known as the Brezhnev Doctrine, was roundly condemned.

Brezhnev's long tenure (1964–1982) brought a return to policies and methods reminiscent of the Stalinist era. State terror was not resumed on a massive scale, but some dissidents were placed in psychiatric hospitals and subjected to chemical and electric shock "therapies"; others were harassed by the secret policy or imprisoned for long periods. This **neo-Stalinism,** as it is sometimes called, was evident in both cultural and economic policy. In the economic sphere, the Brezhnev regime briefly toyed with market-oriented reforms, based on the proposals of Soviet economist Evsei Liberman. But the reforms were soon abandoned in favor of a return to the Stalinist system of central planning with its emphasis on quotas, artificial prices, and top-down management. In the cultural sphere, censorship, which Khrushchev had relaxed in the early 1960s, was restored. In 1968 two writers, Andrei Sinyavsky and Yuli Daniel, were convicted of "anti-Soviet agitation," a political crime under Soviet law that typically carries a penalty of seven years in prison. The trial sent a chill throughout artistic and literary circles in the Soviet Union.

Two events led to the emergence of a human rights movement in the USSR in the late 1960s: the Israeli victory in the Six Day War in 1967 and the Soviet invasion of Czechoslovakia in 1968. The first event inspired Soviet Jews to seek permission to emigrate to Israel (or the West); the second focused attention on repressive Soviet policies both at home and abroad and gave rise to protests (even from devout communists) throughout Eastern and Western Europe. In the Soviet Union, a small but vocal group of dissidents took up the cudgels for liberalization of Soviet politics and culture.

Détente and Decline

The early 1970s witnessed the opening wedge of a dramatic realignment: the United States and Communist China buried the hatchet after more than two decades of hostility. Moscow looked on in dismay but should not have been surprised: one of the oldest principles of international politics—the enemy of my enemy is my friend—was working to bring these strange bedfellows together.

With relations between Washington and Beijing warming up, the Soviet Union decided it was time to seek accommodation with the United States. President Nixon and his foreign policy guru, Henry Kissinger, keen to play off one communist giant against the other, seized the opportunity for a superpower **détente.** In 1972, the two superpowers signed a strategic arms limitation agreement, SALT I. They also moved to improve bilateral trade relations. East-West trade had already developed outside the Soviet-American relationship. In the early 1970s, West Germany, under the center-left government of Chancellor Willy Brandt, pursued an independent foreign policy (*Ostpolitik*) that sharply increased trade and other ties between East and West Germany and between Eastern and Western Europe.

Superpower relations in the 1970s were on a roller-coaster ride. Progress in strategic arms limitation was not matched in other areas. The **Helsinki Accords** in 1975, which obligated the signatories to respect personal rights and civil liberties, gave the Soviet human rights movement a boost. Ironically, it became a new source of tension in east-west relations, however.

One manifestation of the hardening Soviet attitudes toward both the West and internal liberalization (the two policy tracks tended to move in tandem) was a crackdown on dissent. Several prominent human rights activists and so-called refuseniks (Soviet Jews who were refused permission to emigrate) were arrested and put on trial. The most famous, Anatoly Shcharansky, was both a human rights activist and a refusenik, thus symbolizing everything the Brezhnev regime sought to suppress. He was accused not only of anti-Soviet agitation but also of being a spy. The Soviet punishment for treason was death. Shcharansky's life was spared, but he was sentenced to thirteen years in a labor colony. (In 1986 Shcharansky was exchanged for several East German spies, and he now lives in Israel and is a member of Israel's parliament.)

After 1979, Jewish emigration was reduced to a trickle, and the political climate discouraged manifestations of dissent or nonconformity. The Kremlin's neo-Stalinist social and cultural policies were matched by a strict, orthodox approach to economic problems. The prescribed remedies for inefficiency continued to have one common denominator: overcentralized management within the rigid framework of economic planning. (An in-depth analysis of the Soviet economic malady is presented later in this book.) In the early, 1980s, the ossified Soviet system, like its geriatric leaders, showed clear signs of old age.

The ebb and flow of political repression during the Brezhnev years obscured the steady erosion of central authority. Several forces were causing this growing instability. First, the steel sword of Stalin's totalitarian system had been the secret police, or **KGB** (Committee of State Security). After Khrushchev's Secret Speech in 1956, the KGB was demoralized, discredited, and partly defanged. Still formidable, it nonetheless ceased to inspire the kind of fear it had in Stalin's day.

The fact that Western visitors were allowed to enter the country and move about specific "open" cities relatively freely, especially after the Soviet-American détente of the early 1970s, was a symptom of the Kremlin's weakening hold on society. At the same time, more Soviet academicians, scientists, and other professionals were permitted to venture abroad. Accompanying this "travel revolution" was a "communications revolution." With the waves of tourists coming to the USSR came Western ideas, clothing, music, magazines, tapes, records, and gadgets. Some young people learned to speak English by approaching Americans (and other English speakers) on the street and striking up a conversation. They would offer their services as unofficial tour guides, asking only for an opportunity to speak English in return.[21]

Soviet-American relations, always tense and tentative, soured in the late 1970s. The Soviet invasion of Afghanistan in 1979 drove relations between Washington and Moscow to the lowest low point in a decade. (The SALT II treaty, which subsequently stalled in the U.S. Senate, was one of the casualties.) American President Jimmy Carter imposed a retaliatory grain embargo on the Soviet Union and the United States boycotted the Moscow Summer Olympics. The election of Ronald Reagan, a staunch anticommunist, seemed likely to bring a resurgence of the Cold War as the 1980s unfolded.

When Brezhnev died in 1982, former head of the KGB Yuri Andropov succeeded him. Andropov moved quickly to revitalize the Soviet economy, relying primarily on exhortation and admonition; his watchword was discipline. Anyone caught skipping work ("absenteeism"), avoiding work or malingering on the job ("parasitism"), getting drunk or causing a public disturbance ("hooliganism"), dealing on the black market ("speculation"), or engaging in other corrupt practices would be punished to the limits of the law.

Soviet citizens were both optimistic and apprehensive about the new regime. There was widespread recognition that stagnation had set in and that only a strong leader with a clear vision of the future could pull the nation out of its doldrums. But there was also an unspoken fear that Andropov might resurrect the Stalinist police state.

These hopes and fears were for naught, however. Andropov fell ill and died in the spring of 1984. His successor, Konstantin Chernenko, old and frail from the start, died a year later. The Soviet Union had now been without energetic leadership for years. For nearly three decades, one iron-fisted ruler—Joseph Stalin—had held sway in the Kremlin. Now, between 1982 and 1985, the country would have four different "bosses" (Brezhnev, Andropov, Chernenko, and Gorbachev) in one three-year period. Something had to be done about the Soviet gerontocracy. Aging neo-Stalinists whose jaded habits of mind precluded initiative and innovation could not rejuvenate an arthritic economy.

Enter Mikhail Gorbachev. Gorbachev was in his fifties when he took over the reins of power—a youngster by Soviet political standards. Gorbachev's accession in 1985 and Reagan's desire to finish his second term with a flourish set the stage for a second détente. In November 1987, the two superpowers signed a treaty eliminating intermediate-range nuclear forces in Europe. Moscow had made several unilateral concessions in the negotiations. This conciliatory attitude in matters of arms control, combined with Gorbachev's liberal domestic reforms, raised the prospect of a real thaw in the Cold War.

Gorbachev moved boldly on the cultural and economic fronts (see Chapter Six). In the political sphere, he paid lip service to democratization but kept a tight rein on state power. Many observers believed the Soviet Union was on the verge of a new era. In fact, it was approaching its demise.

IDEOLOGY AND POLITICAL CULTURE

An **ideology** is an organized belief system. Like religion, it may be sponsored by the state, promoted by an organization outside the state, or entirely separate from the state.

In the Soviet model, the official ideology was an amalgam of ideas and teachings associated primarily with Marx and Lenin—hence the term **Marxism-Leninism.** Political culture is broader, not only encompassing ideology but also values, attitudes, myths, fears, prejudices, perceptions, and preferences that permeate and condition the political thoughts and actions of society's members. This distinction was especially crucial in the Soviet-bloc countries because the ideology was used as a kind of smokescreen concealing the underlying values that actually motivated political behavior.

The Virtues of Stalinism

Understanding other cultures requires a certain ability to suspend our own ingrained values and habits of mind. Failure to do so inevitably leads to misconceptions. To cite one example, a journalist named Hedrick Smith, posted to Moscow in the 1970s, expected to find that most Soviet citizens remembered Stalin with fear and loathing. He was surprised to discover, however, that "so essential was Stalin to the concept of how Russia should be ruled for many middle-aged and elderly people that they no longer recall their panic at the time of his death."[22] Many ordinary Soviet citizens expressed nostalgia for a time when Russia had a strong boss.

Smith's observations comparing Soviet (and especially Russian) attitudes toward authority with Western (in particular, American) views are worth quoting at some length:

> [There is] a fundamental difference between Russians and Americans, who are often moved to seek similarities in their national characters. They may share an openness of spirit but Russians and Americans differ sharply in their attitudes toward power and authority—and not just because of Soviet Communism. Inbred mistrust of authority is an American tradition. We are wary as a people of bigness when it is accompanied by unchecked power— Big Business, Big Labor, big anything.. . .
>
> Not so the Russians. Bigness and power are admired almost without qualification. Size inspires awe—huge Kremlins, cannons, churchbells under the czars; huge dams, missiles, atom smashers under the Communists. Marxism-Leninism has provided a rationale for large-scale production and concentrated power in the hands of Party leaders and central planners. But six centuries of authoritarian rule from Ivan the Great and Ivan the Terrible forward had made Russians monarchists in their bones long before Lenin and Stalin came along.. . .
>
> So much has been inherited from the past that a Russian takes for granted elements of political despotism that are instantly an affront to a Westerner. History has conditioned Russians differently. The cruel tyranny of Stalin was prefigured by the bloody reign of Ivan the Terrible in the sixteenth century and the iron rule of Nicholas I in the nineteenth century. Peter the Great, celebrated for opening Russia to the West and introducing a more modern Army and state administration, is well known abroad for having also improved the efficiency of authoritarian controls, some of which survive today. It was Peter who set up the first political police administration and who officially instituted censorship and the practice of issuing internal passports to keep Russians from traveling away from their permanent homes without special permission.[23]

The easy assumption that the virtues of democracy are as obvious to Russians as they are to Americans turns out to be a delusion. For reasons deeply rooted in their history, Russians tend to value security more than freedom (which, before Gorbachev's reform campaign, they had never known); at the same time, they often fear disorder more than tyranny.[24]

Part of the Russian aversion to overt forms of disobedience can probably be explained by their history of draconian rule, the resulting absence of democracy, and a natural fear of the unknown. People accustomed to stern discipline are bound to feel insecure and perhaps disoriented when that discipline is reduced or removed. Of course, not all Soviet citizens feared freedom or equated democracy with disorder, but most probably did.

Russians learned to deal with embarrassing facts by hiding them. Western observers are often struck by the Russian penchant for *pokazukha,* putting up a false front. The practice of deliberately disguising unpleasant realities is a time-honored and highly perfected tradition in Russia. This practice became a trademark of Soviet rule. For example, the Soviet travel agency, Intourist, packaged special tours of showcase cities just for foreigners, provided guides (who did double duty as chaperones), and kept visitors' schedules so jam packed with excursions, museums, ballet performances, and the like that there was no time to poke around and explore the darker side of Soviet life.

Russians have long believed that Western nations view them as crude and uncultured. "You like to laugh at our misfortunes" is a common sentiment Russians express toward Americans. (Like many other misperceptions we entertain about each other, this one contains a kernel of truth.) The deep-rooted Russian inferiority complex—manifested, for example, in the proclivity of Russian schoolteachers to challenge American visitors to impromptu poetry-reciting contests—was reinforced by Soviet propaganda during the Cold War. The upshot was a kind of reflexive Soviet patriotism that popped up even in nonthreatening interpersonal encounters with the West. Such reactions may strike Westerners as inappropriate, but they are a natural reflection of a deep-seated Russian sense of inferiority vis-à-vis the West.

Thinly Disguised Nationalism

Patriotism is a universal emotion, but the "blood and soil" Russian variety startles many Western visitors. During the Communist era, Soviet patriotism was really Russian patriotism with a thin Bolshevik veneer. Signs of patriotism were everywhere; some were transparently contrived by the regime for foreign consumption, but many were spontaneous and heartfelt. Hedrick Smith quoted a young Soviet economist: "We learned from our history that to survive, we must band together." Smith also noted that Suvorov, the Russian military commander who defeated both Frederick the Great and Napoleon, used to say, *"Pust khuzhe, da nashe"* ("Let it be worse, but let it be ours").[25]

This attitude is akin to "My country, right or wrong," something the Russians call *kvasnoi patriotizm.* Smith explained it this way:

> Like so many essentials of Russian life, the phrase does not readily lend itself to translation, for one has to know that kvas is a fermented peasant drink made from water dripped through burnt bread. Kvas has a malty flavor, and cheap kvas can be like cold coffee—bitter, the color of muddy water, with grounds at the bottom. In cities all over Russia, white-coated women serve up glass mugs of kvas from large, saffron-colored, mobile

metal kegs in the summertime. Foreigners usually pass up a second mug, but Russians swear by it, and peasants produce their own home brew of kvas. So kvas patriotism represents the earthy peasantry: an intensely Russian brand of patriotism.[26]

The impact of communism on Russian political culture was (and still is) evident in a phenomenon called *blat*—a generic term for the pervasive corruption, cheating, and dishonesty that permeated everyday life in the USSR. Blat assumed myriad forms: theft of state property, bribery, embezzlement, moonlighting, and dealing on the black market. It involved bending, evading, or breaking the rules in all sorts of subtle and not so subtle ways. Almost everybody did it, largely out of necessity, because consumer goods and services were always scarce (and therefore precious) and because prices fixed by the state did not reflect their true (market) value.

Thus the distortions introduced into the Soviet economy by the system of central planning—in particular, the emphasis on heavy industry and defense production at the expense of consumer needs—created a morally ambiguous climate in which widespread dishonesty and underhandedness were rewarded (and tacitly accepted) and honesty and integrity appeared foolish. Moreover, the rigidities of central planning made it expedient for plant managers, too, to cheat, lie, and falsify records on a vast scale, including the use of illegal go-betweens to obtain essential materials on the black market, in a never-ending struggle to fulfill monthly production quotas.

Public morality in the USSR reflected the collectivism that lay at the core of Marxist ethics. This moral propensity contrasted sharply with the individualism so prevalent in countries like France and the United States. In the Soviet Union, the paramount importance of the collective was rarely questioned. Schoolchildren were taught to place group rights above individual rights and to take responsibility for the performance and conduct of their classmates. Similarly, teachers generally held parents responsible for the attitudes and actions of their children in school. Adults were even expected to take responsibility for the conduct of other adults—especially family members, neighbors, and coworkers—to an extent that was startling and alien to Westerners.

The severe erosion of public and private morality in the Soviet Union was one of the bitter fruits of the Stalinist system. The reason we know that to be the case is that what happened in the Soviet Union also happened in all the other countries where the Stalinist (or Soviet) model was installed—an excellent example of how comparative studies can often be used to confirm or refute hypotheses in political science.

EASTERN EUROPE BEFORE 1945

The nations of Eastern Europe have historical roots, but the present states emerged as sovereign entities only in the modern age, after centuries of foreign rule. Hungary regained internal independence in 1867 with the establishment of the dual monarchy (the emperor of Austria was also Hungary's king). Romania became independent in 1878, Bulgaria in 1908, and Albania in 1912. Czecho-slovakia and Yugoslavia emerged as independent states only after World War I and dissolved shortly after the demise of the Soviet Union. Poland was reconstituted as a sovereign state after the war; Russia, Prussia, and Austria had dismantled it in a series of partitions more than a century earlier.

East Germany was a special case. Stalin formed the German Democratic Republic (GDR) from the portion of Germany occupied by Soviet troops after the defeat of Hitler's Third Reich in 1945; it had never aspired to a separate existence, always considering itself part of a single German nation.

Before World War I, four great empires dominated Eastern Europe, all located on the periphery of the region and only one, Russia, anchored in a Slavic culture. By the mid-nineteenth century, the Russian empire encompassed all of the Ukraine, part of Poland, and Bessarabia (now part of Moldova). The Russians, Prussians, and Austrian Hapsburgs partitioned and ruled Poland from the end of the eighteenth century until 1918. Austria's domain included the territories of what are now the Czech Republic, Slovakia, Hungary, Slovenia, and Croatia from the fifteenth century until its defeat and dissolution in World War I. The Ottoman Empire (Turkey) once ruled the Balkans (the bulk southeastern Europe), including Bulgaria, Romania, Bosnia, Serbia, Macedonia, and Albania. Hungary was also under Ottoman rule for a time.

The most important distinction, politically, is between the Eastern European countries once ruled by Austria and Prussia (later Germany) and those ruled by the Ottoman Turks. Most of the former were greatly influenced by Western Europe and made important contributions to the high culture of the West (consider, for example, the impact on classical music of Czech composers such as Dvorak and Smetana or the Polish composer Chopin). The Balkans developed in relative isolation from the West, and hence the cultural contributions of its peoples are generally less widely known outside the region.

Although all Eastern European countries had limited autonomy, the north-ern-tier Slavic nations generally experienced less oppression and abuse than did their neighbors to the south, who endured religious persecution and heavy taxation while benefiting from little or no economic and political development well into the twentieth century.

In the turbulent period between World War I and World War II (1918–1939), many Eastern European governments had a democratic veneer, but only Czechoslovakia was a true democracy. Other nations in the region lacked experience in democratic self-government, although Poland was no stranger to the idea of constitutional (or contractual) limits on kings, regional assemblies, and the principle of the *liberum veto*.* Many also lacked moderate leadership and faced enormous economic and social problems. Anti-Semitism and extreme national-ism were prevalent throughout the region, as were divisions over religion, social reform, and national aspirations. The leaders of Hungary, Romania, and Bulgaria saw the Nazi totalitarian model as a solution to their desperate domestic

---

*Under this rule, each and every member of the assembly has the right to reject legislation—
a form of democratic decision making that obviously goes way beyond majority rule but can
lead to deadlock.

circumstances. (All three countries later joined the Hitler-led Axis.) Widespread hostility to both Russia and communism also reinforced this perverse inclination to embrace Nazi Germany.

All the nations of Eastern Europe lost their independence in World War II. Poland, Czechoslovakia, and Yugoslavia were conquered by Nazi Germany (but in Yugoslavia, Tito's partisans waged a ferocious guerrilla war against the Germans).

In 1939, Hitler and Stalin signed a nonaggression pact under which they split Poland. Two years later, Hitler tore up the agreement, overran Poland, and attacked the Soviet Union. Later, when Stalin turned the tide, the advancing **Red Army** waited on the eastern bank of the Vistula River while German troops crushed the **Polish underground.** (The Polish government in exile had called for the Warsaw uprising in the belief that it would hasten the defeat of the Germans; rather than helping the Polish fighters, Stalin kept his army on the sidelines.) In due time, Soviet troops crossed the Vistula and pursued Hitler's retreating forces into Germany. Ironically, Hitler ended up giving Stalin a golden opportunity to dispatch Soviet troops into Poland. After the war, the Red Army occupied Poland and ensured Soviet domination of that country until 1989.

The story of Poland is tragic but not without precedent. In 1772, Prussia and Russia annexed major portions of Polish territory in the **First Partition of Poland.** According to Ivan Volgyes, "Poland then tried to re-create its former greatness by reforming the obsolete workings of its government." In the Second Partition in 1793, Poland was further reduced. "Even though the Poles, under the brilliant general Tadeusz Kosciuszko, fought valiantly against partition, the dream of Polish independence was brutally crushed by the invading Prussian and Russian armies." The Third Partition, involving the Austrians, in 1795 marked "the end of Poland as a political entity, as a state."[27]

Hungary, Romania, and Bulgaria were first seduced and then subjugated by Hitler. As accomplices of Nazi Germany, they could expect little sympathy from the Allies after the war. (This point is often underemphasized in historical treatments of this period.) Thus the postwar Soviet land grab in Eastern Europe was actually facilitated by the very nations that eventually fell victim to Stalin's megalomania.

One of the most important consequences of World War II was the unification of Eastern Europe into a military and political bloc under the Warsaw Pact, led by the Soviet Union. Thus one Slavic nation, Russia, the nucleus of the USSR, succeeded in bringing Eastern Europe's Slavic peoples under a single political authority for the first time in history. But in so doing, Stalin made the same mistake the czars had made in earlier centuries: he overextended the empire.

SLAVIC BUT *NOT* RUSSIAN: POLAND, UKRAINE, CZECHOSLOVAKIA, AND YUGOSLAVIA

The Soviet grip on Eastern Europe was probably never as firm as it appeared to the West, as periodic revolts in Poland and attempted defections by Hungary and Czechoslovakia revealed. In addition, the "captive nations" (as they were often

MAP 5.2 Russian Federation

called, see Map 5.2) resisted Soviet rule in a number of subtle ways. In the first place, most people seldom paid more than lip service to the official ideology. It was the subject of jokes and sarcasm in private, even as it was treated with mock reverence in public. In the second place, an undercurrent of anticommunist (anti-Russian) sentiment bubbled just beneath the surface throughout Eastern Europe. The extent of this rejection of the communist ideology was dramatically revealed in 1989, as one communist government after another simply abandoned the ship of state.

According to one scholar, "The failure of the Soviet Union to Russify the area and convert the population to its brand of 'Marxism-Leninism' should not overshadow the enormous moral, spiritual, and cultural damage inflicted upon the East European nations." The Soviet model was "superimposed on natural diversity," and no aspect of life was left untouched:

> The extent of damages and the degree of recovery naturally vary from country to country, but in all of them deep-rooted feelings of having been robbed and degraded by an alien superpower are still very live issues. Indeed it is hardly an exaggeration to say that nationalism constitutes

the heart of the challenge to Soviet domination and that external and internal emancipation from the Soviet Union is the central theme of East European political life.[28]

Remarkably, these words were written two decades before the great "emancipation" of which they spoke came to pass.

Widespread anti-Sovietism was reinforced by another universal element in Eastern Europe: ethnic particularism, or nationalism. Each group is highly conscious of its heritage. When the Soviet Union interfered (or worse, intervened) in the internal affairs of the various countries, it stirred strong nationalistic impulses. Moscow's heavy-handed treatment of its satellites in Eastern Europe helped heterogeneous states like Czechoslovakia and Yugoslavia overcome ethnic tensions within their own societies. The dissolution of these states following the Soviet withdrawal from Eastern Europe strongly supports this conclusion.

In the absence of Soviet hegemony, nationalism is again playing a major role in Eastern Europe, both within and between states. Historic rivalries were submerged but never dissolved by ideology or alliance ties. Even during the heyday of the Cold War, these rivalries occasionally came to the fore:

> Witness, for example, the glee with which the East Germans and Poles intervened in Czechoslovakia in 1968, the pressures for military intervention in Poland in 1981 expressed by the East Germans and Czechoslovaks, or the problems between Hungary, on the one hand, and Czechoslovakia and Romania, on the other, regarding the presence of significant Magyar minorities in the latter two states.[29]

One commonality that may have helped ease the pain of adjustment to the Stalinist system after World War II is the tradition of authoritarianism that pervades most of Slavic Europe. The fact that, of all the nations of Eastern Europe, only Czechoslovakia had ever tried democracy with any degree of success has taken on new relevance with the collapse of communism in the region.

In retrospect, the underlying problem throughout the Soviet bloc was more spiritual than material, more psychological than economic. What ultimately determines the success or failure of a society or an economy (especially one endowed with natural resources and the population base necessary for sustained growth and prosperity) is elusive but intangible factors (what is often called "culture") surely plays a role.[30] Japan, for example, achieved its postwar economic miracle even without the natural resources that would seem to be a prerequisite.

Chiang Kai-shek, the pro-West leader of Nationalist China, once described communism as a disease of the heart. In the 1980s, the communist leaders of the Soviet Union and Eastern Europe were forced to confront the fact that Chiang might have been right. As the events of 1989–1991 were to show, the disease was ultimately to prove fatal.

Slavic ("Eastern") Europe encompasses the former Soviet Union west of the Urals, East Central Europe, and the Balkans. We have already examined the USSR in this chapter; here the focus is on Poland and Czechoslovakia in East Central Europe, Yugoslavia in the Balkans, and Ukraine. Much of present-day Ukraine had come under Tsarist (Russian) rule by (or before) the time of Peter the Great (1682–1725); the redoubtable Catherine the Great (1762–1796) grabbed extensive lands in the western Ukraine.

Hungary is also a strong candidate for special consideration in this section. Like the Czech Republic and Poland, Hungary is a relatively homogenous society with a population and government committed to the painful and complex transition from totalitarianism to liberal democracy. Unlike Czech and Poles, Hungarians are Magyars, not Slavs.

Poland and the Czech Republic are now members of the North Atlantic Treaty Organization (NATO) and the European Union (EU). Russia, Serbia, and the Ukraine remain outside of these two groupings. For all five, the challenges of economic and political liberalization are daunting, but Poland and the Czech Republic, along with Hungary and Slovenia, have moved further and faster than the other former Soviet bloc states. At the same time, the difficulties discussed here—restructuring, privatization, corruption, inflation, unemployment, currency convertibility, foreign investment, and external trade—are in many cases magnified in other parts of the region (for example, Moldova and the Ukraine) where efforts to reinvent the state and economy in the 1990s have met with little success.

Poland: Flat Land, Fluid Borders

The origins of the Polish nation, like those of other Slavic nations, are obscure. It is difficult to separate fact and folklore. What it is known is that the first Polish state had come into existence by the middle of the tenth century (see Figure 5.2).

Poland has never had natural boundaries; instead, Polish territory expanded and contracted over the centuries. Indeed, because of the absence of any natural obstacles to invasion, "Poland's shifting boundaries have made her, over the centuries, the only amorphous state in Europe."[31] In the seventeenth century, Poland's eastern frontier stretched to within 90 miles of Moscow. Poland was then the largest state in Europe, except for the emerging but "inchoate" Russian empire.

The Vistula was the "axis of the Polish nation through a thousand years of political vicissitude, a unifying force linking the cities of Warsaw and Cracow and the great estates of Galicia with the Baltic."[32] To Poles, it is more than just a river, much as Mt. Rushmore is more than just a sculpted rock to Americans.

After World War II, the shape of Poland again changed. At the Yalta and Potsdam conferences, Stalin demanded that a large portion of Polish territory be ceded to the Soviet Union; Poland would be compensated with German territory in the west. As a result, the territory between the Oder and the Vistula, including a tributary of the former (the Warta) came into Poland's possession. But "in the east, Poland lost nearly half of the territory which had been shown as Polish on maps of the inter-war period." This painful surgery was "no more than a recent instance of the tragic burden imposed by geography on Poland's past."[33]

For two hundred years prior to World War II, Poland's borders had moved eastward; now they were shifted dramatically in the other direction and without the participation of the Poles themselves. In short, as a result of the 1945 settlement, Poland's eastern frontier shifted 500 miles west of the seventeenth-century boundary. At the same time, Poland moved 150 miles closer to Western Europe (see Map 5.3).

MAP 5.3 Poland

SOURCE: Adapted from the University of Texas Libraries, The University of Texas at Austin.

It was a lot like déjà vu for Poland, which was partitioned three times in the late eighteenth century (1772, 1793, and 1795). With the third and final partition in 1795, the Polish state disappeared from the map of Europe, only to reappear more than a century later at the end of World War I. In brief, having been a great power from the fourteenth to the seventeenth centuries, Poland had vanished from 1795 to 1919, when it had reemerged as an independent state, only to be invaded and occupied by Nazi Germany and Soviet Russia in 1939.

Despite its turbulent history, the Polish nation has preserved a surprisingly clear sense of cultural identity, but shifting frontiers meant that Poland would never be ethnically homogenous. On the fringes of the Polish lands lived Lithuanians, White Russians, and Ukrainians—"predominantly peasant peoples . . . on whom the Polish aristocracy imposed an alien culture."[34] The greatest dynasty ever to rule Poland (the Jagiellon, 1386-1572) was actually Lithuanian in origin. Lithuania was incorporated into Poland in 1569 and only in the 1880s did

960–992 Reign of Mieszko I

Birth of Polish state Mieszko marries Dubrowka of Bohemia, converts to Christianity; makes Christianity religion of all Poland. Establishes boundaries roughly similar to present-day Polish.

996–1370 Piast Dynasty

Wars and invasions place Poland's national survival in jeopardy, but Poland is again culturally and politically unified under Casimir the Great (1333–1370).

1382–1572 Jagiellonian Dynasty

Poland and Lithuanian form alliance through marriage of young Polish Queen Jadwiga and Lithuanian Duke Jagiello; union greatly expands Poland's boundaries; Polish-Lithuanian alliance lasts 400 years. Despite many wars (against Teutonic Knights, Tatars, Russia, and Ottoman Empire), Poland prospers; Renaissance reaches Poland in 16th century; Polish adopted as national language (in lieu of Latin); in 1569, the Polish Parliament, or Sejm, unifies Poland and Lithuania into one state.

1572–1795 Royal Republic

In 1573, the Polish Sejm legislates religious tolerance (Catholics, Jews, Protestants, Orthodox Christians, and Muslims live together peacefully); Poland's capital moves from Krakow to Warsaw. In the "Deluge" (1655-1660), Sweden invades Poland with help of Tartars and Cossacks, Polish cities are burned and plundered; population is repeatedly decimated (population reduced from 10 million to 6 million due to wars, famine and bubonic plague); in the second half of the 18th century, three powerful neighbors (Russia, Prussia, and Austria) vie for control of Poland, leading to the Three Partitions of Poland (1772, 1793, and 1795); kingdom of Poland comes to an end with the abdication of Stanislaus II (1795). Poland disappears as a nation-state for the next 123 years.

1914–1945 Rebirth of the Polish Nation-State

Poland is devastated in World War I but reemerges as an independent country as part of the peace settlement in 1918. Treaty of Versailles (1919) gives Poland western Prussia (formerly part of Germany); Poland takes parts of western Ukraine and Belarus by force in Polish-Soviet War (1919–1920); Poland is devastated in World War II; invaded and occupied by Nazi Germany at the beginning of the war and by the Soviet Union at the end of the war. Some 6 million Poles die in World War II.

1945–1989 Communist Era—Poland under Soviet Domination

Periodic popular uprisings fail to overthrow Soviet-backed one-party system; in 1978, Cardinal Karol Wojtyla becomes Pope John Paul II (first non-Italian pontiff in nearly 500 years); in the 1980s, Solidarity movement led by Lech Walesa wins concessions leading to relaxation of strict police-state controls.

1989–present Independent Polish Democracy

Poland looks westward, joins the Western alliance (NATO) and the European Union (EU).

FIGURE 5.2 Landmarks in Polish History

it experience anything like a national revival. Poles treated Lithuanians with courtesy and respect, but they tended to view White Russians and Ukrainians as inferior. Thus, it is not surprising that in the eyes of Russians and Ukrainians, Poles are Westerners first and Slavs second.

Unlike Russia, Poland is a Roman Catholic country. Unlike the Czechs, Poles never rebelled against the Vatican and did not take part in the Reformation.

MAP 5.4 Ukraine

SOURCE: Adapted from the University of Texas Libraries, The University of Texas at Austin.

Between the 1790s and 1990s, Poland was independent for only twenty years. When Poland was once again partitioned in 1939, it was done by two totalitarian states, Russia and Germany. In 1945, Stalin would make Poland into a Soviet satellite. Not until 1989 would Poland finally become a fully sovereign and independent state.

Poland ruled large chunks of territory that fall within the historical frontiers of Ukraine; today, it is the other way around: territory that fell within the historical boundaries of Poland now forms the western frontier of Ukraine. A glance at the map of Europe reveals that Poland's expansions and contractions could not have occurred without directly effecting Ukraine—and vice versa. Clearly, the histories of Poland and Ukraine are intertwined. Both countries are Slavic or Slavonic (these two terms are identical in meaning).

Both Poland and Ukraine also have a distinctive national identity, culture, and language. Both can look back to a golden age when they were independent and powerful states. Both countries have also been invaded repeatedly, subjugated by neighboring states, and come through it all with a sense of nationhood more or less intact. And finally, both states are now once again independent. We turn next to a brief look at Ukraine, the birthplace of modern Russia.

Ukraine: In Russia's Shadow

Ukraine makes its first appearance in the ancient chronicles of Europe around the middle of the ninth century, at a time when the various Slavic tribes were just beginning to emerge as distinct nations (see Figure 5.3). This early Kievan state

911–988 Establishment of Kievan Rus Empire

Viking Prince Oleg, ruler of Kiev, signs peace treaty with Byzantine Empire (911); Prince Vladimir converts to Christianity (988).

1019–1054 Heyday Kievan Rus State

Prince Iaroslav the Wise. Cathedral of St. Sophia constructed in Kiev.

1055–1240 Decline and Fall of the Kievan State

Civil war. Rise of new threat (the Polovtsy). Mongols invade (1237). Kiev destroyed (1240).

1918 Partial Rebirth (The Soviet Period)

Ukraine reappears on map of Europe as Ukrainian Soviet Socialist Republic (one of the 15 Soviet republics).

1991 Ukrainian Statehood

Ukraine regains its independence (750 years after the Mongols destroyed Kiev!) following the collapse of the Soviet Union.

FIGURE 5.3 Landmarks in Ukrainian History

was ruled by a series of powerful rulers with names like Igor (912–945), Olga (945–964), Sviatoslav (964–972), Iaropolk (972–978), Vladimir I (978–1015), Sviatopolk (1015–1019), and Iaroslav the Wise (1019–1054).

Not much is known about the earliest Kievan Rus monarchs. Indeed, there has long been a lively debate among historians over the origins of the Kievan Rus state. Proponents of the "Norman theory" have long believed that the first rulers of the Kievan Rus were of Scandinavian, not Slavic, origin. But more recent evidence casts doubt on the Norman theory.[35]

More is known about the two greatest Kievan rulers, Saint Vladimir and Iaroslav the Wise. Vladimir I is called "Saint Vladimir" because it was his decision to adopt Christianity (specifically, the Greek Orthodox rite) as the state-sponsored religion of the Kievan Rus sometime around 988. It is difficult to exaggerate the far-reaching consequences of this decision for the future of both Ukraine and Russia. From that point forward until the triumph of the Bolsheviks in the October Revolution (1917) roughly a millennium later, Ukrainian and Russian culture, architecture, art, music, and literature would bear the imprint of the Eastern Orthodox Church. It would never bow to Rome and in time would break with Byzantium (Constantinople) as well, forming the Ukrainian Orthodox and Russian Orthodox rites, but the influences of the Greek Orthodox religion and Byzantine culture were pervasive. This fact goes a long way to explaining why Lenin and his Bolsheviks were hell bent on eradicating every trace of religion from Soviet life after 1917: Lenin knew that it would be impossible to transform Russia without first destroying the moral authority of the church.

The Soviet attack on religion, instigated by Russia's new ruler, was thus a direct challenge to Ukrainians' sense of nationhood. Unsurprisingly, Ukrainians fought the Bolsheviks after World War I, proclaiming a Ukrainian National Republic in 1918. The Bolsheviks eventually prevailed after several years of bitter fighting (the period known as War Communism in history books). In 1922, Ukraine was reincorporated in the Russian empire (renamed the Union of Soviet Socialist Republics).

During several centuries prior to World War I, Russia ruled Ukraine, although the Ottoman Turks seized control of the North Black Sea coast and the Crimea in the late fifteenth century (see Map 5.4). Poles and Lithuanians ruled a large part of the contemporary Ukraine (including Kiev) in the fourteenth and fifteenth centuries. With the rise of Muscovy (the successor to the Kievan Rus) in the sixteenth century, the political center of gravity shifted northeastward and Ukraine once again came to be ruled by eastern Slavs (Russians) rather than western Slavs (Poles) and Lithuanians (Baltic/Indo-European). But Ukrainians would not be masters of their own fate, except for a brief time after World War I, until the Soviet Union self-destructed at the end of 1991.

There is one other major episode that has shaped Ukrainians' sense of who they are, namely, the Mongol invasions of the thirteenth century. Attacking Riazan in 1237, and then Vladimir, the seat of Suzdal's grand prince, the Mongols set about securing the entire territory of the eastern Slavs. They captured Riazan after five days of fierce fighting and massacred everybody. At Vladimir it was the same terrifying story, only on a larger scale. The grand prince himself perished along with his entire army. Over the following eighteen months, the Mongols prepared for the next great campaign while continuing to attack and conquer additional Russian lands. In 1240, the Mongols struck again, this time aiming to conquer lands beyond Russia. In 1242, they stormed Kiev, mass murdered the population, and leveled the city and St. Sophia cathedral. All that remains standing is a remnant of the Golden Gate of Kiev that stood at the entrance to the city.

Some 730 years later, when this writer and his students visited Kiev, a prim and scholarly Intourist guide related the grim details of this massacre at the hands of the Mongol horde (a word used exclusively with reference to the Mongols). Women and children, she told us, had taken refuge in a cathedral in the vain hope that they would escape a cruel fate. But alas no power on earth or in heaven could save them from the Mongols.

Ukrainian history is a rich mixture of fact and folklore. The tragic character of that history did not end with the lifting of the **Mongol yoke** in the fourteenth century, but nothing would equal its devastating impact on the people of the once-mighty Kievan Rus (contemporary Ukraine) until the 1930s, when a state-engineered famine—part of Stalin's murderous economic program designed to catch up with the West in shortest possible time (discussed earlier)—led to the death of an estimated 7–10 million Ukrainians. Shockingly, Stalin forced Ukrainians to make grain deliveries to the state for consumption in cities and for export while Ukrainians themselves starved.

Ukrainian Nationalism   This brief historical sketch ends on a personal note. On a visit to Kiev in the 1980s, I was walking back to my hotel with a purchase I had made at a nearby store. It was the official flag of the Ukrainian Soviet Republic. Two young men stopped me on the street and asked why I had bought that flag and what I thought of it. Trying to be diplomatic, I guardedly replied that it was colorful (bright red and turquoise with a gold hammer and sickle). Then I turned the tables. "What do *you* think of it?" I asked. Without any

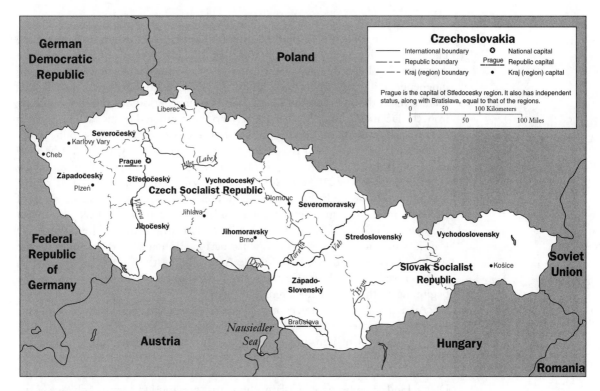

MAP 5.5 Czechoslovakia 1918–1992

SOURCE: Adapted from the University of Texas Libraries, The University of Texas at Austin.

hesitation, one of the young men replied, "We don't like it." It was not the *real* Ukrainian flag, he told me. The real one is blue on top and yellow on the bottom. Ukrainians, they both agreed, did not like the false flag.

I had bought the flag to use as a prop in my classes on Soviet politics; as it happened, the anecdote about my chance encounter with two young Ukrainian nationalists was worth far more than the flag itself. At the time, no one would have guessed that Ukraine would soon become an independent state after some seven and a half centuries of subjugation to foreign rule. But knowing what I did about how Ukrainians have suffered at the hands of outsiders, and having seen for myself that Ukrainian nationalism was alive and well, I had no doubt that given the chance they would choose freedom and independence. As we will see in Chapter Six, after 1991 the question was whether independence would mean freedom—or tyranny in a new guise.

Czechoslovakia: Slavic Outside, Western Inside

Czechoslovakia is located in East Central Europe, bordered by Poland, Germany, Austria, Hungary, and Ukraine. The Poles and Czechs are generally considered to be the most Western-oriented Slavic nations.

The name *Czech* refers to the native inhabitants of Bohemia and Moravia, which were part of the **Great Moravian Empire** in the ninth century (see Figure 5.4). They eventually became part of the Holy Roman Empire under the Austrian Hapsburg dynasty, but not before Bohemia had established a strong independent identity of its own under the **Přemyslid kings** who established themselves as the rulers of the **Czech lands** over a period of the time stretching from the life and death of St. Wenceslas (who was murdered by his own brother) in the first half of the tenth century to the brief reign of Wenceslas III (1305–1306).

Ottakar I (1198–1230) is a major name in Czech history, for it was he who made the Bohemian king a major force in the Central European (and especially German) affairs. In 1212, the Golden Bull (royal decree) of Frederick II recognized the right of the Bohemian nobility to elect its own ruler. The kingdom of Bohemia reached its greatest extension under Ottakar II (1253–1278), and with the opening of the famous silver mines at Stříbro (the name of the town is the Czech word for "silver") during this period Bohemia became one of the wealthiest countries in the later Middle Ages. The death of Ottakar II, however, in a decisive battle with the German king Rudolf of Hapsburg in 1278, marks the beginning of the end of the Přemyslid line.

After a four-year interregnum, John of Luxemburg, son of the Emperor Henry VII, succeeded the last Přemyslid (Bohemian) king but was forced to issue a charter (a kind of constitution) guaranteeing the rights and privileges of the Bohemian nobility and clergy. For the first time, written law limited the powers of Bohemia's king (John, of course, was not Bohemian). In addition, the national Diet, a kind of embryonic legislative body that previously had met only on special occasions, became a regular institution. John was a warrior-king who participated in three major military campaigns. He was killed in the battle of Crécy, fighting on the French side. He had shown little interest in Bohemian affairs, but he had greatly boosted Bohemia standing in international affairs. His greatest legacy to the Czechs, however, was his son Charles.

The reign of Charles I (1347–1378) coincides with a golden age in Bohemian history. As Holy Roman Emperor, he became known to the world as Charles IV. It was Charles who completed the work of creating a Czech nation-state, issuing a series of charters in 1348 that established a clear order of dynastic succession and fixed Bohemia's place in the firmament of the Holy Roman Empire. The king of Bohemia was placed at the head of the list of the empire's electors. Moravia and Silesia, as well as Upper Lusatia, were formally incorporated into the Czech lands. Bohemia's self-governing status within the empire was guaranteed. Charles ruled as an enlightened monarch who promoted constitutionalism and attended to the economic and cultural development of the nation. He published a code of laws, made Prague one of the world's most beautiful cities, and founded the first university in central Europe (named Charles University in his honor).

The first rumblings of the Protestant Reformation occurred in Bohemia, not Germany. The leader was a professor at the university in Prague named Jan (John) Hus (1369–1415), who attacked the sale of indulgences, demanded Church reforms, challenged the Pope's primacy, and stressed the spiritual authority of Holy Scripture. He was also an outspoken Bohemian nationalist. Rome retaliated

9th century Czech Beginnings

10th century to 1337 Era of the Přemyslid Kings

Prince Vaclav (Wenceslas), young heir to Bohemian throne, murdered by half-brother; becomes patron saint of the Czech people (the "good King Wenceslas" in the well-known Christmas carol) in 935; Přemyslid kings establish centralized state, expand Bohemian territory, and bring country under protection of German-based Holy Roman Empire. In 1212, Frederick II makes Bohemia a virtually independent kingdom within the empire.

1310–1378 Czech Golden Age

Reign of Charles I (son of John of Luxembourg); crowned Charles IV, Holy Roman Emperor in 1355; Prague becomes major center of culture and learning. Founding of Charles University (first university in Central Europe). Many of Prague's architectural marvels date from this period.

1415–1526 Hussite Era and George of Poděbrady

Jan Hus leads church reform movement; Hus burned at the stake for heresy (1415). Hussite wars fought (1420–1434). George of Poděbrady (the "Hussite king") became popular ruler of the Czechlands in 1458.

1526–1790 Hapsburg Dynasty to Joseph II

Holy Roman Emperor Rudolf II moves his court back to Prague (1583), ushers in Prague's "Second Golden Age." Protestant uprising against Hapsburg in 1618; defenestration of Prague; Battle of White Mountain (1620); rebellion fails. Czech language and culture repressed for 150 years, known to Czechs as the Dark Age. Maria Teresa (1740–1780) and son, Joseph II (1780–1790) institute reforms, reducing power of Catholic Church, expelling the Jesuits (1783), and granting greater rights to minorities.

1790–1918 Czech National Revival and World War I

Reawakening of Czech national aspirations. World War I spells end of Hapsburg dynasty. Czechoslovakia established as independent state in 1918.

1918–1948 Birth and Death of Independent Czechoslovakia

Czechoslovakia flourishes as parliamentary democracy, independent, prosperous, and free until Nazi takeover in 1939. Soviet Red Army liberates most of the country at the end of World War II. Communists win national elections in 1948, establish one-party communist state.

1945–1989 Communist Era

Communist hardliners subservient to Moscow take charge, nationalize industry, create a centrally planned economy, and crush dissent. Czechs rally around reform communist leader Alexander Dubcek in 1968, attempt to institute "socialism with a human face." Soviet military intervention brings Prague Spring to a tragic end, ushering in two more decades of repressive communist rule.

1989–present Czech Republic

In a "Velvet Revolution," Czechs demand an end to communist rule, rally around dissident playwright Vaclav Havel. Communist rulers go quietly. Havel guides a newly free and independent Czechoslovakia through the process of writing new constitution and creating parliamentary democracy. Czechs and Slovaks split peacefully into separate states (the "Velvet Divorce"). Czechs join NATO and European Union (Slovaks follow suit).

FIGURE 5.4 Landmarks in Czech History

against this heresy by excommunicating Hus. In 1415, the emperor promised him safe conduct to attend the **Council of Constance,** where he hoped to be vindicated. In violation of this promise, Hus was arrested and burned at the stake. After Jan Hus was martyred, his power as a national symbol would be greatly magnified.

Hus's followers would take up the sword against both Rome and foreign rule. The Hussite wars (1420–1433) opened a new chapter in Czech national history. The pope proclaimed a Bohemian Crusade, which united the nation under a brilliant soldier, Jan Ziska, headquartered in the town of Tabor. Ziska won a series of victories between 1420 and 1422. His death did not slow the Hussite armies. Now led by a priest, Procop the Great, the **Hussites** defeated one crusade after another, in the process marching beyond the traditional Czech lands and advancing across Germany as far as the Baltic Sea.

The Hussites were for a brief time the most formidable military force in central Europe, if not all of Europe. The Hussite movement collapsed in civil war in 1434, but the Hussites were not quite finished. In 1448, a young nobleman, George Podiebrad, seized power in Prague and established himself as the leader of the Hussites. He defeated the radical wing of the Hussites at Tabor in 1452 and set about reconciling Catholics and Hussites. In 1459, George Podiebrad was elected king. Although he was a moderate Hussite who pursued a policy of reconciliation with the Vatican, George was technically a heretic. When George died in 1471, having defeated various papal attempts to dethrone him, the question of Bohemia's relations with Rome was unresolved.

In the sixteenth century, the Czech lands fell under the imperial rule of the Austrian Hapsburgs. The official religion in Bohemia and Moravia became Roman Catholic; the official language was German; the political capital of gravity shifted decisively from Prague to Vienna. The Czechs would bend but never break. In 1618, the Thirty Years' War started with the famous **defenestration of Prague,** in which two governor-agents of the Hapsburgs were hurled from a window in the palace of Prague. The Bohemians consummated this act of rebellion by deposing Ferdinand II and electing Frederick V as the new Bohemian king. Frederick V, known in Czech history as the "Winter King," fled to Holland following the **Battle of White Mountain** (1620), which ended in disaster for the Bohemian rebels.

For the next three centuries, Czech nationalism would be suppressed but it would not die. On the contrary, it reawakened with a vengeance in the second half of the nineteenth century as the so-called **Czech National Revival.** World War I delivered a deathblow to the Austro-Hungarian Empire and gave new impetus to the drive for an independent Czech nation-state. A small nation with a proud tradition befitting a much bigger country was about to enter a new era of freedom and self-government—or so it seemed.

The First Slavic Democracy   Czechoslovakia came into being after World War I (see Map 5.5). Established in 1918 as an independent republic, it was the only functioning democracy in Slavic Europe during the interwar period. Dr. Thomas G. Masaryk (1850–1937), Czechoslovakia's principal founder, succeeded in melding the two parts of the country—Bohemia and Moravia, the Czech lands to the west, and

Slovakia in the east—into a single state under a constitution that provided for a freely elected parliament that in turn elected the president. Appropriately enough, Masaryk became Czechoslovakia's first and most beloved president. He was perfect for the job: his father was a Slovak, his mother a Moravian, and his wife an American! A philosopher and teacher by profession, he was an extraordinary leader who displayed both wisdom and moral courage throughout his long life.

Carved out of the Austro-Hungarian Empire, Czechoslovakia was a hybrid state from the beginning. The Czech lands were part of Austria before World War I, and Slovakia was part of Hungary. (Hungary lost one-third of its territory and a significant part of its population to Czechoslovakia and Romania, which still affects relations among these three countries to this day.) The Czechs were more numerous than the Slovaks (by almost two to one), more Western, and industrially more advanced. Although the languages they speak are so similar they have no difficulty communicating with one another (indeed, both use the Roman rather than the Cyrillic alphabet), both Czechs and Slovaks insist that Czech and Slovak are distinct languages rather than one language spoken in slightly different dialects. From the outset, then, the political institutions of Czechoslovakia had to bridge economic, cultural, ethnolinguistic, and geographic divides.

Totalitarianism Right and Left   Czechoslovakia's golden age of democracy ended in 1938 following the infamous appeasement of Hitler by British Prime Minister Neville Chamberlain at Munich. Chamberlain conceded the **Sudetenland,** a part of Czechoslovakia inhabited by 3 million ethnic Germans, to Hitler in return for the Nazi leader's false promise of peace. The Nazi occupation lasted from 1939 to 1945 and helped set the stage for a new kind of totalitarian dictatorship by brutalizing the society and introducing police-state methods into a country that had been governed by good and decent leaders committed to constitutionalism and the rule of law.

After World War II, the fate of Czechoslovakia was in the hands of the Soviet Union, reflecting the fact that the Soviet army had played the largest role in liberating the country from Nazi rule. The communists staged a coup in February 1948, ousting President Eduard Beneš and establishing the Communist People's Republic of Czechoslovakia (changed to Socialist Republic in 1960). Subservient to Moscow from its inception, communist Czechoslovakia became a federal system in 1969 following the Prague Spring uprising, a popular uprising against communist rule put down by invading Soviet forces the previous year. Until the demise of communist rule at the end of 1989, Czechoslovakia had a reputation as one of the most rigidly Stalinist states in the Soviet bloc.

The story of how and why Czechoslovakia committed political euthanasia a few years after the return of democracy belongs to the next chapter. Suffice it to say that the *o* connecting the Czech lands and Slovakia was like a wedding ring that no longer fit.

Yugoslavia: Federation or Tinderbox?

The Balkan region has been aptly described as a tinderbox. For centuries this region (Map 5.6) was a crucible of war and its most important city, Belgrade, was a

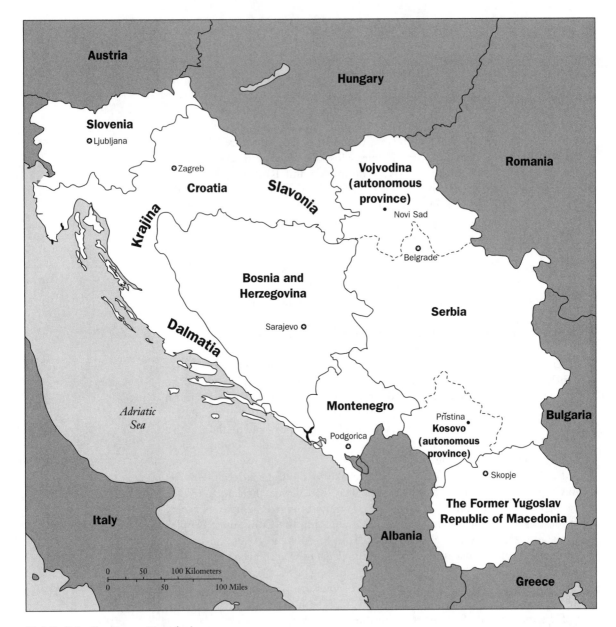

MAP 5.6 The Former Yugoslavia

SOURCE: Adapted from the University of Texas Libraries, The University of Texas at Austin.

prized pawn in a strategic tug-of-war involving the clashing interests and competing religions of various great powers and several empires (see Figure 5.5). In modern times, an independent Serbia did not emerge until the nineteenth century and did not reinvent itself as a country called Yugoslavia until 1929.

The Balkan region was a cauldron of conflict early in the twentieth century and again at the end of the century. In this area, Yugoslavia had long been

7th millennium B.C. Beginnings

Earliest known Neolithic settlement in area of modern Belgrade (Serbian capital).

1st century B.C.E. Roman Period

Romans colonize Singidinum (Belgrade).

441–878 C.E. Invasions and Slavic Conquest

Huns destroy Singidinum (Belgrade) in 441; Byzantine Emperor Justinian I rebuilds Singidinum (535). Avars conquer and sack city (584); Byzantine Empire regains it (592). Avars again destroy Singidinum (7th century). Slavs conquer city around 630 C.E..

9th century Bulgarian Era

Bulgarians control fortress (827). First written record of name "Beograd" or Belgrade (878), meaning "White City." Hungarians attack Belgrade (896).

971–1072 Belgrade in Tug of War

Byzantines regain control of Belgrade in 971; Bulgarians take it back in 976; Byzantines conquer city twice in 11th century (1018 and 1072); Hungarians destroy city in 1096 but Byzantines remain in control.

12th century Tug of War Continues

Byzantines and Hungarians vie for control of Belgrade. Hungarians twice sack Belgrade (1127 and 1182); Byzantines regain city by diplomacy (1185).

1230–1427 Precursor to Modern Serbia

Serbian King Stefan Dragutin takes control of Belgrade (1284); first time the city of Belgrade comes under Serbian rule; Belgrade becomes capital of Serbia (1403).

1427–1688 Tug of War Again

Hungarians repeatedly battle Ottoman Empire for control of Belgrade and Serbia. In 1521, Suleiman the Magnificent conquers Belgrade and establishes period of Ottoman rule.

1688–1841 Between Two Empires

Duke Maximilian captures Belgrade (1688), but Ottomans recapture it two years later; Prince of Savoy captures Belgrade (1717); Treaty of Belgrade (1739) between Austria and Ottoman Empire returns city to Ottoman rule; Belgrade changes hands several more times between 1739 and 1830.

1830–1914 Birth of Modern Serbia

Mahmud II proclaims Serbia autonomous (self-governing) in 1830; Belgrade becomes the capital of the Princedom of Serbia (1841); Great Powers at the Berlin Congress recognize the independence of Serbia (Berlin Treaty, 1878); Kingdom of Serbia proclaimed in1882; World War I puts future of Serbia in doubt; Belgrade becomes capital of the Kingdom of Serbs, Croats, and Slovenes (future Yugoslavia) in 1918.

F I G U R E 5.5 Landmarks in Serbian History

considered the country most likely to disintegrate. That it stayed together for more than four decades after World War II was the result largely of the leadership skills of one man, Josip Broz Tito.

Tito's Fragile State The largely Slavic population of Yugoslavia consisted of eight primary ethnic groups speaking one of four languages (Serbo-Croat, Macedonian, Slovenian, and Albanian) and comprising three distinct religious communities (Eastern Orthodox, Roman Catholic, and Muslim (see Table 5.1).

TABLE 5.1 Composition of the Population of Prebreakup Yugoslavia

Ethnic Group	Share of Population (percent)	Religion
Serbs	37	Eastern Orthodox
Croats	20	Roman Catholic
Bosnian Muslims	9	Muslim
Slovenes	8	Roman Catholic
Albanians	8	Muslim
Macedonians	6	Eastern Orthodox
Montenegrins	3	Eastern Orthodox
Hungarians	2	Roman Catholic

After World War II, Marshal Tito, the popular leader of the communist-inspired **partisans** who fought valiantly against the Axis powers, created one of the most complex political and economic systems anywhere in the world. This complexity was a reflection of the fragile ethnic and historical basis for the Yugoslav state, which came into being after World War I (see Figure 5.6). Tito himself was the glue that held the country together. After his death in 1980, the country began to come apart. Before the violent breakup in 1991–1992, there were six constituent republics and two autonomous provinces (see Table 5.2), each with its own governmental apparatus (presidency, prime minister and cabinet, indirectly elected assembly, and judiciary).

Between East and West   Tito's decision to break with Stalin in 1948 was a turning point in the history of world communism. It ensured that Moscow would use its control over the rest of Eastern Europe to try to isolate Belgrade and force Tito out. This left Tito little choice but to turn to the West for trade and aid.

But how could Tito, a fervent communist, expect a sympathetic hearing in the industrial democracies, particularly the United States? Communism and capitalism are antithetical, and Europe in 1948 was feeling the chill of the Cold War. Tito's solution was to complicate the picture enough so that the leaders of the "free" (noncommunist) world could deal with Yugoslavia without seeming to be consorting with the enemy. To this end, he kept Yugoslavia's borders open and allowed free enterprise on a limited scale (quite unlike the Soviet model). People could leave and return at will. Also, the government did not try to ban Western culture (including rock music, blue jeans, and marijuana) as other communist states did. Yugoslavia was a popular summer destination for tens of thousands of Americans, English was widely spoken, and American fads were quickly adopted by Yugoslav youth. In general, Yugoslavia did not have the look or feel of a communist country.

Tito wanted to show the world (and Moscow) that he could find a way between communism and capitalism that would be a model for the newly emerging nations of Africa and Asia. Indeed, Tito established himself as an early

1918–1929 Birth of Yugoslavia

Kingdom of Serbs, Croats, and Slovenes formed at end of World War I. Croatia, Slovenia, and Bosnia-Herzegovina had been part of Austro-Hungarian Empire. Serbia and Macedonia were independent states; renamed Yugoslavia in 1929.

1945–1980 Tito's Yugoslavia

Following World War II, monarchy becomes a one-party communist state under Marshal Tito (called Federal People's Republic of Yugoslavia). Comprises six "republics" (Serbia, Croatia, Bosnia-Herzegovina, Macedonia, Slovenia, and Montenegro and two provinces Kosovo and Vojvodina). Tito breaks with Stalin (1948). Tito's death in 1980 leaves future of Yugoslav federation in doubt.

1980–1991 Post-Tito Yugoslavia

Without Tito as authority figure and honest broker, tensions between Belgrade and republics/nationalities/ethnic groups mount; Serbian Slobodan Milosevic becomes Serbian Communist leader in 1987, revives dream of Greater Serbia, "elected" president in 1989. Yugoslavia begins to disintegrate.

1991–2000 Milosevic Dictatorship and Breakup of Yugoslavia

Slovenia and Croatia declare independence (June 1991); Macedonia declares independence (January 1992); Bosnia-Herzegovina declares independence and Serbia and Montenegro form "Republic of Yugoslavia" (April 1992). Wars and atrocities ("ethnic cleansing") take a terrible toll on civilian populations; worst violence occurs in Bosnia (1992-1995) and Kosovo (1996-1999). Vojislav Kostunica wins elections in September 2000 but Milosevic refuses to concede. Mass demonstrations in Belgrade force Milosevic to step down, ending last communist dictatorship in former Yugoslavia.

2001–present Democratic Serbia

Milosevic arrested and turned over to international tribunal to be tried for war crimes; rump state of Yugoslavia formally dissolved, replaced by loose federation of Serbia and Montenegro; popular prime minister of Serbia, Zoran Djindjic, assassinated; resurgence of ethnic violence in Kosovo in 2004.

FIGURE 5.6 Landmarks in Yugoslavia's History

leader of the nonaligned movement—Third World nations that sought to avoid choosing sides in the east-west conflict and to redefine global issues along north-south lines (that is, developed versus developing countries).

Building the Workers' Paradise   Tito's reforms were aimed at decentralizing decision-making authority—the antithesis of the highly centralized Stalinist system. One of the first and most dramatic steps in this direction was the introduction of **workers' self-management.** The idea was to give the workers control over production (hence responsibility for it) via freely elected workers' councils and management boards. Even the enterprise manager was to be elected by the workers.

Workers' self-management, Tito reasoned, would remove one major obstacle to labor productivity: workers' alienation. On the positive side, workers would take greater pride in their work, leading to improved quality of goods; they would better understand the problems of management and thus would avoid unreasonable demands and expectations; and they would develop a greater loyalty to the collective—both the enterprise and their co-workers.

TABLE 5.2 Prebreakup Yugoslavia

Republic or Province (capital)	Area (square miles)	Population
Republics		
Bosnia-Herzegovina (Sarajevo)	19,741	4,116,439
Croatia (Zagreb)	21,829	4,578,109
Macedonia (Skopje)	9,928	1,913,571
Montenegro (Titograd)	5,333	583,475
Serbia (Belgrade)	21,609	5,666,060
Slovenia (Ljubljana)	7,819	1,883,764
Autonomous Provinces		
Kosovo (Pristina)	4,203	1,584,558
Vojvodina (Novi Sad)	8,303	2,028,239

Within this system evolved indicative planning to set overall targets for the various sectors of the economy. These targets were guidelines, not obligatory goals. In agriculture, too, the state relinquished direct control: collectivization was halted, and the state reprivatized most farmland in the 1950s.

In the 1960s, the Yugoslav leadership gave greater autonomy to plant managers and further reduced the role of central administrators. As in the West, the market forces of supply and demand set prices, and profitability became the test of efficiency. A state planning agency remained active in Belgrade, but production targets were set at the republic level and were coordinated by the federal agency. Under the impact of these reforms, Yugoslavia developed the most consumer-oriented economy in Eastern Europe.

How well did these reforms work? The results were mixed. While Tito was alive, the economy remained healthy, but in the 1980s a number of chronic problems emerged, including mounting external debt, a falling standard of living, and rising unemployment. In addition, despite workers' self-management, low productivity caused prices to climb and energy costs were high. And even harder times lay ahead.

Centralized Federalism   Economic reforms in Yugoslavia were accompanied by changes in the formal structures of the government. These changes were designed to create the appearance of decentralized, democratic republicanism.

Under Tito, it did not matter much who held what official position. As founder and chief architect of the nation, Tito called the shots, and no one expected otherwise. This extraordinary consensus enabled Tito to experiment with various forms of political power sharing without having to relinquish any personal power. He designed an elaborate set of institutions that shrouded the dominant role of the Yugoslav Communist Party (officially the League of Yugoslav Communists) in the trappings of federalism and democracy. Under this unique system, Yugoslavia had a rotating collective chief executive that consisted of nine persons, one from each of the six republics and the two autonomous provinces, and one ex officio member representing the Communist Party. The Federal Assembly elected a chairman to a one-year term. Under a special constitutional provision, Tito served as president until his death in 1980. The system was therefore never really tested during Tito's lifetime.

The thirty-three-member **Federal Executive Council** (the cabinet) was the functional equivalent of the Council of Ministers in the USSR. The collective presidency nominated a member of the bicameral Federal Assembly to be president of the Federal Executive Council, and the Federal Assembly then voted confirmation. The Yugoslav premier was thus chosen in a manner similar to that of many parliamentary democracies. The council was responsible for the government's day-to-day operations.

The Federal Assembly was a bicameral legislature made up of the Federal Chamber and the Chamber of Republics and Provinces. The electoral process was byzantine in its complexity, but during Tito's lifetime it mattered little because elections were stage managed (and all candidates were screened) by a communist front organization called the Socialist Alliance of Working People of Yugoslavia (SSRNJ). Ultimately, local assemblies chose delegates to the Federal Chamber, and provincial or republic-level assemblies chose delegates to the other chamber.

The basic unit of local government, the commune, had considerable administrative authority and some autonomy in matters not expressly delegated to the federal government, the constituent republics, or the autonomous provinces. Government at this level involved extensive citizen participation. One student of Yugoslav politics reported in 1977:

> The communes have become key local units that have several primary concerns. One of these is economic, including planning, investments, internal trade, and supervision over economic enterprises. Another concern is municipal services, such as water supply, sewers, streets, and public utilities. A third comprises the area of "social management," that is, citizen control over public utilities.[36]

Administration of municipal services and public utilities is certainly relevant to the quality of life, but such matters are trivial compared with the momentous issues that confront whole societies and nations.

Despite the elaborate façade of federalism and democracy, political power remained a Communist Party monopoly to the end. Other political parties were banned, and dissent was kept to a minimum. Marxist-Leninist dogma pervaded the press, the arts, and propaganda. In the final analysis, Yugoslavia was a one-party state.

Nearly a decade after Yugoslavia split with the Soviet Union, Milovan Djilas, Tito's former comrade in arms and perhaps the most famous inside critic of Soviet-style communism in the postwar period, published a book called *The New Class*. (Djilas was in prison at the time for expressing the ideas contained in the book.) "The greatest illusion," he wrote, "was that industrialization and collectivization in the USSR, and destruction of capitalist ownership, would result in a classless society." Instead, he argued, a **new class** emerged in place of the old one:

The roots of the new class were implanted in a special party of the Bolshevik type. Lenin was right in his view that his party was an exception in the history of human society, although he did not suspect that it would be the beginning of a new class. . . . The party . . . is the core of that class, and its base. . . . The new class may be said to be made up of those who have special privileges and economic preference because of the administrative monopoly they hold.[37]

Nonetheless, thanks to Tito, the Yugoslav Communist Party had a stronger bias toward collective leadership than its Soviet counterpart.

Thus, Tito balanced regional and ethnic interests in the top party organs much as he did in the collective presidency and the Federal Executive Council. This system may have ensured representation of the major parts of Yugoslavia's diverse multiethnic society, but it did not constitute a participatory democracy. Nor could such a façade resist the centuries-old resentments of those various ethnic groups after Tito's death.

SUMMARY AND CONCLUSIONS

Slavic Europe has developed along quite different lines from Western Europe. Powerful intellectual and cultural movements such as the Renaissance and Reformation never penetrated deeply into most of Eastern Europe (Poland and the Czech Republic are two notable exceptions). Primarily for reasons of geography and climate, Slavic nations generally developed along very different lines compared to the countries of Western Europe. They lagged behind the West in the development of modern technology and industry. They also failed to develop a strong educated middle class of shopkeepers, entrepreneurs, and professionals (teachers, doctors, and lawyers) in parallel with the West. Finally, in the absence of a rising middle class, most Slavic nations did not develop liberal democratic institutions or traditions before World War II. (Czechoslovakia, however, was a full-fledged parliamentary democracy in the period between the two world wars.)

The history of the region bears scant evidence of fraternal ties among Slavic nations beyond ethnolinguistic similarities. On the contrary, outbreaks of ethnic conflict have been quite common except during the period of Soviet domination. The Soviet Union ruled most of the Slavic world for four decades after World War II; Russia, in turn, dominated the Soviet Union. The nations of Eastern Europe have long histories of foreign domination by imperial powers—Russia, Germany, Austria-Hungary, and the Ottoman Turks.

Five centuries ago, Poland was a great power in its own right. Ukrainians and Czechs can also look back on a golden age when they were prosperous and independent states. Yugoslavia came into being after World War I following centuries of ethnic conflict and subjugation at the hands of powerful neighbors. Serbia, the most powerful state in the Yugoslav federation, was under Ottoman (Turkish) rule from 1521 until the nineteenth century.

In 1989, one communist regime after another fell in a wave of popular discontent and brought an end to the period of *Pax Sovietica* —stability based on Soviet economic and military dominance. In December 1991, the Soviet Union collapsed after an abortive coup by hardliners. In the next chapter we turn our attention to the attempt to transplant Western institutions in predominantly Slavic Europe.

KEY TERMS

autarky

Balkans

Battle of White Mountain

blat

Bolsheviks

Caucasus

central planning

Cheka

collectivization

containment

Council of Constance

cult of personality

Czech lands

Czech National Revival

defenestration of Prague

de-Stalinization

détente

Eastern Orthodox rite

Federal Executive Council

First Partition of Poland

Five-Year Plans

Great Moravian Empire

Great Terror

gulag

Helsinki Accords

Hussites

ideology

Iron Curtain

KGB

Kievan Rus

kolkhoz

kulaki

Marxism–Leninism

Mensheviks

Mongol yoke

Narodnaya Volya ("People's Will")

narodnichestvo

narodniki

neo-Stalinism

new class

New Economic Policy (NEP)

October Revolution

Okhrana

Partisans

Polish underground proletariat

Přemyslid kings

Red Army

Revolution of 1905

Romanov

Russification

Secret Speech

Slavic

Soviet Union

soviets

Stalinism

Sudetenland

virgin lands

War Communism

Warsaw Pact

workers' self-management

SUGGESTED READINGS

Billington, James. *The Icon and the Axe: An Interpretive History of Russian Culture.* New York: Random House, 1994.

Brent, Jonathan, and Naumov, Vladimir P. *Stalin's Last Crime: The Plot against the Jewish Doctors, 1948-1953.* New York: HarperCollins, 2003.

Cohen, Philip J. *Serbia's Secret War: Propaganda and the Deceit of History.* College Station: Texas A&M University, 1996.

Conquest, Robert. *Harvest of Sorrow: Soviet Collectivization and the Terror-Famine.* New York: Oxford University Press, 1987.

Davies, Norman. *God's Playground: A History of Poland.* Rev. ed. New York: Columbia University Press, 2004.

De Madariaga, Isabela. *Ivan the Terrible.* New Haven: Yale University Press, 2005.

Dziewanowski, M. Kamil. *A History of Soviet Russia and Its Aftermath.* Englewood Cliffs, NJ: Prentice-Hall, 1997.

Figes, Orlando. *Natasha's Dance: A Cultural History of Russia.* New York: Henry Holt, 2003.

Leff, Carol. *The Czech and Slovak Republics.* Boulder, CO: Westview Press, 1996.

Lewin, Moshe. *The Soviet Century.* New York: Verso, 2005.

Lieven, Dominic. *Nicholas II.* New York: St. Martin's Press, 1996.

Lukes, Igor. *Czechoslovakia between Stalin and Hitler: The Diplomacy of Edward Benes in the 1930s.* New York: Oxford University Press, 1996.

Martin, Janet. *Medieval Russia, 980–1584.* New York: Cambridge University Press, 1996.

Massie, Robert. *Nicholas and Alexandria.* New York: Random House, 2000.

——— *Peter the Great: His Life and World.* New York: Ballantine Books, 1986.

Montefiore, Simon Sebag. *Stalin: The Court of the Red Tsar.* London: Weidenfeld and Nicholson, 2003.

——— *Potemkin: Catherine the Great's Imperial Partner.* New York: Vintage Books, 2005.

Pipes, Richard. *Russia under the Old Regime.* New York: Viking Penguin, 1997.

Reid, Anna. *Borderland: A Journey through the History of Ukraine.* Boulder, CO: Westview Press, 2000.

Riasanovsky, Nicholas V. *A History of Russia.* 4th ed. New York: Oxford University Press, 1977.

Robson, Roy R. *Old Believers in Modern Russia.* DeKalb, IL: Northern Illinois University Press, 1996.

Thurston, Robert W. *Life and Terror in Stalin's Russia, 1934–1941.* New Haven, CO: Yale University Press, 1996.

Zamoyska, Adam. *The Polish Way: A Thousand Year History of the Poles and Their Culture.* New York: Hippocrene Books, 1997.

WEB SITES

www.departments.bucknell.edu/russian/material.html

www.historywiz.com/russia.htm

www.uni.edu/becker/Russian2.html

members.valley.net/~transnat/

www.uea.ac.uk/his/webcours/russia/links/

www.rootsweb.com/~polwgw/history.html

NOTES

1. Louis J. Halle, *The Cold War as History* (New York: HarperCollins, 1991), pp. 103–104.

2. Alexis de Tocqueville, *Democracy in America* (New York: Knopf, 1945), p. 452.

3. Vadim Medish, *The Soviet Union* (Englewood Cliffs, NJ: Prentice-Hall, 1987), p. 23.

4. Nicholas V. Riasanovsky, *A History of Russia,* 4th ed. (New York: Oxford University Press, 1977), p. 347.

5. Medish, *Soviet Union,* p. 22.

6. See, for example, Paul Kennedy, *The Rise and Fall of the Great Powers* (New York: Vintage Books, 1987), pp. 70–77.

7. Medish, *Soviet Union,* pp. 22–23.

8. Berdyaev, *Origin of Russian Communism,* pp. 8–9.

9. Riasanovsky, *History of Russia,* p. 425.

10. Ibid., p. 426.

11. Robert Conquest, *V. I. Lenin* (New York: Viking Penguin, 1972), p. 32.

12. Isaac Deutscher, *Stalin: A Political Biography* (New York: Vintage Books, 1960), p. 550.

13. In the Stalinist tradition, Five-Year Plans were documents that set forth general economic goals. These plans, drawn up at five-year intervals, provided the framework for the annual plans that prescribed detailed production targets (quotas) for each industrial and agricultural enterprise.

14. See, for example, Robert Conquest, *The Harvest of Sorrow: Soviet Collectivization and the Terror-Famine* (New York: Oxford University Press, 1987); and Adam B. Ulam, *Stalin* (Boston: Beacon, 1989).

15. Riasanovsky, *History of Russia,* p. 551.

16. See Edward Crankshaw, *Khrushchev: A Career* (New York: Viking Penguin, 1966).

17. Deutscher, *Stalin,* pp. 550–551.

18. Alexander Werth, *Russia at War, 1941–1945* (New York: Avon, 1964), pp. 904–906.

19. On the question of forced labor, one eyewitness estimates that at least a million Russian refugees were "perfidiously returned by Allied authorities into Soviet hands" in 1946 and 1947. The same writer records many other instances of mass arrests and banishment to the gulags during this period. See Alexander Solzhenitsyn, *The Gulag Archipelago, 1918–1956* (New York: Harper & Row, 1973), p. 85.

20. Roy A. Medvedev and Zhores A. Medvedev, *Khrushchev: The Years in Power* (New York: Norton, 1978), p. 121.

21. See J. Philip Rogers, *The Future of European Security* (New York: St. Martin's Press, 1993).

22. Hedrick Smith, *The Russians* (New York: Ballantine, 1984), p. 332.

23. Ibid.

24. See David K. Shipler, *Russia: Broken Idols, Solemn Dreams* (New York: Viking Penguin, 1983), p. 200.

25. Smith, *Russians,* pp. 410–411.

26. Ibid., p. 411.

27. Ivan Volgyes, *Politics in Eastern Europe* (Homewood, IL: Dorsey, 1986), pp. 29–30.

28. Paul Lendvai, *Eagles in Cobwebs: Nationalism and Communism in the Balkans* (Garden City, NY: Anchor/Doubleday, 1969), p. 15.

29. Volgyes, *Politics in Eastern Europe,* p. 297.

30. For a provocative theory that purports to explain why some societies succeed and others do not, see Jared Diamond, *Guns, Germs, and Steel: The Fate of Human Societies.* New York: Norton, 1997.

31. Alan Palmer, *The Lands Between: A History of East-Central Europe since the Congress of Vienna* (New York: Macmillan, 1970), p. 2.

32. Ibid.

33. Ibid.

34. Ibid. p. 4.

35. Riasanovsky, *History of Russia,* pp. 25–30; see also David Mackenzie and Michael W. Curran, *A History of Russia and the Soviet Union,* 3rd edition (Belmont, CA: Wadsworth, 1987), pp. 23–29.

36. Richard F. Starr, *Communist Regimes in Eastern Europe,* 5th ed. (Stanford, CA: Hoover Institution, 1988), p. 194.

37. Milovan Djilas, *The New Class* (New York: Praeger, 1957), pp. 37–40.

6

Politics in Eastern Europe
Blending the Old and the New

*F*rom *World War II until the watershed events of 1989, Moscow imposed the Soviet model of* scientific socialism *on its client states in Eastern Europe. That model shaped the region's approach to politics, government, and economy for nearly half a century (longer in Russia and its empire). In many ways, Russia remains an enigma. An immense country with problems to match, post-Soviet Russia has the potential to play a major role in European and global affairs, as it did when it was the great colossus of world communism—the "other" superpower. Will Russia join Europe and reengage in world politics or revert to its old habits of despotism, autarky, paranoia, and xenophobia?*

In this chapter we also take a close look at the transitions occurring in the former Soviet bloc countries. These countries became independent as a result of spontaneous democratic movements that swept across Eastern Europe in 1989. Creating new political institutions, converting centrally planned economies to market economies, and remodeling political cultures are three major problems of transition that faced (and still face) them. Unsurprisingly, some have dealt with these challenges more successfully than others, and none has yet completed the transition or entirely overcome the obstacles that remain as a legacy of the old totalitarian state. It is thus important to understand that transitions are not a given, that they can change directions, or go sideways.

Besides Russia, we again focus on Poland, Ukraine, the Czech Republic, and Serbia (formerly Yugoslavia). Although so far no East European country has caught up economically with Western Europe, Poland and the Czech Republic (along with Hungary, Slovenia, and the Baltic states) have made the fastest progress, whereas Ukraine and Serbia (and, to a lesser extent, Romania and Bulgaria) have lagged behind. A few countries in the region—including Belarus, Moldova, and Albania are impoverished, mired in the past, and going nowhere.

Except for its vast oil and gas reserves, Russia would be at risk of becoming a postcommunist basket case as well. Despite a rapidly declining population and a flaccid economy, Russia continues to possess a vast arsenal of modern weapons. Russia poses no immediate military threat to the West so long as it does not disintegrate. Paradoxically, a failed Russian state would pose a greater potential threat to the West than a successful one. We begin with an in-depth look at Russia today.

To understand where Russia is going, we need to know where it has been. We cannot make sense of politics in contemporary Russia without getting inside the Stalinist political system. As you read what follows, try to imagine how living in such an oppressive society would affect you personally. How might it change your values, work habits, and relationships with family and friends? If you were deprived of the freedom Westerners take for granted, would you be more idealistic, trusting, and ambitious, or less? What would be the cumulative effect on society as a whole? Would it pay to be honest, trustworthy, and hard working, or would deceit and sloth be more rational? Questions of this kind are crucial to an analysis of what's wrong with Russia today, why the Russian economy has fallen into a deep slump, and why democracy gets mixed reviews (at best) from most Russians now.

THE LEGACY OF SOVIET COMMUNISM

The Soviet Constitution proclaimed the Communist Party of the Soviet Union (CPSU) the "leading and guiding force of Soviet society and the nucleus of its political system." As previously noted, the party operated according to the Leninist principle of **democratic centralism** (an oxymoron if ever there was one). The preamble to the party rules unequivocally stated that "monolithic cohesion" and "a high degree of conscious discipline on the part of all Communists are an inviolable law of the CPSU."[1]

Since 1918 the CPSU had been the sole repository of legitimate authority in the Soviet Union and throughout Slavic Europe. For seven decades after the October Revolution of 1917, the party was an all-pervasive presence in Soviet society. Its tentacles reached deeply into four key structures: the state bureaucracy, the secret police (KGB), the economy (a kind of giant corporation), and the military.

The party's leading role was rooted in Leninist ideology, which stressed the need for a **vanguard of the proletariat.** Karl Marx used the word *proletariat* to designate the oppressed working class, which, he theorized, would eventually seize power in a revolutionary takeover. Lenin asserted that strong leadership—in the form of the Communist Party—was necessary to galvanize the masses into revolutionary action. These two seminal ideas—that revolution is the path to working-class power and that the Communist Party is the necessary catalyst—are

TABLE 6.1 Soviet Leaders, from Lenin to Gorbachev[*]

Leader	Years in Power
V. I. Lenin[†]	1917–1924
Josef Stalin[†]	1922–1953
Nikita S. Khrushchev	1953–1964
Leonid I. Brezhnev	1964–1982
Yuri V. Andropov	1982–1984
Konstantin U. Chernenko	1984–1985
Mikhail S. Gorbachev[‡]	1985–1991

[*]All top Soviet leaders, whatever specific title(s) they may have preferred or position(s) they may have held, presided over the Politburo.

[†]As chairman of the Council of People's Commissars, Lenin was the de facto head of the party and the government: although Stalin was named general secretary of the party in 1922, he was unable to assert unquestioned control over the party until after Lenin's death in 1924.

[‡]In 1989, the office of chairman of the presidium of the Supreme Soviet was strengthened and renamed "chairman of the Supreme Soviet." Gorbachev was elected to this new office and served until the Congress of People's Deputies created the executive presidency in March 1990. The office of chairman of the Supreme Soviet remained, but its executive and ceremonial functions were transferred to the executive presidency.

basic tenets of Marxism-Leninism. No Soviet leader before Gorbachev had dared (or cared) to renounce them (see Table 6.1).

Soviet "Democracy" and Potemkin's Ghost

As students of Russian history know, any mention of a **Potemkin village** refers to something that appears to be true or real but in fact is only an illusion. Prince Potemkin (1739–1791) was the favorite minister of Catherine the Great, who, according to a celebrated legend, contrived to please and impress the all-powerful tsarina by showing her a supposedly typical village in the country. But the "village" was a ruse: it consisted of false fronts and a cast of characters in costumes playing well-rehearsed roles—like a Hollywood set. The story of Potemkin's trickery may or may not be true, but it has become part of Russia's rich folklore, and it accurately depicts what Soviet "democracy" was (and was not) all about.

On its face, the Soviet government looked much like Western democracies. All citizens at least 18 years of age were eligible to vote; election to local and regional soviets (or councils) were held every two years, and elections were held every four years for the **Supreme Soviet** (national legislature). The latter functioned like a parliament; its 1500 members were elected to two chambers of equal size, the Soviet of Nationalities and the Soviet of the Union. The Supreme Soviet chose the **Council of Ministers**, which implemented the laws it passed. The same pattern was replicated on lower levels all the way down to the local soviets.

Elections to the Supreme Soviet and thousands of soviets at the republic, provincial, and local levels were held with much fanfare. Everyone was required by law to vote; the government claimed that 99.99 percent of all eligible voters cast ballots in national elections. (According to official figures, one election in the Turkmen SSR was almost perfect: only one voter out of 1.5 million failed to vote!)

But real power resided elsewhere. The Communist Party (CPSU) monopolized control of all key positions in the state bureaucracy, secret police (KGB), and military. This control was exercised through an interlocking directorate made up of two bodies—the **Politburo** and the **Secretariat**. The term *interlocking* is apt here because the same individuals were often members of both groups. The Politburo (or "political bureau") and the Secretariat (comprising party chieftains called secretaries) were actually twin organs of the Communist Party and, in theory, were not part of the government at all. The General Secretary was the most powerful figure in the government (although a premier who presided over the Council of Ministers was the formal head of government and a president "elected" by the Supreme Soviet was the head of state). In practice, a dozen or so party bosses ruled the country. Even the party's own legislative body, known as the **Central Committee,** existed largely to rubber-stamp the Politburo's decisions. Thus, the Soviet regime was an oligarchic dictatorship disguised as a democracy.

The Negation of Economics: How Not to Compete (or Succeed)

Beginning in the 1950s, the Soviet Union forged a kind of East bloc common market called **Comecon**—officially the Council of Mutual Economic Assistance (CEMA). Later in the 1950s, Khrushchev boasted, "We will bury you"—meaning the Soviet Union and the "world socialist system" would race ahead of the West *economically*. But Khrushchev's prediction turned out to be dead wrong.

By the 1980s, there was a major question looming about whether state planning was still appropriate for industrially developed socialist states. The specter of a stagnant workers' state had haunted the Soviet Union and its Warsaw Pact allies at least since the early 1960s, and the East was falling farther and farther behind the West. Recall that Khrushchev had launched a series of ill-starred reforms in industry and agriculture (as well as a radical reorganization of the party-state machinery) before he was ousted in 1964. Later in the decade, Hungary experimented with market-style reforms, and Czechoslovakia tried to introduce multiparty democracy in 1968. In the Soviet Union, Premier Alexei Kosygin tried to restart the stalled reform effort. In so doing, he was guided by the theoretical writings of Soviet economist Evsei Liberman. These early reform episodes reflected a growing awareness that the system was not working.

The **Liberman reforms** were designed to decentralize economic decision making. Managers were to be given considerable discretion in making microeconomic production and investment decisions. Enterprises were even to be charged interest on the capital they used. Given more latitude, "managers were expected to take risks, innovate, reduce costs, and thereby increase the sales and profits of their enterprises."[2] Had Libermanism triumphed, Soviet managers would have had to operate much as Western entrepreneurs do. But it was not to be. The entrenched party-state bureaucracy, at whose expense the reforms would have come, quickly aborted the embryonic reform movement. In retrospect, the failure of the reforms in the 1960s sealed the fate of the Soviet Union and its satellites in Eastern Europe.

Marxism versus the Marketplace

According to the Soviet constitution, the nation's economy was "based on the Socialist ownership of all the means of production," including the land. Two forms of socialist ownership were recognized in the USSR: state ownership and collective, or cooperative, ownership. The former was considered a higher form because it encompassed the entire society, whereas the latter was a lower form because it was limited to relatively few people. This distinction was clearly evident in agriculture, which was divided into **collective farms (*kolkhozy*)** and **state farms (*sovkhozy*).** The farmers themselves technically owned the collective farms, whereas state farms were owned by society at large and were run by the government, which gave them preferential treatment (more funds, better equipment). State farms were huge, averaging well over 90,000 acres—five or six times the size of the average collective farm. They were operated like an assembly line in an industrial enterprise and were managed by professionals trained in such fields as agronomy, animal husbandry, and horticulture. State farmers, like industrial workers, were specialized by function and were paid an hourly wage. In effect, the Soviet government sought to industrialize agriculture.

The state also owned all industrial enterprises, public utilities, banks, transportation systems, and mass-communication facilities as well as most retail outlets and repair shops. As a result, nearly everybody (approximately 85 percent of the work force) worked for the state. Those who did not work for the state belonged to cooperatives or collectives, which, though not state owned, were tightly controlled by the state.

This employment monopoly gave the state enormous control over the individual. Furthermore, a so-called **antiparasite law** made it a crime not to work. If you were fired for any reason (including unauthorized political activity), where could you go to find another job? The employer who dismissed you from one job could bar you from another and at the same time put you on the wrong side of the law—a kind of double jeopardy that very effectively kept Soviet workers in line.

The Concept of Central Planning

The idea of **central planning** is simple enough: decide what society needs, put the people to work, and distribute material benefits fairly. Nobody owns anything but transportable personal possessions—for example, clothing, furniture, and books. (It was possible to own a car in the Soviet Union, but most people either could not afford one and or were put on a waiting list for years.)

Prices are set by the state; they do not fluctuate in response to the market forces of supply and demand, as under capitalism. The Soviet economy—the largest ever to adopt this system—was thus planned and managed from the top, whereas a market economy is driven from the bottom, by consumers.

The State Planning Committee—or **Gosplan**—had primary responsibility for charting the course of the Soviet economy but had to coordinate its work with a number of other bureaucratic entities, including the State Committee on

Prices, the State Bank (Gosbank), the Ministry of Finance, the State Committee on Material and Technical Supplies (Gossnab), and nearly fifty central ministries (as well as 750 in the fifteen union republics) that ran the various industries.

The complicated planning process involved both long-range (five-year) and short-range (one-year) plans. These plans set production growth targets for the various sectors of the economy, which were then translated into output quotas for individual enterprises. The short-range plan contained the growth targets for the whole economy for the current year. The various ministries then broke down this general blueprint into monthly plans with quotas for every factory, plant, enterprise, and association in the Soviet Union. (If you think this process sounds complicated and cumbersome, you are right.) The plan always reflected the political priorities of the top leadership in the interlocking directorates of the Politburo, the Secretariat, and the Council of Ministers. Unlike market-based economies, what it did *not* reflect was popular priorities and consumer preferences.

Such detailed economic planning would be daunting under any circumstances. To keep factories humming and assembly lines moving, it was necessary to determine in advance how many parts, in what exact sizes, would be needed to turn out the quota of, say, tractors at a given plant; how many train cars, trucks, or barges would be needed to deliver the right quantities of iron and steel and other components on schedule; how much energy would be needed to run the plant during different times of the year; and on and on. Innumerable calculations had been made for every single item manufactured or processed.

Under the Stalinist system of economic management, the state planning mechanism made millions of supply-and-demand calculations each year and set prices on hundreds of thousands of industrial and consumer items.[3] Obviously, if material allocations were miscalculated or if suppliers' and producers' timetables were not synchronized or if a key transportation pipeline got disrupted or clogged, the system would break down. Indeed, bottlenecks were one of several generic problems that plagued Soviet central planning. Rare attempts to link producers, suppliers, and consumers more directly failed miserably.

Problems of Planning

The absence of market mechanisms was at the root of many, if not most, Soviet economic problems. Take performance indicators as an example. Output quotas (rather than the profits that drive capitalism) were used to measure success in the Soviet economy. Every factory was expected to fulfill its quota every month. If a factory overfulfilled its quota for the year, its workers and managers were rewarded with pay bonuses. Underfulfillment blocked promotions for plant managers and dashed workers' hopes for a year-end windfall. Thus the primary objective of every plant manager was not to improve efficiency but rather to overfulfill the quotas by a small margin (overfulfilling by large margins would lead to higher quotas the next year, thus creating new pressures).

Plan fulfillment became an all-consuming end. To achieve it, plant managers typically hoarded supplies and deliberately inflated labor requirements to provide a cushion in case vital materials were not delivered on time or it should become

TABLE 6.2 The Shrinking Soviet Economy, 1961–1985 (average annual growth in net material product, percent)

Years	1961–1965	1966–1970	1971–1975	1976–1980	1981–1985
Official statistics	6.5	7.8	5.7	4.3	3.2
CIA* (GNP)	4.8	4.9	3.0	1.9	1.8

*U.S. Central Intelligence Agency.

SOURCE: Anders Aslund, *Gorbachev's Struggle for Economic Reform* (Ithaca:, NY: Cornell University Press, 1991), p. 17.

necessary to speed up production to meet the monthly quota. These widespread practices caused planning distortions and supply bottlenecks.

Moreover, as performance indicators, quotas themselves were problematic. Imagine that a factory produced nails. Nails of all sizes, weights, and types were needed, but there was always a dilemma: if the quota was based on gross weight, the manager had an incentive to produce big, heavy nails rather than small, lightweight ones; but if the quota was based on quantity, the manager would produce lots of little nails.

Another economic fact of life in the USSR was low labor productivity, resulting mostly from the paucity of incentives. Workers were all paid about the same, no matter how much or how little they produced. Everyone was guaranteed a job, and rarely was anyone fired (except for political reasons). In short, the system did little to encourage efficiency.

The collapse of communism was primarily the result of economic failure. Stalin imposed this inefficient system on all the satellite states of Slavic Europe after World War II. Many of the problems these countries face today are rooted in the economic deformities caused by central planning.

The Gorbachev Reforms

Gorbachev inherited an economy that had been declining steadily for at least two decades (see Table 6.2.). By the mid-1980s, Soviet economic growth had fallen to less than 2 percent a year, about half what it had been a decade earlier. One out of every nine industrial enterprises and nearly a third of the farms were losing money, and such essentials as food, housing, medical treatment, and transportation were being heavily subsidized by the state (indeed, these subsidies, it is now clear, had become a crushing burden). The irony of this situation is glaring: Soviet propagandists had long boasted that central planning, the heart and soul of scientific socialism, would solve the problems of boom-and-bust economic cycles, which plagued (and ultimately doomed) capitalism. Indeed, a blustering Nikita Khrushchev, the same Soviet boss who earlier denounced the crimes of Stalin, warned the West that "we will bury you" in the late 1950s. But when Gorbachev walked in Khrushchev's footsteps thirty years later, it was exactly the other way around.

The Soviet Economy before the Crash   In the waning years of Soviet rule, annual increments in food production barely kept pace with population growth, and despite heavy investment in agriculture the Soviet Union continued to spend billions of rubles to import meat and grain (much of which, ironically, came from Moscow's arch-rival, the United States). Even so, the supply of meat and butter was so far short of demand nearly three years after Gorbachev's rise to power that severe rationing of both remained in force in many provincial cities.[4]

Investment priorities in agriculture, ironically, reflected terrible planning. Farm-to-market roads and facilities for storage, processing, packaging, and retailing were woefully neglected. Nearly one-third of Soviet farm output (including a quantity of grain equal to what the government was buying on the world market) spoiled or was eaten by rodents. In 1987, for example, well over half of the entire potato crop rotted in the fields when heavy rains disrupted the harvest (potatoes and bread are the two most important staples in the Russian diet).

General living standards were abysmal compared with those in the industrial democracies of the West. Housing was always in short supply. In the cities, many lived in communal apartments, sharing bathrooms and kitchens with other families.

A growing technology gap with the West accentuated the Soviet economy's downslide. The gap widened in the 1970s and 1980s as the computer revolution, like the Renaissance and the Reformation centuries earlier, eluded the East and energized the West. The consequence, in Gorbachev's own words, was to create "pre-crisis conditions" that forced the USSR to change the way it worked in order to ward off decline and decay. Soviet economists conceded shortly before dissolution of the USSR that "no more than about 10 percent of the country's industrial production measures up to world standards of quality and technological advancement"[5]

Gorbachev Tries Triage   Any type of reform is risky in a country accustomed to repressive rule. Pushing for political change threatens the power and privilege of the ruling class and risks opening the floodgates of popular unrest. By 1990, Mikhail Gorbachev's democratization campaign had gone past the point of no return. Although he certainly never intended to dismantle the whole system, Gorbachev did take dramatic steps to reconstitute the Soviet parliament and to allow the first meaningful elections in Soviet history, at the same time breaking the Communist Party's monopoly and relaxing press censorship.

Gorbachev had apparently decided that a greater measure of popular participation was the price the party had to pay to get the country out of its economic doldrums and lure trade, aid, and investment from the West. His reforms involved converting the Supreme Soviet into an unwieldy new **Congress of Peoples' Deputies,** which elected a smaller, full-time parliament and a president. The president would assume the power previously exercised by the Communist Party leader. (Gorbachev already held both positions.)

The government delivered on its promise to hold multicandidate elections in 1989 and 1990. An open process of nominating candidates sparked an enthusiastic popular response. Meetings, at times, were raucous. Although the Communists won a majority of the seats (as expected), many independents also won and some highly placed Communist officials were, in fact, defeated. Moreover, such outspoken opposition figures as Andrei Sakharov and Boris Yeltsin (who had been removed as Moscow's maverick party chief) were elected handily. Yeltsin, running as an at-large candidate for all of Moscow, won by a landslide. The popular election was followed by a second vote within the Congress to choose members of the smaller Supreme Soviet. When Yeltsin was not elected to this body, such a hue and cry arose from an awakened citizenry that he was quietly given a seat.

For the first time ever, the new Soviet parliament gave voice to an opposition with an agenda of its own, including a demand to end the Communist Party's monopoly on power. This principle was the cornerstone of the monolithic Soviet state—**Article Six** of the constitution guaranteed the Communist Party's "leading and guiding" role. Under mounting pressure from parliament, public opinion, and Western governments, Gorbachev finally renounced this icon of Soviet rule at a historic meeting of the Central Committee in early 1990, fore-shadowing the collapse of Soviet power the following year.

Precisely what Gorbachev meant by "democratization" was always a mystery. He made it clear from the outset that Western-style democracy was not what he had in mind, denouncing attempts to "use democratic rights for undemocratic purposes." As examples, he mentioned efforts aimed at "redrawing boundaries" or "setting up opposition parties."[6]

It is difficult to say whether Gorbachev moved too fast or too slow, whether he willed the complete demise of the Stalinist system or was swept along by swift political currents he could not control. Clearly, he vacillated between accelerating the pace of reform and applying the brakes. His failure to define his terms and detail his policies was perhaps a case of calculated ambiguity. If so, the strategy failed miserably.

The main problem, however, was not political but economic. The model of central planning that Stalin had brutally imposed first on the Soviet Union and, after World War II, on Eastern Europe, did not work. As a consequence, the Communist states were falling further and further behind the capitalist states—the exact opposite of what Marx had predicted. The failure of this prophecy also discredited the prophet.

Perestroika: Deconstructing the Soviet Economy   The conventional wisdom within the Soviet bloc long held that Moscow was the model for the other socialist countries, but with the advent of Gorbachev's "new thinking," the Soviet Union showed a willingness to learn from the experience of other socialist states, especially Yugoslavia, Hungary, and the People's Republic of China (PRC). Gorbachev's dilemma was acute: how to reconstruct the economy without first destroying it.

At a Communist Party meeting in early 1986, Gorbachev endorsed a radical restructuring of the Soviet economy, thus launching the reform drive called **perestroika.** Later in the year, the official gazette of the Supreme Soviet pub-lished a list of thirty-eight measures to be implemented before the end of 1990; the new laws' concerns ranged from voting and plebiscites to economic incen-tives, pricing, the press, governmental reorganization, and the activities of the KGB. In November, the Supreme Soviet approved a law allowing citizens to moonlight for extra cash (many had been doing so illegally for decades).

The **moonlighting law,** which took effect in the spring of 1987, was the first to ease the ban on private enterprise since Lenin's short-lived New Economic Policy in 1921. Any Soviet citizen could now ask local authorities for permission to start what would amount to a small business. However, the Kremlin warned that it was not sanctioning "free-enterprise activities." Its ostensible aim was to tap the energies of Soviet citizens who were not in the work force, including housewives, pensioners, invalids, and students.

This new attitude toward private initiative was in truth an attempt to alleviate the woeful lack of services in the Soviet Union. Moreover, it represented a first tentative step toward recognition of individuals' economic rights by a regime long hostile to the idea of private property. But envy proved to be a serious problem, for many Russians—long exposed to a steady barrage of anti-capitalist propaganda—resent entrepreneurs who make a lot of money. In this and other ways, the political culture spawned by Marxist-Leninist ideology and a cradle-to-the-grave system of social welfare impeded efforts at economic reform.

The 1987 **Law on Soviet Enterprise** provided the legal framework for perestroika by mandating major changes in the management of state-owned enterprises. The changes were aimed at simulating market conditions without actually creating a free market. In 1988, another new law permitted individuals to produce and sell consumer goods for a profit at free-market prices. By the end of 1988, thousands of new businesses were operating. Although these new cooperatives typically produced consumer goods of better quality than those made by state-run enterprises, shoppers complained that the prices were prohibitively high. The cooperatives in turn complained that government policies (including high taxes) made it impossible to lower prices. In addition, petty bureaucrats unaccustomed to dealing expeditiously (or even courteously) with the citizenry often refused to grant permission to start a new business.

Gorbachev promised to decentralize the Soviet economy further by changing the regulations governing external trade. Many industrial enterprises and even some governmental departments were empowered to make deals with foreign firms. (Previously, all international commerce was conducted through a state monopoly.) Moreover, these enterprises and departments were to be allowed to retain some of their profits.

In the end, Gorbachev's halting economic reforms were too little too late to stop the avalanche he had triggered from burying the decaying Stalinist system he had inherited. Perestroika turned out to be a series of halfway measures that had the effect of disrupting the centrally planned economy without laying the foundations for a true market economy. In short, the economy was in limbo and Gorbachev was to blame.

Worse, the Soviet economy showed no signs of reviving. During the first half of 1989, for example, productivity rose less than 3 percent, according to official Soviet figures. Against a backdrop of unprecedented inflation and all-too-familiar empty shelves, Soviet consumers complained bitterly that the shortages were worse than at any time since World War II, despite a looming foreign trade deficit that threatened to bankrupt the state.

Glasnost: Building a Civic Culture   Perestroika was overshadowed in the late 1980s by **glasnost** ("openness") and democratization, which eased the political controls that were the hallmark of Communist Party rule. Even before the landmark political reforms of 1989–1990, Gorbachev had allowed greater public candor. This new freedom of expression was an integral part of Gorbachev's strategy for economic revitalization, but it carried considerable risks.

"Each citizen must undergo a personal perestroika," Gorbachev declared, "to unleash the latent human potential necessary to make national restructuring a success."[7] That would necessitate a fundamental change in the social psychology of a nation unaccustomed to personal freedom or individual initiative, encumbered by a discredited ideology, and inhibited by centuries of political and religious oppression. There was a "cultural fear of spontaneity here dating back to the czars, a tendency to see Western-style individual freedom as the first, inevitable step toward anarchy."[8] Breaking this pattern without breaking up the political system—that was the challenge. Far from abandoning the system, Gorbachev hoped to breathe new life into it.

Glasnost was thus a kind of grand experiment in behavioral engineering. Soviet society became a giant laboratory for testing new forms of cultural expression and political activity. Writers and books long banished were "rehabilitated." Many films and documentaries that had been blocked by the censors for decades were cleared for Soviet audiences in 1987 and 1988. Even previously banned American films began appearing in Soviet movie theaters.[9]

The Soviet press also enjoyed a new openness, publishing articles on such previously taboo subjects as prostitution, drug abuse, homosexuality, and even the misuse of psychiatry to punish dissidents. Embarrassing statistics about infant mortality and life expectancy, withheld for years by Soviet authorities, were again made available. Negative news—crime statistics, industrial accidents, traffic mishaps, and official corruption—began to transfigure the Soviet mass media: the old formula combining Pollyanna and propaganda gave way to accuracy, honesty, and realism.

Reform This . . .   Westerners tend to assume that people everywhere want democracy. The reality is not so simple. In fact, Russians have good reason to be skeptical of government, pessimistic about progress, wary of reforms, and indifferent to democracy. Russians' fear of anarchy often overshadows any yearning for democracy.[10] Russians "repeatedly remind a foreigner" that Russian history "is replete with illustrations that authority cannot be eroded only a little but is swept away completely when weakened and overwhelmed. . . . And in the milieu of Russia's upheaval and chaos, revolutions have been made."[11]

There are also pragmatic reasons why people were cynical about reforms. Reformers in the Soviet Union had always failed. Furthermore, the surface changes associated with glasnost "failed to bring any substantial change in the everyday life of people or the functioning of the system."[12] On the contrary, the first effects of perestroika were to bring a cut in pay for many workers, price increases for food and other state-subsidized essentials, and the disturbing possibility of unemployment. Suddenly the great advantage of state-centered socialism—security—gave way to a new and nagging sense of precariousness. This problem persists right down to the present and has, if anything, worsened with the passage of time.

In sum, to succeed in revitalizing the Soviet economy, Gorbachev had to revitalize Soviet society; to succeed in revitalizing society, he had to overcome widespread fear that radical reforms would only mean longer food lines and emptier shelves. Gorbachev's successors faced the same challenge. Democratization paradoxically deepened popular cynicism in Russia thanks to (1) a moribund economy, (2) pervasive corruption in both government and business, (3) collusion between the two, and (4) the rise of a new class of Russian robber barons and mafia-style (organized crime) bosses.

Why Gorbachev Failed

As the architect of the reforms that vanquished Stalinist rule, dissolved the Soviet empire, ended the Cold War, and ushered in a new era, Gorbachev's place in world history is secure. But his place in *Russian* history is a different story. Many Russians still blame Gorbachev for the country's current problems. Very few express any sympathy for what he tried to do. What he actually did, as they see it, was to destroy the old order, which for all its flaws was better than the new one. But Russians (understandably) tend to see things from a personal rather than a systemic perspective.

Even Gorbachev's most high-minded efforts often met with public resistance and anger. For example, when he tried to deal head on with the alarmingly high incidence of alcoholism in the Soviet society—a problem with devastating human and economic consequences—he risked open rebellion. (One colleague relates a personal story about a Russian taxi driver who said he was going to kill Gorbachev for launching his anti-alcohol campaign.) This well-intentioned but ill-conceived policy, carried out from 1985 to 1987, illustrates a recurrent pattern in the Soviet politics during this period—namely, the boomerang effect of Gorbachev's reform efforts.

Looking at the big picture, Gorbachev inherited an arthritic and debilitated economy, as we have already seen. Stalinist central planning had the great advantage of giving the state total control over the economy. As a result, the command economies of the Soviet bloc generally experienced very low inflation (see Table 6.3.). Only in the 1980s did this begin to change significantly in certain countries; until the late 1980s, price stability was a given in the Soviet Union, East Germany, Czechoslovakia, and Romania.

However, as we have already seen, the advantages of central planning were offset by even bigger disadvantages. For example, growth rates slowed perceptibly between 1951 and 1988 (see Table 6.4), not only in the Soviet Union but also in its satellite states. This downward trend in the face of dynamic market economies in Western Europe, Asia, and North America forced Gorbachev's hand. In a real sense, then, in embracing economic reforms he was simply making a virtue of necessity.

In addition, Gorbachev faced formidable opposition, not least from within his own "party" and the government he headed. Take the mammoth Soviet state

T A B L E 6.3   **Comecon Inflation Rates, 1970–1990 (percent)**

Country	1970	1975	1980	1985	1990
Soviet Union	0.0	0.1	0.1	1.0	10.0
Bulgaria	–0.4	0.3	14.0	1.7	64.0
Czechoslovakia	1.7	0.7	2.9	2.3	10.0
East Germany	–0.3	0.2	0.5	0.0	–3.0
Hungary	1.3	3.8	9.3	7.0	28.3
Poland	1.2	2.3	9.4	15.1	584.7
Romania	0.4	0.2	1.5	–0.4	4.7

SOURCE: Domenico Mario Nuti, "Perestroika," *Economic Policy* 3 (October 1988), p. 369; Vienna Institute for Comparative Economic Studies, ed., *Comecon Data 1988* (London: Macmillan, 1989), p. 157; Vienna Institute for Comparative Economic Studies, ed., *Comecon Data 1990* (London: Macmillan, 1991), p. 159.

bureaucracy, for example. At the upper echelons, bureaucrats constituted a privileged elite under Stalinism. Of course, they had little to gain and much to lose under the Gorbachev reforms. As part of the planned restructuring, half of these functionaries would be fired as ministries consolidated and streamlined. Party bureaucrats also felt threatened. The party's power was inseparable from its watchdog function in all areas of Soviet life—social, cultural, political, economic, and military.[13]

Ethnic diversity was another obstacle in the path of Soviet reform. The Soviet state encompassed eleven time zones, one-sixth of the earth's surface, 120 official languages, and over a hundred separate nationalities. Russians constituted a bare majority (52.4 percent) of the total Soviet population at the time the union splintered apart. For decades, the Russian-dominated and highly centralized Soviet government had suppressed expressions of cultural and linguistic particularism.

T A B L E 6.4   **Sinking Together: Comecon at a Glance, 1951–1988 (annual average GDP expansion at constant prices, percent)**

Country	1951–1973	1974–1982	1983–1988
Soviet Union	5.0	2.1	1.9
Bulgaria	6.1	2.4	1.4
Czechoslovakia	3.8	1.8	1.8
East Germany	4.6	2.6	2.1
Hungary	4.0	1.9	1.4
Poland	4.8	0.5	4.2
Romania	5.9	3.7	2.9

SOURCE: International Monetary Fund, *World Economic Outlook*, May 1990 (Washington, DC: Author, 1990), p. 65; International Monetary Fund, *International Financial Statistics Yearbook 1991*, vol. 54 (Washington, DC: Author, 1991), pp. 160–163; Development Centre of the Organization for Economic Cooperation and Development, *The World Economy in the 20th Century* (Paris: Author, 1989), p. 36.

Marxist-Leninist ideology was a convenient (though not very satisfactory) substitute for the various cultures contained within this vast empire.

Gorbachev's policies unwittingly aroused nationalistic rumblings all over the Soviet periphery. In the Baltic States, Latvians, Estonians, and Lithuanians looked back nostalgically to the period before World War II, when they were self-governing. In the Transcaucasus, Azerbaijanis, Georgians, and Armenians retained a strong sense of national identity; ethnic tensions in Nagorno-Karabakh, a part of Azerbaijan populated mainly by ethnic Armenians, touched off violent clashes, mass demonstrations, and bloody rioting in 1988–89.[14] In the Ukraine, with a population nearly equal to that of France or Great Britain, nationalism and separatism were reinforced by a rich cultural legacy, a history that predates the Muscovite era, and a long-standing resentment of Russian dominance. Finally, in Soviet Central Asia, Turkmen, Kirghiz, Uzbek, Kazakh, and Tajik nationalities continued to observe their own customs and practices, despite Soviet efforts to "modernize" them; all except the Tajiks speak Turkic languages, and all are Muslim.

Nationalism and the rekindling of old ethnic rivalries gave rise to violence in various places. For a brief time, Gorbachev attempted to contain these conflicts and to demonstrate that the center (Moscow) was still strong enough to maintain law and order wherever and whenever necessary. Then, in August 1991, an event of seismic proportions suddenly threw the door to independence wide open.

The August Coup: Prelude and Aftermath

The rebellious mood of the republics posed a danger to the survival of Gorbachev's reform movement and ultimately to the union. The other danger lurking in the background was the faltering economy, as Soviet GNP started to shrink in 1990 and plunged sharply in 1991. Ominously, the state budget deficit escalated during this period and inflation reached near-panic levels as Soviet printing presses stamped out ruble notes around the clock.[15] Meanwhile Soviet debt to the West mushroomed, leaving the Kremlin in the humiliating position of owing tens of billions of dollars to its capitalist Cold War rivals and being too broke to keep up the interest payments.[16]

Gorbachev's failure to revive the economy had two immediate consequences. First, it brought further hardships to long-suffering Soviet consumers who, thanks to glasnost, now had a voice. In 1990 and 1991, Gorbachev faced growing public hostility to perestroika; as his popularity plummeted, the danger of a coup by hardliners rose commensurately. Second, Gorbachev's vacillation on the conversion to a free-market economy damaged his prestige in the West. The combination of disaffection at home and disillusionment abroad made Gorbachev vulnerable. His carefully cultivated public image had been his greatest political asset; now that image was badly tarnished.

It was the unresolved **nationalities problem** that proved to be Gorbachev's Achilles' heel (see Map 6.1). In the spring of 1991, Gorbachev convened a conference at which he concluded a compact with the nine participating republics, granting them internal autonomy under a proposed new constitution that would establish the "Union of Soviet Sovereign [rather than

Comparative Ethnic Groups in the Former Soviet Union, 1989

Country	Titular Ethnic Group (percent)	Russian (percent)	Minor Ethnic Group (percent)		Other (percent)	Total Population (thousands)*
Russia	-	82	Tatar	4	15	147,553
Estonia	62	30	Ukrainian	3	5	1,573
Latvia	52	34	Belorussian	5	9	2,678
Lithuania	80	9	Polish	7	4	3,695
Belarus	78	13	Polish	4	5	10,195
Ukraine	73	22	Jewish	1	4	51,578
Moldova	64	13	Ukrainian	11	9	4,359
Georgia	70	6	Armenian	8	16	5,431
Armenia	93	2	Azeri	3	2	3,326
Azerbaijan	83	6	Armenian	6	5	7,092
Kazakstan	40	38	German	6	16	16,580
Turkmenistan	72	9	Uzbek	9	10	3,572
Tajikistan	62	8	Uzbek	24	6	5,182
Uzbekistan	71	8	Tajik	5	16	20,094
Kyrgyzstan	52	21	Uzbek	13	14	4,308

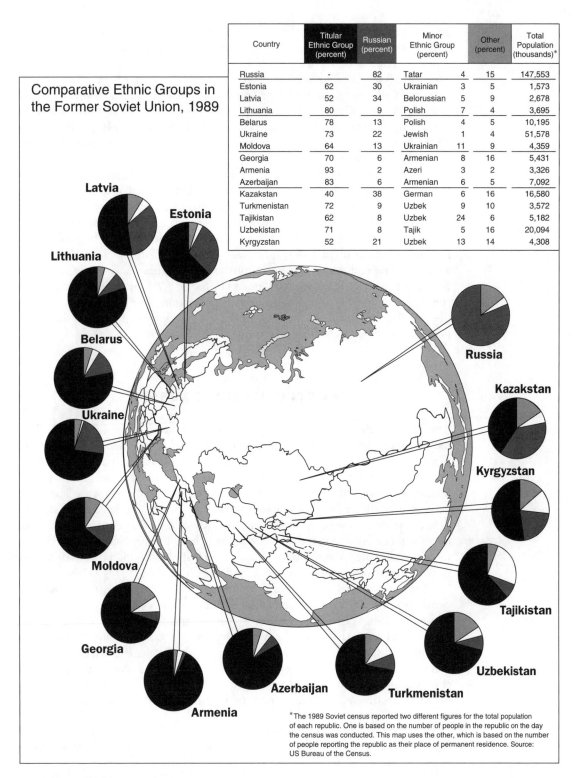

*The 1989 Soviet census reported two different figures for the total population of each republic. One is based on the number of people in the republic on the day the census was conducted. This map uses the other, which is based on the number of people reporting the republic as their place of permanent residence. Source: US Bureau of the Census.

M A P 6.1   Russian Nationalities

SOURCE: Adapted from the University of Texas Libraries, The University of Texas at Austin.

Socialist] Republics." Gorbachev was to meet with the nine republics to sign the new union compact on August 20; Kremlin hardliners tried to preempt this action by staging a coup on August 18.

Gorbachev failed to heed the warning signs and paid a high price: he was kidnapped and placed under house arrest at a retreat in the Crimea. The figure best positioned to challenge Gorbachev for preeminence was Boris Yeltsin, a popular figure who had been elected president of the Russian Republic in June 1991. Now Yeltsin alone stood between the conspirators and control of the tottering Soviet state.

Yeltsin moved quickly into the breach, rallying the nation and emerging from the crisis a national hero. Displaying personal bravery and brilliant timing, he climbed onto a tank at a crucial moment and read a ringing proclamation of defiance against the would-be destroyers of Russia's fledgling democracy.

The August coup quickly fell apart. Ironically, it accelerated the processes of national decay. With the now politically bankrupt Gorbachev standing alone against the republics, the dissolution of the Soviet Union was only a matter of time (four months, to be exact). Unlike Gorbachev, Yeltsin claimed the right to rule Russia as a result of winning a legitimate election. The formal dissolution of the USSR, accompanied by Gorbachev's ignominious departure from the political scene, left Yeltsin in sole charge of Russia's destiny.

POSTCOMMUNIST RUSSIA

The **Russian Federation** is easily the largest and most powerful remnant of the old Soviet empire. Russia's population numbers roughly 143 million, or about half that of the former USSR. The Ukraine, with a population of some 50 million, is the other large successor state. Both have witnessed a net population loss caused largely by out-migration in recent years. In terms of territory, Russia occupies 76 percent of the former USSR and continues to be the world's largest state in geographic size. Governing such a vast territory is a challenge under the best of circumstances; governing it democratically is an even bigger challenge. In trying to meet this challenge, the authors of Russia's current constitution borrowed features from the French, German, American, and British models, among others.

During Boris Yeltsin's tenure as president (1991–1999), Russia was governed democratically but not very effectively. The present constitution, adopted in December 1993, came in the wake of a bitter struggle between Yeltsin and his opponents (opposed to radical reform), which culminated in an abortive coup attempt by leaders of the Yeltsin opposition in the Supreme Soviet. These dramatic events were televised by CNN and watched by a world audience. The climax came when the army decided to back Yeltsin, staging an artillery attack (!) on the Russian White House (parliament building) and killing several dozen people in the process.

It is quite possible that Yeltsin's willingness to use deadly force in this crisis may have staved off other attempts by communist diehards to turn back the clock.

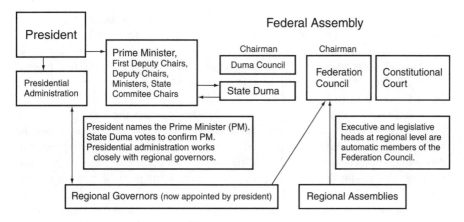

FIGURE 6.1 Russia's "Presidential Republic"

In any event, Russian voters subsequently elected a new parliament and approved Yeltsin's proposed new constitution. (However, some critics accused the Yeltsin camp of ballot-box tampering.)

The Yeltsin constitution (see Figure 6.1) buttressed presidential powers at the expense of the legislature and gave the central government enhanced authority over Russia's twenty-two republics and sixty-eight regions. The new political system, which Yeltsin called a "presidential republic," most closely resembles that of the French Fifth Republic.

A Strong President (Getting Stronger)

As in France, a directly elected president appoints a government—headed by the prime minister (officially, the Government Chairman)—which must maintain the confidence of the parliament to stay in power. The Russian president also has the right to dismiss the prime minister (again, as in the French system). Moreover, the president can dissolve the parliament (lower house) if it rejects his choice of prime minister three times in a row. This "hammer" is only available in certain circumstances. The parliament cannot be dissolved in the first year of its election, or after it has filed impeachment charges against a sitting president, or once a state of emergency has been declared, or, finally, in the last six months of a president's term.

The Russian president can veto laws, although the legislature can override the veto with two-thirds majorities in both houses. (Here a page was taken from the American system of checks and balances.) Moreover, the president may declare martial law or a state of emergency and may rule by decree with legislative approval. The president can also issue decrees (laws, for all practical purposes). Presidential decrees, however, must meet two tests: (1) they must not violate existing laws; and (2) they must have enough support within the parliament to avoid a vote to override.

The parliament, in turn, can bring down a government (as in other parliamentary systems) but with this caveat: *it takes not one but two no-confidence votes to force the president's hand* (the president can ignore the first one). If the government loses on a second vote of confidence, the president must either dissolve parliament (and set new elections) or dismiss the government. Also, parliament can impeach the president if a two-thirds majority in both the upper and lower houses vote to do so. The process also involves Russia's two highest courts (the Supreme Court and the Constitutional Court) and is therefore similar (but not identical) to that used in the United States.

In at least one other respect, Russia's presidency under the 1993 constitution reminds us of France's under the Fifth Republic. Like France's Charles de Gaulle, Yeltsin avoided any direct association with a political party. (French presidents after de Gaulle, however, did not follow this precedent.) Yeltsin's successor, Vladimir Putin, also did not run as the candidate of any particular political party (although he endorsed a coalition of liberal reformers called the Union of Right Forces). This precedent in Russia is likely to continue until the Russian political party system evolves into one more nearly resembling Western models—that is, having relatively few parties (say, five or six) with a clear identity and enough financial and popular support to survive for more than one or two elections.

A Weak Parliament (Getting Weaker)

The Federal Assembly comprises two chambers, the **Federation Council** (upper house) and the **State Duma** (lower house). The Council has 176 members (two from each of the republics and regions) and the State Duma has 450 members. Putin moved to gain control over the upper house in December 2004 by pushing through a new law giving the president power to appoint regional governors (they were previously elected by the people). Regional governors play a key role in choosing members of the Federation Council.

Half the State Duma is elected by proportional representation (but parties must get at least five percent of the total votes cast to win any seats); the other half is chosen by the "first past the post" system (simple-majority voting in single-member districts) used in the United States and Great Britain. Note that the dual system of electing delegates resembles that used today in Germany, as does the indirect way the upper house is constituted (in contrast to the U.S. Senate, for example, which is directly elected).

The two houses of the **Federal Assembly** (parliament) differ greatly in the way they are chosen and how they operate. The lower house (State Duma) initiates most legislation (the exceptions are enumerated in the Constitution and apply to certain policy areas of special importance to the regions represented by the Federation Council). When a bill passes in the Duma, it is sent to the upper house (Federation Council). If the upper house rejects the bill, it goes back to the Duma, where a commission (similar to a "conference committee" in the U.S. Congress) tries to iron out any differences. Where the differences cannot be resolved, the Duma may override the Federation Council's action (if it can muster a two-thirds majority) and send the bill directly to the president.

When a bill clears the parliament, it goes to the president to be signed. The president, as mentioned earlier, may refuse to sign a bill into law (veto), instead sending it back to the Duma with proposed changes. The Duma can either accept the presidential version of the bill and approve it by an absolute majority, or reject the president's amendments (override) by a two-thirds majority vote. The measure then goes to the Federation Council, which has essentially the same options (approve by a simple majority or reject by two-thirds).

The Duma has occasionally overridden presidential vetoes and more often overrides Federation Council rejections. Generally, the president and parliament have sought to avoid provoking a constitutional crisis, although the State Duma initiated impeachment proceedings against Yeltsin in 1998 based on rather extravagant charges including treason (for his role in dissolving the USSR in 1991), violating the constitution (illegally waging war in Chechnya and illegally dissolving the Russian Congress and Supreme Soviet in 1993), destroying Russia military capabilities, and committing genocide against the Russian people by implementing ruinous economic policies. Ultimately, none of the charges got the required 300 votes (two-thirds) but the Chechen War charge failed by only 16 votes.

A Figurehead Prime Minister

The new Russian government combines features of presidential democracy with features of parliamentary democracy. Russia has borrowed sparingly from the British model. Thus, for example, the prime minister is the formal head ("chair") of government and he (she) is responsible to the parliament (that is, subject to approval and removal by the lower house). There are obvious differences even here, however. First, the Russian prime minister has no popular mandate and is not automatically chosen by being the head of the party that wins parliamentary elections (as in Great Britain). Second, the Russian prime minister can be dismissed by either the president or by the parliament.

Because Russia does not have two large political parties that alternate in power, the prime minister is unlikely to have a strong power base either within the parliament or within the electorate. That leaves only the bureaucracy itself as a potential source of leverage. At least two of Yeltsin's five prime ministers—Victor Chernomyrdin and Yegenii Primakov—had risen to the top ranks of the state administration prior to becoming prime minister, but Yeltsin dismissed both when he saw fit. For its part, the Duma twice rejected Chernomyrdin when Yeltsin tried to give him a second chance.

Given the fact that the Russian constitution (like its French counterpart) does not clearly define the relationship between the two executives or who (which one) can do precisely "what, when, and how," it is possible that a future prime minister will be able to play a more assertive role in the policy process than past prime ministers have played so far. At present, the prime minister takes the lead in managing the economy and bureaucracy while the president concentrates on internal security, foreign policy, and national defense. President Putin is clearly the boss of the Kremlin and as such he can intervene in any area of policy at any time. What it means in practice is that Russian presidents can use prime ministers as sacrificial lambs when problems arise in hopes of deflecting the blame.

The relationship between the two chief executives will continue to evolve and the position of prime minister could be strengthened relative to that of both president and parliament after Putin's departure. As myriad upstart political parties of the early democratic period are winnowed out and replaced by a few parties with staying power, the Russian parliament might yet become a counterweight to executive power. Clearly, however, the trend under Vladimir Putin is toward a more powerful presidency and a weaker legislative branch. So long as the Russian political party system remains fragmented, there is little likelihood that a rival party leader—that is, one at odds with the president and having a solid majority in the State Duma—will become prime minister. If a rival party does happen to win a clear majority, however, and if the president refuses to go along with the Russian parliament's choice of prime minister, he (she) would run the risk of provoking a constitutional crisis. Thus, the French experience in "cohabitation" is one of several possible faces of Russian democracy in the future.

Putin's Meteoric Rise to Power

Yeltsin named Putin, a former KGB officer and political unknown, to be his new prime minister in August 1999. None of Yeltsin's first four prime ministers had lasted long in office, so Putin's sudden elevation to this post might have been no big deal. In fact, it was a big deal: eight months later, Putin was the newly elected president of Russia. The story of Putin's meteoric rise to power says a great deal about the promise and unpredictability of Russia's experiment in democracy.

As background, President Yeltsin's second term proved to be only slightly less turbulent than the first. His continuing problems with the economy and a dirty war in Chechnya (discussed later) were compounded by episodes of serious illness. Through it all, Yeltsin somehow managed to cling to power. His daughter and other members of his personal entourage (called the "Family" by political insiders) were instrumental in keeping the ship of state afloat when Yeltsin himself was incapacitated. Miraculously, he always bounced back. In retrospect, Yeltsin's decision to make Putin prime minister was the first scene in the final act of a drama that had begun almost a decade earlier. To the end, Yeltsin displayed an extraordinary sense of political theater.

If Yeltsin's plan was to position Putin for succession to the presidency, the December 1999 parliamentary elections were critical. Putin, for his part, did two things that bolstered his standing with the voters. First, he quickly won over many Russians with a "get tough" approach to the conduct of the war in Chechnya after a long period of dithering and indecision on the part of his predecessors (and, of course, President Yeltsin). Second, he boldly endorsed two upstart political parties—**Unity** (also called Medved, which means Bear), a last-minute coalition with no known program, and the **Union of Right-Wing Forces,** a party of liberal reformers. Unity nearly finished in first place, only slightly behind the front-running Communists, while the Union of Right-Wing Forces finished a respectable fourth. Together these two parties garnered about one-third of the popular vote and just a few seats fewer than the Communists in the new Duma. For the first time, the Russian parliament had two blocs—one on the left and one right on the right—facing each other. Was the Russian political party system at long last becoming less chaotic, perhaps even normal?

Normal is hardly the word for what happened next. At the first meeting of the newly elected Duma, the Communists and Unity (the main pro-Putin party) struck a deal, dividing up the chairs of the key committees between them. The Communists came out best, retaining the post of Duma speaker (leader) and getting nine committee chairs, but in return pledged to support the new government—in other words, to accept Putin's choice of prime minister and reform program. The opposition parties cried foul (one former prime minister, Yevgeny Primakov, called the deal a "desecration"). Nonetheless, the arrangement was a first for Russia's young democracy.

In sum, Russia's new constitution looks democratic. The real test, however, is not how a constitution looks on paper but how it works in practice. We will examine how well Russian democracy is meeting this test later.

EASTERN EUROPE: FROM STALINISM TO PLURALISM

From 1945 to 1989, Eastern Europe comprised nine sovereign nations: Albania, Bulgaria, Czechoslovakia, East Germany, Hungary, Poland, Romania, Yugoslavia, and the USSR. After World War II, the Red Army occupied all of them except Albania and Yugoslavia. By 1948, Stalin had imposed the Soviet model everywhere; in Yugoslavia, Marshal Tito rebuffed Stalin but in many ways imitated Stalinism. Monolithic rule prevailed until an avalanche of popular demands for democratic reforms swept it away in 1989 and 1990—and more than doubled the roster of nations in the Slavic Europe.

Stalin insisted that the governments of the Soviet Union's **outer empire** be modeled on his own, featuring these four elements:

- Communist party dictatorship
- Government apparatus democratic in appearance but highly centralized and hierarchical
- Socialist command economy in which patterns of production and consumption reflect political priorities rather than market forces
- Foreign policy based on fraternal relations with other socialist states

Eastern Europe during the Cold War

Throughout Eastern Europe, the Communist Party dominated politics. In some cases, other political parties existed (for example, in Poland and Hungary), but they were empty shells designed to hide the fact that the ruling party was all powerful.

Party organization in Eastern Europe mirrored Soviet practice. The size of party membership in each country was kept at 6 percent to 12 percent of the total population, ensuring that the party remained an elite organization. Elitism was apparently necessary for party morale, political recruitment, ideological integrity, and internal discipline.

Communist parties in Eastern Europe also imitated the Soviet insistence on political and intellectual conformity. Like the Communist Party of the Soviet Union (CPSU), they were intolerant of dissent and used censorship, surveillance, intimidation, coercion, and incessant propaganda to suppress freedom of artistic and literary expression as well as political free speech.

Czechoslovakia, East Germany, Bulgaria and Romania were hard-line Stalinist regimes. Poland and Hungary were the two most permissive communist regimes (not counting Yugoslavia). Hungary actually attempted to break away from Moscow in 1956, as did Czechoslovakia in 1968. Both attempts came to grief when the Soviet Union sent in tanks and troops to restore communist rule. Yugoslavia was the one major exception to this portrait of Soviet domination over Eastern Europe.

Moscow's Clones

Government structures in the Eastern European nations differed superficially from the Soviet model, but in all of them executive authority was centralized and the state apparatus was subservient to the party. In these countries, as in the Soviet Union, responsibility for day-to-day administration rested with the premier and a council of ministers handpicked by the party leadership. Rubber-stamping was the primary function of Eastern European parliaments, much as the Supreme Soviet legitimized Politburo decisions in the Kremlin.

Cloned Economies, Too

Following World War II, Moscow imposed Stalinist economic as well as political structures on Eastern Europe. Hence the entire region simultaneously embarked on the adventure of central planning, nationalization of industry, and collectivization of agriculture. Only in Poland did stiff peasant resistance keep most land in private hands.

In design and function, the command economies of Eastern Europe were clones of the Soviet economy. Developmentally, however, they lagged behind the Soviet Union (which itself fell further and further behind the West, as we have already noted). Moscow was content to buy raw materials from these countries and sell manufactured goods back to them—not exactly a good deal for the Eastern European satellites. To add insult to injury, Soviet manufactures were relatively expensive, and the quality was notoriously poor.

The problem with central planning, in a nutshell, was that the system did not produce prosperity anywhere and, as a result, an ever-widening gap opened up between standards of living on opposite sides of the so-called Iron Curtain. That central planning was fundamentally flawed was most vividly illustrated by divided Germany where the capitalist western part blossomed—an "economic miracle," it was said—in stark contrast to the prevailing gloom in the Stalinist eastern part.

Rulers who kept popular discontent at bay only by police-state vigilance became one of the hallmarks of Cold War. Not surprisingly, reform was in the air long before Gorbachev gave it Moscow's stamp of approval. First Hungary and then other countries (especially Poland) began experimenting with market mechanisms. These experiments were cautious and tightly controlled, but they suggested that the Stalinist model was a major impediment to economic growth and technological progress.

Why did Eastern Europeans wait so long before finally scrapping a system that did not work? In a word, fear. When Hungary tried to break away in 1956, the Kremlin dispatched tanks and troops to crush the rebellion, executing its popular leader as a traitor to the cause of socialism. When another reform-minded leader promised "socialism with a human face" in Czechoslovakia during the ill-fated **Prague Spring** of 1968, the Soviet Union again launched a brutal military intervention, ousting the reformers and restoring neo-Stalinists to power. Soviet pressures on the Polish government to crack down on dissent in 1956 and again in 1980 and 1981 did not go unnoticed in the other satellite states either.

One of the bitter lessons of Hungary, Czechoslovakia, and Poland was that Moscow would not allow any Eastern European member state to withdraw from the Warsaw Pact; Hungary had tried and failed. Nor would the Soviet Union allow opposition parties to exist. Czechoslovakia's move in this direction in 1968 jeopardized the Party's monopoly on power. That, in turn, led to the Soviet invasion and the enunciation of the **Brezhnev Doctrine,** which asserted Moscow's right to intervene in Eastern Europe to defend socialism against "counterrevolution." Finally, the Soviet Union would not tolerate independent power centers (such as the Solidarity trade-union movement in Poland in the early 1980s) that threatened or challenged the party's monopoly on power. As the events of 1989 demonstrated, Soviet domination was the only glue holding the so-called **socialist commonwealth** together.

The Revolutions of 1989

The year 1989 was a turning point in the long struggle between two irreconcilable ideologies—communism and capitalism. As it happened, Eastern Europe was the stage for Act I of this great drama. The year began with steps toward free elections in Poland and Hungary; it ended with the ouster of East Germany's communist dictator, the subsequent opening of the intra-German border (and the dismantling of the Berlin Wall), the resignation of the communist leadership in Czechoslovakia, and the overthrow of a particularly corrupt and brutal tyrant in Romania.

During 1989, Poland and Hungary introduced a series of political reforms aimed at democratization. In Poland, the independent trade union **Solidarity,** banned for eight years, was relegalized. The government allowed relatively free elections in June. Solidarity was allowed to contest all the seats for the Senate (upper house) and won an overwhelming majority in that body. It also won all seats it was allowed to contest in the Sejm (lower house). Although the Communists enjoyed a guaranteed majority in the Sejm (nearly two-thirds of the seats), the June elections were a ringing mandate for the opposition (mainly Solidarity). In August, the Polish parliament chose the first noncommunist prime minister in a Soviet-bloc country.

In a similar move, the Hungarian parliament voted to allow freedom of association and assembly in January 1989. The following month the ruling Hungarian Socialist Workers' Party (HSWP) approved formation of independent political parties. Hungary thus became the first Eastern European state since the Stalinist takeover to relinquish the Communist Party's monopoly position and embrace a competitive multiparty system. In May 1989, Hungary dismantled the barbed-wire fence separating it from neutral Austria—an act of immense symbolic significance in a country where freedom of movement was so long denied to its citizens. The end of the communist era in Hungary was rapidly drawing to a close.

The communist regimes of East Germany, Czechoslovakia, and Romania tumbled in a kind of chain reaction. The crisis in the German Democratic Republic (GDR) began with the flight of East Germans, vacationing in Hungary, to West Germany. Soon East Germans were clamoring for freedom to emigrate, freedom of speech, freedom of assembly—in a word, for democracy. Some fled through Poland; others sought refuge in the West German embassy in Prague, Czechoslovakia. Spectacular mass demonstrations occurred in Leipzig, East Berlin, and other East German cities throughout the fall of 1989. Under intense popular pressure and increasingly isolated (even Gorbachev offered no support), the Communist Party leadership replaced its hard-line chief. In a further effort to placate a society now in open revolt, the beleaguered GDR first gave Prague permission to allow thousands of East Germans in Czechoslovakia to go west and then caved completely, throwing open the intra-German border and allowing East Germans to travel freely to West Germany.

Next came one of the twentieth century's unforgettable moments: People from both halves of Berlin, a city divided for nearly three decades, began tearing down the Berlin Wall, first with hand tools, then with heavy equipment, celebrating around the clock atop the wall, in the streets, and at popular gathering places. People came from all over the world to celebrate with them, and millions more joined the party via satellite television. German youths on unscheduled holiday from school danced and sang, laughed and cried. Strangers embraced. For anyone who had grown up during the Cold War, it was an unforgettable scene.

In short order, the East German government resigned. In the elections held soon thereafter, the Communists suffered a humiliating defeat, as East Germans endorsed an early merger of the two German states—the key plank in the winning Christian Democrats' platform. Unification came quickly (in October 1990).

In neighboring Czechoslovakia, the conservative Communist government steadfastly resisted major economic and political reforms until it was swept away by popular discontent in late 1989. In an amazing role reversal, Vaclav Havel, a dissident writer languishing in a Czech prison at the beginning of the year, accepted the presidency in December.

Romania was the last domino to fall. It had had the most repressive regime in Eastern Europe. There, a spontaneous revolution against the brutal and corrupt dictatorship of Nicolae Ceauşescu started in the town of Timişoara and spread across the country. It would be the bloodiest domino of all. The army captured its fleeing dictator and his wife (an accomplice in his crimes), staged a perfunctory trial, and executed them on the spot. Romania's new leaders—so-called reform communists—set up the Council of National Reconciliation to run the country until free elections could be held. Critics denounced the new government for including former members of the fallen dictator's inner circle and for operating too much like the old government.

Oddly enough, the last dictatorship to fall in Eastern Europe was in Yugoslavia, the only communist country in Europe that had successfully pursued an independent course and remained friendly toward the West throughout the Cold War. Indeed, Yugoslavia (Serbia and Montenegro) would not be rid of Slobodan Milosevic's tyranny for another decade.

In the first half of 1990, East European voters rejected not only the Communists but also other parties of the left and center-left (most notably the Social Democrats). So-called **reform communism** failed to rally large numbers of voters in most countries, but the PDS (successor to the old ruling communist party) in the former German Democratic Republic (GDR) played—and continues to play—an important role as a repository of popular discontent in eastern Germany. The surprising popularity of center-right parties touting free enterprise reflected widespread disillusion with the Stalinist system of central planning. Rising expectations associated with market reforms, however, put the new leaders under the gun to produce quick results.

Nor is communism quite dead yet. Communists have never relinquished power in Belarus and were voted back into power in Moldova (2001). Communist parties still have significant popular bases in Russia and the Czech Republic. In Bulgaria, the Communist Party (BKP) is part of an octagonal electoral alliance that polled the largest vote total (34%) in the 2005 parliamentary elections.

Also, recycled communist parties (resembling Western-style social democratic parties) have won elections in Poland, Hungary, and elsewhere. The leaders and elected representatives of these parties are firmly committed to constitutional modes and methods now, but the fact remains that many of them were avowed communists before 1989. In Hungary, for example, a conservative Budapest newspaper exposed Prime Minister Peter Medgyessy as a former communist secret agent—a spy—shortly after his Socialist Party won the 2002 elections. So even though communism in Eastern Europe is certainly down (and downplayed), it is not exactly out.

The transition from communism to constitutional democracy has not been easy or painless anywhere. Czechoslovakia quietly split in 1992. The relatively homogeneous societies of Poland and Hungary were in no danger of breakup, but they displayed a common set of weaknesses that added up to a kind of post-communist syndrome—official corruption, weak civic cultures, and badly fragmented party systems. Even so, emerging democracies with few exceptions abolished the old Stalinist order, moved to create a free press, extended civil liberties, and held free parliamentary elections. At the same time, antidemocratic regimes in Yugoslavia, Ukraine, and Belarus would resist the mighty forces of change and in effect attempt to turn back the tide of history.

CASE STUDIES: POLAND, UKRAINE, CZECH REPUBLIC, SERBIA (FORMERLY YUGOSLAVIA)

Czechoslovakia and Yugoslavia both suffered a similar fate after 1989—both split apart into separate entities. Unlike Yugoslavia, Czechoslovakia was able to accomplish the separation without great turmoil and entirely without bloodshed. Poland pioneered in **shock therapy**—jumping out ahead in the race to see which former communist state would be the first to complete the great transition. The Ukraine, on the other hand, did not enter the race at all, and Yugoslavia descended into civil war.

POLAND: FREE AT LAST

In December 1989, Poland launched a bold reform program designed to transform the Polish economy rapidly from centrally planned to free-market, adopted a constitutional amendment that abolished the "leading role" of the Communist Party, and proclaimed the new Republic of Poland. The Polish United Workers' (Communist) Party ceased to exist in January 1990, and most of the property of the former ruling party was turned over to the state. Local elections held in May 1990 were entirely free, but voter turnout was low (slightly over 40 percent). Holdovers from the communist era—including the ministers of defense and the interior (secret police)—were replaced in a cabinet reshuffle in mid-1990.

In December, Lech Walesa, the leader of the Solidarity movement in the 1980s, became the first popularly elected president of Poland. Poland's new constitution, which was approved by a national referendum in May 1997, reflects the country's strong commitment to democratic norms. It establishes checks and balances among the president, prime minister, and parliament, and provides for judicial review as a final line of defense against arbitrary legislative or executive action. It also guarantees a full range of civil rights, including the right to free speech, press, and assembly.

Poland's governmental structure is a cross between the American presidential and the British parliamentary models. The council of ministers or cabinet is typically formed from a majority coalition in the bicameral legislature's lower house. The prime minister heads the cabinet. The president is directly elected to a five-year term. The prime minister is the head of the government, and the president is head of state. Thus, like France, Poland has a dual executive, but despite this outward resemblance Poland's president does not enjoy the high profile or the prestigious trappings of the French presidency. Even so, being directly elected, he or she has a potential connection with the voters that heads of state in most parliamentary systems lack. And when push comes to shove, Poland's president does not lack the power under the present constitution to throw his or her weight around.

One of the president's key functions is to nominate the cabinet (government) and prime minister in consultation with the Sejm, which accepts or rejects the president's recommendations by majority vote. If the Sejm reject the president's

---

B O X   6.1   Poland's Not-Quite-French Presidency

Under Poland's "Little Constitution," the president designates the prime minister and appoints the cabinet upon consultation with the prime minister, but the Sejm must approve the new government within two weeks (by a simple majority). If the government is not approved, the Sejm then has the responsibility to choose its own candidate, again by a majority vote. If the Sejm fails, the president has another chance, but this time the vote in favor requires only that more deputies vote yes than no. If the president's choice fails a second time, the Sejm can try again by the lesser vote. If no government can be confirmed, the president can either dissolve parliament or appoint an interim government (for up to six months), during which time the Sejm must either come to an

agreement on forming a government or parliament is automatically dissolved.

The president's legislative prerogatives include the right to propose legislation; to veto acts of parliament; to ask the Constitutional Tribunal to rule on the constitutionality of legislation; and to take whatever measures are necessary and proper for the implementation of the laws. The president also plays a key role in the ratification of international agreements. Finally, the president can declare martial law, mobilize the nation, and introduce a state of emergency for a period of up to three months, which can be extended for up to three months with the approval of the National Assembly (both houses).

---

first choice, the second nominee needs only a simple majority with half the deputies present and voting. This procedural rule came into play in the spring of 2004 when Prime Minister Leszek Miller resigned and President Aleksander Kwasniewski had to find a one-year replacement before the next scheduled parliamentary elections in 2005 (see Box 6.1).

The parliament consists of a 460-member **Sejm** (lower chamber) and a Senate (100 members). All deputies in both houses are directly elected in constituencies (voting districts) since 2001, when revisions in the election law abolished the national list and introduced a new proportional representation (PR) system aimed at calculating seats by a more equitable method. Among other things, the new law stipulated that with the exception of guaranteed seats for small ethnic parties, only parties garnering at least 5 percent of the total vote can be represented in parliament. Under this new system, seven parties gained parliamentary representation in the 2001 elections (see Table 6.5).

Former **Democratic Left Alliance (SLD)** leader Kwasniewski was elected to a second term as president in October 2000, receiving 53.9% of the popular vote. Following the September 2001 parliamentary elections, the center-left SLD headed a coalition government with the Polish Peasant Party (PSL) and leftist **Union of Labor (UP).** The kaleidoscopic nature of Polish politics was evidenced by the fact that the former ruling "party"—a center-right coalition known as **Solidarity Electoral Action (AWS)**—went into total eclipse, winning not a single parliamentary seat in 2001!

But the PSL quit the ruling coalition in March 2003. Later that same month, 22 SDL MPs quit the SLD and formed the Polish Social Democratic Party (SdPl). As noted earlier, Leszek Miller resigned in May 2004. President Kwasniewski chose a former finance minister, Marek Belka, to head an SLD-led minority government. The Sejm confirmed Belka in June; in October, he faced a no-confidence motion but survived. With both presidential and parliamentary elections scheduled for 2005, the question hanging in the air was whether Poland could or

TABLE 6.5   Political Parties in Poland's Parliament in 2005

SLD = Democratic Left Alliance*

PO = Citizens Platform

SO = Self-Defense

PiS = Law and Justice

PSL = Polish Peasant Party

LPR = League of Polish Families

UP = Union of Labor

SdPl = Polish Social Democratic Party

*A faction broke away from the SLD in 2003 and formed a new party, the Polish Social Democratic Party (SdPl).

would continue to move forward despite the drag effect of fractious parties, corrupt politicians, and an apathetic electorate.

UKRAINE: THE LONG WINTER

With the end of the Cold War, warm winds of change produced a rapid thaw in Poland and other former communist countries. In Ukraine, however, there was little change in the political climate despite the fact that breakup of the Soviet Union had open the door to a new and long-awaited era of independence from Moscow. In one sense, it was a dream come true for the Ukrainian people; in another sense, it was like awakening from a bad dream only to discover that reality was worse.

Like Poland and France, Ukraine has a hybrid political system of government combining features of both the parliamentary and presidential models. The president, who is popularly elected and serves a five-year term, exercises important constitutional powers and prerogatives, including control of the security forces. Also, surveillance is permitted for reasons of national security. This police power sounds ominous (especially in a country with a Stalinist past) but in fact is hardly different from the United States under the PATRIOT Act. Despite legal and constitutional protections, the government has not always shown due respect for free speech and freedom of the press. In particular, the failure of the government to conduct a full and proper investigation into the disappearance and murder of a well-known independent journalist (31-year-old Gyorgy Gongadze) in 2000 further damaged Ukraine's badly tarnished international image. To make matters worse, then President Leonid Kuchma and other high officials were widely suspected of being involved in the crime.

As in Poland, the president nominates the prime minister, who must be confirmed by the parliament. The main law-making body is the 450-member is a unicameral parliament called the **Supreme Rada.** The parliament, whose members are elected to four-year terms, also ratifies international agreements and approves the budget. Half of the seats in the Supreme Rada are chosen from party lists by proportional vote, the other half from individual constituencies. Under a new law passed in 2004, however, all seats in the 2006 parliamentary elections will be chosen from party lists.

Following free elections in December 1991, Leonid M. Kravchuk, a former chairman of the Rada, was elected president. At the same time, voters endorsed a referendum on independence by an overwhelming majority (90 percent). Unfortunately, that auspicious start led into a blind alley.

In the 1990s, the government of the newly independent Ukraine gained an international reputation for criminality and corruption. Ex-communists reinvented themselves as "elected" officials or business impresarios (called oligarchs in Ukraine as well as Russia). Bribery, extortion, embezzlement, and massive kickbacks were all part of the picture. Cliques of wheeler-dealers with connections to organized crime (the Ukrainian mafia) gained control of virtually all the country's previously state-owned assets through under-the-table privatization deals that created instant multimillionaires and even billionaires. Nor were the oligarchs content to control the economy. Oligarchic clans also sought to control the government by creating and financing off-the-shelf political parties beholden only to themselves.[17]

Ukrainian political parties include former communists, socialists, agrarians, liberals, nationalists, and various independent groupings. After the collapse of Soviet power, Ukraine adopted a multiparty system, extended basic guarantees of civil and political rights to national minorities, and adopted a new democratic constitution (in 1996).[18] But all the trappings of democracy could not conceal the reality of a corrupt government in league with criminals and crooks.

Kuchma was elected as Ukraine's second president in July 1994 and reelected to a second five-year term in November 1999. International observers criticized the election, pointing especially, among other things, to slanted media coverage, but the outcome was not challenged. The parliamentary elections held in the spring of 2002, though flawed, nonetheless set the stage for the **Orange Revolution** in 2004. A Kuchma-backed bloc, **For a United Ukraine,** won the largest number of seats, followed by a reformist bloc called **Our Ukraine**—the political formation backing former Prime Minister (and now President) Viktor Yushchenko.

The 2004 presidential election campaign was marred by foul play on the part of the government, including intimidation of the opposition and the independent media, abuse of state power, slanted state-controlled media coverage, and the like.[19] According to the official tally, the two major candidates— Prime Minister Viktor Yanukovych (Kuchma's candidate) and opposition leader Yushchenko—garnered equal shares of the popular vote (39–40 percent), setting up a winner-take-all second round. The November 21 runoff election was a sham. Widespread violations were reported, including multiple voting by busloads of people, fraudulent absentee ballots, a suspiciously large number of mobile ballot box votes, and the like. The biggest bombshell of all was the story behind Yushchenko's mysteriously disfigured face. Sometime during the fall, as the campaign heated up, Yushchenko had been poisoned with dioxin. He survived, but the devastating effect of the poison was clear for all to see. Once again, Kuchma and his cronies in the security forces were credibly implicated. Sustained mass demonstrations in support of Yushchenko occurred in Kiev and other cities. The crisis was building to a dramatic showdown and the whole world was watching.

To no one's surprise, the official observers of the Organization for Security and Cooperation in Europe (OSCE) found that the election "did not meet a considerable number of OSCE commitments and Council of Europe and other European standards for democratic elections." The government "displayed a lack of will to conduct a genuine democratic election process." Other impartial monitoring agencies were equally critical.

When the Ukraine's official Central Election Commission (CEC) declared Yanukovych the winner by a narrow three-point margin (49.46 to 46.61 percent) on November 24, 2004, the United States and Europe refused to accept the result as legitimate. European leaders went to Kiev to mediate a political solution. Three days later, the Ukrainian parliament (Rada) passed a resolution denouncing the election results. On December 1, the Rada passed a vote of "no confidence" in the government. Ukraine's Supreme Court also got into the act on December 3 when it invalidated the runoff "results" and mandated a repeat of the second-round vote.

An agreement mediated by the European leaders led to new legislation in early December that closed loopholes in the electoral law. The constitution was amended to curtail the powers of the president, and parliament also sought to devolve some powers to regional councils.

The December 26 revote went off without a hitch. According to OSCE observers, "campaign conditions were markedly more equal, observers received fewer reports of pressure on voters, the election administration was more transparent and the media more balanced than in previous rounds . . . in our collective view Ukraine's elections have moved substantially closer to meeting OSCE and other European standards." When the results were tabulated, Yushchenko was declared the winner with 51.99 percent of the votes against 44.20 percent for Yanukovych. Yushchenko was inaugurated on January 23, 2005.

Is it a story with a happy ending? Not necessarily: this election revealed a huge fault line splitting the country along an east-west axis. The eastern region of Ukraine is conservative (against liberal reforms) and pro-Russian; the western region is pro-Western, in favor of reforms, and eager to join the European Union (EU). There was even talk of secession in the eastern Ukraine. Meanwhile Russia's President Putin, a potential spoiler, made no bones about his displeasure at the turn of events in a country that many Russian nationalists still consider a province of Russia. Worse still, as we will see in Chapter Seven, rifts, rivalries and scandals have ruined a golden opportunity to get the country moving in the right direction. Sadly, a few at the top have dashed the hopes of the many at the bottom without whom there would have been no Orange Revolution.

CZECH REPUBLIC: REINVENTING DEMOCRACY

At the end of 1989, after the Soviet-installed regimes in Poland, Hungary, and East Germany had fallen, Czechoslovakia also rose up against its communist rulers. But the Czech uprising was mild compared with what occurred in other communist countries.

The Velvet Revolution

The leaders of the **Velvet Revolution** (as the name implies) were opposed to violence. Without question, Vaclav Havel was the major inspirational force behind the uprising. Alexander Dubcek, a Slovak who had spearheaded the ill-fated attempt to reintroduce democracy in 1968, was another key figure.

That earlier episode ironically helped seal the fate of Czechoslovakia's rulers. Having crushed the 1968 reform movement and conducted widespread purges of reformers (ultimately affecting half a million party members) from 1969 to 1971, the perpetrators of these draconian policies could not easily jump on the reform bandwagon even if they had wanted to do so. Thus, in March 1987 President Gustav Husak declared, "No one is forcing Soviet ideas on Czechoslovakia." When Husak was replaced as party leader in December 1987, Gorbachev publicly urged his successor to proceed with the "democratization of public and political life." Gorbachev's perestroika campaign had put Czechoslovakia's communist leaders on the defensive.

A Cumbersome Constitution

The new short-lived **Czech and Slovak Federal Republic (CSFR)** created in 1990 as the successor to the Soviet-style federal state formed in 1969, inherited a cumbersome constitution ill-suited to the new era. At a meeting with the leaders of **Civic Forum,** a flash-in-the-pan opposition party hastily created to negotiate the transition to democratic rule in late November 1989, the tottering dictatorship agreed to delete all references to the Communist Party's "leading role" and a few other provisions. For the most part, however, the government after 1989 continued to operate within the preexisting constitutional structure. (A new constitution was being drafted, but it turned into a race against the clock as the two halves of the CSFR started splitting apart in 1991.) The big difference, of course, was that the communist rulers treated the constitution as an ornament, whereas the new democratic leaders were obliged to take it seriously.

The system set up by the inherited constitution created a division of powers between the federal government on one hand and the two national governments on the other. It established Prague as the capital of the Czech Republic and Bratislava as the seat of government in the Slovak Republic. Each republic was had its own **National Council** (legislature) and executive (prime minister and cabinet), which operated concurrently with the federal government in Prague.

The bicameral **Federal Assembly,** consisting of the **Chamber of Nations** and the **Chamber of the People,** was the highest organ of state power (although in practice, of course, the Communist Party enjoyed a de facto power monopoly until 1989). The Federal Assembly elected a president (under the communists this was pro forma), who in turn appointed a head of government and cabinet. Hence Czechoslovakia had both a head of state (the president) and a head of government (the prime minister), an arrangement common elsewhere in Europe. The Federal

Assembly chose the Supreme Court judges, and the National Councils chose judges for regional and district courts.

The federal structure was more complicated than the unitary systems of Western Europe, but it was necessary because of the ethnic makeup of Czechoslovakia. The federation's political problems after 1989 were to some degree attributable to procedural difficulties built into the inherited constitution.

One State, Three Governments

Under Czechoslovakia's original 1918 constitution, a three-fifths majority in the Federal Assembly elected the president. This stringent majoritarian requirement was no doubt adopted to ensure that the president would have a clear mandate and could therefore speak with moral authority. It was not a problem in 1918: Thomas Masaryk was the unchallenged leader of the country. (He was elected to a seven-year term and exempted from the constitutional ban against self-succession.) But the three-fifths majority rule was a potential problem in the future. A fragmented Federal Assembly might not be able to agree on a worthy candidate, which could lead either to a constitutional crisis or the election of a weak compromise candidate. In some circumstances, it might even result in the election of a demagogue (that is, a politician who panders to public opinion to gain power but does not believe in democracy).

The inherited constitution also prescribed legislative procedures that made it relatively easy for opposition parties in a fragmented parliament to block legislation and in general play an obstructionist role. Both legislative chambers had to approve legislation before it could become law—not an unreasonable rule. The 150 seats in the Chamber of the People were allocated in proportion to population (giving the Czechs a two-to-one advantage); the 150 seats in the Chamber of Nations were split equally between the two republics. The Chamber of Nations also voted in a peculiar way: the two parts voted separately. Legislation had to be approved not only in both chambers but also in both parts of the Chamber of Nations. Hence a relatively small opposition (as few as thirty-eight members) in one part of this chamber could block all government policy and federal legislation, which meant that the will of the majority in the Federal Assembly could be thwarted by one-eighth of its delegates. Moreover, certain actions (such as election of a president) required a three-fifths majority in both houses of the Federal Assembly. In this case, it took not only 180 votes total for approval but also forty-five members in both parts of the Chamber of Nations: in other words, 31 members (10 percent of the whole body plus one) could kill a measure.

Finally, the existence of the two National Councils created an institutional-ized tug-of-war between three governments of more or less equal weight (although the political balance shifted decisively against the federal government in 1992). In such a compact country (about 15 million people inhabiting a territory the size of New York State), it was an open invitation to a schism between the federal government in Prague and the Slovak National Council in Bratislava. Intended by the communist regime to give the appearance of autonomy to Czechs and Slovaks, it had the effect of magnifying the points of contention

MAP 6.2 The Czech Republic

SOURCE: Adapted from the University of Texas Libraries, The University of Texas at Austin.

between the two parts of the country once the communists were gone and paving the way for two separate nation-states.

The Velvet Divorce

The **Velvet Divorce**—a term used in the news media to refer to the nonviolent breakup of Czechoslovakia in 1992 (effective on January 1, 1993)—came about despite efforts described earlier to satisfy the national aspirations of both Czechs and Slovaks. There are several reasons why the attempt to create a government on the model of a federal republic (such as Germany or the United States) did not work. In the first place, although Czechs and Slovaks speak a very similar language, they did not share a common culture or history until the period after World War I—quite recently, in other words. When Czechs rhapsodize about the great heroes of Czech history or the world-class contributions Czechs have made in music, literature, and science, they seldom if ever mention any Slovaks. Slovakia was long part of the kingdom of Hungary, whereas Bohemia and Moravia (the Czech lands) were either ruled by indigenous kings, foreign kings who moved the royal court to Prague, or Hapsburg (Austrian) kings. In other words, Czechs and Slovaks had a very different political history prior to the twentieth century.

Second, economic development in the two segments of Czechoslovakia diverged: the Czech part was on a faster track than the Slovak part. The Czech economy was based on manufacturing; the Slovak economy was geared toward agriculture and mining (raw materials). During the communist period, there was a significant net transfer of resources from "rich" Bohemia and Moravia to "poor" Slovakia—a fact that Czechs were not inclined to forget and Slovaks did not care to remember. As is so often the case, this type of unequal relationship bred resentment on both sides. And despite the steady redistribution of wealth in Czechoslovakia, Czech GDP was 20 percent higher than Slovak GDP in the early 1990s (though in recent years Slovakia's economy has outpaced the Czech Republic's). Money transfers from the Czech budget to Slovakia were halted in January 1991. Money was not the only reason for this divorce, but it would be naïve to suggest that it was not an issue.

Finally, personalities and political ambitions also played a role. Czechs and Slovaks did not decide to split up; Czech and Slovak *politicians* made this decision. Polls showed that the public on both sides was split evenly. Had the issue been put to a vote of the people, it is quite possible that the country called Czechoslovakia would still exist.

The fate of Czechoslovakia after 1989 illustrates the practical obstacles to implementation of a federal republic in a European context—that is, in a region where nationalism is so deeply rooted. It is worth noting that federations also did not outlast communist rule in the former Soviet Union or Yugoslavia.

One Government, Two Heads

The breakup of Czechoslovakia necessitated the drafting of new constitutions. It is important to get things right at this stage both because it can be very difficult to *amend* a constitution and because any attempt to do so is often acrimonious.

The Czech constitution establishes a parliamentary system with an indirectly elected president who appoints the prime minister—both can lay serious claim to the role of chief executive. The constitution also creates a bicameral legislature, but political foot dragging delayed creation of the upper house (Senate). As a result, several years after the Czech Republic came into being there were still major unresolved constitutional issues affecting the basic functions of government. Nevertheless, seen through Western eyes, the Czechs adopted a reassuring charter because it is admirably concise and democratic, offers a broad spectrum of human rights guarantees, and protects private property rights.

The president of the Czech Republic is elected by the parliament for a five-year term and can hold office for no more than two terms in succession. The president has the power to appoint and dismiss the prime minister and cabinet as well as to dissolve the **Chamber of Deputies** (lower house). These presidential powers only become operative, however, when (1) the parliament fails to pass a measure the government considers a matter of confidence, or (2) the parliament itself initiates a no-confidence vote and passes it by an absolute majority of all the deputies. The Czech president thus does not have the discretionary power of, say, the French president to dismiss the prime minister at will. If the Chamber of Deputies fails to approve the president's choice of prime minister after two attempts, the president must appoint the prime minister proposed by the chairman of the Chamber of Deputies—the reverse of the rule in the Russian constitution.

The president's powers of appointment are extensive but, with few exceptions, not exclusive. The president has impressive powers of judicial intervention as well. Thus, he can issue pardons, reduce penalties, preempt or discontinue criminal proceedings, and nullify punishments. In addition, he has the right to grant amnesty.

Under Article 63, the president represents the Czech Republic in the world and "concludes and ratifies international treaties." The president is also the "supreme commander of the armed forces." In general, presidential powers in the foreign policy arena would appear to be extensive, but Article 63 later stipulates that "Decisions by the President of the Republic made in accordance with Paragraphs (1) and (2) require for their validity the co signature of the Prime Minister or another member of the government entrusted by him." Thus, the president's hands can effectively be tied in the exercise of the powers enumerated in Article 63 if the prime minister chooses to tie them.

The real substance of executive power for the most part resides in the prime minister, who, under Article 77, organizes the activity of the government, chairs it meetings, acts on its behalf, and carries out the duties entrusted by the constitution and law. Article 67 (1) makes it clear that "The government is the supreme organ of executive power"; Article 67 (2) further states, "The government consists of the Prime Minister, deputy prime ministers and ministers." Under Article 74, the prime minister has the real power to form a government; the president's apparent power to appoint and recall ministers under Article 62 turns out to be a mere formality.

Although the constitution appears to give the president extensive powers, these powers on closer examination are rather illusory. Another way to view the executive powers under the Czech constitution is to recognize the ambiguities (perhaps deliberate) surrounding the president's role and the built-in tensions (almost certainly deliberate) between the roles of president and prime minister. The precedent set by President Havel gives the prime minister virtually a free hand in the conduct of the country's domestic affairs, whereas responsibility for diplomacy and foreign policy is divided between the president's office and the foreign ministry.

The dual executive came under attack in the late 1990s, when the Czech parliament passed a law aimed at drastically reducing the powers of the president. Former Prime Minister Vaclav Klaus, leader of the opposition **Civic Democratic Party (ODS)** party and Havel's main nemesis, instigated the action (but in league with the ruling Social Democrats). The next move was President Havel's, who challenged the law's constitutionality, placing the matter in the hands of the Czech Constitutional Court, which, in the end, ruled in Havel's favor. Ironically, Klaus would eventually succeed Havel as president, thereby benefiting from his own defeat.

Slavic Italy?

The Social Democrats (ČSSD) won the most parliamentary seats in the 2002 elections but faced opposition from both the hard right (ODS) and the hard left (the Communists). ČSSD could only form a government with the help of other parties, but the resulting coalition was vulnerable from the start. When ČSSD did poorly in EU parliamentary elections in 2004 (the first such elections Czechs could vote in), Prime Minister Vladimir Spidla resigned. His successor, Stanislav Gross, was forced to resign soon thereafter (in the spring of 2005) as a result of scandal involving the financing of his luxury apartment in Prague. Thus, the Czech government would have three different heads (prime ministers) in the span of a single year.

Intuitively, it would seem that this type of instability is a bad thing (and it certainly can be), but one advantage parliamentary democracies have over American-style presidential systems is the ability to change leaders without changing ruling parties or policies. However, frequent changes at the top, though not necessarily crisis inducing, are often associated with ineffective government. In this regard, polls in the Czech Republic indicated that three out of four Czechs did not expect the new prime minister, Jiři Paroubek, to succeed in solving the country's problems.

SERBIA: THE LONG ROAD AHEAD

In one of contemporary Europe's great ironies, Yugoslavia would become a pariah state—a throwback to the Stalinist era—after 1989. Recall that during the Cold War Yugoslavia under Tito defied the Soviet Union and established a relatively liberal form of communist rule. In 1989, however, President Slobodan Milosevic, riding a wave of nationalist fervor, resisted democratization, choosing instead to fight efforts to break up the **Yugoslav Federation.** As we are about to discover, despite Milosevic's grim determination and brutal tactics, Yugoslavia self-destructed in the 1990s.

The Failed Experiment Called Yugoslavia

Yugoslavia broke with Moscow in 1948 and looked westward for friendship and assistance. Recall that Yugoslavia was the only Eastern European state not occupied by Stalin's armies in World War II, having had the good fortune not to share a border with the Soviet Union.

Yugoslavia's pioneering efforts to decentralize administration and to institute workers' self-management as well as its welcoming approach to trade with the West were widely admired.[20] **Workers' councils** constituted the cornerstone of the Yugoslav experiment from 1950, when Tito promised "factories to the workers" as the first step toward repudiating the Stalinist model. The councils were intended to ensure management from below at the enterprise level in order to avoid the stultifying effects of party-state control.

But in the 1950s, reality failed to catch up with the rhetoric of **self-management.** In the 1960s, reformers made repeated attempts to spur reforms. They sought "to end arbitrary political intervention in the economy in order to allow the market to work freely."[21] Self-management finally came of age in the 1970s, by which time Yugoslav workers, at least in theory, gained the right to manage the means of production and make decisions about product distribution. The social and political significance of this system was once described as follows:

> Within Yugoslavia, self-management provides the foundation for
> the "democratization of social life" and the "construction of a political
> system" that expresses the plurality of interests in society and allows
> contradictions inherent in such a society "to be resolved democratically
> by dialogue and consultations." . . . Self-management affects almost every
> facet of Yugoslav life.[22]

In Search of the Workers' Paradise: "Self-Management"

Up to 1989, Yugoslavia was, at least on the surface, the most innovative state in Eastern Europe. Yet its experimentation with market-oriented, pseudodemocratic reforms failed to revitalize its lethargic economy or solve its political problems. The attempt to combine a free-market economy (including free emigration and free trade) with socialism and a one-party state foundered. Efforts to close unprofitable factories threatened workers with unemployment even as soaring inflation reduced purchasing power. Austerity measures implemented in 1987, including price increases and a wage freeze, led to widespread strikes.

Social unrest, spurred by ethnic tensions, was nothing new in Yugoslavia. The rivalry between Serbs and Croats was legendary. But in the 1980s, conflict between Serbs and Yugoslavia's ethnic Albanians broke out. In 1981, thousands of young Albanians demonstrated in the Serbian province of Kosovo, chanting anti-Yugoslav slogans and demanding political emancipation from Serbia. Such subnational particularism was never far below the surface in Yugoslavia, but the upheaval in Kosovo also had economic causes: Yugoslavia had piled up a huge multibillion-dollar foreign debt, price inflation was spinning out of control, and unemployment was in double digits.[23]

Yugoslavia's economic outlook remained bleak throughout the decade, although it did manage to reduce its foreign debt (thanks to trade surpluses in the mid-1980s). But evidence of remaining structural problems was easy to find: inflation approached triple digits, one worker in seven could not find a job, and state control was increasing.[24]

Almost predictably in this economic climate, ethnic strains reached crisis levels. Milovan Djilas, Yugoslavia's most famous dissident, aptly summed up the situation: "We now face a choice. Either we go forward, become freer and join the rest of Europe, or we will fall backward and become the underdeveloped state we were before World War II."[25]

Yugoslavia's Last Stand

By 1992, Slovenia, Croatia, Bosnia and Herzegovina, and Macedonia all seceded from Yugoslavia. Serbia renamed this new truncated state the **Federal Republic of Yugoslavia (FRY),** though in reality Yugoslavia was neither federal nor a republic. Despite the trappings of federalism and representative government, Serbia's leader, Slobodan Milosevic, ruled the rump state of Yugoslavia as a dictator. The breaking away of Slovenia, Croatia, Macedonia and Bosnia-Herzegovina at the outset of the 1990s left only Serbia and Montenegro in the phony federation.

The 1992 constitution provided for a directly elected federal assembly consisting of a **Chamber of Citizens** (120 members chosen by proportional representation) and a **Chamber of Republics** (with an equal number of deputies for Serbia and Montenegro). The presidents of Serbia and Montenegro were elected by popular vote, but the assembly elected the federal president, who was a virtual figurehead. In theory, both member states are equal, with a guarantee that if the president is from one republic, the prime minister will be from the other. In reality, Serbia continued to dominate the "federation," and the promise of parity was cynically ignored.

When the autocratic Milosevic reasserted Belgrade's authority over the autonomous provinces of Kosovo and Vojvodina, the Albanians in Kosovo agitated for separation from the Republic of Serbia. That decision would boomerang, leading to Milosevic's overthrow in 2000 (see Chapter 7). In December 2000, a coalition of 18 parties calling itself the **Democratic Opposition of Serbia (DOS)** won in a landslide, gaining 176 out of 250 parliamentary seats. The leader of this movement, Zoran Djindic, became the new prime minister. He promised long overdue democratic reforms. In March 2002, the heads of the federal and republican governments signed the **Belgrade Agreements,** which set forth the framework for a redefinition of Montenegro's relationship with Serbia within a single state. In February 2003, the assembly ratified a new constitution that, among other things, changed the name of the country from Yugoslavia to **Serbia and Montenegro** (see Map 6.3).

Toward a New Political Order

Under the new constitution, most governing powers devolved to the republic level. The president of Serbia and Montenegro has largely ceremonial and formal functions. The real chief executives are the prime ministers of the two republics. Both republics are parliamentary democracies that bear a general resemblance to the familiar British model. We will focus on Serbia here because Serbia is the senior partner in the new state of Serbia and Montenegro and because the two republics both operate under the same constitutional rules.

The law-making body for Serbia and Montenegro is the 250-member union Parliament, which is a unicameral body. The two republics also have popularly elected parliaments and each has its own president, prime minister, and deputy prime minister (like the arrangement between Czechs and Slovaks before the

MAP 6.3 Serbia and Montenegro

SOURCE: Adapted from the University of Texas Libraries, The University of Texas at Austin.

breakup in 1992). The federal government has a president (as already noted) and five federal ministers—for defense, foreign affairs, external economic relations, intern economic relations, and minority and human rights. Significantly, there is *no federal prime minister* and the power to tax and spend exists at the republic rather than the federal level. But note that there is a federal ministry of minority and human rights—in effect, it is Serbia's "ministry of redemption," designed to signal the world that in the future (unlike the past) minority groups and the two autonomous provinces of Vojvodina and Kosovo will receive fair treatment.

Today, Serbia is a multiparty democracy on paper and in practice, but the road ahead is still impeded by the wreckage of the past. In March 2003, just one month after the new constitution went into effect, Prime Minister Zoran Djindjic was assassinated. The Serbian and union governments declared a state of emergency and ordered a massive crackdown on organized crime that led to the arrest of

TABLE 6.6 Serbia's Parliamentary Elections, December 2003

Party*	Seats	Percentage
SRS	82	28%
DSS	53	18%
DS	37	13%
G-17 Plus	34	12%
SPO/NS	22	8%
SPS	22	7%

*SRS = Serbian Radical Party; DSS = Democratic Party of Serbia; DS = Democratic Party; G-17 Plus = Group of 17 Plus; SPO/NS = Serbian Renewal Party/New Serbia; SPS = Socialist Party of Serbia (former Communist Party).

more than 4000 people. The new government, however, was to be plagued by a series of scandals in the second half of 2003, which in turn prompted it to call for early elections.

In 2002, two rounds of presidential elections Table 6.6) had failed because of low turnout (Serbian law required participation by at least 50 percent of registered voters for a valid election). In November 2003, the presidential election in Serbia was declared invalid for the same reason—voter apathy had again dealt the cause of Serbian democracy an embarrassing defeat. Parliamentary elections in Serbia held the following month produced a new minority government headed by Vojislav Kostunica (see Table 6.6). The fate of the government depended on the stability of a three-party coalition including the Democratic Party of Serbia (DSS), G-17, and the Serbian Renewal Movement/New Serbia (SPO/NS). The Socialist Party of Serbia (SPS) also pledged its support but did not formally join the government.

In June 2004, after amending the law that required a 50% turnout of registered voters for a valid election, Boris Tadic, leader of the Democratic Party (DS), was elected President of Serbia. Although DS did not join the governing coalition, it was committed to democratic reforms.

The new state of Serbia and Montenegro is undertaking the kind of reforms necessary for eventual admission to NATO and the European Union. The country faces many perils, including the constant threat of another volcanic eruption in Kosovo. In the meantime, it appears likely that Montenegro will soon severe its ties with Serbia.

SUMMARY AND CONCLUSIONS

With few exceptions, the former communist states of Eastern Europe, predominantly Slavic nations with little previous experience in democratic self-government, have made major strides toward the creation of open societies with Western-style (liberal) political and economic systems. Poland, the Czech Republic, tiny Slovenia, Hungary, and the Baltic states led the way after 1989, but Ukraine and Serbia continued to be ruled by communist-style dictators in the

1990s. Both countries have recently overthrown dictators and instituted liberal reforms, but they have a lot of catching up to do. Romania and Bulgaria are in between the most and least advanced "emerging democracies" in Eastern Europe, and Belarus, Moldova, and Albania are at the back of the pack.

Russia remains a wild card in Europe. Having jettisoned the institutional forms of Stalinism, Russia has kept much of the substance, including a thinly masked "presidential" dictatorship and a state-centered economy. Russia lost precious time under the erratic rule of President Boris Yeltsin, who allowed a few corrupt individuals (the so-called "oligarchs") to profit hugely from bogus efforts to privatize the economy. The staggering transfer of wealth from the public to the private sector associated with this phony privatization left the few with fabulous fortunes and the many without anything—including hope. It also undermined public support for "democracy and gave rise to understandable cynicism about politics in general.

In fairness, Yeltsin's successor, Vladimir Putin, inherited a mess—a corrupted and stalled economy, a disillusioned society, and a political system in disarray (and facing a major secessionist challenge in Chechnya). The "dirty war" in Chechnya continues, despite Putin's iron resolve and willingness to countenance brutal means (including extensive civilian collateral damage) to suppress it. The economy has shown signs of reviving under Putin's guidance, showing modest positive growth rates, but most of the good news is attributable to a single factor—oil. Russia is blessed with an abundance of "black gold" and is highly dependent on proceeds from the export of oil and natural gas. This dependency is dangerous—it means a windfall in hard currency in times of skyrocketing crude oil prices, but, as we will see in the next chapter, it also places Russia at great risk. Russia's immediate neighbors in Eastern Europe (the former Soviet satellite states) have a particularly keen interest in Russian prosperity and stability.

KEY TERMS

antiparasite law

Article Six

Belgrade Agreements

Brezhnev Doctrine

Central Committee

central planning

Chamber of Citizens

Chamber of Deputies

Chamber of Nations

Chamber of Republics

Chamber of the People

Civic Democratic
    Party (ODS)

Civic Forum

collective farms
    (*kolkhozy*)

Comecon

Congress of Peoples'
    Deputies

Council of Ministers

Czech and Slovak Federal
    Republic (CSFR)

democratic centralism

Democratic Left
    Alliance (SLD)

Democratic Opposition
    of Serbia (DOS)

Federal Assembly (Czech
    Republic)

Federal Assembly
    (Russia)

Federal Republic of
    Yugoslavia (FRY)

Federation Council

For a United Ukraine

glasnost

Gosplan

Law on Soviet Enterprise

Liberman reforms

moonlighting law

National Council

nationalities problem

Orange Revolution

Our Ukraine

outer empire

perestroika

Politburo

Potemkin village

Prague Spring

reform communism

Russian Federation

Secretariat

Sejm

self-management

Serbia and Montenegro

shock therapy

socialist commonwealth

Solidarity

Solidarity Electoral
Action (AWS)

State Duma

state farms (*sovkhozy*)

Supreme Rada

Supreme Soviet

Unity

Union of Labor (UP)

Union of Right-Wing
Forces

vanguard of the
proletariat

Velvet Divorce

Velvet Revolution

workers' councils

Yugoslav Federation

SUGGESTED READINGS

Aslund, Anders. *Gorbachev's Struggle for Economic Reform*. Ithaca, NY: Cornell University Press, 1991.

Dedek, Oldrich, ed. *The Break-up of Czechoslovakia: An In-Depth Economic Analysis*. Brookfield, VT: Ashgate, 1996.

Dragnich, Alex N. *Serbs and Croats: The Struggle in Yugoslavia*. San Diego, CA: Harcourt Brace, 1992.

Dunn, Elizabeth C. *Privatizing Poland: Baby Food, Big Business, and the Remaking of Labor*. Ithaca, NY: Cornell University Press, 2004.

Gagnon, V. P., Jr. *The Myth of Ethnic War: Serbia and Croatia in the 1990s*. Ithaca, NY: Cornell University Press, 2004.

Goldman, Marshall. *The Piratization of Russia: Russian Reform Goes Awry*. New York: Routledge, 2003.

Glenny, Misha. *The Fall of Yugoslavia: Yugoslavia at War*. New York: Viking Penguin, 1993.

Jones, Lynne F. *Then They Started Shooting: Growing Up in Wartime Bosnia*. Cambridge, MA: Harvard University Press, 2004.

Karahasan, Dzevad. *Sarajevo, Exodus of a City*. New York: Kodansha America, 1994.

Kullberg, Judith S. *Legislative Politics in Russia: From Soviets to Parliaments*. Armonk, N.Y.: Sharpe, 1997.

Laquer, Walter. *The Long Road to Freedom: Russia and Glasnost*. New York: Macmillan, 1990.

Lebor, Adam. *Milosevic: A Biography*. New Haven, CT: Yale University Press, 2004.

McRaul, Michael; Mikolai Petrov; and Andrei Ryabov. *Between Dictatorship and Democracy: Russian Post-Communist Political Reform*. Washington, DC: Carnegie Endowment for International Peace, 2004.

Pontuso, James F. *Vaclav Havel: Civic Responsibility in the Postmodern Age*. Lanham, MD: Rowman & Littlefield, 2004.

Rothschild, Joseph. *Return to Diversity: A Political History of East Central Europe since World War II*. New York: Oxford University Press, 1989.

Satter, David. *Darkness at Dawn: The Rise of the Russian Criminal State.* New Haven, CT: Yale University Press, 2003.

Shevtsova, Lila. *Yeltsin's Russia: Myths and Realities.* Washington, DC: Carnegie Endowment for International Peace, 1999.

WEB SITES

www.columbia.edu/cu/sipa/REGIONAL/ECE/homepage.html

www.ceo.cz/

members.valley.net/~transnat/

www.rferl.org/

www.ucis.pitt.edu/reesweb/

NOTES

1. Gordon B. Smith, *Soviet Politics: Continuity and Contradictions* (New York: St. Martin's, 1987), p. 365.

2. Stanley Rothman and George W. Breslauer, *Soviet Politics and Society* (St. Paul, MN: West, 1978), p. 242; see also E. G. Liberman, *Economic Methods and Effectiveness of Production* (White Plains, NY: International Arts and Sciences Press, 1971).

3. Robert Gillette, "Perestroika: Bold Shift in Economy," *The Los Angeles Times,* October 27 1989, p. 1. (This article can be accessed electronically at www.latimes.com.)

4. Ibid.

5. Ibid.

6. Paul Quinn-Judge, "Gorbachev Presses for a Rollback of Party's Power," *Christian Science Monitor,* June 29, 1988, p. 1.

7. Dan Fisher and William J. Eaton, "Rumbles of Change Stir Soviet Union," *Los Angeles Times,* Oct. 25, 1987, p. 1.

8. Ibid.

9. Dan Fisher, "Glasnost: Soviets Try to Open Up," *Los Angeles Times*, Oct. 29, 1987, p. 1.

10. See Hedrick Smith, *The Russians* (New York: Ballantine, 1984), pp. 320–362; see also, David Shipler, *Russia* (New York: Viking Penguin, 1983), pp. 301–346.

11. Shipler, *Russia,* p. 326.

12. Alex Goldfarb, "Testing Glasnost: An Exile Visits His Homeland," *New York Times Magazine,* Dec. 6, 1987, p. 49.

13. Shipler, *Russia,* p. 324. The pervasiveness of the surveillance system nurtured and maintained by the party since 1917 was suggested in this sardonic (and thoroughly Russian) condensation of the Soviet constitution: "Whatever is not forbidden is compulsory."

14. Bill Keller, "Riots' Legacy of Distrust Quietly Stalks a Soviet City," *New York Times,* Aug. 31, 1989, p. 1.

15. Paul Hofheinz, "Let's Do Business," *Fortune*, Sept. 23, 1991, p. 62; Amy Kaslow, "Swedish Adviser Says Soviet Republics, West Are Squandering Chance to Solve Problems," *Christian Science Monitor*, Oct. 23, 1991, p. 1; Gerald F. Seib and Alan Murray, "IMF Effort to Reform Soviet Economy Runs Many Daunting Risks," *Wall Street Journal*, Oct. 15, 1991, p. 1.

16. Seib and Murray, "IMF Effort to Reform Soviet Economy. . . ."

17. Adrian Karatnycky, "Ukraine's Orange Revolution, *Foreign Affairs*, March-April 2005, Vol. 84, No. 2, pp. 38–40.

18. Although the constitution guarantees freedom of religion, religious organizations must register with local authorities and with the central government—a carryover from the communist era. Ukrainian is the only official state language, but minority rights are protected under a 1991 law. At least in theory, ethnic minorities can use national languages in schools and cultural facilities, as well as in conducting personal business. In Crimea and parts of eastern Ukraine—areas with large ethnic Russian minorities—local and regional governments allow the use of Russian in official correspondence.

19. Ibid., pp. 35–52.

20. See Bogdan Denitch, "The Relevance of Yugoslav Self-Management," in *Comparative Communism: The Soviet, Chinese, and Yugoslav Models*, Gary K. Bertsch and Thomas W. Ganschow, eds. (New York: Freeman, 1976), pp. 268–279.

21. April Carter, *Democratic Reform in Yugoslavia: The Changing Role of the Party* (Princeton, NJ: Princeton University Press, 1982), p. 5.

22. Wayne S. Vucinich, "Major Trends in Eastern Europe," in *Eastern Europe in the 1980s*, Stephen Fischer Galati, ed. (Boulder, CO: Westview, 1981), p. 5.

23. Darko Bekic, "Yugoslavia's System in Crisis: Internal View," *Problems of Communism*, Nov.-Dec. 1985, p. 71.

24. Jackson Diehl, "Yugoslavia's New Leader Has Yet to Take Hold," *Washington Post*, Dec. 8, 1986, p. A17.

25. William Echikson, "Top Dissident Now Free to Go Abroad: Yugoslavia 'Faces a Choice,'" *Christian Science Monitor*, Jan. 22, 1987, p. 12.

Eastern Europe Today
The Long (But Wide Open) Road West

E astern Europe is still far behind the West but has the potential to become the stage for most dynamic economies on the Continent in the first half of the twenty-first century. *Low labor costs are a major competitive advantage, but this plus is offset by several minuses: inadequate infrastructure (roads, bridges, power grids), the need for heavy capital investment to modernize (or replace) existing plants and equipment, and languorous work habits associated with the communist era. Nonetheless, prospects for Eastern Europe—especially the countries that joined the EU in 2004—have improved greatly since 1989 and are likely to continue on an upward glide path.*

Russia is a potential spoiler. Russia does not pose a military threat to the West as the Soviet Union once did, nor are Russia and the United States ideological rivals as they were during the Cold War. On the other hand, the fact that Russia is no longer a source of security, subsidies and cheap energy for the governments of Eastern Europe as it was before 1989 poses a challenge for the former Soviet satellite states and also for the West. Membership in the European Union can compensate for these losses, but in the meantime Eastern Europe remains highly energy dependent on Russia. The smoldering secessionist movement in Chechnya continues to drain away precious moral and material resources. Except for oil exports, there are few bright spots in the Russian economy. Nor has the danger posed by Russia's huge cache of nuclear weapons been entirely removed now that the era of east-west strategic confrontation has ended. In the event of a social upheaval or a government crisis, who or what would prevent weapons of mass destruction from falling into the wrong hands?

Thus, Eastern Europe, with few exceptions, has opted to join the West—good news for East Europeans, perhaps, but bad news for Russia. So far, Russia has grudgingly (though not always graciously) accepted this rejection, but whether it will accept isolation is another matter. If Russia's increasing isolation is bad for Europe in general, it is likely to be even worse for Eastern Europe because of historic and geographic proximities that are too close for comfort. One of the big questions looming in Europe's future, therefore, is whether Russia will join Europe or attempt to go it alone. The latter course is a foreign policy mired in the past; a foreign policy for the future involves opening up Russia to Europe—and vice versa.

The east-west conflict that split Europe apart after 1945 unraveled in 1989 and came completely undone with the collapse of the Soviet Union at the end of 1991. Europe's cleavage was a result of politics and ideology, not geography. Nonetheless, as we have seen, cultural, linguistic, ethnic, and economic differences existed long before the onset of the Cold War.

Before World War II, no nation in Eastern Europe, with the single exception of Czechoslovakia between 1919 and 1939, had any direct experience in democratic self-government. Nor had the Reformation in the sixteenth century penetrated the Slavic world (again with the exception of the Czech lands). The Slavic languages of Eastern Europe sounded strange to Westerners accustomed to hearing Romance languages (Italian, French, Spanish, and Portuguese) or English. German and Scandinavian languages were somewhere in between—not as baffling to Western ears as Slavic tongues, but still foreign. Religiously, Eastern Europe also differed from Western Europe: in the East, the established church generally derived from the **Eastern Orthodox** rite or Islam; in the West, it was almost exclusively Roman Catholic or Protestant.

The economic contrasts between East and West were no less glaring. The industrial revolution transformed the societies of Western Europe—rendering them urban, modern, and mechanized—while Eastern Europe's peasant masses remained largely unchanged—illiterate, land-poor, and tradition-bound. During the Cold War, opposing modes of economic organization and operation served to magnify preexisting differences in relative levels of economic development. West European economies, spurred by the energizing effects of free markets and competitive enterprise, recovered quickly from the devastation of World War II and then raced ahead of Eastern Europe's centrally planned economies, which were impeded by the onerous weight of a monolithic bureaucratic state and a Stalinist welfare model that made people utterly dependent on the state for benefits and subsidies while paying them little in wages and salaries. A popular Soviet working-class joke went as follows: "We live in a make-believe world—we pretend to work and they pretend to pay us."

But the concepts of "East" and "West" as applied to Europe had often given rise to a major fallacy—namely, that there is no middle ground between East and West and that the East is all one color (solid red before 1989) and the West is all

another color. On closer examination, no part of Europe is (or ever was) mono-
chromatic, including the part on the "wrong" side of the Iron Curtain.

Czechs and Poles, for example, are Western in fundamental ways, including
national orientation, culture and religion. By *national orientation* we mean that in
external affairs Czechs and Poles tend to look west rather than east. Thus, very
few Czechs or Poles migrated East in the nineteenth century, whereas waves of
East Europeans (far more Czechs and Poles than any others) were heading west
(mostly to the United States). Poland, as we know, is a Roman Catholic country,
and the Czechs actually anticipated the Reformation, revolting against the Vatican
before it became fashionable in Germany, Holland, the Scandinavian countries,
and even France.

Even linguistically the differences between East and West are not as clear cut
as we might think. Czechs and Poles do not use the Cyrillic alphabet, which is
what makes Russian and Ukrainian, for example, appear so strange and unin-
telligible to Westerners. Romanian is actually a Romance language (derived from
Latin), and Hungarian (Magyar) belongs to the Finno-Ugric language family, as
does Estonian. Lithuanian and Latvian are Baltic languages. Finally, German is a
kind of buffer-zone language—neither Slavic nor Romance.

Invidious comparisons that make Slavs out to be inferior to West Europeans
are based on ignorance and prejudice, an extreme example being the Nazi ideology that held that Slavs were *Untermenschen* (subhuman). Unfortunately, as is so
often the case, the stereotype does have some credence in the eyes of many in the
West. As a result, Slavic peoples frequently express an odd mixture of envy and
resentment toward Western Europe, and West Europeans often express pity or
disdain toward Slavic countries.

Generally speaking, except for the Russians (who remain wary), East Europeans are eager to join the West (especially the North Atlantic Treaty Organization and the European Union), whereas Western governments, understandably,
first demand solid evidence of reforms. What this means, in a nutshell, is that
Eastern Europeans are put in the humiliating (but familiar) position of having to
prove themselves to the West. Only now more than ever, proving themselves
means emulating Western Europe. And so long as Russia chooses to stand apart, it
also means having to choose between Russia and the West.

Most of the former communist states (including the former Soviet republics)
have made this choice without wavering. Many of the former communist states
are now members of NATO, and eight of them (plus Cyprus and Malta) joined
the EU in 2004. As noted earlier, Ukraine has been badly split on the question of
Europe versus Russia (although the outcome of the Orange Revolution appears
to have settled that question once and for all). On the other hand, authoritarian

president of Belarus, Alexander Lukashenko, has sided unequivocally with Russia. Whether most Belarusians agree or are simply too scared to oppose him is impossible to prove, but one thing is certain: the people of Belarus have never had a chance to vote in a free and fair election. Politically and economically, Lukashenko's Belarus has more in common with Mubarak's Egypt than with neighbors like Poland and Lithuania, or even Yushchenko's Ukraine.

If Eastern Europe is eager to join the EU and Western Europe is amenable but wary, what accounts for the difference in ardor between the two sides? We don't have to look very far for the answer. Economically, Eastern Europe lags way behind the West. Slovenia, with the highest per capita GDP in Eastern Europe, trails the two West European countries with the lowest per capita GDP, Greece and Portugal. Compared to the EU as a whole, Slovenia's per capita GDP in 2004 was 72 percent of the EU's, while Poland's was a mere 42 percent and Lithuania's a paltry 39 percent. Even the relatively well-off Czechs fell way short of the EU average (60 percent). In short, Eastern Europe has everything to gain and nothing to lose by joining the exclusive EU club; Western Europe also stands to gain in the long run, but the risks and costs are considerable.

For the single-market concept to work, the rich EU countries must help the poor countries catch up. That means, among other things, providing regional aid (making net transfers of resources from the EU budget from Western Europe to Eastern Europe). But Western Europe is facing huge internal and external problems of its own. Why would it voluntarily take on this additional burden?

In international politics nations rarely act out of purely altruistic motives. The EU (correctly) decided that the evolution of liberal democracies and healthy market economies in the East is good not only for Europe as a whole but also for individual member states in the West. The EU has proven to be a great catalyst for economic growth—that is a reason for optimism. But the new East European democracies still have a lot to prove—to themselves, above all.

RUSSIA: NEITHER EAST NOR WEST

Russia's economic problems did not evaporate with the passing of the Soviet Union. Nor did the prospects for Russia or the other former Soviet republics suddenly improve—for the vast majority, things went from bad to worse during President Boris Yeltsin.

The Unplanned Economy: A Dismal Decade

At the very outset, the Russian Federation found itself in an economic crisis. In January 1992, consumers rioted in many cities, protesting against the lifting of

TABLE 7.1 Russian Per Capita Consumption, 1990–1993 (kilograms)

Product	1990	1991	1992	1993
Meat	75	69	60	56
Milk	386	347	281	279
Eggs (number)	297	288	263	246
Fish	20	16	13	10
Sugar	47	38	34	35
Vegetable oil	10	8	7	8
Potatoes	106	112	118	114
Vegetables	89	86	77	83
Grain products	119	120	125	130

SOURCE: Official statistics; see U.S. Central Intelligence Agency, *Handbook of International Economic Statistics* (Washington, DC: Author, September 1995), pp 34–35.

price controls. It was a harbinger of things to come. As the year wore on, the economy continued its tailspin, incomes and output plummeted, inflation soared, and the government was powerless to reverse the trends. Meanwhile, it appeared as though only profiteers and criminals were prospering while millions of law-abiding citizens were once again forced to wait in long lines for sugar, flour, and other staples (see Table 7.1). It was the disappointment of democracy—the fact that it brought hardship rather than hope—that quickly became paramount in the minds of the vast majority of Russians.

Russia teetered on the brink of hyperinflation, in part because of reckless monetary policies. Massive government subsidies to failing state enterprises were financed by a flood of freshly printed rubles. The inflation rate reached such dizzying heights by the end of 1992 that the ruble was in dire jeopardy. The **ruble crisis** pointed to the perils of switching to free-market prices in economies previously based on state-owned industries and strict price controls. This crisis seriously tarnished Yeltsin's image and, arguably, doomed any hopes of seeing a true Russian democracy blossom for at least a generation.

With paltry foreign reserves (gold and convertible currency), the Kremlin was forced to seek a moratorium on repayment of its external debt. The International Monetary Fund (IMF) agreed to extend a new multibillion-dollar loan to Russia in April 1993 but made the deal conditional on implementation of market reforms. Meanwhile, Russia was also running up large multibillion-dollar trade deficits and foreign debts to Germany, the United States, and other Western countries. Russian nationalists found it humiliating for Moscow—still a nuclear superpower, after all—to be financially dependent on the West. Small wonder that Yeltsin was no longer a hero to most Russians.

Under enormous cross-pressures from the international community on one hand and from his domestic critics on the other, Yeltsin temporized. After the hardliners' last stand in 1993, Yeltsin turned over management of the economy to his prime minister Viktor Chernomyrdin, who adopted a pragmatic monetary

TABLE 7.2   Russia: Selected Economic Indicators

Indicator	1991	1992	1993	1994
GDP, 1991–1994 (percent change)				
Real growth	−13.0	−19.0	−12.0	−15.0
Per capita real growth	−13.0	−19.0	−11.0	−15.0
Industrial output (change in total)	−8.0	−19.0	−16.2	−22.8
Agricultural output (change in total)	−5.0	−8.0	−2.0	−9.0
Energy				
Oil (thousand BPD)	—	7,880	6,935	6,320
Natural gas (billion m$^{3)}$	—	639	618	607
Coal (million MTS)	—	329	296	271
Electricity (billion kWh)	—	1,002	950	876

SOURCE: Official statistics; see U.S. Central Intelligence Agency, *Handbook of International Economic Statistics* (Washington, DC: Author, September 1995), pp. 34–35.

policy aimed at restricting growth of the money supply and curbing consumer demand. The inflation rate fell sharply after that, although it was still exceedingly high by Western standards in the mid-1990s.[1]

Yeltsin was understandably reluctant to shut down many of the country's woefully inefficient medium-size and large factories, knowing that to do so would cause massive layoffs. His dilemma was the greater because under the old communist system everybody (except "parasites") had a job, unemployment was anathema, and nobody was ever fired. As a result, in the first three years of Yeltsin's presidency, industrial growth rates in Russia actually fell faster than the GNP as a whole (see Table 7.2).

The price of Yeltsin's ambivalence was a failing economy. For example, light industry declined overall by almost one-third, and the chemicals sector (including petrochemicals) fell by nearly one-fourth. Agriculture production also dropped steadily during this period. Russia's per capita GNP in 1995 was roughly a tenth of Belgium's and barely half of Hungary's.

Thus, when Yeltsin ran for reelection in 1996, he was courting a voter whose average wages (about $150 per month) and living standards had fallen during his first term in office. However, the economy was showing some signs of reviving thanks in part to fresh loans from the International Monetary Fund (IMF); inflation decelerated; the value of the ruble stabilized; and foreign investors were beginning to take notice. Russians were not better off than they had been four years earlier, but there was new hope. That plus a well-timed lull in the war in Chechnya proved to be enough to put Yeltsin over the top one more time as he trounced Gennady Zyuganov, the Communist Party's lackluster candidate, in a runoff election. Russia's great campaigner had done it again.

Russia's economy perked up in 1996-97 but plummeted again in 1998 (see Table 7.3). The reversals were due in part to external circumstances—lower oil prices and a crisis that started in Asia's emerging markets and spread. But

TABLE 7.3 Russian Economic Performance, 1992–2004 (percentage annual change)

	1992	1994	1996	1998	2000	2002	2004
GDP	−14.5	−12.6	−6.0	−5.0	9.0	4.1	5.7
Inflation	2323	202	21.8	82.0	20.2	14.9	10.8

SOURCE: World Bank and "Emerging Market Indicators," *The Economist,* July 1, 2000, December 7, 2002, and March 27, 2004.

Yeltsin was also to blame. In return for financing his campaign, Yeltsin allowed a few tycoons to gain a stranglehold on the commanding heights of the economy—banking, energy, and mining, among others. These so-called oligarchs demanded (and got) all sorts of special privileges, including "privatization on favorable terms, and a virtual tax holiday which starved the exchequer and kept interest rates high."[2] Yeltsin proved in spades that skilled politicians do not always make good presidents.

Putin to the Rescue (?)

Yeltsin's successor, Vladimir Putin, is cut from different cloth. Tough and energetic in dealing with terrorism, the secessionist movement in Chechnya, and **oligarchs** (billionaire entrepreneurs) who dare to venture into politics, Putin has nonetheless shown far less resolve in his efforts to reform or revitalize the economy. Instead, his boldest moves have been to seize or reshuffle key assets—especially in the energy industry. In failing to take full advantage of the country's windfall profits from oil and gas exports in recent years, Putin has lost precious time—and perhaps the last best opportunity to turn Russia's economy around. After the disastrous 1990s, strong medicine was needed to put the country on the highway to economic health.

Under Putin, Russia's economic picture brightened considerably, thanks largely to the steep rise in oil prices. Russia's oil dependent economy is dangerously dependent on the price of raw materials—especially oil and natural gas—on the world market. About half the total growth in Russia's GNP during Putin's tenure is attributable to energy exports alone. "Oil and gas account for 20 percent of Russia's total GNP, 55 percent of Russia's export earnings, and 40 percent of its total tax revenues."[3] Russia is the world's only **petrostate** with a nuclear arsenal. A petrostate is characterized by oil dependency, lack of economic diversity, highly concentrated wealth amidst widespread poverty, and weak social and civic institutions. The volatile combination of a demoralized society and a huge arsenal of mass destruction weapons (WMD)—including nuclear, biological, and chemical capabilities—poses a danger to Russia, Europe, and the world.

Why are many Russians demoralized? Here are a few of the sobering facts of life if you live in contemporary Russia. First, your life expectancy is very low by European standards: "A boy born in Russia today can expect to live just to the age of fifty-eight, younger than if he were born in Bangladesh. No other educated, industrialized state has suffered such a prolonged, catastrophic growth in death rates."[4] According to most estimates, Russia's population will decline by one-third to one-half by the middle of the present century because of a plummeting birthrate, ill health (heart disease, alcoholism, tuberculosis, and AIDs take an alarming toll in today's Russia), and emigration. In addition to disease, the effects of environmental poisons are a major threat facing Russia.

The implications for Russia's future could hardly be more profound. Although Russia's armed forces are far smaller than under the Soviet armies of yesteryear, Russia still has a million men in arms. With exposed borders stretching for thousands of miles from St. Petersburg in the west across the vast expanses of Central Asia all the way to Vladivostok in the east, Russia has long considered a large army essential for self-defense. Russians never forget how often Russia has been invaded (Mongols from the east; Poles, French, and Germans from the west). Fear of invasion remains a driving force in Russian military planning; fear of having to fight a two-front war is Russia's recurring nightmare—hence the desire to keep a formidable army. After 2005, however,

> the number of seventeen- and eighteen-year-olds eligible for military duty will decline sharply, the result of the baby bust of the late nineteen-eighties and early nineties. Soldiers are at much higher risk for H.I.V. than other members of society; young men are prone to risky sexual behavior, often relying upon prostitutes during long tours of duty away from home, and drug use is common. In 2002, only eleven percent of the men called to serve were considered fit for duty; five thousand draftees tested positive for H.I.V. and were turned away.[5]

Despite these daunting problems, Putin's popularity ratings have remained surprisingly high. One reason: he has brought some of Russia's powerful oligarchs down, using the police and legal system to intimidate or drive them into exile. Putin's decision to arrest and jail Mikhail Khodorkovsky, Russia's wealthiest man, in October 2003 on charges of fraud and tax evasion has been widely condemned in the West as a gross violation of Khodorkovsky's civil rights, but most Russians see it differently.[6] They consider the oligarchs to be greedy robber barons. Seen in this light, Putin is a kind of Robin Hood—though a very selective one who has "robbed" from only a few of the superrich and done little for the poor. (Khodorkovsky, who was sentenced to nine years in prison in 2005, reportedly had political ambitions of his own—if so, that might explain why Putin had Khodorkovsky put away while sparing other oligarchs who have wisely stayed out of politics.)

Arguably, Russia's biggest problem—one that permeates and undermines the society, economy, and political system alike—is corruption. In the Stalinist era, stealing, cheating, bribery, black market trading, and, in general, beating the system became a way of life. To a large extent, petty crime became a necessity. When everybody's doing it, breaking the rules becomes the norm. The problem was inherent in the system—there were constant shortages of staples (meat, fruits, and vegetables), and when these items were available people had to stand in long lines for hours, often in freezing cold, hoping to get lucky. Luck was necessary because there was never any guarantee that stocks of whatever was on sale would not run out before one made it to the head of the line—unless a friend or family member happened to work in the shop. Connections and bribes on all levels were the lubricants that kept the machinery of the planned economy from grinding to a halt. When it finally did break down, the machinery was discarded (or privatized), but the old habits did not die. Unfortunately, when it comes to efforts aimed at curbing corruption, Putin has talked a better game than he has played.

To be sure, obstacles to eradicating this problem in today's Russia are enormous. To his credit, Putin personally has not been implicated in financial and business scandals. Nonetheless, on his watch corruption has continued to erode Russia's image abroad. Worse still, it has given democracy a bad name where it matters most—at home. Surveys show (not surprisingly) that many Russians are cynical and disillusioned with democracy. They no longer believe that freedom can change things for the better. Most shockingly, Russians consider police, politicians, civil servants, and government ministers to be in more corrupting professions than thieves, conmen, drug dealers, and terrorists.[7]

Even so, Putin has ruled Russia with a strong and steady hand. In particular, he has taken steps to control inflation, balance the budget, improve Russia's trade relations, and attract foreign investment. On paper, Russia's economic performance has improved. In 2004, the Russian economy grew at brisk 6–7 percent (but, as noted, most of that momentum was due to soaring oil and gas prices on the world market). Also, domestic inflation was relatively tame by Russian standards (around 12 percent).

However, a closer look reveals that nearly all Russia's recent economic growth is attributable to a single factor: gas and oil exports. High oil prices have been a bonanza for an otherwise lame and limping economy. Then, too, Putin's increasingly heavy hand raises troubling questions about Russia's future. What does it mean for how Russia will be ruled or the role of the state in the economy? Will the tender shoots of Russian democracy be crushed, as many close observers believe is happening?[8] Will Russia revert to a state-controlled economy? Many of Putin's closest confidantes—perhaps 50 to 70 percent of the Kremlin's staff—come from the ranks of the old Soviet secret police (KGB).[9] Putin's harsh (and highly selective) reprisals against certain oligarchs and rivals combined with his personal affinity for coercive instruments of the state are troubling to many friends of constitutional democracy, as is Putin's lament over the collapse of the Soviet Union— "the greatest geopolitical catastrophe of the twentieth century," he called it in his annual state-of-the-nation address in April 2005.[10]

Putin has moved systematically to consolidate his power. Having crafted a solid majority in the lower house of the Duma in December 2003, he asked parliament to take a number of steps to recentralize power: first, abolishing popular election of Russia's eighty-nine regional and provincial governors in favor of presidential appointment; second, changing the way representatives to the parliament are elected by abolishing individual candidacies, having voters vote instead for party lists, and using a proportional representation (PR) system to distribute seats (thus giving party bosses and Putin himself more control over the process); third, giving the president a major role in the nomination of federal judges. In general, the overall effect of these and other (earlier) changes Putin has pushed through are to shrink liberal democracy, freedom of the press, and political opposition and, conversely, to expand the powers of the presidency.

Russia's Nettlesome Nationalities

Post–Soviet Russia remains a multiethnic Eurasian empire stretching from the Gulf of Finland to the Sea of Japan. By itself, it still boasts roughly three-fourths of the total land area of the former Soviet Union and one-half of its population. Although over four-fifths of the Russian Federation's population consists of ethnic Russians, many ethnic minorities (including Tatars, Ukrainians, Chechens, Germans, and Poles, among others) live there as well. Under the old Bolshevik structure (which survives intact), Russia comprises twenty constituent republics representing relatively large ethnic groups and a plethora of smaller administrative entities.

The nationalities issue is closely linked to a virulent strain of Russian nationalism characterized by xenophobia. In early November 2005, one thousand ultranationalists staged an anti-immigration march in central Moscow. With hate crimes against immigrants from the former Soviet republics on the rise, such manifestations of racial bigotry pose an obvious danger to public safety. Three weeks later, police broke up a counterprotest of anti-fascist marchers on the same street and arrested some of the organizers. A series of dueling rallies occurred in the ensuing weeks.[11] Meanwhile, it was unclear where President Putin stood on two key questions. Who has a right to assemble in post-Soviet Russia? Will the police protect non-Russian minorities who are victims of hate crimes, or look the other way? In a larger sense, the overarching question, one that remains unanswered after fourteen years of post-Soviet rule, is the status of civil rights—or simply freedom—in the new Russia.

The War in Chechnya

In Chechnya, a bid for independence in November 1991 triggered a crisis and led eventually to a protracted war. When Yeltsin decreed a state of emergency in the rebel area and dispatched special Interior Ministry troops to enforce it, a majority in the Russian parliament refused to back this move and called instead for negotiations under parliamentary auspices.

The opponents of Yeltsin's action charged it was no different from Gorbachev's failed attempts to settle ethnic conflicts by force, and defenders warned that if Yeltsin failed to act decisively, Russia would suffer the same fate as the disintegrating Soviet Union. The issue split the party bloc known as **Democratic Russia,** a pillar of Yeltsin's political support. "In the ensuing uproar," wrote one reporter, "the Russian government backed down, leaving an uneasy truce in which the Chechen government issues statements as if it were independent and the Russian government ignores them."[12] This secessionist movement, which culminated in a ferocious war a few years later, was a stark reminder that the new Russia would face some of the same problems that had undone the old Soviet order.

Unlike his predecessors (including Gorbachev), when President Yeltsin decided to get tough in Chechnya, he had to justify the use of force to the press, the parliament, and the public. His inept handling of the ensuing war in the mid-1990s nearly cost him the presidency; worse, the war badly divided Russian society and threatened to crack the very foundations of Russia's none too sturdy democratic institutions. During the course of that conflict, with horrific battle scenes being broadcast around the world on satellite television, Yeltsin vacillated between the extremes of conciliation and vengeance. As a result, he appeared indecisive, alienating doves and hawks alike, while the international community widely condemned the Kremlin's brutal intervention.

After a bloody two-year war that left the diminutive Chechnya in ruins but unconquered—a war that exposed Russia's weakness to an incredulous world—Yeltsin decided to negotiate a settlement. As a result, free elections were held in Chechnya in January 1997. Chechnya's leadership continued to demand full independence from Russia, but Moscow remained publicly silent on this all-important question, despite having signed the peace agreement.

The silence was broken in the fall of 1999 with bombs and artillery fire: in the twilight of his presidency, the ever-unpredictable Yeltsin launched a second war in Chechnya. But this time the military operations were better planned and executed. As noted earlier, Yeltsin put Vladimir Putin, his new prime minister, in charge of the war effort. Putin ruthlessly directed a massive assault against Chechnya's rebel strongholds, and the Russian public responded with a patriotic outpouring of gratitude. Putin's surging popularity in the polls was the immediate result.

Although Putin had subdued Chechnya and installed a puppet government, low-intensity conflict continued. Rebels resorted to guerrilla-style tactics, sniper fire killed Russian soldiers daily, and Chechen leaders, including the ousted president, remained at large. After the September 11, 2001, President George W. Bush's "war on terrorism" appears to have emboldened Putin to intensify Moscow's military solution to the Chechen problem, which he portrayed as a Russian war on terrorism. But the rebels refused to surrender.

In October 2002, Chechen fighters seized a Moscow theater and held 700 people inside hostage. After a standoff that lasted for two and half days, Russian commandos moved in, using a presumably nonlethal poison gas to render the hostage takers (and the hostages) unconscious. But when the gas killed many of the hostages, the government refused to name the gas (allegedly for security reasons) and would not tell doctors how to treat the victims. The incident further incited hatred on both sides.

A Russian-choreographed referendum the following spring adopted a new constitution and formally declared Chechnya part of Russia, but it settled nothing. In the summer of 2003, a suicide bomber drove a truck packed with explosives into a Russian military hospital, killing many of the hospital's staff and patients. In September 2004, Chechen rebels seized Middle School Number One in Beslan (North Ossetia), holding the children and teachers hostage for more than two days. The tragedy ended in a bloodbath as some 200 hostages were killed and many hundreds more injured. (Russian commandos killed twenty-seven hostage takers.)

The Kremlin put all the blame for these (and other) incidents on Chechen rebels and likened them to the perpetrators of the 9/11 terrorist attacks on America. By linking Moscow's Chechen problem with Washington's war on terrorism, Putin gained the diplomatic leverage he needed to keep Western powers from protesting the Russian army's brutal efforts to crush the Chechen rebellion.

The two Chechen wars pushed Moscow's troubled relations with other minorities off the stage. In 1992, the Tatars voted yes in a referendum on independence. But Tatarstan's dispute with Moscow, unlike Chechnya's, ended peacefully in February 1994, when the two sides signed an autonomy agreement. Tensions between Russia and other former Soviet republics remain as well. Flash points include Georgia, where the South Ossetians wanted to secede to join Russia, Moldova, where ethnic Russians were fighting native Romanians in a Russian-majority enclave in the Dnestr region, and Nagorno-Karabakh, a relatively large chunk of territory that is legally part of Azerbaijan but politically and militarily controlled by Armenia.

Russian or Citizen?

Russia has an endemic federal problem that the United States does not have. Although the majority of its population is ethnic Russian, Russia remains a multiethnic empire. The distinction between **Russkye** (ethnic Russians) and **Rossianiye** (citizens of Russia) in the vernacular reflects this diversity. When the parliament proposed calling the country just plain "Russia," objections were raised on the grounds that this name refers only to the *Russkye*—the *Rossianiye* would have been left out. This may seem like an abstruse point to outsiders, but the ethnic wars in the former Yugoslavia, as well as Russia's war in Chechnya, serve as grim reminders that in this part of the world such matters are anything but academic.

As its name declares, the Russian Federation is a federal (rather than unitary) system. The Soviet Union was also a federation in name, but the key to its survival for more than seven decades was the existence of a monopoly of force at the center rather than any division of powers between the center and the provinces. By contrast, the rulers of the current Russian Federation are duty bound to accept constitutional constraints on the power they exercise. Such constraints are often severely tested in times of crisis (even for well-established federal republics)—especially if a secession movement provokes the crisis. The American Civil War is a case in point. In the United States, constitutional rules have always been restored (and often strengthened) following conflicts and crises. Whether Russia's fledgling and fragile democracy will slide into dictatorship as it faces an uncertain future remains to be seen.

India and Nigeria are two other countries where federalism has been adopted as a solution to the problem of governing a diverse population scattered over a large territory. Significantly, in both countries (and also in Canada) the spirit of secession has at one time or another shattered the calm. The United States put that issue to rest nearly a century and a half ago. India and Nigeria have still not done so, and neither has Russia.

EASTERN EUROPE: HEADING WEST

The tidal wave of popular uprisings that rolled across Eastern Europe in 1989 swept away communist regimes in Poland, Hungary, East Germany, Czechoslovakia, and Romania. (Communist governments in Bulgaria and Albania soon fell by the wayside as well.) In East Central Europe, new leaders with popular mandates moved rapidly to democratize the political processes and reorient domestic and foreign policies. But the pace of change in Poland, Czechoslovakia, and Hungary was not matched in Russia, the Ukraine, or the Balkans (Romania, Bulgaria, and Yugoslavia). In the former Soviet Union, the old order was replaced by a new disorder. As a consequence, the east-west conflict quickly faded from the vernacular of European politics, but the Slavic world rapidly divided into parts going in different directions at different speeds.

Chapter Five highlighted the distinctive religious, ethnic, and cultural experiences of the Slavic nations, but they all have at least one thing in common: although the Iron Curtain has fallen away, the lingering effects of Stalinist rule remain throughout the region. Many of the problems facing the former communist states are the product of rigid economic policies that stifled all initiative for more than four decades.

New political systems cannot be implemented overnight, nor can ruined economies be easily restored, but hopeful signs of an economic revival have appeared from Lithuania in the north to Slovenia in the south. In Poland, the Czech Republic, and Slovakia, the winds of change have brought in foreign investment—the vital seeds of growth for emerging markets. But in other countries such as Serbia, Romania, and the Ukraine the fruits of reform (like the reforms themselves) are slow to materialize or non-existent.

The Baggage Problem

Economically, Slavic Europe lagged behind Western Europe long before there was a Soviet Union or an Iron Curtain. After World War II, the chasm continued to widen. Kremlin boss Nikita Khrushchev's boast, "We will bury you," (by which he meant that socialism would prove itself to be superior to capitalism in the long run), turned out to be one of the least accurate predictions of the twentieth century: In the mid-1990s, the German economy alone dwarfed the combined gross domestic product of the entire Slavic world. To embark on the road west, the ex-communist states would first have to jettison a lot of old baggage.

After 1989, euphoria quickly gave way to the sobering realities of economic life in postcommunist societies. The challenge was different from that facing

Europe after World War II in at least one fundamental way: the economies in question were intact. Eastern Europe at the end of the Cold War did not have war-devastated infrastructures and factories. They were not starting from scratch, so to speak. They had railroads, bridges, power grids, highways, and factories, but most of these assets were part of the problem: by and large, they were obsolescent or decaying or both. The task at hand was thus to salvage what could be salvaged, to shut down what could not be, and to build the new (literally in some cases) alongside the old.

As previously noted, the impediments included a rigid system of central planning, a domestic climate generally inhospitable to technological innovation and foreign investment, and a lingering Cold War rivalry that barred Soviet-bloc countries from full participation in the global economy. After 1989, the leaders of Poland, Hungary, and Czechoslovakia moved quickly to replace the police state organs that underpinned communist rule for four decades. The movement toward a free-market economy was now unhampered by ideological strictures or the threat of Soviet intervention. In Poland, the government boldly adopted a strategy called shock therapy—austerity measures (budget cuts, wage restraints, reduced state subsidies), an end to price controls, and rapid privatization of the economy. In Czechoslovakia, an alternative strategy aimed at a less jarring—but no less complete—transition to a free market.

In the Balkans, however, the pace of change was much slower and the ghost of totalitarianism lingered longer. Any hope of a peaceful evolution toward a new order was shattered by the bloody civil war in Yugoslavia, where tens of thousands of people were killed, and millions more were left homeless. The war, which was sparked by ethnic hatred in Bosnia-Herzegovina, gave rise to a kind of déjà vu in the West. (Recall that World War I was triggered by the assassination of Archduke Ferdinand of Austria at Sarajevo, the capital of Bosnia, by a Bosnian-Serb nationalist in June 1914.) No sooner was the "dirty war" in Bosnia brought to a bitter end than another one broke out in Kosovo, a province of Serbia inhabited mainly by ethnic Albanians.

Outsiders (including the United States and its NATO allies) were reluctant to intervene in Yugoslavia's civil war even after reports of atrocities and human rights violations (especially by the Serbs) in Bosnia-Herzegovina were reported in the press and condemned by the United Nations. The Western powers were particularly anxious not to do anything that might provoke the Russians into intervening on the side of the Serbs (as they did in World War I). That was high unlikely, as long as Yeltsin—a man with a history of alcoholism and heart disease—remained in power. Even so, in the chaos and uncertainty enveloping Russia, one danger was that Russian generals would join forces with extreme nationalists (including old-guard communists) and take action with or without Yeltsin's approval. Who could forget that the Balkan tinderbox had triggered World War I? Who could say for certain that history was not repeating itself?

That instability in one country would spill over into neighboring countries, possibly causing cross-border conflicts, was a danger not to be lightly dismissed. Wars often give rise to sudden mass migrations as people flee from the fighting. The resulting refugee problems can destabilize neighboring states not directly involved in the hostilities—a potential nightmare for Western Europe. Although the nightmare did not come to pass, ethnic conflicts in the former Yugoslavia left nearly 600,000 refugees in limbo after nearly a decade of fighting—300,000 from Bosnia and 296,000 from Serbia and Montenegro. (Germany had a total refugee population approaching 1 million (960,000) in 2003, the United Kingdom had over a quarter of a million (276,000), and the overcrowded Netherlands had 140,000. In countries already facing a mounting crisis in public finance related to pensions, unemployment benefits, and a wide range of other social programs, the additional burden on tax revenues arising from an influx of refugees was most unwelcome.

The push of war (or famine) is one cause of migration; the pull of opportunities and higher living standards is another. During the Cold War, the Soviet Union kept the populations of Eastern Europe (the "captive nations") from migrating to the West—precisely the reason why the Soviet Union and East Germany built the Berlin Wall in 1961. When the Cold War ended, many West Europeans feared a mass influx of East European immigrants in search of jobs. A rich country is a natural magnet for people from poor countries. (This phenomenon explains how the American Wild West was populated—that is, by land-poor peasants from rural areas in Europe who immigrated to America and became the frontier farmers we know as settlers and pioneers.)

The turmoil resulting from the collapse of the Soviet empire occasioned a great debate in the West. According to one theory, stability in Eastern Europe and the Balkans, as well as in the former Soviet Union itself, was purely a function of Moscow's hegemony (dominance) in the region. When Mikhail Gorbachev pulled the props from under the structures that his predecessors had built (the Warsaw Pact, Comecon), the whole thing collapsed like a house of cards. Those who subscribed to this theory tended to be pessimistic about the long-term prospects for peace in the region.

A more optimistic theory held that instability in Slavic Europe was a manifestation of economic failure and the human hardships that went with it. Thus, the solution to ethnic strife and social unrest was primarily economic. Correct policies, infusions of capital from the West, and access to Europe's **single market** (the EU) would turn things around. Which side was right? There was (is) truth on both sides. Strong economies are more likely to produce contented societies than weak economies. But strong economies require stable political systems and sound policies.

The consequences of the Soviet withdrawal are obvious, but cause and effect are much more difficult to establish. For example, Yugoslavia was never under Soviet domination and might well have disintegrated even if the Cold War had not ended. Significantly, Czechoslovakia went through a bloodless breakup very different from Yugoslavia's violent one. Moreover, the Slavic nations are not alone in fighting wars with neighboring states—witness the innumerable conflicts in Western Europe following the emergence of the nation-state system in the sixteenth century.

For all the turmoil in the first decade after the fall of communism, there are clear signs that a stable order is emerging in Eastern Europe. With the partial

TABLE 7.4 Elections and Parties: The Early Winnowing Effect

Country	Election Date	Number of Parties in Election	Number of Parties in the Parliament
Bulgaria	October 13, 1991	37	5
Czech Republic	June 5, 1992	21	6
Hungary	March 26, 1990	45	7
Poland	October 27, 1991	67	29
Romania	September 27, 1992	7	7*
Slovakia	June 5, 1992	5	5

*Excludes thirteen seats for national minorities.

exception of Poland, a **winnowing effect** narrowed the number of viable political parties in the early 1990s (see Table 7.4), thus reducing the danger of parliamentary fragmentation and governmental paralysis. Given the long period of enforced conformity they went through, it is not surprising that the former socialist countries are having some difficulty containing pent-up collective emotions, coping with newfound liberties, and reaching consensus on the best solutions to the problems that are the legacy of communist rule.

Preparing for Takeoff

Many of the problems plaguing the former Soviet Union are also present elsewhere in Eastern Europe. The dilemmas and dislocations associated with making the transition from central planning to the free market are regionwide. Ethnic animosities kept in check by police-state controls before 1989 have resurfaced in various places. But despite these nagging problems, Poland, Hungary, the Czech Republic, and Slovakia (as well as the Baltic states) set about creating a **competitive market** by freeing prices, privatizing large parts of the economy, and shutting down inefficient state-owned industries. The immediate effect was a sharp drop in industrial output in the early 1990s. It was the kind of painful but necessary adjustment that can easily undercut public support for **market reforms** if it failed to produce tangible benefits. (Economists generally agree that state-owned enterprises generally wasted labor and energy, produced inferior goods, and excessively polluted the environment, but East Europeans associated them with full employment and lifelong job-security.)

Although direct foreign investment in the region rose sharply in the early 1990s, the wait-and-see attitude of Western and Japanese investors impeded rapid economic recovery. During the nineties, Hungary and Poland attracted the lion's share of all foreign investment in the region. The Czech Republic and Slovenia were next in line, followed distantly by the others. In attracting foreign capital, a clear commitment to private enterprise and evidence of political stability were (are) the two most important factors. For example, in the mid-1990s, when a newly elected Polish president (and an ex-communist) gave reassurances that he

TABLE 7.5 Emerging Markets in 1999–2000: A Performance Comparison*
(percentage of change from a year earlier)

	GDP	Industrial Production	Consumer Prices
Asia			
China	8.1	11.5	0.1
India	5.8	12.2	5.5
Indonesia	3.2	34.8	1.2
Malaysia	11.7	18.6	1.2
Thailand	5.2	4.2	1.7
Latin America			
Argentina	0.9	5.8	−1.0
Brazil	3.1	3.3	5.3
Chile	5.5	2.9	3.6
Mexico	7.9	5.1	9.3
Eastern Europe			
Czech Republic	4.4	2.8	3.7
Hungary	6.8	20.3	9.1
Poland	6.0	12.3	10.0
Russia	7.5	10.6	19.4

*The precise reporting periods represented in this table vary slightly from country to country, but the data all pertain to the one-year period 1999–2000, and therefore provide a reasonable basis for a comparison of relative economic performance.

SOURCE: "Emerging Market Indicators," *The Economist,* July 1, 2000, p. 116.

intended to a continue Poland's market reforms, foreign investors responded by pouring about $2 billion into Poland's reviving economy.[13] By contrast, in the Czech Republic hopes of enticing private foreign investors were momentarily set back in 1997, when scandals and a currency crisis brought down the conservative government of then Prime Minister (now President) Vaclav Klaus.

A comparison with other emerging markets suggests that Poland, Hungary, and the Czech Republic were on the right track at the end of the 1990s (see Table 7.5). Slovenia was another bright spot in the region; Slovakia, still playing catch-up, was showing signs of vitality, too. More recently, the Baltic states have come on strong; in fact, in 2002, Lithuania had the fastest growth rate in Europe (nearly 7 percent), followed closely by Latvia and Estonia. As a result, all of these countries were admitted to the European Union in 2004.

Macroeconomic statistics can be misleading, however, because national economies vary greatly in size and stage of development. Given the right conditions (investment capital, tax incentives, a skilled labor force) a small economy like Lithuania will often grow a lot faster than a large economy like Germany but the actual value of the increment to the nation's wealth will still be greater in the large economy. (For example, 10 percent of a thousand dollars is a tiny amount

TABLE 7.6 **After Communism: Economic Performance in Eastern Europe, 1990–1998**

Country	Average Annual Real Growth (percent)	Average Annual Inflation Rate (percent)
Bulgaria	−1.8	117
Croatia	0.5	131
Czech Republic	−0.2	14
Hungary	0.9	22
Poland	4.4	27
Romania	−0.6	114
Slovakia	1.1	11
Slovenia	4.4	27

SOURCE: International Bank for Reconstruction and Development, *World Bank Atlas 2000* (Washington, DC: Author, 2000).

compared to 2 percent of a million dollars.) Hence it is always important to put GNP growth rates into perspective.

To further illustrate this point, Brazil's GNP in the late 1990s was twice the size of Russia's, according to World Bank statistics. It was also roughly seventeen times larger than Hungary's, fourteen times the size of the Czech Republic's, and five times larger than Poland's. Hence Brazil's growth rates, although slower than, say, Poland's in 1999, were nonetheless more impressive than they seem at first glance, whereas the Czech Republic's were just the opposite.

Membership in the EU provides a major incentive for these countries to work for change and stability simultaneously. It may also help governments facing vociferous opposition parties to encourage pragmatism and moderation rather than ideological posturing and confrontation.

Overall, Poland and Slovenia achieved the highest average annual economic growth rates in the region during the decade of the nineties, followed by Hungary and Slovakia (see Table 7.6). Czechs, however, enjoyed single-digit inflation and low unemployment, in contrast to Poland and Hungary, where unemployment remained a serious problem. On the negative side, many formerly state-owned enterprises in the Czech Republic continued to keep redundant and inefficient workers on the payroll—a short-term solution impeding the long-term process of adjustment to a competitive business environment. We turn first to Poland.

POLAND: THE SHOCK TREATMENT

In the 1990s, Poland led the way in making the transition from communism to capitalism. Both terms are used loosely in this case because Poland was never a full-blown communist state and after 1989 it did not shed all the attributes of the

Stalinist state—particularly state ownership of the "commanding heights" of the economy. A decade after implementation of the shock therapy measures designed to force the pace of market reforms in Poland, three-quarters of country's tangible assets, including mines, steel mills, and factories, remained in state hands although "most of Poland's GDP comes from the private sector." With few exceptions, communist-era enterprises are "deep in debt and bleeding money. Only one in ten . . . is turning a profit."[14]

Unlike other Soviet-dominated East European countries, Poles managed to preserve a private sector alongside the centrally planned economy Stalin's Polish puppets imposed after World War II. Polish farmers (smallholders, that is) resisted collectivization and shopkeepers were allowed to own and operate small businesses. In the last decade of communist rule, the private sector accounted for 5–10 percent of economic activity. Thus the connection to private enterprise was never completely broken, which helps explain why Poland set the pace when the time came time to introduce market reforms.

And set the pace it did. As the lid came off the market and the profit motive was given free play, the moribund Polish economy sprang to life again, bouncing back from dismal double-digit GDP contractions at the beginning of the decade to positive growth in the range of 5 percent between 1993 and 2003. At the same time, austerity measures associated with the shock therapy drove down inflation from a high of nearly 600 percent (!) in the early 1990s to less than 5 percent a decade later. It was projected to fall below 2 percent in 2006.

That was the good news. The bad news was that Poland's public finances were in serious disarray, as indicated by the fact that the deficit in 2001 was projected at 11 percent of GDP (compared to an average of slightly less than 3 percent for the euro area in 2004) for the coming year. Moreover, unemployment continued to hover around 20 percent in 2003.

Why? What happened to take the bloom off the flowering Polish reform program so quickly? Even more than the welfare states of Western Europe, the Polish government remains heavily committed to a full range of cradle-to-the-grave social benefits. Paying for this extensive state-funded safety net means that social security contributions in Poland are among the highest in Europe. The number of Poles claiming disability benefits (including many cheaters) is very high as well. These chronic budget imbalances were accompanied by an economic slowdown in the late 1990s, prompting some observers—including former finance minister Leszek Balcerowicz, the governor of Poland's central bank—to connect the two. There were other causes—external to Poland—that probably had more to do with the slowdown there, including the sluggish German economy and another ruble crisis in Russia. Nonetheless, there was no denying that consumer confidence was falling and Poles were spending less than they had just a year or two earlier before the central bank raised interest rates in order to keep inflation under control.

Besides budget deficits and tighter credit, there were other signs that all was not well. As noted earlier, high unemployment is one of the biggest problems facing the Polish government in recent years, rising from 10 percent in 1998 to 20 percent in 2003. An OECD concluded that Poland's labor market was the worst

T A B L E 7.7 **Employment in Four Ex-Communist States in 2004 (working-age population holding jobs)***

Czech Republic	65%
Hungary	56%
Slovakia	58%
Poland	51%

*To put these figures into perspective, slightly over 75 percent of the white working-age population held jobs in the United Kingdom in 2003 and 62.4 percent of the total working-age population held jobs in the United States in 2005.

among its thirty rich member countries; moreover, it was also outshined by some of its ex-communist neighbors (see Table 7.7).

Poland continues to suffer from structural defects that are a legacy of the communist era when workers were poorly paid but everybody was guaranteed a job. But so do other former communist states. So why does Poland have a bigger job-creation problem than, say, the Czech Republic or Hungary?

If you want to set up a new factory in Poland or keep an old factory going, you face high payroll taxes, a high minimum wage (little less than the average wage), and various obstacles to firing workers (including job-protection clauses in privatization contracts). Obviously, anything that creates (or perpetuates) disincentives to hiring new workers prevents the jobless rate from falling. To make matters worse, new jobseekers are entering the labor market in larger numbers now thanks to Poland's baby boom of the early 1980s. This situation, in turn, causes at least one next-door neighbor already hard hit by unemployment and labor disputes namely, Germany—to worry that Polish workers will cross the border in large numbers in search of jobs.

Agriculture still accounts for roughly 16 percent of Poland's total labor force (the ratio for developed market economies is normally below 3 percent). At the same time, Poland's total farm production contributes only about 3 percent to the nation's annual GDP. "Getting rural folk into more productive jobs could add 30% to Polish output," according to the OECD.[15]

Not all Poland's problems are economic in nature. Poles are well aware that corruption is widespread but fixing the problem is another matter. Official corruption is far and away the worst kind because it probably means that the individuals who are responsible for enforcing the laws and protecting the public interest have dirty hands themselves. Small wonder, then, that Poles—like Czechs, Russians, and others living in an ex-communist state—are often very cynical about politics. Unlike many Americans, people in this part of the world do not automatically equate prosperity with democracy or capitalism. According to a former Polish science minister, "To admit that life is good is seen in some circles as almost indecent."[16] Many Poles in all walks of life express similar sentiments.

This disillusionment is expressed in various ways, but perhaps the most damaging expression for the vitality of Poland's new democracy takes the form of apathy. In 1990, when the mustachioed hero of Poland's fabled Solidarity movement, Lech Walesa, was elected president, only 53 percent of eligible voters bothered to cast a ballot. (Poland requires a 50 percent turnout; anything less invalidates the vote.)

Voter apathy and official corruption contribute to a political environment that is less than conducive to good government or governmental stability—the two are obviously interrelated. Poland's ever-changing political landscape reflects the shallowness and fragility of the country's democratic roots. Power has shifted left and right in a kaleidoscopic succession of shaky coalition governments sometimes lacking a majority in the Sejm. Poland had seen no fewer than ten prime ministers come and go by the time of the 2005 elections. The number of political parties fell from about a hundred competing in the 1991 elections to a dozen or so viable ones a decade later (seven of which managed to qualify for seats in the parliament in 2001). Ideally, the winnowing effect eliminates fringe parties, rationalizes the process by giving voters a manageable number of viable alternatives, and forces serious parties to seek broad public support rather than appealing to narrow special interests or single-issue groups. But, as Poland's still-fragmented political party system attests, theory and practice are two different things.

Between 1989 and 2005, there were four rounds of parliamentary elections— in 1989, 1993, 1997, and 2001. Each time the pendulum of power made a sweeping swing to the other side of the political spectrum. In 1989, a center-right coalition led by Solidarity formed a government; in 1993, the pendulum swung to the left; four years later, the pendulum swung back to the right; finally, in 2001, voters repudiated the Solidarity Electoral Alliance (AWS), handing power back to the left. In 2001, AWS failed to win a single seat (despite having controlled a commanding 201 seats in the previous parliament), while the victorious Democratic Left Alliance (SLD) saw its representation in Sejm jump from 164 seats to 216. But despite these gyrations, governments have been surprisingly steadfast in the pursuit of economic reforms, as well as membership in NATO and the European Union.

Nonetheless, two parties in particular illustrate the volatility of Polish politics and the potential for surprises on both the left and the right. The first is a populist party called **Self-Defense** (*Samoobrana* in Polish). Led by a former boxer by the name of Andrzej Lepper known to keep a punching bag in his office, Self-Defense had a broad popular following (20–30 percent) in 2004. What was Lepper advocating that so many Poles liked so much? George W. Bush, he said, should be put on trial for invading Iraq. Poland should quit the European Union unless it can get a better deal. Half the reserves in the Polish Nation Bank should be used to subsidize low-interest loans to farmers and homebuyers. If the value of the zloty (Poland's currency) falls, so what? It will boost Polish exports.

Self-Defense is a left-wing populist party founded in the early 1990s to fight for the interests of small farmers. It has evolved into a party that appeals directly "to the millions who feel they have lost out in the transition from communism to capitalism. It promises to halve unemployment in four years, to increase social-security payments, to launch a big public-works program, and to preserve what remains of state-controlled industry."[17]

Rivaling Self-Defense on the right are two newcomers to the political scene–**Civic Platform** (PO), or Platforma, and **Law and Justice** (PiS).

The PO, an upstart party that did not even exist until a few months before the election, won an impressive 13 percent of the vote in 2001. It is a business-friendly centrist party embracing classical liberal principles. Self-defense and Civic Platform both support EU membership but criticize what they see as flaws in the proposed EU constitution. These criticisms had helped put the outcome of Poland's referendum on that question in doubt even before voters in France and Holland made it moot. The Law and Justice Party is even more harshly critical of the proposed EU constitution. In the 2005 election (discussed later), the party campaigned on a platform that condemned waste in government spending and corruption, a message that resonated with many Polish voters.

When Marek Belka replaced Leszek Miller as prime minister in May 2004, it was doubtful whether he would get confirmed or, if confirmed, how long he could hang on as head of a minority government. Belka did manage to hang on, surviving a no-confidence vote later in 2004. He was helped by an economic upturn in 2004, which saw GDP rise by 4–5 percent (Poland's best showing since 1997).

Nonetheless, the center-right parties again swept back into power in the fall of 2005, as two right-wing parties—Law and Justice and Civic Platform—won 288 out of 460 total seats (155 and 133, respectively), while the outgoing Alliance of the Democratic Left (SLD) won only 55 seats. Once again, the pendulum had swung in the other direction, a sign that voter dissatisfaction remains high in Poland.

The center right also dominated the presidential elections in October 2005. Aleksander Kazyński, leader of the Law and Justice Party, won a runoff election against Civic Platform's Donald Tusk. Another sign that all is not well in the eyes of the electorate: more than half the eligible voters did not bother to vote on the first ballot.

In sum, Poland has made great strides since the days of one-party dictatorship and foreign domination. There is no Polish economic miracle in the making, but the trajectory of the economy is a gradually ascending curve. Entrance into the EU does not guarantee anything, but it does hold out the prospect of faster growth in the years to come. Poland is a big country with big problems. To compete within the huge and highly competitive single market (the EU) it must rationalize and modernize its communist-era factories. To do that, it must attract foreign investment, which in turn means keeping public finances in balance and inflation under control. Lowering corporate and payroll taxes would lure foreign capital, but Poland also has a strong commitment to social justice (the welfare state). In the final analysis, success in all these areas depends on political and governmental stability.

More than two centuries after once-mighty Poland was dismembered and following four decades in a kind of collective bondage, Poland has a new lease on life. With the Cold War over and Russia no longer a military threat, Poland's pivotal position in Central Europe is once again an asset rather than a liability. It also makes Poland a particularly valuable asset to NATO and the EU.

We turn next to Ukraine, a country nearly twice the size of Poland and boasting a considerably larger population (37 million compared to 48 million). That is about all Ukraine had to boast about—until the winter of 2004–2005.

UKRAINE: GEOGRAPHY IS DESTINY . . .
OR MAYBE NOT

"In Europe, geography no longer equals destiny"—at least in the view of NATO's secretary general, who made this bold assertion in April 2004.[18] Few in Poland or the Baltic States would dispute this assertion, but Ukrainians might well have questioned it at the time. As if to get a definitive answer, they would test whether "geography no longer equals destiny" at the end of the year in a presidential election that pitted an authoritarian old guard backed by Moscow against an opposition candidate who promised to tilt the country toward the West.

When pro-Russian candidate Prime Minister Viktor Yanukovich, the personal choice of outgoing President Leonid Kuchma, was declared the winner, Russia's President Putin endorsed the outcome, while leaders in the West, including President Bush, backed the opposition claim that the election was rigged.[19] Putin appeared to be "insisting that the lines defining Moscow's sphere influence . . . hold firm at Ukraine's western border."[20] Suddenly Ukraine found itself on the fault line as the tectonic plates beneath Europe's post–Cold War political order shifted.

Ironically, it was Ukraine's own internal east-west divide that set the stage for this drama. Support for opposition candidate (now president) Viktor Yushchenko was strong in western Ukraine, which had been part of eastern Poland before 1939. Many people there still speak Polish rather than Ukrainian or Russian. Although some secretly long to be reunited with Poland, the vast majority desire at the very least to join the European Union and NATO (as Poland has done). Yushchenko was the first serious candidate for president to come out unequivocally in favor of this tilt westward. Support for Yanukovich came primarily from predominantly Russian-speaking eastern Ukraine. Many inhabitants of eastern Ukraine are ethnic Russians and even Ukrainians there look at western Ukraine as un-Ukrainian and untrustworthy. Throughout Slavic Europe, people are aware of the stigma associated with the word "eastern" by Westerners. It is true in Germany today, it was true in the former Czechoslovakia before the breakup in 1992, and it is true of Ukraine. It is also, of course, true of Europe as a whole.

Now that so many former Soviet satellite states have joined the West, it is easy to forget that without Moscow's acquiescence it might not have happened—or if it did, might not have been accomplished peacefully. When the Soviet Union crumbled, Russia remained. No longer a superpower, Russia was nonetheless in possession of a superpower-sized nuclear arsenal. No one familiar with the awesome power of these weapons will doubt that Russia can still put its foot down, and it looked as though Putin was determined to do so. But that was before the Orange Revolution—a nonviolent, spontaneous act of mass defiance— changed the stakes.[21]

Thousands of Ukrainians streamed into the streets of Kiev, the capital, to protest the rigged election of Viktor Yanukovich, then camped out in the center of the city, braving the cold Ukrainian winter, until Rada (parliament) passed a vote of no confidence in the Yanukovich government; outgoing President

Kuchma acceded to opposition demands for a second runoff election; and Russian President Vladimir Putin backed away from the brink. The protestors refused to disperse and go home until Viktor Yushchenko was declared the official winner of the second runoff election in late December.[22] After the Constitutional Court dismissed a specious challenge by Yanukovich, Yushchenko was sworn in and Ukraine appeared set to turn a new page in its history.

Turning that page, however, would be easier said than done. The country that had once been a breadbasket had become a basket case. In 2004, Ukraine's gross national product was only 60 percent of what it had been before the Soviet collapse. Yushchenko faces the daunting task of reviving one of the most dilapidated economies on the Continent. In 2004, Ukraine's per capita GDP was less than two-fifths that of Bulgaria, Romania, or Turkey—countries that are candidates for EU membership but rank among the poorest in Europe. Ukraine's GDP stood at a miniscule $55 billion, about one-tenth the size of the Netherlands' economy, though Ukraine's population is four times larger. Even Russia, with three times more people, a floundering reform program, and the same Stalinist legacy to overcome, is doing considerably better than Ukraine.

On the positive side, Ukraine's economy was growing. As prime minister for eighteen months in 2000–2001, Yushchenko had taken bold steps to straighten out the country's public finances by collecting taxes, and going after privatization accounts receivable, and recouping "more than $1 billion that had been siphoned off by energy oligarchs."[23] The economy responded by growing 6 percent in 2000 and over 9 percent in 2001. Ukraine's economic recovery continued on a positive trajectory even after Kuchma sacked Yushchenko in 2001. Although the growth rate slowed in 2005, it had hit a peak of 12.5 percent the previous year.[24]

It may turn out that one legacy of the Orange Revolution is to open the West to Ukraine, and vice versa. If so, Ukraine's economy will soon begin to benefit from the stimulating effects of trade and investment with Europe's richest countries The potential exists: Ukraine has vast fertile lands, coal, iron ore, large deposits of various minerals, and timber. Major farm products include grain, sugar beets and sunflower seeds. Heavy industry in Ukraine is woefully inefficient and mismanaged, but there is a lot of it. Ukraine produces metals, coke, fertilizer, airplanes, turbines, metallurgical equipment, diesel locomotives, and tractors. In addition, oil and gas transport is a major source of foreign exchange, mainly from Russian fuel exports flowing through pipelines that cross Ukraine en route to Western Europe.

In sum, the east-west faceoff in late 2004 over Ukraine's future did cause tremors in Europe, but fortunately not the earthquake some observers feared. Constitutional changes in the Ukraine's political system designed to strengthen the parliament and prime minister at the expense of the president were set in motion before the election. What, if any, lasting effect these changes will have on Ukraine's inchoate democracy remains to be seen.

The early signs give little cause for optimism. Scandals and a deep split between the top two leaders of the Orange Revolution left Ukraine's fledgling democracy teetering precariously on the edge of a precipice in the fall of 2005. With rumors and accusations flying in all directions, Yushchenko sacked the government headed by Yulia Timoshenko, his confederate in the Orange Revolution and now his bitter rival. A key member of Yushchenko's own inner circle, his chief of staff Oleksandr Zinchenko, resigned, charging that other close advisors had organized an "information blockade" around the president in order to keep him in the dark while they grabbed assets and settled old scores.[25] The charge had the ring of truth.

The citizens of the new Ukraine at long last are free to choose whether to make a clean break with the past or continue on the same path that brought the country to the brink of ruin. Whatever the future holds, Ukrainians can no longer blame geography—or Russia—if things go awry.

THE CZECH REPUBLIC: CHALLENGES AHEAD

The big question in 1992 was whether Prague would continue to be the capital of a federal state with two republics or whether Bratislava would become the capital of an independent Slovak state. A decade later, few Czechs or Slovaks expressed nostalgia for a bygone time when they were all part of one not-so-happy "family."

The Best of the Worst

Before 1989, Czechoslovakia and East Germany had been the two most rigidly Stalinist states in the Soviet bloc. They also had the healthiest economies in the communist world. In the early 1990s, about one-half of the Czechoslovak labor force was employed in industry, producing machinery and machine tools, chemical products, textiles, and glassware. The principal crops were wheat, potatoes, barley (a prime ingredient in beer, for which the Czechs are famous), and sugar beets. Czechoslovakia had been a net exporter of food since the early 1970s.

By 1980, economic tremors prompted the government to call for greater efficiency, cuts in subsidies to state enterprises, the gearing of wages to productivity, and advances in quality control to boost Czechoslovak imports to the West. But economic performance during the 1980s resembled a roller-coaster ride.

Economic figures do not tell the whole story, however. Anyone who had spent a few days in Moscow or Leningrad (St. Petersburg) and then visited Prague could see the sharp contrast in living standards. In Prague, unlike Moscow, one did not see people waiting in long lines to buy food and other necessities. Nor did one see empty shops or bare shelves. Czechs and Slovaks generally ate and dressed well, possessed various household appliances, frequented pubs and restaurants, and attended the theater, cinema, and concerts. Most Czech and Slovak families owned an automobile, whereas most Russians could only dream of having a private car. And the national health system in Czechoslovakia was much better than in the Soviet Union.

In sum, if the Czechoslovak economy was not vibrant in the 1980s, neither was it bleak. To the extent that economic factors contributed to public disenchantment with communism, it probably reflected the fact that the Western-oriented

Czechoslovaks tended to use the West rather than the East as a yardstick for comparison. The fact that Czechoslovakia shared a border with prosperous West Germany might well have been a contributing factor (as it certainly was in East Germany). Also relevant is the famous J-curve theory, which holds that the greatest danger of mass revolt occurs not during progressively worsening conditions, as one might expect, but rather when steadily improving conditions are followed by a leveling off or a downturn. As living standards improve, there is a natural surge of rising expectations; if those expectations are not met, disappointment may be manifested in the spirit of rebellion.

Czechs without Slovakia

The Czech and Slovak republics formally split into two separate states at the end of 1992. The separation was accomplished peacefully but not painlessly. For many Czechs and Slovaks, the **Velvet Divorce** was unwanted. Polls showed that a majority in both republics opposed it. There were many wrenching issues to resolve, including how to divide Czechoslovakia's assets and liabilities (including military facilities and weapons, foreign reserves, the external debt, and foreign embassies); what to do about the flag, anthem, and other important symbols of the former nation; and whether or not to create a customs union or retain a common currency.

Nonetheless, the breakup occurred without lasting bitterness between the two former partners and the country called Czechoslovakia soon became a fading memory. Slovakia was always the junior partner, living within the shadow of the bigger and richer Czech lands. The loss of subsidies from Prague was a sharp blow to the Slovak economy and a corresponding boost to the Czech Republic. By the same token, Czechs benefited from the stabilizing effect of the soft-spoken, internationally acclaimed President Vaclav Havel. By contrast, inept leadership and acrimonious politics hampered Slovakia's economic rebuilding program until the defeat of the combative and controversial prime minister Vladimir Meciar in 1998.

A Botched Privatization

Despite the disruptive effects of the breakup, Czechoslovakia's GDP stabilized in 1992 and began rising again. Led by conservative Prime Minister Vaclav Klaus, the Czech Republic initiated an ambitious privatization scheme during this period. The objectives of this plan were to abolish the huge, inefficient state-owned enterprises of the Communist era, make ordinary Czechs shareholders in new companies, and create a competitive free-market economy. Unfortunately, the plan fell victim to corruption, mismanagement, opposition, and obstruction from various quarters. Nor was the nation's top policy maker blameless. Prime Minister Klaus was at best inconsistent (at worst cynical), extolling the virtues of free enterprise and striking Thatcherlike poses in public but letting expedience rather than principle be his guide in practice.

In early 1997, the country was rocked by a financial crisis with multiple causes, including the bungled privatization program, a continuing succession of bank failures, government scandals, and a general economic malaise. In July 1997, the Czech Republic, along with Poland and Hungary, was formally invited to join the NATO alliance at the Madrid summit meeting, but this historic event was overshadowed by a natural disaster—the worst flooding in Czech history. One-third of the country was deluged and several dozen people were killed. Many towns and villages were awash; early estimates of the damage put the total at a billion and a half dollars or higher.

By the end of the year, the public mood had turned from sour to bitter amid a scandal involving the campaign finances of the ruling ODS party. Prime Minister Klaus denied any personal involvement, but as party leader he could not escape responsibility. At the end of 1997, the laconic Klaus was forced to step down in the face of mounting public criticism and crumbling support within the government's party coalition in parliament.

Winners Not Quite In, Losers Not Quite Out

With Klaus out and no other party leader in parliament willing or able to form a new government, President Havel appointed a caretaker pending preparation for new elections in mid-1998. The Social Democrats led by Milos Zeman gained more popular votes and parliamentary seats than Klaus's ODS, but fell far short of a clear majority. The inconclusive outcome of the election left the key questions unanswered. Would Zeman (or anybody else) be able to form a government? If so, would it be able to govern? Zeman's options were severely limited: a coalition of the left that included the Communists or a partnership with small center-right parties. The first option was undesirable and the second proved to be impossible. That left only one possibility for the Social Democrats—a minority government dependent on a benign opposition. But would the former prime minister in defeat make a deal?

Klaus pledged not to play the role of spoiler, but ODS would not become the junior partner in a coalition government either. As the opposition, ODS would freely criticize but not obstruct the new government, this was the essence of the so-called **Opposition Agreement.** In return, Zeman obviously had to resolve not to pursue a policy course or press for legislation unpalatable to the center-right. The result was a government with a gun held to its head by the opposition. Klaus was holding the gun, of course, but there was always the danger that it would backfire: if he pulled the trigger, would he look like an alternative or an assassin? Would the electorate reward or punish his party at the next election?

The Opposition Agreement: A Stab at Stability

Not surprisingly, the Zeman government stayed the course, undertaking few new initiatives and banking on a reviving economy to boost the Social Democrats' popular support. There was more common ground between government and opposition than might have been expected. Zeman, an economist by training, pursued privatization with no less vigor (and arguably more) than Klaus had. In general, his economic policies had the effect of reassuring potential foreign investors.

In foreign policy, too, Zeman followed the course charted by his predecessor. As leader of the opposition, Zeman had been cool to the idea of NATO membership; as leader of the nation he put any earlier doubts aside. He also continued to press for entry into the European Union, but on terms that would protect new members' fragile emerging markets.

Perhaps the most important long-term consequence of the Opposition Agreement was a cooperative effort to scrap the existing system of proportional representation in favor of an Anglo-American first-past-the-post system (single-member districts, plurality vote) and to weaken the office of the presidency. Remember that this type of system weakens the link between popular votes and parliamentary representation and tends to favor large parties while shutting out small ones altogether. Obviously, the Social Democrats and ODS stand to gain the most from this change. Alarmed by this development, the smaller parties in parliament formed a four-party coalition in an attempt to stop the political freight train bearing down on them.

It is easy to question the motives behind these two changes in the Czech Republic's political system. Discriminating against small parties appears to violate the spirit of political fair play and the intent of democracy—to give voters the right to choose among meaningful alternatives. On the other hand, governmental stability—or even paralysis—is the price societies often have to pay for such a wide-open system. The confusion, disarray, and improvisation that characterized Czech government in 1997-98 provide a classic case in point.

A bizarre episode at the end of 2000 provided new evidence that all was not well in the Czech transition to democracy. When a council established by parliament named a new head of the Czech state television network (ČETA), journalists at the facility—unhappy with the choice—barricaded themselves inside. They argued that the new director was unfit for the position because of his close ties to former Prime Minister Vaclav Klaus. The issue, they insisted, was journalistic independence and integrity, not personalities. Normal programming was disrupted (for example, there was virtually no news or weather presented) and the disgruntled employees broadcast an alternative news show every night accessible to about 10 percent of Czech households with satellite and cable television. Apparently, many Czechs agreed—every night for weeks on end crowds gathered in Wenceslas Square or at the television station on the outskirts of Prague to demonstrate solidarity with the strikers. And, in traditional Bohemian fashion, people brought food and drink to the rebels who hoisted it up to second-story windows in plastic buckets.

Following the 2002 elections, the Social Democrats joined with two smaller parties to form a fragile coalition government. The coalition had a razor thin one-seat majority in parliament, and even that disappeared in July 2003 when a disgruntled MP announced he was leaving the Social Democratic Party's parliamentary caucus. Whether the government could limp along without a majority until the next elections was seriously in doubt. The government's disarray would likely play into the hands of the unreformed Communists, the third largest party in the Czech parliament. Many older Czechs especially could not help but remember that the Communists had come to power after World War II as a result of winning

T A B L E   7.8   **Central Europe's Brightening Prospects: Forecasted Growth in Real GDP (percentage of annual change)**

Country	2000	2004	2006 (estimate)
Czech Republic	2.6	4.3	4.4
Hungary	5.6	3.8	4.0
Poland	5.0	3.9	4.1

SOURCE: "Emerging Market Indicators," *The Economist*, October 14, 2000, p. 148 and "The World in 2006," *The Economist*, April 9, 2005, p. 90.

an election. Meanwhile, the Czech Republic was due to join the EU in 2004—a major milestone that placed a premium on firm leadership.

The *economic* consequences of political instability for Europe's emerging democracies cannot be ignored. The stakes for these countries, including the Czech Republic, are extremely high. When it comes to enticing foreign investment, vital for rapid economic redevelopment, the first hurdle is political, not economic. By the same token, few things are more important to trade expansion in this part of the world than access to Europe's huge single market, but full membership in the EU (including the single currency) will depend, above all, on solid evidence of democratic maturity.

The Czech Republic's transition to a market economy remains incomplete, but not without its successes. It has not only managed to keep both inflation and interest rates at moderate levels but also has partially restructured the economy while avoiding mass worker dislocations. By the end of the decade, GDP growth was modest but steady and industrial output was rising more steeply. Economic forecasts for 2006 were slightly rosier (Table 7.8).

Czechs have enjoyed the second highest per capita GDP in the region (first-ranking Slovenia is far ahead, however). Inflation has been very low (1–2 percent in 2004-2005), and foreign companies have begun investing heavily in the Czech economy. Productivity and wages are going up, but budget deficits, a legacy of the communist era, remain a chronic problem.

Overall, Eastern Europe was gradually emerging from the economic doldrums. There were no model democracies to be found, perhaps, but the dictatorships of the past were long gone, with few exceptions. One of the last countries to oust a dictator was Yugoslavia—oddly enough, the very country that had been closest to the West during the Cold War.

SERBIA (FORMERLY YUGOSLAVIA): REJECTING DICTATORSHIP

Freedom of the press is guaranteed by the constitution, but under Slobodan Milosevic the government often treated civil liberties, including free speech, with disdain. Indeed, Milosevic tightly controlled the news media and the leading newspapers were strictly censored. *Vreme*, an independent newsweekly, was the one major exception. In all probability, Milosevic allowed this single bastion of free speech to exist as a way to mollify or confound his critics.

A virtual dictator, Milosevic was totally out of step with the times, preferring force and intimidation to persuasion, negotiation, and compromise. But he had a keen instinct for personal political survival. In the postcommunist era, he managed to hang onto power longer than others who played by the rules of democracy. Ultimately, he failed to keep even the rump state he inherited united, but in that he was not alone. No East European leader succeeded in maintaining a national consensus during the difficult transition from communist dictatorship to democracy. However, the bitter legacy of Milosevic's rule is not only dissension and disunity but also an economy in ruins and a society with a badly tarnished reputation in the world.

Into the Abyss

Ever-increasing economic problems—including hyperinflation (more than 1,000 percent for a time in 1989–1990)—accelerated Yugoslavia's disintegration. On July 2, 1990, democratically elected governments in Slovenia and Macedonia declared their independence ("full sovereignty") within Yugoslavia, and Croatia approved constitutional changes having basically the same effect. On the same day, a majority of Serbs approved a referendum on a new constitution that made the formerly autonomous provinces of Kosovo and Vojvodina parts of Greater Serbia (in violation of the federal constitution). Meanwhile, the Kosovo assembly approved a measure making Kosovo a sovereign republic within Yugoslavia. Serbia then dissolved the Kosovo legislature.

Former communists won by landslides in Serbia and Montenegro but lost decisively in Bosnia-Herzegovina. Ethnic tensions were thus reinforced by a political and ideological rift between the Serbs and Montenegrins on one hand and the rest of the crumbling Yugoslav federation on the other. (A similar phenomenon occurred in Czechoslovakia in 1992, with the Czechs being led by free-market enthusiasts and the Slovaks by a leftist politician who opposed rapid privatization.) The Serbian government further exacerbated the situation by issuing, without National Bank approval, $1.4 billion in new money to ease its own financial straits. Branded as "stealing from the other republics," this action triggered the beginning of the end for the Yugoslav federation.

A bitter civil war—more like a series of civil wars—soon broke out. The first round pitted tiny Slovenia against the Yugoslav National Army (YNA) in the summer of 1991. Slovenia won the **Ten Day War** and seceded from the federation. Now Belgrade braced for the secessionist tsunami that was about to hit Yugoslavia.

Round two pitted Serbia against Croatia. The fighting brought extensive loss of life and damage to Croatia; when the smoke cleared, Serbia had annexed Krajina (formerly part of Croatia). Many towns and cities, including Vukovar and Dubrovnik, had endured heavy bombing and artillery attacks by the Yugoslav (Serbian) armed forces. International mediation and a United Nations peace-keeping force brought a ceasefire but not a settlement.

Tragically, there was no containing the conflict. Bosnia-Herzegovina was to be the next battleground.

A Dirty War: Bosnia

In Bosnia-Herzegovina the tragedy was compounded by the fact that Bosnian Muslims, although numerically the largest ethnic group there, were caught in the crossfire between Serbs and Croats. After months of bloody fighting and a particularly brutal artillery assault on Sarajevo, the capital, Serbs (31 percent of Bosnia's population) controlled 65 percent of the territory, and Croats (17 percent of the population) held about 30 percent. That left the Muslim population (44 percent of the total) with only 5 percent of the territory.

Some well-informed observers feared that the upshot of the war would be to divide Bosnia between Serbia and Croatia, leaving the Bosnian Muslims a nation without a state (not unlike Palestinians). Worse, it was not entirely clear who was doing what to whom. The **Yugoslav National Army (YNA)** made a pretense of neutrality, but it was widely reported that the army was supplying Serbian guerrillas with arms and ammunition. Although Yugoslav forces were withdrawing from Slovenia, Croatia, and Macedonia in April 1992, the army was reluctant to withdraw from Bosnia-Herzegovina because 65 percent of its arms industry and installations were concentrated there.

The war in Bosnia worsened in 1992 and 1993. Egregious human rights violations by all three warring sides—Bosnian Muslims and Croatians as well as Bosnian Serbs—characterized the conflict from the beginning. Reports of ethnic cleansing—the systematic deportation or slaughter of Muslims by Bosnian Serbs, allegedly with the covert support of Belgrade—caused outrage in the West and led to calls (especially in the United States) for economic sanctions, no-fly zones, and even military intervention. As stories of atrocities (concentration camps reminiscent of the Holocaust and the systematic rape of Muslim women) piled up, pressures built for effective measures to punish the Serbs, who nonetheless remained defiant in the face of growing diplomatic isolation.

Former U.S. Secretary of State Cyrus Vance and former British Foreign Secretary David Owen, representing the United Nations and the European Union, respectively, attempted to broker a ceasefire based on a proposed division of Bosnia into ten autonomous regions, some controlled by Serbs, some by Croats, and some by Bosnian Muslims—all supervised by a United Nations peacekeeping force. But the warring sides rejected this **cantonization** plan, and the Bosnian Serbs continued their relentless ethnic cleansing in the widening areas under Serb military control. Fears that Macedonia and Kosovo would be the next battlegrounds added to the sense of alarm in the international community.

The war in Bosnia dragged on despite continuing efforts by United Nations peacekeepers, the European Union, and the United States to mediate. Nor did NATO air strikes stop it. Serbia was widely condemned for its role in aiding and abetting the Bosnian Serbs. The effects of the Yugoslav war and the international trade embargo against Serbia were devastating. Critical shortages of many food staples forced the Serbian government to introduce rationing. Inflation reached a million percent in 1993, prompting Belgrade to adopt a new currency, the super dinar, in January 1994. In the summer of 1994, two-thirds of all working-age Serbs were unemployed, mainly because of plant closings caused by the embargo.

When the war finally ended in 1995, there was still a big question mark over Bosnia's future and, ironically, over Serbia's as well. Only the fate of the old Yugoslavia was beyond question: its existence was now nothing more than a fiction maintained solely for the self-gratification of Serbian nationalists.

Whistle While You (Skip) Work: Serbia in Revolt

The government of Slobodan Milosevic, Serbia's authoritarian president faced mounting popular discontent in 1996. In November, a mass anti-government movement emerged in response to Milosevic's decision to cancel the results of local elections after opposition candidates won in fourteen communities. With national elections just around the corner, Milosevic and his followers had good reason for concern. In Belgrade, thousands of peaceful demonstrators streamed into the streets, ignoring the government's warnings, threats, and entreaties.

Milosevic was especially loath to relinquish the state monopoly of the mass media. A swelling tide of protesters began to drown out the government's lies by going outside or simply opening a window and banging on pots, pans, and garbage-can lids every evening during the censored nightly news broadcasts on state television. They also began blowing whistles. Soon the whistle became a symbol and a badge, as well as the weapon of choice. People of all ages, including schoolchildren, started wearing whistles around their necks. The din and roar of the movement literally overwhelmed the voice of official authority.

Finally, Milosevic made a concession, allowing some of his opponents to take office. In one such community south of Belgrade, police barricaded themselves in local radio and television stations in January 1997 to prevent these facilities from falling into the hands of the duly elected officials. Miraculously, incidents of violence between police and protesters had so far been few. But how much longer the tension could continue to build up without erupting was anybody's guess.

Another Dirty War: Kosovo

In November 1995, the United States brokered the Dayton peace accord, which halted the fighting in Bosnia-Herzegovina. The Serbian government played a constructive role, finally accepting the principle of a separate Bosnia and Croatia. In return, the United States lifted economic sanctions against Serbia. Notwithstanding, there remained a serious question whether—or how long—conflict in the neighborhood of the former Yugoslavia could be contained. Would Bulgaria, Romania, Hungary, Albania, Greece, and Turkey stand by if Belgrade attempted to incorporate more territories of the former Yugoslavia into a **Greater Serbia**? For example, hundreds of thousand of Hungarians live on the wrong side of the border with Hungary (in a region of Serbia called Vojvodina) as well as in Slovakia and Romania. By the same token, some 2 million Albanians live in Kosovo (part of Serbia). Macedonia also has a large Albanian minority.

The answer was, unfortunately, not long in coming. Another war in the name of Greater Serbia broke out, this time in Kosovo, a province of Serbia inhabited mostly ethnic by Albanians but highly prized for historical and cultural reasons by the Serbs. The Serbian army cracked down brutally in Kosovo after Kosovars (ethnic Albanians) revolted. The **Kosovo Liberation Army (KLA)** offensive was spurred by Serbian refusal to grant an acceptable degree of autonomy to the province.

But Serbian arms were far superior and the Serbian army showed no mercy in Kosovo. Quite the contrary: Serbian forces began systematically driving Kosovars out of their homes, villages, and, ultimately, Serbia (Kosovo, that is) into neighboring Macedonia, Albania, and other neighboring states. The aim of this strategy, to the world's horror, appeared to be "ethnic cleansing." Faced with this unfolding human tragedy and an uncompromising Milosevic, NATO (bolstered by the United Nation) initiated a bombing campaign—belatedly, in the opinion of critics—against Serbia in the spring of 1999. By the time NATO's intervention finally brought the Milosevic government to its knees, well over a million Kosovars (roughly three-fifths of the entire ethnic Albanian population) had been driven from their homes.

The joyless end of the fighting was accompanied by an imposed "peace." The United Nations put its own interim administration in charge with NATO troops on the ground as a kind of police force. The declared aim was "substantial autonomy and self-government" for the province, whatever that meant. The UN-NATO regime disarmed the KLA and promised to protect the tiny (5 percent) Serbian minority in Kosovo against recriminations by angry ethnic Albanians. It was a promise not perfectly kept, as many Serbians in Kosovo were attacked or threatened.

In sum, nothing was settled. There was no end in sight for the UN protectorate so long as Milosevic was in power. For all its good intentions, the United Nations once again proved itself ill equipped to govern. UN administrators were unfamiliar with local customs and struggled with a baffling language barrier. NATO forces now in the odd role of protecting Serbians met with hostility from the outraged Kosovars. Meanwhile, there was an institutional and legal vacuum with neither laws, nor courts, nor local police to fight ordinary (and not so ordinary) crime.

Milosevic the Loser

The economic impact of the war on Serbia was devastating. After years of enduring economic sanctions imposed by the United Nations and the European Union, the effects of NATO bombing raids against infrastructure and strategic industries were severe. Serbs had grown accustomed to a relatively high standard of living during the previous decades of the Cold War but were now facing hardships and shortages. Nonetheless, the Serbian people were divided politically. Because Milosevic blamed the West all along for interfering in Serbia's domestic affairs, the NATO air raids against Serbia and the imposed "peace" in Kosovo that followed fed the government's propaganda machine. On the other hand, many Serbs who wanted the kind of democratic reforms that had been realized elsewhere in Eastern Europe opposed Milosevic's dictatorial rule. That Milosevic was a dictator could not be denied: he controlled the press, rigged elections, and dealt harshly with all manifestations of opposition. The upshot was a divided and ambivalent populace leading to a dangerously volatile situation.

Milosevic was forced to back down in Kosovo but was not humbled. It was not long before new war clouds were gathering over Montenegro, the only one of the original Yugoslav republics still tied to Serbia. Taking a cue from Milosevic's eroding support in the aftermath of the fiasco in Kosovo, Montenegro's popularly elected president sought closer ties to the West and posed as a counterweight to Milosevic. The possibility of yet another dirty war in the Balkans once again set off alarm bells in Western capitals.

Meanwhile, Milosevic attempted to boost his popularity by promising an election in the fall of 2000—an election that he probably expected to win (by hook or crook), but in fact lost. Although his opponent, Vojislav Kostunica, clearly won the election, Milosevic refused to step down. He now claimed Kostunica had gotten just under the 50 percent needed to win outright and called for a runoff. Serbs knew what that would mean: Milosevic would do a better job of stuffing ballot boxes the second time around.

So Serbs surged into the streets. Riot police had little or no deterrent effect on anti-government demonstrators who gathered in Belgrade's main Republic Square by the thousands. Milosevic was also under tremendous pressure from abroad. When the Serbian Army decided to back Kostunica and Russian President Vladimir Putin even deserted him, Milosevic bowed to the inevitable, defiantly telling the Serbian people in a televised address that he was conceding defeat but not getting out of politics.

What followed was a bizarre drama in which remnants of the fallen government, including the interior minister (who controls the national police in Serbia), refused to give up their posts. But the newly elected president, buoyed by a wave of enthusiastic popular support and backed by Western governments, stood firm. And when general elections were held in December 2000, a coalition of eighteen parties, the **Democratic Opposition of Serbia (DOS)** led by Zoran Djindic, won easily, gaining 176 out of 250 parliamentary seats. The election removed all doubt about the extent of the former dictator Milosevic's unpopularity—his disgraced Communists captured only 14 percent of the popular vote. So now Serbia at long last had a popularly elected president, parliament, and prime minister, but little else. The economy was in a shambles and the government was stalemated.

Belgium and the Czech Republic both have populations almost identical in size to Serbia's, but the Serbian economy is only about one-fourth the size of the Czech economy and one-twentieth the size of the Belgian economy. The gravity of Serbia's plight becomes clearer when one looks at cross-country comparisons of per capita GDP adjusted for differences in purchasing power (called purchasing power parity). By that measure, Serbia ranks with Angola, Cameroon, and Mongolia.

The prospects for Serbia remain highly uncertain, but the departure of Milosevic created the possibility for a new beginning. It would not be easy, however. Yugoslavia's current problems can be seen as an extension of the policy failures of the past. Milosevic pursued reckless and misguided policies aimed at self-aggrandizement in terms of both personal and national power. He did so at the expense of constitutional integrity, economic development, and international respectability.

The Yugoslavia Milosevic bequeathed was physically smaller, economically poorer, and militarily weaker than the one he inherited. Moreover, Milosevic's mania for creating a Greater Serbia at all costs made Belgrade the capital of a pariah state in the eyes of world—a world to which his successor(s) would have to turn for trade concessions, investment, and other favors. In April 2001, he was arrested and extradited to the Netherlands to stand trial for war crimes.

SUMMARY AND CONCLUSIONS

The Soviet state developed an elaborate set of highly centralized political institutions. The Communist Party—including the Politburo, Secretariat, and the Central Committee apparatus—was the organizational backbone of the Stalinist system. An all-encompassing state bureaucracy carried out the will of this monolithic party. Under Stalin's rule, the secret police (KGB) kept a tight lid on political dissent, art, and literature. Little escaped Soviet censors.

This draconian system remained largely intact until Mikhail Gorbachev's accession to power in 1985. By that time, the Soviet Union's planned economy had stagnated. Gorbachev called for new thinking and launched a series of bold economic and political reforms. His own vacillations; resistance from vested interests within the party, state bureaucracy, secret police, and military; and the sheer magnitude of the tasks combined to bring the reforms to grief. The "outer empire" came unraveled in 1989; the "inner empire" disintegrated in 1991 after an abortive coup by hardliners.

Russia is no longer a totalitarian state, but many Russians still face hardships, and the nation must overcome a wide array of obstacles if freedom is to survive. The former Soviet-bloc countries in Eastern Europe have also adopted liberal constitutions. Although Poland and Hungary have successfully made the transition to democratic rule, the Czech Republic is the most stable, liberal, democracy in the region. Ukraine has been among the least liberal, but the Orange Revolution at the end of 2004, which brought a reform-minded opposition candidate to power, appeared to be a harbinger of political and economic change. Serbia (formerly Yugoslavia), by contrast, remained an ill-disguised authoritarian regime until 2000–2001 and, though now ruled democratically, has a yet to deal successfully with the problem of Kosovo or to revive the torpid economy.

The former communist states of Europe are going through a difficult transition period from central planning and police-state controls to market economies and multiparty democracy. In Russia, as elsewhere in the former Soviet Union, this process has been tumultuous, and the outcome remains indeterminate. In a few ex-communist states, market reforms have progressed rapidly but not always smoothly. Poland, Hungary, and the Czech Republic, along with Slovenia, have managed the smoothest transitions in the region. In recent years, the Baltic states have also shown signs of economic vitality. All seven (plus Slovakia, Cyprus and Malta) joined the EU in 2004.

Years of communist rule engendered a deep distrust of politics. Building a new relationship between government and society is crucial to the long-term success of Eastern Europe's emerging democracies.

The former Yugoslavia was torn asunder by ethnic conflict and civil war in the 1990s, but NATO intervention in Bosnia and Kosovo and the subsequent ouster of Serbian dictator Slobodan Milosevic in 2000 brought an end to the fighting. Serbia now has a new democratically elected government, but the Serbian economy is still a basket case.

The problem of ethnic conflict is not confined to the Balkans. Despite a brutal military response, Russia has not succeeded in suppressing the secessionist movement in Chechnya. Even more troubling, Russia's continued economic recovery is heavily oil dependent. A collapse in world oil markets could thus have a highly destabilizing effect on Russian society, possibly even calling the present system of government into question. Turning Russia's economy around will take time; eradicating corruption and turning Russia's demoralized society around will take even longer.

KEY TERMS

cantonization

Civic Platform Party

competitive market

Democratic Opposition of Serbia (DOS)

Democratic Russia

Eastern Orthodox

Greater Serbia

Kosovo Liberation Army (KLA)

Law and Justice Party

market reforms

oligarchs

Opposition Agreement

petrostate

Rossianiye

ruble crisis

Russkye

Self-Defense Party

single market

Ten Day War

Velvet Divorce

winnowing effect

Yugoslav National Army (YNA)

SUGGESTED READINGS

Bugajski, Janusz. *Cold Peace: Russia's New Imperialism.* New York: Praeger, 2004.

Dedek, Oldrich, ed. *The Break-up of Czechoslovakia: An In-Depth Economic Analysis.* Brookfield, VT: Ashgate, 1996.

De Nevers, Renée. *Comrades No More: The Seeds of Change in Eastern Europe.* Cambridge: MIT Press, 2002.

Jack, Andrew. *Inside Putin's Russia: Can There Be Reform without Democracy?* New York: Oxford University Press, 2004.

Lo, Bobo. *Vladimir Putin and the Evolution of Russian Foreign Policy.* Oxford: Blackwell, 2003.

Petro, Nicolai N. *Crafting Democracy: How Novgorod Has Coped with Rapid Social Change.* Ithaca, NY: Cornell University Press, 2004.

Phillips, John. *Macedonia: Warlords and Rebels in the Balkans.* New Haven, CN: Yale University Press, 2004.

Primakov, Yevgeni. *Russian Crossroads: Toward the New Millenium.* New Haven, CN: Yale University Press, 2004.

Shevtsova, Lila. *Putin's Russia.* Washington, DC: Carnegie Endowment for International Peace, 2004.

Stojanovic, Svetozar. *Serbia: The Democratic Revolution.* New York: Humanity Books, 2003.

Trenin, Dmitri and Aleksei Malashenko, with Anatol Lieven. *Russia's Restless Frontier: The Chechnya Factor in Post-Soviet Russia.* Washington, DC: Carnegie Endowment for International Peace, 2004.

WEB SITES

www.columbia.edu/cu/sipa/REGIONAL/ECE/homepage.html

www.ceo.cz/

members.valley.net/~transnat/

www.rferl.org/

www.ucis.pitt.edu/reesweb/

NOTES

1. "Emerging Market Indicators," *The Economist,* June 1, 1996, p. 102.

2. "Russia's Flawed Reformer," *The Economist,* January 8, 2000, pp. 19–21.

3. Moisés Naím, "If Geology Is Destiny, Then Russia Is in Trouble, *The New York Times,* December 4, 2003. (Electronic edition)

4. Michael Specter, "The Devastation," *The New Yorker,* October 11, 2004, p. 58.

5. Ibid., p. 68.

6. See for example, "Vladimir III?" *The Economist,* December 11, 2004 p. 46–47.

7. "Corruption in Russia: Blood Money," *The Economist,* October 22, 2005, pp. 53–54.

8. "Frozen out," *The Economist,* December 3, 2005, p. 47.

9. Marshall I. Goldman, "Putin and the Oligarchs," *Foreign Affairs,* November/December, vol. 83, no. 6, 2004, p. 41.

10. Quoted in "Hindrance or Help," *The Economist,* December 3, 2005, p. 11; see also BBC News on the Internet at this URL: http://news.bbc.co.uk/2/hi/europe/4480745.stm.

11. Andrew E. Kramer, "Moscow Rally Held to Protest Growing Rate of Hate Crimes," *The New York Times,* December 19, 2005. (Electronic edition)

12. Daniel Sneider, "Yeltsin Struggles to Keep Russian Federation Intact," *The Christian Science Monitor,* Mar. 25, 1992, p. 1.

13. "Tinker, Tailor, Soldier, Party Leader . . ." *The Economist,* Feb. 3, 1996, p. 43.

14. Matthew Valencia, "Limping towards normality: A survey of Poland," *The Economist,* October 27, 2001, p. 12. (Survey are published as inserts and numbered separately.)

15. "Central Europe's Economies: A Rising Tide," *The Economist* July 17, 2004, p. 54.

16. Valencia, "Limping," p. 4.

17. "Poland's Unruly Politics: When Populism Trumps Socialism," *The Economist,* May 8, 2004, p. 47. (Note: British spelling has been amended to American in the quote.)

18. Craig R. Whitney, "The New East-West Divide," *The New York Times,* November 28, 2004, "Week in Review" (Section 4), p. 1.

19. You be the judge: The Central Election Commission claimed that the turnout for the November 21st runoff was 96.65% of registered voters, or about 20% above the turnout in the first round, and that Yanukovich won 96.2% of the votes to 2% for Yushchenko. See C. J. Chivers, "Premier's Camp Signals A Threat to Ukraine Unity," *The New York Times,* November 29, 2004 (electronic edition).

20. Ibid.

21. For a detailed and insightful account of the Orange Revolution, see Adrian Karatnycky, "Ukraine's Orange Revolution," *Foreign Affairs,* March/April 2005, pp. 35–52.

22. C. J. Chivers, "Yushenko Wins 52% of Vote; Rival Vows Challenge," *The New York Times,* December 28, 2004 (electronic edition).

23. Adrian Karatnycky, "Ukraine's Orange Revolution," *Foreign Affairs,* March/April 2005, vol. 84, no. 2, p. 41.

24. Ibid., p. 49.

25. "Orange Fades," *The Economist,* September 10, 2005, p. 49.

PART III

The European Union

Member states in 2005 (total = 25): Austria, Belgium, Britain, Cyprus, Czech Republic, Denmark, Estonia, Finland, France, Germany, Greece, Hungary, Ireland, Italy, Latvia, Lithuania, Luxembourg, Malta, the Netherlands, Poland, Portugal, Slovakia, Slovenia, Sweden, and Spain

EU population: 447 million

EU total GDP (2005 estimate): $14 trillion

EU average GDP per capita (2005 estimate): $31,320

Highest GDP per capita (2006 estimate): Ireland, $52,940; Denmark, $51,610

Lowest GDP per capita (2006 estimate): Latvia, $6,100

Highest projected growth rates (2006): Latvia, 6.5 percent; Estonia, 6.4 percent Slovakia, 5.5 percent; Lithuania, 5.4 percent

Lowest projected growth rates (2006): Portugal, 1.0 percent; Italy, 1.1 percent; Germany, 1.6 percent; France, 1.7 percent

Highest inflation rate (Fall, 2005): Hungary, 3.2 percent

Lowest inflation rate (Fall, 2005): Sweden 0.8 percent

Euro zone countries: Austria, Belgium, Finland, France, Germany, Greece, Ireland, Italy, Luxembourg, Netherlands, Portugal, and Spain.

Euro zone population: 306 million

Euro zone GDP growth (2006 estimate): 1.8 percent

Euro zone inflation (2004): 2.1 percent

Euro zone unemployment (2004): 8.9 percent

SOURCE: Estimates and projections are from *The World in 2006*, an annual publication of *The Economist*, pp. 91–94 and *The World in 2005*, pp. 87–91; highest and lowest inflation rates are from *The Economist*, December 3, 2005, pp. 96 and 98.

8

Beyond East and West

What Is Europe?

The theme of Chapter Eight is captured in the title: Is it possible to go beyond the Europe of the Cold War or the Europe of nation-states? Europe faces two contradictory categorical imperatives, a term first used by philosopher Immanuel Kant (1724–1804) in an essay entitled "Perpetual Peace" (1795). First, there is a need for peace, prosperity, and stability—the fruits of unity. Second, there is a need for independence, self-identity, and competition—the fruits of diversity. The first impulse—toward cooperation—is fed by a dread of war, and the second—toward rivalry and conflict—is a natural outgrowth of nationalism. In the last two chapters of this book we come full circle, returning to the theme of Chapter One.

The idea of a unified Europe is not new. In fact, it has been the pet project of many of Europe's most illustrious thinkers—not to mention an assortment of dreamers and schemers—for centuries.[1] In the mid-1960s, after the Common Market had become a reality but before it had expanded beyond the original six members, a noted scholar wrote, "It has been possible to unify France, Germany, and Italy, but not Europe, and not even Austria-Hungary. The organizing principle of modern Europe has not been the unity of federalism, but the independence of nationalism."[2]

Nationalism acquired a bad name in the twentieth century as a result of two shockingly destructive world wars; its association with right-wing totalitarianism in Germany, Italy, and elsewhere; and, finally, its links to social unrest running the gamut from ethnic conflict and secessionist movements to terrorism-prone insurgencies after World War II, not only in Europe but also in the former colonial areas. (Ironically, it fell out of favor morally and ideologically in Europe even as it was coming into its own in the Middle East, Africa, and Asia.) But there is another side to nationalism, one that is now only dimly perceived by the public and seldom mentioned by politicians, journalists and other close observers. As Professor David Calleo has written,

> Nationalism might more properly be defined in its normal healthy, rather than occasionally diseased, form. It is [a] theory of the state which holds that consensus can be achieved successfully only within the community of identity established by a *national* culture.... The nationalist [sought] ...a degree of common identity and civic spirit that would rally the contentious elements of society towards rational cooperation within [a] generally accepted constitutional framework.[3]

Moreover, as Calleo notes, "modern democracy has almost never been established outside the context of a national state."[4]

Thus, the importance of nationalism in modern European history can be exaggerated only with difficulty, but its positive side is easily overlooked or denigrated. Indeed, nation building on the Continent was the major preoccupation of old and new states alike in the nineteenth century.[5] This point is a key to understanding the paradox of contemporary Europe—integrating into a single economy while simultaneously subdividing into a larger number of sovereign states than ever before in its history.

Lingering nationalism is still ubiquitous at the start of the twenty-first century, but that does not necessarily mean that a politically united Europe is impossible. European history stands as testimony to this startling truth: if something can be imagined, it can be accomplished—for better or worse—given the right set of circumstances. The rise of totalitarian tyrannies in Stalin's Russia and Hitler's Germany in the first half of the twentieth century proved the negative; the emergence of the European communities in the second half of the twentieth century, culminating in the recent birth of the European Union, proves the positive.

Europe's greatest thinkers have imagined Europe as a single political unit at least since the time of the Roman Empire; in the modern era, ideas on the unity of Europe can be traced back to the fourteenth century, to Dante and Pierre DuBois, counselor to Philip the Fair.[6] Thereafter, the list of luminaries favoring a united Europe would grow through the centuries—King George Podiebrad of Bohemia, Emeric Cruce, the Duc de Sully, Comenius, William Penn, the Abbe de Saint Pierre, Count Henri de Saint-Simon, Jeremy Bentham, Victor Hugo, and P.-J. Proudhon (to name but a few).[7]

The two world wars gave the European movement new impetus and, during the second of these, a sense of urgency.[8] In the darkest days of 1940, Winston Churchill actually offered to merge the British and French governments![9] At the end of the war, Churchill and de Gaulle both embraced the idea of confederation, but by this time ardent federalists had stolen a march on the politicians.

In 1944, representatives from nine European countries met in secret at a villa in Geneva, Switzerland, to make common cause against Hitler's Germany. It was imperative, they admonished, "to supersede the dogma of absolute state sovereignty by joining together in a single federal organization."[10] Noting that "in the space of a single generation Europe has been the epicenter of two world conflicts due primarily to the existence of thirty sovereign states on this continent," they declared: "This anarchy must be ended by the creation of a federal Union among the peoples of Europe."[11]

The impetus for a united Europe did not end in 1945, when the guns finally fell silent. On the contrary, across the Continent "a multitude of movements, groups, associations and leagues committed to the idea of federation" sprang up. A meeting at Montreux (Switzerland) in 1947 led to the convening of the **Congress of Europe** at The Hague (the Netherlands) in the spring of 1948— the beginning of the European project now known as the European Union.[12] As this essay underscores, however, it is a project that, for all its remarkable achievements, remains far from completion. Moreover, despite the formidable obstacles that have had to be overcome, it is fair to say that what has been accomplished up to now, is the easy part, relatively speaking. The hard part—political amalgamation—remains a distant goal, one that is not shared by all Europeans or viewed in the same way even by those who do.[13]

WHAT MAKES EUROPEANS EUROPEAN?

What *do* Europeans have in common? Europe's rich heritage in philosophy, science and the fine arts is a colorful tapestry of contributions from all the nations huddled together on that small "continent".[14] No single country can claim to have created European civilization. Nor is demographic or geographic size a reliable guide to the relative value of each nation's contribution in a given field. For example, the Czech contribution to Europe's treasury of classical music far exceeds that nation's diminutive size, and the Dutch have produced a similar disproportion of great artists. Indeed, calling something a "Rembrandt" is a universal form of flattery, and not only in aesthetic matters.

Europe's creativity and dynamism is apparent in the material world of industry and technology, as well.[15] It was, of course, Europe that launched the Industrial Age in the 18th century. Before that, advances in maritime and military technology propelled Europe into the era of the so-called Great Discoveries that preceded the drive to colonize most of the non-European world.[16] In the first half of the twentieth century, the very same dynamism revealed its dark side in catastrophic wars and totalitarian revolutions.

Europeans also share a common religious tradition and political history replete with similar (if not identical) institutions, from papacy to monarchy. But kings divided Europe more successfully than popes united it. In the final analysis, politics trumps religion in Europe. For obvious reasons, Europe's kings cultivated one other value that today's Europeans share (in a paradoxical way): nationalism. The problem, of course, is that there is a separate brand of nationalism for every nation in Europe.

Nationalism was once indispensable to kings facing the challenge of building modern states from the ground up, so to speak. Today, however, it is the major obstacle to the reconstitution of Europe as a single superstate, federal or otherwise. Does this mean that a federation of European states is out of the question? Not necessarily. What it *does* mean is that any political union will remain a pipedream unless or until a new European political culture and consciousness—in effect, a new European nation—emerges. There is no guarantee that will ever happen nor is it certain that it would be the Promised Land for Europe if it did.

For centuries the focus of Europe's visionary unifiers was on the desired *product*. After World War II, however, a new breed of **Eurocrats** gained the ascendancy and shifted attention decisively toward the *process*.

Theoretically, the only two schemes that make any sense in the European context are a confederation or a federation. The idea of confederation has attracted many adherents over the centuries. As recently as the 1960s, French President Charles de Gaulle tried unsuccessfully to sell such a plan to France's Common Market partners.[17]

European federalists often distrust executive power, be it wielded by kings or presidents (modern-day kings). According to one scholar, the dream of a unified Europe "is powered not only by the drive to build Europe, but by the desire to propose a substitute for that form of presidential government which has come increasingly to predominate within the modern national state."[18] They take a dim view of **power politics** in general and typically emphasize economic relationships rather than military might. As technocrats by temperament and training, they are also far more comfortable dealing with domestic problems than international conflict.[19]

This belief in **technocracy**—rule by technocrats* —is a key understanding the theory and practice of European integration in the postwar period. Its basic tenet is "that many of the problems that presently plague humankind could be solved if only decisions could be left to impartial, scientifically trained experts whose efforts were not continually distorted by the emotional and hasty generalizations of mass politics."[20] In the eyes of the Eurocrats, presidents typically appeal to mass politics in order to circumvent or checkmate a recalcitrant legislature or simply to whip up patriotism in times of crisis. Europeans did not survive centuries of autocratic rule and, more recently, decades of totalitarian tyranny only to give supreme power to a popularly elected king.

---

*The concept combines the words *bureaucrat* and *technician*. It follows that a technocrat is a civil servant with technical expertise in a profession such as agronomy, biochemistry, or mechanical engineering.

To describe this attitude is to suggest the wide gap between America's political traditions and Europe's emerging political culture. The latter is not based on a formal ideology but rather on an informal set of core values embraced in varying degrees by most Europeans depending on the specific value and the issues associated with it.

In the following pages I elucidate these core values and pinpoints some sources of tension within and between them. I also examine how abstract values are expressed in the concrete issues and controversies that animate European politics today. Throughout, I give special emphasis to the challenges posed by the historic expansion of the EU to include the ex-communist states in Eastern Europe and the Balkans, as well as Cyprus, Malta and, at some future date, perhaps even Turkey.

The Embrace of Liberty

At the dawn of the twentieth century, most Europeans had still never voted in a meaningful election and, with few exceptions, existing constitutions did little to limit royal powers or protect individual rights. Indeed, the very idea of *civil* society as a web of relationships among citizens independent of the state had not yet taken root.

How Europe has changed! Following the collapse of communist rule, a wave of democracy rolled across the eastern flank of the Continent in the 1990s. Today, even Russia, long a synonym for political oppression, is ruled by a popularly elected president whose powers—however broad—are defined by a new constitution and functioning legislature. In Europe, the triumph of the West was, above all, the triumph of liberal democracy.

It is difficult to exaggerate the importance of this development. What divided Europe, politically and ideologically, since the French Revolution was not only nationalism but also the idea of liberty. This subversive idea was the antithesis of absolute monarchy in the nineteenth century and of totalitarianism in the twentieth century. The twenty-first century promises to be utterly different in this all-important respect.

Europeans of all nationalities have suffered in one way or another from the actions of tyrants; in modern Europe, oppression and aggression are both closely related to the absence of constitutional constraints on power. Thus, Europeans understand even better than most Americans that freedom and security are indivisible. Now that the vast majority of Europe's peoples have won the right to vote, to dissent and, if all else fails, to emigrate, it is highly unlikely that any of them will give up these rights willingly. Europe's age of liberty, after two centuries in the offing, has finally dawned.

The experience of liberty may be relatively new to some 360 million Europeans who lived on the "wrong side" of the Iron Curtain during the Cold War (1945–1989), but the idea itself is definitely not.[21] The pedigree and geographical proximity of this idea means that democracy had a head start in Eastern Europe in the 1990s in comparison with Africa, the Middle East, and Asia.

Hungarians may not have experienced constitutional democracy until the 1990s, but they have long known about it (and occasionally fought for it).[22]

As we will see, freedom is about the only political value that does not divide Europeans today. Other values, even those that most Europeans hold dear, cause divisions based on nation, social class, or religion. This broad embrace of liberty, then, is a key element in the new European political culture, one that gives a measure of cohesion to an otherwise highly contentious community of nation-states. Ironically, critics of the European Union have often decried what they call a "democratic deficit"—namely, the absence of any direct connection between voters and decision-making institutions or processes within the EU.[23]

Rising Expectations

Europeans associate liberty with *prosperity*. Significantly, only states that are stable democracies with open societies and market economies are considered for membership in the European Union. The decision to admit ten new members in 2004 (discussed later) attests to the continuing importance of these criteria, as well as the widespread belief that membership in the EU is the best guarantee of a prosperous future.

Of course, people everywhere desire prosperity and Europeans are no different, except that, like Americans, they have come to *expect* it. Income disparities among social classes, age groups, nations, and regions in Europe can cause envy and inevitably give rise to clashes of interest that undermine efforts to broaden and deepen economic integration.

Significant disparities in wealth and living standards in Western Europe still exist. These disparities give rise to clashes of interest and complicate the political process within the EU. In the **Europe of the Fifteen,** for example, Portugal, Greek, Spain, and Ireland were still relatively poor in the late 1990s by comparison with the other eleven members. Nor does wealth exclusively correlate with size: Lilliputian Luxembourg and diminutive Denmark are the wealthiest countries in the EU, followed by Ireland (see Table 8.1).

The relative position of national economies does not change overnight, and it often happens that the rich get richer and the poor stay poor. Historically, the dynamism of the European Union and the sheer size of its market have meant that new members get a boost upon entry, but membership in the EU can also be a double-edged sword because domestic producers often find it daunting to compete on a playing field that is home to so many world-class multinational corporations. Gaining ground in this competitive arena is not easy, as a snapshot of the EU in 2005 reveals (see Table 8.2).

Nonetheless, even the poorest EU members are far richer than the former communist states; Slovenia, the richest, had a per capita GNP slightly lower than that of Portugal in the late 1990s. Eastern Europe as a whole remains far behind the EU countries by any standard of comparison (see Table 8.3). Next to Slovenia, the Czech Republic is the richest country in Eastern Europe, but it still lags far behind "poor" Portugal in GDP per capita. The Ukraine, the second largest East European state, remains abysmally poor by EU standards.

TABLE 8.1 **GNP in the European Union: A Country Comparison Excluding the 2004 Expansion States**

Country	GNP (billions US$)	Per Capita GNP (thousands US$)	Population
Austria	320	39,130	8,200,000
Belgium	378	36,430	10,400,000
Denmark	264	48,920	5,400,000
Finland	199	37,740	5,300,000
France	2,220	36,630	60,600,000
Germany	2,930	35,450	82,700,000
Greece	216	20,210	10,700,000
Ireland	200	48,250	4,100,000
Italy	1,830	31,410	58,100,000
Luxembourg	28	60,475	463,000
Netherlands	640	38,950	16,400,000
Portugal	184	17,680	10,400,000
Spain	1,100	26,660	41,300,000
Sweden	394	43,480	9,100,000
United Kingdom	2,350	38,670	60,670,000
Total EU GNP (2005) = $13.25 trillion			

SOURCE: "Countries: The World in Figures," *The World in 2005*, Economist Intelligence Unit (a subsidiary of *The Economist*).

Poland's GDP was bigger than that of Portugal or Greece, the poorest EU members prior to 2004, but its per capita GDP was only about one-third as much. Overall, the per capita gross domestic product of the ten expansion countries in 2001 (the most recent EU figures available) was about $5,500 compared to $23,000 for the fifteen already in the club.[24] The addition of Poland, Hungary, Slovenia, Slovakia, the Czech Republic, and the three Baltic states (Latvia, Lithuania, and Estonia) plus Cyprus and Malta in 2004 increased the EU population by 20 percent (or 75 million people), its territory by 25 percent, but its gross domestic product by only about 5 percent.[25]

In 1998, the combined GDP of the EU's fifteen members was over $8.3 trillion (it had risen to over $9 trillion by 2003). The combined GDP of the ten new members was only about $322 billion—considerably smaller than that of the Netherlands alone. Except for Malta, Cyprus and Slovenia, the accession states have a dismal GDP per head of between 16% and 26% of the EU average. As a consequence, EU development funds will "eventually flow east rather than south."[26] Accordingly, in December 2005, after months of wrangling over the budget, EU heads of state agreed to a controversial plan to cut the British rebate by roughly £1 billion a year between 2007 and 2013 and re-channel the money to Eastern Europe (see Chapter Nine for a more detailed account). Not surprisingly,

TABLE 8.2   The Rich and Not So Rich: Selected EU Countries in 2005 Ranked by Per Capita GDP

Rank	GDP per capita	GDP growth	Inflation
Denmark	$48,920	2.5%	2.0%
Ireland	$48,250	4.9%	2.2%
Sweden	$43,480	2.7%	1.6%
Austria	$39,130	2.4%	1.7%
Netherlands	$38,950	2.0%	1.5%
United Kingdom	$38,670	2.3%	1.8%
Finland	$37,740	3.0%	1.3%
France	$36,630	2.4%	1.9%
Germany	$35,450	1.9%	1.5%
Italy	$31,410	1.8%	2.0%
Spain	$26,660	3.0%	2.5%
Greece	$20,210	3.4%	2.9%
Slovenia	$17,700	3.7%	3.0%
Portugal	$17,680	2.3%	2.2%
Czech Republic	$11,960	4.1%	2.4%
Hungary	$11,210	4.0%	4.7%
Estonia	$ 9,310	6.0%	3.2%
Slovakia	$ 8,940	5.1%	5.7%
Poland	$ 7,300	4.5%	3.3%
Lithuania	$ 7,110	6.5%	1.6%
Latvia	$ 5,800	5.5%	3.5%

SOURCE: "Countries: The World in Figures," *The World in 2005,* Economist Intelligence Unit (a subsidiary of *The Economist*). These numbers are estimates.

the Portuguese, who have been among the main beneficiaries of regional development aid since joining the EU in 1986, are far less enthusiastic about the prospect of EU expansion than voters in several other small EU states.[27]

A Cherished Diversity

Is it possible to be for economic integration and against moves to strengthen the European Union? Perhaps the best answer to this question is found in the writings, speeches, and policies of General Charles de Gaulle, the founder of France's Fifth Republic and its first president. That de Gaulle placed an indelible mark on French politics is well known. What is less often remembered is that he also played a major role in the shaping of modern Europe. Indeed, during the first decade after the signing of the Rome Treaty (1958) that launched the Common Market, nobody was more assertive in promoting a particular vision of Europe than President de Gaulle.

TABLE 8.3 Europe's Emerging Markets in EU Perspective: Eight New Member States Admitted in 2004

Member State	GDP (billion US$)
Poland	$279
Czech Republic	$122
Hungary	$112
Slovakia	$49
Slovenia	$36
Lithuania	$24
Latvia	$13
Estonia	$12
Total	**$647 billion**
EU 15 (2005)	**$13.25 trillion**

SOURCE: "Countries: The World in Figures," *The World in 2005*, Economist Intelligence Unit (a subsidiary of *The Economist*). These numbers are estimates.

De Gaulle is best remembered as a staunch nationalist. In the mid-1960s, he was the only major political leader in Europe who spoke out in praise of nationalism.[28] But he was by no means a voice in the wilderness. As one close observer wrote, "he seems sufficiently formidable to freeze the movement towards European federal unity, and, if he lives long enough, to wreck it."[29] In fact, De Gaulle did not live long enough to wreck "the movement towards European federal unity," but he did slow it down. By providing an alternative vision of Europe, he posed a challenge to all who dreamt of a Europe without nation-states or "old-fashioned" nationalism.

De Gaulle was vehemently opposed to supranationalism. He did not think nationalism was old-fashioned or outmoded. Quite the contrary: he argued compellingly that there is no substitute in the modern world for the nation-state as an instrument of political authority or as an effective actor in the arena of international politics.

But de Gaulle was no war-mongering reactionary. He favored the creation of a European confederation based on a Franco-German entente that would institutionalize cooperative ties and coordinate economic policies among existing national governments.[30] His plan, in other words, was to leave the sovereignty of states intact while facilitating trade and commerce and building trust at the grass roots level. To have an effective state, de Gaulle believed, it is necessary, above all, to have a "moral entity sufficiently living, established and recognized to obtain the congenital loyalty of its subjects . . . and, if it should happen, that millions of men would be willing to die for it."[31]

De Gaulle, the professional soldier, was especially scornful of the federalists' pet project in the early 1950s—namely, the creation of a **European Defense Community.** It would not be a European Army, he asserted, but merely "the army called European" probably under the command of an American![32]

Wars are not fought simply by Pentagons, by GHQs, by Shapes, or NATOs. Wars are fought with the blood and souls of men. Neither European nor Atlantic defense can be built except on the basis of realities and those realities are national. There are no others, except, of course, in the formulations of politicians.[33]

Following De Gaulle's personal campaign against the European army, which was defeated in the French National Assembly in 1954, he withdrew from politics to write his *Memoirs*.

When de Gaulle returned in 1958, it was not for the purpose of losing the nation he had just rescued in a nebulous Europe. Nonetheless, de Gaulle never abandoned his commitment to European unity. But de Gaulle talked about unity in the context of the real Europe, not the Europe of the federalists' dreams. In the real Europe, states were "very different from one another, each has its own spirit, its own history, its own language, its own misfortunes, glories and ambitions." They alone "have the right to order and the authority to act." To imagine otherwise "is a dream."

As previously noted, de Gaulle's gave his proposal for a European confederation concrete expression in the so-called Fouchet Plan in 1961. One of the plan's key features was a de Gaulle trademark: it called for a popular referendum in the member states to legitimate the whole enterprise. De Gaulle's fondness for this device—reminiscent of Napoleon Bonaparte—was controversial and certainly one of the reasons why the **Fouchet Plan** failed to win the approval of the other Common Market states.

At this point the reader might be asking, "Why dwell on an idea put forward so long ago that failed?" The question is fair enough, but the answer is surprisingly simple. De Gaulle was obviously out of step with many of Europe's politicians and intellectuals in the 1960s, but time has proven he was essentially correct in his assessment. More than four decades after the Fouchet Plan failed, the dream of a European federation remains just that—a dream. For all Europe's success in economic integration (always high on de Gaulle's list of desirable outcomes), the European Union has *at best* made only modest and faltering progress toward political federation.

The Stillborn Constitution   Fast-forward now to 2003: The EU was preparing to bring ten new members (75 million people) under the big tent in the next year. Ironically, the circus analogy would have struck many Europeans, including many of the 105 delegates to the **Convention on the Future of Europe,** as entirely appropriate. After sixteen months of debate and deliberation, the convention had finally produced a draft of what it hoped would eventually become Europe's first constitution.

A reporter for the *New York Times* summed it up this way: "The process has been awkward and unpredictable, ambitious and timid, as delegates from the 15 member nations of the European Union and the 10 that are to join next year fight to protect their countries' national interests even as they agree to cede bits of sovereignty."[34] Similarly, one of two vice presidents of the convention expressed dissatisfaction with the result, complaining:

> Too many member states are defending themselves instead of sharing power at the European level to make things better. It's each state beyond the constitution. That's why I'm not even sure we are entitled to call it a constitution. [35]

The process itself spoke volumes: as a showcase of Europe's deep-rooted cultural and political diversity, it would have come as no surprise to Charles de Gaulle. But the process did not end in Brussels. The next step involved formal presentation of the draft at a summit meeting of the EU heads of state in Greece, followed by an intergovernmental review giving each member state one last chance to demand changes. Finally, each national parliament—including those of the ten new members—must ratify the document before it comes into force. Some countries (Ireland and Denmark, for example) have a constitutional rule that requires a national referendum for approval of any new step of this kind. But, as we already know, voters in France and the Netherlands rejected the proposed constitution in May 2005, leaving it in limbo.

The issues that surfaced at the EU constitution-drafting convention in Brussels vividly illustrate the sense in which political and cultural diversity remains a vibrant fact of life in contemporary Europe. As the American founders discovered at the Philadelphia Convention, federalism juxtaposes the interests of big and small states in the starkest form. Hence, at Brussels, France and other big states favored a strong president from a large country—"an idea that is anathema to the smaller states."

The chairman of the convention, former French President Giscard d'Estaing, attacked the existing principle that each member state is entitled to a Commissioner and a vote: "His aides point out that in an enlarged EU of 25 countries, the seven smallest ones representing a paltry 1.5% of the EU's GDP will have more voting weight in the European Commission than the six largest countries with 82% of the Union's GDP."[36] (The EU's institutions and current modes of operation are discussed in Chapter Nine.) Giscard d'Estaing also proposed making seats in the European Parliament more proportional to population and extending the tenure in office of the EU president to as much as five years.[37] (Under the existing system the presidency rotates among all the member states every six months.) These and other proposed changes had a common purpose: to adjust the workings of a complex and expanding organization comprising twenty-five sovereign member states. The need for adjustments—whether of the kind Giscard d'Estaing proposed or some other kind—was widely acknowledged. Whether the adjustments necessary to prevent political gridlock and institutional paralysis would prove to be possible was the all-important question.

From a geopolitical perspective, Europe is a region of small nations historically dominated by a few big ones. The great majority of EU member states—nineteen out of twenty-five—are small states with a strong tendency to weigh matters of national interest on the same scale. The average size of the nineteen small states is only about 5 million, ranging from 15.7 million (the Netherlands) to a mere 377,000 (Malta). The total population of the nineteen is only about 20 percent larger than that of Germany.

Not surprisingly, the small states within the EU generally oppose attempts by big states like France to gain political advantage or special treatment based on population size. Thus, for example, they favor retaining the principle of equality in the EU Commission.

By the same token, the stand taken on key policy and procedural issues by two middle-sized states, Spain and Poland, could become decisively important in the future because these two member states, each with a population of slightly under 40 million, are not as big as Germany, France, Italy, and Great Britain nor as small as the others. As we will see in Chapter Nine, one vital procedural question that has been a source of friction involves the weighted-voting formula in the Council of Ministers. Spain has fought against changing the voting rules that "give it power disproportionate to its population" (and almost equal to that of Germany even though Germans outnumber Spaniards by two to one).[38]

Rising Euroscepticism   Some EU members remain deeply skeptical about any steps toward political federation. The British government, for example, insists on the right of any member to veto decisions on foreign policy and taxation—two areas that cut to the very core of national sovereignty. Germany, on the other hand, has obvious historical reasons for seeking to allay its neighbors' fears and no reason to fear a federation in which it would be the biggest constituent part.[39] These differences are merely illustrative: a catalogue of national concerns would be just that—a catalogue. And the catalogue would be the size of a phone book.

Of course, not all the contentious issues at the Brussels convention were tied to the big state–small state split. Some issues go to the very heart of democracy itself. For example, decision making within the EU is not transparent even to members of the European Parliament (much less the public).[40] But for avid Eurocrats and supranationalists, there is a democratic dilemma that confounds benign intentions: making decisions more transparent will further complicate an already cumbersome process. Imagine having French farmers protesting over agricultural policy set in Brussels! How would Paris deal with that kind of a predicament?

De Gaulle recognized that for a European superstate to exist there would have to be a leader (or leaders) capable of inspiring loyalty in the hearts of Europeans of every nationality—a supernation. The delegates at Brussels agreed that the EU needs a single foreign minister to speak on behalf of Europe. Member states agreed to create such a post but Europe will continue to have national foreign ministries (and ministers) as well. How effectively or authoritatively a future EU foreign minister can speak for Europe under these circumstances is a wide open question.

What good is a foreign policy without an army? Simply to ask the question is to suggest how far Europe is from anything resembling a self-sufficient political union—one, that is, capable of standing on its own militarily and standing up to the United States in disputes over the use of force (such as the invasion of Iraq in 2003). The shelved European constitution talks vaguely of "structured cooperation" in the realm of defense, but goes no further. It does not pledge member states to commit resources to a European army and does not dare to mention the possibility of creating a European nuclear deterrent or seeking a seat at the United Nations. The latter would probably require the United Kingdom and France to give up the seats they hold as permanent members of the Security Council.

The Brussels constitution was published in eleven languages in 2003 and no fewer than twenty-one languages the next year with the accession of ten new members. Even the Czechs and the Slovaks who were part of a single state (Czechoslovakia) for most of the twentieth century would require two separate languages. If he had still been around, it would probably have been enough to make even the chiseled face of Charles de Gaulle break into a smile.

A Sense of Unity

So far, we have seen that Europe is a region of great cultural diversity in which nationalism has not been extinguished despite a half-century of progress toward a full economic integration over an ever-larger area. Indeed, extinguishing nationalism has never been a realistic expectation for the European Union. So why call it a "union" or aspire to create a "common foreign and security policy"? This is the language of unity, but perhaps it is wishful thinking. Perhaps the underlying reality is that Europe remains a fractious and volatile region.

No. Europe has moved away from its war-prone past. It is a very different place from the Europe of a half-century ago when the **European Coal and Steel Community (ECSC)**—the first small step toward a single economy— came into being. War is still a possibility, of course, but war is no longer what Europe is about.

Europe has not had the luxury of following a well-worn path. Rather, it has had to blaze a trail from the old European "war system" to the new Europe, in which war is widely rejected as an instrument of foreign policy. The fact that getting from the old to the new Europe meant passing through a protracted period when the Continent was politically and economically divided by an Iron Curtain makes the achievements that culminated in the Europe of the twenty-five all the more remarkable.

As we noted earlier, Europeans proudly share a common heritage, one that is unique to West. We will not repeat what has already been said elsewhere, but it is important to note that Europe's ethnic and linguistic differences are counter-balanced by religious and artistic commonalities. The latter have not precluded national rivalries and interstate wars, but it is equally true that the former have not drowned out voices calling for European unity since as far back as the Middle Ages. It was only after the catastrophe of World War II, however, that Europeans began taking the concrete steps that have made this desire for unity without uniformity more than wishful thinking. The result is plain to see: the European Union now has a population of 450 million citizens, exceeded in sheer mass only by China and India, and a super-economy roughly equal in size to that of the United States (about $12 trillion in 2005).

For the general public, the desire for unity in the context of European history is, above all, a desire for peace. This point can hardly be exaggerated, but it is easily overlooked now that the last great European war for the vast majority of EU citizens exists only in history books. In 1952, the coal and steel community (ECSC) brought together six countries—France, Germany, Belgium, the Netherlands, Luxembourg, and Italy—that had been enemies in World War II. In addition to the economic rationale of coordinating investment in two basic industries, the ECSC was intended "to reduce the risk of war between historic enemies by integrating industries essential for war production."[41] The fundamental importance of energy and iron products in the creation of national military capabilities is well documented in scholarly literature on international politics and clearly illustrated by modern European history.[42] In sum, for Europeans who had been in the middle of the maelstrom in both world wars to take this dramatic step in the early 1950s was, above all, an attempt to avert the worst consequence of disunity, namely another major war.

Stressing the strong desire for peace as a motive force in postwar European politics is not to diminish the importance of prosperity as a reason for greater unity. Europeans see a logical three-way connection between peace and prosperity, prosperity and unity, and unity and peace. The **functionalists** who worked so hard to establish the original European communities in the 1950s believed that this dynamic could be best by kick-started by promoting economic integration.[43]

Is it true? Does unity (integration) promote prosperity or were European functionalists making a leap of faith that has no basis in reality? It is easy to demonstrate that prosperity in Europe does correlate positively with economic integration, but a correlation does not necessarily prove cause and effect. There is no way of knowing, for example, whether Portugal would have a significantly lower standard of living today if it had not joined the EU in 1986 or if it would be significantly higher had Portugal joined in 1958.

Some European countries that do not belong to the EU are more prosperous than countries that do. Norway, for example, which does not belong to the EU, is Europe's richest country. It had a per capita GDP of $48,380 in 2004. Sweden, Norway's next-door neighbor and a member of the EU since 1995, has a much lower per capita GDP ($38,720 in 2004). But Norway is the exception, not the rule, because it has a small population and a fantastic source of wealth available to few European countries, namely, oil—lots of it. (Norway shares the rich North Sea oil fields with the United Kingdom; the petrodollar bonanza has to be spread much thinner in the U.K. than in Norway, population 4.6 million.)

Similarly, Switzerland would be the wealthiest country in the EU (except for tiny Luxembourg) if it belonged but has chosen to stay out. Denmark, which has chosen not to be a part of the euro currency zone, ranks right behind Switzerland on the roster of Europe's richest countries.

Nonetheless, there is a widespread *belief* that membership in the EU is a ticket on the gravy train. Economists agree that large open markets encourage efficiency through competition and economies of scale, a more rational allocation of resources (including both labor and capital), comparative advantage, and the like.

Logic and evidence are two different things, but the evidence *does* suggest that economic integration has promoted growth and dynamism in Europe even though it is equally clear that you can be rich and not belong to the club.

The EU itself is a monument to the fact that political elites in Europe place a high premium on unity. Major political parties sometimes appeal to voters to reject certain policies under consideration in Brussels but rarely, if ever, advocate withdrawing from the EU or, in the case of new applicants, not joining.[44] The British, for example, have always been more skeptical of federal schemes and more reluctant to relinquish sovereignty over key areas of national policy than many of the other member states, but neither of the two major parties has ever advocated getting out of the EU. Like the British, Denmark, Sweden, and Greece opted to stay out of the Euro zone when it was launched in 1999, but Greece joined in 2001. (Sweden voted no in a national referendum in September of 2003.)

Political elites frequently have different ideas on the major issues of the day than the general public. What politicians and bureaucrats cook up is not always in step with public opinion. This observation would seem to apply with special force to a kind of **protostate** like the EU. By the term *protostate* we mean that the EU is somewhat more than an international organization of sovereign states but much less than a sovereign state in its own right. Given the fact there is little direct connection between European citizens and the institutions of European Union, it would be surprising if ordinary people from countries as different as Portugal and Poland or France and Finland expressed patriotic feelings toward the EU.

As we have seen, the trappings of the EU are democratic, but actual decision-making processes within the EU are neither democratic nor transparent. If the process had been made more democratic, however, it would probably have slowed the pace of integration or perhaps blocked it altogether. This democratic dilemma makes it all the more remarkable that most Europeans until recently generally backed the EU, both in public opinion polls and in the voting booth. Some more than others: citizens of the original six members were generally more supportive than citizens of Great Britain and Denmark. Overwhelming majorities expressed positive attitudes toward the EU in France, Germany and Italy, but Danish voters said no to converting to the euro and in 2003 Prime Minister Tony Blair reaffirmed London's intention to stay out of the euro zone indefinitely, as well.[45]

Further signs of popular support for the EU (and thus for European unity) in 2003 were the overwhelming yes votes in national referenda in Eastern Europe. In Poland, for example, 77 percent voted in favor of joining the EU.[46] Voters in the Czech Republic also strongly endorsed the accession, as they had earlier in Lithuania, Slovakia, and Hungary.[47] Estonia and Latvia followed suit later in the year.

The question "What is Europe?" was once again on the front burner in 2005 when twenty-five EU member states began the tortuous process of ratifying or rejecting the proposed EU constitution. It is too soon to say whether the negative verdict of voters in France and the Netherlands on the proposed EU constitution in 2005 signals a more general turning away from the idea of a unified Europe toward greater **Euroscepticism.** We take a closer look at the EU—its evolution, operation, and expansion—in the final chapter.

SUMMARY AND CONCLUSIONS

Europeans are akin to a quarrelsome family with a history of fratricidal warfare who have learned the hard way that they have a lot to gain by getting along together—and too much to lose not to. At the same time, Europeans—no less than Americans and Canadians, for example—prefer to speak the national language and exhibit a robust "love of one's own" in architecture, music, manners, sports, food, and the like. In short, the desire for unity coexists, at times uneasily, with the reality of diversity. Finally, what makes future successes of the EU possible—though by no mean inevitable—is that Europeans from the Atlantic to the Urals are governed more or less democratically; that they want freedom, peace and prosperity; and that they associate all three with integration.

Nonetheless, the road ahead is bumpy, at best. In the final analysis, the future of Europe hinges on whether or not Europeans decide to continue down the path of integration—a path set by Monnet, Schuman, and Spaak at a time when Europe's past appeared to be the major impediment to its future.

KEY TERMS

Congress of Europe (1948)

Convention on the Future of Europe

Eurocrats

European Coal and Steel Community (ECSC)

European Defense Community

Europe of the Fifteen

Euroscepticism

Fouchet Plan

functionalists

power politics

protostate

technocracy

SUGGESTED READINGS

Calleo, David. *Europe's Future: The Grand Alternatives.* New York: W. W. Norton, 1967.
De Rougemont, Denis. *The Meaning of Europe.* New York: Stein and Day, 1965.
Delanty, Gerard. *Inventing Europe: Idea, Identity, Reality.* New York: St. Martin's Press, 1995.
Guéhenno, Jean-Marie. *The End of the Nation-State.* Minneapolis, MN: University of Minnesota Press, 1995, translated by Victoria Elliot
Pagden, Anthony. *The Idea of Europe: From Antiquity to the European Union.* Cambridge, UK: Cambridge University Press, 2002.

Rifkin, Jeremy. *The European Dream: How Europe's Vision of the Future Is Quietly Eclipsing the American Dream*. New York: Tarcher/Penguin, 2004.

Rose, Richard. *What Is Europe?* New York: HarperCollins, 1996.

Shore, Cris. *Building Europe: The Cultural Politics of European Integration*. London: Routledge, 2000.

Smith, Anthony. *Nationalism: Theory, Ideology, History*. Cambridge, UK: Polity Press, 2001.

Tilly, Charles, ed. *The Formation of the National State in Western Europe*. Princeton, NJ: University of Princeton Press, 1975.

WEB SITES

europa.eu.int/index_en.htm

www.state.gov/www/regions/eur

www.jeanmonnetprogram.org/TOC/index.php

www.eu-history.leidenuniv.nl/

aei.pitt.edu/

vlib.iue.it/hist-eur-integration/Index.html

NOTES

1. David Calleo, *Europe's Future: The Grand Alternatives* (New York: W.W. Norton, 1967), p. 23.
2. Ibid.
3. Ibid. pp. 25–16.
4. Ibid.
5. Ibid. p. 27.
6. Denis de Rougemont, *The Meaning of Europe* (New York: Stein and Day, 1965), p. 68.
7. Ibid. pp. 68–80.
8. Ibid. p. 81. See also Calleo, *Europe's Future*, pp. 29–32.
9. Calleo, *Europe's Future*, pp. 31.
10. Ibid.
11. Ibid. (The author's citation of the complete text for this declaration is found on page 88.)
12. Ibid. pp. 82–85.
13. See, for example, Richard Rose, *What Is Europe?* (New York: HarperCollins, 1996), pp. 12–17. The author posits that the state is still the pivotal feature of European politics and, though not denying the growing role of interdependence, notes "the politics of the European Union emphasizes disagreements." See also Calleo, *Europe's Future,* pp. 35–36. A span of some thirty years separated the appearance of these books, but the two authors' assessment of Europe's prospects for federation are remarkably similar. Thus, Calleo wrote (p. 37): "While federalism as an ideal has

gained many ardent enthusiasts in modern times, federalism as a process seeking to convert the national states into a new order has made little progress."

14. According to a famous description by Paul Valéry, Europe is "a kind of promontory of the ancient continent, a western appendix of Asia" rather than a continent apart. Similarly, the *Geographie universelle* of Mantelle and Brun, published in Paris in 1816, refers to Europe as "This narrow peninsula, which appears on the map as no more than an appendix of Asia." Quoted in de Rougemont, *Meaning of Europe*, pp. 13–14.

15. It is this dynamism and sense of adventure that defines Europe, according to some scholarly observers. See, for example, de Rougement, *Meaning of Europe*, pp. 11–28.

16. Ibid. pp. 17–24.

17. Known as the Fouchet Plan, this arrangement would have institutionalized regular meetings among European heads of state with the purpose of hammering out common policies "at the summit". For an excellent (and rather sympathetic) discussion of this idea, see Calleo, *Europe's Future*, pp. 128–133.

18. Ibid. p. 74.

19. Ibid. pp. 73–75.

20. Ibid. p. 75

21. The number of Europeans who did not experience democracy directly prior to the 1990s is roughly equal to the number who did. Approximately 360 million people inhabit the former communist countries of Eastern Europe and the Balkans; the total population of the fifteen members of the European Union in the 1990s was about 375 million, but that number includes some 17 million former East Germans who belong on the other side of the line in this comparison. The only noteworthy exception is Czechoslovakia, which functioned as a full-blown parliamentary democracy between the two world wars.

22. Witness the Hungarian Revolution of 1956, when a spontaneous popular uprising would have swept away communist rule but for a brutal Soviet intervention.

23. Shirley William, "Sovereignty and Accountability in the European Community," in Robert O. Keohane and Stanley Hoffman, eds., *The New European Community: Decisionmaking and Institutional Change* (Boulder, CO: Westview Press, 1991), pp. 175–176; see also Juliet Lodge, "The European Parliament," in Sven S. Andersen and Kjell A. Eliassen, eds., *The European Union: How Democratic Is It?* (London: Sage Publications, 1996), pp. 187–214.

24. Frank Bruni and Anthee Carassava, "For Europe, the Messages Differ on the State of the Union," *The New York Times*, June 22, 2003 (electronic edition).

25. "Europe moves east," The World in 2003, *The Economist*, p. 14.

26. Ibid.

27. "Eurobarometer," *The Economist*, September 9, 2000. See also Thomas M. Magstadt, *Nations and Governments* (Boston: Bedford/St. Martin's Press, 2002), p. 172.

28. Calleo, *Europe's Future*, p. 81.

29. Ibid.

30. Ibid., p. 82. De Gaulle, according to Calleo, "has been unyieldingly hostile to the supranational pretensions of the Common Market, but he has energetically encouraged European economic integration. . . . He would build Europe around the

existing national states rather than a new federal center. De Gaulle's union would work to coordinate national policies wherever possible while leaving the political sovereignty of the states intact."

31. Ibid., pp. 85–86. De Gaulle made this observation in a press conference on February 25, 1953, at a time when his own political future, and that of France, was clouded and uncertain.

32. Ibid., p. 87. De Gaulle speech, November 4, 1951.

33. Ibid. De Gaulle press conference, December 21, 1951.

34. Elaine Sciolino, "Seeking Unity, Europe Drafts a Constitution," *The New York Times,* June 15, 2003 (electronic edition).

35. Ibid. See also "Tidying up or tyranny?" *The Economist,* May 31, 2003, pp. 51–52.

36. "Tidying up or tyranny?" pp. 51–52.

37. Ibid.

38. Ibid.

39. Sciolino, "Seeking Unity . . ."

40. Ibid. A British delegate to the Brussels convention and the European Parliament, Gisela Stuart, complained, "Right now, if my prime minister goes to Brussels and makes decisions behind closed doors, I as a parliamentarian cannot hold him to account because I only know the outcome, I don't know the process. It's the same with the ministers. They can tell me anything."

41. Rose, *What Is Europe?* p. 40. Similarly, Calleo writes how "to Frenchman long devoted to the European cause, Robert Schuman, the Foreign Minister, and Jean Monnet, the Father of Europe," produced what must surely be one of the most imaginative diplomatic solutions in modern history, the European Coal and Steel Community. It was impossible, they argued to tie together France and Germany through classical diplomatic arrangements. The basic problem was that neither could afford to concede much to the other without feeling its own security and prosperity endangered, and thus the old cycle of competition and fear had continued endlessly. The only solution was to fuse the two countries in such a way that each would lose its independent power to do mortal harm to the other. They could then cooperate without fearing that what benefited one invariably threatened the other." Calleo, *Europe's Future,* p. 48.

42. For a recent analysis of the role of these factors in determining the power capabilities of the main actors in international politics, see John Mearsheimer, *The Tragedy of the Great Powers* (New York: W. W. Norton, 2001), pp. 55–82.

43. See David Mitrany, *A Working Peace System* (Chicago: Quadrangle Books, 1966). Mitrany developed the first comprehensive functionalist theory in the 1940s as a practical way to use international organizations as vehicles for developing the habit of cooperation on the part of states far more accustomed to competition. For an analysis of the connection between the functionalists and European supranationalists, see David Wood and Birol Yesilada, *The Emerging European Union* (New York: Longman, 2002), pp. 13–17.

44. One exception is President Vaclav Klaus, former leader of the opposition center-right party in the Czech Republic, who expressed doubts prior to the national referendum in June 2003, saying that he thought Czechs deserved more time to enjoy sovereignty after a long period of Soviet tutelage prior to 1989. But even Klaus, "the only leader

of a candidate country not to strongly support membership, has compared the outcome of the Czech vote to a lump of sugar dropped into a cup of coffee." See wire service article, "Czechs Ratify EU Membership," *Washington Post*, June 15, 2003, p. A25.

45. "What a Pity. What a Relief," *The Economist*, June 14, 2003, p. 46.

46. See, for example, "Back into the Fold," *The Economist*, June 14, 2003, pp. 45–46.

47. "Come On, Try and Get Excited," *The Economist*, June 7, 2003, p. 45. Lithuania's referendum resulted in a resounding 91 percent yes vote with a 63 percent turnout.

9

The United States of Europe

Inevitable or Impossible?

*T*his chapter traces the evolution of the European Union, briefly describes its basic institutions, and explains how it makes decisions. It also looks at the attempt to write a constitution for Europe and sees the recent setbacks as a pause along the way rather than the end of the trail. Next, it assesses contemporary Europe's strengths and weaknesses, changing relations with the United States, and role in the evolving global system. It closes with a brief commentary on the distinction between integration, which is compatible with a community of sovereign national governments, and federation, which is not, and concludes that Europe is not likely to make the leap to a qualitatively different form of political organization for a long time to come—if ever.

We begin by considering Europe's improbable economic merger and asking whether a half-century of supranational institution building will eventually lead to creation of a new European superpower. Two bestsellers published in 2004 said yes.[1] The author of one of these books, T. R. Reid, summarizes the argument in the following way:

> In the jargon of the political scientists, the kind of power that a nation accrues through military strength is known as "hard power." The influence that comes from economic strength, from cultural and political influence, from leadership in international organizations, is known as "soft power." Along with the rest of the world, the European Union has essentially conceded global dominance in the field of "hard power" to the United States and its unmatchable military forces. But the EU is betting that it can become an actor of equal importance on the world stage—in short, the world's next superpower—through the "soft power" it is consistently enhancing. Indeed, the Europeans argue that hard power is so costly to maintain—and so likely to generate hatred

from those who are weaker—that soft power amounts to greater power.[2]

Since the 1950s, Western Europe has moved toward ever tighter economic integration. In the 1990s, the European Community (EC) was transfigured into the European Union (EU) when its members voted in steps for full economic unification complete with a common European currency, the **euro.** In 2003, the European Union comprised 15 countries (Austria, Belgium, Britain, Denmark, Finland, France, Germany, Greece, Ireland, Italy, Luxembourg, the Netherlands, Portugal, Spain, and Sweden), compared to six at its modest beginning. Ten more countries joined in 2004, including Latvia, Lithuania, Estonia, Poland, the Czech Republic, Slovakia, Hungary, and Slovenia, plus Malta and Cyprus, increasing the EU total population from 370 million to 450 million (see Map 9.1). It is the world's largest trading bloc and rivals the United States as an economic superpower.

But some say Europe lacks military efficacy (or hard power). Traditionally, a great power had to be capable of fielding mighty armies or navies (or both). Today, a superpower must have an army, navy, and air force with global reach. If the United States is taken as the model of what a superpower must or should be, then there is surely only one in existence: no other state or grouping of states in the world can rival the United States in hard power capabilities.

However, the notion that Europe is weak, as some suggest, is a misconception.[3] Europe does not lack hard power or the economic and technological wherewithal to create more of it over time if there is a political will or urgent need to do so. Though it is true that EU countries continue to spend far less on military security (or national defense) than the United States, they have a bigger population base, well-trained troops, modern weapons and communications systems, a pivotal geographic position close to several key strategic chokepoints, and (often oddly overlooked) not one but two nuclear strike forces (British and French). In other words, the European democracies possess the basic elements of a global military power. What they lack is a set of integrated political-military structures and a common foreign and security policy (CFSP).

Eurosceptics stress what Europe (meaning the EU) lacks. They point out that Europe has several dozen national governments and that these governments are still sovereign entities—that is, they alone decide whether to accept or reject rules made in Brussels. They also point out that Europe still has no unified military command structure apart from NATO, which remains an American-led alliance. Both points are well taken and would have been indisputable as recently as the 1980s. But as we know, Europe has changed a great deal since the collapse of communism at the end of the decade. And as we are about to discover, the most visible changes are interlaced with major changes in the way the EU does business—changes that are

MAP 9.1   The European Union in 2006

largely "below the radar" for most Americans but nonetheless of critical importance to a true understanding of what is happening on the other side of the Atlantic. We begin with a thumbnail sketch of the European Union today.

BECOMING EUROPE: THE EU AS CATALYST

These days, the terms *Europe* and *EU* are often used synonymously. When people talk about global issues or current events, they often make comments that imply a single European political will: "Europe favors multilateralism," or "Europe opposes military intervention unless the United Nations authorizes it." What they mean is that the EU (as well as public opinion in the EU countries) favors multilateral diplomacy and opposes military action that violates international law. No one refers to Asia in the same way, for example. It would be nonsensical to say, "Asia opposes the Kyoto Treaty," for example, but not, "Europe supports the Kyoto Treaty" (it does). Obviously, there is no EU equivalent in Asia or any other region of the globe (except North America, where thirteen former colonies metamorphosed into a single nation of fifty states).

Europe is old, but what is happening there is new and unprecedented, which perhaps explains why the world has been slow to recognize its significance. To appreciate how much Europe has changed, we need to take a closer look at how it has evolved since the early 1950s and where the process stands at the moment.

The EU encompasses the three separate legal entities dating back to the 1950s: the European Coal and Steel Community (ECSC), the European Economic Community (EEC), and the European Atomic Energy Community (Euratom). The EEC—popularly known as the Common Market—is the heart of the new Europe.

First Things First: Integration before Federation

After World War II, Belgium's foreign minister Paul-Henri Spaak advocated a federal approach, but most of his counterparts "subscribed to a vague notion of solidarity and transnational cooperation."[4] Other high-profile European leaders, including Robert Schuman, the French foreign minister, and Jean Monnet (often called the "Father of Europe"), nonetheless favored steps toward some form of union. Great Britain was the major holdout (although Winston Churchill gave rhetorical support to European unity, his deeds in the end did not match his words).

If the British were ambivalent about Europe, the Americans were not. Thus, the Marshall Plan quite publicly and deliberately prodded the European democracies toward cooperative action. In a famous June 1947 speech at Harvard University, Secretary of State Marshall spoke bluntly: "It would be neither fitting nor efficacious for this Government to undertake to draw up unilaterally a program designed to place Europe on its feet economically. This is the business of the Europeans. The initiative, I think, must come from Europe.... The program should be a joint one, agreed to by a number, if not all, European nations."[5]

The emphasis on a "joint" program "agreed to by a number, *if not all,* European nations" made it crystal clear that the Truman administration expected the recipients of Marshall Plan aid to collaborate. The first step would be to collaborate in creating a structure for collaboration. The direct result was the formation of the Organization for European Economic Cooperation (OEEC). The indirect result was a nudge toward economic integration within a new set of supranational structures.

Ideally, these structures would have been all inclusive, but the British balked and Moscow barred the East Europeans countries under its boot heel. NATO (established in 1949) initially included the North Atlantic democracies minus Sweden, and the Council of Europe (also formed in 1949) encompassed nearly all the countries of Western Europe. However, NATO was not strictly a *European* organization—in fact, it was run not from Paris (later Brussels) but from the Pentagon on the American side of the Atlantic. For its part, the Council of Europe was quickly eclipsed, as a more narrowly based "community" became the fulcrum of a pioneering effort to integrate two strategic sectors of six separate economies.

The European Coal and Steel Community

The idea of forming a coal and steel community was the brainstorm of two Frenchmen, Robert Schuman and Jean Monnet.[6] It was Schuman who in his official capacity as French foreign minister first proposed the idea to Europe, but it was Monnet who proposed it to Schuman. When Schuman unveiled the plan that was to become the European Coal and Steel Community on May 9, 1950, he linked it to a grand design for European integration, promising that it would "lay the first concrete foundation for a European Federation which is so indispensable to the preservation of peace."[7] More than half a century later, the adoption of a common currency (the euro), the expansion eastward, and the signing of a pact to create a constitution that provides for a president and foreign minister make the words Schuman spoke on that spring day sound prophetic.

Significantly, Schuman did not pair federation with prosperity, but with "the preservation of peace." The **Schuman Plan** exemplified the French technocratic approach to economic development—the approach universally associated with Jean Monnet. As in the French "indicative planning" model, it created a High Authority that would, in effect, imitate the French planning office, where technocrats would direct and cajole but not dictate or control. The six economies of the coal and steel community would be integrated piece by piece, a sector at a time, moving crabwise toward European union rather than rushing headlong into it.[8] The fate of the plan depended in no small measure on American approval, which was swift and enthusiastic.

Occupied Germany's acceptance was never in doubt. Indeed, Chancellor Adenauer had actually proposed a Franco-German union two months earlier, but neither France nor Europe was ready to embrace Germany to that extent yet in 1950. At this point, when the coal and steel community was still two years from becoming a reality, the Federal Republic of Germany had itself only just been formally launched and would not become a member of the fledgling NATO alliance until 1954. No one in West Germany—formally named the Federal

Republic of Germany or FRG—knew at that point whether or when Germans would be welcomed back into the European family of nations.

Under the circumstances, the initiative taken by the French government in 1950 can be seen as either proactive or preemptive, or both. With the Americans pushing for strong cooperation among the European democracies and the West Germans eager for redemption, France could either act decisively to shape Europe's future (and its own place therein) or take a pass and live to regret it. British aloofness from the Continent was another important factor in France's decision to seize the initiative.

For France, however, unstable government was a chronic problem during the Fourth Republic (1946–1958). Fortunately, the French foreign ministry was more stable than French governments as a whole; foreign ministers did not come and go nearly as frequently as prime ministers. Thus, either Georges Bidault or Robert Schuman was in charge of France's foreign policy for more than a decade. It so happened that Schuman occupied that post in 1950 and that he had come round to the view, still far from universally held in France a scant five years after the end of the war, that reconciliation with Germany as an essential first step toward European union was profoundly in France's national interest.

Schuman and Monnet were pioneers who not only imagined a united Europe but invented practical ways of moving toward that goal. Monnet envisioned a much more supranational coal and steel community than the one that eventually came into being. In his first draft treaty, he had called for a **High Authority,** a parliament (or assembly), and a court. The High Authority, the lynchpin of the ECSC system under this plan, would have directed the affairs of the community with the help of a small supranational staff—a centralized, top-down model. But that plan was not acceptable to the other parties, most notably the Dutch, who sought successfully to curb the powers of the High Authority by insisting that ESCS decision making be primarily intergovernmental rather than supranational.[9] The Dutch were not alone in fearing Franco-German dominance. Thus, Monnet was forced to acquiesce in the creation of a Council of Ministers—what would be, in effect, the intergovernmental traffic cop and gatekeeper of the new community—as the price of securing six signatures to the first integration treaty in European history.

What was required for security (war prevention) was anathema to sovereignty (national independence)–there was no escaping this hard reality. But in the early 1950s, the abhorrence of war prevailed over the atavistic impulse to fall back on narrow nationalism. In the Belgian stance, for example, "there was no trace of idealism about the wider advantages to mankind of European integration. . . . It was taken for granted that peace between France and Germany was essential for Belgium's security, and that this was the strongest reason for accession to the treaty."[10]

Two potential stumbling blocks involved French insistence on the breakup of the huge German conglomerates in the Ruhr and the German demand that France give control of the Saar back to Germany. Voting weights, language, and location were among the practical problems that had to be addressed. The first question was resolved when Germany acceded to a French demand for voting equality; the second was resolved by agreement to make each country's language official but to make French the working language of the community;

and the third—the location of community institutions—was resolved by putting the Council of Ministers in Brussels, the High Authority temporarily in Luxembourg, and the assembly in Strasbourg.

All the evidence points to the conclusion that security trumped any calculations about the economic benefits of creating a coal and steel community. Most experts agree that the ECSC had relatively little economic impact (the fifty-year ECSC treaty expired in 2002).[11] What it did, however, was provide an early success story in the epic struggle to overcome the cycle of violence associated with European nation-state system. In the process, in bringing the ECSC negotiations to a successful conclusion the six original European community members proved that it was possible to overcome a wide range of economic and political—as well as technical—problems.

France had played the key role in bringing the coal and steel community into existence. Here, too, the reasons had more to do with the French national security than with economic factors. First, France had every incentive to make Germany's treasure trove of coal and iron ore a "community" asset, thus ensuring its own access not only to the resources of the Ruhr and but also to information about German coal and steel production. Second, France had a strategic interest in creating a European counterweight to American economic and military power on the Continent. Knowing full well that it could not hope to rival the American colossus by itself, France exhibited a strong proclivity toward creation of supranational institutions in which France and a pliant West Germany would play the leading role. But this strong proclivity was at odds with French nationalism. The result, reinforced by the institutional frailties of the Fourth Republic, was an ambivalence that burst like a stray bombshell on the floor of the French National Assembly (parliament) in 1954.

The European Defense Community

The idea of a supranational European army was closely associated with the French initiative to create a coal and steel community, essentially two sides of the same coin. Both originated in Paris and both were inspired by France's fear of Germany. Perhaps more than any other foreign-policy issue of the times, the European Defense Community (EDC) tested the limits of Franco-German relations and strained Franco-American relations. The antagonism between France and the United States over the invasion of Iraq in 2003 is reminiscent of this early episode in the Cold War, as is the British decision to side with the United States against France.

The background to the EDC drama, like the 2003 crisis in trans-Atlantic relations, also involved a war the United States was fighting in another part of the world. The Korean War brought the politically explosive issue of German remilitarization to the fore. The Truman administration, pressed to spend huge sums rearming against the perceived Soviet threat in Europe and simultaneously fight a major war in Asia, favored the rapid political rehabilitation of West Germany, including restoration of full sovereignty to the Bonn government and the creation of large German armored divisions. Reconstituting the German army meant admitting West Germany to NATO, a move the United States favored. France did not.

It was primarily France's fear of Germany that inspired the initiative to create a European army, not fear of the Soviet Union or communism. For the United States, in the grip of a rising anticommunist hysteria, "godless Communism" personified by Josef Stalin and embodied in a totalitarian one-party state possessing a multimillion-man army, made all other conceivable threats pale by comparison. Although the French Communist Party was a major political force at that time and the French did not dismiss the Soviet threat, Paris was understandably focused on the danger closer to home. It was Germany, not Russia, that had attacked France three times in the last eight decades. By contrast, Russian troops entered France only once—in 1814, after the war of attrition and ultimate defeat of Napoleon, whose armies had invaded Russia in 1812 and marched all the way to Moscow, leaving the city in ruins.[12] Even then, Tsar Alexander and his victorious army stayed only long enough to negotiate the treaty that sent Napoleon into exile. Seen in this light, it is no wonder that France continued to see Germany as a greater threat than Russia in the immediate aftermath of World War II.

France's first gambit—in October 1950—came in the form of a plan that called for creation of small German infantry units integrated into a supranational European army. Both the Americans and the German rejected the so-called Pleven Plan (named for the French prime minister *de jour*)—the Germans because it was inequitable and left the larger question of a timetable for restoring West German sovereignty unresolved, the Americans because it would have kept the FRG from achieving its full potential as a Western ally in the Cold War and because Washington was loathe to allow Paris to set Europe's security agenda. After the Pleven Plan ran into a diplomatic brick wall, the six parties to the ECSC then in progress started parallel intergovernmental talks aimed at modifying the plan—clearly, the idea of creating a defense community was far from dead at that point. Once again, the British government, now with Winston Churchill and the Tories back in power, declined to get involved.

Elsewhere as well, proponents of the EDC were fighting an uphill battle, not only in France, where the Gaullists and the Communists both bitterly opposed it (for different reasons), but also in West Germany, where the Socialists opposed any move toward remilitarization on pacifist grounds. Not surprisingly, Moscow did its utmost to derail the EDC talks, at one point in March 1952 sending around a diplomatic note that called for Four Power talks to conclude a German peace treaty. The Soviet proposal contemplated two principles—German unification and neutrality—calculated to have wide appeal across Europe. Moscow obviously hoped to head off German remilitarization—a goal shared by the French, who were nonetheless in danger of becoming isolated within NATO on the German question.

Despite all this controversy, Adenauer and the Pleven government pressed ahead, now with the full support of Washington. The plan that emerged from these negotiations resembled the now familiar European community model—a commission, a Council of Ministers, and an assembly. The European army would comprise military forces from all the member states, including division-sized German units, as Adenauer and the Americans favored, but in deference to France and the FRG's other neighbors there would be no German defense ministry or general staff.

The other five signatories to the EDC treaty ratified it in due course, leaving France, where the debate was still raging in June 1954 when the government changed hands, as the only holdout. Pierre Mendès-France enjoyed considerable prestige thanks largely to his success in extricating France from Indochina after a disastrous war there, but it was not enough to carry the day against a rising tide of parliamentary opposition from both the left and the right.

Charles de Gaulle, in temporary retirement, gave a high-profile press conference in November 1953 denouncing the EDC treaty and its unnamed "inspirer," Jean Monnet.[13] When the adroit Pierre Mendès-France became prime minister in mid-1954, he decided to settle the issue for once and for all: the opposing sides would slug it out in on the floor of parliament and the measure would then be put to a do-or-die. It was a bruising debate marred by much taunting and melodrama. Edward Herriot, a former prime minister, warned darkly that the joining the EDC would be "the end of France." Others portrayed the EDC proposal as an attack on the army and the empire, two pillars of France's glorious past. Pro-EDC speakers, including Christian Democrats, centrists, and some moderate Socialists, were shouted down. In the end, the treaty was defeated on a procedural motion by a tally of 319 to 264, with the Communists and the Gaullists—the strangest of bedfellows—standing solidly against it.

The defeat of the EDC also foredoomed the now all but forgotten European Political Community, the pet project of Italy's Prime Minister Alcide de Gasperi. The proposed political community was to have provided an embryonic federalist framework to encompass the defense community and the coal and steel community, as well as any future "communities" not yet in the works. But it was not to be—at least not in 1954 or in the next half century.

The Mother of All Common Markets

What happened at Rome in 1957 has been described in countless books and is now common knowledge—at least in Europe.[14] Suffice it to say that what people most often remember is that the main Treaty of Rome (there were actually two treaties) gave rise to the Common Market—formally called the European Economic Community or EEC. The fact that the name is still in use as though there is only one "common market" in the world and that everyone knows it is often treated as a synonym for the European Union testifies to the success of this grand experiment.

At the Rome meeting, the Six set three ambitious and interrelated goals:

1. Immediate action to create a customs union—all tariffs and other obstacles to trade among the EEC members would be removed and all goods coming into the EEC would be subject to the same customs duties and controls.

2. Eventual creation of a single or common market for labor, goods and services, and money within the Community—to achieve this goal, member states would strive toward a uniform set of rules governing competition, state subsidies, the breakup of monopolies and cartels, and social benefits including health and safety standards.

3. Development of a common agricultural policy—farm price guarantees aimed
   at stabilizing agricultural markets, assuring food prices, and getting the
   politically potent farmers (especially in France) on board.

Of the three, the first was achieved with relative ease, the second proved hardest
to accomplish, and the third nearly brought the EEC to a standstill in the early
1960s, when President de Gaulle threatened to block further progress unless the
other member states agreed to the Common Agricultural Policy (CAP) on
France's terms.

De Gaulle personified France's profound ambivalence toward the EEC. As a
fervent nationalist, de Gaulle naturally favored intergovernmental agreements
(treaties) that left France's prized sovereignty unsullied. But as a clear-eyed realist,
de Gaulle knew that France alone could not act as a counterweight to the American superpower. Paradoxically, only by forging tight bonds that tied German
economic might to Europe rather than America could France hope to play a role
commensurate with its self-image as a great power.

Basically, de Gaulle wanted to start building Europe from the ground up
rather than create a kind of skeletal superstate with no content, and he wanted
France to be in the driver's seat (recall that Britain did not join the Common
Market and that Germany and Italy, stigmatized by the hideously immoral war
they had started and lost, were in no position to assert themselves). In time,
however, the strategy of weaving a web around Germany and Italy would weave
one around France as well.

This web was precisely what the British sought to escape when they declined
to attend the Messina conference and expressed disdain for the whole idea of
economic integration, eventually choosing instead to join the European Free
Trade Association (EFTA) formed in 1959. When the British finally realized they
had made a mistake and asked to join the EEC, de Gaulle put his foot down.
Why? First, de Gaulle knew that British membership would dilute France's power
within the EEC. Second, de Gaulle did not trust the British to side with Europe
against America in future disputes—hence his renunciation of the "special relationship" between the Great Britain and the United States. Third, de Gaulle
knew that the British would seek concession for members of the Commonwealth
and would side with West Germany on EEC agricultural policy. Thus, keeping
the British out was arguably good for France but not for Europe.

Coming of Age: Beyond the Common Market

Britain would finally join the European Community, along with Denmark and
Ireland, in January 1973. That brought the membership in the Common Market
to nine—on its way to a total of twenty-five in 2004 (see Table 9.1). The EC-EU
expansion to include most of the Continent in the relatively short span of roughly
half a century can be explained quite simply: nothing succeeds like success.
Success in this case is defined mainly in economic rather than political or military
terms. Economically, there can be no question that integration has been good for
Europe.

TABLE 9.1   The Widening Net: EU Enlargements 1957–2004

Original Members	Enlargements				
1957	1973	1981	1986	1995	2004
Belgium	Britain	Greece	Spain	Austria	Cyprus
France	Denmark		Portugal	Finland	Czech Republic
Germany	Ireland			Sweden	Estonia
Italy					Hungary
Luxembourg					Latvia
Netherlands					Lithuania
					Malta
					Poland
					Slovakia
					Slovenia

The European Union is the world's largest single economy. Even without the ten new members admitted in 2004, the EU, with only about 6 percent of the world's population, accounted for over 28 percent of global GNP by the end of the twentieth century.[15] The EU had also become the biggest trading bloc, accounting for nearly two-fifths of world exports, double the value of exports within the North American Free Trade Association (NAFTA). Several dozen European companies are on the Fortune 100 list of the top multinational corporations (MNCs), including BP Amoco, DaimlerChrysler, Fiat, Royal Dutch/ Shell, Siemens, and Volkswagen. These companies benefit greatly from access to global markets, but they have the additional good fortune to be anchored inside the EU, the largest single market on earth.

In the mid-1980s, three decades after its founding, the European Community (EC) was well on its way to becoming an economic superpower, despite the fact that the second goal of the Rome Treaty—creation of a single market—remained elusive. The Single European Act, signed in 1986, called for completion of the common market in fact as well as name by 1992. Despite Western Europe's impressive economic success in the preceding decades, there were clear warning signs of a long-term slowdown in economic growth rates, and there was even talk of stagnation.

In a word, the European Community stood at the crossroads. The choice was clear: either move forward or run in place as the rest of the world changed. Running in place might well mean missing an opportunity—possibly the last—to remake Europe and keep the Eurofederalists' dream alive. The collapse of communism in 1989 and China's extraordinary economic upsurge in the 1990s created a heightened sense of drama and left little doubt that the pace of change in Western Europe would have to accelerate to keep up with the changes elsewhere.

TABLE 9.2 European Union: Six Milestones

Treaty	Date	Significance
Rome	1957–58	Launched the Common Market
Single European Act	1986	Aimed at achieving a single EC economy
Maastricht	1991–92	Launched the European Union; called for economic and monetary union by 1999
Amsterdam	1997	Extended qualified majority voting (QMV) Moved toward a common foreign and defense policy
Nice	2001	Adjusted voting weights in Council and extended QMV
Brussels	2004	Proposed European Union constitution would extend QMV; elect presidents of the European Council and the European Commission; establish the position of EU foreign minister; and move toward a common foreign and defense policy

It was in these circumstances that the twelve EC members decided to launch the European Union in 1992 at a meeting in Maastricht, the Netherlands. The Treaty of Maastricht called for an Economic and Monetary Union by 1999, adoption of a common foreign and security policy, and greater cooperation on justice and home affairs, among other things. This treaty would be followed up with three additional treaties in the coming years, each taking the European Union farther down the road to a single economy governed by a supranational political authority (see Table 9.2).

The Single European Act signed in 1986 set an ambitious agenda for the European Community, one that was reaffirmed and extended at Maastricht in 1992. Nobody could have guessed how much the political map of Europe would change in the interim. The sudden disappearance of the Iron Curtain, the breakup of the Soviet Union, Czechoslovakia, and Yugoslavia, the restoration of full sovereignty and independence to the former Soviet "satellite" states in Eastern Europe—all these changes would transform Europe in the 1990s with or without a boost from Brussels. But what was a merely set of goals for the EC in 1986 had taken on new urgency. Either Brussels would seize the initiative in recasting Europe or Europe would recast itself. Seen in this light, the launching of the European Union in 1992, which in effect revitalized the European project, takes on new meaning.

Putting the Euro in Europe

The Maastricht Treaty unlocked the door to European federation but it did not open it. The ratification debates brought Europe's anti-federalists (often called the Eurosceptics) out in force and revealed much popular dissatisfaction with the complexity and stupefying language of the treaty.[16] There was also a good deal of resistance to the treaty's centerpiece—an economic and monetary union (EMU). To appreciate how bold this proposal really was, recall that the American colonies under the Articles of Confederation used different forms of currency and that removing this impediment to interstate commerce was one of the primary reasons for calling a constitutional convention at Philadelphia in 1787. Now imagine that an American presidential candidate were to come out for abandoning the dollar in favor of a new unit of currency called the "naft" (named after the North American Free Trade Association or NAFTA) to compete with the euro (the new EU currency). Would the American people elect a candidate who wanted to get rid of the dollar with all that it symbolizes?

The exchange rate question had been a preoccupation of the EEC long before the Maastricht meeting. In the 1960s, exchange rate instability, by the weakening of the U.S. dollar, threatened the survival of the Common Market and represented a major obstacle in the path of a future European union. In 1969, West German Chancellor Willy Brandt called for creation of a European monetary union—a first. The following year West Germany presented a formal plan for such a union, but it was overtaken by events, namely, the postwar international monetary system adopted at the historic Bretton Woods Conference in July 1944. In 1972, the United States cut the tie between gold and dollar (the so-called gold exchange standard) because the huge volume of dollars in the world economy, coupled with chronic U.S. balance of payments deficits, imperiled America's dwindling gold reserves.

A system of floating exchange rates replaced the old fixed-exchange rate system ("fixed" did not means exchange rates were never adjusted, only that the rules forbid adjustments unrelated to objective or "structural" economic conditions). The new system provided far less exchange-rate stability or certainty and posed major problems for intra-bloc EC trade. A scheme to stabilize exchange rates in the early 1970s called "the snake in the tunnel" lasted less than a year. (The tunnel represented the margin in which EC currencies were allowed to fluctuate; the snake was the float of the EC currencies in relation to one another.) In 1973, the snake left the tunnel. After that, until 1979, rates floated freely except for a "floating snake" that involved West Germany and four small neighboring member states (Belgium, the Netherlands, Luxembourg, and Denmark).

By 1979, it was clear to all that the system of floating exchange rates involved way too much floating and not nearly enough system to be a workable solution for a community that equated success with burgeoning trade. The exchange rate problem brought the shortcomings of the Common Market into high relief and raised serious questions about the possibility of stopping halfway on the road to economic integration. Could a glorified customs union whose participants were constantly bickering over an issue as basic as the value of the various currencies used in intracommunity trade succeed in the long run? Was creation of a single economy not the logical (and declared) goal of economic integration? There was no possibility of achieving such a union unless the EC could find a solution to the money puzzle.

Thus, something had to be done to save the EC from itself, but the member states were not yet prepared to go all the way to complete monetary union in 1979, in large part because of insufficient economic convergence. Instead, they adopted something called the Exchanged Rate Mechanism (ERM), which was to be the centerpiece of a newly launched European Monetary System (EMS). The ERM was based on an accounting device called the European Currency Unit (ecu). The fond hope of the Eurofederalists was that the ecu would stabilize EC currencies and pave the way psychologically and politically for a single currency. That currency, the euro, now exists, of course—it replaced the national currencies of a dozen countries in January 2002. Its use is currently confined to Western Europe, but it will eventually become the main medium of exchange in most of the former Soviet bloc countries as well.

The road, however, would not be without hazards and hairpin curves: indeed, Britain and Italy would eventually pull out of the ERM and Spain, Portugal, and Ireland would devalue. Nonetheless, a crucial lesson was learned, one that would later be applied to great effect after the historic Maastricht meeting: namely, that the pace of integration in the final analysis is a function of the overall progress toward economic convergence

Perhaps nothing better illustrates the progressive ambivalence that had been the hallmark of the European Community since its founding than the fact that during a time when the EC could not agree on a monetary union, its members agreed to set a deadline for establishing an economic union! In early 1986, the EC heads of state signed the Single European Act in Luxembourg. In theory, the act created the world's largest market instantaneously; in practice, between 1987, when it was ratified by all twelve member states, and 1992, when the European Union was formally launched, it eased or lifted various controls on the flow of goods, services, capital and labor within the EC area. Another pattern peculiar to the European integration project is evident in the steps taken at Luxembourg in 1986 and at Maastricht in 1992, namely, a tendency of national governments to get ahead of the populations and electorates they represent—in other words, to lead rather than follow, to move on to the next stage rather than wait for public opinion to catch its breath and get too comfortable.

Remarkably, however, none of these setbacks and sources of resistance stopped Europe's national leaders from moving forward—not until 2005, that is. But by that time the European Union was a *fait accompli*.

The Apparatus of Integration: EU Institutions

The EU functions like a government in many respects, but it is a government of a different kind. Like federal systems, the EU shares power with the units (member states) that comprise it. But unlike true federations, the component parts are not subordinate to the body they comprise; in fact, it is the other way around. In truth, the EU is a creature of twenty-five national governments. As we will see, there is a parliament but it cannot make laws by itself and in some key policy areas not at all. There is an executive but not a prime minister or a "government" chosen by the majority in parliament. There are two presidents but neither is popularly elected. Consequently, there is really no EU chief executive worthy of the title.

The **Council of Ministers** long had final decision-making authority over major new initiatives, and still does except in the areas now governed by co-decision (see below). As the name implies, it is a body composed of national ministers (often, but not always, foreign minister). All members great and small have a veto in matters that involve any significant transfer of powers from national governments to the EU. (Contrast the power of a small state like Portugal or Denmark to kill a proposal in the Council of Ministers with the weak position of the biggest American states—say, Texas or California—vis-à-vis the federal government). But in all other matters, the EU has adopted a form of majority rule. Voting power in the Council of Ministers is now weighted according to population, Germany ranks first; France, Italy, and the United Kingdom share the second rank; then Spain; and so on. Unanimity was long the rule in the Council. Today, **qualified majority voting (QMV)** is used in deciding many matters before the Council, but the unanimity rule still applies to new initiatives in the areas foreign and security policy, asylum, immigration, taxation, and economic policy. Since 1997 (Amsterdam), **constructive abstention** makes it possible for a member state to let the EU go ahead with a new rule or set of arrangements while exempting itself. It was through this device, for example, that the euro was launched in 2002 without the participation of Britain, Denmark, and Sweden.

The **European Commission** is the administrative arm. Its members (two each from France, Germany, Italy, Spain, and the United Kingdom; one from each of the other member states) are pledged not to think or act as representatives of a nation, in other words, to be independent and impartial in carrying out the duties of the Commission. It is accountable to the **European Parliament,** which can dismiss the commission by a vote of censure (but so far it has never done so, although it was prepared to do so on one occasion).[17] It initiates proposals but must obtain the prior approval of the Council of Ministers before taking action on any new measures. The parliament shares the power of the purse with the Council of Ministers and has the right to reject the budget—a power it exercised in 1979 and 1984 because it disagreed with the Council's spending priorities.

A representative assembly was envisioned in the original treaties setting up the Common Market, but the first election of members of the European Parliament (MEPs) did not take place until 1973. Previously, delegates were appointed from their national parliaments. MEPs were directly elected for the first time in 1979. In 1984, the second EU direct elections involved 120 million voters in ten countries—60 percent of eligible voters. Turnout varies greatly, ranging from a high of 92 percent in Belgium (where voting is compulsory) to a low of 32 percent in the United Kingdom (where the electorate has always been lukewarm toward the EU).

The European Parliament is truly European. Its administrative arm is located in Luxembourg, weeklong plenary sessions take place monthly (alternating between Strasbourg and Brussels), and the eighteen specialized committees normally meet for two weeks each month in Brussels. The proceedings in full

TABLE 9.3 The European Parliament: One Germany = Six Denmarks

Germany	99	Netherlands	25
United Kingdom	87	Sweden	22
France	87	Austria	22
Italy	87	Denmark	16
Spain	64	Finland	16
Belgium	25	Ireland	15
Greece	25	Luxembourg	6
Portugal	25		

sessions and in committees are simultaneously translated into the EU's nine official languages: English, Danish, Dutch, French, German, Greek, Italian, Spanish, and Portuguese. MEPs sit and vote not as national delegations but as parliamentary factions based on political aims and ideological compatibility. (Table 9.3 shows how seats are apportioned in the European Parliament.)

The Single European Act (SEA), signed and put into effect in 1986–87, called for greater use of majority voting in the Council of Ministers as well as a limited increase in the European Parliament's powers. It gave the latter the right to reject or amend legislation in policy areas designated for **codecision.** The Council of Ministers can override the European Parliament in these areas, but only by a unanimous vote.

The member states also formally recognized the importance of coordinating policy in foreign affairs and environmental protection. Today, institutions common to all, including the European Parliament, European Council, Council of Ministers, European Commission, Court of Justice, and Court of Auditors, play a role in the formulation of EU policies and rules. But that is not all: in 1999, the **European Monetary Union (EMU)** went into effect creating a single currency, the **euro,** and a new institution, the **European Central Bank (ECB),** headquartered in Frankfurt, Germany. Three of the fifteen member states (Britain, Denmark, and Sweden) opted out, and Greece was deemed unready. But the eleven governments that were ready and willing boldly went ahead without the other four. (Greece adopted the euro in 2001.)

States and Weights: Qualified Majority Voting

As noted earlier, the Council of Ministers now conducts most of its business by qualified majority voting (QMV). In other words, the EU appears to be incrementally moving away from a unanimity-based decision-making model (stressing the primacy of national sovereignty) toward a majoritarian one (stressing the primacy of community). Because the member states vary in size from tiny countries like Luxembourg and Malta to big countries like Britain, France, Germany, and Italy, any method of decision making must take differences in population and wealth into account. The EU has attempted to finesse this politically delicate issue by adopting a system of **weighted voting.**

The weights assigned to different states must be worked out jointly and each state must agree (at least in principle) to accept the outcome of future votes based on whatever formula is adopted. Obviously, the precise formula will have major implications that cannot be fully understood without doing the math. When all decisions taken by the Council of Ministers required unanimity, as was the case for roughly three decades, any member state no matter how small could block any new initiative it did not like.

In 1987, after the EU ratified the **Single European Act,** qualified majority voting became the preferred decision-making mechanism used to achieve the act's primary objective of creating a single market. The significance of this decision transcended economics or mathematics. By abolishing the unanimity rule in one policy area it established the principle that state sovereignty does not always trump EU authority. At the same time, the EU moved cautiously, retaining the requirement for unanimity on such politically sensitive issues as taxes, border controls, immigration, and labor-management relations.

During the 1990s, QMV decision making in the Council of Ministers remained more or less frozen in place, despite important measures that expedited EU enlargement and established the Economic and Monetary Union (EMU). The **Treaty of Amsterdam** (1997) modified arrangements agreed upon at Maastricht five years earlier whereby the Council of Ministers and the European Parliament would share legislative powers in certain areas (a procedure the EU calls *codecision*). The net effect of the codecision procedure was to give the European Parliament a significant role in the EU legislative process for the first time in its history.

In anticipation of a major enlargement that would soon bring ten more members into the EU, the **Treaty of Nice** (2000) adopted new rules for choosing the EU Commission and changed the QMV system in the Council (see Table 9.4). Prior to the Nice Summit, the QMV weighting system gave the small and medium-sized states (many) an advantage over the large states (few). Spain was potentially the holder of the balance: if Spain joined the small states, they had an absolute majority of 47 votes to 40 votes for the big states; if Spain voted with the big states, the balance shifted 48 to 39 against the small states. Although voting in the Council of Ministers does not necessarily break down along big state versus small state lines, nonetheless the decision-making arithmetic says a lot about the continuing importance of the sovereignty issue.

The Nice summit occurred at a time when the EU was expecting to add ten new members. The impending enlargement was certain to change the dynamics (and mathematics) of decision making within the Council—still the supreme legislative body in the EU. The Nice formula increased the ratio of votes between big and small states in favor of big states, but two medium-sized countries—Spain and Poland—were favored the most. Of course, Poland was not yet a member, but the changes to the QMV formula anticipated the next EU expansion, which was not far off. When Poland and the other new members were admitted in 2004, there was little practical difference in the weights assigned to the six most populous

TABLE 9.4 Qualified Majority Voting (QMV)*

Member State	Pre-Nice	Citizens per vote	Post-Nice	Citizens per vote
United Kingdom	10	5,950,000	29	2,050,000
Germany	10	8,210,000	29	2,830,000
France	10	5,860,000	29	2,020,000
Italy	10	5,760,000	29	1,990,000
Poland	—	———	27	1,410,000
Spain	8	4,920,000	27	1,460,000
Netherlands	5	3,160,000	13	1,220,000
Belgium	5	2,040,000	12	850,000
Czech Republic	—	———	12	850,000
Greece	5	2,100,000	12	880,000
Hungary	—	———	12	830,000
Portugal	5	2,000,000	12	830,000
Sweden	4	2,220,000	10	890,000
Austria	4	2,020,000	10	810,000
Denmark	3	1,770,000	7	760,000
Finland	3	1,730,000	7	740,000
Ireland	3	1,230,000	7	530,000
Lithuania	—	———	7	490,000
Slovakia	—	———	7	770,000
Cyprus	—	———	4	200,000
Estonia	—	———	4	330,000
Latvia	—	———	4	576,000
Luxembourg	2	200,000	4	100,000
Slovenia	—	———	4	500,000
Malta	—	———	3	130,000

*Romania (14 votes) and Bulgaria (10 votes) are expected to join the EU in 2007.

member states (Germany, Britain, France, Italy, Spain, and Poland) even though the largest, Germany, dwarfed the smallest, Poland. (Germany's population is more than twice the size of Poland's; its economy is roughly eleven times bigger).

But there was more to the new QMV formula than met the eye. In fact, it involved not one majority but three. First, a qualified majority was defined as 72 percent of the total votes. Second, approval required an absolute majority of member states (thirteen after 2004). Third, when requested by a member state, a measure had to be sanctioned by member states representing at least 62 percent of the EU population (as well as a qualified majority of 72 percent of the total votes in the Council).

The upshot was to further complicate an already too complicated decision-making procedure in the EU. France would not accept fewer votes than Germany was assigned, Belgium did not want to settle for fewer votes than the Netherlands, and so on. Most of all, though the agreement to adopt the euro and admit ten new members showed how far the EU had come, the wrangling over the QMV system highlighted how far it still had to go to become something more than a confederation of economically integrated but politically separate and sovereign states.

In 2003, as the EU was preparing to bring ten new member states on board and hammer out a constitution, a momentous event outside Europe—the American-led invasion of Iraq—demonstrated how empty the rhetoric in Brussels about a common foreign and security policy (CFSP) really was. Recall that the trans-Atlantic dispute over Iraq in 2003 pitted the United States, backed primarily by Great Britain and Spain, against France, Germany, and (to a lesser extent) Belgium. In addition, Poland sided with the United States, whereas Turkey balked at letting Washington use its territory as a springboard for the invasion. Nothing in post–Cold War era cast the EU's lack of a common foreign policy into sharper relief than the bitter dispute in the Atlantic community and within the EU itself over war against Iraq.

Acrimony over the war jeopardized the fragile consensus among the EU members over the wisdom of pushing ahead with the proposed new constitution, which would have to be ratified by all twenty-five countries. Competing and potentially incompatible national interests resurfaced. The QMV formula adopted at the Nice Summit, among other things, came under renewed attack, but the argument stopped short of a free-for-all. Work on the new constitution resulted in a consensus that the cumbersome triple majority method (the Nice formula) should be simplified. At the Paris Summit in October 2004, heads of state agreed that a qualified majority would be defined as follows: at least fifteen member states representing 65 percent of the EU population. If and when the membership goes to twenty-eight, the number 15 will be replaced by 55 percent of the Council votes, except on votes involving measures that do not originate in the Commission or the EU Ministry of Foreign Affair. (For such measures, the number 15 becomes 72 percent of the Council votes representing 65 percent of the population.)

A related procedural question is what constitutes a **blocking minority.** To satisfy the majority and allay fears of big-state domination, it was agreed at Paris that it would take at least four member-states to block action in the Council. In other words, three of the four biggest states (most likely France, Germany, and Italy) alone could not block Council action (even though they have a combined population of about 200 million, roughly 45 percent of the EU total).

Qualified majority voting is now used in all but the most politically charged issue areas (for example, foreign policy, taxation, and the environment) where unanimity is still required. With continuing EU enlargement, the QMV formula will most likely continue to be reviewed and revised from time to time, giving rise to potential frictions whenever changes are deemed necessary. Obviously, any majority voting system—qualified or not—is at odds with the jealously guarded national rights and privileges of ancient sovereign states. Any change in relative voting weights is thus bound to be politically sensitive.

The Three Pillars of the New Europe

In retrospect, the series of historic EU summits in the 1990s were in a real sense all about attempting to answer that question without directly addressing it. The Maastricht and Amsterdam Treaties divided the EU into **three pillars**—the European Community (the internal market), the Common Foreign and Security Policy (CFSP), and Justice and Home Affairs. The **first pillar** dealt with the heart of the European project, namely economic integration. The two-pronged strategy involved "widening and deepening" integration, which also became the mantra for Eurofederalists. Widening, of course, referred to the enlargements that were anticipated in the coming years. Deepening referred, above all, to the creation of a common currency (the euro), as the jewel in the crown of the projected new **European Monetary System (EMS).** The latter would include a **European Central Bank (ECB)** responsible for EU monetary policy (setting interest rates and fighting inflation). The ECB opened its doors in June 1998. Remarkably, the EMS would be fully operational within a decade—the euro was formerly launched in January 2002.

The need for a coordinating mechanism in foreign policy was evident in the Bosnian crisis in the mid-1990s and Iraq invasion in 2003. In the latter case, four of the five biggest EU states lined up on opposite sides—the United Kingdom and Spain backed the U.S. decision to invade, whereas France and Germany wanted to give the United Nations more time to resolve the dispute (over weapons inspections) peacefully.

These two crises focused new attention on the **second pillar** (the CFSP). It had become apparent to many Europeans that failure to present a united front to the world had effectively deprived Europe of a place at the global table. No single European state could speak for Europe; the EU alone had the potential to do so. But as matters stood, the EU had no effective voice at the United Nations or in Washington or anywhere else in the world. In the late 1990s, EU leaders made ringing declarations and began to lay the foundations for a European foreign policy. Still, that the CFSP existed only in theory was clearly demonstrated in 2002-2003, when the EU was singularly incapable of speaking with one voice as the war of words between Washington and Baghdad escalated.

The proposed constitution (discussed later) addressed this problem head on by consolidating two preexisting foreign-affairs posts in the Commission into one. (The reference here is to the Commissioner for External Affairs and the Commissioner for Enlargement. The EU Secretary-General, who heads the Council's Secretariat, and the President of the Commission each play a role in making, explaining, and carrying out EU foreign policy as well.) Thus, if the intent of the constitutional treaty were put into practice, the EU foreign minister would become the voice of Europe in world politics.

The "war on terror" also lent a new sense of urgency to the **third pillar**—Justice and Home Affairs.[18] This pillar involves issues related to law enforcement, including asylum, immigration, fugitive criminals, terrorism, and drugs. In general, it is up to the interior ministers of the member states to coordinate national policies in these areas. National laws still operate, but the Council of Ministers can adopt conventions that define new rules and procedures for the EU as a whole by a qualified majority vote in a wide range of policy areas. Theoretically, functions can be shifted from the third pillar to the first pillar (the EC) by a unanimous vote in the Council.

The terrorist attacks on the World Trade Center and the Pentagon on September 11, 2001, had law enforcement repercussions in Europe as well as the United States. Up to that point, national police, investigative bodies, intelligence services, and criminal courts continued to operate under procedural rules and criminal codes set at the national level, not in Brussels. Following 9/11, President George W. Bush threw down the gauntlet, declaring, "You are either with the us or with the terrorists." This challenge (like the terrorist threat itself) conveniently handed Eurofederalists a case for accelerating the effort to expand the EU's law enforcement powers as well as seeking closer coordination of police and intelligence functions in Brussels.[19]

The shelved EU constitution would have created a category of serious cross-border crimes (for example, corruption, fraud, and child trafficking).[20] Standardization of national criminal codes dealing with these specific felonies is one necessary step. Another step is to broaden the EU's powers in the areas of immigration and internal security, two policy areas that have hitherto been too politically sensitive for Brussels to touch. Washington's "war on terrorism" had the effect of spurring the EU toward greater integration of security policies and procedures. It is possible that these efforts will go forward despite the EU's setbacks in 2005.

MOTHER OF ALL TREATIES:
THE EUROPEAN CONSTITUTION

In early 2002, the EU embarked on one of its most ambitious projects to date: to draft a constitution for Europe. The legal status of such a charter, once adopted, would make it the supreme law in all countries belonging to the EU—higher than existing *national* constitutions.

But here's the catch: The proposed European constitution assumed the form of a *treaty*—a point of enormous symbolic and practical importance. Treaties have always been used to frame the EU's structures and define its powers, beginning with the Treaty of Rome of 1958 and culminating in the Treaty of Amsterdam in 1997. What was different about this treaty? It rolled all the previous treaties into one charter document, making it the mother of all EU treaties.

From the start, this venture was a huge roll of the dice—a political gamble against steep odds. To go into effect, the proposed charter had to be ratified in all twenty-five member states. Even a tiny member state like Luxembourg (population: 427,000) or Malta (population 377,000) could theoretically have blocked this treaty (and therefore the constitution) from going into effect. The results of the referenda in France and Holland (discussed later) ended speculation about who or what might stand in the way of success. What happens next was still unclear at the end of 2005.

Because there is still a possibility that some key features of the discredited constitution will be put into effect on a piecemeal basis, it is worth taking a closer look. As noted, the plan contemplated simplifying the qualified majority voting system in the Council. Other important changes included the following:

- National vetoes would be removed from several additional policy areas.

- The Commission would eventually (by 2014) have fewer commissioners (making it less unwieldy).

- The president of the Council would serve for two and a half years (changed from six months).

- There would be a single EU foreign minister (one chief diplomat instead of two, as before).

In a sense, these revisions represented a natural evolution calibrated to the quickened pace of change, especially the EU's rapid post–Cold War expansion in the 1990s. They were also an attempt to legitimize and codify institutional change. There was (is) ultimately no escaping the question: What kind of Europe is most desirable, a Europe of sovereign states or a federal Europe? It was a question that had never been put to the supreme test—a vote of the people. That test finally came in 2005, more than half a century after the European project made its debut.

The Constitutional Fiasco

One recurring criticism leveled at Brussels revolves around something scholars and pundits often call the *democratic deficit*. Critics say that too many EU decisions are made behind closed doors. In this view, rules and regulations generated within the bowels of the EU bureaucracy are displacing national policies without ever being put to a vote in the countries where this creeping revolution is occurring. The language and laws of the EU are so arcane and complicated (the proposed constitution itself is over 200 pages long), it is often said, that no one except Eurocrats and lawyers can possibly understand what it all means.[21] The critics have a point: The body of EU law and standards known as the ***acquis communitaire*** is enormous and constantly growing, totaling 80,000 pages by 2004.

"The EU has long excelled at high politics, cutting deals in smoke-filled rooms—but has always failed at popular politics," according to *The Economist,* an influential British newsweekly with a worldwide circulation.[22] The pseudonymous author of this article warned that pushing the EU too fast down the road to federation was placing the whole integration project in peril. "What if voters stopped accepting that EU-driven reforms are technocratic exercises for the general European good, and began to see them as highly political decisions over which they have little democratic control? What if politicians started to pander to such feeling by attacking unpopular EU decisions rather than endorsing them with a wink and a shrug?" The article also pointed out that the percentage of EU citizens who considered membership in the Union a "good thing" had dropped from 72 percent in the early 1990s to 54 percent in 2003.

As noted, the proposed constitution must be ratified by all twenty-five member states for it to take effect. The national governments decide what method of ratification to use (referendum or parliamentary vote). Most countries planned to do it the "easy" way–by parliamentary vote. At least ten countries chose to put the matter to a popular vote. Spain held the first referendum (February 2005). To no one's surprise, Spanish voters gave a resounding yes to the new constitution. By this time, the parliaments of three other countries had also approved it. Did the auspicious start mean that the EU train had picked up so much momentum that nothing could derail or sidetrack it? Hardly.

Two big question marks were France and the Netherlands, two key countries where, as in Spain, the constitution would be put to a popular vote. In France, polls indicated that public enthusiasm was waning in early 2005, in part because of controversy over the wisdom of admitting Turkey (recall that France has a large Muslim population and that xenophobia has been on the rise there in recent years). In the Netherlands, public opinion was said to be souring because the Dutch contribute more per capita to the EU budget than any other member state. As we know, both the French and the Dutch voted decisively against the constitution.

But several other countries that planned to hold referenda, including Poland, the Czech Republic, Denmark, Ireland, and the United Kingdom, were unde-cided. In Poland, any election or referendum with less than 50 percent turnout is invalid. In the Czech Republic, President Vaclav Klaus declared that he was "100 percent against" the constitution. In both Denmark and Ireland, voters have rejected EU treaties in the past. British voters, finally, are considered the most Eurosceptic of all.[23]

Generally speaking, the British electorate is "skeptical about creating any-thing that looks like a European state," and demands "the absolute right ... to veto decisions on foreign policy and taxation."[24] This is not to say that the British are opposed to the single market, but they have so far remained out of the euro zone and they remain deeply skeptical of efforts to go beyond economic inte-gration into realms that are not clearly related to the internal market. Not surprisingly, at the constitutional convention in Brussels, Britain objected to the inclusion of the word *federal* to describe the way the union would function.[25] The British objection was reflected in the final draft, which substituted innoc-uous phrases (to wit: "united in ever closer union") for the unmentionable *f* word.[26]

The referenda in France and the Netherlands let the British off the hook, so to speak. Tony Blair's government lost no time in shelving plans for a British vote.

Whither Europe?

Europeans understand that the world has changed and that, in a real sense, it left the former Great Powers behind. Spain was the first to fall by the wayside centuries ago. Austria lost its place at the Great Power table after World War I. Russia temporarily vacated its place as well. Great Britain and France fell into second-rank status as a consequence of World War II, and Germany was utterly defeated and occupied. That left only a resurgent Russia (in the guise of the Soviet Union) as a first-rank power in Europe. There was only one other first-rank power in the world, of course: the United States.

Recalling that the world from 1945 to 1989 was bipolar is not to belabor the obvious because now that the Cold War is over it is so easily overlooked. The legacy of that era remains deeply etched in the face of politics and public opinion in contemporary Europe. The very existence of the European Union is conspicuous evidence of Europe's continuing quest for a place in the new world order; its search for an alternative to the "war system" that had twice turned the Continent into a blood-drenched battlefield between 1914 and 1945; and its recognition that at a minimum peace and prosperity depend on economic integration. Paradoxically, the experience of the EU also illustrates the nation-state's lingering hold on hearts and minds of Europeans, including many who embrace the internal market (economic unity) but remain deeply attached to the symbols of substance of sovereignty (including the national flag, anthem, military forces, police, courts, diplomatic corps, foreign policy, and the like).

Two other factors that touch a very sensitive nerve in every country are the national currency and the mother tongue. The way the EU handled the currency question says a lot about Europe's ambivalence toward Brussels as a node of authority. In order to move the internal market forward, it was necessary to create a single currency and a European Central Bank. But for that to happen, the member states had to agree unanimously to abolish existing national currencies and to sell this idea to the voters back home. But it was *not* unanimous. Several member states did not want to participate, but no government wanted to be the one to kill a plan the majority favored. All fifteen member states agreed on at least one thing: respect for national authority (sovereignty) dictated that on a measure of such high emotional and political impact member states must be allowed to stay out of the EMU without being evicted from the club. This was the genesis of the constructive abstention mentioned earlier. The EU also refrained from creating a European Finance Minister because any such proposal would undoubtedly have met with strong resistance from many quarters.[27]

The European Central Bank (ECB) opened its doors in Frankfurt in 1998. Four years later, the EU began using the new euro. Three countries—Great Britain, Denmark, and Sweden—opted out. Was it a model for future EU steps toward the dream of "ever closer union"? Quite possibly it was, particularly after the derailing of the EU constitutional treaty in 2005.

The language issue also remains a potential bone of contention in the EU. It is one thing to take orders from a new boss; it is quite another to take orders from a new boss who does not even speak your language. Nothing illustrates the emotional side of politics more vividly than the language question. In the United States, the idea of bilingual education, for example, is extremely controversial. The famous American melting pot effect owes much to the fact that immigrants soon discover they cannot succeed unless they learn English.

B O X 9.1 Tongue-Tied in Europe

The desire to protect and promote its language is a threat that runs through France's policy in the Union. For instance, longstanding efforts to develop a common EU patent-law have been stymied because France cannot accept English as the sole language for patents; and if French is made valid for EU patents, then the Germans, Italians and Spanish insist that their tongues should also be included. France has also consistently fought to prevent the EU gaining control of trade policy relating to "cultural industries," lest this impede efforts to protect French-language films and music. And the French government has keenly

championed Romania as a candidate to join the Union because of "la Francophonie." ...

The more realistic French officials acknowledge that however much cash and energy are put into the promotion of French within the Union and elsewhere, it is a losing battle. "This is a real trauma for France," says Mr [Bruno] Dethomas [one-time spokesman for former EU Commission president Jacques Delors]. "Our only revenge is that the English language is being killed by all these foreigners speaking it so badly."

SOURCE: Excerpted from Charlemagne, "The Galling Rise of English," *The Economist,* March 31, 2003, p. 50.

A crucial difference between the United States of America and the potential United States of Europe is that the citizens of the new Europe are not immigrants. They have not chosen to leave family and friends, to seek a new life in a new land, to learn a new language and new way of seeing things. On this issue, France is one of the most adamant about the importance of preserving its national identity (see Box 9.1). One senior French official at EU headquarters in Brussels put the matter succinctly: "It's not so much a single language that I fear but the single way of thinking that it brings with it."[28]

There is a possibility that the language issue will rekindle the ancient cross-channel rivalry between the British and the French. For several centuries, French, not English, was the diplomatic language of Europe. It has also been the main language of the EU—until recently. Now French is being challenged by English within the EU as a result of the addition of two new Nordic member states (Sweden and Finland) in 1995 and the ten expansion states in 2004. In all these countries, as elsewhere in Europe, far more people speak English than French as a second language. This trend will likely accelerate given the fact that "over 92% of secondary-school students in the EU's non-English-speaking countries are studying English, compared with 33 percent learning French and 13% studying German."[29]

Ambitious young Europeans are often keen to get a degree from a British or American university, where they are obviously exposed to ideas many Europeans consider anathema. The French official quoted earlier, for example, questions whether "it is possible to speak English without thinking American."[30]

Naturally, France is the most vocal on this issue, but it is not alone in wishing to protect its linguistic heritage. Czechs, for example, are not averse to learning foreign languages, but are often impatient with foreigners in their midst who do not speak Czech. Foreigners who take up temporary residence in the Czech Republic are often chided (and occasionally humiliated) for not speaking Czech or not speaking it well enough.[31] No doubt the point is equally valid for most of the other EU member states—not to mention the United States.[32]

To summarize, most Europeans today, including many who support the EU as presently constituted, would strongly oppose the creation of a European superstate.[33] A solid majority in the United Kingdom, Denmark, and possibly elsewhere would also oppose any steps they believed might eventually lead to creation of a federal Europe. Yet there is a sophisticated and persistent cross-national minority of Eurofederalists, Europhiles, and Eurocrats who remain committed to a political union. In the words of one prominent Eurofederalist: "The antidote to nationalism and chauvinism whether based on race or class, and ultimately to the totalitarian dictatorships which are its inevitable product in this century, is to hold federalist beliefs and put them into practice. It is to establish unity in diversity, an organic balance between local freedoms and communal obligations, and the pooling of 'sovereign' rights which none of our countries is able to exercise alone in the present-day world."[34]

But, although the heirs of Jean Monnet will keep the hope of one Europe alive, the reality of Charles de Gaulle's *Europe des patries* shows no signs of fading any time soon. In short, Europe will not imitate the American model of federalism because it cannot and because Europe has always been about exploration and discovery—Europe innovates, it does not imitate. In addition, Europeans continue to be highly ambivalent about Americans, admiring America's wealth and power but disdaining what they see as America's lack of cultural sophistication, its crass commercialism, its political immaturity, and, in recent times, its trigger-happy use of military force. Nonetheless, the Europe of the twenty-first century will be very different from the one America rescued in World War II. No longer artificially divided, the EU will continue to expand, and it will vie with America for bragging rights as the world's largest and most dynamic single economy. But can Europe break away from military-political dependence on the United States?

IS EUROPE WEAK?

One of history's ironies is that the United States wanted to break away from Europe in the eighteenth century, endeavored to keep Europe out of the Western Hemisphere (the Monroe Doctrine) in the nineteenth century, and was pulled back into Europe in the twentieth century. After World War II, with Soviet dictator Josef Stalin's massive armies poised and forward-based in Poland and East Germany, the United States vowed to defend democracy in the part of Europe it had liberated by defeating another dictator, Adolph Hitler. In 1949, Washington institutionalized that commitment, creating the North Atlantic Treaty Organization (NATO), which bound the United States and the democracies of Western Europe in a new **Atlantic Community.** American military muscle and West European weakness made this community possible, and fear of an imminent Soviet bid for hegemony in Europe made the NATO alliance necessary.

In effect, the United States assumed the burden of Western Europe's defense after World War II because the war-devastated economies of the Continent were not capable of taking it on themselves. The American strategy was two pronged:

to stimulate a rapid economy recovery (hence the Marshall Plan in 1948) through an infusion of foreign aid and to promote economic prosperity through trade liberalization and, ultimately, creation of a large market similar to that in the United States. Thus, Washington encouraged the Schumann Plan (coal and steel community) and the Treaty of Rome (common market) in the 1950s while maintaining a strong military presence in Germany and Italy as well as the North Atlantic and the Mediterranean.

For the duration of the Cold War, two international organizations—the European Community (EC) and NATO—framed interstate relations within the Atlantic Community. It was a paradox of historic proportions that the success of the one made Western Europe an economic powerhouse at the same time that the other perpetuated its military weakness. So long as American taxpayers were willing to protect Western Europe (and pick up most of the tab), America's NATO allies had little incentive to invest heavily in their own defense. The fact that the U.S. assumed the burden of Japan's defense after World War II, freeing Japan to concentrate on economic expansion and flood foreign markets with its exports, is frequently remarked. That the United States performed much the same service for Western Europe is often overlooked.[35]

The United States spent unprecedented sums during the formative first decades of the Cold War, prompting this admonition from President Dwight Eisenhower: "The problem in defense spending is to figure how far you should go without destroying from within what you are trying to defend from without." U.S. military expenditures absorbed 9–10 percent of the total federal budget in the 1950s and 1960s, fell to about 5 percent in the post-Vietnam gloom of the 1970s, and climbed again to around 6 percent in the 1980s. "And in real terms it ran at $400 billion annually, in 1996 dollars, during Korea, Vietnam, and the second half of the 1980s, when it contributed to overall budget deficits."[36]

In hindsight, it is clear that one of the ironic consequences of the decision to create NATO—whether intended or unintended—was to ensure that Western Europe would remain weak militarily *because* the United States was strong. Free Europe knew that Washington would come to its defense in a crisis (as it had already done twice in the first half of the twentieth century). In exchange, Washington insisted on a dominant role in all matters affecting trans-Atlantic security (NATO's supreme commander is always an American). Western Europe, not unlike Japan, also benefited from being able to spend far less on defense than the United States was (and is) spending. America's NATO allies rarely spend more than 3 percent of GNP on defense; in the 1990s, this figure fell to around 2 percent on average, and for Germany it was only 1.5 percent. Amazingly, U.S. arms outlays after 9/11 exceeded the *combined* military budgets of the world's next fourteen biggest defense spenders.[37]

Power in the Postmodern Age

The enlarged EU is bigger by far than the United States demographically. It is roughly America's equal economically. The EU's military *potential* is thus enormous but its member states, collectively speaking, command only modest military capabilities. The reason is no mystery: They spend a combined total of about $140 billion on defense. By comparison, U.S. military spending in 2003 will probably fall somewhere in the range of $400 billion. What this means in relative terms is that Americans will be spending almost three times as much on defense as Europeans. In research and development, the Pentagon spends $28,000 per soldier annually—four times more than Europe spends.[38]

One prominent scholar argues that this wide divergence in military capabilities naturally created a difference in "strategic cultures" and in the theoretical framework of foreign policy in Europe and America. Americans, in this view, tend to see problems as black and white and the world politics as a contest between and evil. Europeans believe they are more sophisticated and see nuances that Americans often fail to see. Americans tend to be impatient and given to military action, whereas Europeans take a longer view, are more inclined to negotiate rather than fight, and trust persuasion more than coercion as an approach to problem-solving.[39]

Europe's inability to act independently on the world stage or to stand up to the United States was on display when the U.S. (backed by the U.K.) invaded Iraq in 2003. France, Germany, Belgium and Turkey opposed the American decision, which they considered premature. Secretary of Defense Donald Rumsfeld expressed the anger of the Bush administration when he disparaged France and Germany as the "old Europe" and praised the "new Europe" (America's partners in the coalition against Iraq).

But are the traditional Great Powers of Europe really over the hill? France and Germany rank third and fourth in the world, economically, behind only the United States and Japan. They have a combined population of about 141 million, roughly equivalent to that of Russia. Germany and France are the twin anchors of the EU, which is now running neck and neck with the United States in the race to be the world's largest economic organism.

Britain, too, has a strong economy, a relatively large population, and a full range of military capabilities, including nuclear weapons. The United States cannot automatically count on British support. The United Kingdom under British Prime Minister Tony Blair has been solidly in the American camp in the "war on terror" and Iraq, but whether London will always choose the United States over Europe is an open question. There are strong historic and economic forces at work pulling Great Britain deeper and deeper into Europe's single economy.

Finally, Russia is a wild card in the new Europe. With the Poles, Czech, Slovaks, Hungarians, Lithuanians, Latvians, and Estonians all members of the EU now, the old barriers to travel, trade and commerce that separated the Soviet Empire (Stalinist Russia and its vast fringe territories) from the West are down. Russia is an economic midget, but a nuclear giant (see Table 9.5). Russia's economy, still staggering after decades of Stalinist mismanagement, has benefited greatly from high oil prices (Russia is a major energy exporter) but shows few signs of internal vitality. Most experts agree that what Russia's ailing economy needs most is a stiff dose of competition—the kind of therapy the EU is designed to deliver.

TABLE 9.5   The European Balance of Power

	Potential Power (2005)		Actual Power (2000)	
	GNP ($)	Population	Size of Army	Number of Nuclear Warheads
United Kingdom	2.35 trillion	61 million	301,150	185
France	2.22 trillion	61 million	411,800	470
Germany	2.93 trillion	83 million	516,500	0
Italy	1.83 trillion	58 million	164,900	0
Russia	330 billion	143 million	348,000	10,000

SOURCE: GNP and Population figures are from "The World in 2005," Economist Intelligence Unit. Figures for army size are from IISS, Military Balance, 2000/2001, pp. 58, 61, 67, 80, 120–21. Figures on nuclear weapons are from Robert S. Norris and William M. Arkin, "French and British Nuclear Forces, 2000" and "Russian Nuclear Forces, 2000," *Bulletin of the Atomic Scientists* 56, no. 5 (September–October 2000), pp. 69–71.

So far, Moscow has been content to remain on the outside, but that, too, could change. Does it sound preposterous to suggest that Russia seek membership in the EU at some point? Perhaps. But not long ago it would have sounded no less preposterous to suggest that the Soviet Union would break up, that democracy would replace Stalinist dictatorship in Eastern Europe, and that the Cold War itself would become history.

Should the United States begin to take steps to wean Europe away from its dependency on American military protection now that the east-west conflict has ended? Europe does have the material wealth, human resources, and technological know-how to defend itself. To be sure, a militarily self-reliant, economically unified, and solidly democratic Europe, would pose a challenge to the United States, but not a threat. Quite on the contrary, such a Europe would be a far better strategic partner for the United States, more capable of managing conflicts in its own backyard with or without U.S. involvement, and able to share the burden of conflict management beyond the frontiers of Europe.[40] Such a Europe would not require (nor desire) a continued American troop presence. At the same time, a Europe self-reliant in matters of foreign and security policy might come to see the world more as Americans see it—namely, as an arena where anarchy rules and the ever-present potential for conflict requires vigilance and a powerful punch.

Soft Power versus Superpower

The emerging Europe is not a flash in the pan. The EU is an economic powerhouse, and it is growing in both physical size and wealth. The question is not whether Europe will become a superpower, but what *kind* of superpower it will be. Europe will not try to imitate the United States. Indeed, divergent views over what meaning and proper uses of power in the contemporary world has been a major source of transatlantic tensions and misunderstanding in recent years. Europeans emphasize trade, aid diplomacy, and international law—sometimes called **soft power**—and criticize America for being too ready to resort to military force. For example, Europe is the biggest aid donor in the world (accounting for 55 percent of the total). Washington, the biggest defense spender, does not deny the importance of soft power but continues to rely primarily on **hard power** (armed intervention, economic sanctions, covert action). Many Europeans bridle at what they see as an American penchant for unilateral policies; many Americans counter that Europe has long been the beneficiary of American military might (in World War I, World War II, and the Cold War) and see Europeans who criticize the United States as ungrateful.

Who is right? Both sides have a point. The truth lies somewhere in the middle. Soft power is here to stay because the world has changed and the new threats (terrorism, illegal drug trafficking, global warming, AIDS and other deadly epidemics, air and water pollution, and so on) cannot be defeated by conventional military means. (The belief that terrorism is susceptible to military solutions is being sorely tested in Iraq and elsewhere—and the results so far are not encouraging.)

But hard power is still a fact of life because the world remains a perilous place. As long as there are rogue states, incompatible cultures, and clashing interests, Western-style democracies will need to have ample hard power at the ready. At the same time, unless democracies use hard power sparingly, they will undermine the moral values and discredit the very institutions that give democracy its universal appeal.

Europe and America: Partners or Rivals?

Will the United States and an enlarged European Union become rivals rather than partners? As the European Union has evolved and expanded, trade disputes between Brussels and Washington have multiplied. Some of the most widely publicized sources of friction are connected with agriculture, a political hot potato on both sides of the Atlantic. Here are some examples of recent EU-U.S. disputes in the headlines in recent years:

- U.S. imposes so-called safeguard duties on steel imports from the EU.
- EU protests the new U.S. farm bill as protectionist.
- EU wins a $4 billion judgment against the U.S. over "foreign sales corporations" tax provisions aimed at helping U.S. exporters.
- U.S. challenges the EU's Common Agricultural Policy.
- U.S. denounces Airbus subsidies.
- EU bans U.S. biotech commodity exports.
- U.S. calls for the removal of "nonscientifically based barriers" to U.S. biotech commodity exports.
- U.S. lawmakers warn Europe on arms sales to China.[41]

These differences are real and not easily resolved. Nonetheless, they have not led to a trans-Atlantic trade war for the simple reason that both sides have too much at stake. Europe is no longer under any plausible military threat.

Economically, the EU and the United States are equals. Military dependence has given way to economic interdependence. The value of two-way trade and investment each year now totals some $2 trillion dollars. In the words of one high-ranking U.S. trade official:

> It grows steadily and is usually quite balanced, affected only by business cycle trends on both sides of the Atlantic. Our capital markets are closely linked and increasingly integrated. European companies own firms we consider American icons such as Chrysler, Shell, Brooks Brothers, or Burger King. American firms own and are building viable futures for such European firms as Jaguar and Volvo.[42]

The market-based economies of Europe and North America are intermeshed in ways that go well beyond trade policies and interstate relations, it is true, but there are some signs of a loosening of trans-Atlantic economic ties as well. Hence the relative importance of the EU as a market for American goods has steadily declined over the past twenty years, from a peak of more than 30 percent in 1982 to slightly less than 12 percent in 2001.[43] This shift reflects the rapid growth of U.S. farm exports to Canada and Mexico in the 1990s following the birth of the **North American Free Trade Association (NAFTA),** and to East Asia, as well as an overall drop in exports to the EU.

A prominent U.S. economist underscored "the mammoth size of U.S. exports to East Asia" and noted that in 2001, "precisely a quarter of United States' total exports of goods went to the Pacific Rim."[44] The value of these exports totaled a stunning $182 billion, which "was identical to the value of the United States' exports to Europe." In 2002, the share of U.S. merchandise exports to the Pacific Rim (26 percent of the total) actually exceeded Europe's share (24 percent).[45]

Nonetheless, the United States imported a record $8.1 billion in EU farm products in 2000, adding $1.8 billion to the bulging U.S. trade deficit.[46] The picture was basically unchanged through 2001, but a falling American stock market, weakening dollar, and faltering economy in 2002–2003 reduced demand for imports and gave U.S. exports a boost, illustrating the extent to which trans-Atlantic trade relations are subject to the vicissitudes of the larger world economy and market forces.

Critics of U.S. trade policy decry the growing **economic regionalism** in the global economy.[47] They argue that Washington gave this trend a big boost by creating NAFTA in the early 1990s. At present, 37 percent of U.S. merchandise exports go to Mexico and Canada, more than to Europe or Asia, but not by a huge margin. By contrast, two-thirds of exports from EU member states stay within European Union, and Japan's exports are similarly concentrated in the Asian region.[48] These facts suggest that regionalism itself is becoming a global issue. If so, the implications for West—both Europe and America—could be enormous.

The Limits of Europe

The EU has avoided a crackup by avoiding showdowns on certain key questions; by allowing member states to opt out of certain arrangements; and by carefully

---

B O X 9.2 **Tightening the Knot: The Treaties of Europe's Union**

Founding Treaties	In Force	Signatories	Main Points
European Coal and Steel Community Treaty (Treaty of Paris, 1951)	1952	Belgium, France, Germany, Italy, Luxembourg, Netherlands	Limited pooling of sovereign powers, first supranational High Authority
European Economic Community Treaty (Treaty of Rome, 1957)	1958	As above	Wide-ranging treaty fixing principles of a common market for goods, plus common farm and trade policies
European Atomic Energy Community Treaty (Rome, 1957)	1958	As above	Institutions and policies regulating nuclear industry
Later Treaties			
Single European Act (Luxembourg, 1986)	1987	As above, plus Denmark, Greece, Ireland, Portugal, Spain, and the United Kingdom	Extension of qualified majority voting; abolition of last internal barriers to trade
Treaty on European Union (Maastricht Treaty, 1992)	1993	As above	Blueprint for monetary union; launch of common foreign and security policy
Treaty of Amsterdam, 1997	1999	As above, plus Austria, Finland, Sweden	Rules on freedom of movement incorporated into EU treaty law
Treaty of Nice, 2000	2001	As above	New rules for choosing commission and voting in council; treaty base for common defense policy

---

balancing the danger of trying to go too fast against the hazards of going too slow.[49] Keeping the EU going has been likened to riding a bicycle: difficult to get started, easiest when in motion, hard to balance standing still.

One secret to the success of the EU is its remarkable dynamism. Hence, the European communities have expanded no fewer than five times in less than fifty years. Then, too, member states have entered into a series of treaties aimed at strengthening and tightening the ties that bind them (see Box 9.2).[50] In the past two decades, the balance between national and European legislation has shifted dramatically. In 2003, a prominent London-based weekly canvassed the major Brussels institutions and embassies and reported: "Of those prepared to offer a number, all reckoned that EU legislation now accounts for more than 50% of new laws."[51]

But despite this rapid growth in EU legislation, there are still major areas of national policy that remain largely off limits to the EU Commission and the European Parliament. In the words of one commentator, "The EU may account for more than half of all legislation across the Union, but it tends to deal with the boring stuff. The issues that get people marching in the street—pensions, welfare benefits, education—are still largely run at a national level, although the EU is beginning to nibble at the edges."[52]

Perhaps the most revealing single statistic about the contrast between rapid progress toward a single market—integration—and the fitful movement toward a common foreign and security policy—federation—is the relative size of the EU budget. The EU budget was a paltry one percent of its members' total GDP in 2002–2003; by comparison, the federal budget in United States was about 24 percent of GDP.[53]

Until (or unless) the European Union can levy taxes directly on property, sales, incomes, and profits, all talk of a federal Europe is either wishful thinking or paranoia. As we have seen, there's been plenty of both—wishful thinking and paranoia—associated with the EU's evolution since the early 1950s.

SUMMARY AND CONCLUSIONS

This chapter explored the challenges Europe will face in the coming years and assessed the future of the European Union as a response to these challenges. It also examined the changing relationship between the United States and Europe in light of dramatic changes in the global power balance resulting from the collapse of the Soviet Union, the spread of democracy and free markets, and the subsequent incorporation of many ex-communist states into NATO and the EU.

When the Common Market was established in 1958, it had only six members, a limited scope (abolishing tariffs on trade among its members), and no record of proven results. Since 2004, the European Union has encompassed twenty-five states in both halves of Europe in a single economy. It is impossible to talk about the problems and prospects for individual European states at present without taking into account whether they belong to the EU or not and, if not, whether (and when) they are likely to be admitted. The EU advanced down the path of ever greater integration so far and fast after 1987 that its members have had to renegotiate the basic rules governing its operation several times (see Box 9.1).

In terms of population, the EU is a far larger single market than the United States, and the combined GNP of the current fifteen members is almost as large. There is no end in sight to the EU's growth in membership or economic might, depending on the political will of member countries. The family fight over the European Monetary System (EMS), which created the single currency (the euro), is a preview of the political obstacles to a deeper and wider Europe. Voters in Sweden rejected a government-sponsored proposal to join the euro zone in September 2003; Danish voters earlier rejected the EMS in a similar referendum; and the United Kingdom, one of the EU heavyweights, has shown no inclination to join—these facts raise the distinct possibility that the old-fashioned politics of nationalism will impede follow-up steps toward further economic integration and preclude any move toward federation. These three countries joined the ten new EU members admitted in 2004 as part of a non-euro bloc, which meant that the euro bloc was actually outnumbered 13 to 12 at least temporarily. (There are no optouts for new member states, however, so they will be required to join the euro zone as soon as they can meet the criteria for entry.)

In retrospect, Ireland's initial rejection of the Nice Treaty (later reversed) appears to have been a harbinger of hardening public attitudes toward Brussels—and not just in Ireland. On the Continent as well, there has been evidence that a soft nationalism (that is, nationalism not tied to militarism or aggressive aims but rather to self-interest) is on the rise. The negative votes on the EU constitution in France and the Netherlands in 2005 may be a sign that a harder form of nationalism is germinating, bolstered in some instances by more extreme forms manifested as xenophobia, anti-globalism, and anti-Americanism. An intriguing question is whether Brussels itself might become the lightning rod for a renascent nationalism in Europe—a possibility that weighed heavily on the minds of Europe's leaders in the summer of 2005.

For the time being, the dream of European federation remains just that—a dream. Decisions are still made by a torturous process that combines bureaucracy and diplomacy and often produces complicated legislation that bewilders the public. National leaders are understandably reluctant to relinquish the sovereignty they are sworn to protect. Moreover, many Europeans view the Commission and Council as undemocratic. A voter backlash—in the case of France, directed against an unpopular prime minister and president as well as the EU constitution—appears to have put any new initiatives on hold.

Fear and the force of habit are the natural enemies of innovation and change. Western Europe has triumphed over these internal enemies to a remarkable degree in the past fifty years. But increasingly nettlesome national problems—some endemic to Europe's postmodern societies, others growing out of post–Cold War changes in the global system—are likely to hinder regional prospects in the years to come.

KEY TERMS

acquis communitaire

Atlantic Community

blocking minority

codecision

constructive abstention

Council of Ministers

economic regionalism

euro

European Commission

European Monetary System (EMS)

European Monetary Union (EMU)

European Parliament

first pillar

hard power

High Authority

North American Free Trade Association (NAFTA)

qualified majority voting (QMV)

Schuman Plan

second pillar

Single European Act

soft power

three pillars

Treaty of Amsterdam

Treaty of Nice

weighted voting

SUGGESTED READINGS

Beach, Derek. *The Dynamics of European Integration: Why and When EU Institutions Matter.* New York: Palgrave Macmillan, 2005.

De Grazia, Victoria. *Irresistible Empire: America's Advance through Twentieth-Century Europe.* Cambridge, MA: Harvard University Press, 2005.

Dinan, Desmond. *Europe Recast: A History of European Union.* Boulder, CO: Lynne Rienner, 2004.

Fabrini, Sergio, ed. *Democracy and Federalism in the European Union and the United States: Exploring Post-national Governance.* New York: Routledge, 2005.

Howorth, Jolyon, and John Keeler (editors). *Defending Europe: The EU, NATO, and the Quest for European Autonomy.* New York: Palgrave Macmillan, 2005.

Lord, Christopher. *A Democratic Audit of the European Union.* New York: Palgrave Macmillan, 2004.

Leonard, Mark. *Why Europe Will Run the 21st Century.* New York: Fourth Estate, 2005.

Martin, Andrew, and George Ross. *Euros and Europeans: Monetary Integration and the European Model of Society.* Cambridge, UK: Cambridge University Press, 2004.

Norman, Peter. *The Accidental Constitution: The Story of the European Convention,* 2nd ed. Brussels: EuroComment, 2005.

Redwood, John. *Superpower Struggles: Mighty America, Faltering Europe, Rising Asia.* Palgrave Macmillan, 2005.

Reid, T.R. *The United States of Europe: The New Superpower and the End of American Supremacy.* New York: Penguin Press, 2004.

Sweet, Alec Stone. *The Judicial Construction of Europe.* New York: Oxford University Press, 2004.

WEB SITES

See this section at the end of Chapter Eight, plus the specific sites listed below.

www.eurunion.org/infores/resguide.htm

www.eurunion.org/legislat/agd2000/agd2000.htm

http://europa.eu.int/index_en.htm

www.europarl.eu.int/home/default_en.htm

www.ecb.int/home/html/index.en.html

www.euro.ecb.int/en.html

NOTES

1. See T. R. Reid, *The United States of Europe: The New Superpower and the End of American Supremacy* (New York: Penguin Press, 2004); see also, Jeremy Rifkin, *The European Dream: How Europe's Vision of the Future is Quietly Eclipsing the American Dream* (New York: Penguin/Tarcher, 2004).

2. Reid, *United States of Europe,* pp. 195–196.

3. Robert Kagan, "Power and Weakness," *Policy Review,* no. 113, June 2002 (accessed electronically at http://www.policyreview.org/JUNE)@/kagan.html). See also John Harper's incisive critique of Kagan's thesis in the "Letters" section of the October 2002 issue, http:///www.policyreview.org/OCT02/letters.html

4. Desmond Dinan, *Europe Recast: A History of European Union* (Boulder, CO: Lynne Rienner, 2004), p. 14.

5. The full text is available at http://www.usaid.gov/multimedia/video/marshall/marshallspeech.html

6. For a fresh look at the role these two giants played in launching postwar Europe, as well as Winston Churchill's vision of a "United States of Europe," see T. R. Reid, *The United States of Europe: The New Superpower and the End of American Supremacy* (New York: Penguin Press, 2004), chap. 2, especially pp. 31–45.

7. For the text of the Schuman Declaration in English, see Peter M. R. Stirk and David Weigall, eds., *The Origins and Development of European Integration: A Reader and Commentary* (London: Pinter, 1999), pp. 75–76.

8. The famed international economist Charles Kindleberger, who served as an official in the U.S. Department of State in the late 1940s used this term. See his "Memo for the Files: Origins of the Marshall Plan," July 1948, in Charles P. Kindleberger, *Marshall Plan Days* (Boston: Unwin and Allen, 1987), p. 27.

9. See Hans-Peter Schwarz, *Konrad Adenauer: A German Politician and Statesman in a Period of War, Revolution and Reconstruction,* vol. 1: From the German Empire to the Federal Republic, 1876–1952 (Oxford: Berghahn Books, 1995), p. 613.

10. Alan Milward, *The European Rescue of the Nation-States,* 2nd ed. (London: Routledge, 2000), p. 82–82.

11. John Gillingham, *Coal, Steel and the Rebirth of Europe, 1945–1955* (Cambridge: Cambridge University Press, 1991), ix.

12. Exactly who set fire to the Russian capital, the defenders or the invaders, remains unclear, but most historians agree that the Russians most likely did it to deprive the French of desperately needed food, shelter and supplies. See, for example, Hugh Seton-Watson, *The Russian Empire 1801–1917* (New York: Oxford University Press, 1989[1967]), pp. 134–35.

13. Charles de Gaulle, *Memoires d'Espoir, suivi d'un choix d'allocutions at messages sur la Vie et la Ve Republiques* (Paris: Plon, 1994), p. 564. Cited in Dinan, *Europe Recast,* p. 60.

14. Unfortunately, the average American knows little about Europe or any other part of the world. A Gallup Poll Survey in 2004 found that "Americans are largely uninformed about the … 25 countries that now comprise the European Union. Only one in five profess to know a great deal or fair amount about the EU; three-quarters admit to knowing little or nothing about it. A knowledge question confirms this finding; only 20% correctly estimate the EU's population relative to that of the United States, saying the EU is larger." In fact, the population of the EU was roughly 50 percent larger than that of the United States in 2004. Accessed on the Internet at http://www.gallup.com/poll/content/login.aspx?ci=12043 on December 5, 2004. Similarly, a CBS News poll taken in 2002 found that only 2 percent of the American people could name the head of Canada's government in 2004, despite the fact that Jean Chrètien had held that position since 1993, longer than any other prime minister in Canadian history.

15. These numbers are from the World Development Indicators Database. See the World Bank website at http://www.worldbank.com. Figures are for 1999.

16. The anti-federalists (known as the Eurosceptics) are discussed elsewhere in this book. In general, antifederalists and Eurosceptics are one and the same. Most members of the European Parliament (MEPs) belong to one of two centrist party groups—slightly left and slightly right—who support wider and deeper integration. But within the various member states, there are parties and individuals on both the far right and the far left that continue to oppose the EU on ideological grounds (patriotism, anti-immigration, class struggle, et cetera). In addition, there are many Eurosceptics of a more moderate bent—for example, in Great Britain, Denmark, and Sweden—who support economic integration but oppose what they see as the steady accumulation of political power over national governments in Brussels.

17. In 1999, an investigatory report from a special committee of "Wise Men" found widespread nepotism and mismanagement in the commission. Rather than facing censure, the College of Commissioners resigned.

18. Ibid.

19. Exactly how to give Brussels more central control in the area of border inspection without opening up a Pandora's box has apparently proved to be all too perplexing. One U.S. scholar has advocated the wholesale transfer of European security policy to the EU and even creation "if necessary [of] a single EU security service and border-control force." But having proposed this move, he then demonstrates unwittingly how unrealistic it is, given the divergent views and interests of big states versus small states, and the like. See Barry Eichengreen, "Putting It Together: The Foibles and Future of the European Union," [Review Essay] *Foreign Affairs,* July/August 2003, pp. 198–199.

20. Eurosceptics greeted the proposal to create a European Public Prosecutor with alarm. See, for example, "Nothing like good enough, so far," *The Economist,* May 31, 2003, p. 14.

21. Lead editorial, "Europe's Proposed Constitution: Where to File It," *The Economist,* June 21, 2003, p. 10.

22. Charlemagne, "The Perils of Political Europe," *The Economist,* June 28, 2003, p. 56.

23. "Vote Early, Vote Often," *The Economist,* February 26, 2005, p. 49.

24. Eliane Sciolino, "Seeking Unity, Europe Drafts a Constitution," *The New York Times,* June 15, 2003. (Electronic edition).

25. Frank Bruni and Anthee Carassava, "For Europe, the Messages Differ on the State of the Union," *The New York Times,* June 22, 2003. (Electronic edition). Thus, Prime Minister Costas Simitis of Greece said the evolving draft constitution reflected a shared belief in "a federal kind of Europe," whereas British Prime Minister Tony Blair insisted it aimed at "a Europe of nations, not a federal superstate."

26. Sciolini, "Seeking Unity."

27. The new constitution also will apparently not address this issue, although some delegates to the Brussels convention favored it. See "Your Darkest Fears Addressed, Your Hardest Questions Answered" [Special report: Europe's constitution], *The Economist,* June 21, 2003, p. 52.

28. Charlemagne, "The Galling Rise of English," *The Economist,* March 31, 2003, p. 50.

29. Ibid.

30. Ibid.

31. As a Fulbright Lecturer in the Czech Republic in the mid-1990s, this author speaks from first-hand experience. Of course, Czechs have as much right to expect

American visitors there to speak Czech as Americans do to expect foreigner visitors to speak English. The point is simply that people everywhere have too much invested in their native tongue to give it up without a fight, and that poses problems for a multilingual political entity like the EU.

32. This observation has to be qualified because there are some exceptions: the Netherlands is virtually bilingual (Dutch and English), whereas Belgium has three official languages.

33. As John Gillingham points out repeatedly in his recently published history of the European Union, the governments of the EU member states reflect this popular sentiment and continue to resist proposals to pool sovereignty even on a limited basis. See John Gillingham, *European Integration 1950–2002: Superstate or New Market Economy?* (New York: Cambridge University Press, 2003.).

34. de Rougemont, *Meaning of Europe,* p. 112.

35. Japan spends on average only about 1 percent of its GNP on defense; the figure for Western Europe is closer to 3 percent.

36. Jeremy Isaacs and Taylor Downing, *The Cold War: An Illustrated History* (New York: Little, Brown, 1998), online at www.cnn.com/SPECIAL/cold.war/episodes/24/epilogue/.

37. Steven Erlanger, "Military Gulf Separates U.S. and European Allies," *The New York Times,* March 16, 2002 (electronic edition).

38. Ibid.

39. Robert Kagan, "Power and Weakness," *Policy Review,* no. 113, June/July 2002. The reader can find this article online at www.policyreview.org. Kagan acknowledges his intellectual debt to John Harper (*American Visions of Europe*). However, Harper takes issue with Kagan's assessment of Western Europe's military weakness, which Harper thinks Kagan overstates. See Harper's letter to the editor in *Policy Review,* no. 115, October–November, 2002.

40. Erlanger, "Military Gulf." Erlanger reports, "European governments sense that they are increasingly becoming second-rank powers, unable to affect American foreign policy goals because they can bring too few assets to the table." He notes NATO's Secretary General, Lord Robertson, has warned Europeans they will have to choose "modernization or marginalization" and US Ambassador to NATO Nicholas Burns expressed fear that the alliance will become "so unbalanced that we may no longer have the ability to fight together in the future."

41. Thom Shanker and David E. Sanger, "U.S. Lawmakers Warn Europe on Arms Sales to China," *The New York Times,* March 2, 2005 (electronic edition).

42. Charles Ries, Principal Deputy Assistant Secretary for European and Eurasian Affairs, "The U.S.-EU Trade Relationship: Partners and Competitors." Speech in Miami, Florida, November 14, 2002 (online at www.state.gov/p/eur/rls/rm/2002/1549/pf.htm).

43. These figures are obtained from the ERS/USDA Briefing Room: European Union: Trade, Economic Research Service, US Department of Agriculture at www.ers.usda.gov/Briefing/EuropeanUnion/trade.htm accessed on June 26, 2003.

44. Bernard K. Gordon, "A High-Risk Trade Policy," *Foreign Affairs,* vol. 82, no. 4, July/August 2003, p. 109.

45. Ibid.

46. Ibid. The trade deficit resulted from a steady growth in overall farm imports in the 1990s.

47. Ibid. This is the point of Gordon's article.

48. Ibid., p. 111.

49. According to Jeffrey Gedmin, director of the Berlin-based Aspen Institute, "The Germans will say that the union is like a bicycle, and if you don't keep pedaling forward, you fall off. The British will say that you can stop and park a bicycle from time to time without getting off it." Quoted in Frank Bruni and Anthee Carassava, "For Europe, the Messages Differ."

50. "Union Pauses for Breath," *The Economist,* February 12, 2002, p. 27.

51. Charlemagne, "Snoring while a Superstate Emerges?" *The Economist,* May 10, 2003, p. 46. According to this article, Austrians estimated that 60–70 percent of their laws were being generated in Brussels, whereas a study by the *Conseil d'Etat* in Paris in the early 1990s put the figure for France at 55 percent.

52. Ibid.

53. Ibid.

Index

nonaggression pact, 208
outer empire policy, 253
pact with Hitler, 61
Polish policy, 211
post-WW II planning, 197
power of, 203
purges, 194
rise of, 193
Secret Speech on, 239
support for, 204
U.S. aid refusal by, 196–197
Stalinism
central planning under, 238
characterization, 193
in Eastern Europe, 253
effects of, 234
precursors to, 192
repudiation of, 244
virtues of, 204–208
Stanislaus II (Poland), 213
State Duma, 250–251
State Planning Committee, 237–238
State terror, 68
Statutory laws, 88
Stefan Dragutin, 223
Strait of Gibraltar, 70
Strategic Arms Limitation Talks (SALT),
201, 202
Stribro, 218
Strikes, 152–153, 165
Suárez, Adolfo, 128, 129, 130
Sudetenland, 57, 221
Suffrage, 11, 67
Suleiman the Magnificent, 223
Supranationalism, 17–18, 325
Supreme Rada, 260
Supreme Soviet, 235–236
Sviatopolk (Ukraine), 215
Sviatoslav (Ukraine), 215

T

Tangentopoli, 127, 168
Taxes
raising, 153
value added, 114
welfare state and, 138–139
Technocracy, 105, 320
Technology, 136, 240
Ten Day War, 306
Terrorism
Irish, 147
in Italy, 125–126
in Spain, 173
Thatcher, Margaret, 12, 125, 152, 157
anti-Europe stance, 148
election victories, 96
Falkland Islands and, 98
free market policy, 86, 145–146
ministerial conflicts and, 95
organized labor and, 100
policies of, 96–97, 149, 176
Thirty Years' War, 28, 57, 220
Timoshenko, Yulia, 301
Tito, Josip Broz
approach to communism, 224–226, 228, 253
elections under, 227
government of, 226–227
leadership skills of, 223
Soviet break by, 200, 224
World War II role, 208, 224
Tory Party
doctrine, 96–97
economic polities, 146
elections, 98
evolution of, 47
leadership, 96
U.S. equivalent, 90

Totalitarianism
Czech, 221
impact of, 318
nationalism and, 19
rise of, 22–24
Trade
Atlantic routes, 45–46
maritime, 13
North American, 347, 349, 367
transatlantic, 366–367
Zollverein and, 59
Trade unions. *See* Labor unions
Trimble, David, 147
Trotsky, Leon, 194
Truman, Harry, 80, 196, 197
Tsushima Strait, battle of, 190
Turkey, 19
Tutelage system, 105
Two-ballot system, 103
Two-party system, 90

U

UCD. *See* Democratic Center Union (UCD)
UDR. *See* Union of Democrats for the Republic
(UDR)
Ukraine
Bolsheviks opposition by, 215
communist-style rule in, 272–273
constitution, 260, 300
corruption in, 261
East-West divide, 299
economy, 187, 300
elections, 261–262, 299–300
emergence of, 214–215
famine, 195
government structure, 260–262
historical landmarks, 215
Mongol invasion, 216
nationalism in, 216–217
natural resources, 300
Orange Revolution
impact of, 279
legacy of, 299
precursors to, 261
Poland and, 214
political parties, 261
political reforms, 260–262
political system, 300–301
population, 248
prime minister, 260
profile, 181
Russian relations, 210, 299–300
Uliva, 167
Ulster, 147
Ultranationalism, 140
Ulyanov, Alexander Ilyich, 191
Ulyanov, Vladimir Ilyich. *See* Lenin, Vladimir
Umberto (Italy), 65
UMP. *See* Union for the Presidential Majority
(UMP)
Unemployment. *See also* Employment
in Britain, 144–145
in France, 156
in Germany, 161
immigration and, 84–85, 111–112, 156
increases in, 83
in Spain, 171, 172
welfare state and, 140
Union for the Presidential Majority (UMP),
112
Union of Democrats for the Republic (UDR),
108
Union of Labor (UP), 259
Union of Right-wing Forces, 252
Union of Soviet Socialist Republics. *See* Soviet
Union
Unitary systems, 89, 105

United Kingdom, 35
Armada defeat by, 75
capital, 41
corporatist model, 100
decline of, 360
defense policy, 148–149
democratic traditions, 47–48
devolution of, 148
economy
free market, 145
New Labor and, 149
politics of, 145–146
post-WW II malaise, 144–145
Tory policies, 145–146
electoral system, 90, 98–99
ethnicity of, 42
EU membership, 47
Eurosceptics, 46
foreign policy, 148–149
geography, 43
geopolitical advantage of, 43
historical landmarks, 44
honest broker role, 21
invasions of, 46
legal system, 88–89
Muslims in, 150–151
naval power of, 43, 45–46
Northern Ireland, 146–147
North Sea oil, 144
parliament
administration, 95–96
cabinet system, 89–90, 93–95
characteristics, 89–90
committee system, 92
desolving of, 93, 99
election of, 98–99
evolution of, 88–90
legislative process, 91–93
loyal opposition in, 92
origins of, 46–47
permanent secretary, 96
prime minister's role, 93–95
PR system, 99
Westminster and, 90–93
political parties, 47, 96–98, 148
postmodern issues, 144–151
pressure groups, 100
profile of, 41
public opinion, 100
relative power of, 40
terrorism in, 146–147, 150–151
unification of, 43
U.S. relationship with, 87, 148, 364
United States
Articles of Confederation, 349
Bosnian War intervention by, 307
Cold War cost, 363
constitutional democracy in, 11
constitutional rules, 288
containment policy, 198
de Tocqueville on, 186
early economic cooperation, 80
economic dominance of, 26
economic power of, 22
EDC and, 343–344
entitlements, 141
EU disputes with, 366–367
European gap and, 320
French relations with, 154, 155
GDP redistribution, 86
language issues, 361
mass immigration to, 8
military in Europe, 362–363
national character of, 204
Philadelphia Convention, 327
political origins of, 29
post-WW II hopes, 25
post-WW II role of, 80